STAR WARS®

OMNIBUS

SHADOWS OF THE EMPIRE™

STAR WARS

OMNIBUS

SHADOWS OF THE EMPIRE™

DARK HORSE BOOKS®

cover illustration Hugh Fleming
publisher Mike Richardson
series editors Bob Cooper, Peet Janes, Suzanne Taylor, Ryder Windham, Chris Warner
collection editor Randy Stradley
assistant editor Freddye Lins
collection designer David Nestelle

Special thanks to Elaine Mederer, Jann Moorhead, David Anderman, Leland Chee, Sue Rostoni, and Carol Roeder at Lucas Licensing.

Star Wars® Omnibus: Shadows of the Empire

This volume collects *Star Wars: Shadows of the Empire* #1–#6; *Star Wars: Mara Jade—By the Emperor's Hand* #1–#6; extra pages from the *Star Wars: Mara Jade—By the Emperor's Hand* TPB collection; and *Star Wars: Shadows of the Empire—Evolution* #1–#5.

Published by Dark Horse Books
A division of Dark Horse Comics, Inc.
10956 SE Main Street
Milwaukie, OR 97222

darkhorse.com | starwars.com

To find a comics shop in your area, call the Comic Shop Locator Service toll-free at 1-888-266-4226

publisher Mike Richardson • executive vice president Neil Hankerson • chief financial officer Tom Weddle • vice president of publishing Randy Stradley • vice president of business development Michael Martens • vice president of marketing, sales, and licensing Anita Nelson • vice president of product development David Scroggy • vice president of information technology Dale LaFountain • director of purchasing Darlene Vogel • general counsel Ken Lizzi • editorial director Davey Estrada • senior managing editor Scott Allie • senior books editor Chris Warner • executive editor Diana Schutz • director of design and production Cary Grazzini • art director Lia Ribacchi • director of scheduling Cara Niece

Library of Congress Cataloging-in-Publication Data

Star wars omnibus : shadows of the empire. -- 1st ed.
    p. cm.
 "This volume collects Star Wars: Shadows of the Empire #1-#6; Star Wars: Mara Jade-By the Emperor's Hand #1-#6; extra pages from the Star Wars: Mara Jade-By the Emperor's Hand TPB collection; and Star Wars: Shadows of the Empire- Evolution #1-#5."
 Shadows of the Empire story by John Wagner, pencils by Kilian Plunkett and John Nadeau, inks by P.Craig Russell, colors by Cary Porter, letters by Dave Cooper -- Mara Jade: By the Emperor's Hand, story by Timothy Zahn and Michael A. Stackpole, art by Carlos Ezquerra, color design by James Sinclair, color rendering by James Sinclair and Chris Chuckry, letters by Michael Taylor -- Shadows of the Empire: Evolution story by Steve Perry, pencils by Ron Randall, inks by Tom Simmons and Ron Randall, colors by Dave Nestelle, letters by Steve Dutro
 ISBN 978-1-59582-434-9
1. Star Wars fiction--Comic books, strips, etc. 2. Graphic novels. I. Wagner, John, 1949- II. Zahn, Timothy. III. Perry, Steve.
 PN6728.S73S7338 2010
 741.5'973--dc22
                    2009034607

First edition: January 2010
ISBN 978-1-59582-434-9

10 9 8 7 6 5 4 3 2 1
Printed in China

As the war for the galaxy peaks, Luke Skywalker and the Rebel Alliance fight not only Darth Vader and the Emperor, but also members of the vast criminal underworld that hide in the shadows of the Empire and resist the Rebels' attempts to restore peace.

CONTENTS

Shadows of the Empire | Illustration by Hugh Fleming

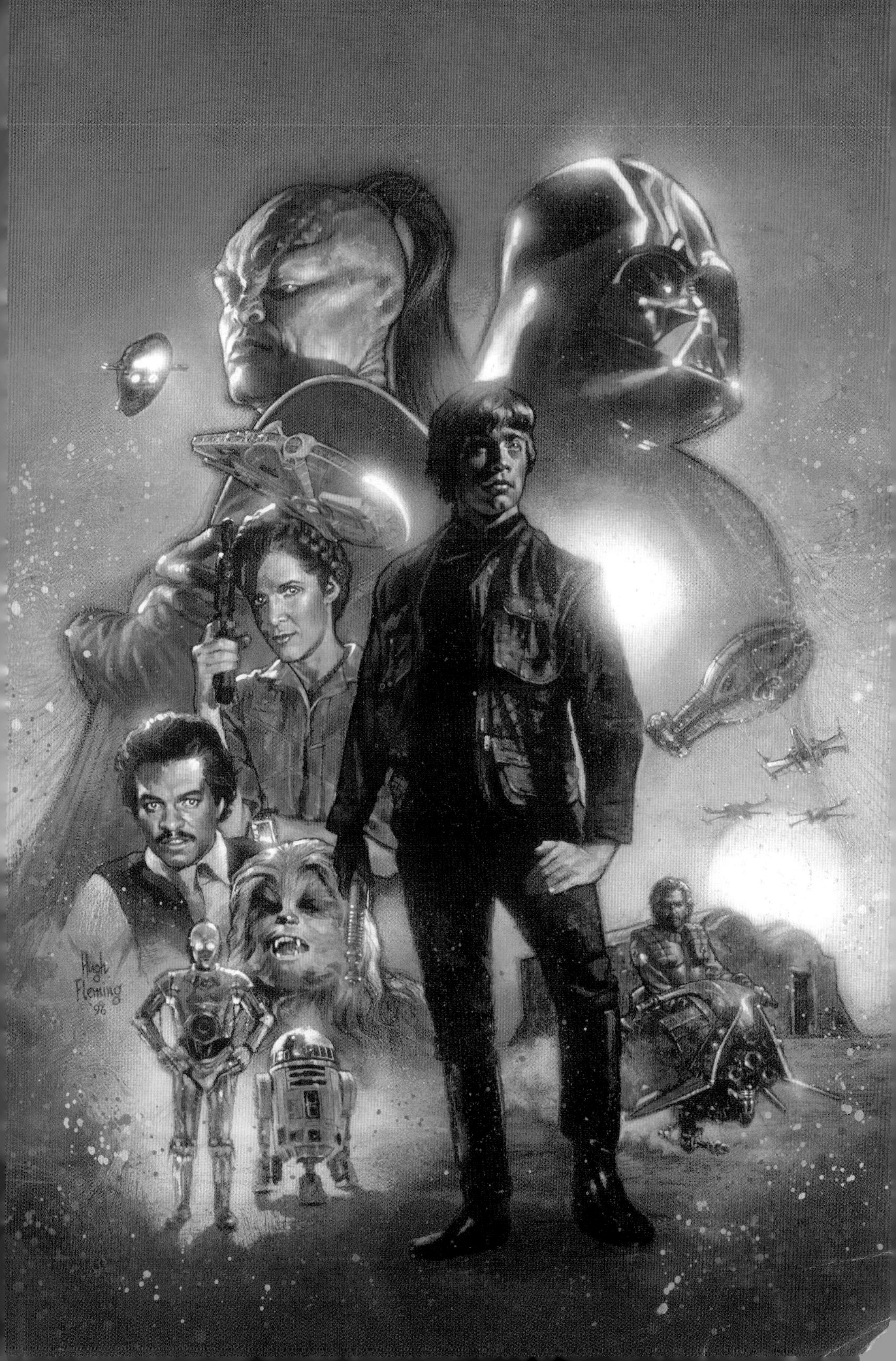
Hugh
Fleming
'96

APPROXIMATELY THREE AND A HALF YEARS
AFTER THE BATTLE OF YAVIN . . .

script by John Wagner
pencils by Kilian Plunkett and John Nadeau
inks by P. Craig Russell
colors by Cary Porter
letters by Dave Cooper

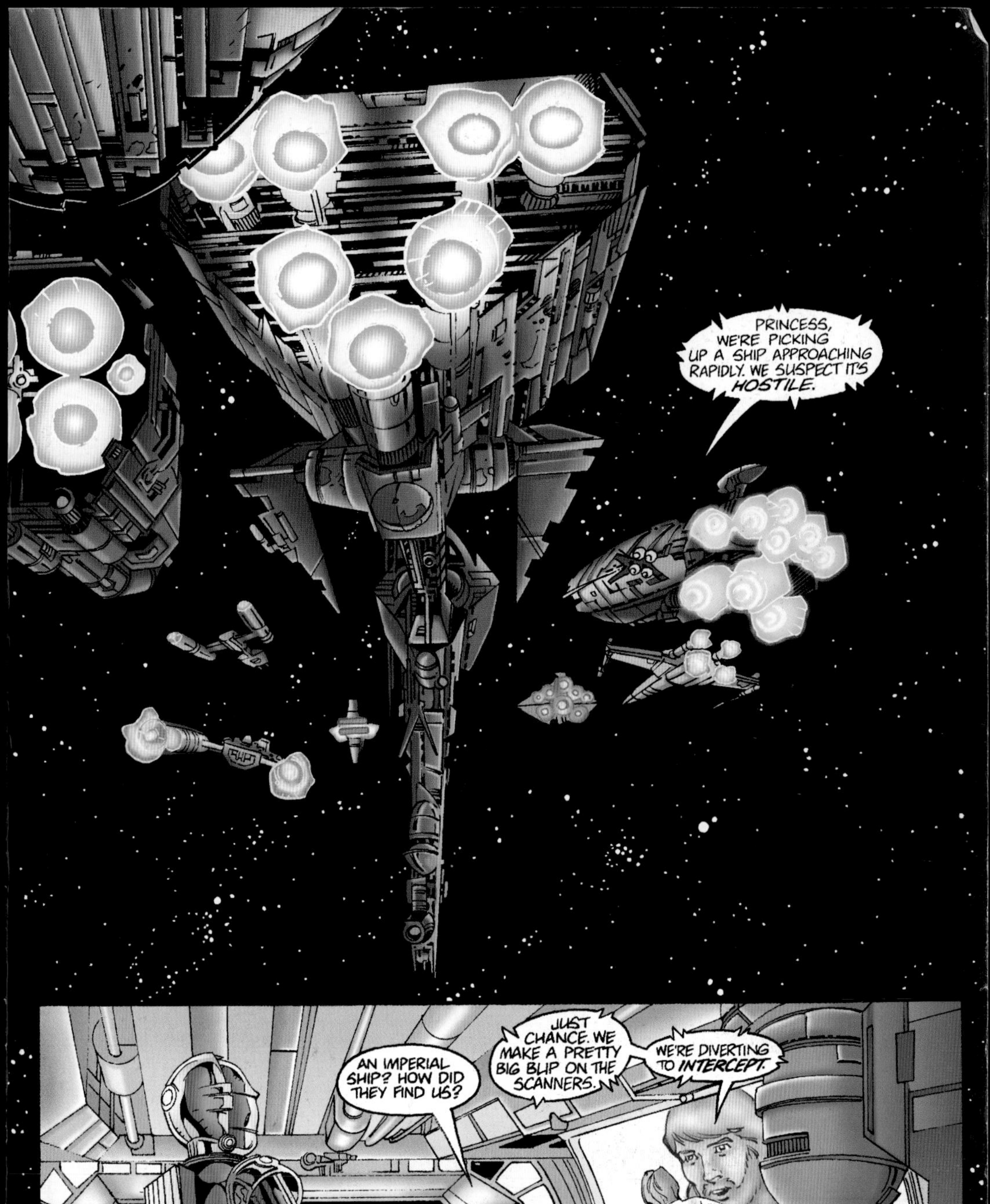
PRINCESS, WE'RE PICKING UP A SHIP APPROACHING RAPIDLY. WE SUSPECT IT'S HOSTILE.

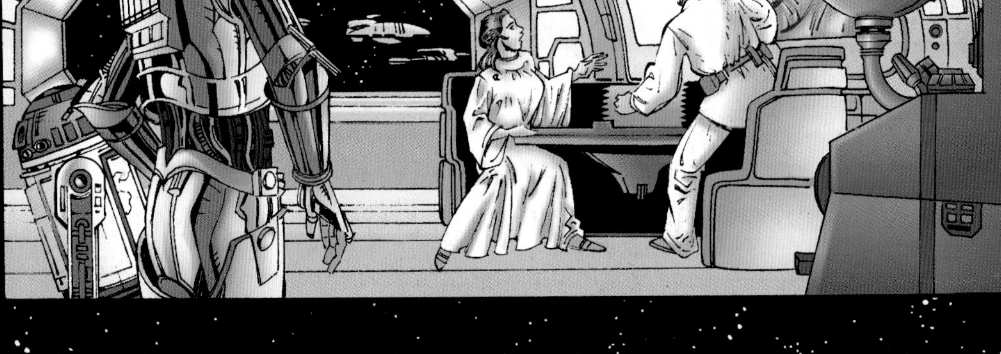
AN IMPERIAL SHIP? HOW DID THEY FIND US?
JUST CHANCE. WE MAKE A PRETTY BIG BLIP ON THE SCANNERS.
WE'RE DIVERTING TO INTERCEPT.

C'MON, ARTOO—!

LUKE! WHERE ARE YOU GOING?

I'M NEEDED, LEIA!

MASTER LUKE, THIS IS MOST INADVISABLE! YOU'VE HARDLY RECOVERED FROM YOUR INJURIES! AND BESIDES, IT WILL BE SOME TIME BEFORE YOU'VE MASTERED THAT NEW PROS-THESIS...

IF YOU MEAN MY HAND, IT'S FINE--

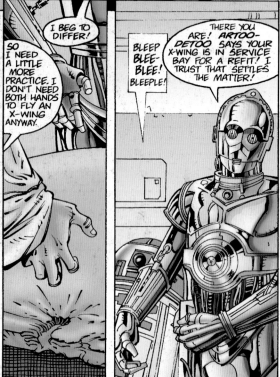

I BEG TO DIFFER!

SO I NEED A LITTLE MORE PRACTICE. I DON'T NEED BOTH HANDS TO FLY AN X-WING ANYWAY.

BLEEP BLEE-BLEE! BLEEPLE!

THERE YOU ARE! ARTOO-DETOO SAYS YOUR X-WING IS IN SERVICE BAY FOR A REFIT! I TRUST THAT SETTLES THE MATTER!

THREEPIO'S RIGHT, LUKE. YOU HAVE TO REST, REGAIN YOUR STRENGTH. WEDGE ANTILLES AND ROGUE SQUADRON ARE WITH THE FLEET...

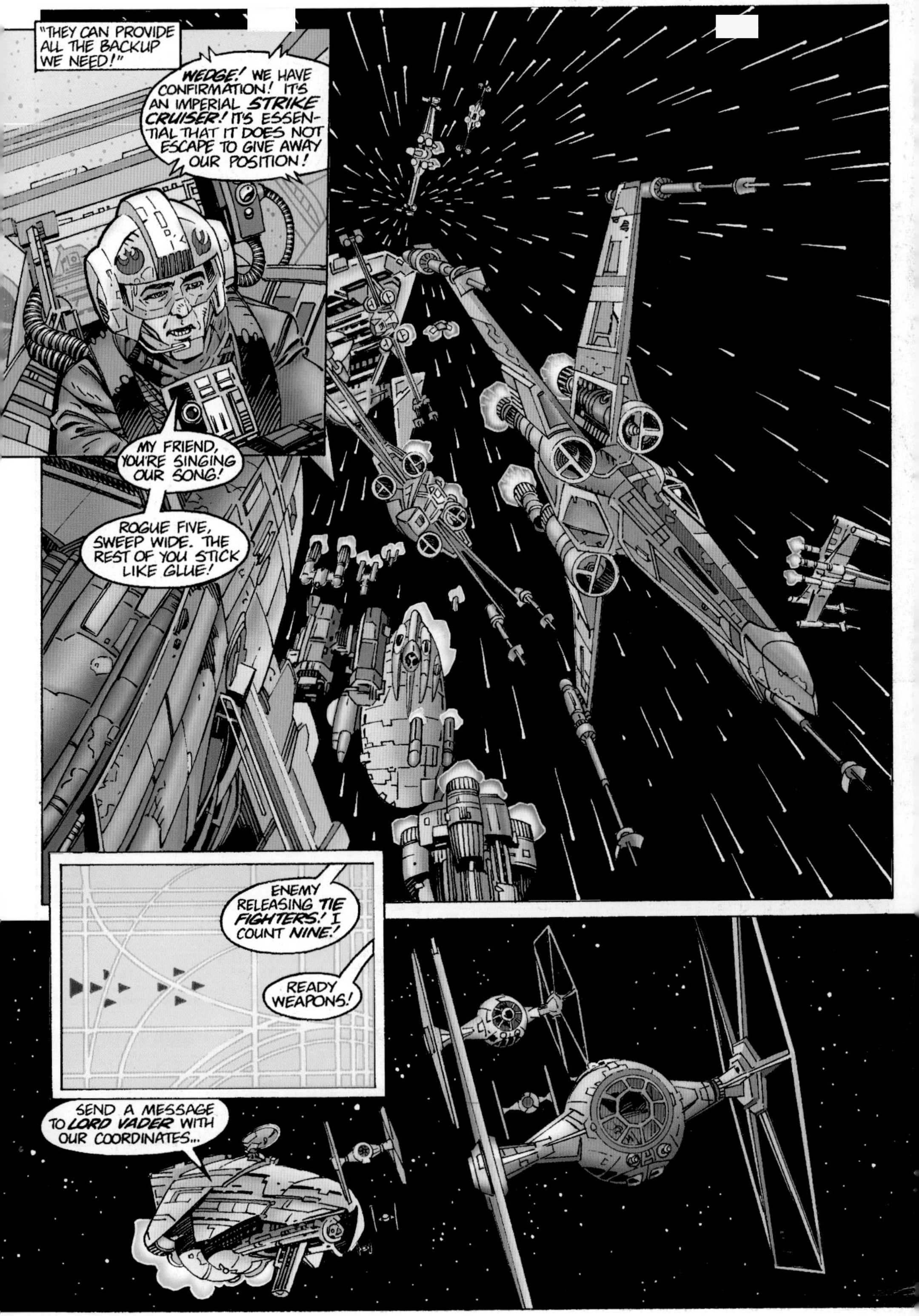
"THEY CAN PROVIDE ALL THE BACKUP WE NEED!"
WEDGE! WE HAVE CONFIRMATION! IT'S AN IMPERIAL STRIKE CRUISER! IT'S ESSENTIAL THAT IT DOES NOT ESCAPE TO GIVE AWAY OUR POSITION!
MY FRIEND, YOU'RE SINGING OUR SONG!
ROGUE FIVE, SWEEP WIDE. THE REST OF YOU STICK LIKE GLUE!
ENEMY RELEASING TIE FIGHTERS! I COUNT NINE!
READY WEAPONS!
SEND A MESSAGE TO LORD VADER WITH OUR COORDINATES...

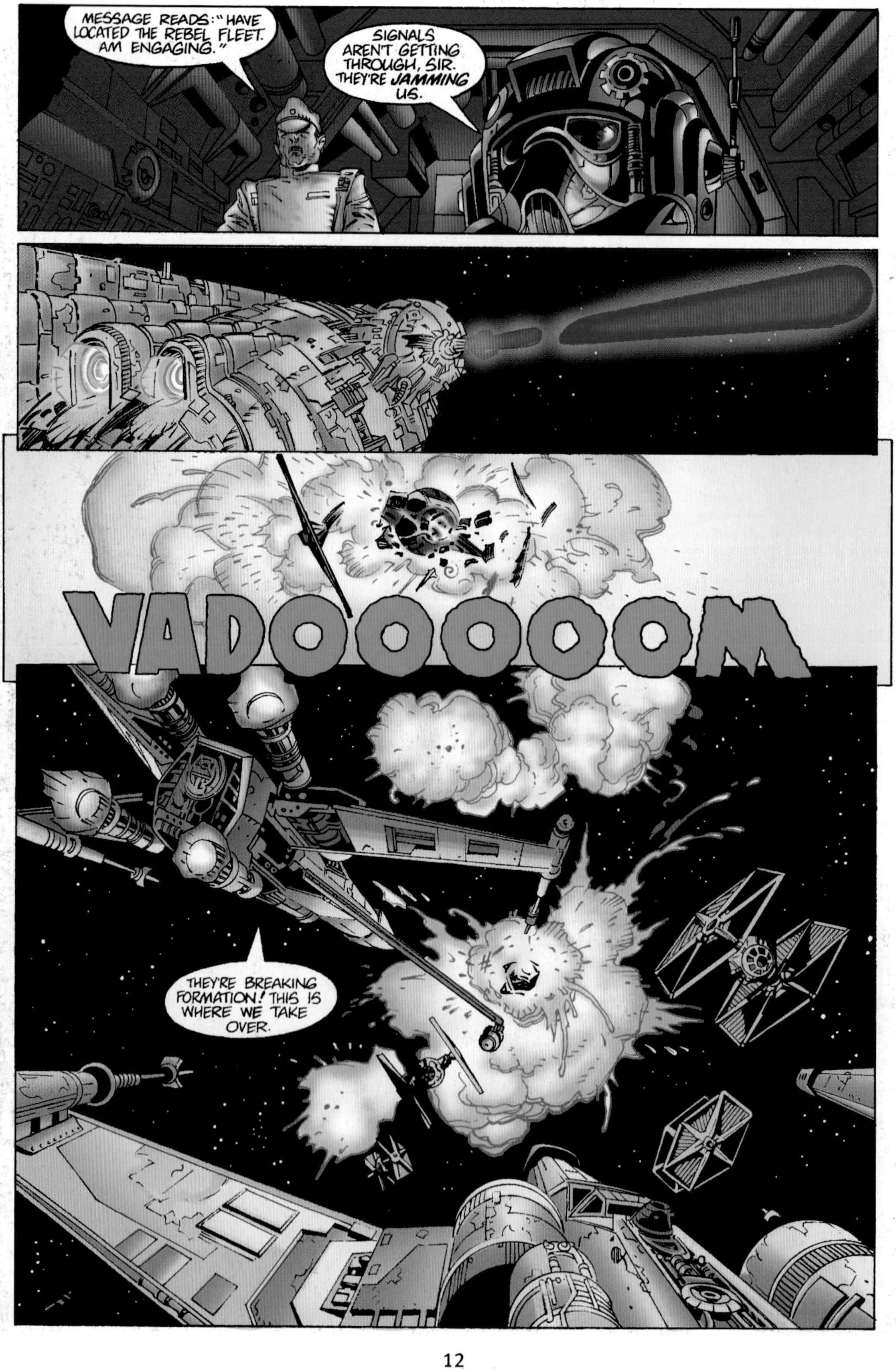
MESSAGE READS: "HAVE LOCATED THE REBEL FLEET. AM ENGAGING."
SIGNALS AREN'T GETTING THROUGH, SIR. THEY'RE JAMMING US.
VADOOOOOM
THEY'RE BREAKING FORMATION! THIS IS WHERE WE TAKE OVER.

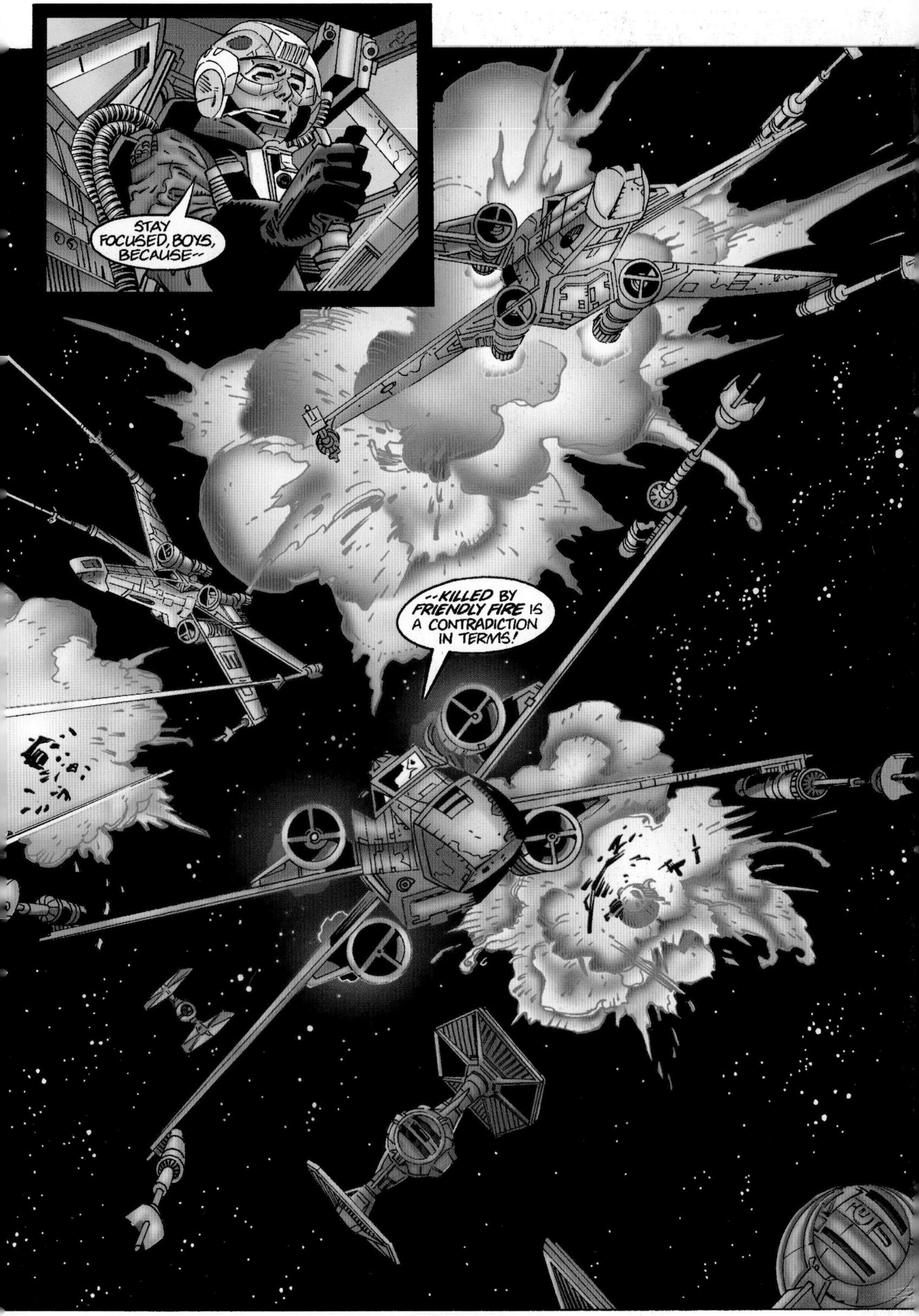
STAY FOCUSED, BOYS, BECAUSE--
--KILLED BY FRIENDLY FIRE IS A CONTRADICTION IN TERMS!

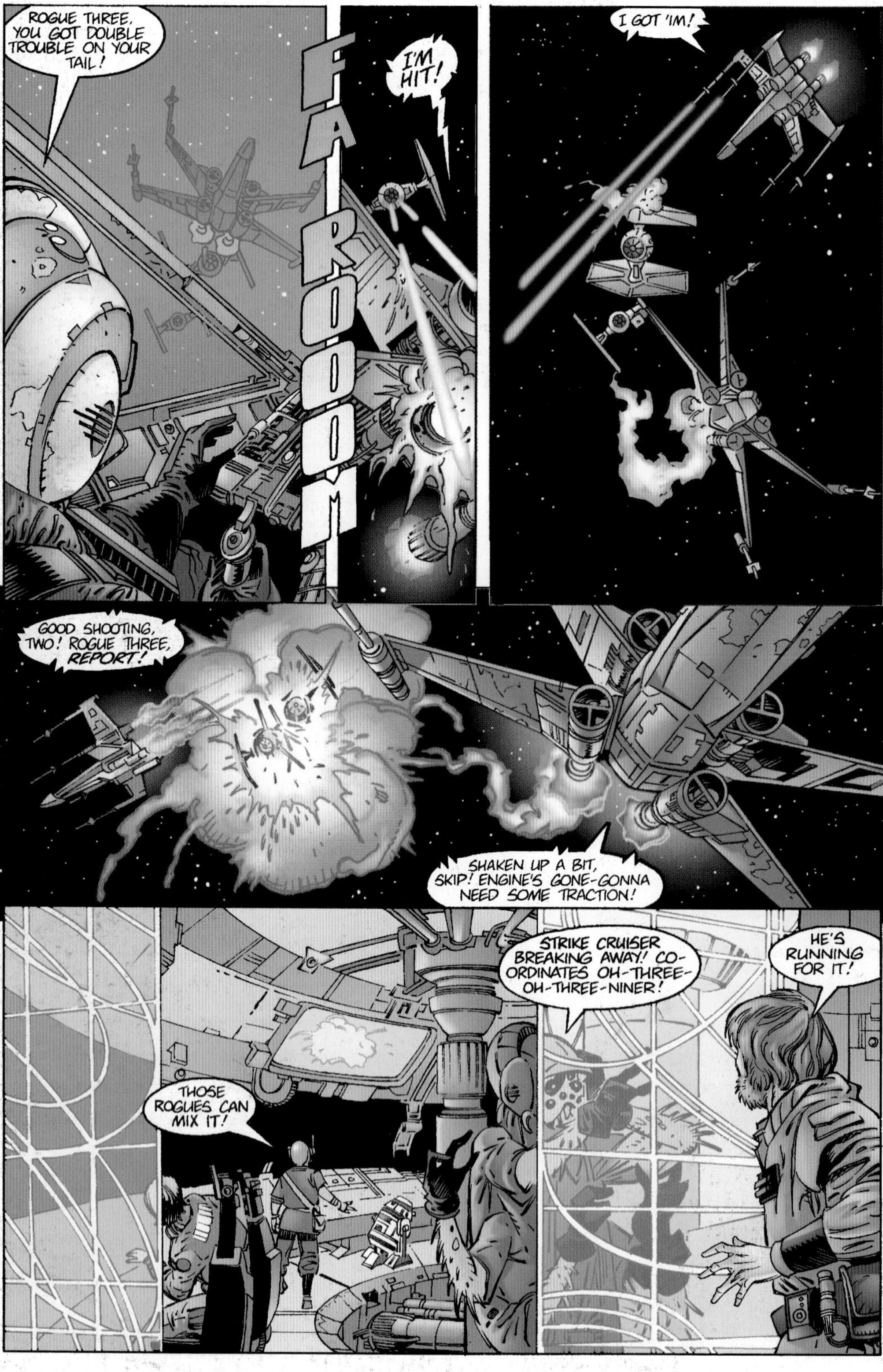
ROGUE THREE, YOU GOT DOUBLE TROUBLE ON YOUR TAIL!
FAROOOOM
I'M HIT!
I GOT 'IM!
GOOD SHOOTING, TWO! ROGUE THREE, REPORT!
SHAKEN UP A BIT, SKIP! ENGINE'S GONE-GONNA NEED SOME TRACTION!
THOSE ROGUES CAN MIX IT!
STRIKE CRUISER BREAKING AWAY! CO-ORDINATES OH-THREE-OH-THREE-NINER!
HE'S RUNNING FOR IT!

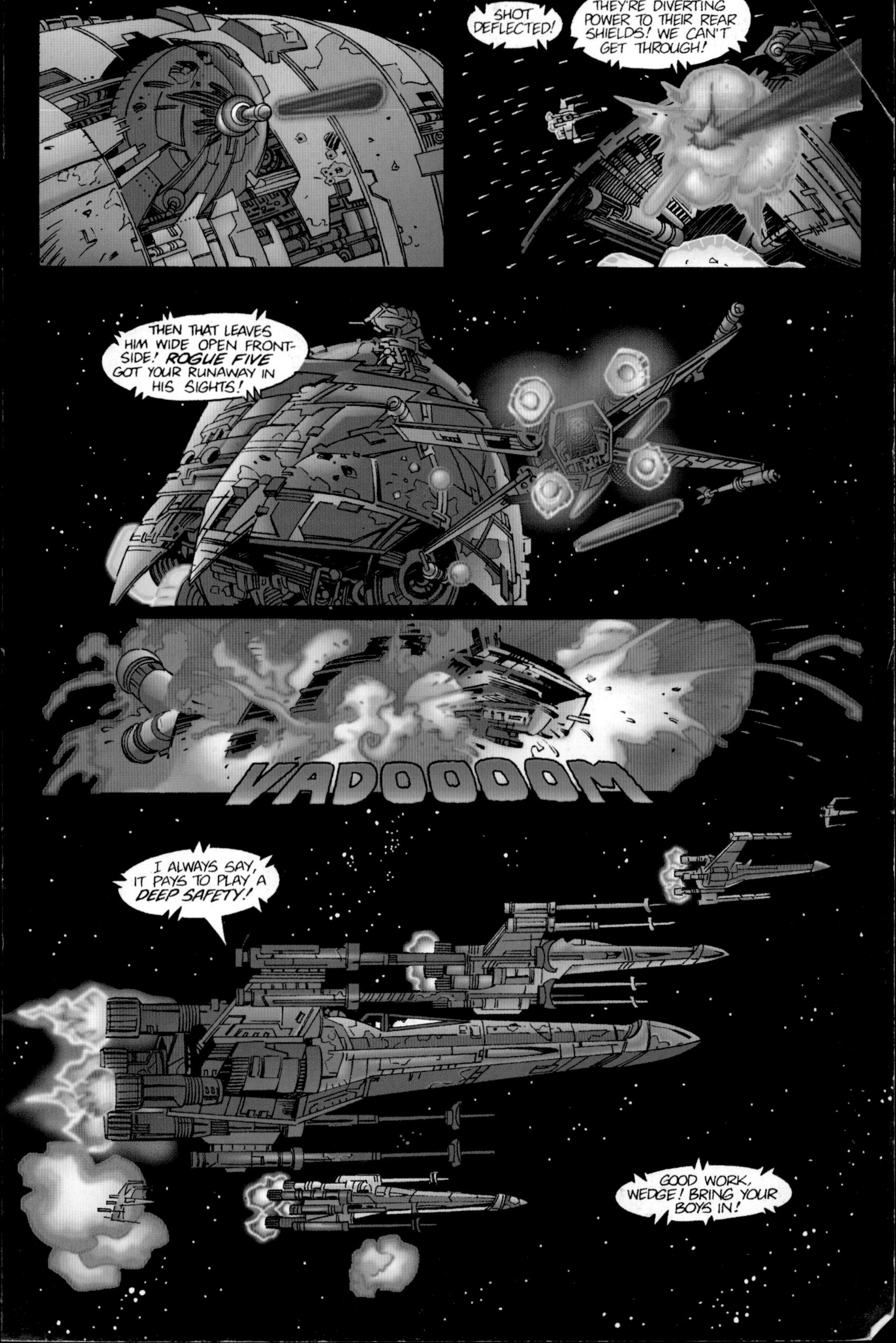
SHOT DEFLECTED!
THEY'RE DIVERTING POWER TO THEIR REAR SHIELDS! WE CAN'T GET THROUGH!
THEN THAT LEAVES HIM WIDE OPEN FRONT-SIDE! ROGUE FIVE GOT YOUR RUNAWAY IN HIS SIGHTS!
VADOOOOM
I ALWAYS SAY, IT PAYS TO PLAY A DEEP SAFETY!
GOOD WORK, WEDGE! BRING YOUR BOYS IN!

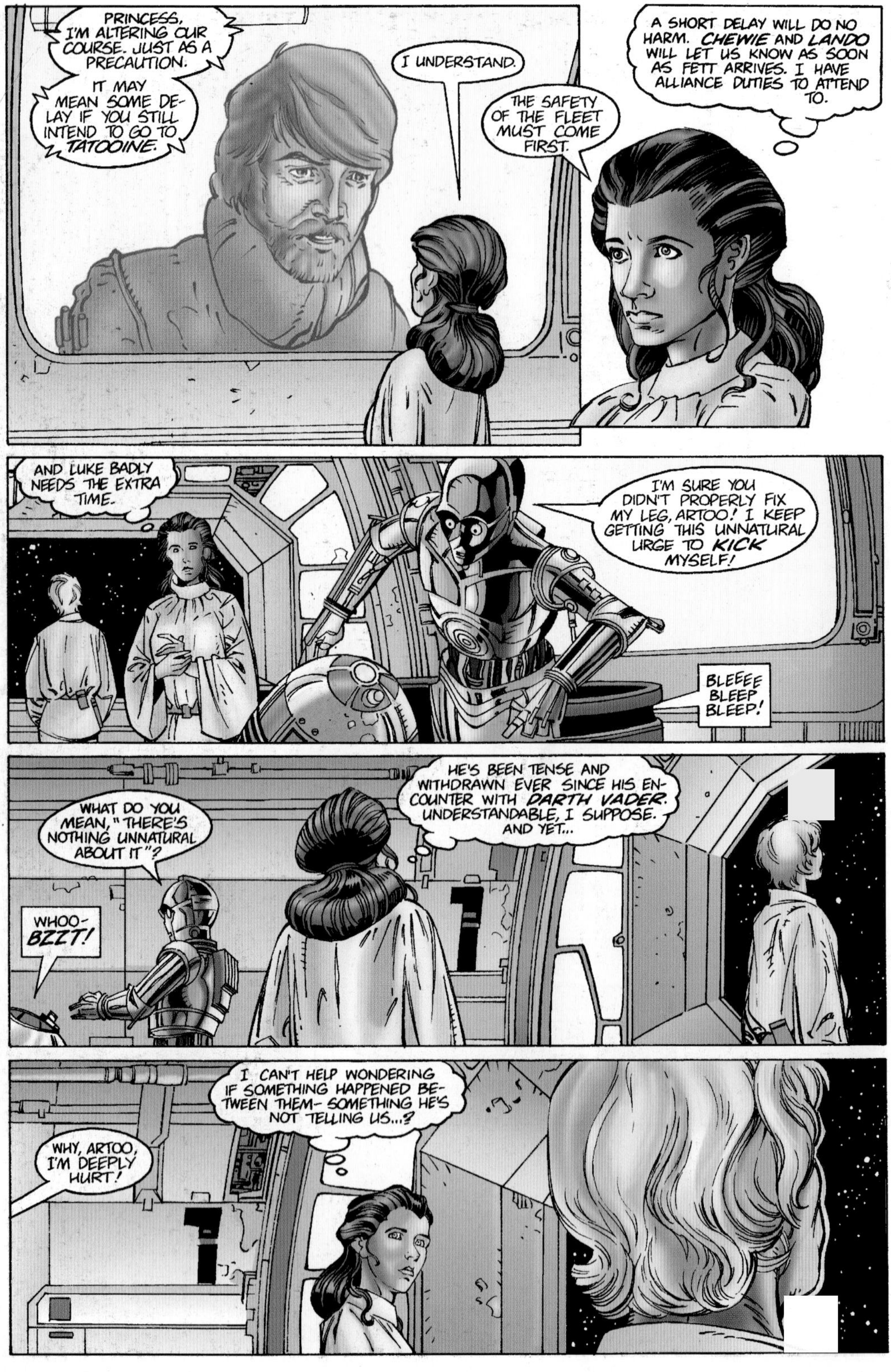
PRINCESS, I'M ALTERING OUR COURSE. JUST AS A PRECAUTION.
IT MAY MEAN SOME DELAY IF YOU STILL INTEND TO GO TO TATOOINE.
I UNDERSTAND.
THE SAFETY OF THE FLEET MUST COME FIRST.
A SHORT DELAY WILL DO NO HARM. CHEWIE AND LANDO WILL LET US KNOW AS SOON AS FETT ARRIVES. I HAVE ALLIANCE DUTIES TO ATTEND TO.
AND LUKE BADLY NEEDS THE EXTRA TIME.
I'M SURE YOU DIDN'T PROPERLY FIX MY LEG, ARTOO! I KEEP GETTING THIS UNNATURAL URGE TO KICK MYSELF!
BLEEEE BLEEP BLEEP!
WHAT DO YOU MEAN, "THERE'S NOTHING UNNATURAL ABOUT IT"?
HE'S BEEN TENSE AND WITHDRAWN EVER SINCE HIS ENCOUNTER WITH DARTH VADER. UNDERSTANDABLE, I SUPPOSE. AND YET...
WHOO-BZZT!
I CAN'T HELP WONDERING IF SOMETHING HAPPENED BETWEEN THEM- SOMETHING HE'S NOT TELLING US...?
WHY, ARTOO, I'M DEEPLY HURT!

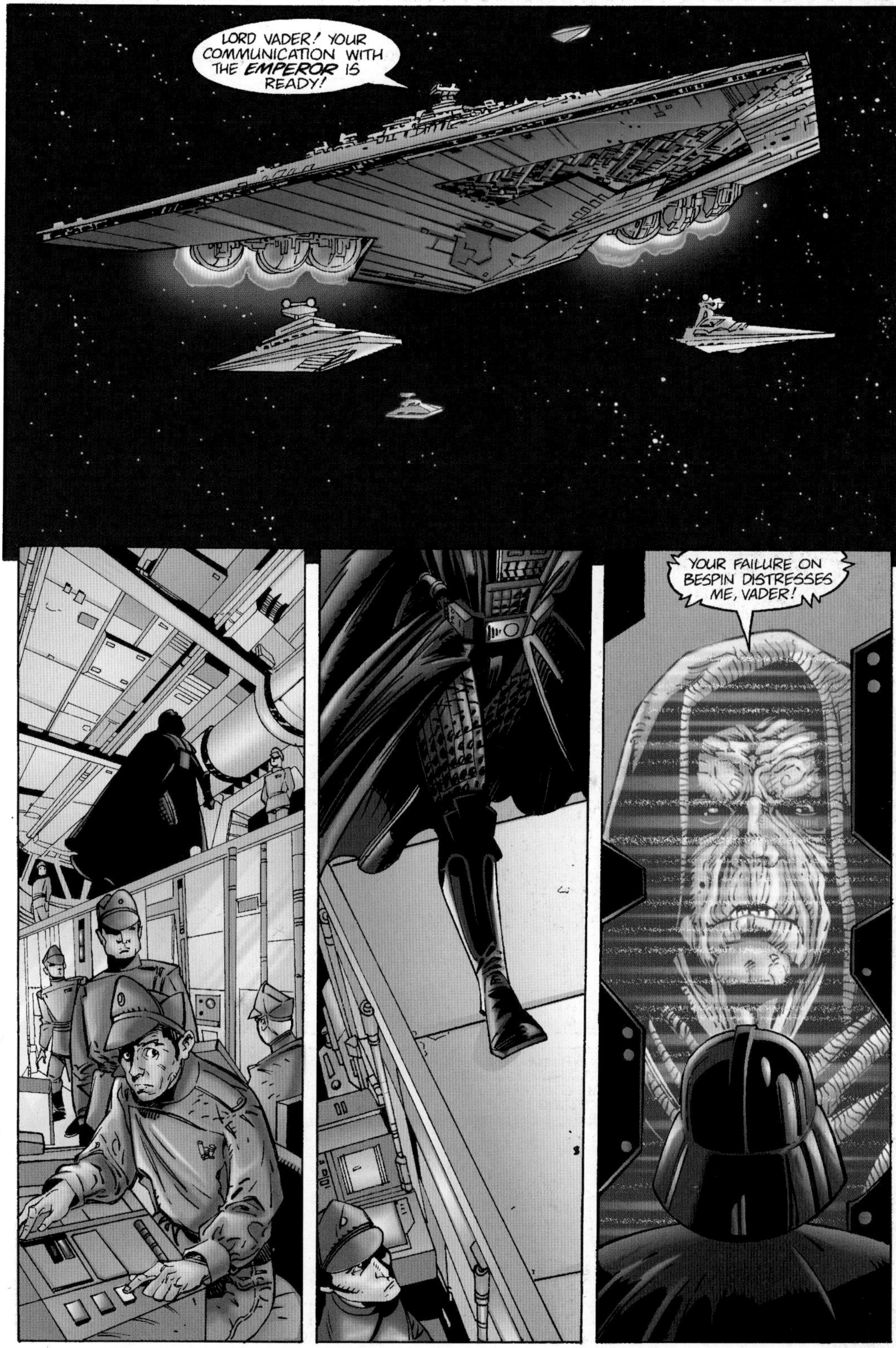
LORD VADER! YOUR COMMUNICATION WITH THE EMPEROR IS READY!
YOUR FAILURE ON BESPIN DISTRESSES ME, VADER!

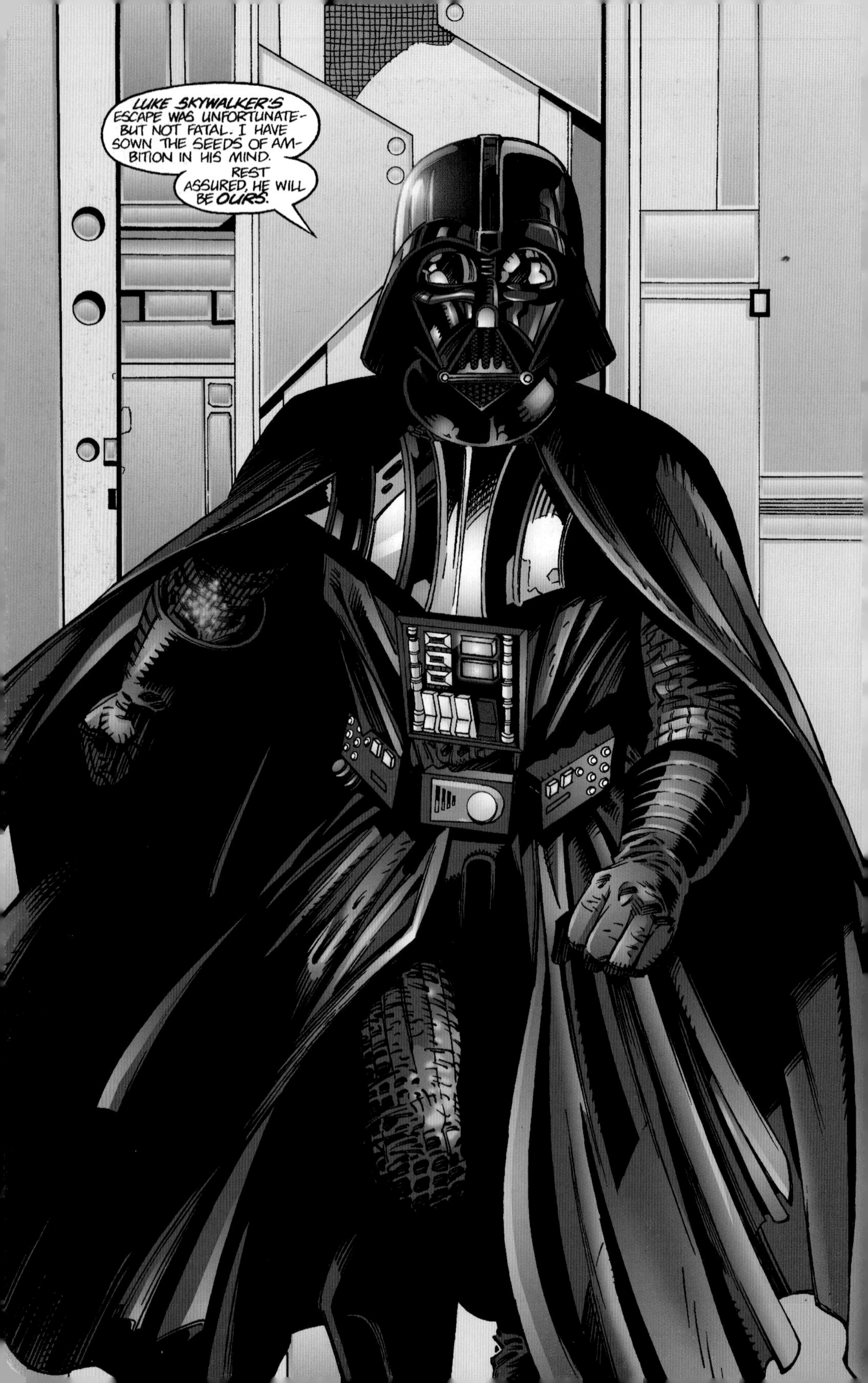
LUKE SKYWALKER'S ESCAPE WAS UNFORTUNATE-BUT NOT FATAL. I HAVE SOWN THE SEEDS OF AMBITION IN HIS MIND.
REST ASSURED, HE WILL BE OURS.

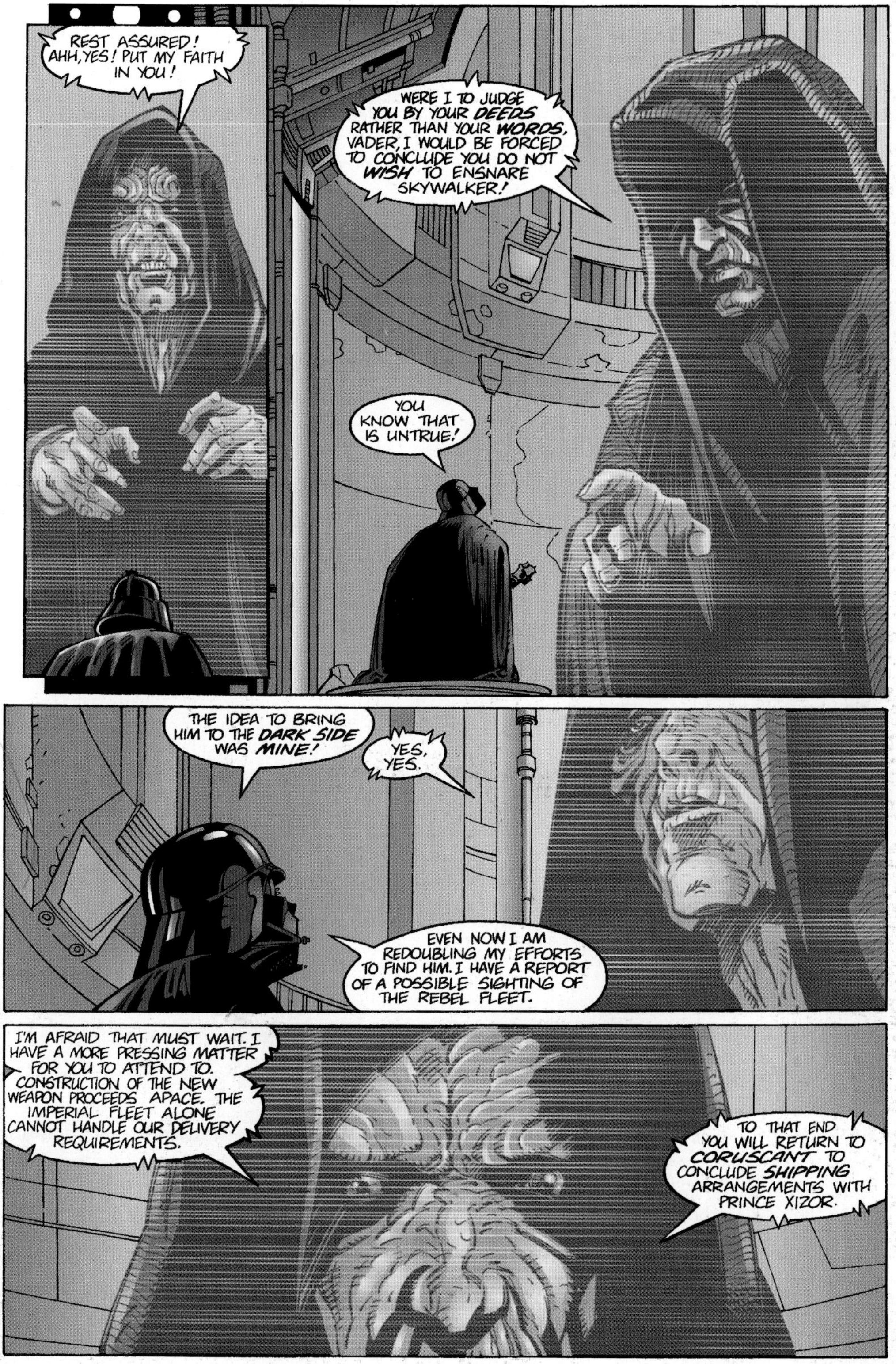
REST ASSURED! AHH, YES! PUT MY FAITH IN YOU!
WERE I TO JUDGE YOU BY YOUR DEEDS RATHER THAN YOUR WORDS, VADER, I WOULD BE FORCED TO CONCLUDE YOU DO NOT WISH TO ENSNARE SKYWALKER!
YOU KNOW THAT IS UNTRUE!
THE IDEA TO BRING HIM TO THE DARK SIDE WAS MINE!
YES, YES.
EVEN NOW I AM REDOUBLING MY EFFORTS TO FIND HIM. I HAVE A REPORT OF A POSSIBLE SIGHTING OF THE REBEL FLEET.
I'M AFRAID THAT MUST WAIT. I HAVE A MORE PRESSING MATTER FOR YOU TO ATTEND TO. CONSTRUCTION OF THE NEW WEAPON PROCEEDS APACE. THE IMPERIAL FLEET ALONE CANNOT HANDLE OUR DELIVERY REQUIREMENTS.
TO THAT END YOU WILL RETURN TO CORUSCANT TO CONCLUDE SHIPPING ARRANGEMENTS WITH PRINCE XIZOR.

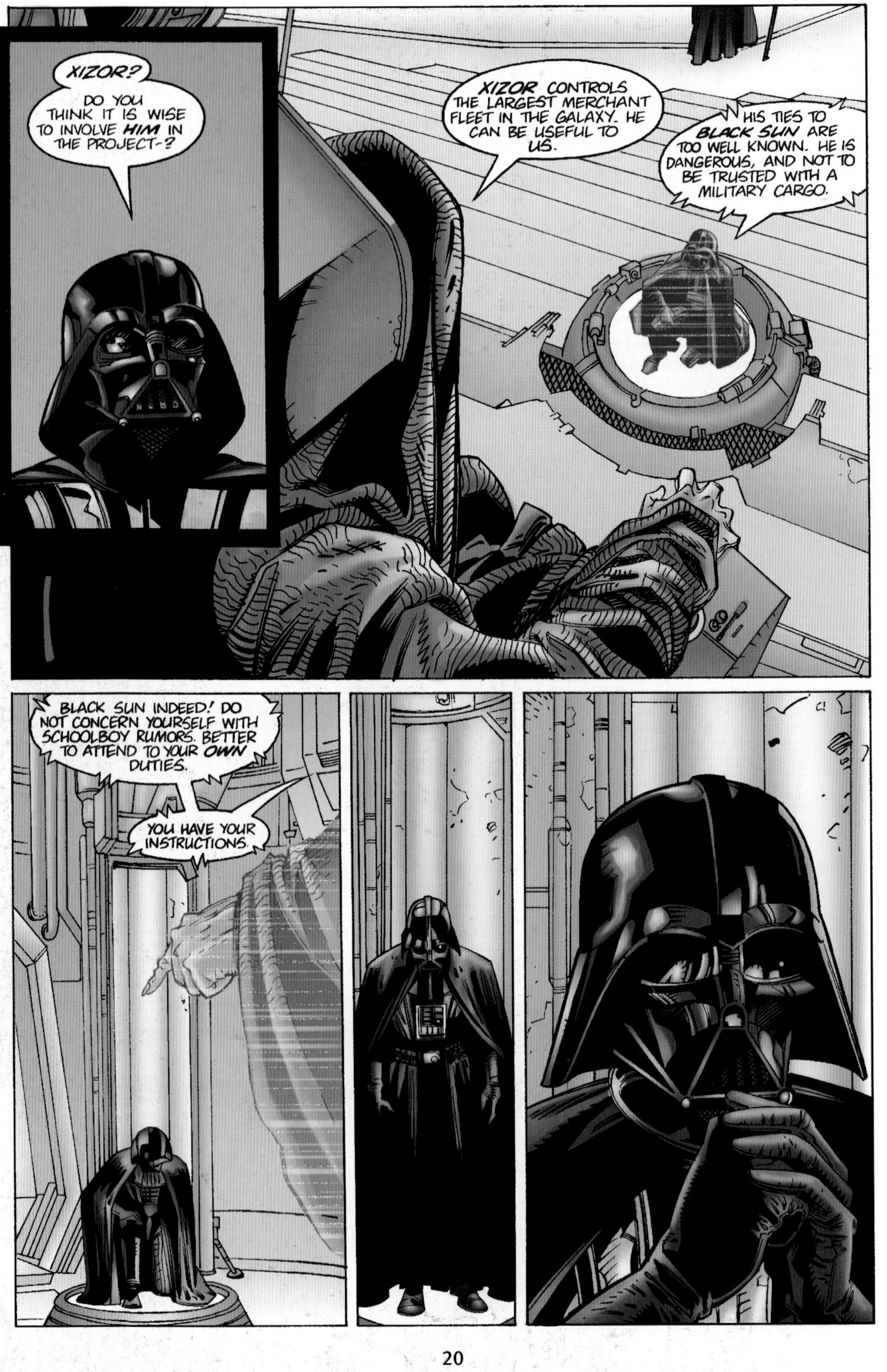
XIZOR?
DO YOU THINK IT IS WISE TO INVOLVE HIM IN THE PROJECT-?
XIZOR CONTROLS THE LARGEST MERCHANT FLEET IN THE GALAXY. HE CAN BE USEFUL TO US.
HIS TIES TO BLACK SUN ARE TOO WELL KNOWN. HE IS DANGEROUS, AND NOT TO BE TRUSTED WITH A MILITARY CARGO.
BLACK SUN INDEED! DO NOT CONCERN YOURSELF WITH SCHOOLBOY RUMORS. BETTER TO ATTEND TO YOUR OWN DUTIES.
YOU HAVE YOUR INSTRUCTIONS.

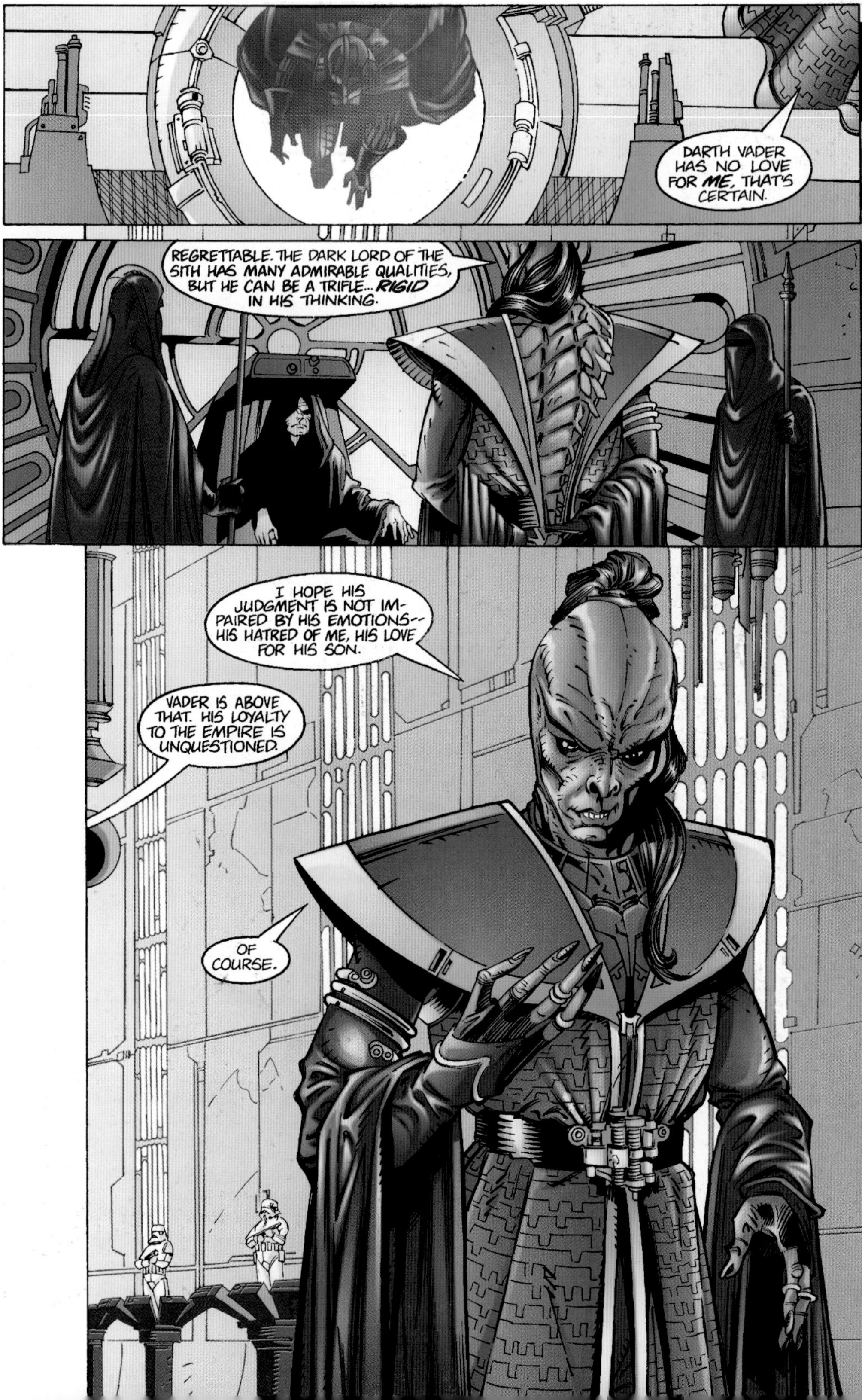
DARTH VADER HAS NO LOVE FOR *ME*, THAT'S CERTAIN.
REGRETTABLE. THE DARK LORD OF THE SITH HAS MANY ADMIRABLE QUALITIES, BUT HE CAN BE A TRIFLE... *RIGID* IN HIS THINKING.
I HOPE HIS JUDGMENT IS NOT IMPAIRED BY HIS EMOTIONS-- HIS HATRED OF ME, HIS LOVE FOR HIS SON.
VADER IS ABOVE THAT. HIS LOYALTY TO THE EMPIRE IS UNQUESTIONED.
OF COURSE.

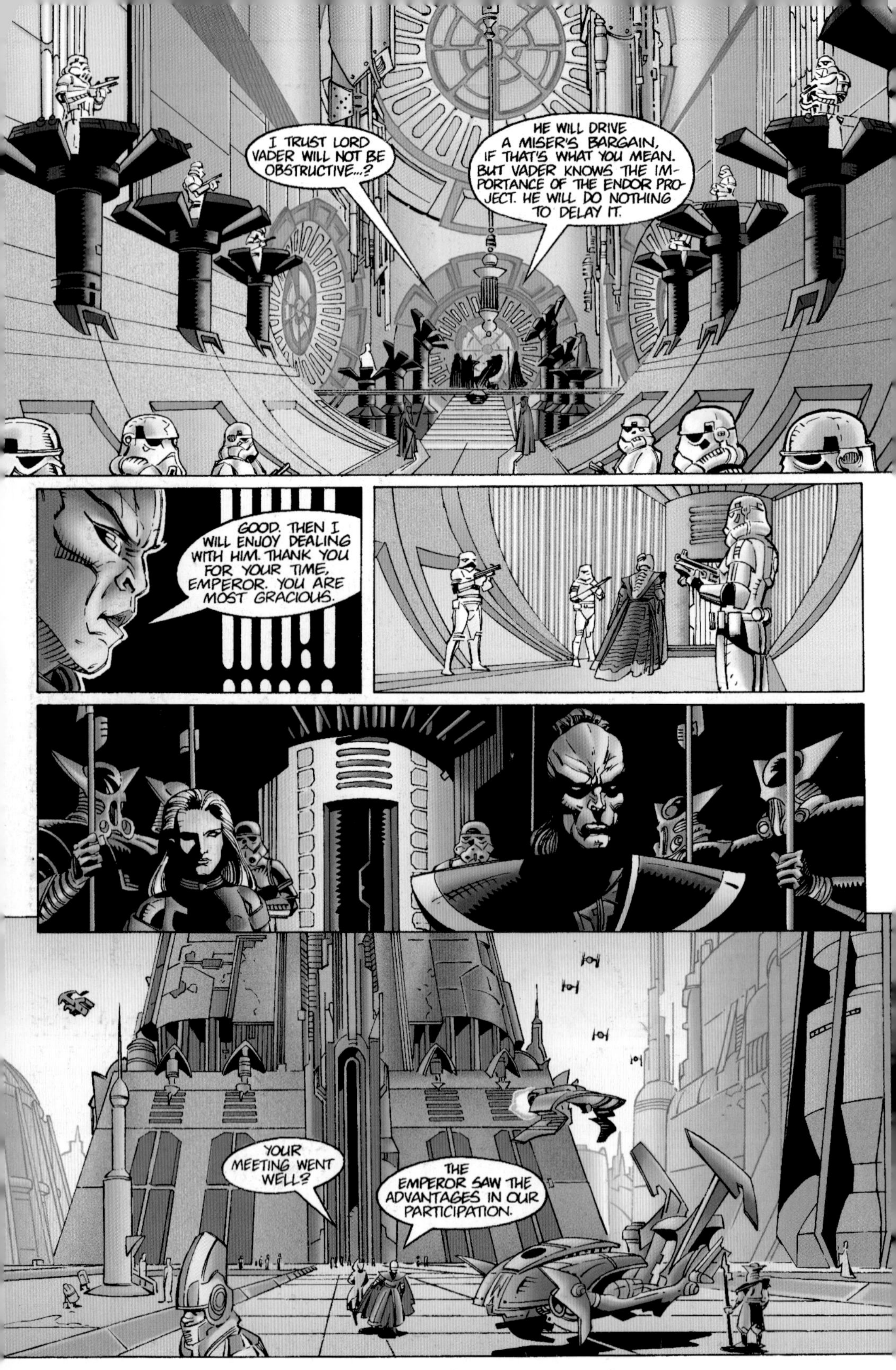
I TRUST LORD VADER WILL NOT BE OBSTRUCTIVE...?
HE WILL DRIVE A MISER'S BARGAIN, IF THAT'S WHAT YOU MEAN. BUT VADER KNOWS THE IMPORTANCE OF THE ENDOR PROJECT. HE WILL DO NOTHING TO DELAY IT.
GOOD. THEN I WILL ENJOY DEALING WITH HIM. THANK YOU FOR YOUR TIME, EMPEROR. YOU ARE MOST GRACIOUS.
YOUR MEETING WENT WELL?
THE EMPEROR SAW THE ADVANTAGES IN OUR PARTICIPATION.

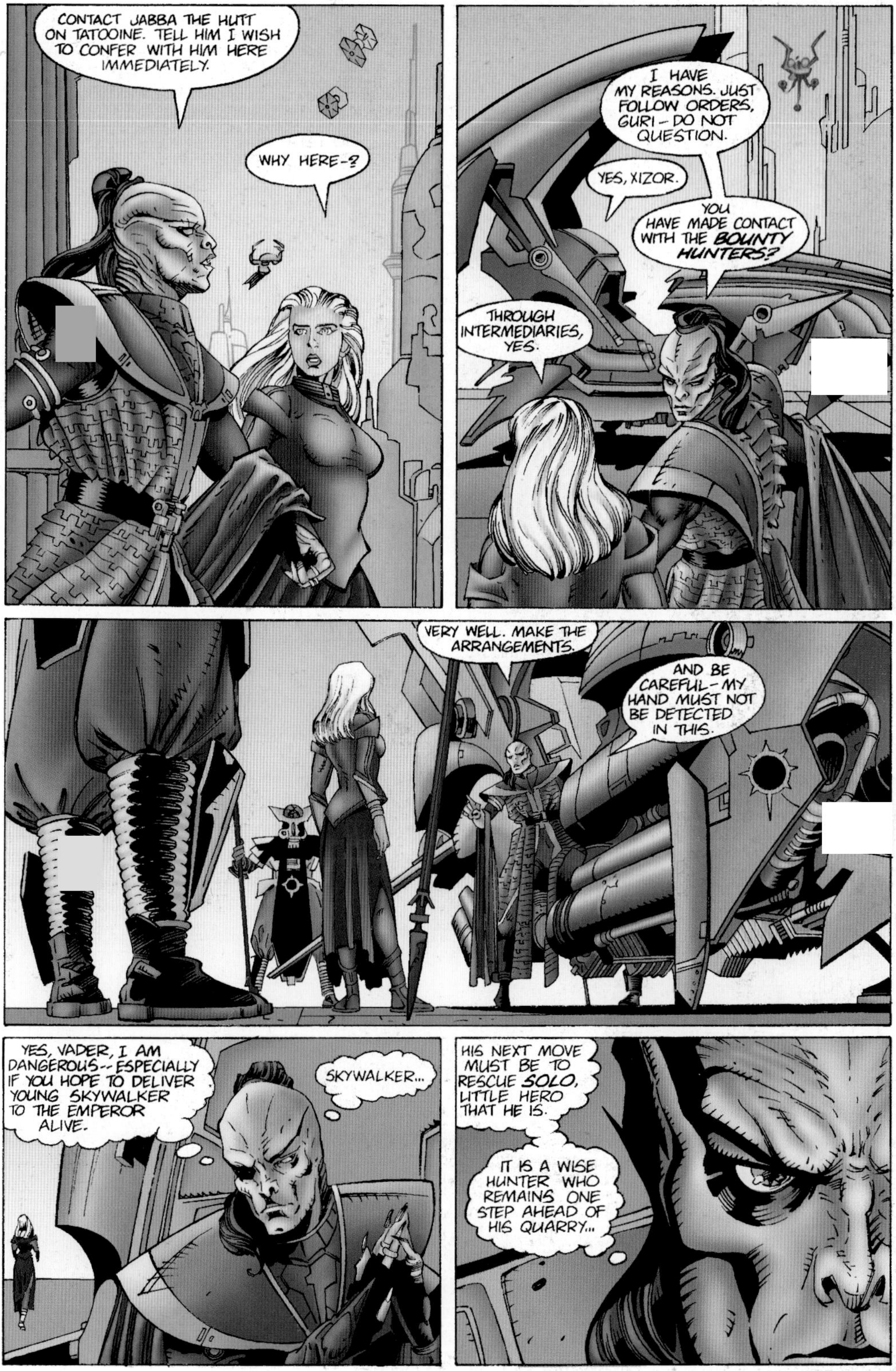
CONTACT JABBA THE HUTT ON TATOOINE. TELL HIM I WISH TO CONFER WITH HIM HERE IMMEDIATELY.
WHY HERE-?
I HAVE MY REASONS. JUST FOLLOW ORDERS, GURI-DO NOT QUESTION.
YES, XIZOR.
YOU HAVE MADE CONTACT WITH THE BOUNTY HUNTERS?
THROUGH INTERMEDIARIES, YES.
VERY WELL. MAKE THE ARRANGEMENTS.
AND BE CAREFUL-MY HAND MUST NOT BE DETECTED IN THIS.
YES, VADER, I AM DANGEROUS--ESPECIALLY IF YOU HOPE TO DELIVER YOUNG SKYWALKER TO THE EMPEROR ALIVE.
SKYWALKER...
HIS NEXT MOVE MUST BE TO RESCUE SOLO, LITTLE HERO THAT HE IS.
IT IS A WISE HUNTER WHO REMAINS ONE STEP AHEAD OF HIS QUARRY...

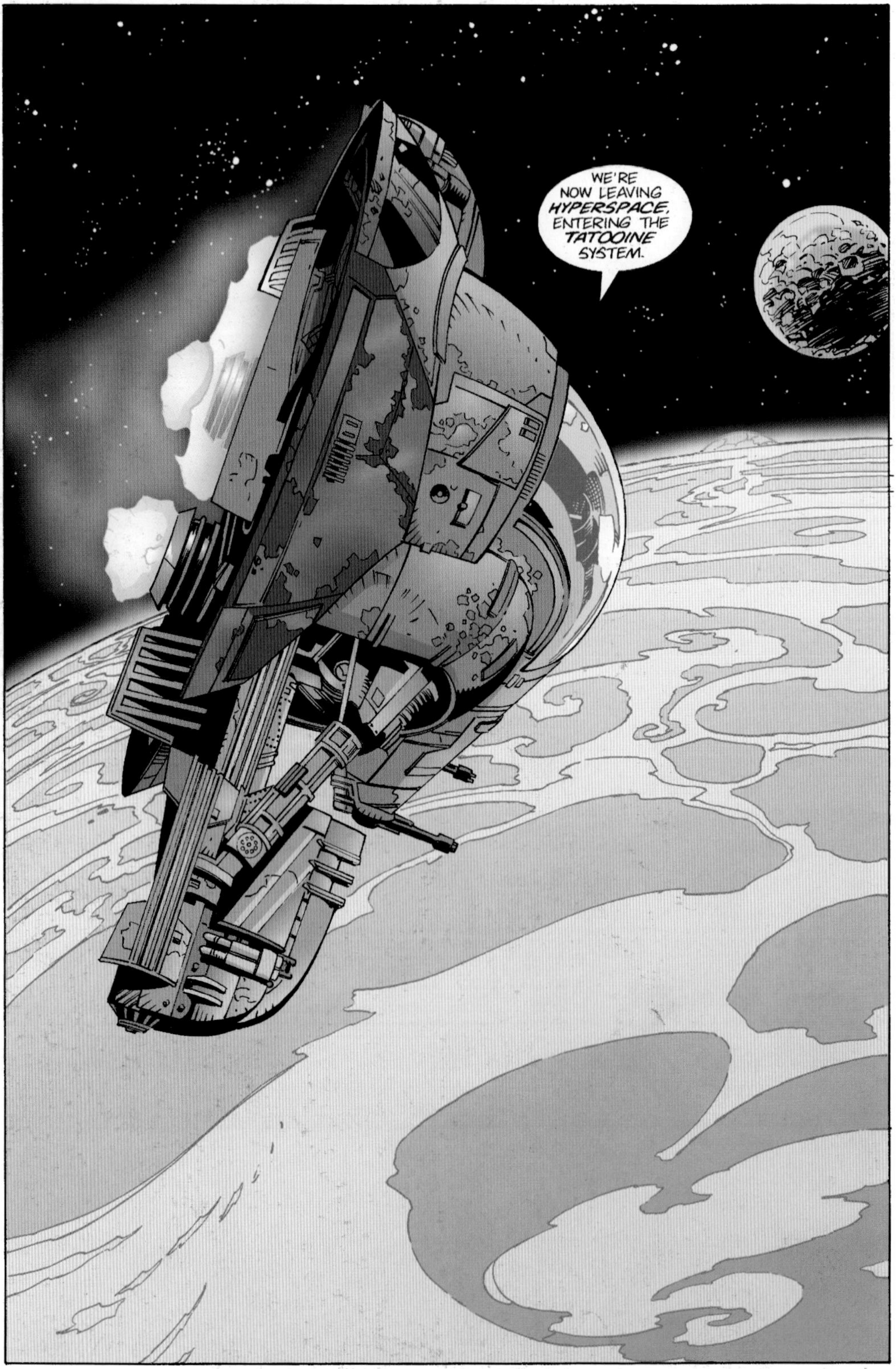
WE'RE NOW LEAVING HYPERSPACE, ENTERING THE TATOOINE SYSTEM.

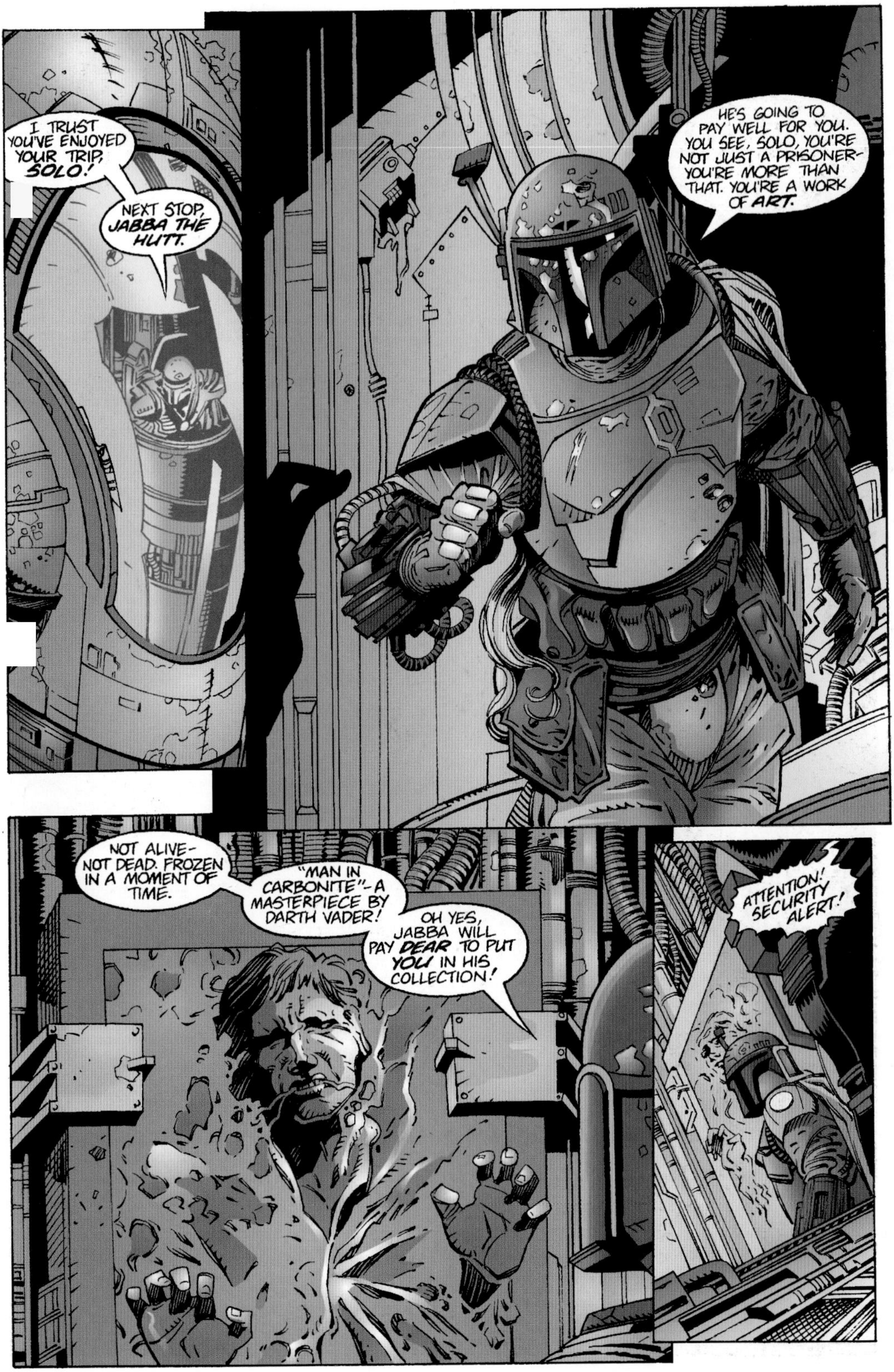
I TRUST YOU'VE ENJOYED YOUR TRIP, SOLO!
NEXT STOP, JABBA THE HUTT.
HE'S GOING TO PAY WELL FOR YOU. YOU SEE, SOLO, YOU'RE NOT JUST A PRISONER-- YOU'RE MORE THAN THAT. YOU'RE A WORK OF ART.
NOT ALIVE-- NOT DEAD. FROZEN IN A MOMENT OF TIME.
"MAN IN CARBONITE"-- A MASTERPIECE BY DARTH VADER!
OH YES, JABBA WILL PAY DEAR TO PUT YOU IN HIS COLLECTION!
ATTENTION! SECURITY ALERT!

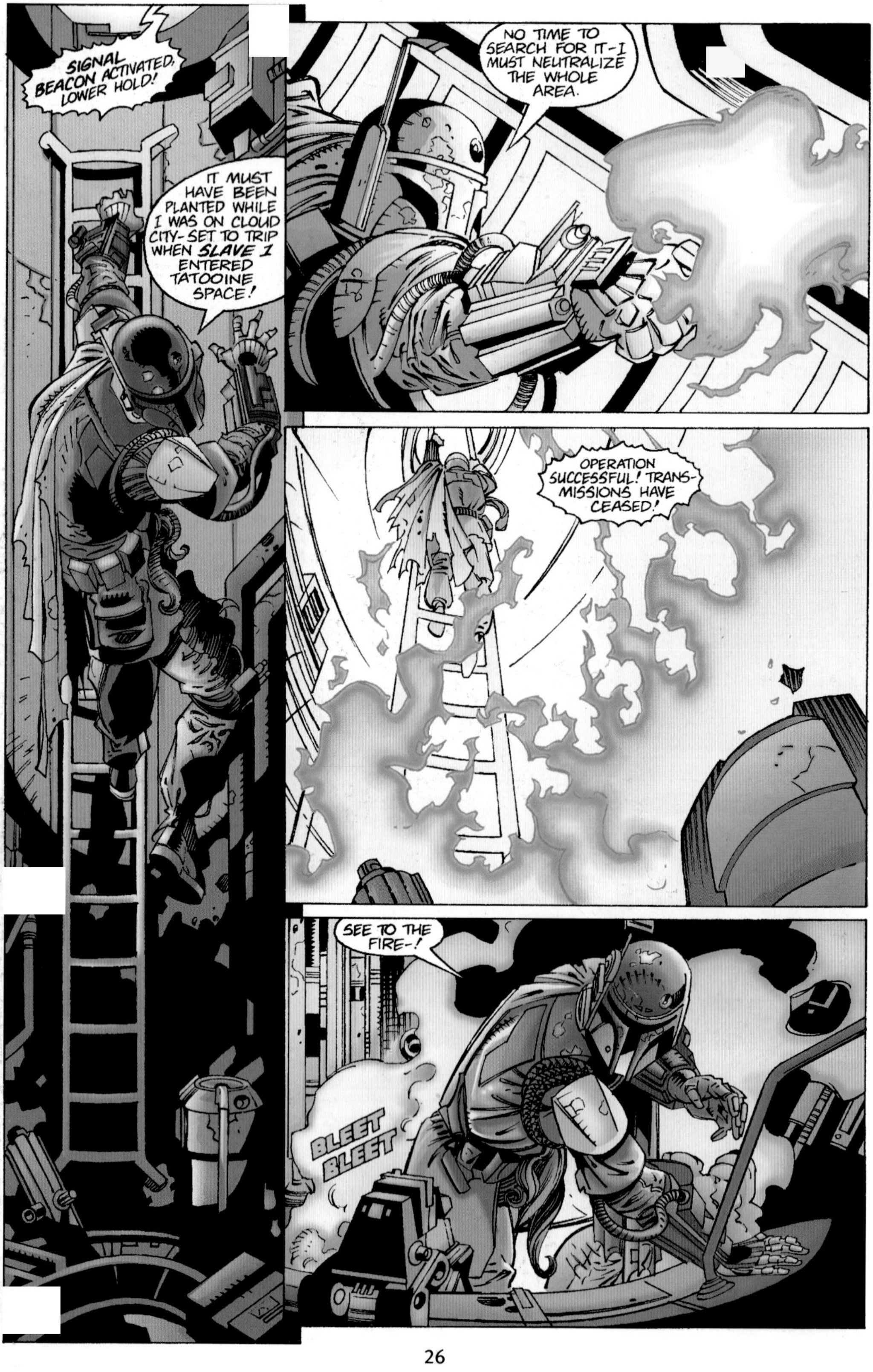
SIGNAL BEACON ACTIVATED, LOWER HOLD!
IT MUST HAVE BEEN PLANTED WHILE I WAS ON CLOUD CITY- SET TO TRIP WHEN SLAVE 1 ENTERED TATOOINE SPACE!
NO TIME TO SEARCH FOR IT- I MUST NEUTRALIZE THE WHOLE AREA.
OPERATION SUCCESSFUL! TRANSMISSIONS HAVE CEASED!
SEE TO THE FIRE-!
BLEET BLEET

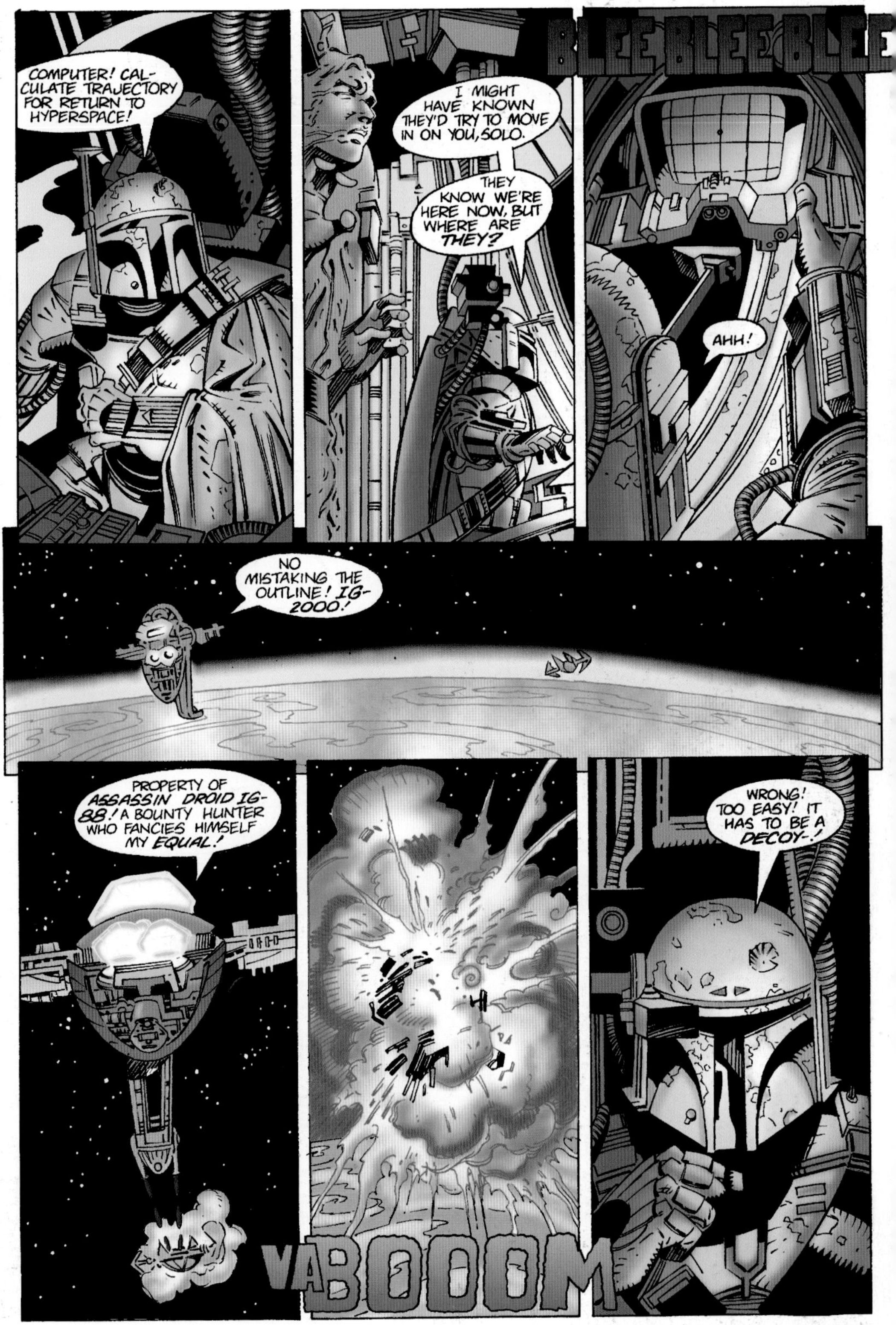
BLEE BLEE BLEE
COMPUTER! CALCULATE TRAJECTORY FOR RETURN TO HYPERSPACE!
I MIGHT HAVE KNOWN THEY'D TRY TO MOVE IN ON YOU, SOLO.
THEY KNOW WE'RE HERE NOW, BUT WHERE ARE THEY?
AHH!
NO MISTAKING THE OUTLINE! IG-2000!
PROPERTY OF ASSASSIN DROID IG-88! A BOUNTY HUNTER WHO FANCIES HIMSELF MY EQUAL!
VABOOOM
WRONG! TOO EASY! IT HAS TO BE A DECOY-!

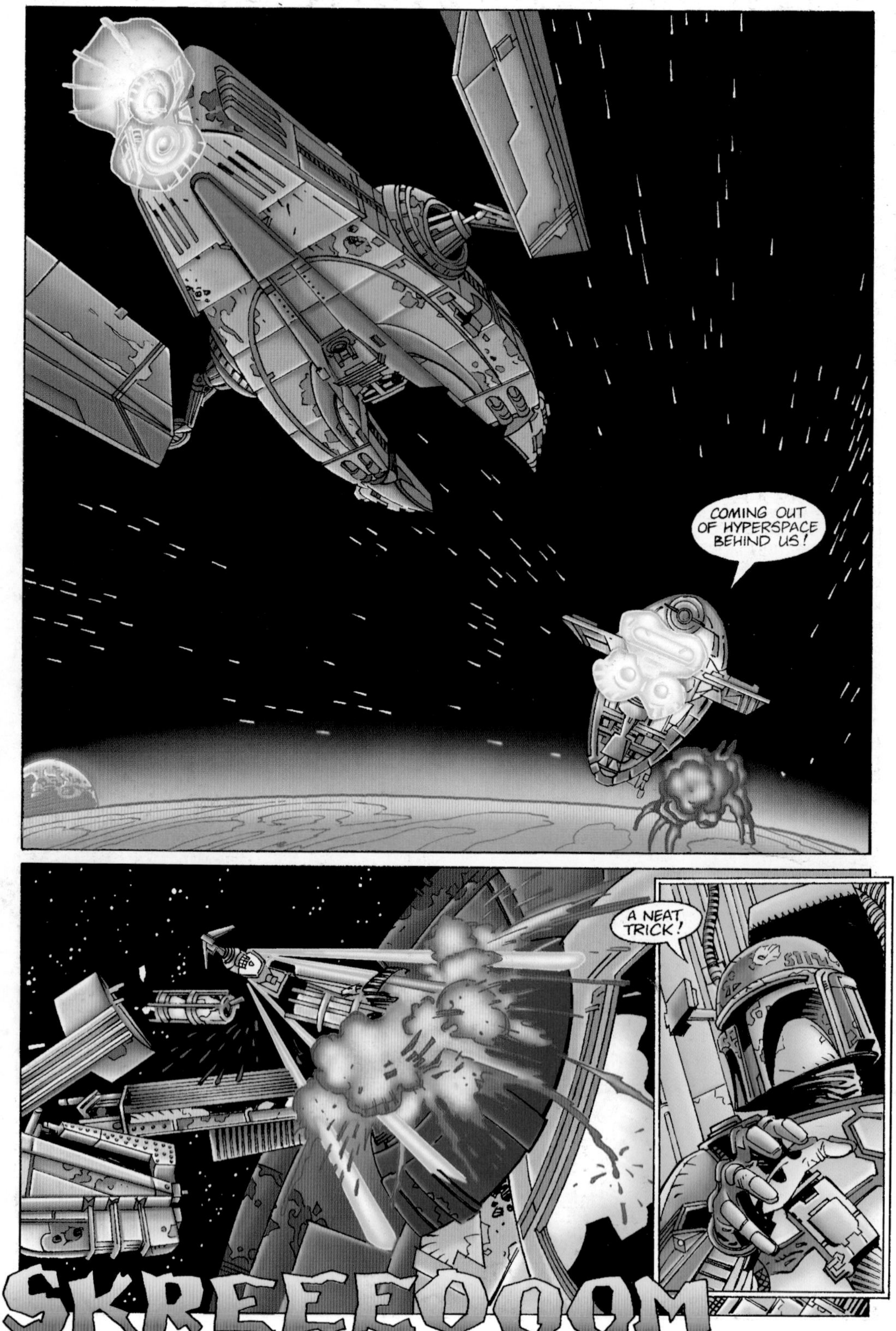
COMING OUT OF HYPERSPACE BEHIND US!
A NEAT TRICK!
SKREEEOOOM

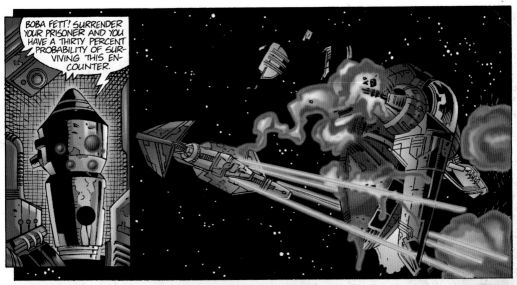

BOBA FETT! SURRENDER YOUR PRISONER AND YOU HAVE A THIRTY PERCENT PROBABILITY OF SURVIVING THIS ENCOUNTER.

YES, HE IS GOOD, THE DROID! BUT HE HAS A PROBLEM. DESTROY ME AND HE MAY LOSE YOU TOO, SOLO.

I AM FAR MORE CAPABLE OF WITHSTANDING THE GRAVOMETRIC PRESSURES THAN YOU. THIS TACTIC HAS A ZERO PROBABILITY CURVE FOR SUCCESS.

INERTIAL DAMPERS ON!

UNNNNHHHH!

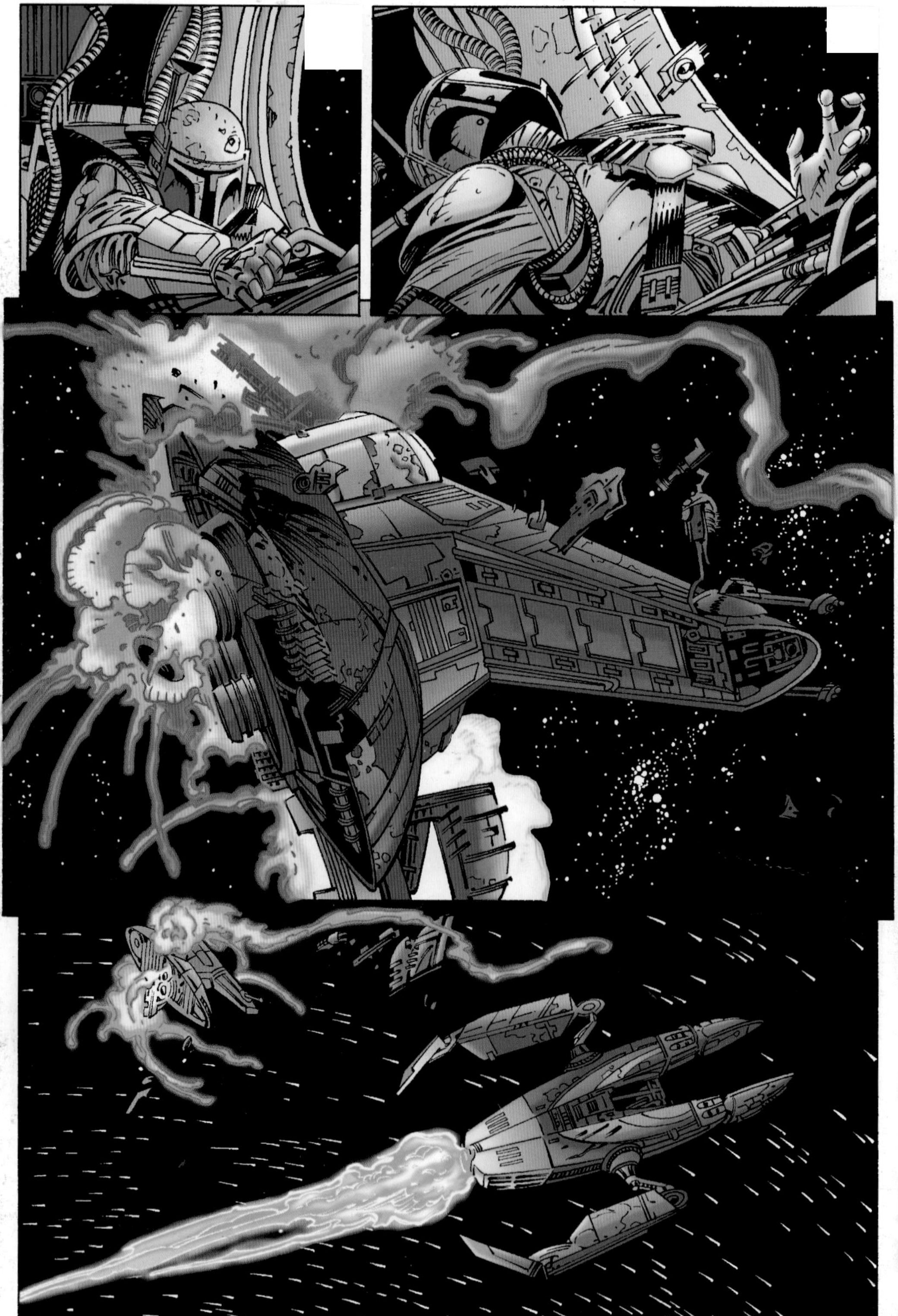

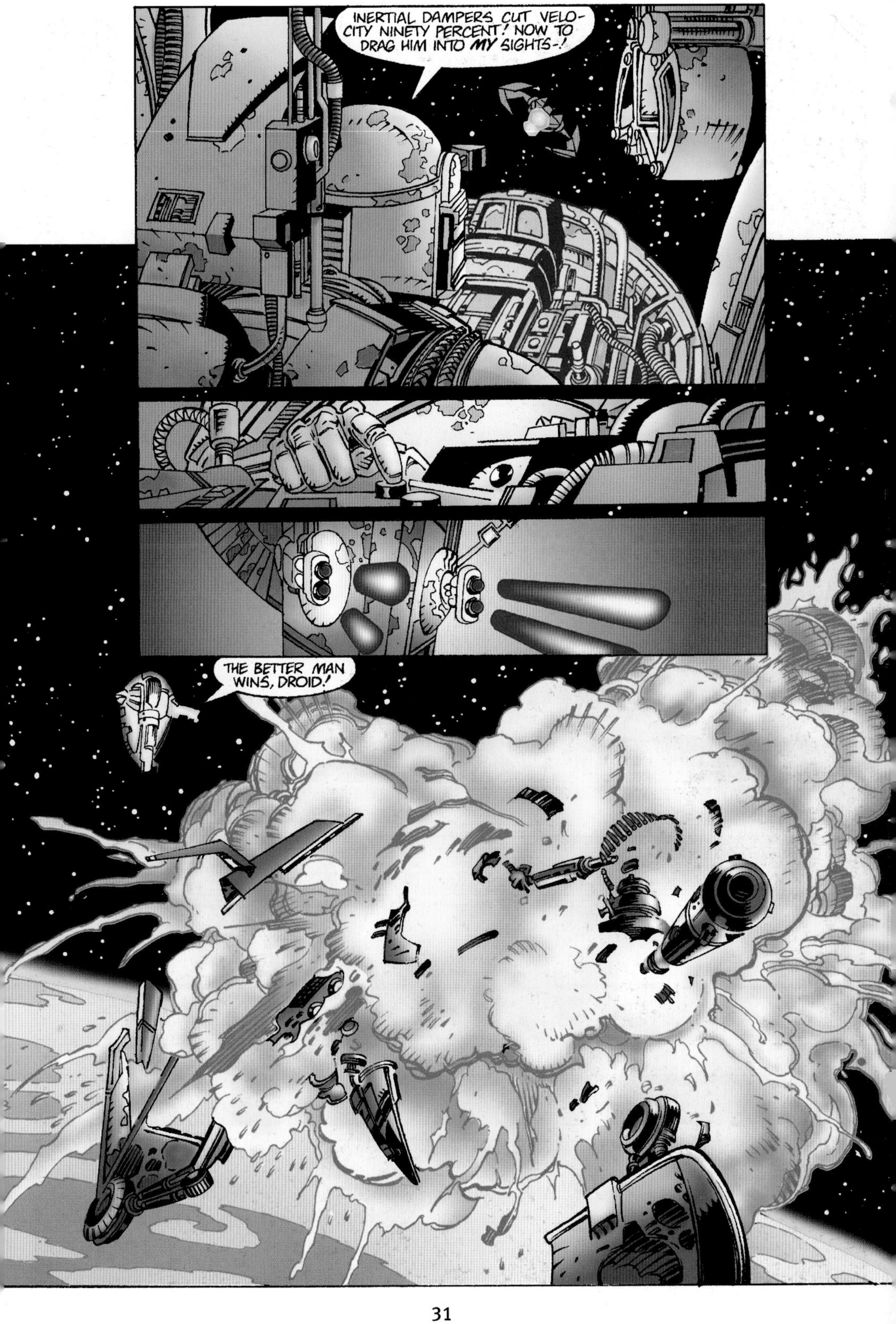
INERTIAL DAMPERS CUT VELOCITY NINETY PERCENT! NOW TO DRAG HIM INTO MY SIGHTS-!
THE BETTER MAN WINS, DROID!

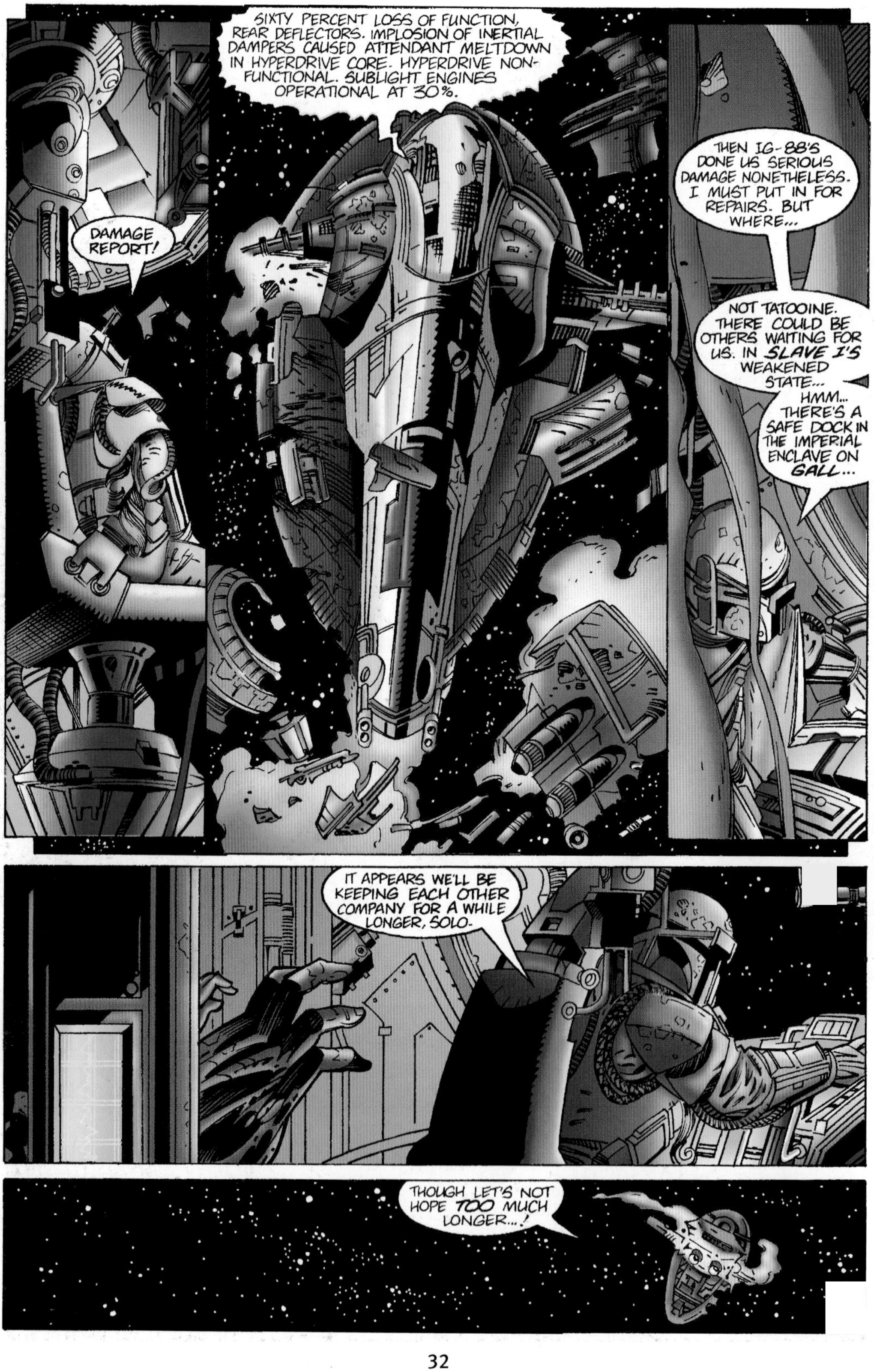
DAMAGE REPORT!
SIXTY PERCENT LOSS OF FUNCTION, REAR DEFLECTORS. IMPLOSION OF INERTIAL DAMPERS CAUSED ATTENDANT MELTDOWN IN HYPERDRIVE CORE. HYPERDRIVE NON-FUNCTIONAL. SUBLIGHT ENGINES OPERATIONAL AT 30%.
THEN IG-88'S DONE US SERIOUS DAMAGE NONETHELESS. I MUST PUT IN FOR REPAIRS. BUT WHERE...
NOT TATOOINE. THERE COULD BE OTHERS WAITING FOR US. IN SLAVE I'S WEAKENED STATE...
HMM... THERE'S A SAFE DOCK IN THE IMPERIAL ENCLAVE ON GALL...
IT APPEARS WE'LL BE KEEPING EACH OTHER COMPANY FOR A WHILE LONGER, SOLO.
THOUGH LET'S NOT HOPE TOO MUCH LONGER...!

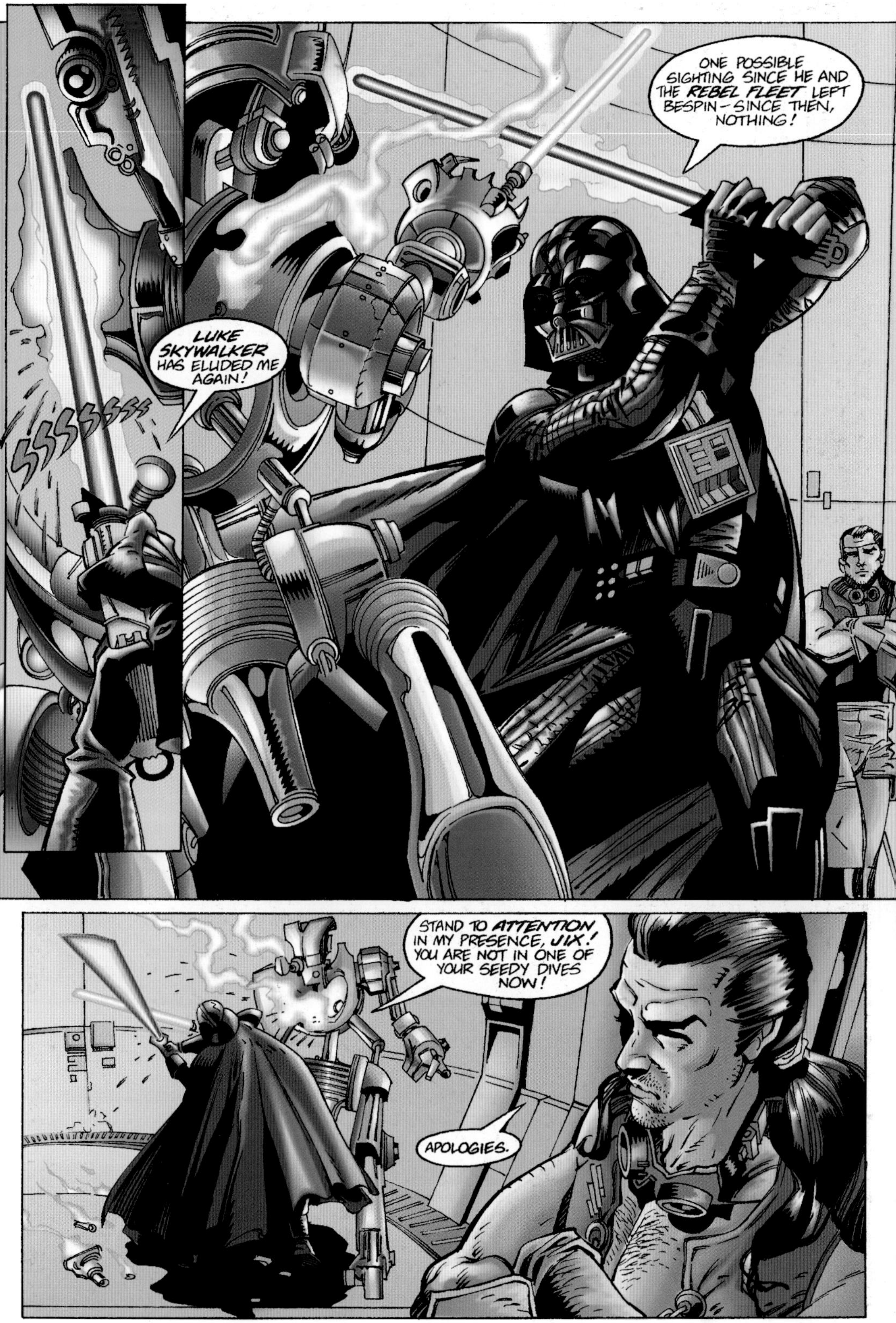
LUKE SKYWALKER HAS ELUDED ME AGAIN!
SSSSSSSSS
ONE POSSIBLE SIGHTING SINCE HE AND THE REBEL FLEET LEFT BESPIN-- SINCE THEN, NOTHING!
STAND TO ATTENTION IN MY PRESENCE, JIX! YOU ARE NOT IN ONE OF YOUR SEEDY DIVES NOW!
APOLOGIES.

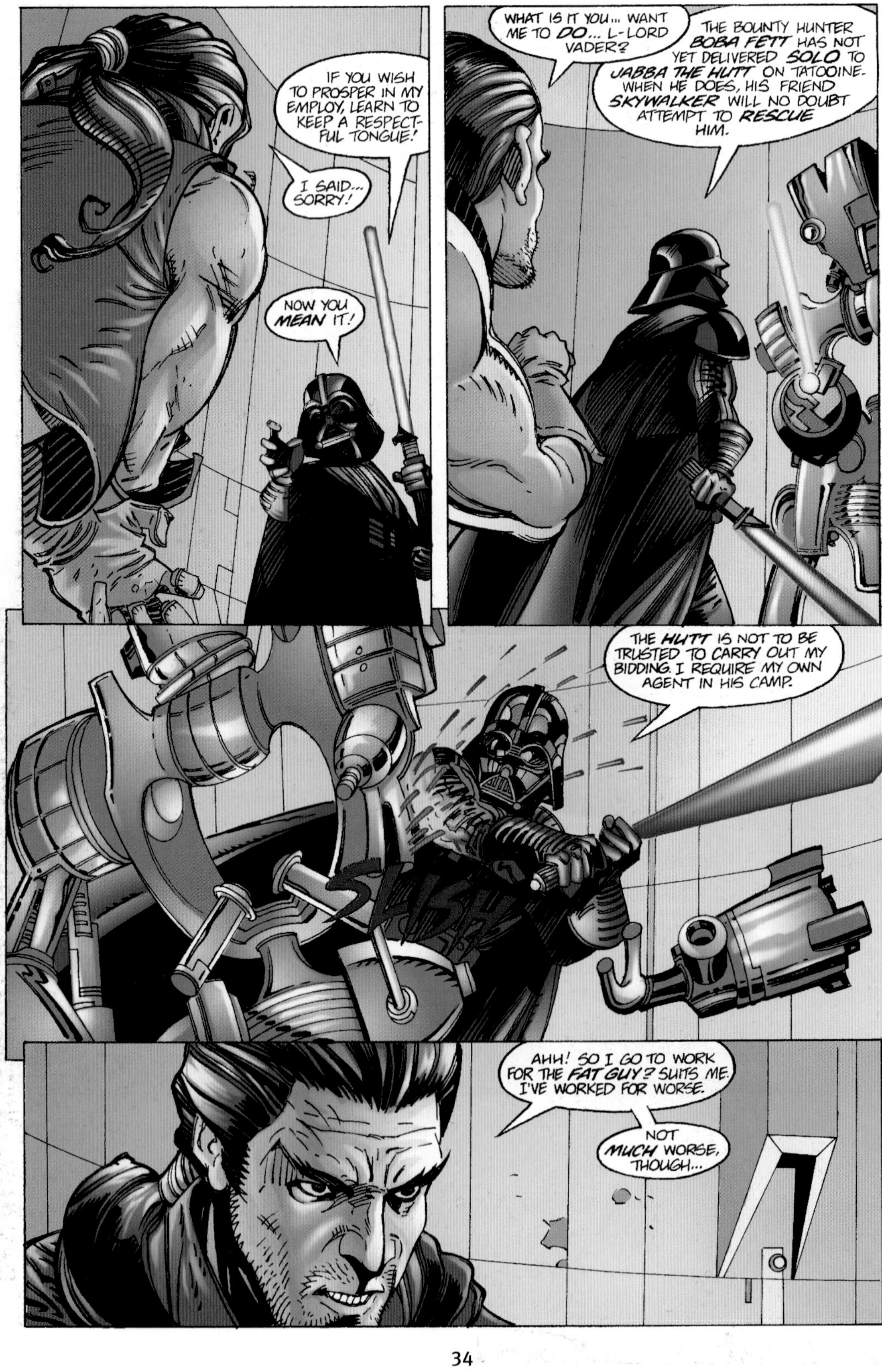
IF YOU WISH TO PROSPER IN MY EMPLOY, LEARN TO KEEP A RESPECTFUL TONGUE!
I SAID... SORRY!
NOW YOU MEAN IT!
WHAT IS IT YOU... WANT ME TO DO... L-LORD VADER?
THE BOUNTY HUNTER BOBA FETT HAS NOT YET DELIVERED SOLO TO JABBA THE HUTT ON TATOOINE. WHEN HE DOES, HIS FRIEND SKYWALKER WILL NO DOUBT ATTEMPT TO RESCUE HIM.
THE HUTT IS NOT TO BE TRUSTED TO CARRY OUT MY BIDDING. I REQUIRE MY OWN AGENT IN HIS CAMP.
AHH! SO I GO TO WORK FOR THE FAT GUY? SUITS ME. I'VE WORKED FOR WORSE.
NOT MUCH WORSE, THOUGH...

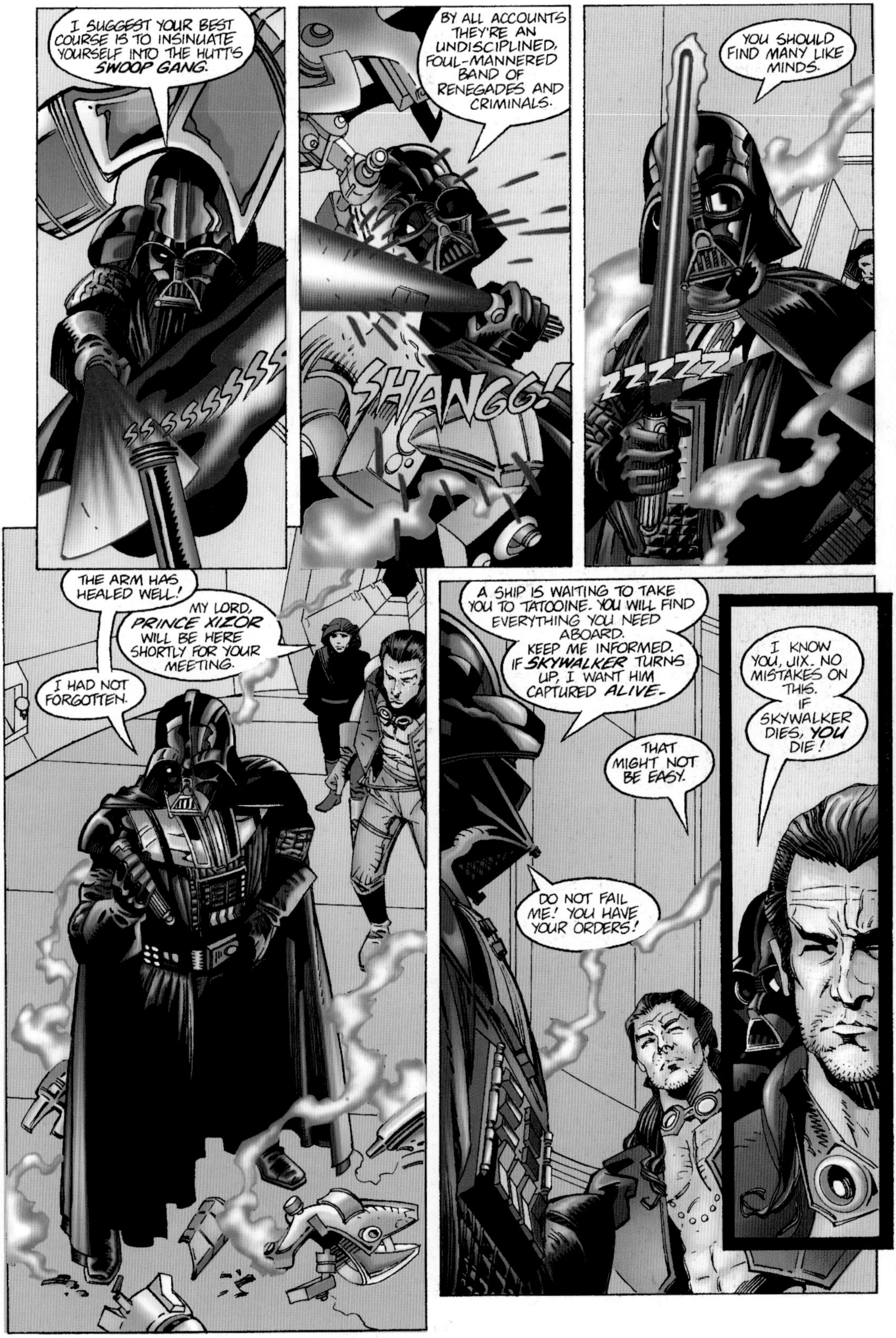
I SUGGEST YOUR BEST COURSE IS TO INSINUATE YOURSELF INTO THE HUTT'S SWOOP GANG.
SSSSSSSSSSSS
BY ALL ACCOUNTS THEY'RE AN UNDISCIPLINED, FOUL-MANNERED BAND OF RENEGADES AND CRIMINALS.
SHANGG!
YOU SHOULD FIND MANY LIKE MINDS.
ZZZZZ
THE ARM HAS HEALED WELL!
MY LORD, PRINCE XIZOR WILL BE HERE SHORTLY FOR YOUR MEETING.
I HAD NOT FORGOTTEN.
A SHIP IS WAITING TO TAKE YOU TO TATOOINE. YOU WILL FIND EVERYTHING YOU NEED ABOARD.
KEEP ME INFORMED. IF SKYWALKER TURNS UP, I WANT HIM CAPTURED ALIVE.
THAT MIGHT NOT BE EASY.
DO NOT FAIL ME! YOU HAVE YOUR ORDERS!
I KNOW YOU, JIX. NO MISTAKES ON THIS. IF SKYWALKER DIES, YOU DIE!

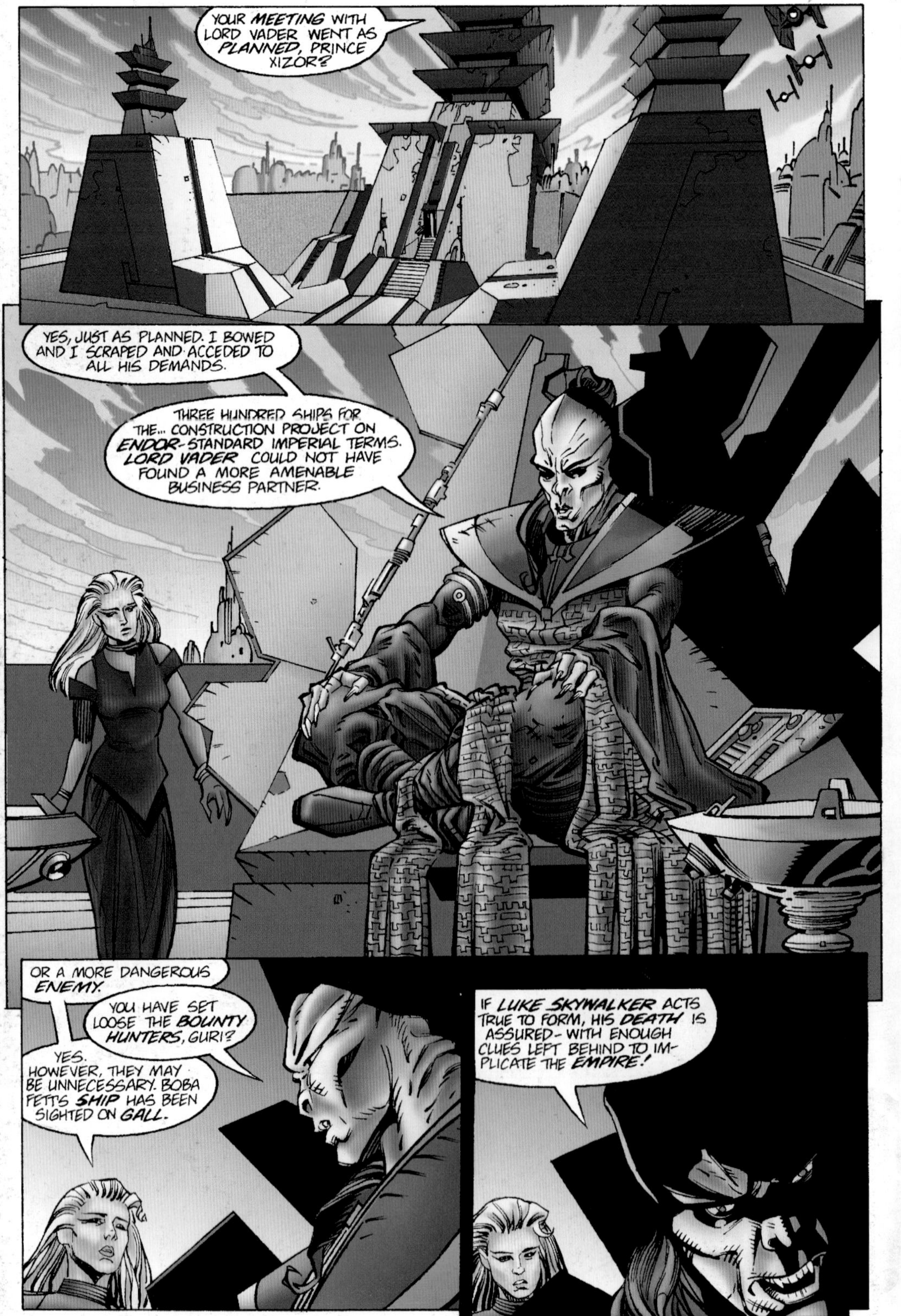
YOUR MEETING WITH LORD VADER WENT AS PLANNED, PRINCE XIZOR?
YES, JUST AS PLANNED. I BOWED AND I SCRAPED AND ACCEDED TO ALL HIS DEMANDS.
THREE HUNDRED SHIPS FOR THE... CONSTRUCTION PROJECT ON ENDOR-STANDARD IMPERIAL TERMS. LORD VADER COULD NOT HAVE FOUND A MORE AMENABLE BUSINESS PARTNER.
OR A MORE DANGEROUS ENEMY.
YOU HAVE SET LOOSE THE BOUNTY HUNTERS, GURI?
YES. HOWEVER, THEY MAY BE UNNECESSARY. BOBA FETT'S SHIP HAS BEEN SIGHTED ON GALL.
IF LUKE SKYWALKER ACTS TRUE TO FORM, HIS DEATH IS ASSURED- WITH ENOUGH CLUES LEFT BEHIND TO IMPLICATE THE EMPIRE!

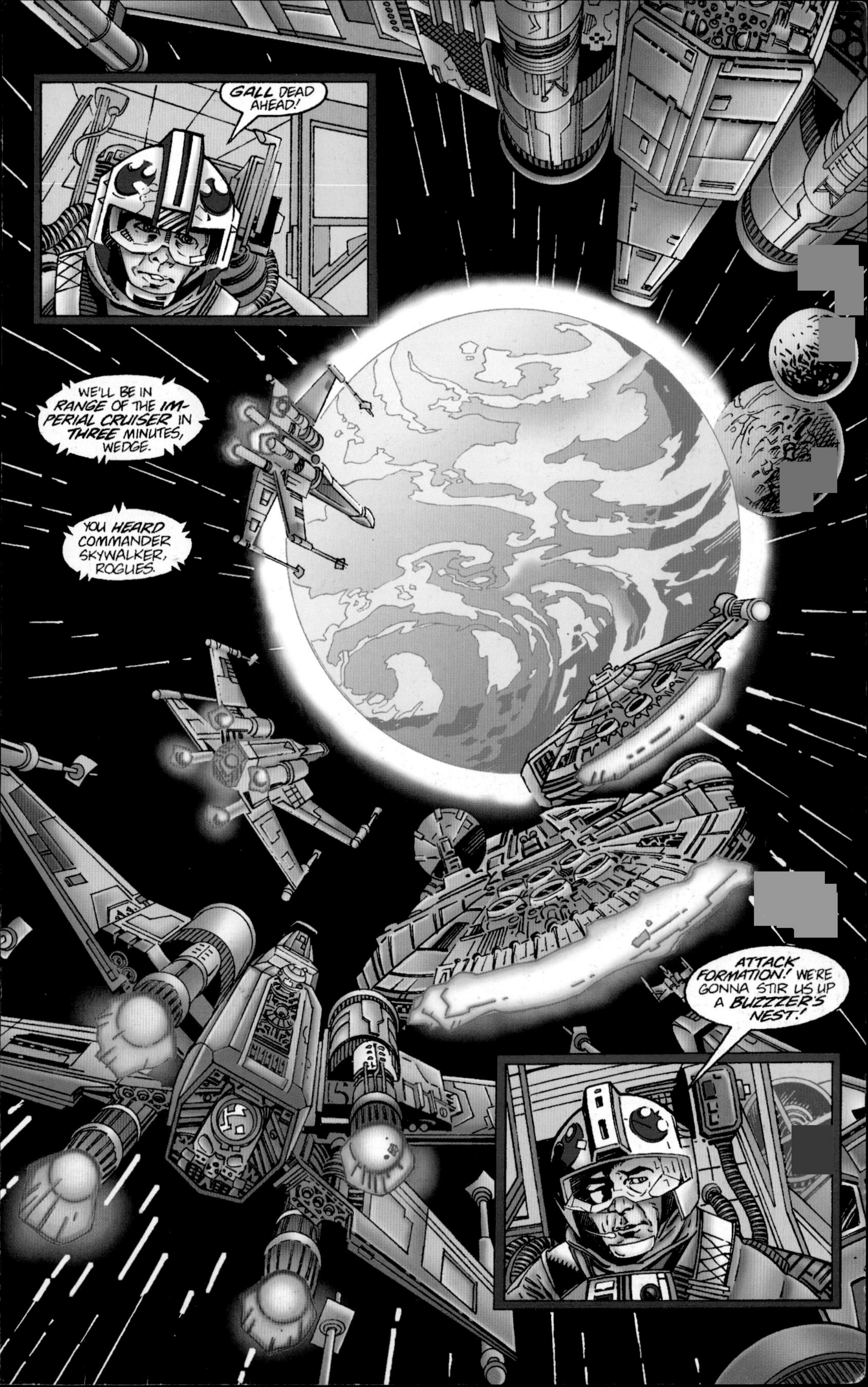
GALL DEAD AHEAD!
WE'LL BE IN RANGE OF THE IMPERIAL CRUISER IN THREE MINUTES, WEDGE.
YOU HEARD COMMANDER SKYWALKER, ROGUES.
ATTACK FORMATION! WE'RE GONNA STIR US UP A BUZZZER'S NEST!

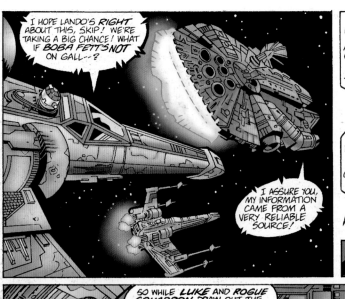

I HOPE LANDO'S *RIGHT* ABOUT THIS, SKIP! WE'RE TAKING A BIG CHANCE! WHAT IF *BOBA FETT'S NOT* ON GALL--?

I ASSURE YOU, MY INFORMATION CAME FROM A VERY RELIABLE SOURCE!

FETT WAS ON HIS WAY TO DELIVER *HAN* TO *JABBA* WHEN ANOTHER BOUNTY HUNTER ATTEMPTED A LITTLE SMASH-GRAB! FETT'S SHIP *SLAVE I* WAS BADLY DAMAGED. THE SAFEST PLACE TO MAKE REPAIRS WAS THE *IMPERIAL ENCLAVE* ON *GALL* -- IT BEING HEAVILY FORTIFIED.

THAT THOUGHT FILLS US WITH GREAT COMFORT, LANDO.

SO WHILE *LUKE* AND *ROGUE SQUADRON* DRAW OUT THE OPPOSITION, WE JUST SNEAK IN THE BACK WAY, FIND *SLAVE I*, AND TAKE *HAN*.

OH, DEAR! THIS ALL SOUNDS MOST DANGEROUS!

ANY RISK IS WORTH TAKING FOR *HAN*. THE... THE ALLIANCE NEEDS HIM.

GRROUARRHH.

OF COURSE THE PRINCESS LOVES HAN, *CHEWIE*. WE *ALL* LOVE HIM.

SURE-- IN OUR OWN DIFFERENT WAYS!

TIME TO PART COMPANY, LUKE! HAPPY HUNTING!

BE CAREFUL, LANDO! MAY THE *FORCE* BE WITH YOU!

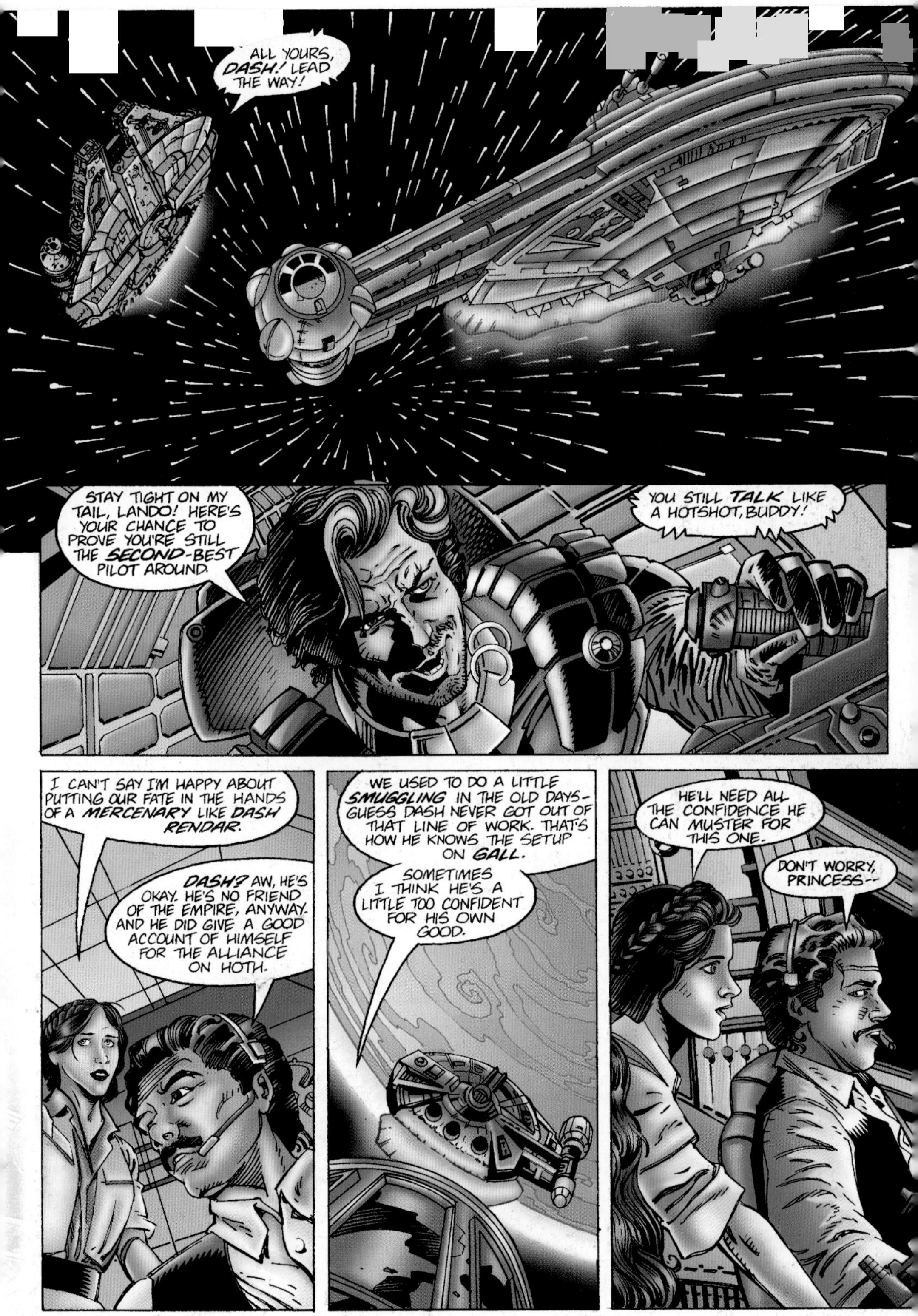
ALL YOURS, DASH! LEAD THE WAY!
STAY TIGHT ON MY TAIL, LANDO! HERE'S YOUR CHANCE TO PROVE YOU'RE STILL THE SECOND-BEST PILOT AROUND.
YOU STILL TALK LIKE A HOTSHOT, BUDDY!
I CAN'T SAY I'M HAPPY ABOUT PUTTING OUR FATE IN THE HANDS OF A MERCENARY LIKE DASH RENDAR.
DASH? AW, HE'S OKAY. HE'S NO FRIEND OF THE EMPIRE, ANYWAY. AND HE DID GIVE A GOOD ACCOUNT OF HIMSELF FOR THE ALLIANCE ON HOTH.
WE USED TO DO A LITTLE SMUGGLING IN THE OLD DAYS-- GUESS DASH NEVER GOT OUT OF THAT LINE OF WORK. THAT'S HOW HE KNOWS THE SETUP ON GALL.
SOMETIMES I THINK HE'S A LITTLE TOO CONFIDENT FOR HIS OWN GOOD.
HE'LL NEED ALL THE CONFIDENCE HE CAN MUSTER FOR THIS ONE.
DON'T WORRY, PRINCESS--

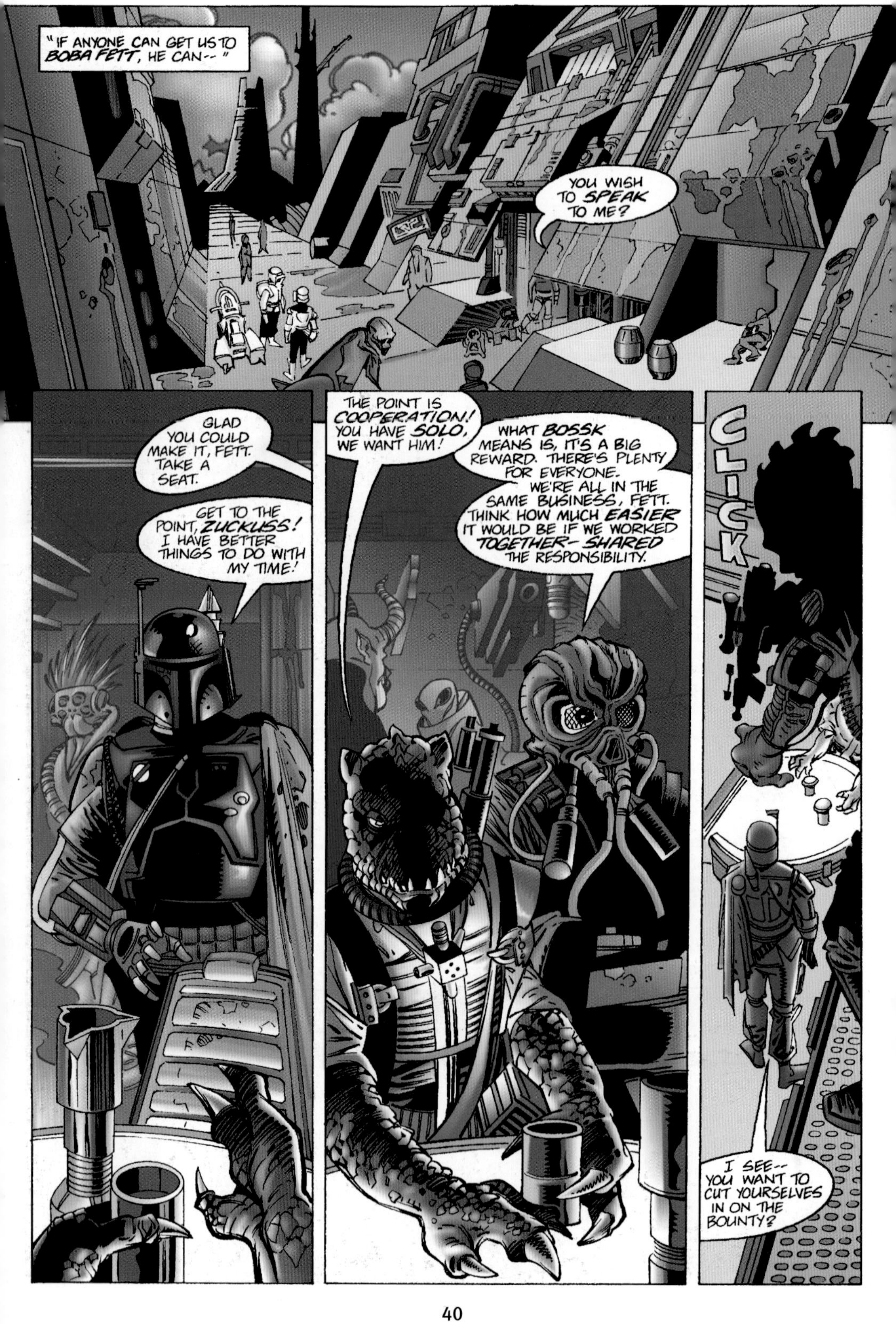
"IF ANYONE CAN GET US TO BOBA FETT, HE CAN--"
YOU WISH TO SPEAK TO ME?
GLAD YOU COULD MAKE IT, FETT. TAKE A SEAT.
GET TO THE POINT, ZUCKUSS! I HAVE BETTER THINGS TO DO WITH MY TIME!
THE POINT IS COOPERATION! YOU HAVE SOLO, WE WANT HIM!
WHAT BOSSK MEANS IS, IT'S A BIG REWARD. THERE'S PLENTY FOR EVERYONE. WE'RE ALL IN THE SAME BUSINESS, FETT. THINK HOW MUCH EASIER IT WOULD BE IF WE WORKED TOGETHER- SHARED THE RESPONSIBILITY.
CLICK
I SEE-- YOU WANT TO CUT YOURSELVES IN ON THE BOUNTY?

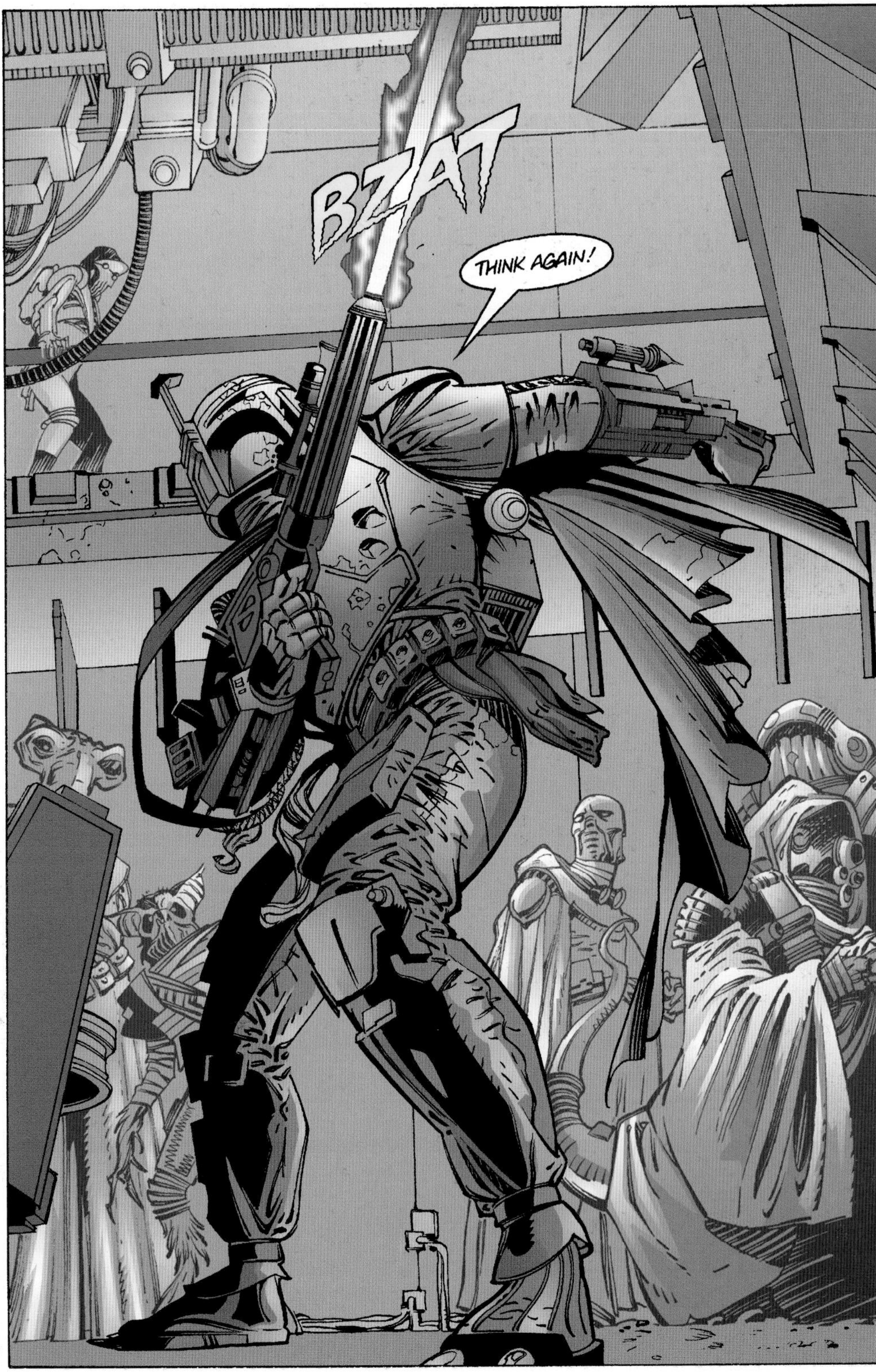
BZAT
THINK AGAIN!

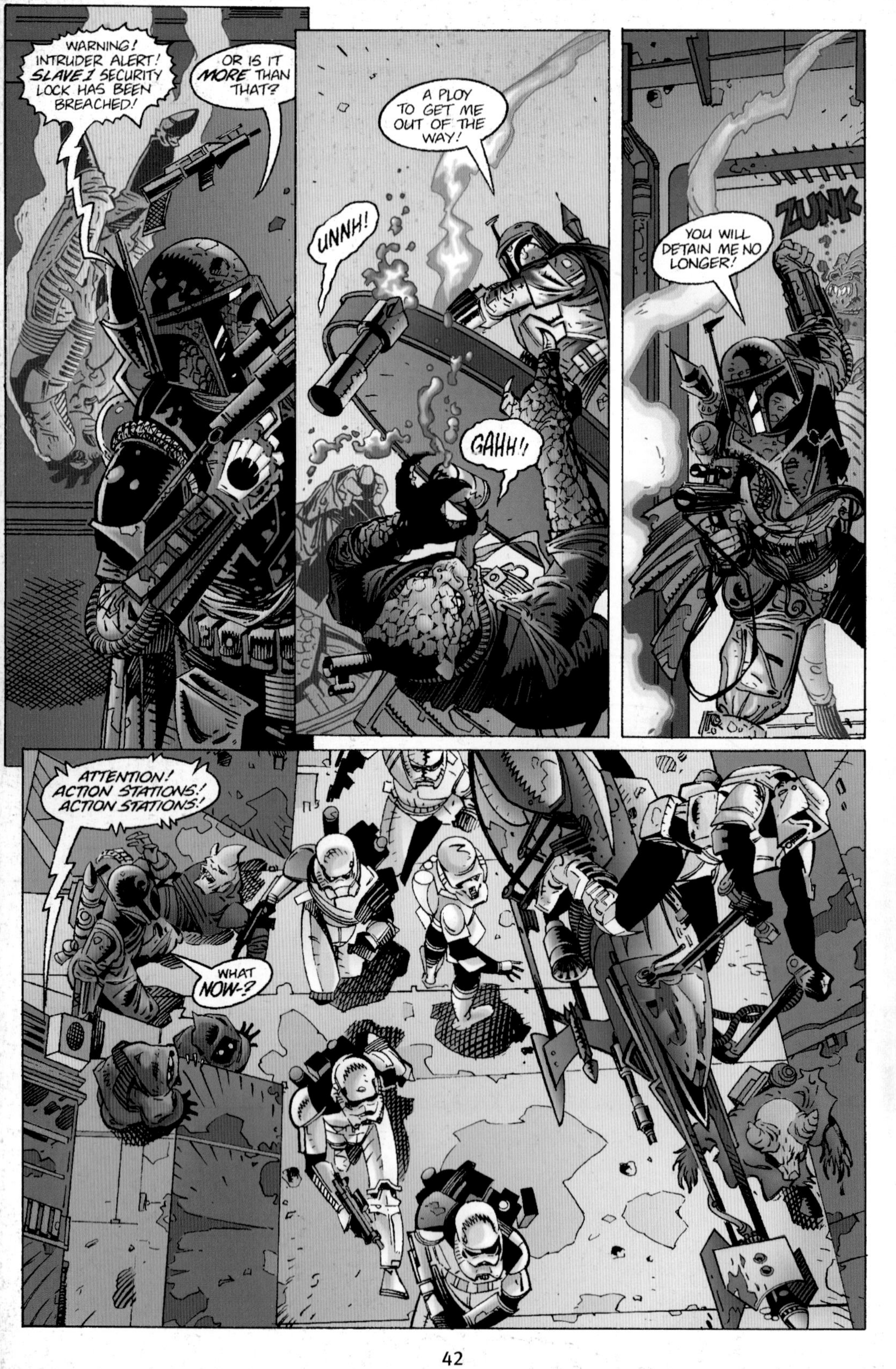
WARNING! INTRUDER ALERT! SLAVE I SECURITY LOCK HAS BEEN BREACHED!
OR IS IT MORE THAN THAT?
A PLOY TO GET ME OUT OF THE WAY!
UNNH!
GAHH!!
ZUNK
YOU WILL DETAIN ME NO LONGER!
ATTENTION! ACTION STATIONS! ACTION STATIONS!
WHAT NOW-?

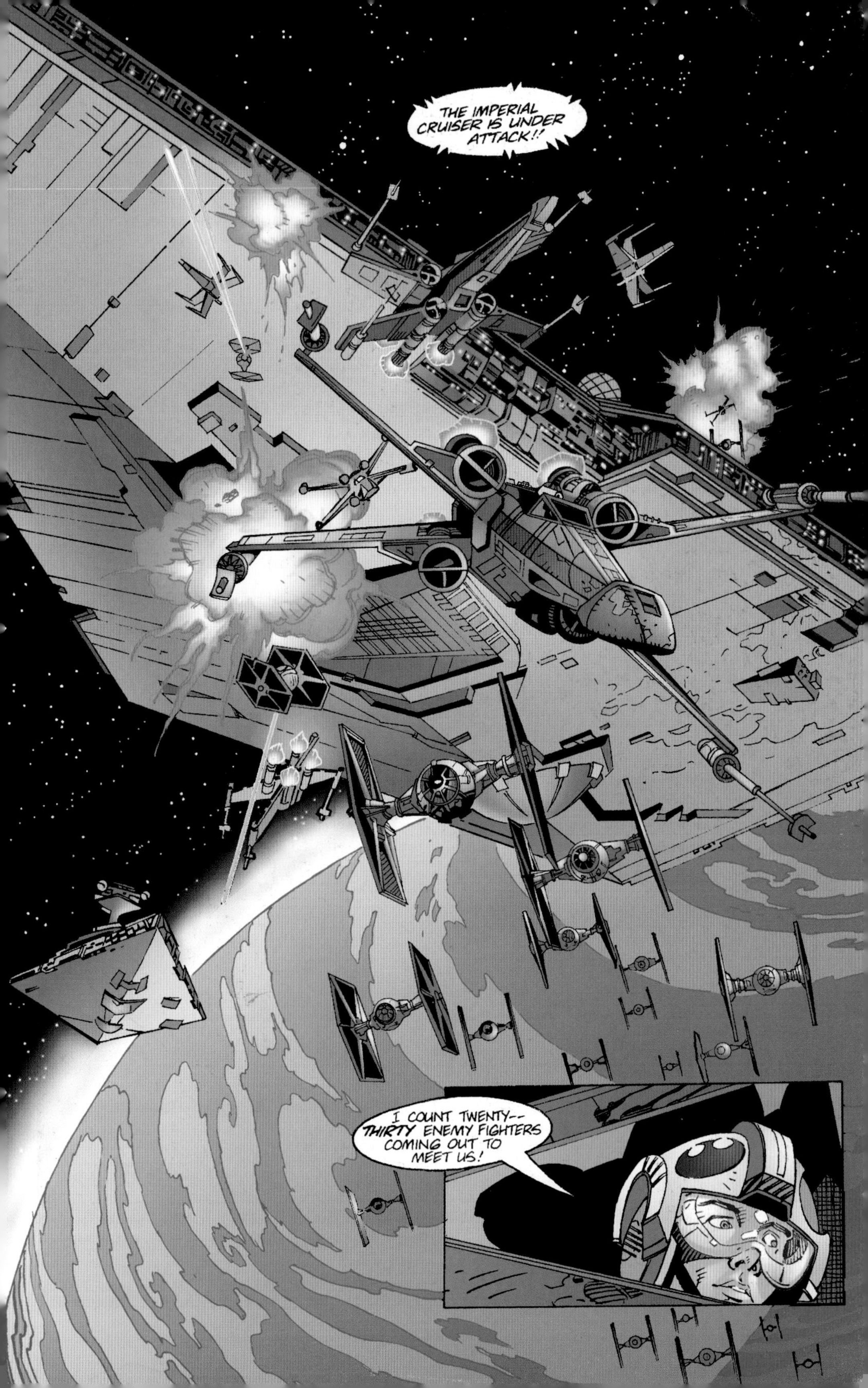
THE IMPERIAL CRUISER IS UNDER ATTACK!!
I COUNT TWENTY-- THIRTY ENEMY FIGHTERS COMING OUT TO MEET US!

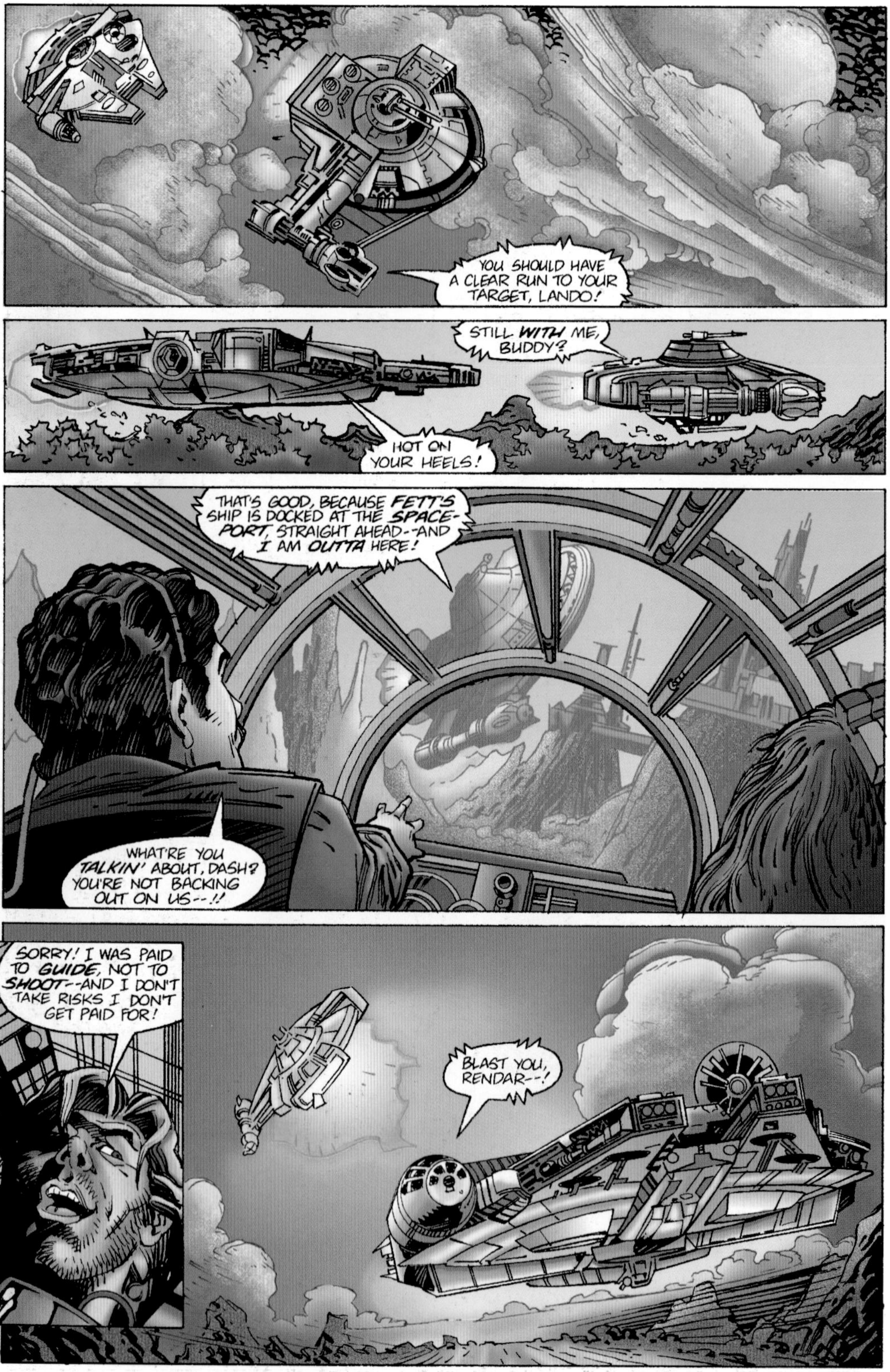
YOU SHOULD HAVE A CLEAR RUN TO YOUR TARGET, LANDO!
STILL WITH ME, BUDDY?
HOT ON YOUR HEELS!
THAT'S GOOD, BECAUSE FETT'S SHIP IS DOCKED AT THE SPACE-PORT, STRAIGHT AHEAD--AND I AM OUTTA HERE!
WHAT'RE YOU TALKIN' ABOUT, DASH? YOU'RE NOT BACKING OUT ON US--!!
SORRY! I WAS PAID TO GUIDE, NOT TO SHOOT--AND I DON'T TAKE RISKS I DON'T GET PAID FOR!
BLAST YOU, RENDAR--!

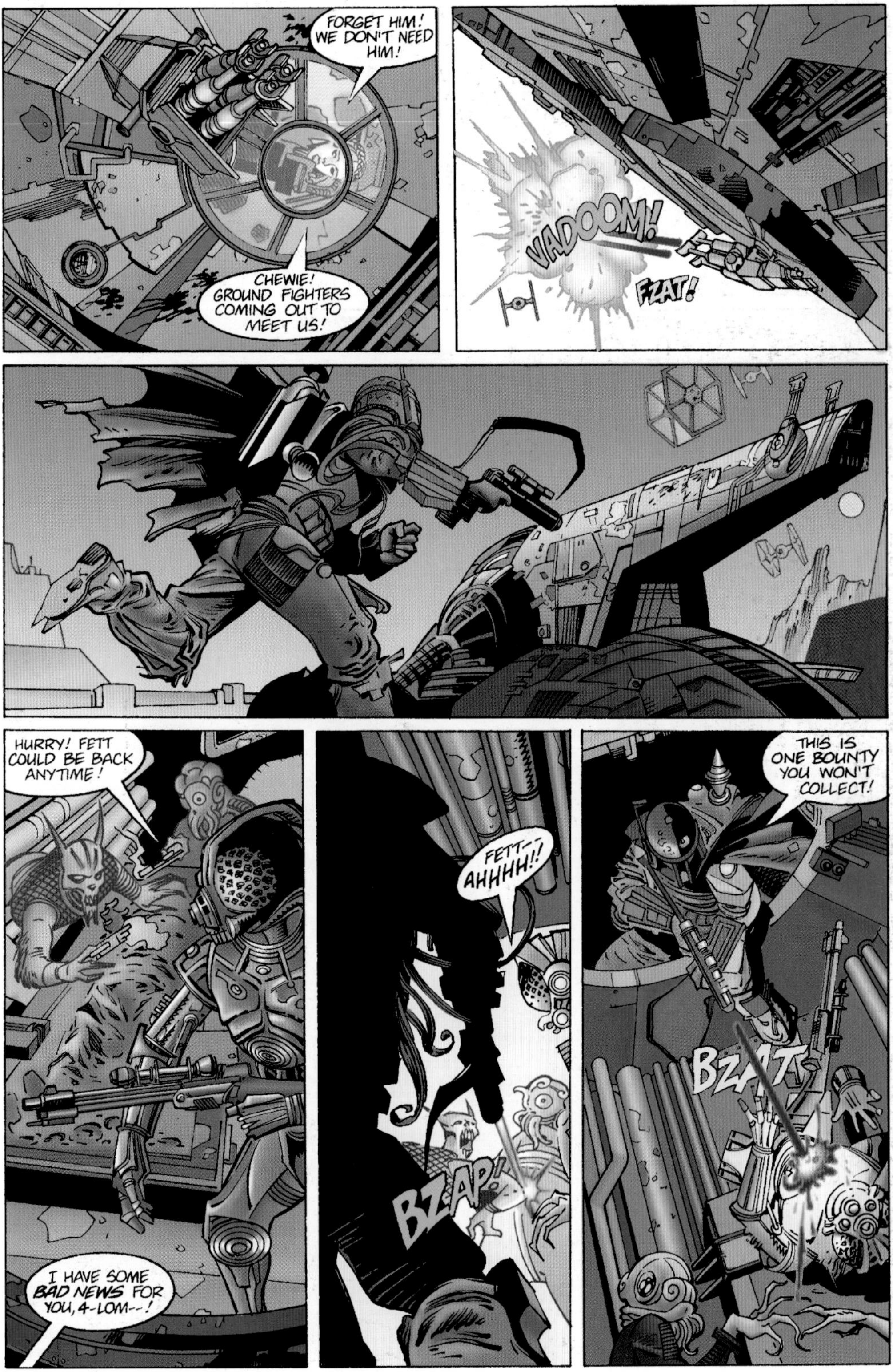
FORGET HIM! WE DON'T NEED HIM!
CHEWIE! GROUND FIGHTERS COMING OUT TO MEET US!
VADOOM!
FZAT!
HURRY! FETT COULD BE BACK ANYTIME!
I HAVE SOME BAD NEWS FOR YOU, 4-LOM--!
FETT--AHHHH!!
BZAP!
THIS IS ONE BOUNTY YOU WON'T COLLECT!
BZAT!

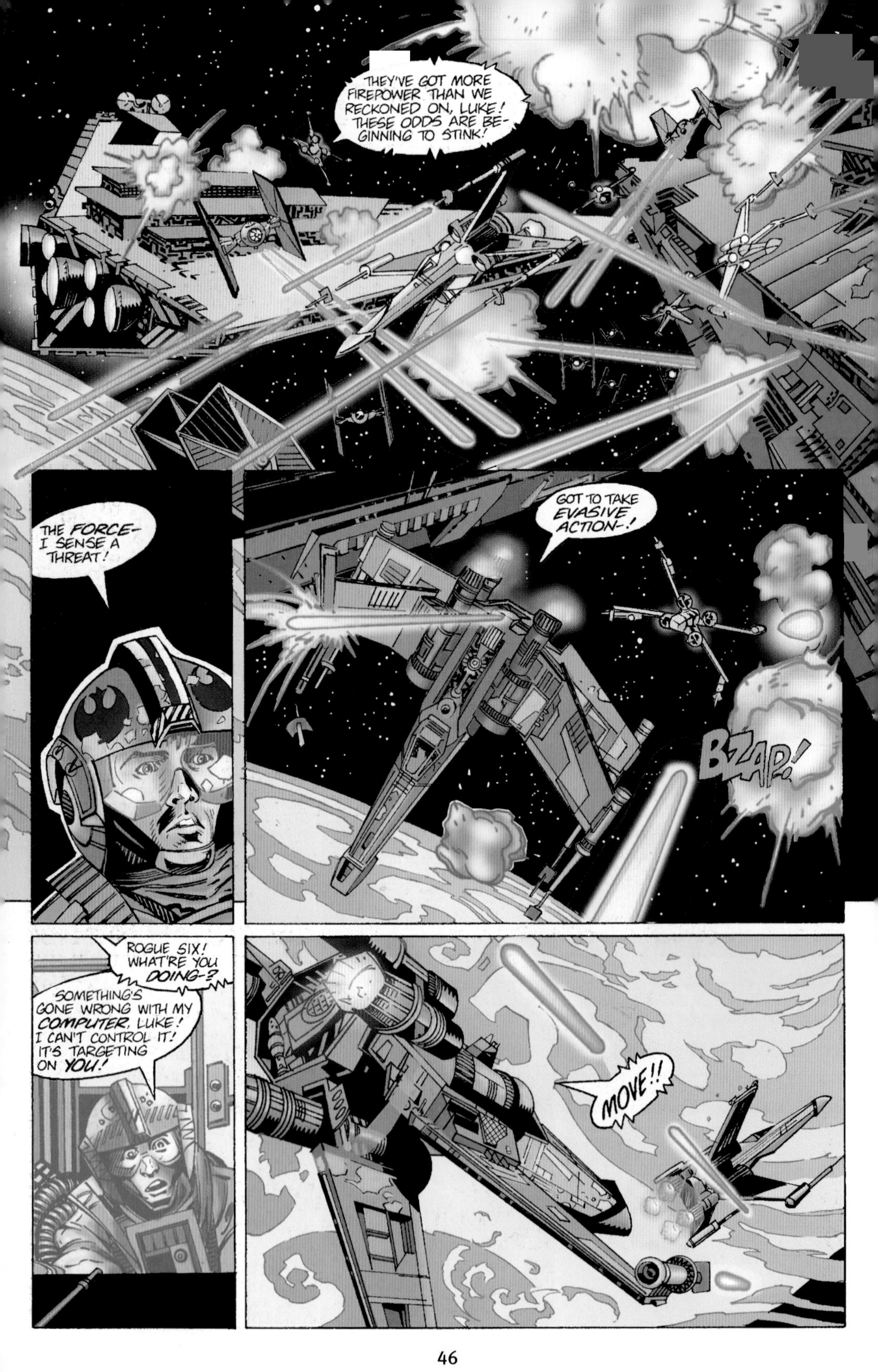
THEY'VE GOT MORE FIREPOWER THAN WE RECKONED ON, LUKE! THESE ODDS ARE BEGINNING TO STINK!
THE FORCE- I SENSE A THREAT!
GOT TO TAKE EVASIVE ACTION-!
BZAP!
ROGUE SIX! WHAT'RE YOU DOING-?
SOMETHING'S GONE WRONG WITH MY COMPUTER, LUKE! I CAN'T CONTROL IT! IT'S TARGETING ON YOU!
MOVE!!

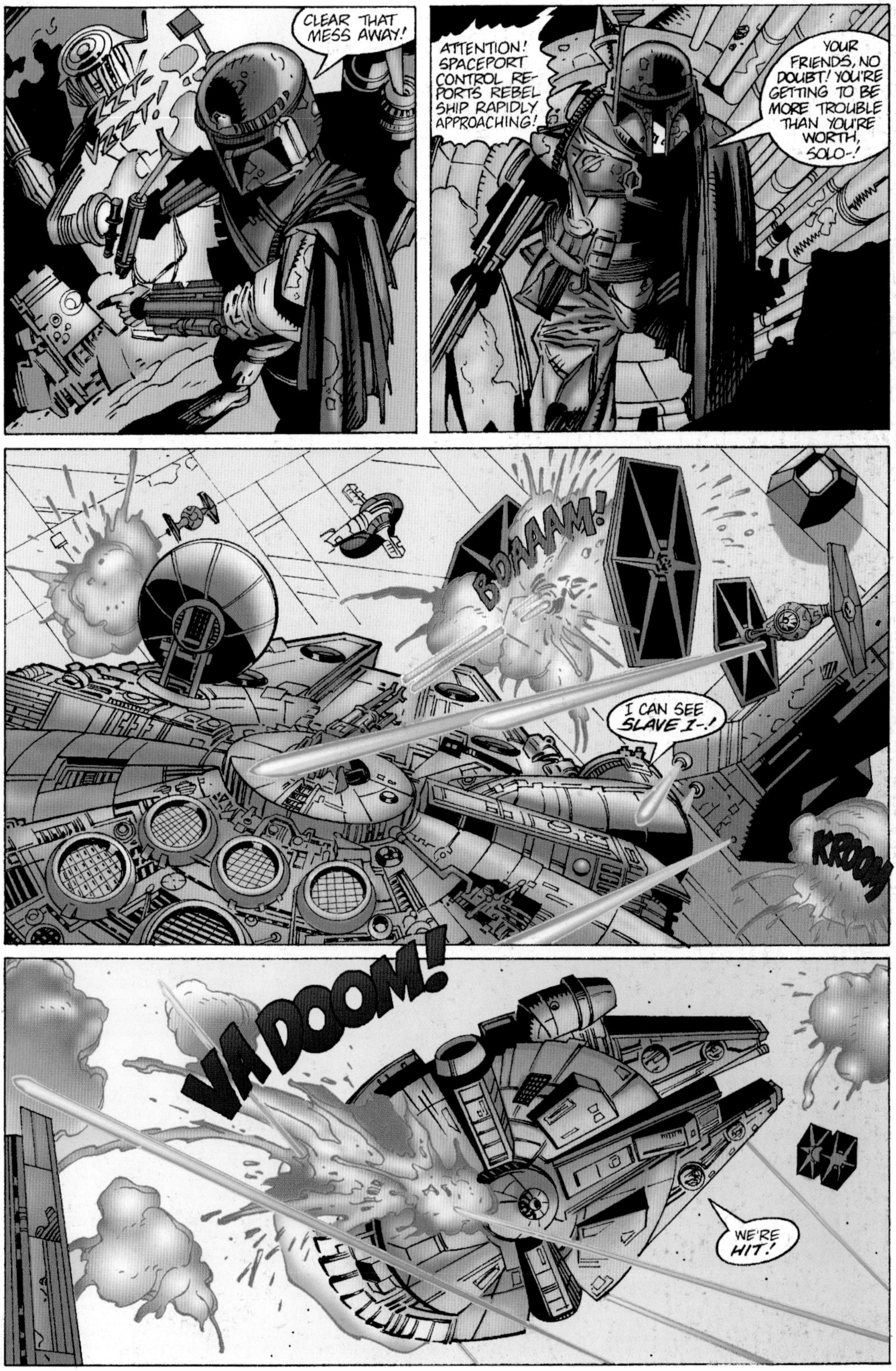
CLEAR THAT MESS AWAY!
VZZZT-VZZZT!
ATTENTION! SPACEPORT CONTROL REPORTS REBEL SHIP RAPIDLY APPROACHING!
YOUR FRIENDS, NO DOUBT! YOU'RE GETTING TO BE MORE TROUBLE THAN YOU'RE WORTH, SOLO-!
BDAAAM!
I CAN SEE SLAVE I-!
KROOM
VADOOM!
WE'RE HIT!

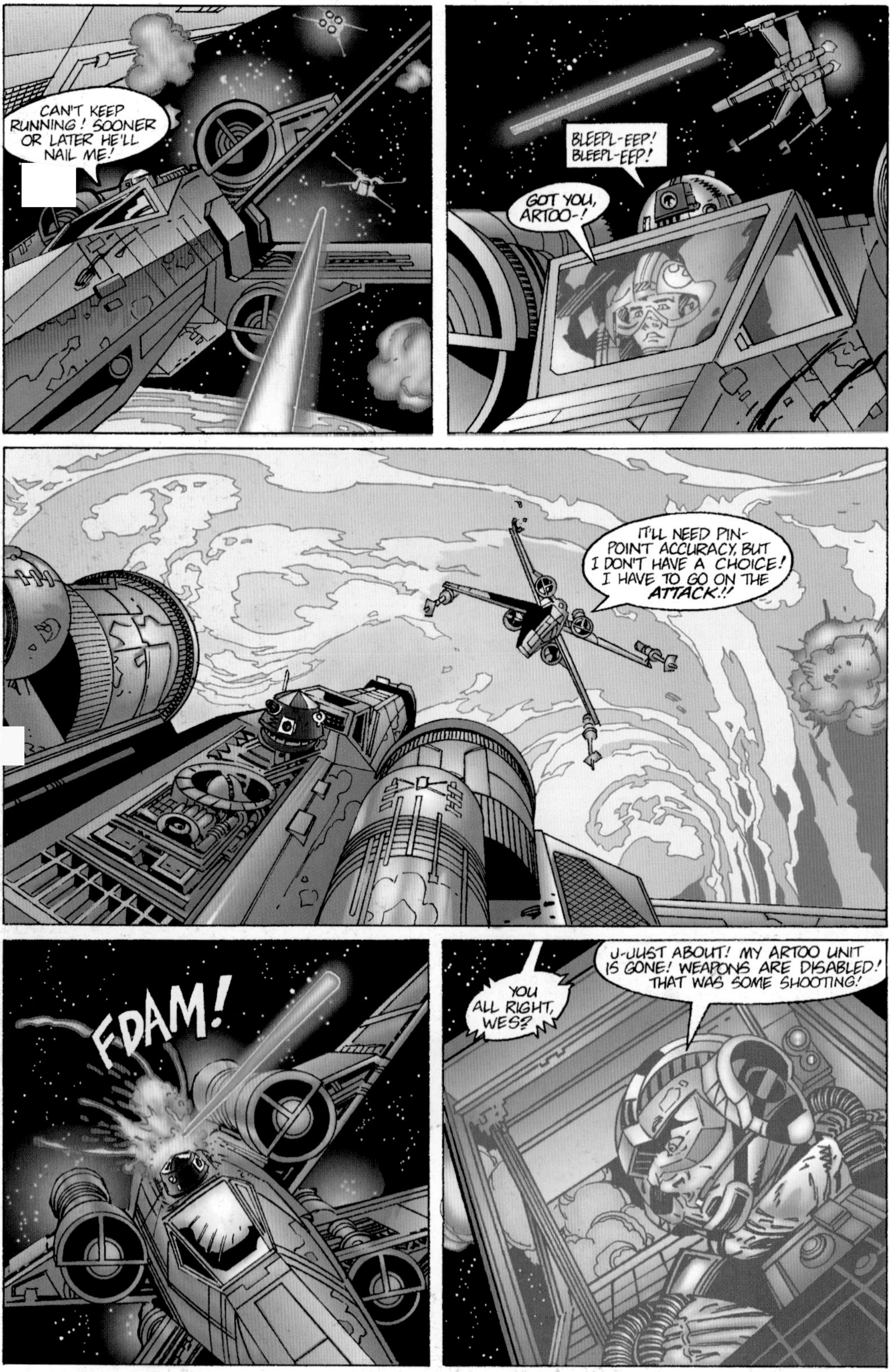
CAN'T KEEP RUNNING! SOONER OR LATER HE'LL NAIL ME!
BLEEPL-EEP! BLEEPL-EEP!
GOT YOU, ARTOO-!
IT'LL NEED PIN-POINT ACCURACY, BUT I DON'T HAVE A CHOICE! I HAVE TO GO ON THE ATTACK!!
FDAM!
YOU ALL RIGHT, WES?
J-JUST ABOUT! MY ARTOO UNIT IS GONE! WEAPONS ARE DISABLED! THAT WAS SOME SHOOTING!

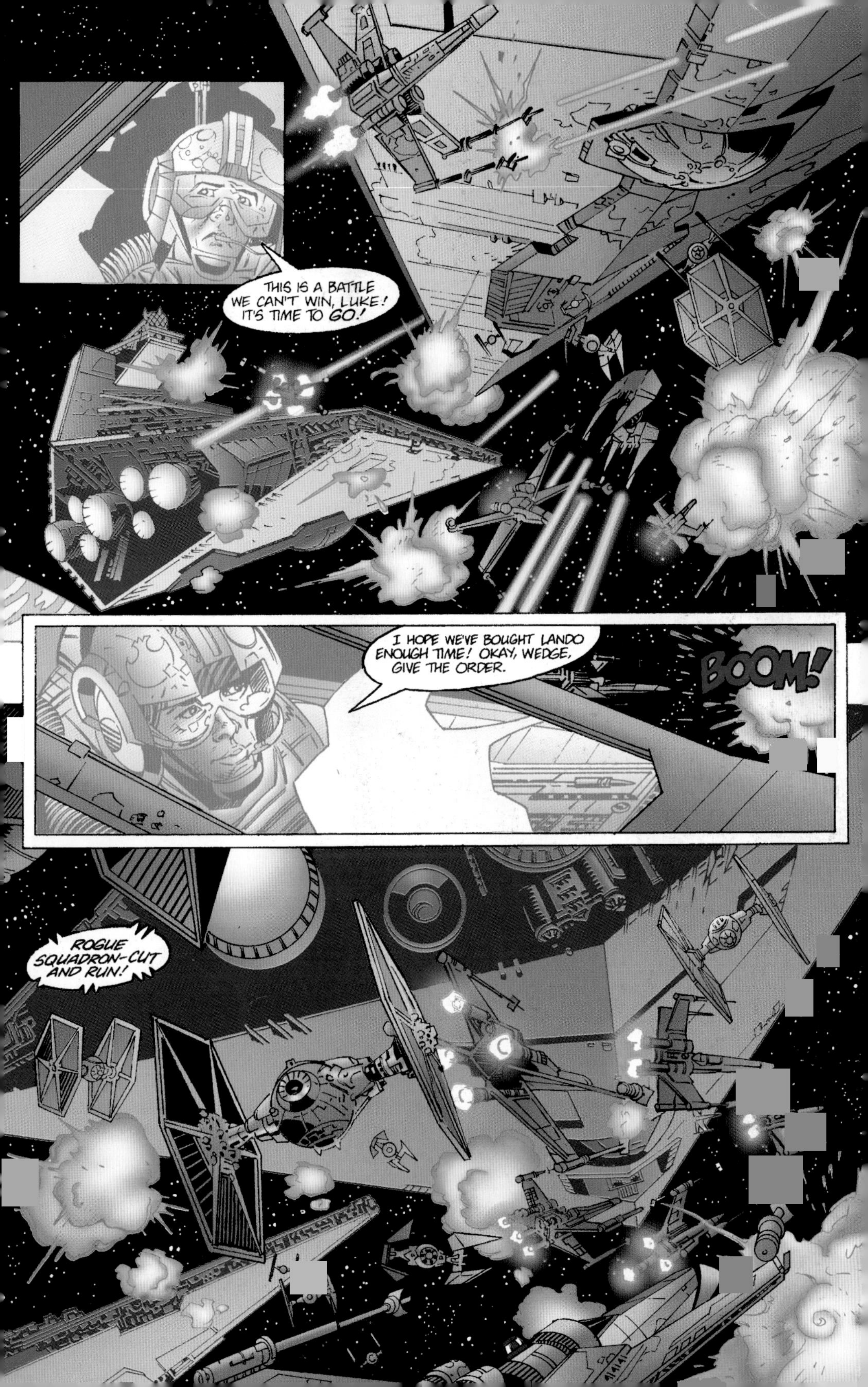
THIS IS A BATTLE WE CAN'T WIN, LUKE! IT'S TIME TO GO!
I HOPE WE'VE BOUGHT LANDO ENOUGH TIME! OKAY, WEDGE, GIVE THE ORDER.
BOOM!
ROGUE SQUADRON-CUT AND RUN!

SLAVE 1 IS LIFTING OFF!

WHAT DAMAGE, LANDO?

WEAPONS SYSTEMS ARE DOWN! WE'VE LOST EXTERNAL COMMUNICATIONS, TOO!

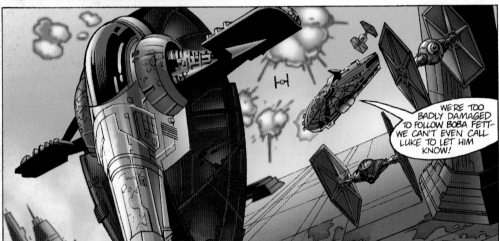

WE'RE TOO BADLY DAMAGED TO FOLLOW BOBA FETT— WE CAN'T EVEN CALL LUKE TO LET HIM KNOW!

ALL WE CAN DO NOW IS RUN!

VERY WELL! THERE'S NO ALTERNATIVE— BREAK OFF THE ATTACK!

GET US OUT OF HERE!

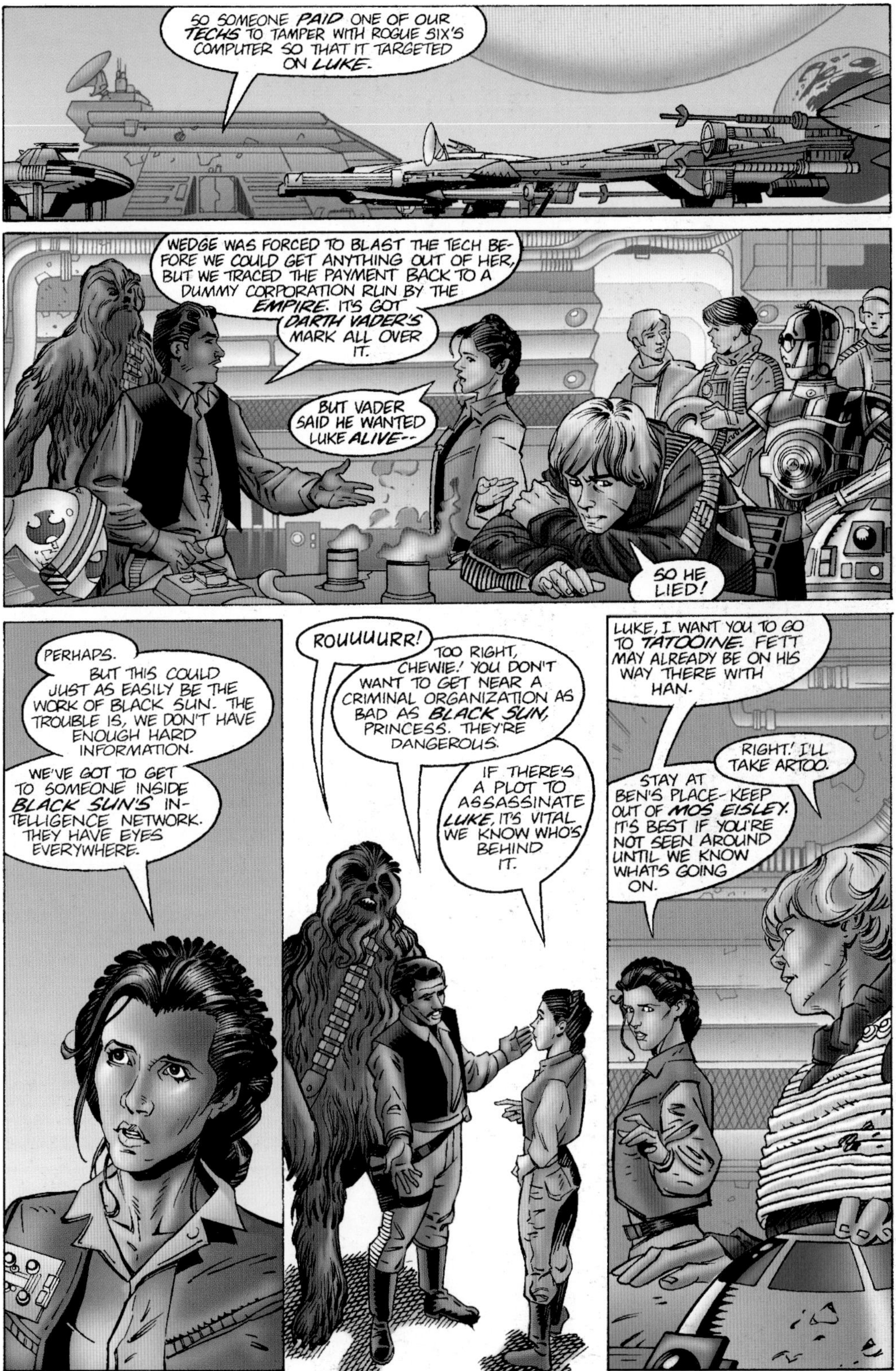
SO SOMEONE PAID ONE OF OUR TECHS TO TAMPER WITH ROGUE SIX'S COMPUTER SO THAT IT TARGETED ON LUKE.
WEDGE WAS FORCED TO BLAST THE TECH BEFORE WE COULD GET ANYTHING OUT OF HER, BUT WE TRACED THE PAYMENT BACK TO A DUMMY CORPORATION RUN BY THE EMPIRE. IT'S GOT DARTH VADER'S MARK ALL OVER IT.
BUT VADER SAID HE WANTED LUKE ALIVE--
SO HE LIED!
PERHAPS.
BUT THIS COULD JUST AS EASILY BE THE WORK OF BLACK SUN. THE TROUBLE IS, WE DON'T HAVE ENOUGH HARD INFORMATION.
WE'VE GOT TO GET TO SOMEONE INSIDE BLACK SUN'S INTELLIGENCE NETWORK. THEY HAVE EYES EVERYWHERE.
ROUUUURR!
TOO RIGHT, CHEWIE! YOU DON'T WANT TO GET NEAR A CRIMINAL ORGANIZATION AS BAD AS BLACK SUN, PRINCESS. THEY'RE DANGEROUS.
IF THERE'S A PLOT TO ASSASSINATE LUKE, IT'S VITAL WE KNOW WHO'S BEHIND IT.
LUKE, I WANT YOU TO GO TO TATOOINE. FETT MAY ALREADY BE ON HIS WAY THERE WITH HAN.
RIGHT! I'LL TAKE ARTOO.
STAY AT BEN'S PLACE- KEEP OUT OF MOS EISLEY. IT'S BEST IF YOU'RE NOT SEEN AROUND UNTIL WE KNOW WHAT'S GOING ON.

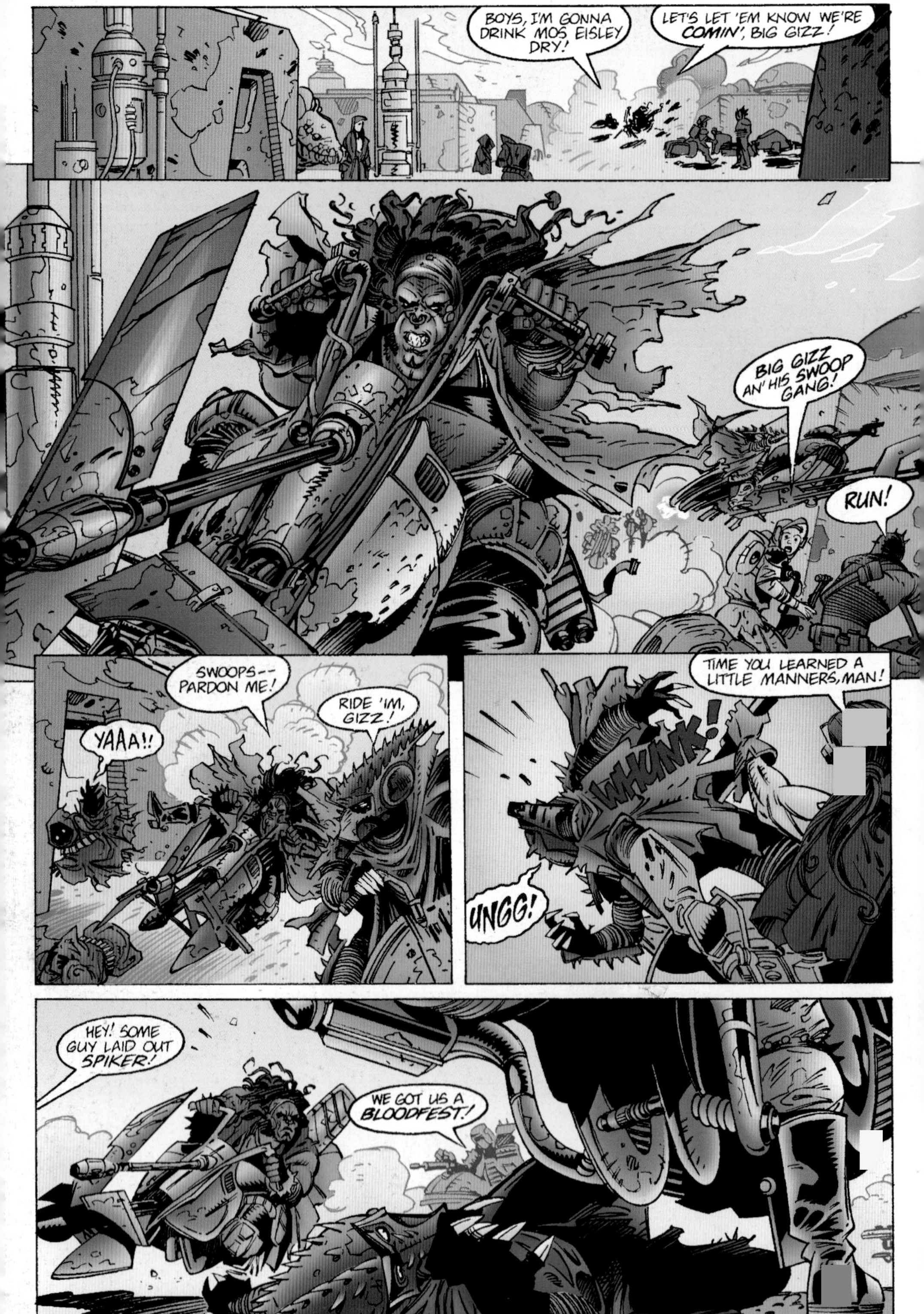
BOYS, I'M GONNA DRINK MOS EISLEY DRY!
LET'S LET 'EM KNOW WE'RE COMIN', BIG GIZZ!
BIG GIZZ AN' HIS SWOOP GANG!
RUN!
SWOOPS-- PARDON ME!
RIDE 'IM, GIZZ!
YAAA!!
TIME YOU LEARNED A LITTLE MANNERS, MAN!
WHUNK!
UNGG!
HEY! SOME GUY LAID OUT SPIKER!
WE GOT US A BLOODFEST!

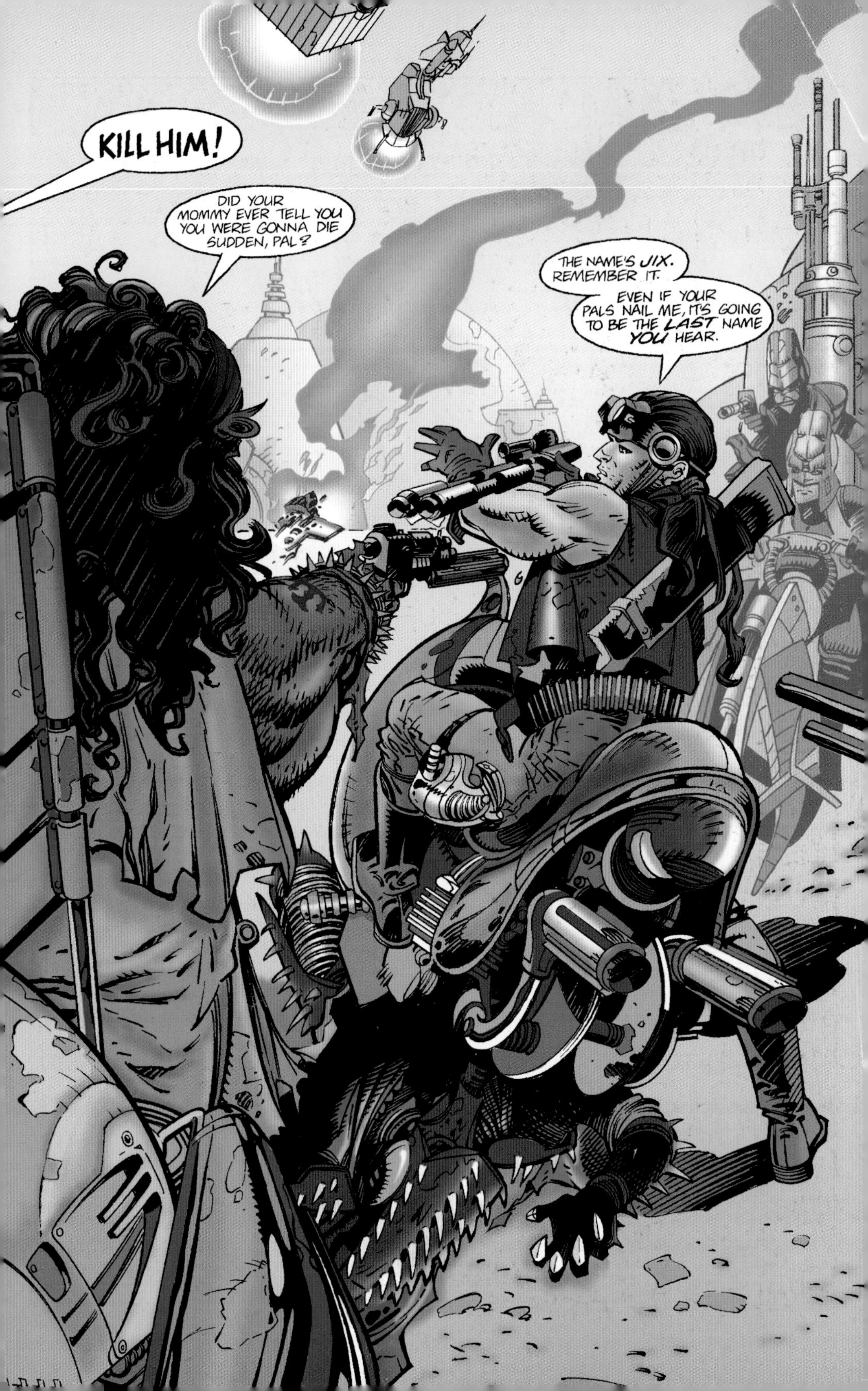
KILL HIM!
DID YOUR MOMMY EVER TELL YOU YOU WERE GONNA DIE SUDDEN, PAL?
THE NAME'S JIX. REMEMBER IT.
EVEN IF YOUR PALS NAIL ME, IT'S GOING TO BE THE LAST NAME YOU HEAR.

HE TALKS PRETTY BIG, DON'T HE, BOYS? RIDES A MEAN *MACHINE*, TOO.

YOU MAKE THIS THING *COOK*, PALLY?

BETTER THAN YOU BUNCH OF AMATEURS, THAT'S FOR SURE.

YESSIR, YOU TALK REAL BIG! TELL YOU WHAT-- GONNA GIVE YOU A CHANCE TO PROVE YOU AIN'T ALL MOUTH~!

YOU AN' ME- ROUND THEM BIG DISHES AN' BACK THROUGH THE TRESTLES. YOU MAKE IT FIRST, MAYBE WE SETTLE FOR JUST BREAKIN' YOUR BONES.

JUST THE KIND OF STUNT I'D EXPECT FROM A BIG DUMB LUNK LIKE YOU.

WHAT ARE YOU WAITING FOR?

HE'S GOT THE JUMP!

GET HIM, GIZZ!

VADER'S MACHINE'S GOT HIM MATCHED FOR SPEED ON THE STRAIGHT!

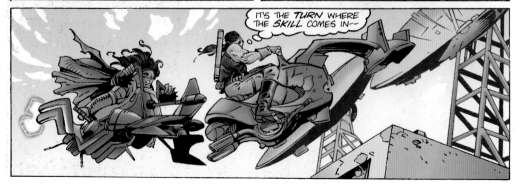

IT'S THE *TURN* WHERE THE *SKILL* COMES IN--

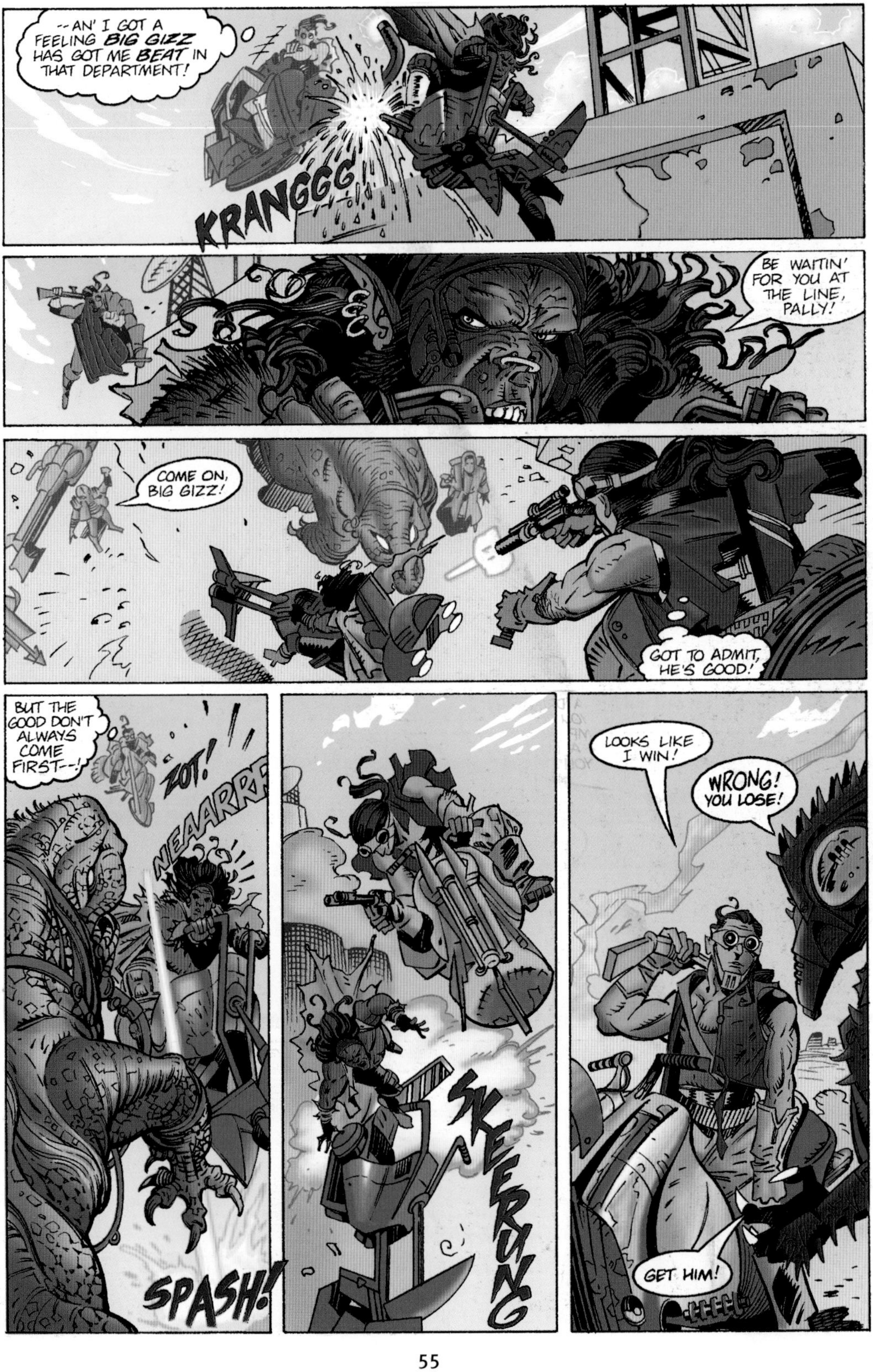
--AN' I GOT A FEELING BIG GIZZ HAS GOT ME BEAT IN THAT DEPARTMENT!
KRANGGG
BE WAITIN' FOR YOU AT THE LINE, PALLY!
COME ON, BIG GIZZ!
GOT TO ADMIT, HE'S GOOD!
BUT THE GOOD DON'T ALWAYS COME FIRST--!
ZOT!
NEAARRR
SPASH!
SKEERUNG
LOOKS LIKE I WIN!
WRONG! YOU LOSE!
GET HIM!

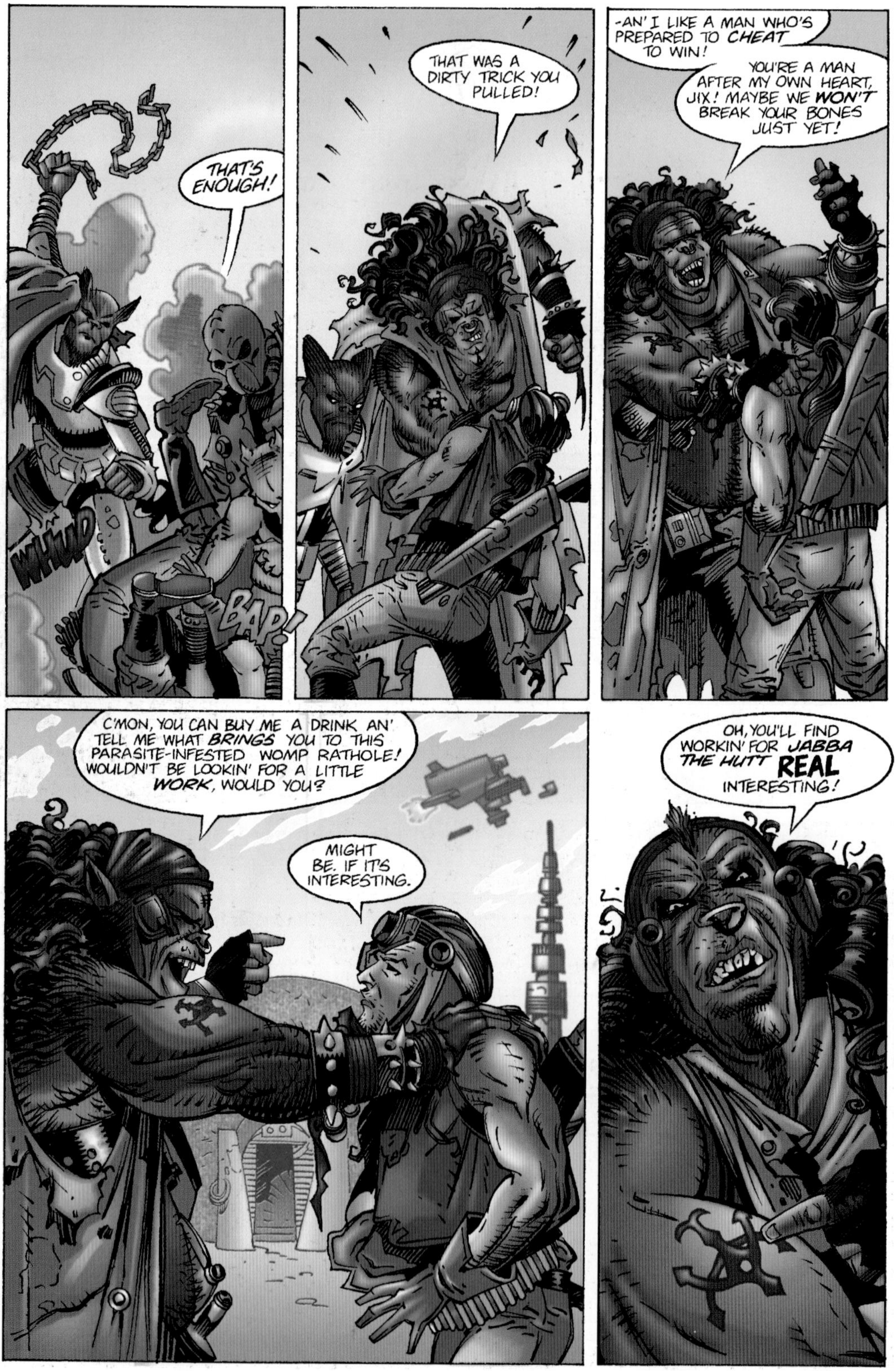
THAT'S ENOUGH!
WHUD
BAP!
THAT WAS A DIRTY TRICK YOU PULLED!
-AN' I LIKE A MAN WHO'S PREPARED TO CHEAT TO WIN!
YOU'RE A MAN AFTER MY OWN HEART, JIX! MAYBE WE WON'T BREAK YOUR BONES JUST YET!
C'MON, YOU CAN BUY ME A DRINK AN' TELL ME WHAT BRINGS YOU TO THIS PARASITE-INFESTED WOMP RATHOLE! WOULDN'T BE LOOKIN' FOR A LITTLE WORK, WOULD YOU?
MIGHT BE. IF IT'S INTERESTING.
OH, YOU'LL FIND WORKIN' FOR JABBA THE HUTT REAL INTERESTING!

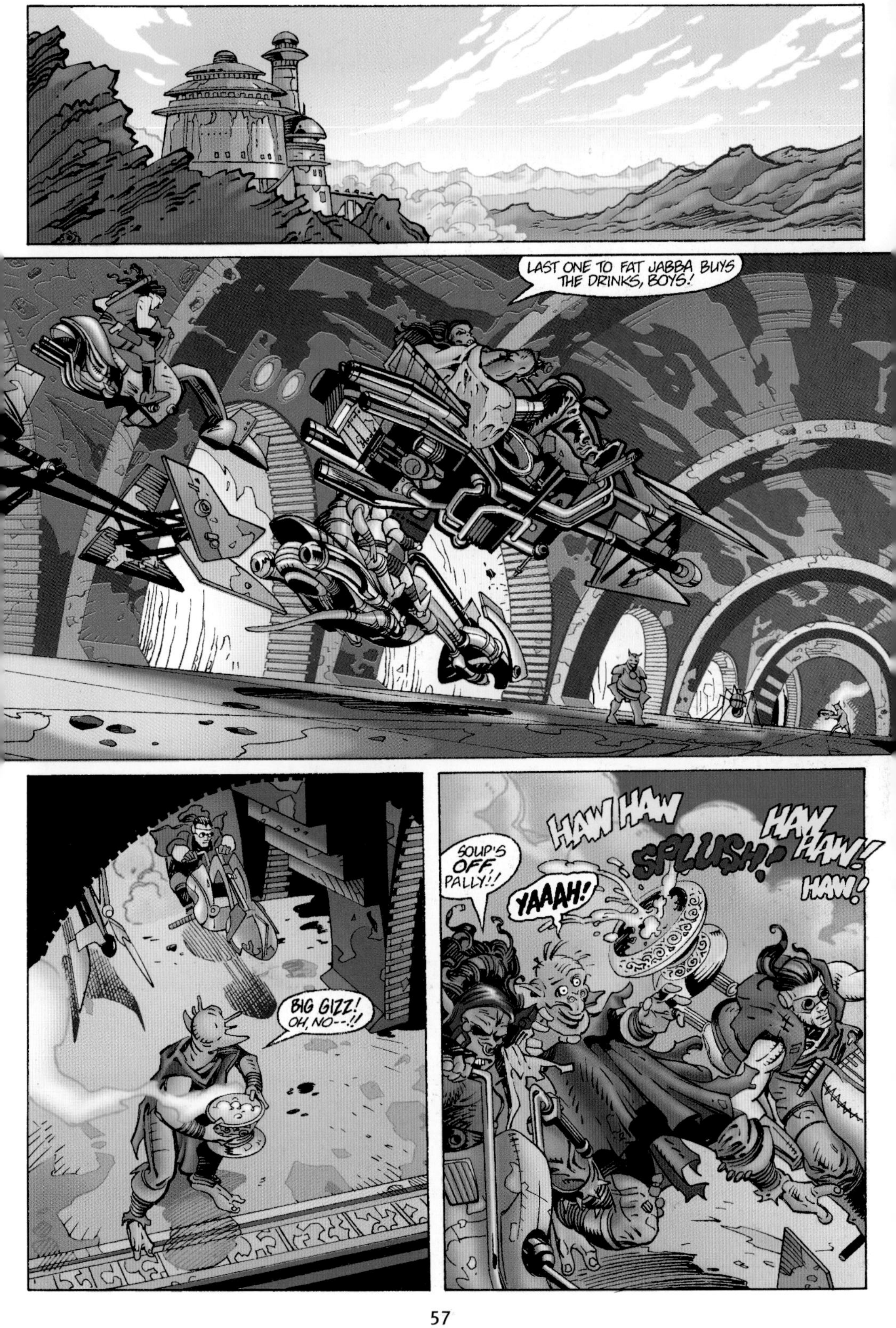
LAST ONE TO FAT JABBA BUYS THE DRINKS, BOYS!
BIG GIZZ! OH, NO--!!
HAW HAW
SOUP'S OFF, PALLY!!
YAAAH!
SPLUSH!
HAW HAW!
HAW!

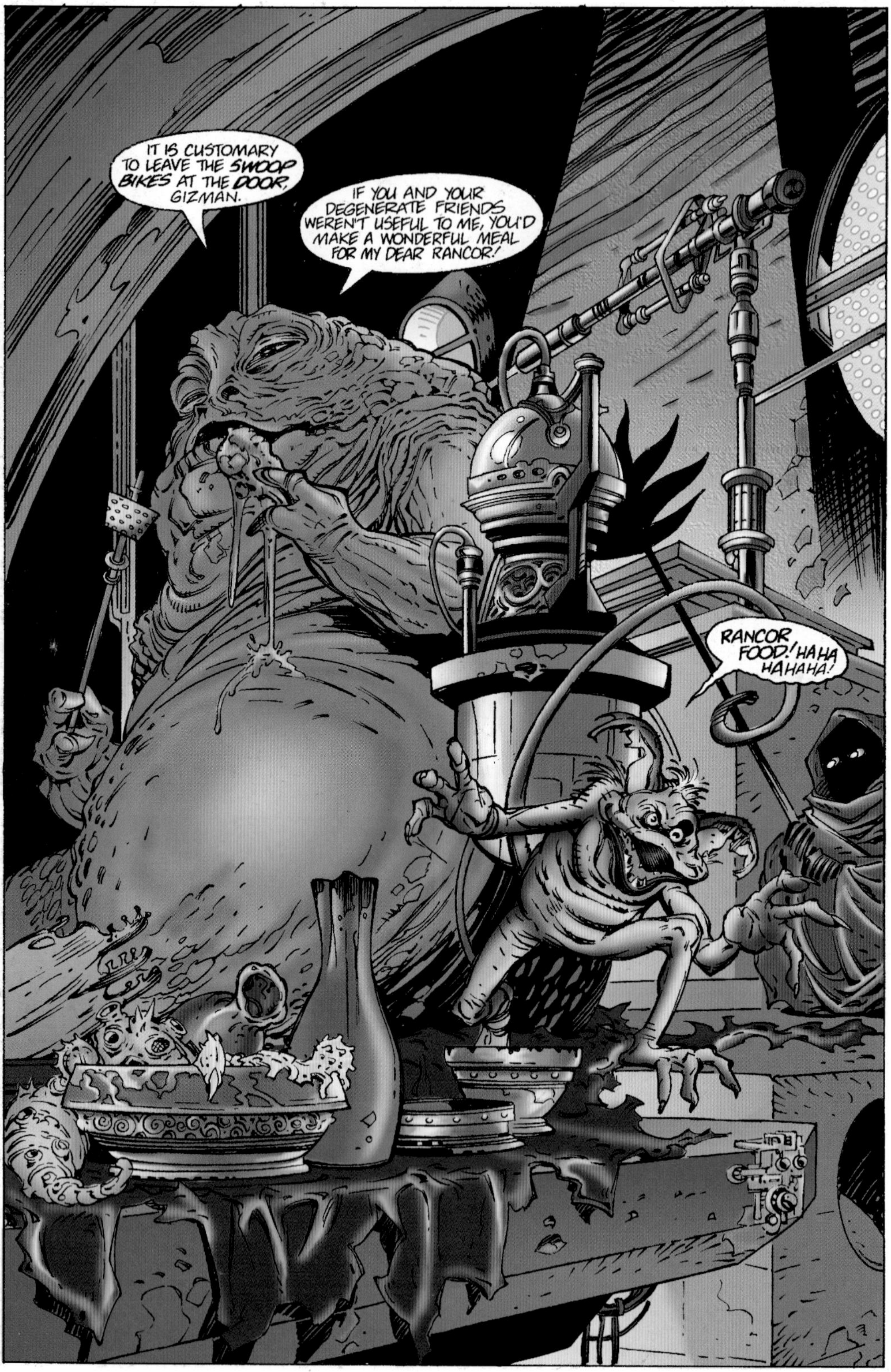
IT IS CUSTOMARY TO LEAVE THE SWOOP BIKES AT THE DOOR, GIZMAN.
IF YOU AND YOUR DEGENERATE FRIENDS WEREN'T USEFUL TO ME, YOU'D MAKE A WONDERFUL MEAL FOR MY DEAR RANCOR!
RANCOR FOOD! HAHA HAHAHA!

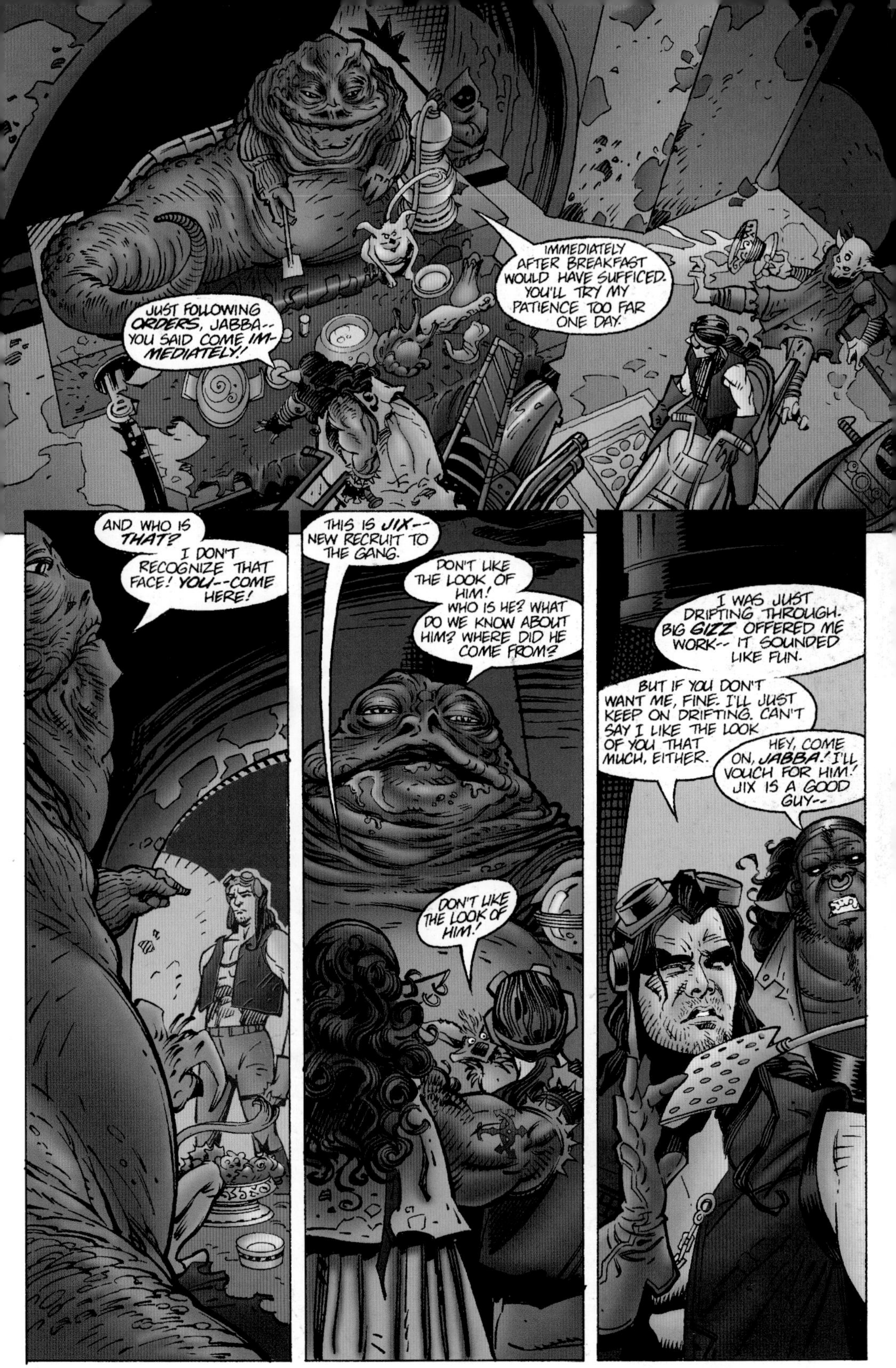
JUST FOLLOWING ORDERS, JABBA-- YOU SAID COME IMMEDIATELY!
IMMEDIATELY AFTER BREAKFAST WOULD HAVE SUFFICED. YOU'LL TRY MY PATIENCE TOO FAR ONE DAY.
AND WHO IS THAT? I DON'T RECOGNIZE THAT FACE! YOU--COME HERE!
THIS IS JIX-- NEW RECRUIT TO THE GANG.
DON'T LIKE THE LOOK OF HIM! WHO IS HE? WHAT DO WE KNOW ABOUT HIM? WHERE DID HE COME FROM?
DON'T LIKE THE LOOK OF HIM!
I WAS JUST DRIFTING THROUGH. BIG GIZZ OFFERED ME WORK-- IT SOUNDED LIKE FUN.
BUT IF YOU DON'T WANT ME, FINE. I'LL JUST KEEP ON DRIFTING. CAN'T SAY I LIKE THE LOOK OF YOU THAT MUCH, EITHER.
HEY, COME ON, JABBA! I'LL VOUCH FOR HIM! JIX IS A GOOD GUY--

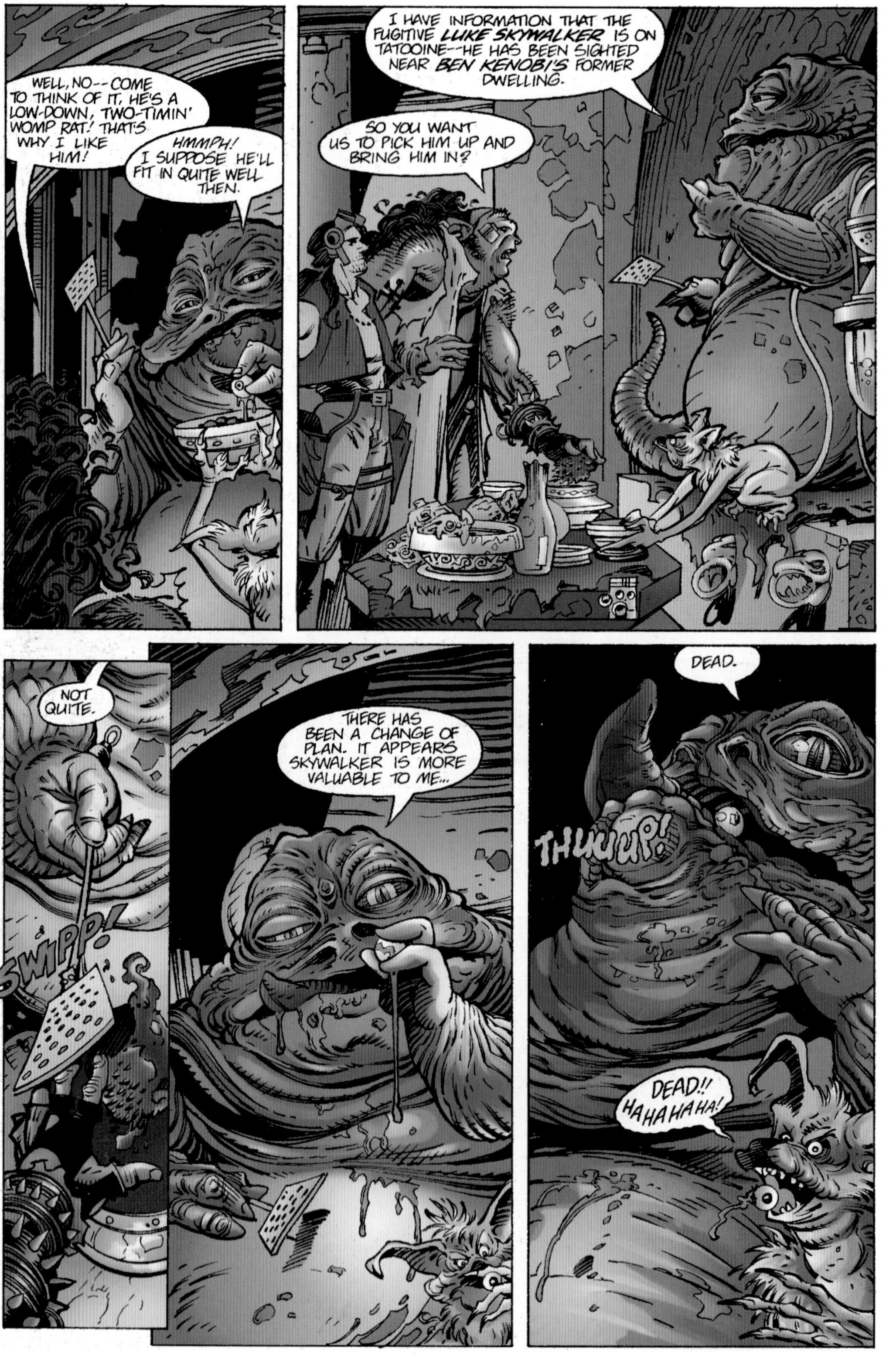
WELL, NO--COME TO THINK OF IT, HE'S A LOW-DOWN, TWO-TIMIN' WOMP RAT! THAT'S WHY I LIKE HIM!
HMMPH! I SUPPOSE HE'LL FIT IN QUITE WELL THEN.
I HAVE INFORMATION THAT THE FUGITIVE LUKE SKYWALKER IS ON TATOOINE--HE HAS BEEN SIGHTED NEAR BEN KENOBI'S FORMER DWELLING.
SO YOU WANT US TO PICK HIM UP AND BRING HIM IN?
NOT QUITE.
SWIPP!
THERE HAS BEEN A CHANGE OF PLAN. IT APPEARS SKYWALKER IS MORE VALUABLE TO ME...
DEAD.
THUUUP!
DEAD!! HAHAHAHA!

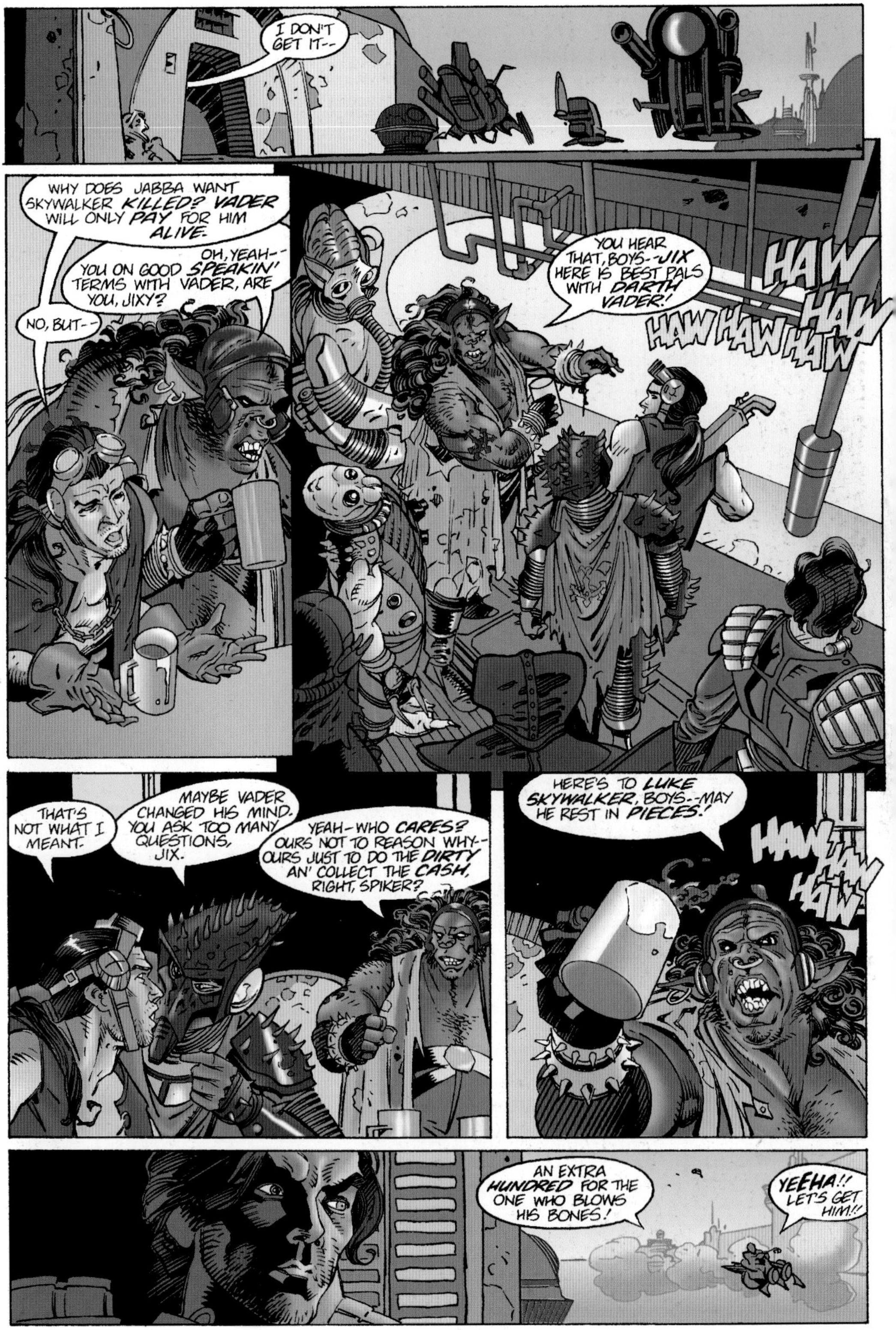
I DON'T GET IT--
WHY DOES JABBA WANT SKYWALKER KILLED? VADER WILL ONLY PAY FOR HIM ALIVE.
OH, YEAH-- YOU ON GOOD SPEAKIN' TERMS WITH VADER, ARE YOU, JIXY?
NO, BUT--
YOU HEAR THAT, BOYS--JIX HERE IS BEST PALS WITH DARTH VADER!
HAW HAW
HAW HAW HAW
THAT'S NOT WHAT I MEANT.
MAYBE VADER CHANGED HIS MIND. YOU ASK TOO MANY QUESTIONS, JIX.
YEAH-WHO CARES? OURS NOT TO REASON WHY-- OURS JUST TO DO THE DIRTY AN' COLLECT THE CASH, RIGHT, SPIKER?
HERE'S TO LUKE SKYWALKER, BOYS--MAY HE REST IN PIECES!
HAW HAW HAW
AN EXTRA HUNDRED FOR THE ONE WHO BLOWS HIS BONES!
YEEHA!! LET'S GET HIM!!

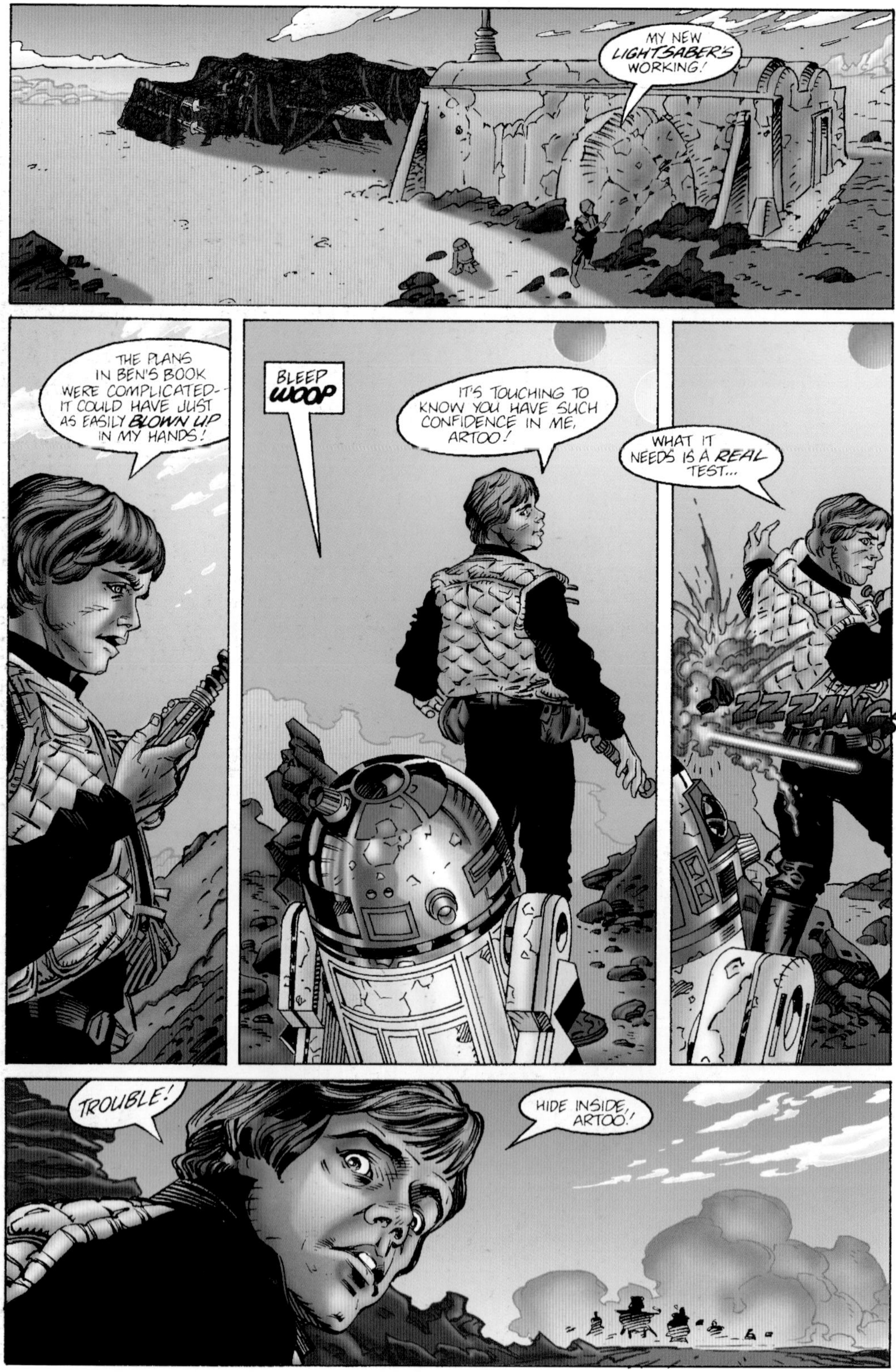
MY NEW LIGHTSABER'S WORKING!
THE PLANS IN BEN'S BOOK WERE COMPLICATED-- IT COULD HAVE JUST AS EASILY BLOWN UP IN MY HANDS!
BLEEP WOOP
IT'S TOUCHING TO KNOW YOU HAVE SUCH CONFIDENCE IN ME, ARTOO!
WHAT IT NEEDS IS A REAL TEST...
ZZZANG
TROUBLE!
HIDE INSIDE, ARTOO!

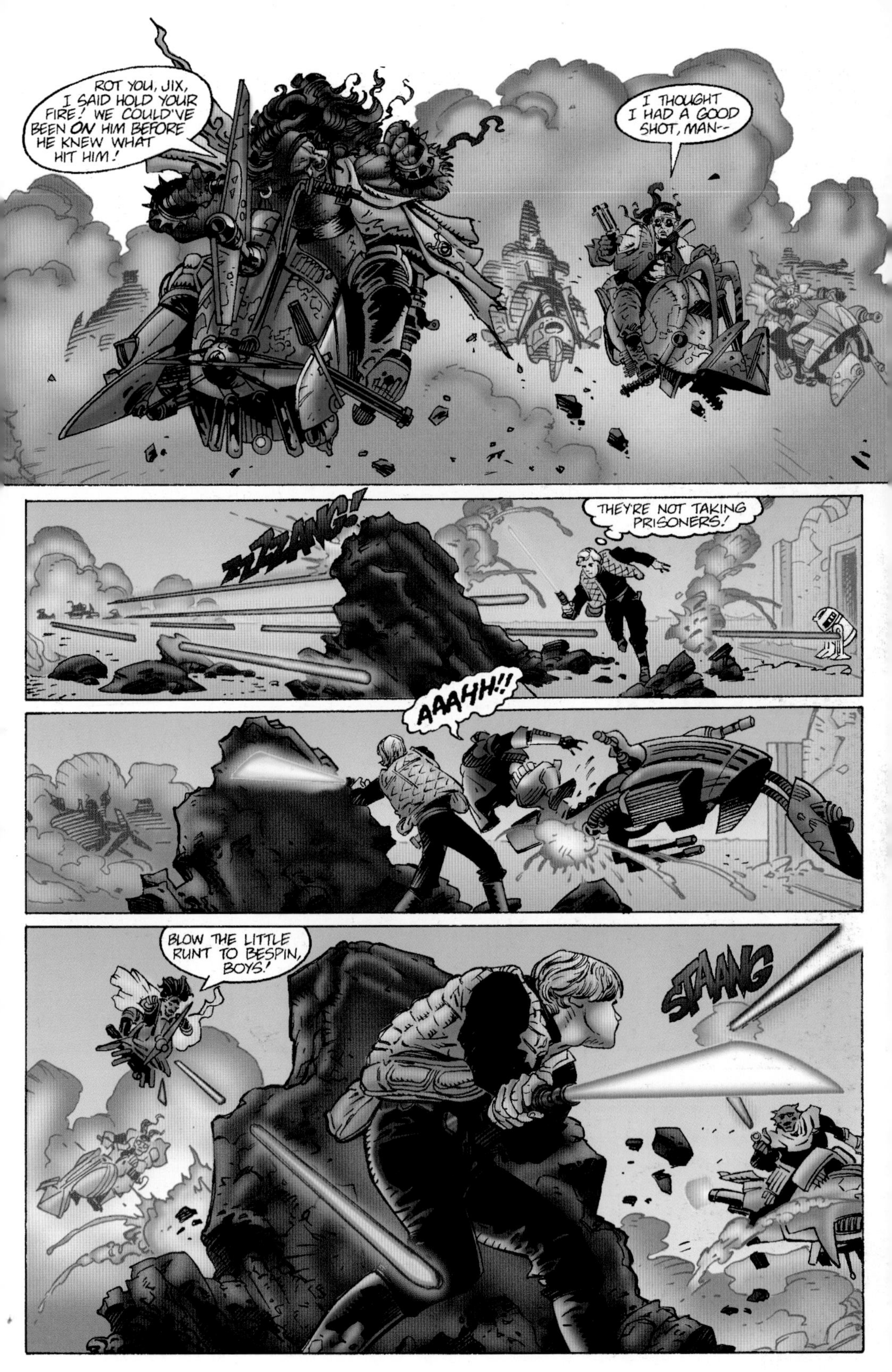
ROT YOU, JIX, I SAID HOLD YOUR FIRE! WE COULD'VE BEEN ON HIM BEFORE HE KNEW WHAT HIT HIM!
I THOUGHT I HAD A GOOD SHOT, MAN--
ZZZANG!
THEY'RE NOT TAKING PRISONERS!
AAAHH!!
BLOW THE LITTLE RUNT TO BESPIN, BOYS!
SJAANG

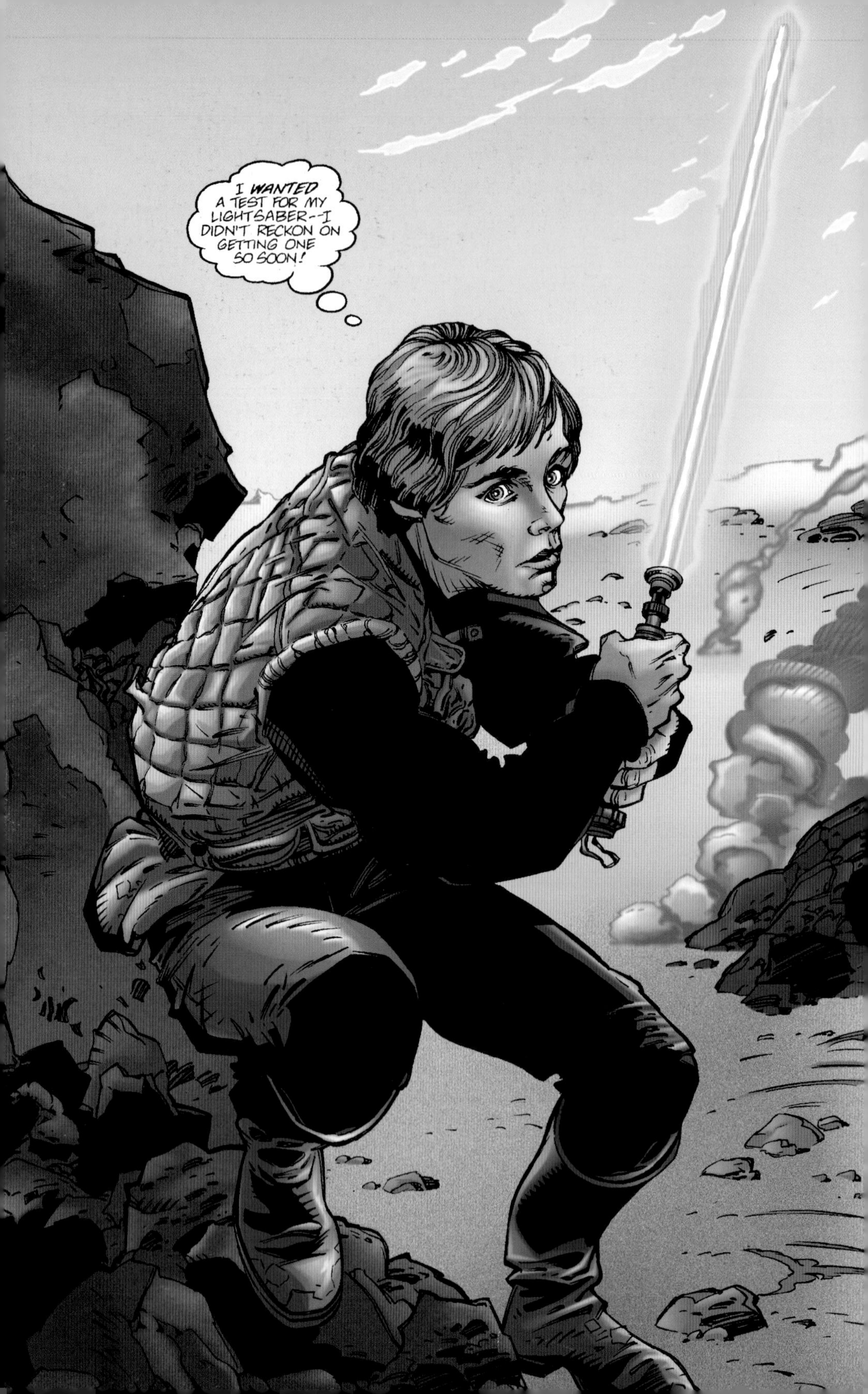
I *WANTED* A TEST FOR MY LIGHTSABER--I DIDN'T RECKON ON GETTING ONE SO SOON!

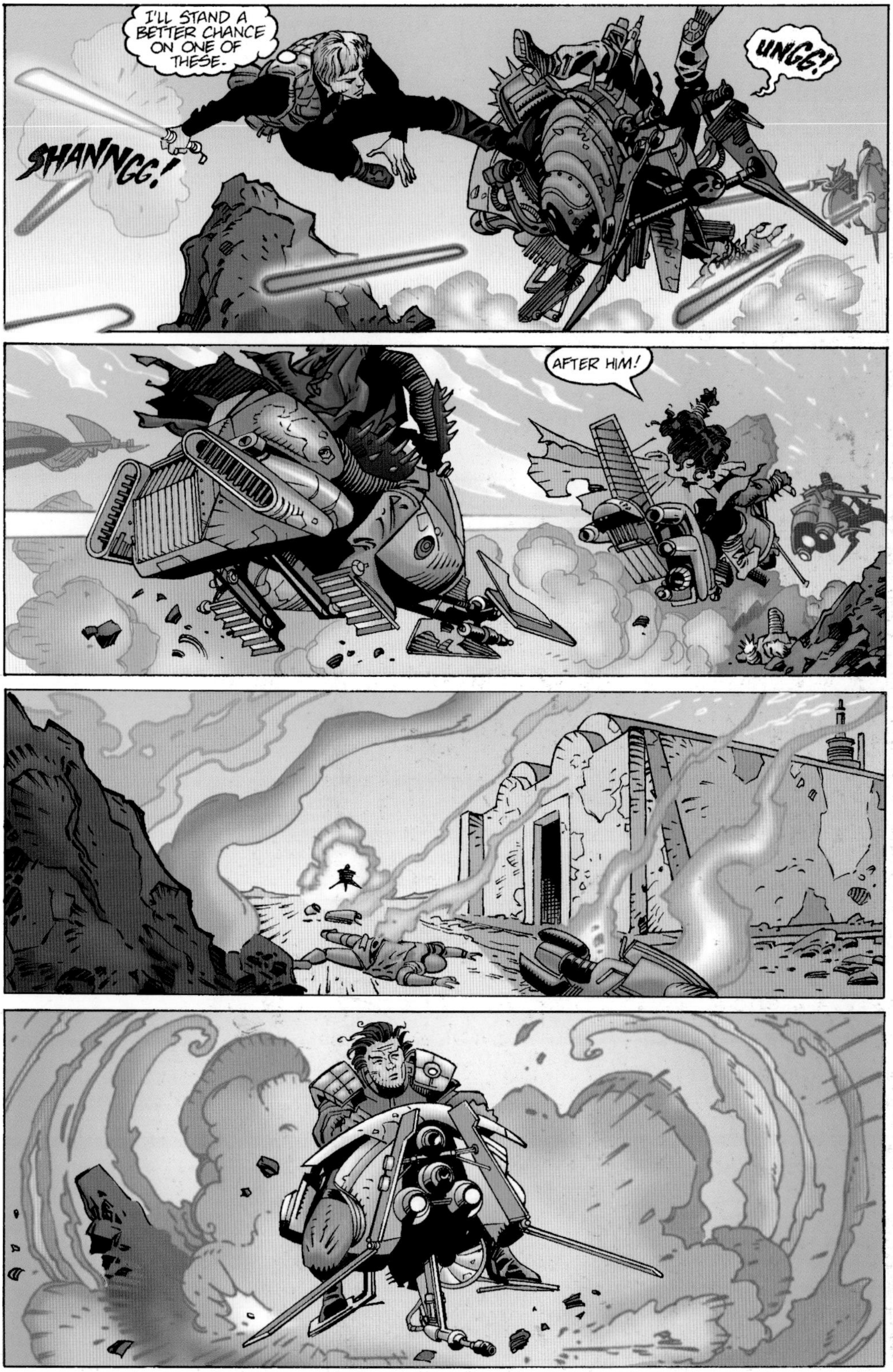
I'LL STAND A BETTER CHANCE ON ONE OF THESE.
SHANNGG!
UNGG!
AFTER HIM!

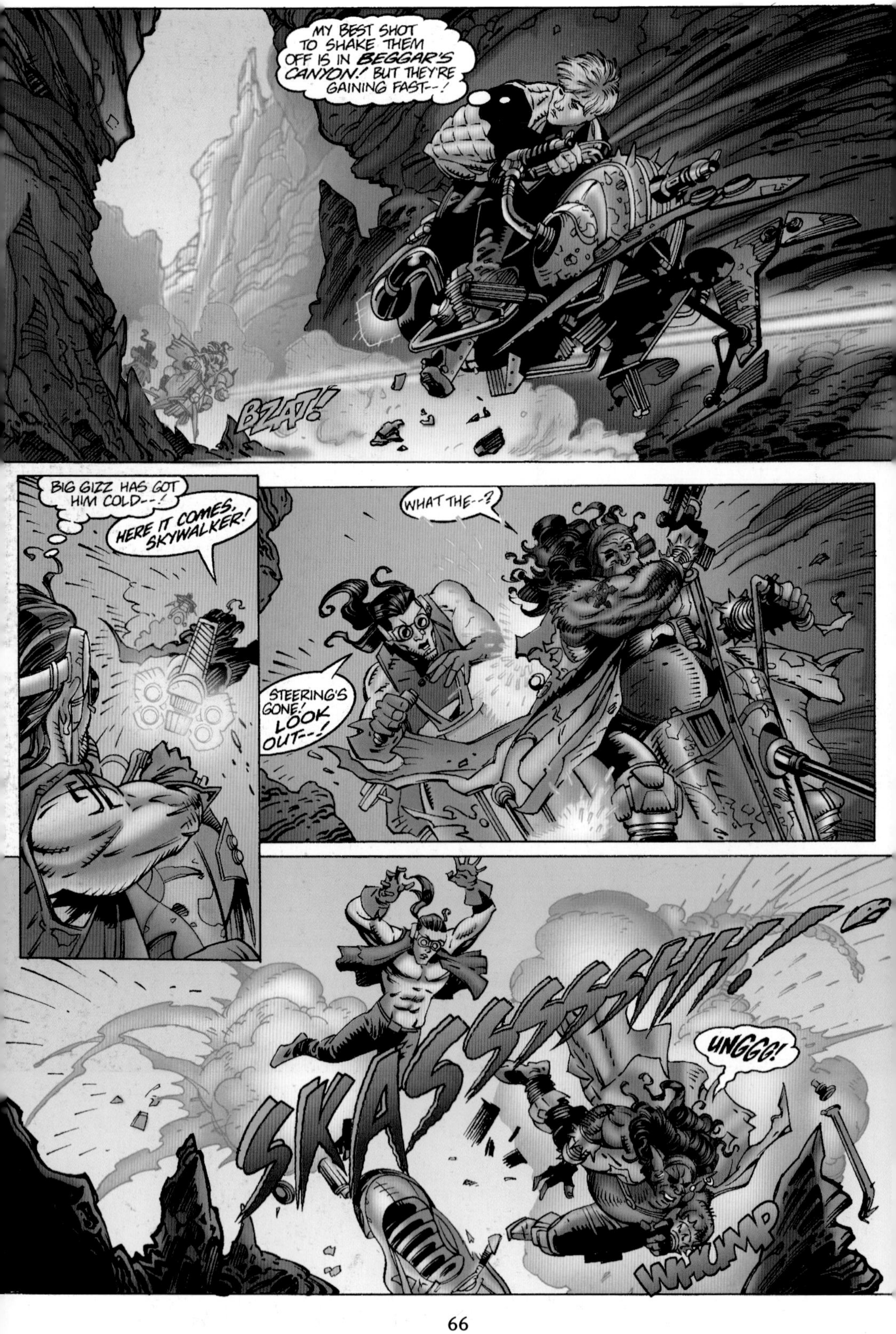
MY BEST SHOT TO SHAKE THEM OFF IS IN BEGGAR'S CANYON! BUT THEY'RE GAINING FAST--!
BZAT!
BIG GIZZ HAS GOT HIM COLD--!
HERE IT COMES, SKYWALKER!
WHAT THE--?
STEERING'S GONE! LOOK OUT--!
SKASSSSSHH!!
UNGGG!
WHUMP

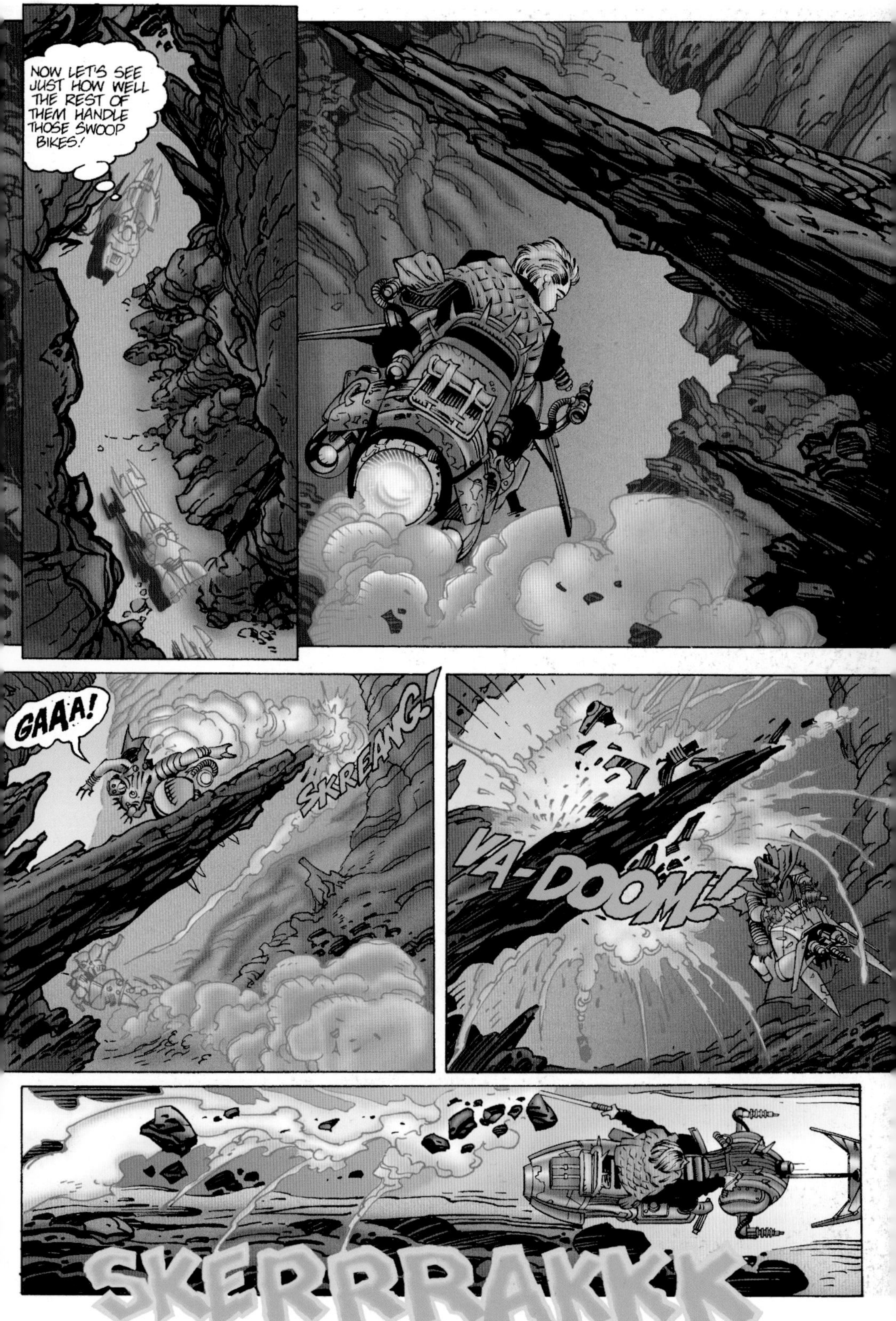
NOW LET'S SEE JUST HOW WELL THE REST OF THEM HANDLE THOSE SWOOP BIKES!
GAAA!
SKREEANG!
VA-DOOM!
SKERRRAKKK

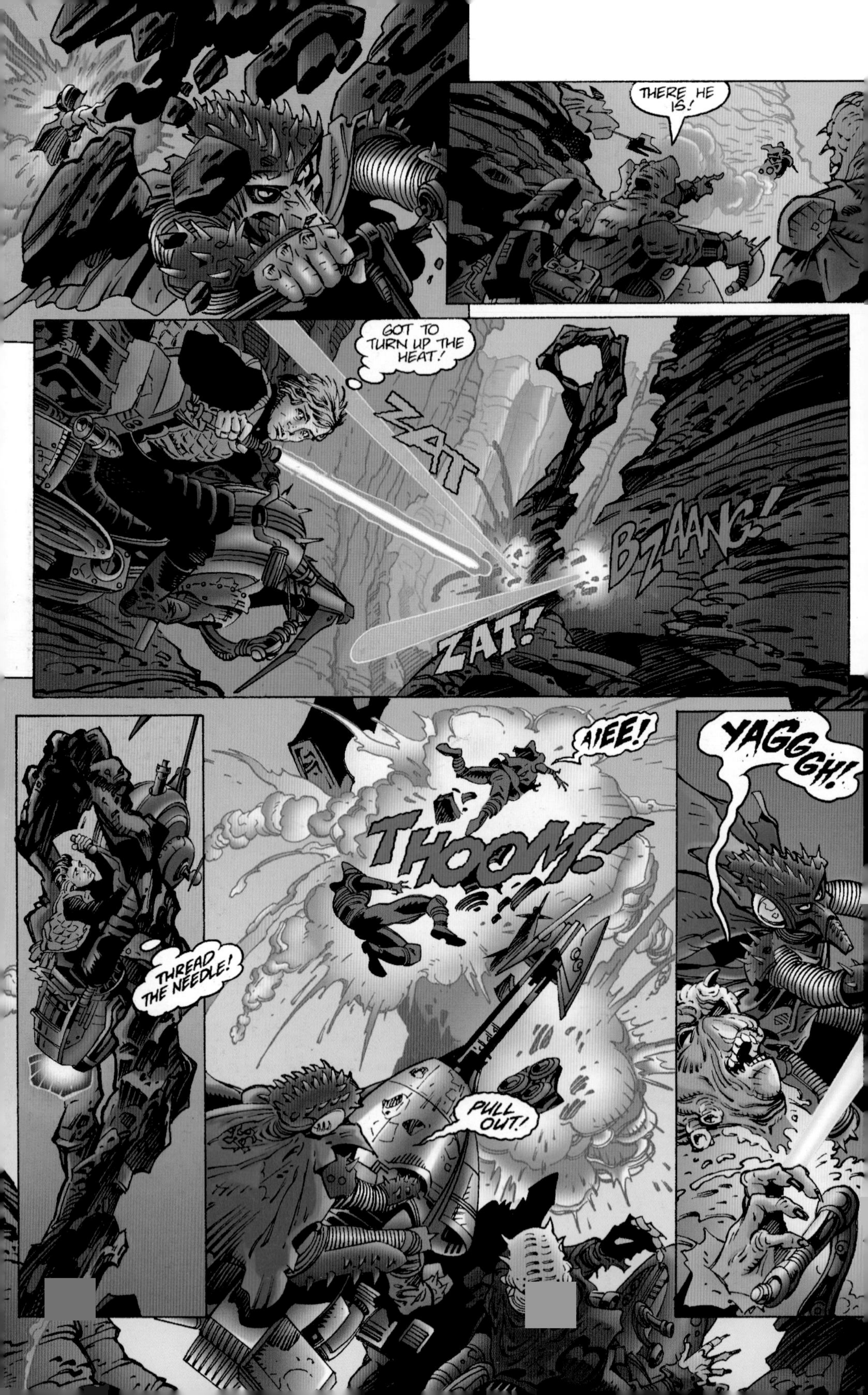
THERE HE IS!
GOT TO TURN UP THE HEAT!
ZAT
BZAANG!
ZAT!
THREAD THE NEEDLE!
AIEE!
THOOM!
PULL OUT!
YAGGGGH!

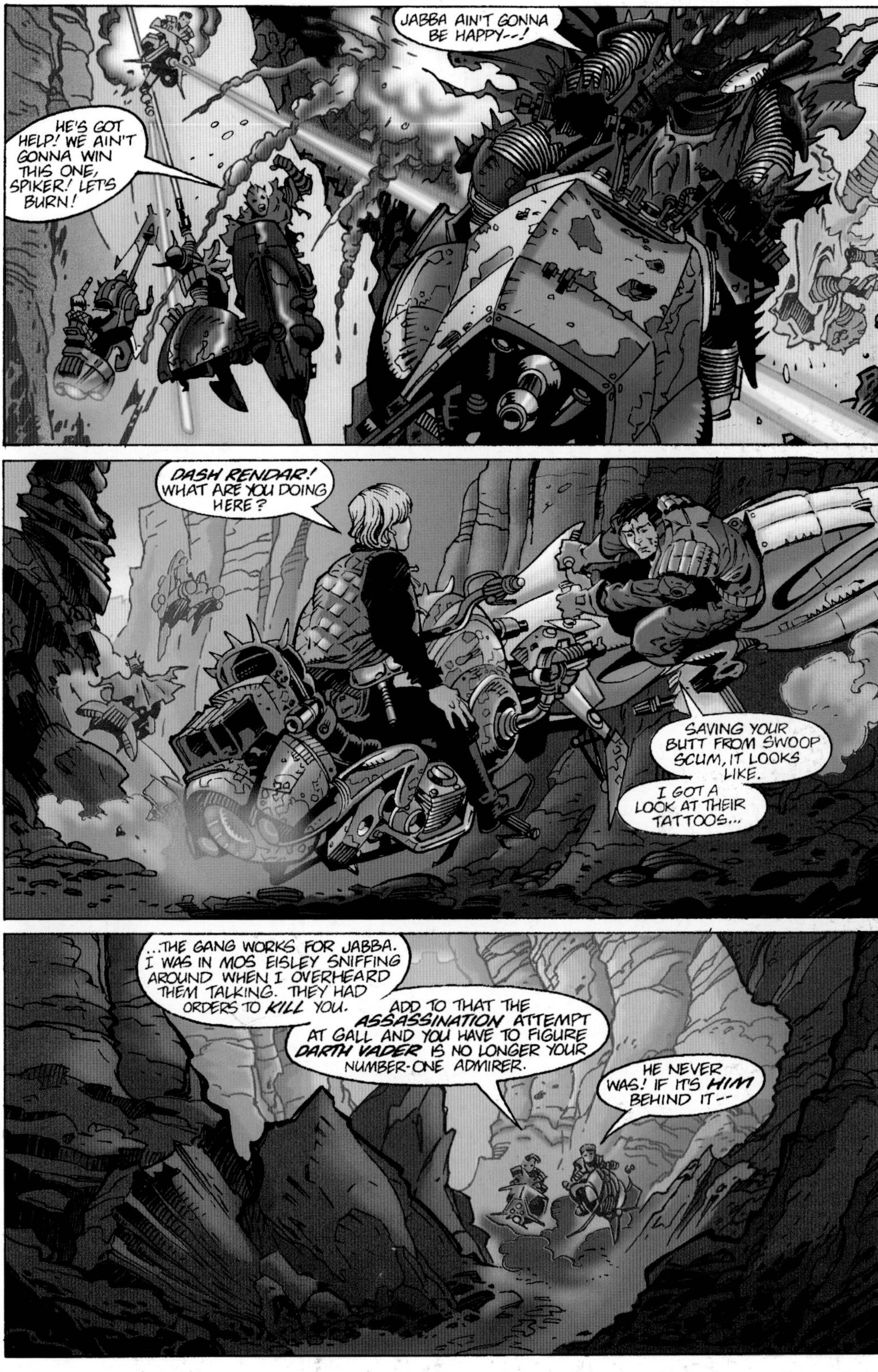
JABBA AIN'T GONNA BE HAPPY--!
HE'S GOT HELP! WE AIN'T GONNA WIN THIS ONE, SPIKER! LET'S BURN!
DASH RENDAR! WHAT ARE YOU DOING HERE?
SAVING YOUR BUTT FROM SWOOP SCUM, IT LOOKS LIKE.
I GOT A LOOK AT THEIR TATTOOS...
...THE GANG WORKS FOR JABBA. I WAS IN MOS EISLEY SNIFFING AROUND WHEN I OVERHEARD THEM TALKING. THEY HAD ORDERS TO KILL YOU.
ADD TO THAT THE ASSASSINATION ATTEMPT AT GALL AND YOU HAVE TO FIGURE DARTH VADER IS NO LONGER YOUR NUMBER-ONE ADMIRER.
HE NEVER WAS! IF IT'S HIM BEHIND IT--

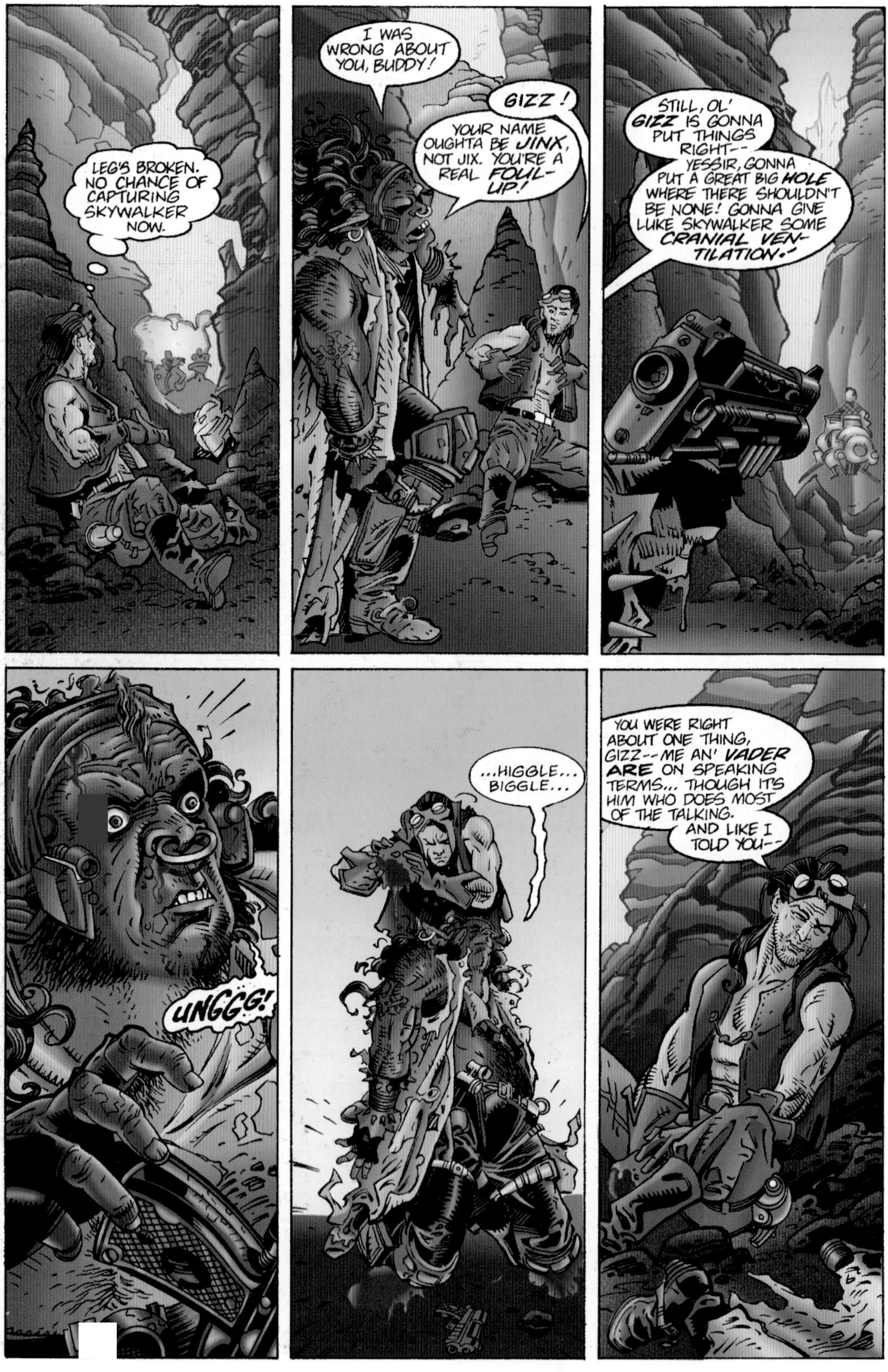
LEG'S BROKEN. NO CHANCE OF CAPTURING SKYWALKER NOW.
I WAS WRONG ABOUT YOU, BUDDY!
GIZZ!
YOUR NAME OUGHTA BE JINX, NOT JIX. YOU'RE A REAL FOUL-UP!
STILL, OL' GIZZ IS GONNA PUT THINGS RIGHT--
YESSIR, GONNA PUT A GREAT BIG HOLE WHERE THERE SHOULDN'T BE NONE! GONNA GIVE LUKE SKYWALKER SOME CRANIAL VEN-TILATION-
UNGGG!
...HIGGLE... BIGGLE...
YOU WERE RIGHT ABOUT ONE THING, GIZZ--ME AN' VADER ARE ON SPEAKING TERMS... THOUGH IT'S HIM WHO DOES MOST OF THE TALKING.
AND LIKE I TOLD YOU--

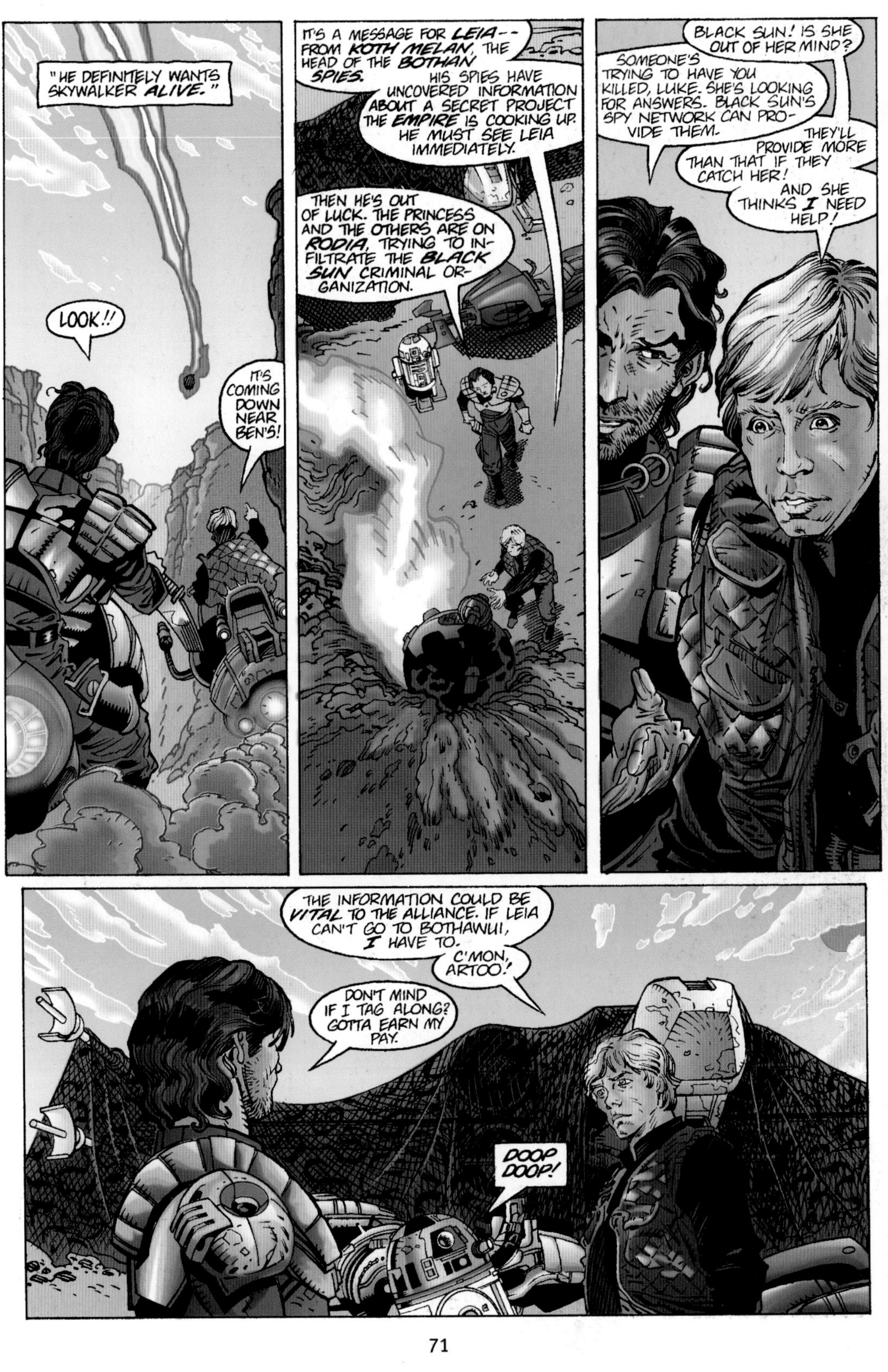

"HE DEFINITELY WANTS SKYWALKER ALIVE."
LOOK!!
IT'S COMING DOWN NEAR BEN'S!
IT'S A MESSAGE FOR LEIA-- FROM KOTH MELAN, THE HEAD OF THE BOTHAN SPIES.
HIS SPIES HAVE UNCOVERED INFORMATION ABOUT A SECRET PROJECT THE EMPIRE IS COOKING UP. HE MUST SEE LEIA IMMEDIATELY.
THEN HE'S OUT OF LUCK. THE PRINCESS AND THE OTHERS ARE ON RODIA, TRYING TO INFILTRATE THE BLACK SUN CRIMINAL ORGANIZATION.
BLACK SUN! IS SHE OUT OF HER MIND?
SOMEONE'S TRYING TO HAVE YOU KILLED, LUKE. SHE'S LOOKING FOR ANSWERS. BLACK SUN'S SPY NETWORK CAN PROVIDE THEM.
THEY'LL PROVIDE MORE THAN THAT IF THEY CATCH HER!
AND SHE THINKS I NEED HELP!
THE INFORMATION COULD BE VITAL TO THE ALLIANCE. IF LEIA CAN'T GO TO BOTHAWUI, I HAVE TO.
C'MON, ARTOO!
DON'T MIND IF I TAG ALONG? GOTTA EARN MY PAY.
DOOP DOOP!

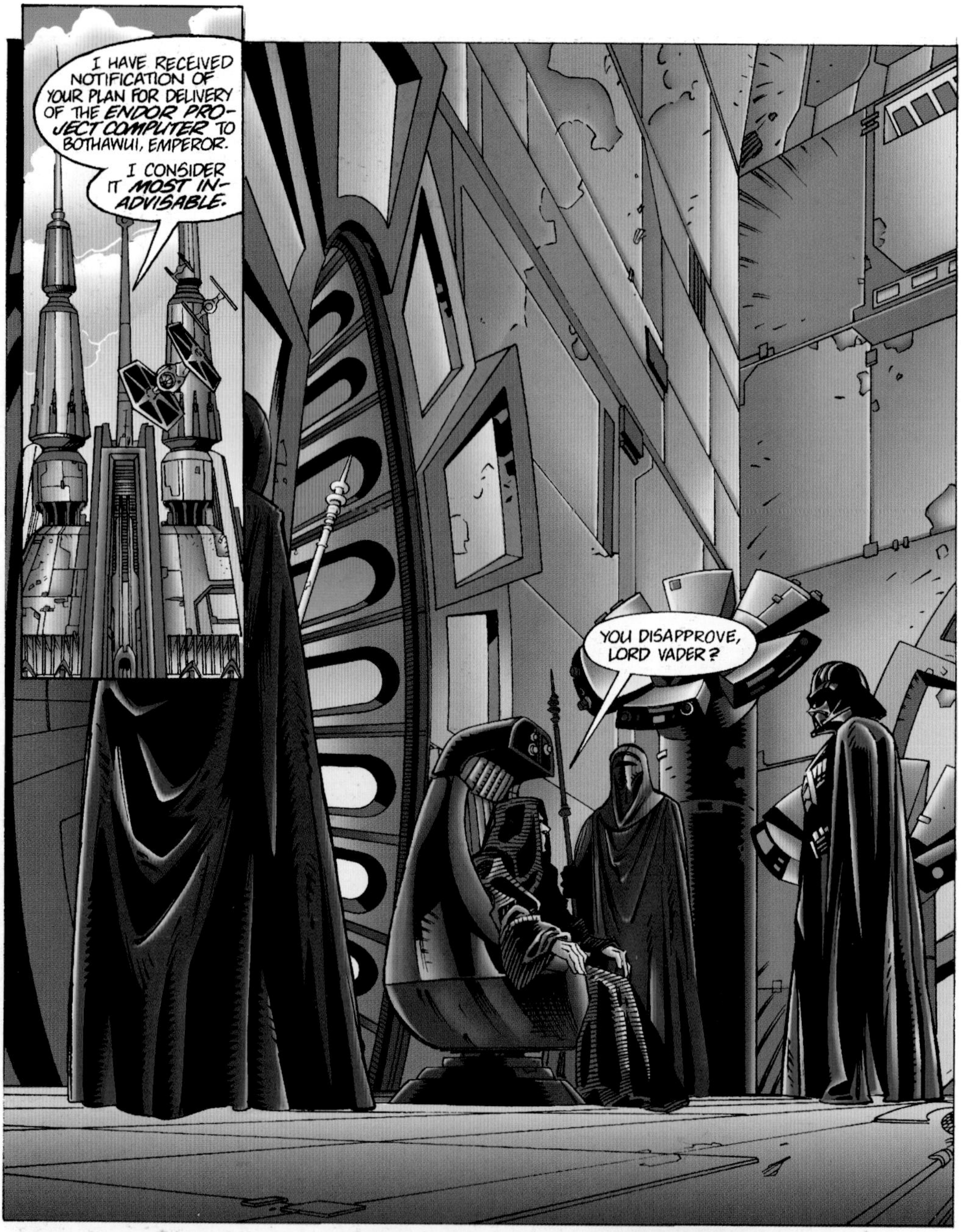
I HAVE RECEIVED NOTIFICATION OF YOUR PLAN FOR DELIVERY OF THE ENDOR PROJECT COMPUTER TO BOTHAWUI, EMPEROR.
I CONSIDER IT MOST INADVISABLE.
YOU DISAPPROVE, LORD VADER?

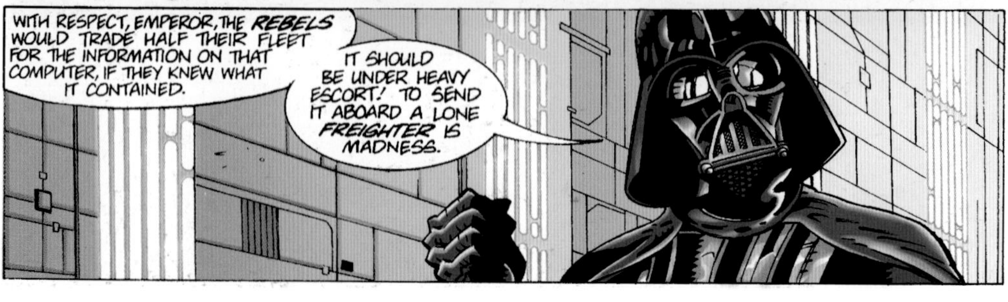
WITH RESPECT, EMPEROR, THE REBELS WOULD TRADE HALF THEIR FLEET FOR THE INFORMATION ON THAT COMPUTER, IF THEY KNEW WHAT IT CONTAINED.
IT SHOULD BE UNDER HEAVY ESCORT! TO SEND IT ABOARD A LONE FREIGHTER IS MADNESS.

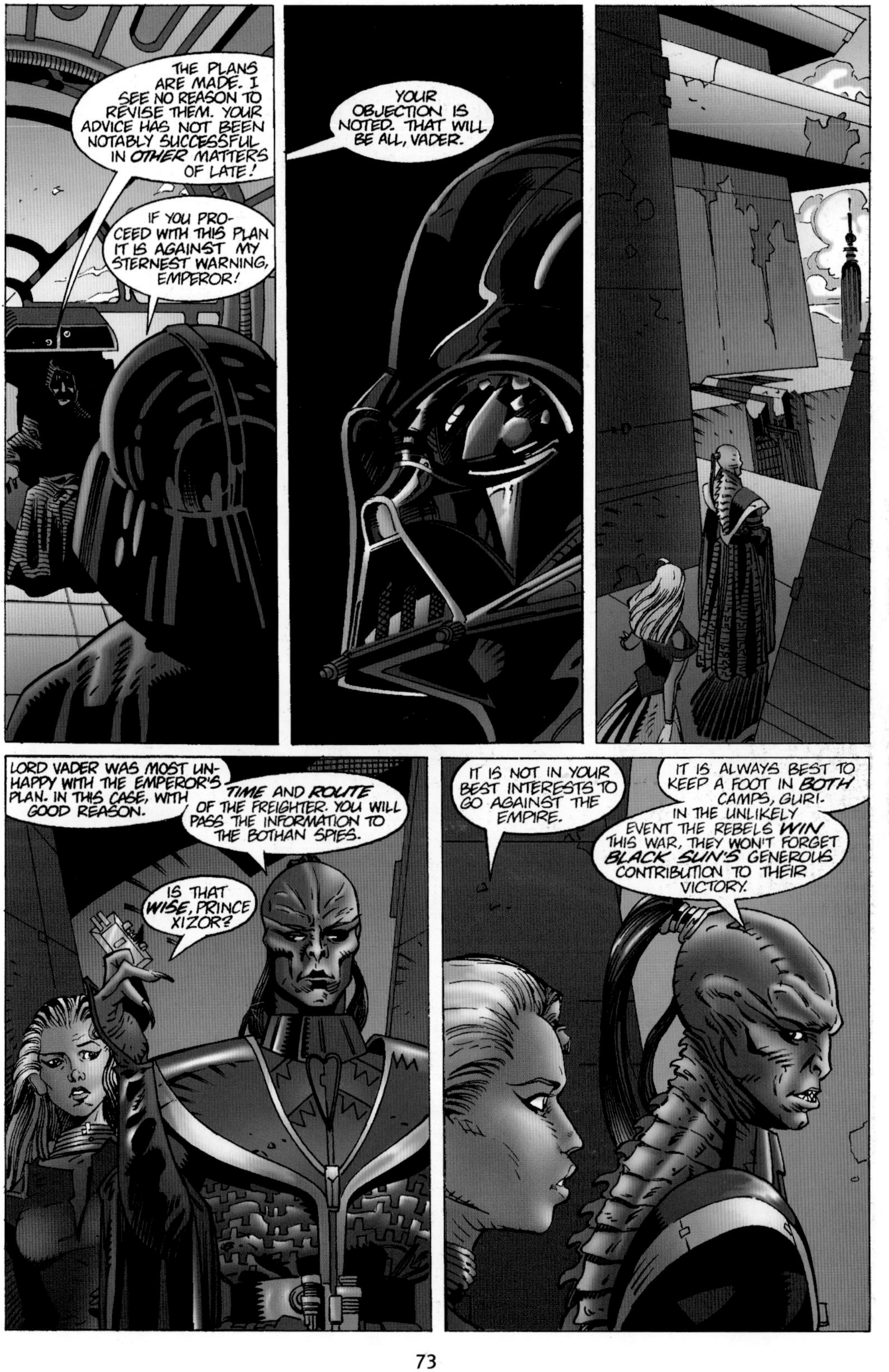
THE PLANS ARE MADE. I SEE NO REASON TO REVISE THEM. YOUR ADVICE HAS NOT BEEN NOTABLY SUCCESSFUL IN OTHER MATTERS OF LATE!
IF YOU PROCEED WITH THIS PLAN IT IS AGAINST MY STERNEST WARNING, EMPEROR!
YOUR OBJECTION IS NOTED. THAT WILL BE ALL, VADER.
LORD VADER WAS MOST UNHAPPY WITH THE EMPEROR'S PLAN. IN THIS CASE, WITH GOOD REASON.
TIME AND ROUTE OF THE FREIGHTER. YOU WILL PASS THE INFORMATION TO THE BOTHAN SPIES.
IS THAT WISE, PRINCE XIZOR?
IT IS NOT IN YOUR BEST INTERESTS TO GO AGAINST THE EMPIRE.
IT IS ALWAYS BEST TO KEEP A FOOT IN BOTH CAMPS, GURI.
IN THE UNLIKELY EVENT THE REBELS WIN THIS WAR, THEY WON'T FORGET BLACK SUN'S GENEROUS CONTRIBUTION TO THEIR VICTORY.

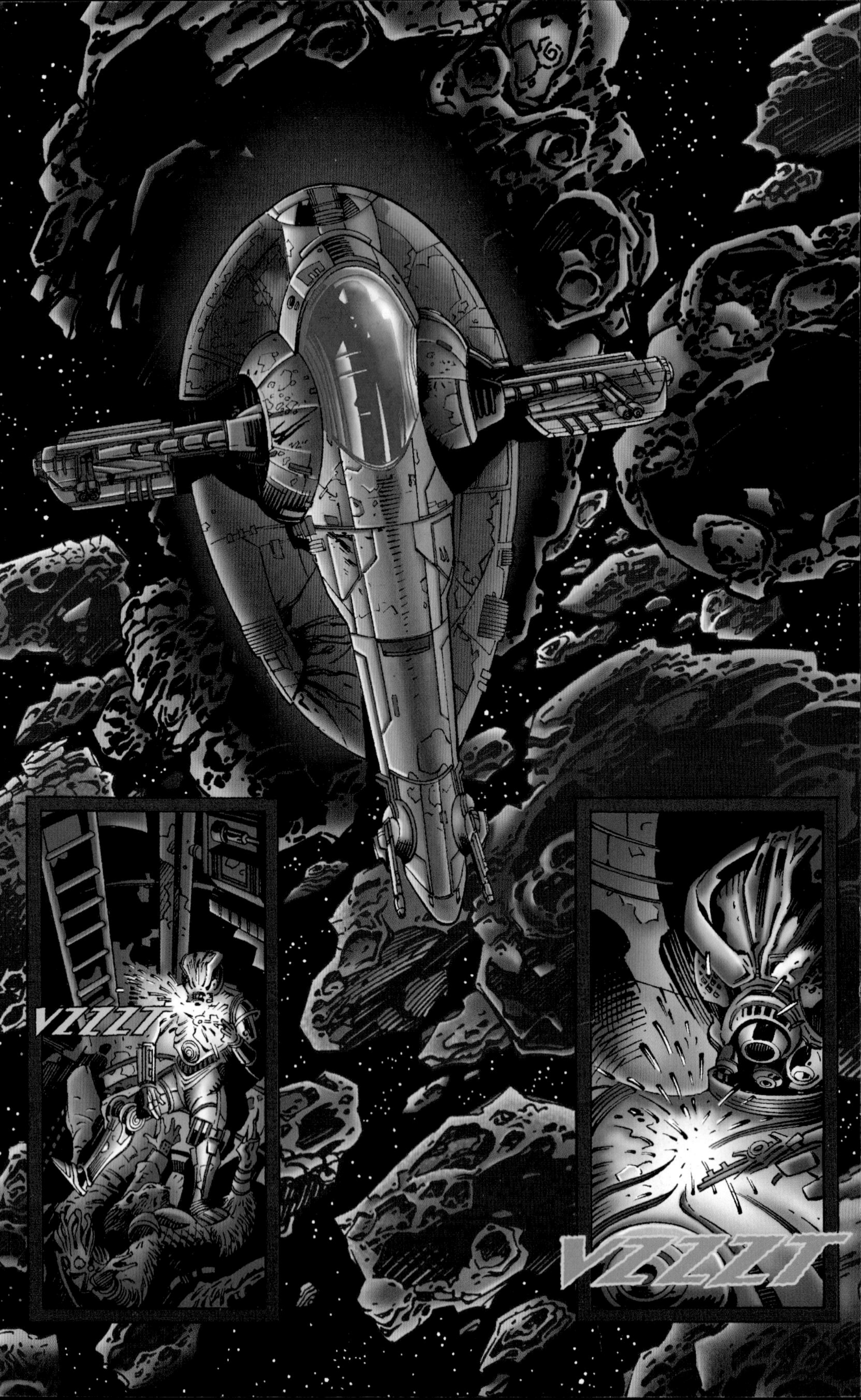
VZZZT
VZZZT

A FINE PREDICAMENT THIS IS, SOLO! HIDING FROM *REBELS* AND *BOUNTY HUNTERS* ALIKE! ALL BECAUSE OF YOU!

WHAT TO *DO* WITH YOU?

TATOOINE, YES... GET YOU TO TATOOINE, CLAIM *JABBA'S* REWARD AND BE *RID* OF YOU.

YET THEY'LL BE WATCHING FOR US, MY FELLOW BOUNTY HUNTERS! I'LL BE LUCKY TO GET YOU THERE IN ONE PIECE!

NOT THAT *YOU* CARE, EH, SOLO? BELIEVE ME, YOU'RE MORE TROUBLE AS A LUMP OF FROZEN CARBONITE THAN YOU EVER WERE IN THE FLESH!

VZZZT-TT

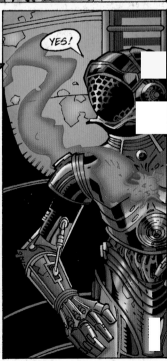

YES!

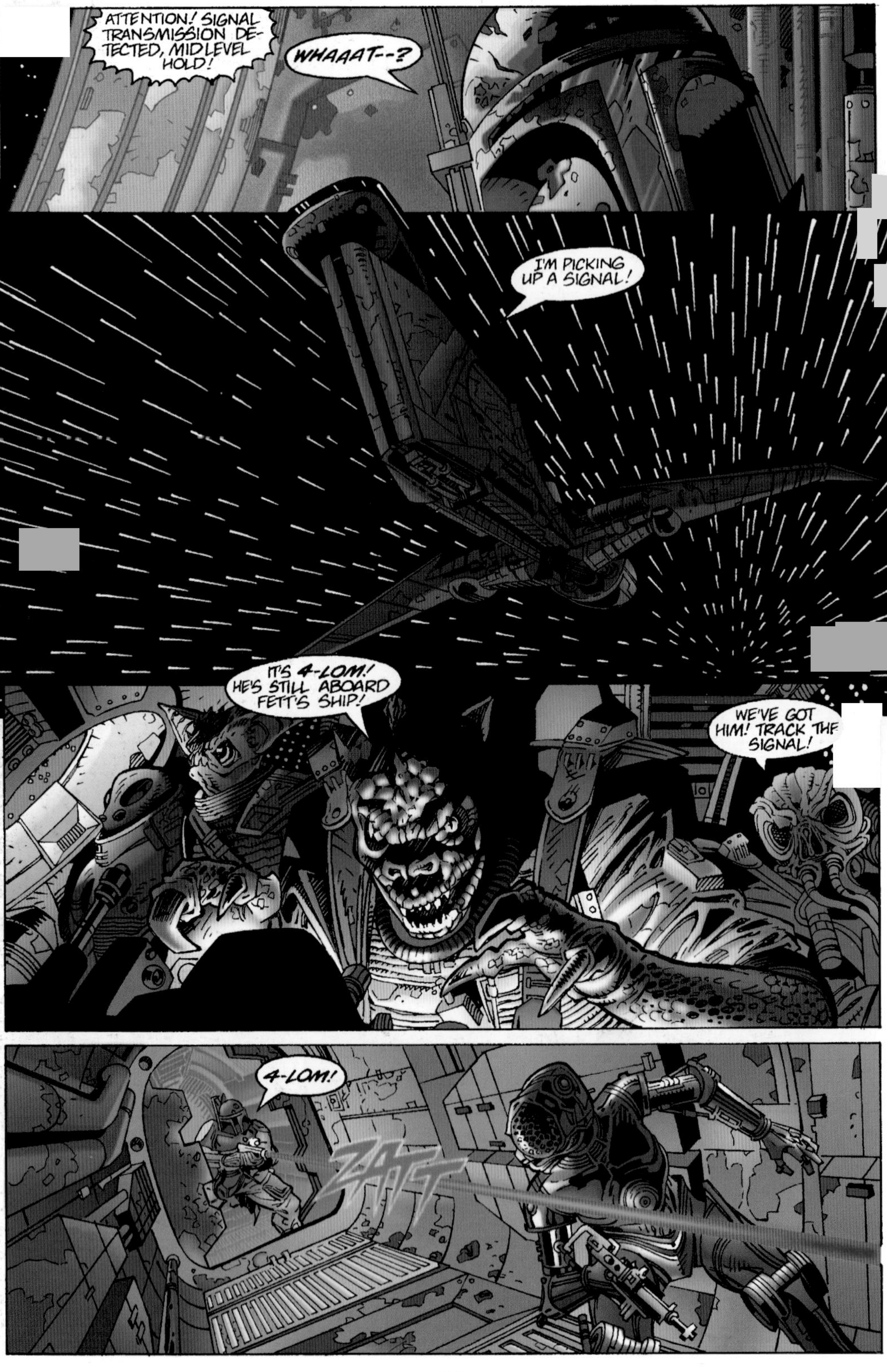
ATTENTION! SIGNAL TRANSMISSION DETECTED, MID LEVEL HOLD!
WHAAAT--?
I'M PICKING UP A SIGNAL!
IT'S 4-LOM! HE'S STILL ABOARD FETT'S SHIP!
WE'VE GOT HIM! TRACK THE SIGNAL!
4-LOM!
ZATT

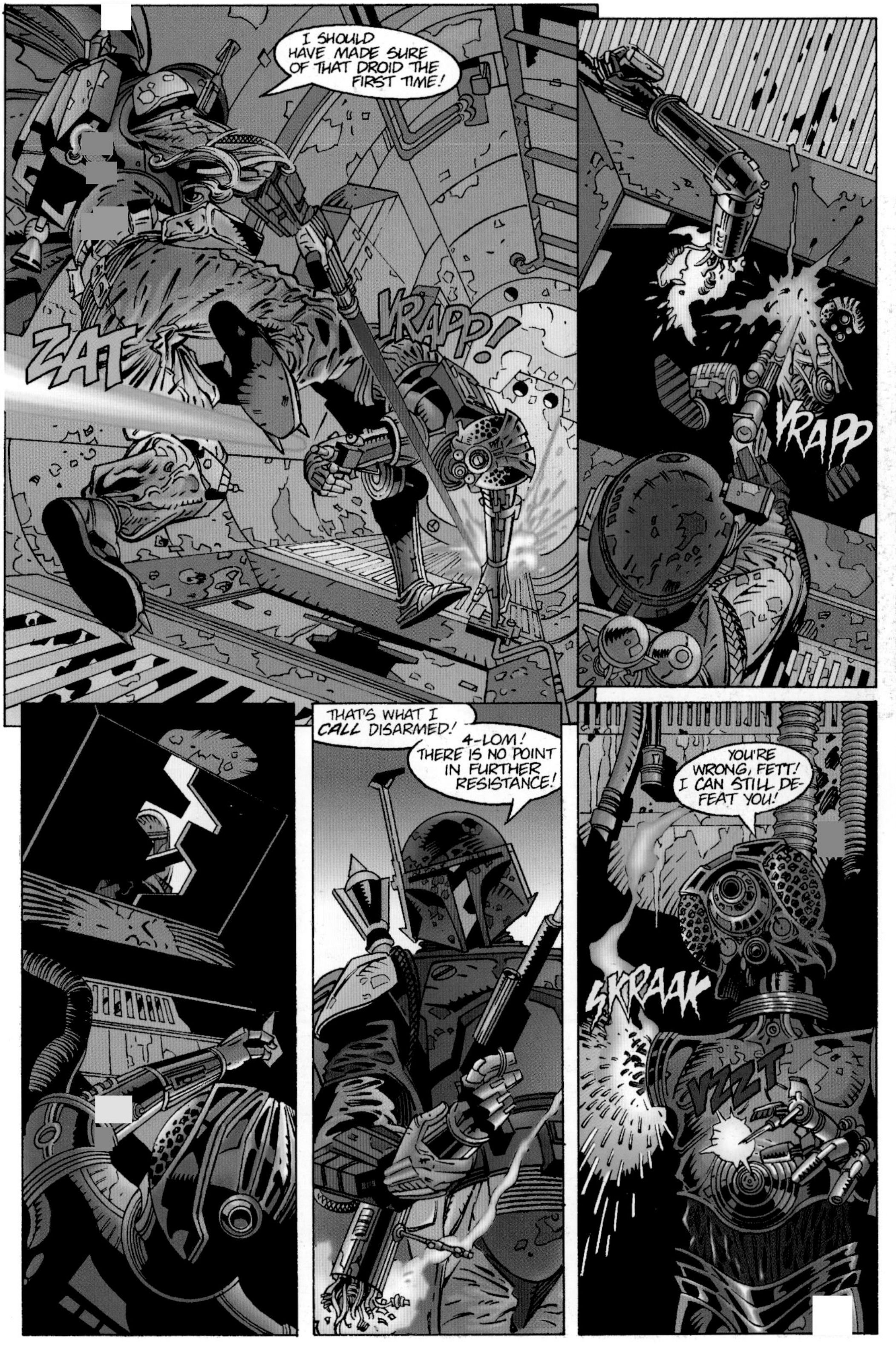
I SHOULD HAVE MADE SURE OF THAT DROID THE FIRST TIME!
ZAT
VRAPP!
VRAPP
THAT'S WHAT I CALL DISARMED!
4-LOM! THERE IS NO POINT IN FURTHER RESISTANCE!
YOU'RE WRONG, FETT! I CAN STILL DEFEAT YOU!
SKRAAK
VZZT

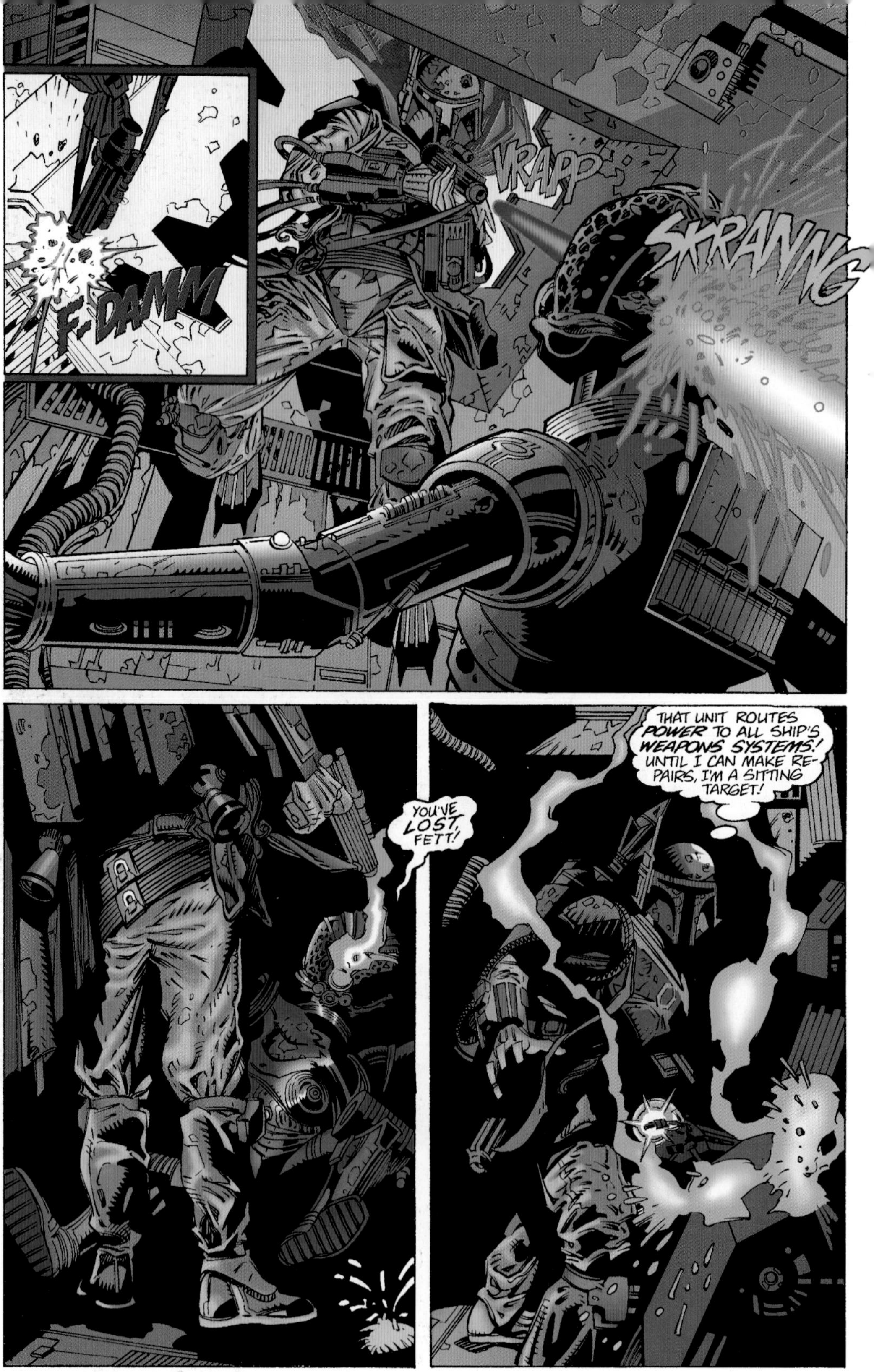
F-DAMM
VRAPP
SKRANNG
YOU'VE LOST, FETT!
THAT UNIT ROUTES POWER TO ALL SHIP'S WEAPONS SYSTEMS! UNTIL I CAN MAKE REPAIRS, I'M A SITTING TARGET!

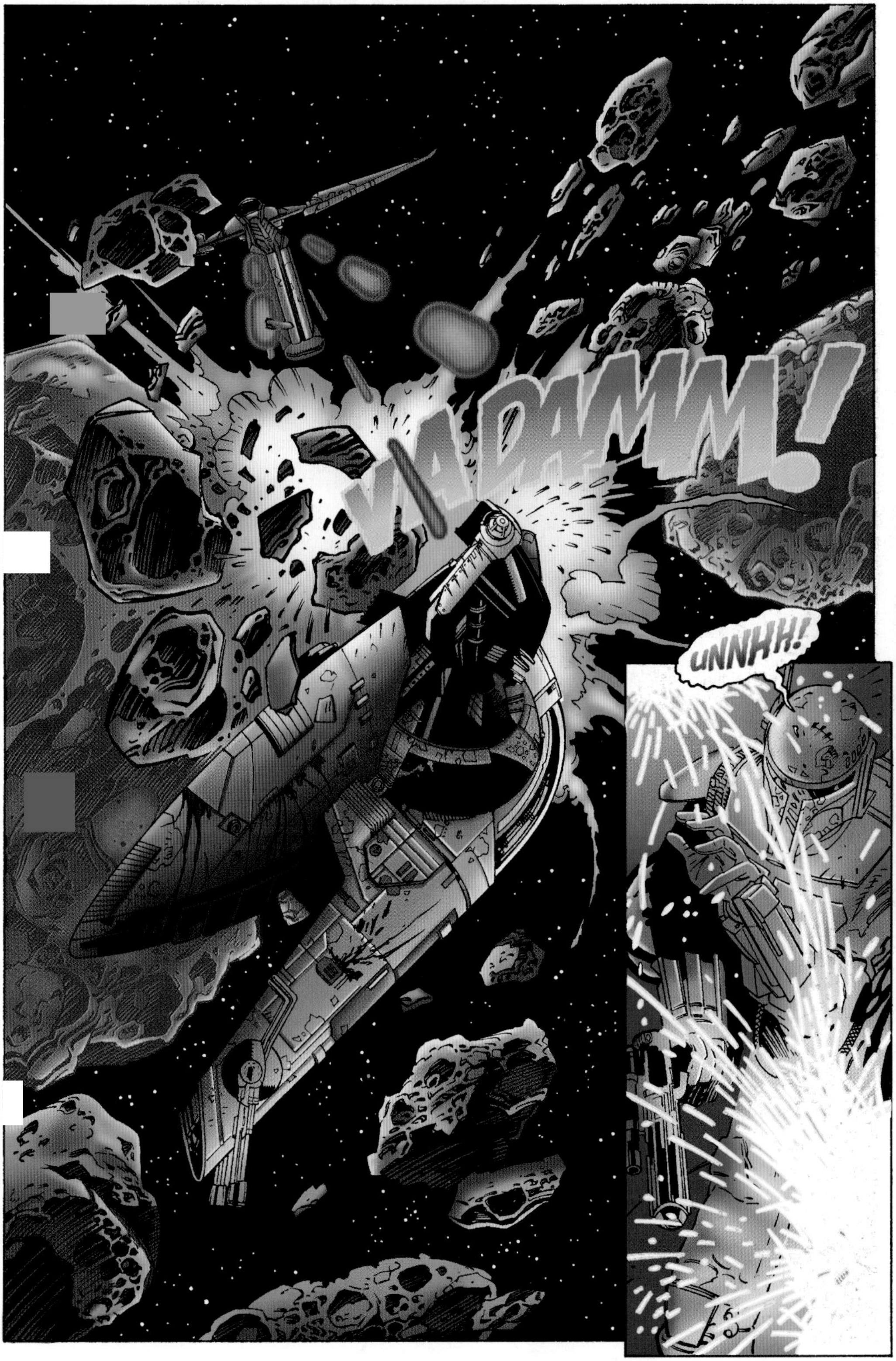
VADAMM!
UNNHH!

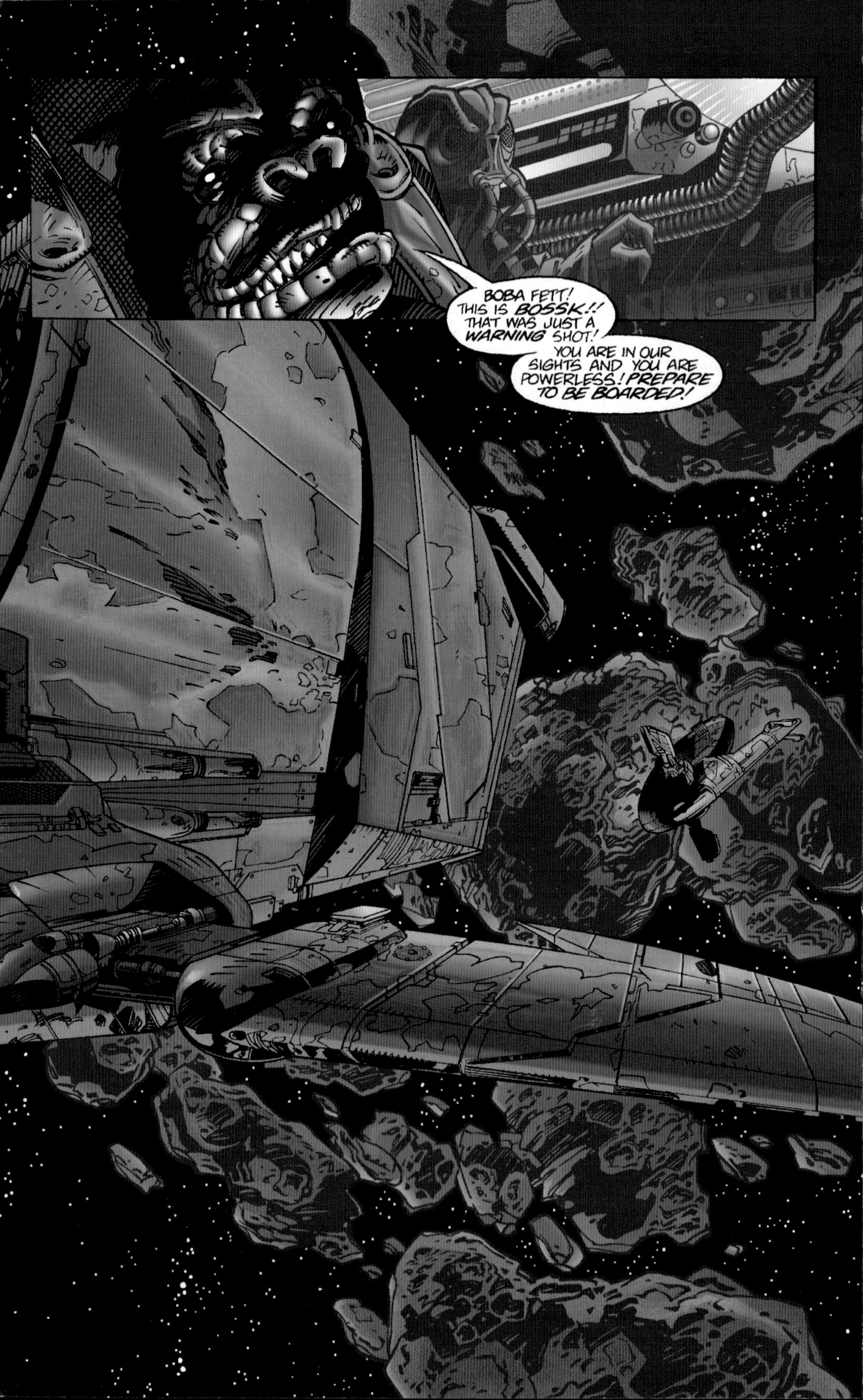
BOBA FETT! THIS IS BOSSK!! THAT WAS JUST A WARNING SHOT! YOU ARE IN OUR SIGHTS AND YOU ARE POWERLESS! PREPARE TO BE BOARDED!

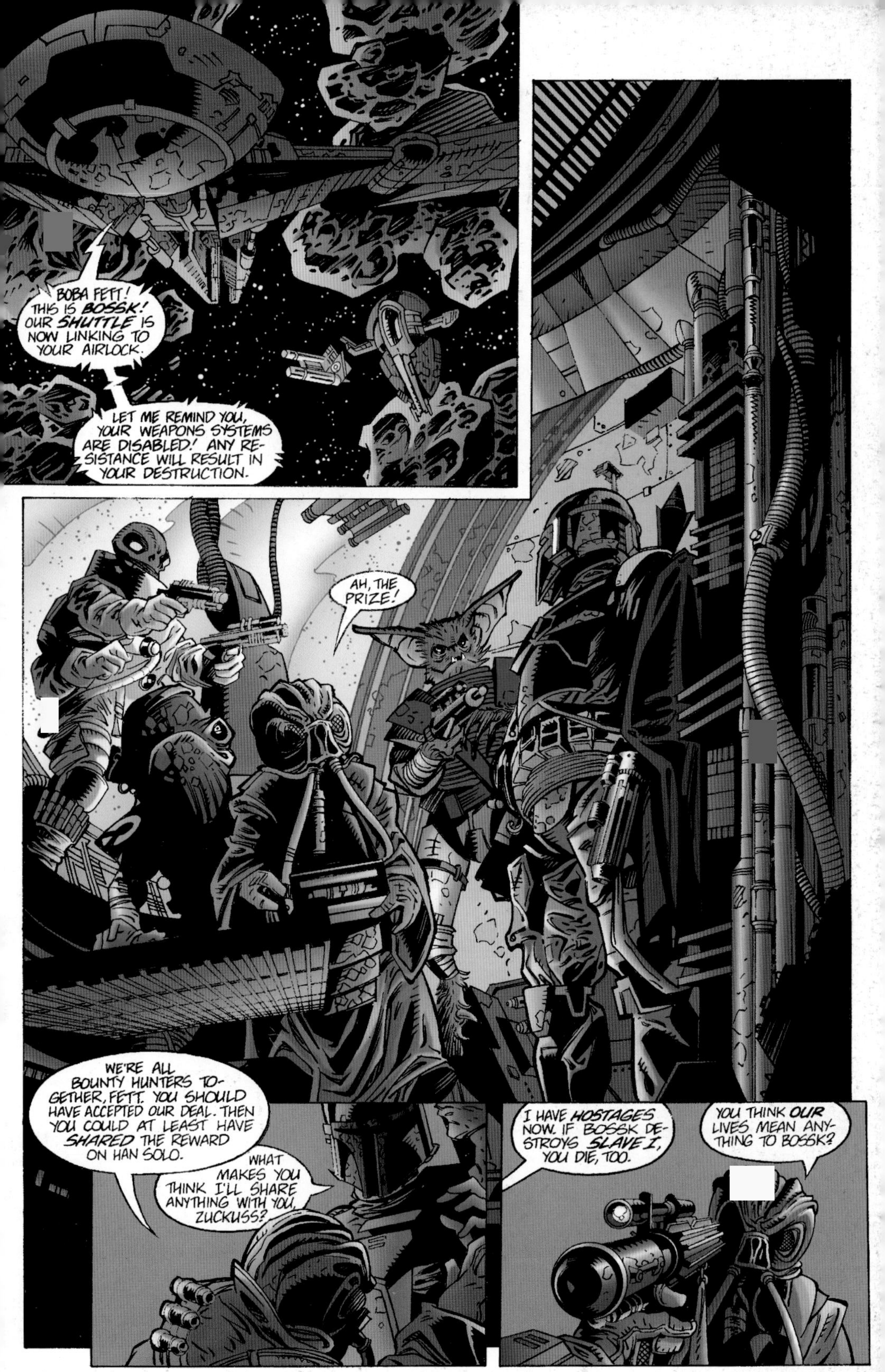
BOBA FETT! THIS IS BOSSK! OUR SHUTTLE IS NOW LINKING TO YOUR AIRLOCK.
LET ME REMIND YOU, YOUR WEAPONS SYSTEMS ARE DISABLED! ANY RESISTANCE WILL RESULT IN YOUR DESTRUCTION.
AH, THE PRIZE!
WE'RE ALL BOUNTY HUNTERS TOGETHER, FETT. YOU SHOULD HAVE ACCEPTED OUR DEAL. THEN YOU COULD AT LEAST HAVE SHARED THE REWARD ON HAN SOLO.
WHAT MAKES YOU THINK I'LL SHARE ANYTHING WITH YOU, ZUCKUSS?
I HAVE HOSTAGES NOW. IF BOSSK DESTROYS SLAVE I, YOU DIE, TOO.
YOU THINK OUR LIVES MEAN ANYTHING TO BOSSK?

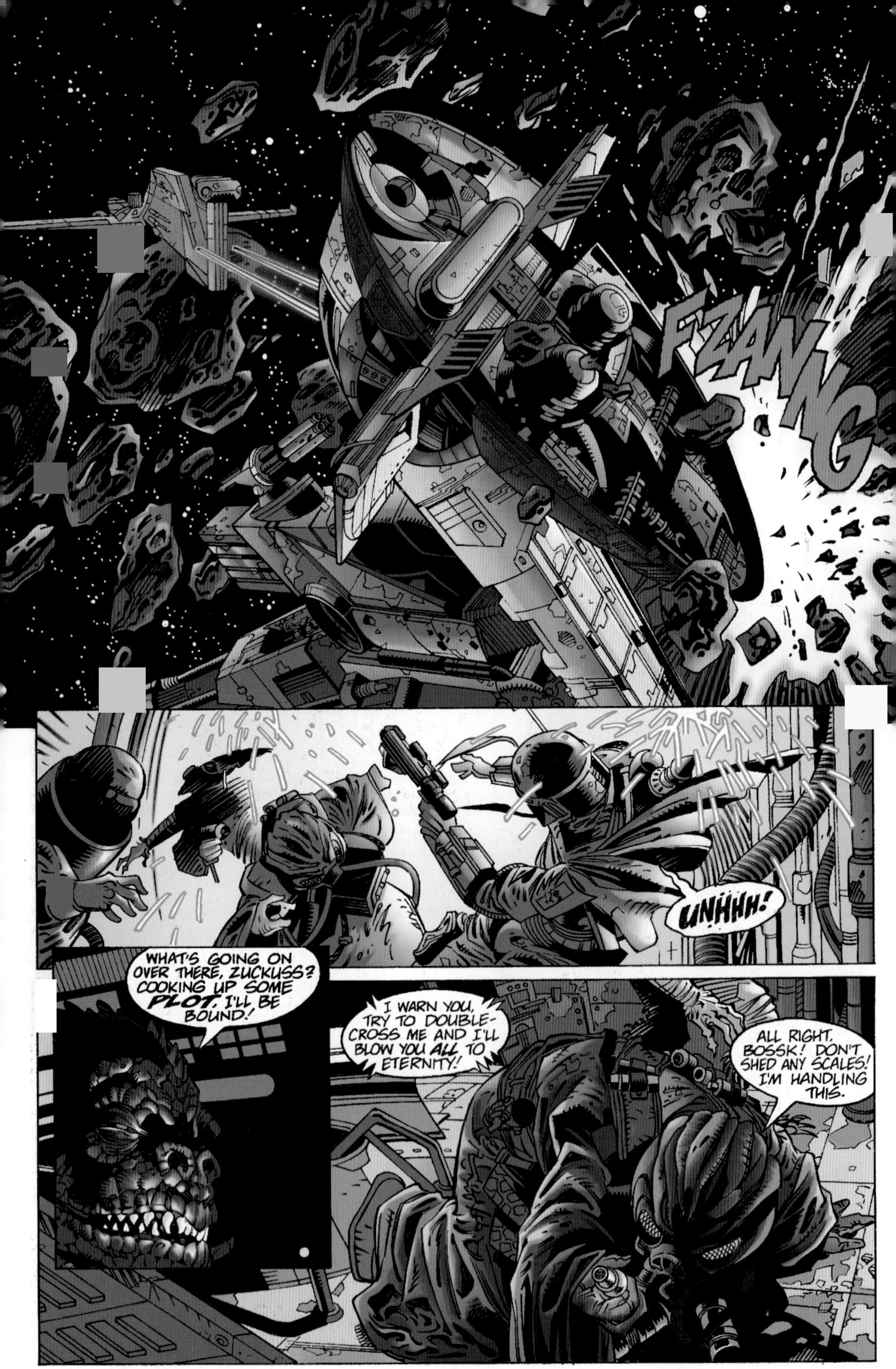
FZANNG
UNHHH!
WHAT'S GOING ON OVER THERE, ZUCKUSS? COOKING UP SOME PLOT, I'LL BE BOUND!
I WARN YOU, TRY TO DOUBLE-CROSS ME AND I'LL BLOW YOU ALL TO ETERNITY!
ALL RIGHT, BOSSK! DON'T SHED ANY SCALES! I'M HANDLING THIS.

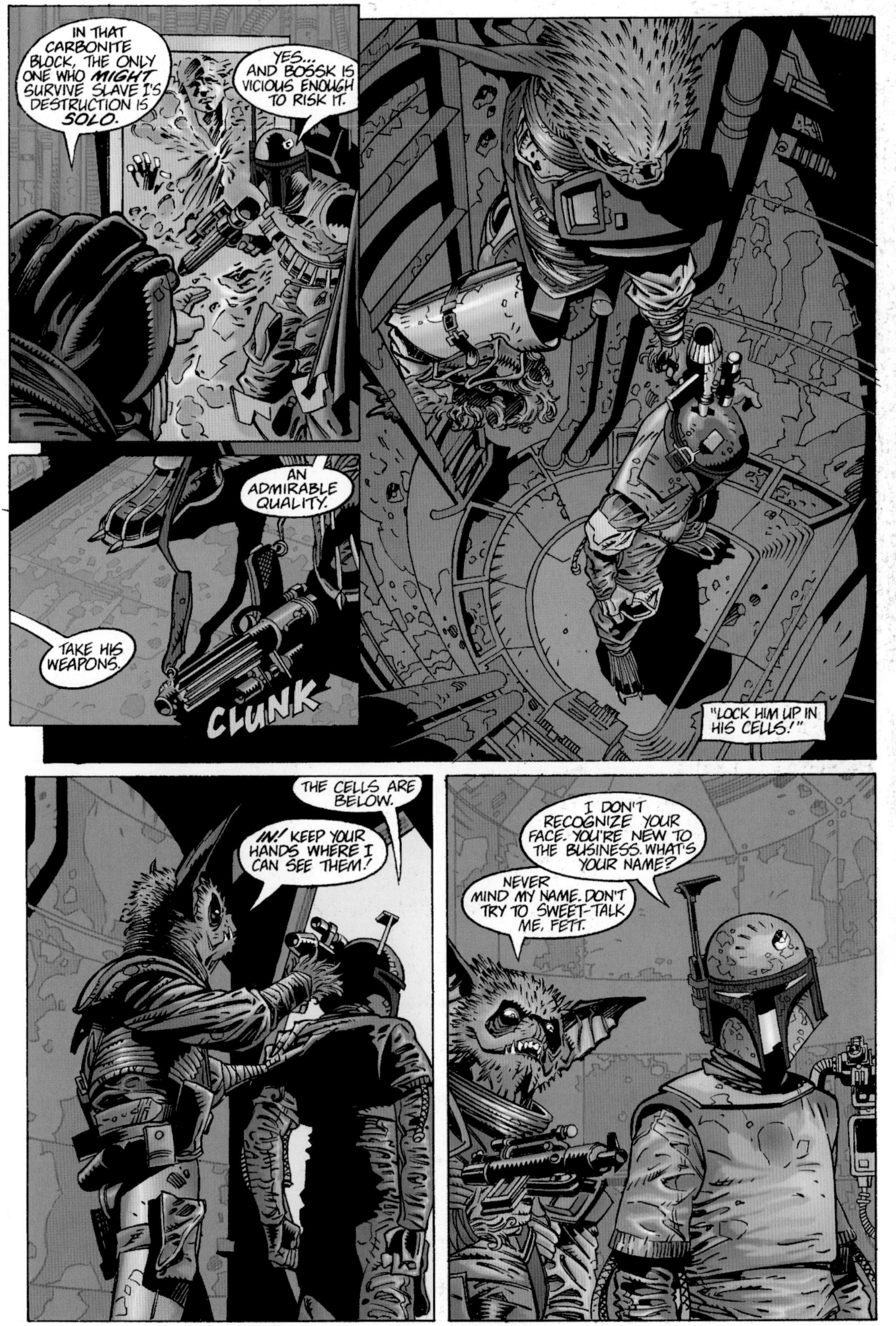
IN THAT CARBONITE BLOCK, THE ONLY ONE WHO *MIGHT* SURVIVE SLAVE I'S DESTRUCTION IS *SOLO*.
YES... AND BOSSK IS VICIOUS ENOUGH TO RISK IT.
AN ADMIRABLE QUALITY.
TAKE HIS WEAPONS.
CLUNK
"LOCK HIM UP IN HIS CELLS!"
THE CELLS ARE BELOW.
IN! KEEP YOUR HANDS WHERE I CAN SEE THEM!
I DON'T RECOGNIZE YOUR FACE. YOU'RE NEW TO THE BUSINESS. WHAT'S YOUR NAME?
NEVER MIND MY NAME. DON'T TRY TO SWEET-TALK ME, FETT.

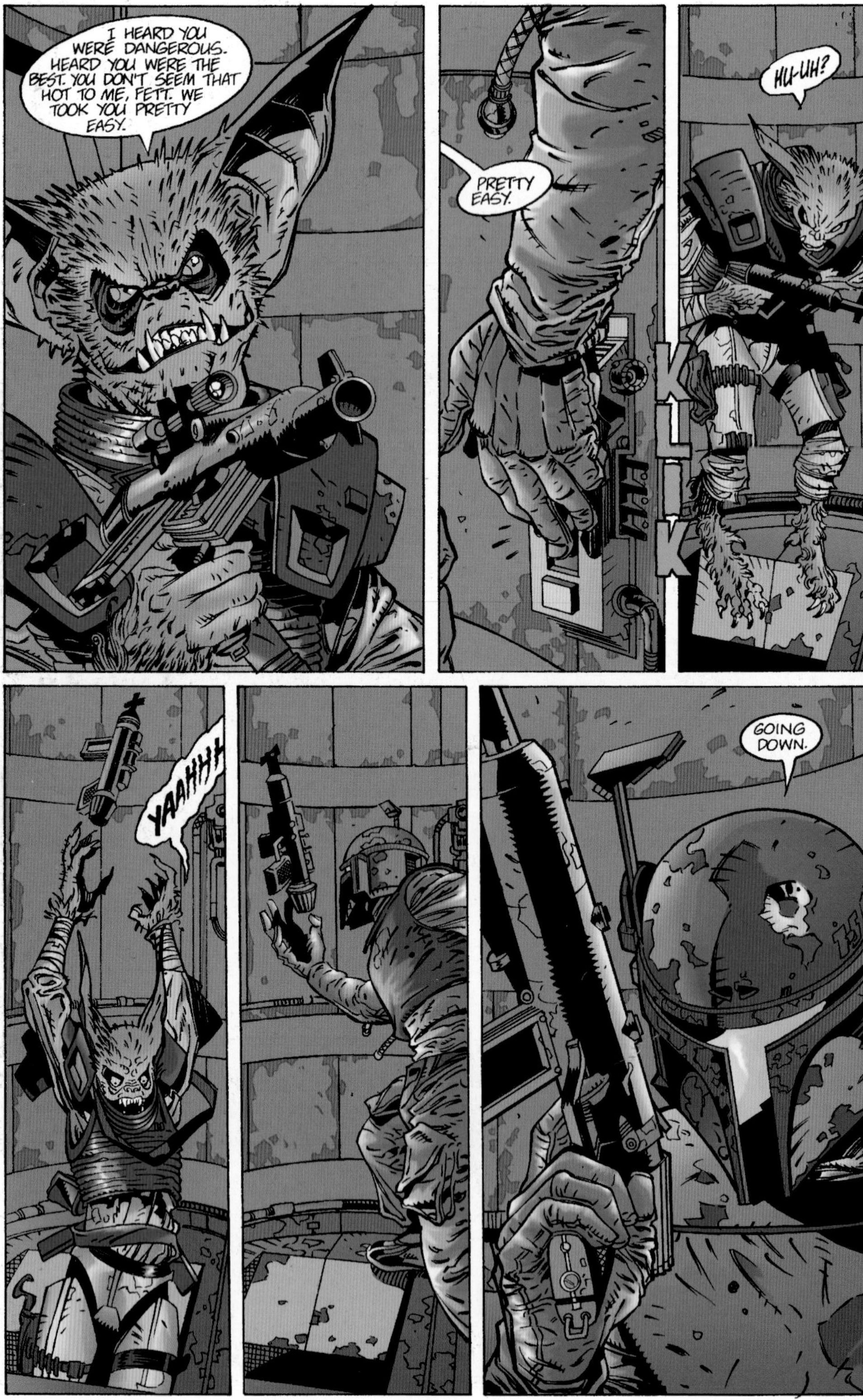
I HEARD YOU WERE DANGEROUS. HEARD YOU WERE THE BEST. YOU DON'T SEEM THAT HOT TO ME, FETT. WE TOOK YOU PRETTY EASY.
PRETTY EASY.
KLIK
HU-UH?
YAAHHH
GOING DOWN.

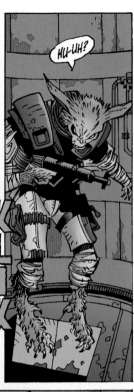

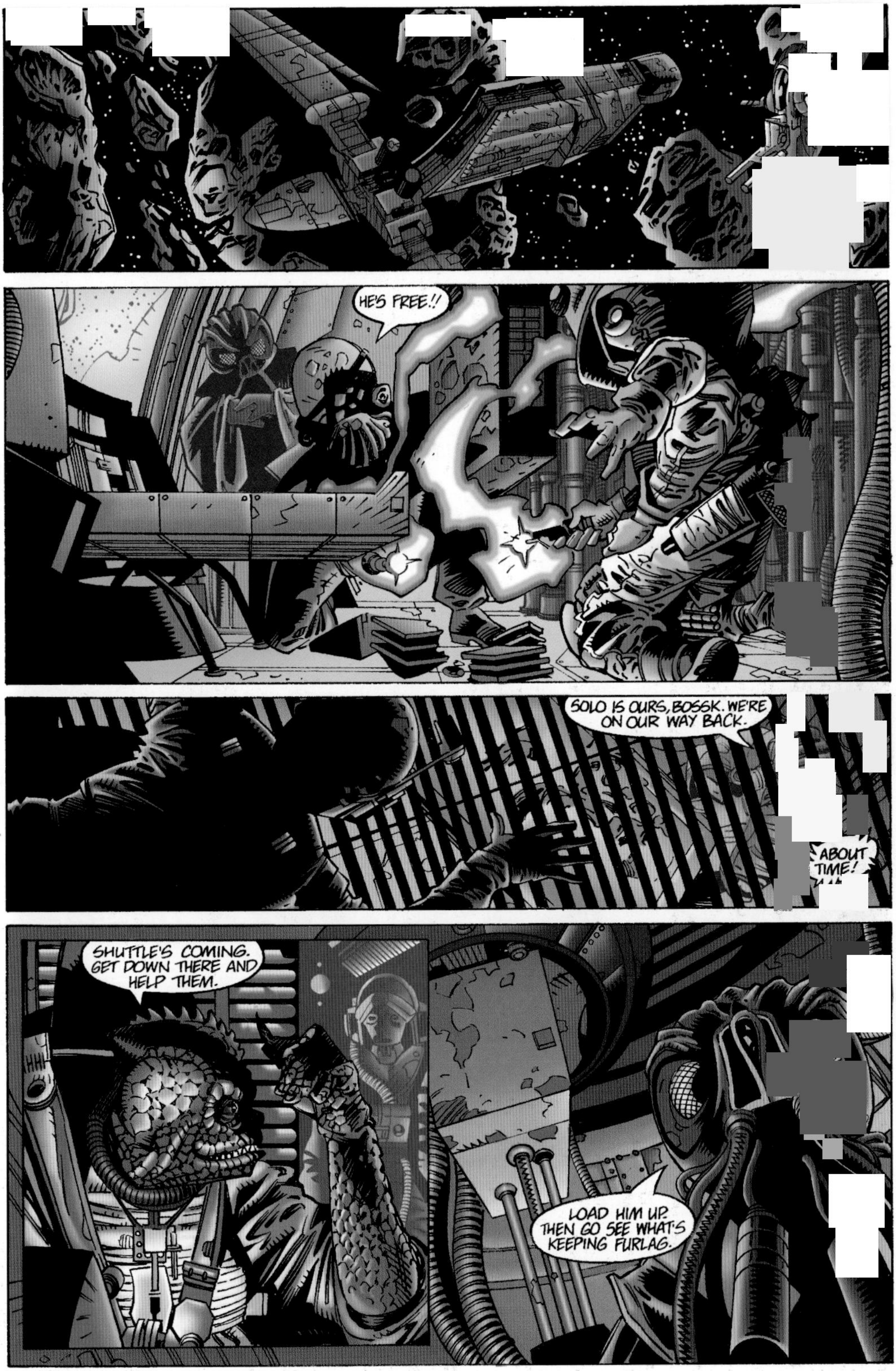
HE'S FREE!!
SOLO IS OURS, BOSSK. WE'RE ON OUR WAY BACK.
ABOUT TIME!
SHUTTLE'S COMING. GET DOWN THERE AND HELP THEM.
LOAD HIM UP. THEN GO SEE WHAT'S KEEPING FURLAG.

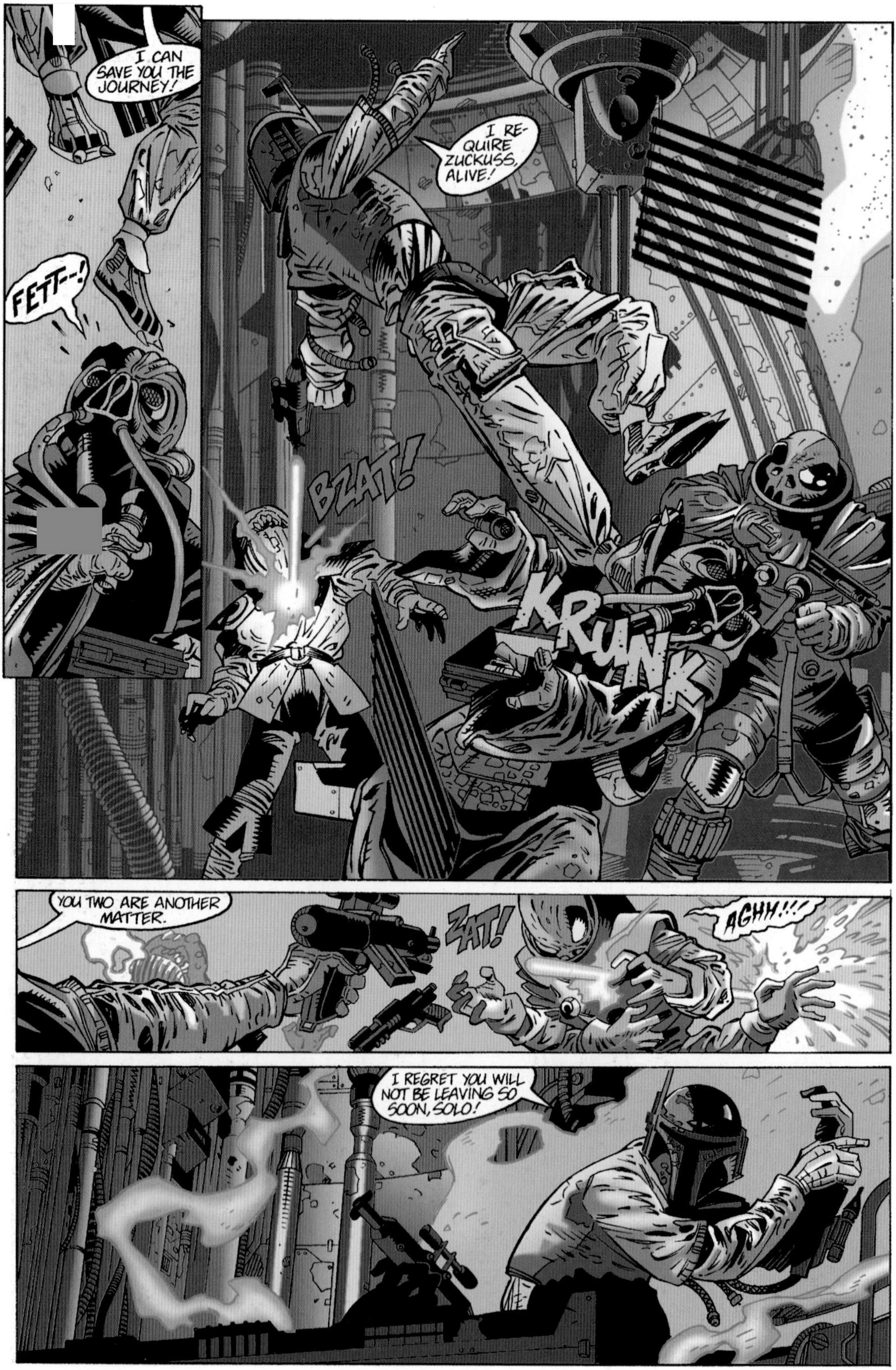
I CAN SAVE YOU THE JOURNEY!
FETT--!
I RE-QUIRE ZUCKUSS, ALIVE!
BZAT!
KRUNK
YOU TWO ARE ANOTHER MATTER.
ZAT!
AGHH!!!
I REGRET YOU WILL NOT BE LEAVING SO SOON, SOLO!

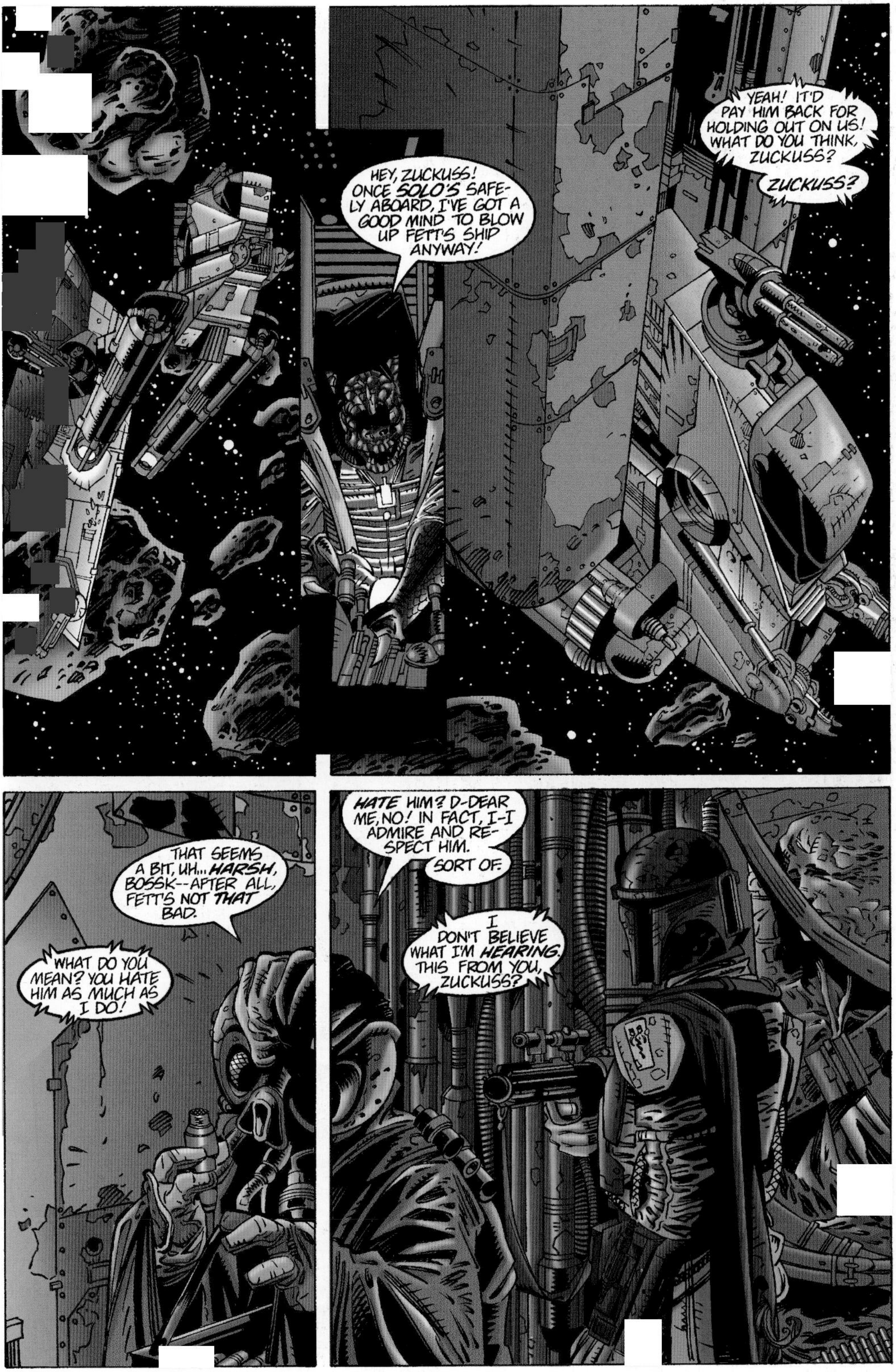
HEY, ZUCKUSS! ONCE SOLO'S SAFELY ABOARD, I'VE GOT A GOOD MIND TO BLOW UP FETT'S SHIP ANYWAY!
YEAH! IT'D PAY HIM BACK FOR HOLDING OUT ON US! WHAT DO YOU THINK, ZUCKUSS?
ZUCKUSS?
THAT SEEMS A BIT, UH... HARSH, BOSSK--AFTER ALL, FETT'S NOT THAT BAD.
WHAT DO YOU MEAN? YOU HATE HIM AS MUCH AS I DO!
HATE HIM? D-DEAR ME, NO! IN FACT, I-I ADMIRE AND RESPECT HIM.
SORT OF.
I DON'T BELIEVE WHAT I'M HEARING. THIS FROM YOU, ZUCKUSS?

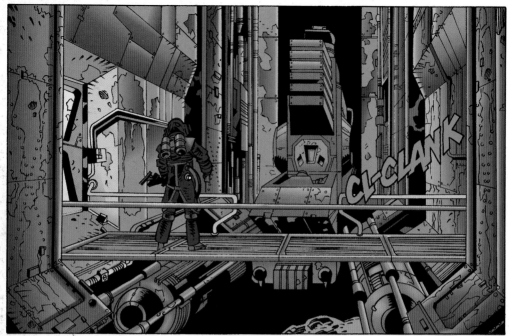

CL-CLANK

COMPUTER! CALCULATE TRAJECTORY FOR EMERGENCY RE-TURN TO HYPER-SPACE.

YEAH, WHY NOT? IT WOULDN'T DO MY *REPUTATION* ANY HARM!

THE BOUNTY HUNTER WHO KILLED BOBA FETT-- THAT'D MAKE *ME* NUMBER-ONE.

I HAVE SOME BAD NEWS FOR YOU, BOSSK.

F-FETT-?

OH, NO--

NEE

NEE

NEE

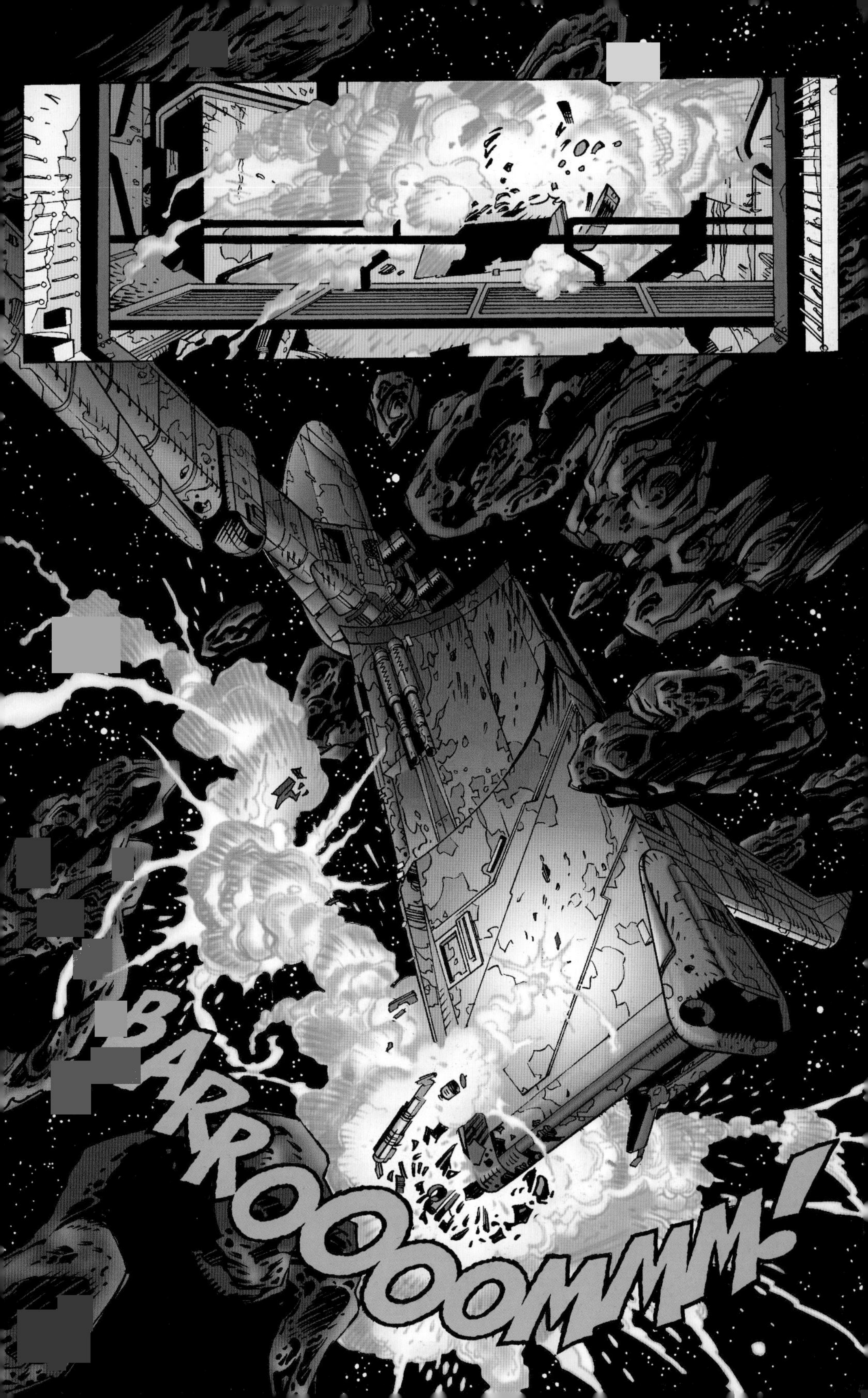
BAROOOOMMM!

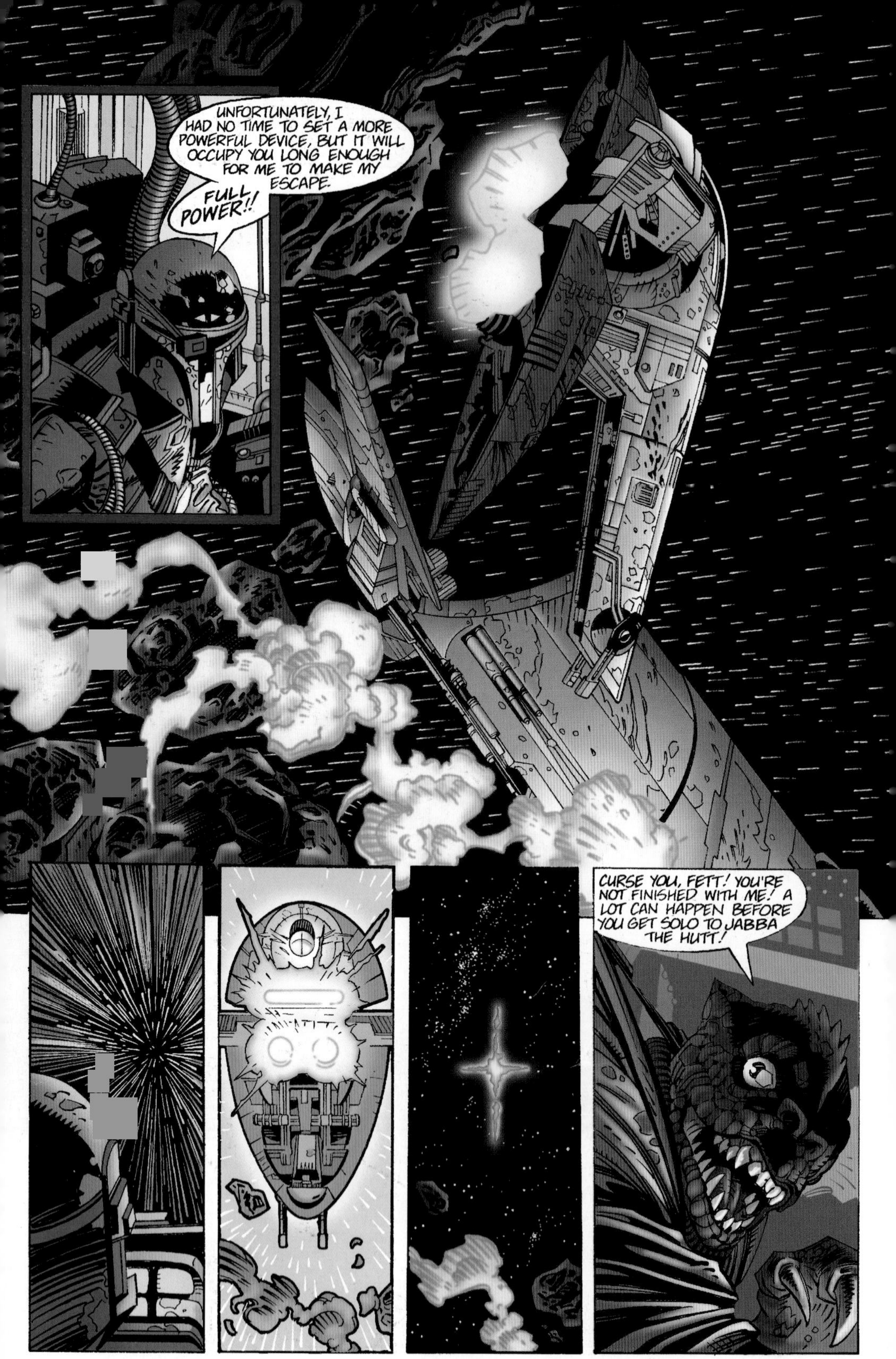
UNFORTUNATELY, I HAD NO TIME TO SET A MORE POWERFUL DEVICE, BUT IT WILL OCCUPY YOU LONG ENOUGH FOR ME TO MAKE MY ESCAPE.
FULL POWER!!
CURSE YOU, FETT! YOU'RE NOT FINISHED WITH ME! A LOT CAN HAPPEN BEFORE YOU GET SOLO TO JABBA THE HUTT!

TELL ME AGAIN HOW *SKYWALKER* ESCAPED YOU.

SKYWALKER GOT LUCKY, JABBA-- THAT'S ALL.

YOUR LEADER DEAD-- HALF YOUR SWOOP GANG GONE? FOR ONE MAN, THAT'S AN ENORMOUS AMOUNT OF LUCK!

WE DID OUR BEST.

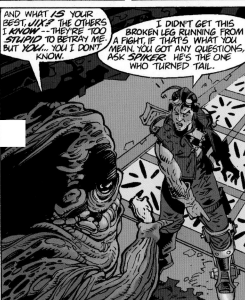

AND WHAT *IS* YOUR BEST, *JIX?* THE OTHERS I *KNOW*--THEY'RE TOO *STUPID* TO BETRAY ME. BUT *YOU*... YOU I DON'T KNOW.

I DIDN'T GET THIS BROKEN LEG RUNNING FROM A FIGHT, IF THAT'S WHAT YOU MEAN. YOU GOT ANY QUESTIONS, ASK *SPIKER.* HE'S THE ONE WHO TURNED TAIL.

YOU CALLIN' ME YELLOW? ROT YOUR GUTS, *JIX--!*

CEASE!

AS FAR AS I AM CON- CERNED, YOU'RE *ALL* AT FAULT! NO AMOUNT OF YOUR SQUABBLING WILL BRING VADER'S REWARD NOW!

DARTH VADER OFFERED THE REWARD? BUT EVERY- BODY KNOWS HE WANTS SKYWALKER *ALIVE.*

APPARENTLY, THINGS HAVE CHANGED.

SKYWALKER HAS OBVIOUSLY INCURRED LORD VADER'S DIS- PLEASURE.

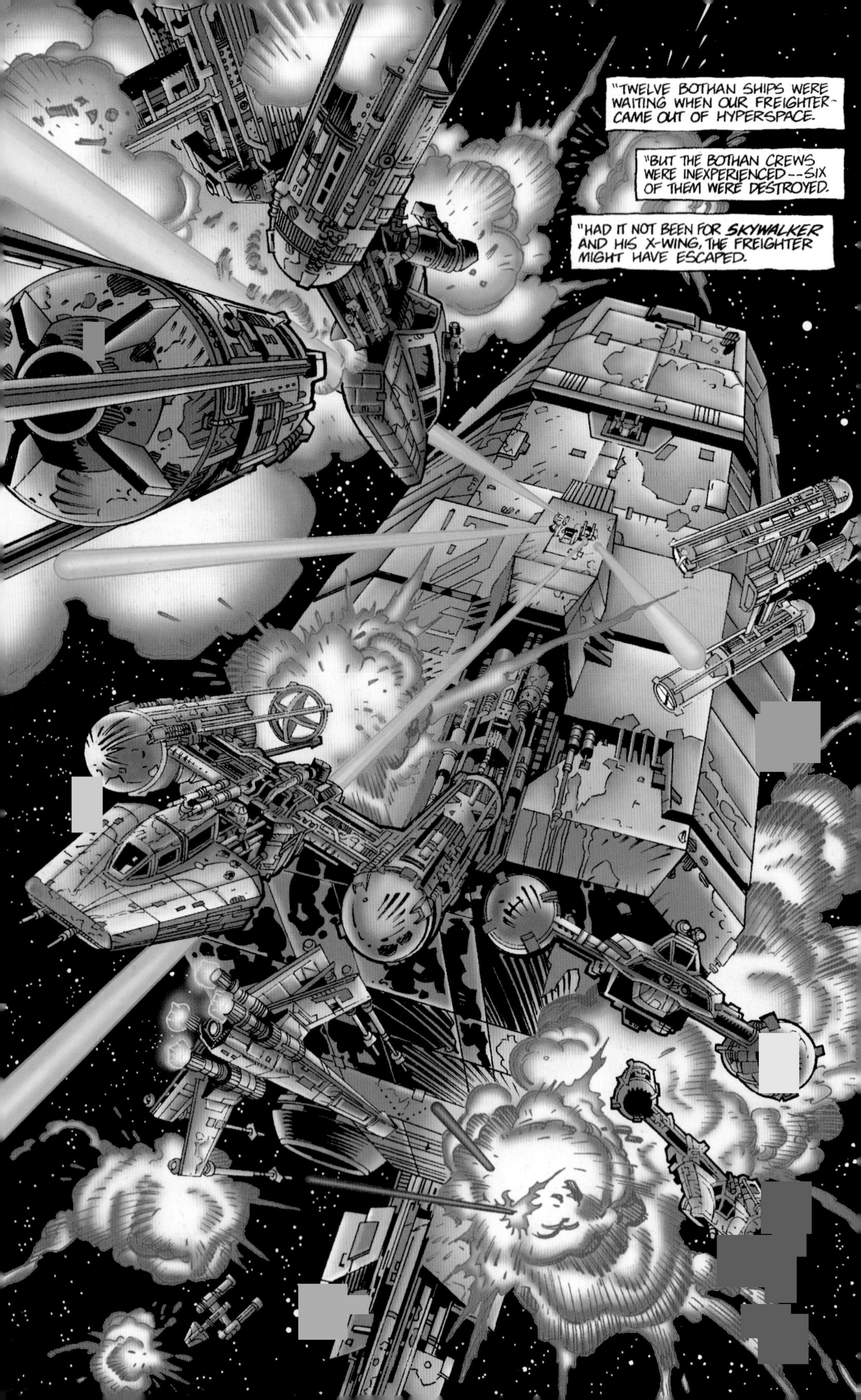
"TWELVE BOTHAN SHIPS WERE WAITING WHEN OUR FREIGHTER-CAME OUT OF HYPERSPACE.
"BUT THE BOTHAN CREWS WERE INEXPERIENCED--SIX OF THEM WERE DESTROYED.
"HAD IT NOT BEEN FOR SKYWALKER AND HIS X-WING, THE FREIGHTER MIGHT HAVE ESCAPED.

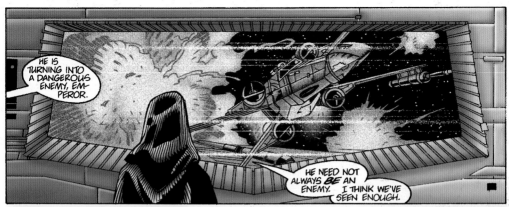

HE IS TURNING INTO A DANGEROUS ENEMY, EM-PEROR.

HE NEED NOT ALWAYS *BE* AN ENEMY. I THINK WE'VE SEEN ENOUGH.

IT WENT EXACTLY AS PLANNED, EMPEROR. WE DIDN'T WANT THE REBELS' VICTORY TO SEEM TOO EASY.

I HOPE YOU KNOW WHAT YOU ARE DOING, PRINCE XIZOR.

IT WAS ON *YOUR* ADVICE I ALLOWED THE COMPUTER CARRYING THE PLANS FOR THE *DEATH STAR* TO FALL INTO REBEL HANDS. YOU HAD BEST BE RIGHT.

I AM, MY MASTER.

ONCE THE REBELS FIND OUT EXACTLY WHAT IT IS THEY HAVE BEEN GIVEN, THEIR TRUST IN ME WILL BE COMPLETE.

I WILL DELIVER THE REBELLION-- AND YOU CAN *CRUSH* IT AT YOUR PLEASURE.

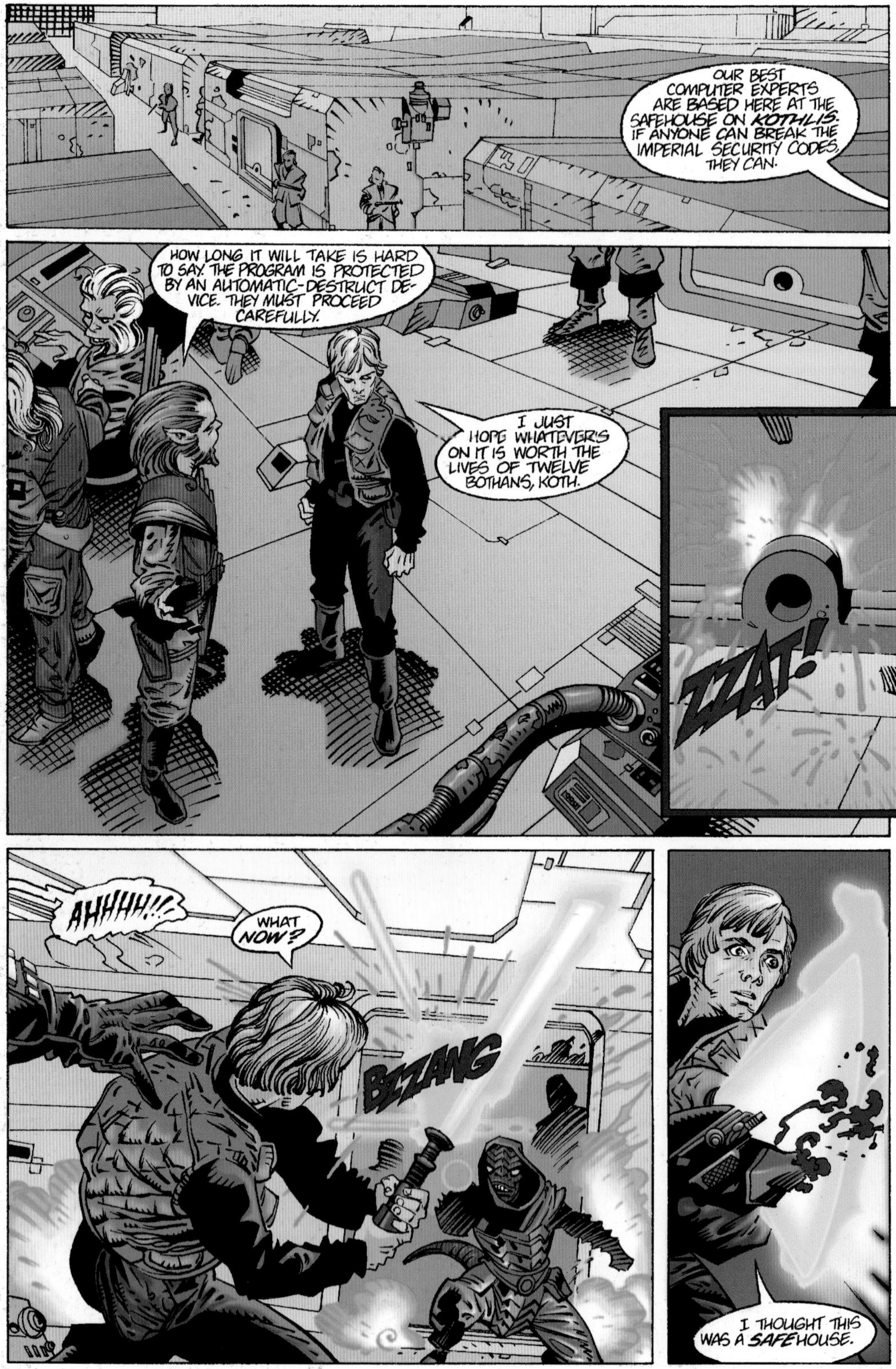
OUR BEST COMPUTER EXPERTS ARE BASED HERE AT THE SAFEHOUSE ON KOTHLIS. IF ANYONE CAN BREAK THE IMPERIAL SECURITY CODES, THEY CAN.
HOW LONG IT WILL TAKE IS HARD TO SAY. THE PROGRAM IS PROTECTED BY AN AUTOMATIC-DESTRUCT DEVICE. THEY MUST PROCEED CAREFULLY.
I JUST HOPE WHATEVER'S ON IT IS WORTH THE LIVES OF TWELVE BOTHANS, KOTH.
ZZAT!
AHHHH!!!
WHAT NOW?
BZZANG
I THOUGHT THIS WAS A SAFE HOUSE.

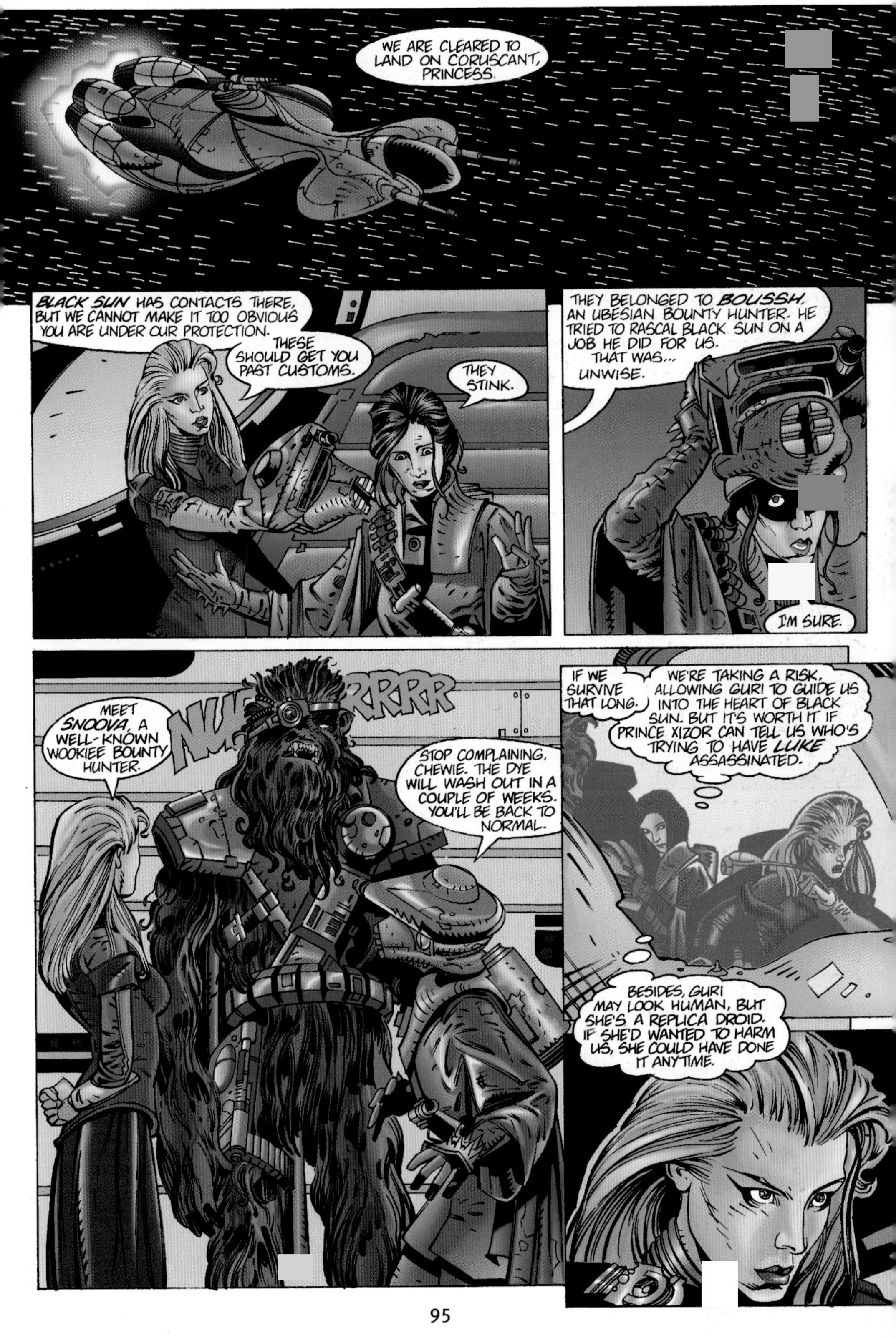
WE ARE CLEARED TO LAND ON CORUSCANT, PRINCESS.
BLACK SUN HAS CONTACTS THERE, BUT WE CANNOT MAKE IT TOO OBVIOUS YOU ARE UNDER OUR PROTECTION.
THESE SHOULD GET YOU PAST CUSTOMS.
THEY STINK.
THEY BELONGED TO BOUSSH, AN UBESIAN BOUNTY HUNTER. HE TRIED TO RASCAL BLACK SUN ON A JOB HE DID FOR US.
THAT WAS... UNWISE.
I'M SURE.
MEET SNOOVA, A WELL-KNOWN WOOKIEE BOUNTY HUNTER.
NU RRRRR
STOP COMPLAINING, CHEWIE. THE DYE WILL WASH OUT IN A COUPLE OF WEEKS. YOU'LL BE BACK TO NORMAL.
IF WE SURVIVE THAT LONG.
WE'RE TAKING A RISK, ALLOWING GURI TO GUIDE US INTO THE HEART OF BLACK SUN. BUT IT'S WORTH IT IF PRINCE XIZOR CAN TELL US WHO'S TRYING TO HAVE LUKE ASSASSINATED.
BESIDES, GURI MAY LOOK HUMAN, BUT SHE'S A REPLICA DROID. IF SHE'D WANTED TO HARM US, SHE COULD HAVE DONE IT ANYTIME.

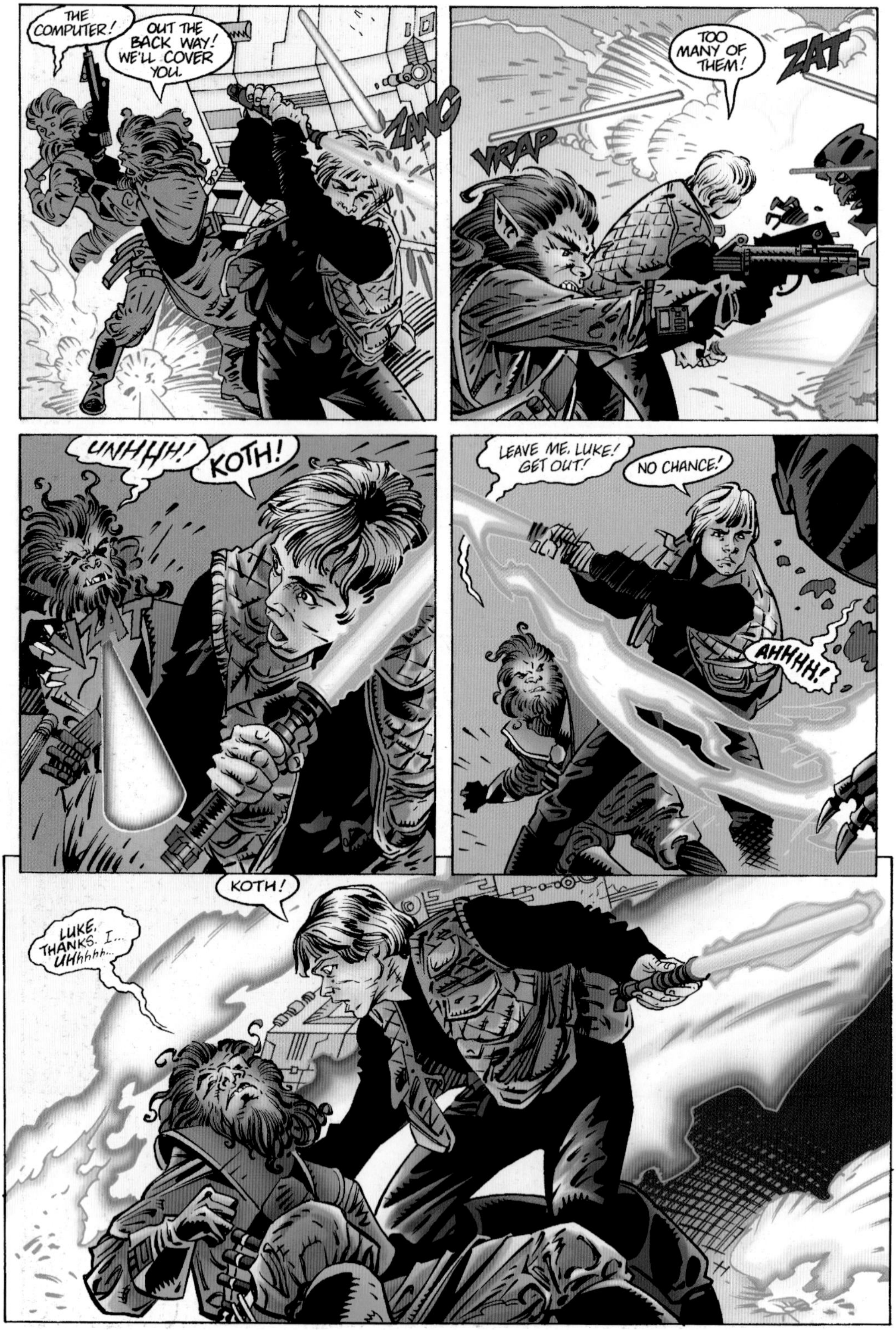
THE COMPUTER!
OUT THE BACK WAY! WE'LL COVER YOU.
ZANG
TOO MANY OF THEM!
ZAT
VRAP
UNHHH!
KOTH!
ZAT
LEAVE ME, LUKE! GET OUT!
NO CHANCE!
AHHHH!
KOTH!
LUKE, THANKS. I... UHhhhh...

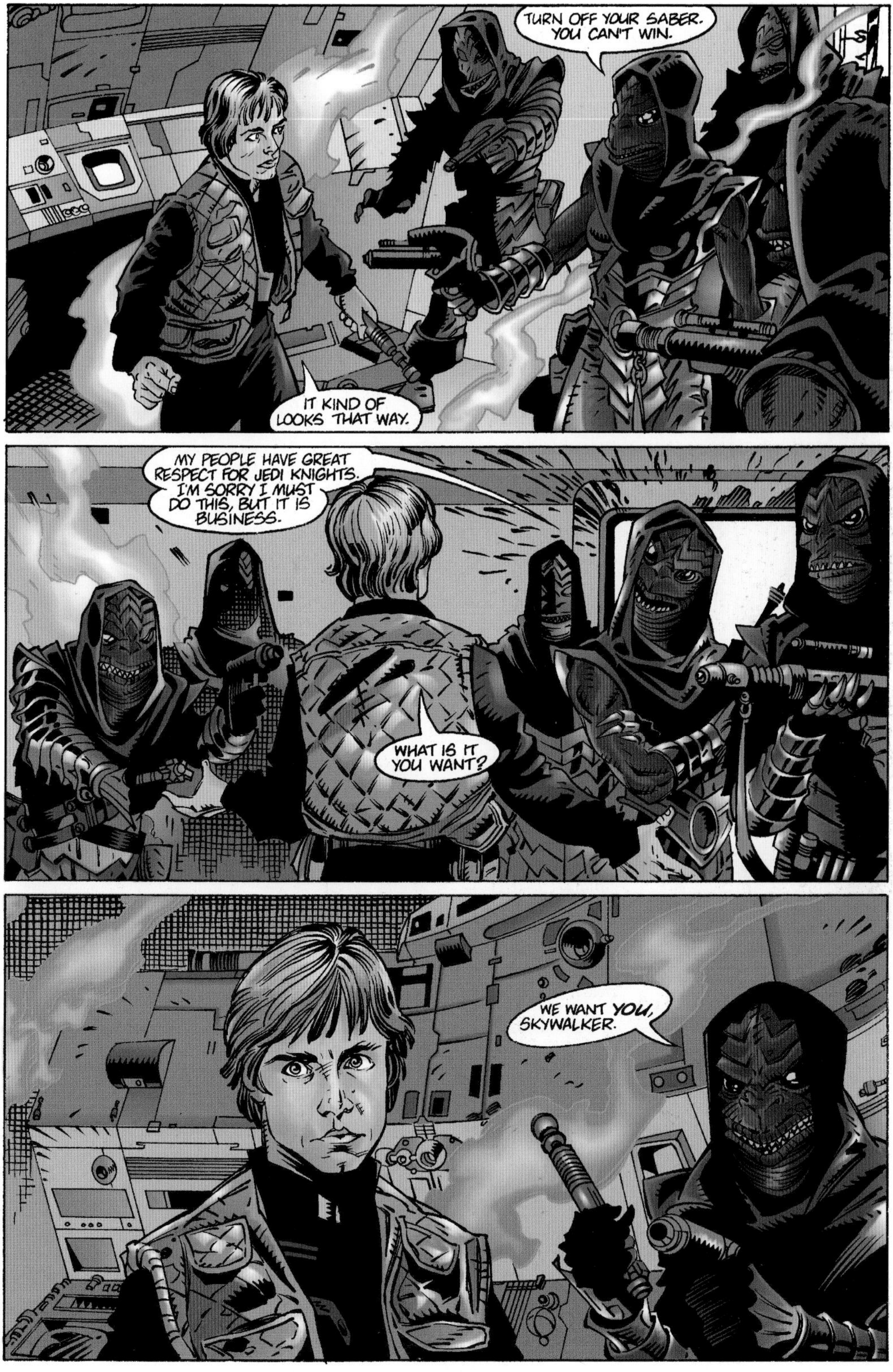
TURN OFF YOUR SABER. YOU CAN'T WIN.
IT KIND OF LOOKS THAT WAY.
MY PEOPLE HAVE GREAT RESPECT FOR JEDI KNIGHTS. I'M SORRY I MUST DO THIS, BUT IT IS BUSINESS.
WHAT IS IT YOU WANT?
WE WANT YOU, SKYWALKER.

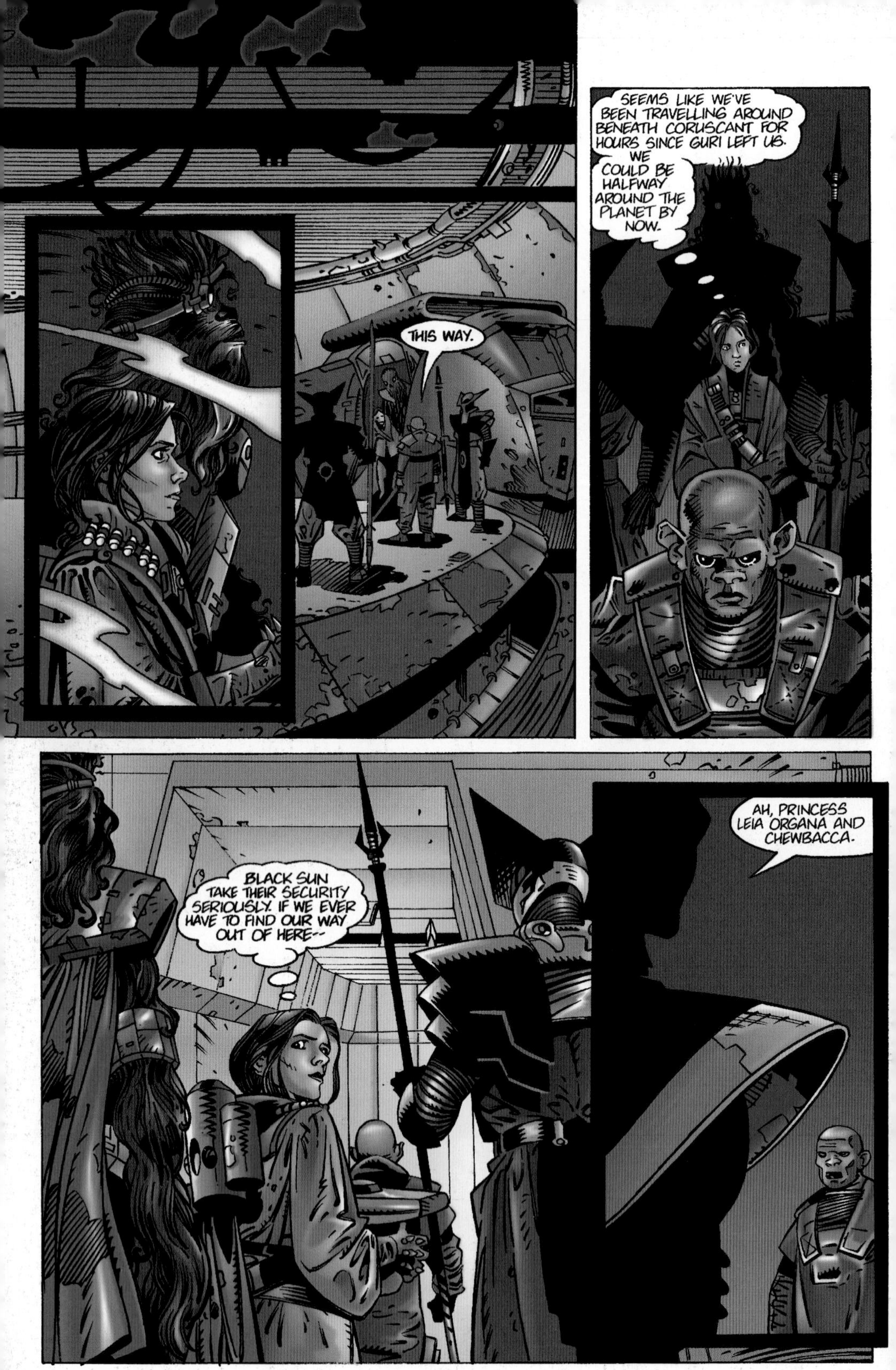
THIS WAY.
SEEMS LIKE WE'VE BEEN TRAVELLING AROUND BENEATH CORUSCANT FOR HOURS SINCE GURI LEFT US.
WE COULD BE HALFWAY AROUND THE PLANET BY NOW.
BLACK SUN TAKE THEIR SECURITY SERIOUSLY. IF WE EVER HAVE TO FIND OUR WAY OUT OF HERE--
AH, PRINCESS LEIA ORGANA AND CHEWBACCA.

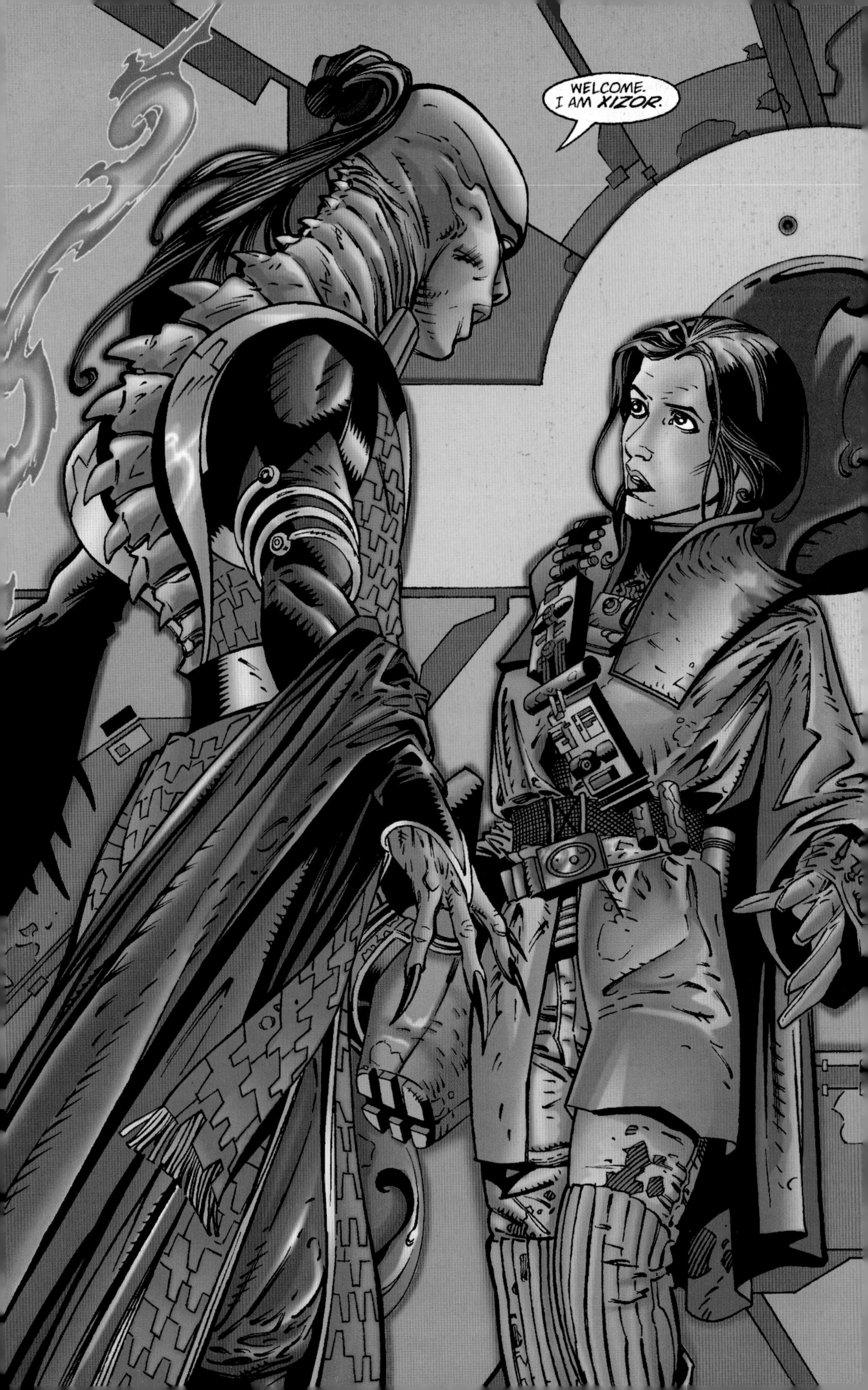
WELCOME. I AM XIZOR.

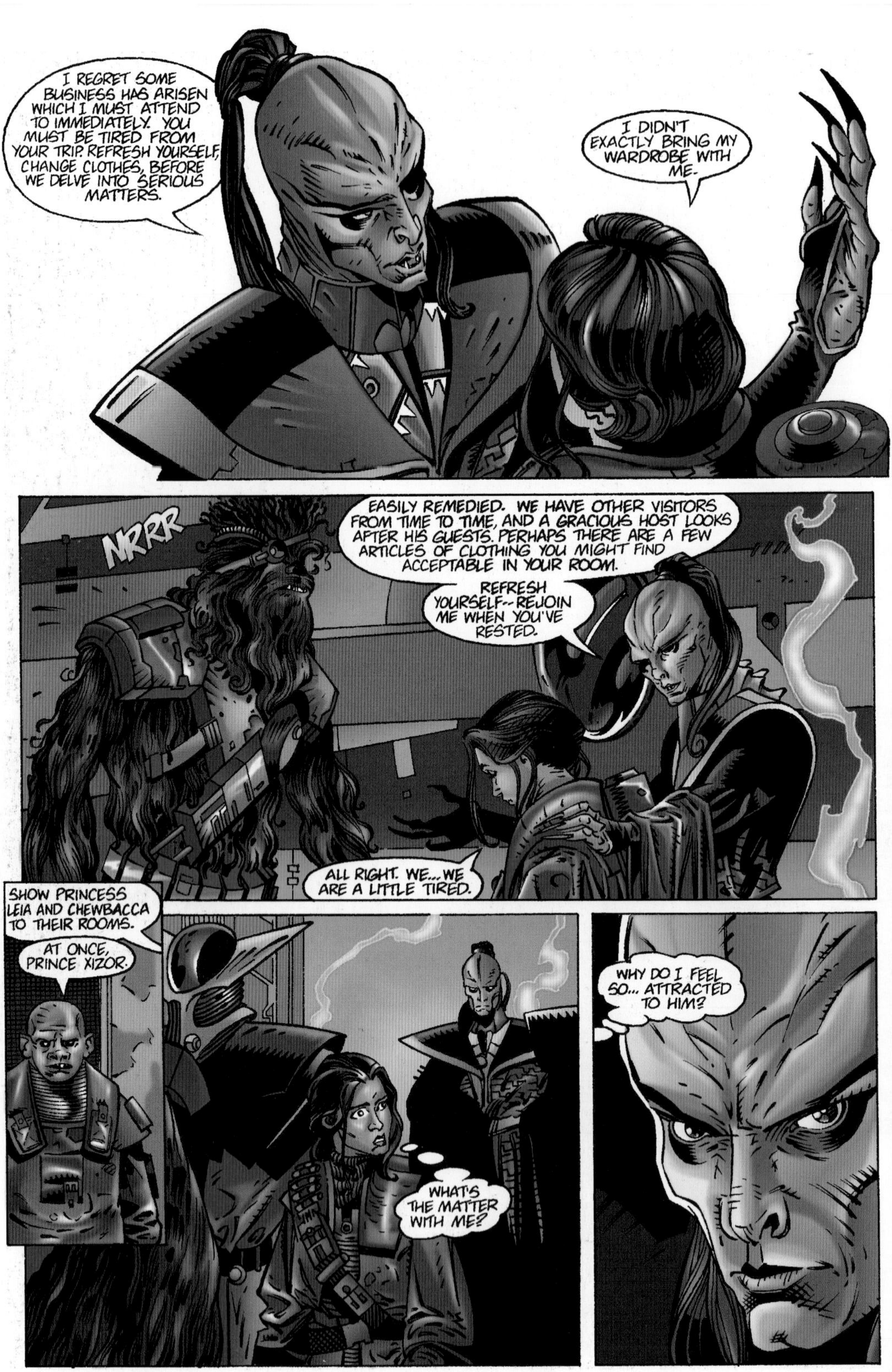
I REGRET SOME BUSINESS HAS ARISEN WHICH I MUST ATTEND TO IMMEDIATELY. YOU MUST BE TIRED FROM YOUR TRIP. REFRESH YOURSELF, CHANGE CLOTHES, BEFORE WE DELVE INTO SERIOUS MATTERS.
I DIDN'T EXACTLY BRING MY WARDROBE WITH ME.
NRRR
EASILY REMEDIED. WE HAVE OTHER VISITORS FROM TIME TO TIME, AND A GRACIOUS HOST LOOKS AFTER HIS GUESTS. PERHAPS THERE ARE A FEW ARTICLES OF CLOTHING YOU MIGHT FIND ACCEPTABLE IN YOUR ROOM.
REFRESH YOURSELF--REJOIN ME WHEN YOU'VE RESTED.
ALL RIGHT. WE... WE ARE A LITTLE TIRED.
SHOW PRINCESS LEIA AND CHEWBACCA TO THEIR ROOMS.
AT ONCE, PRINCE XIZOR.
WHAT'S THE MATTER WITH ME?
WHY DO I FEEL SO... ATTRACTED TO HIM?

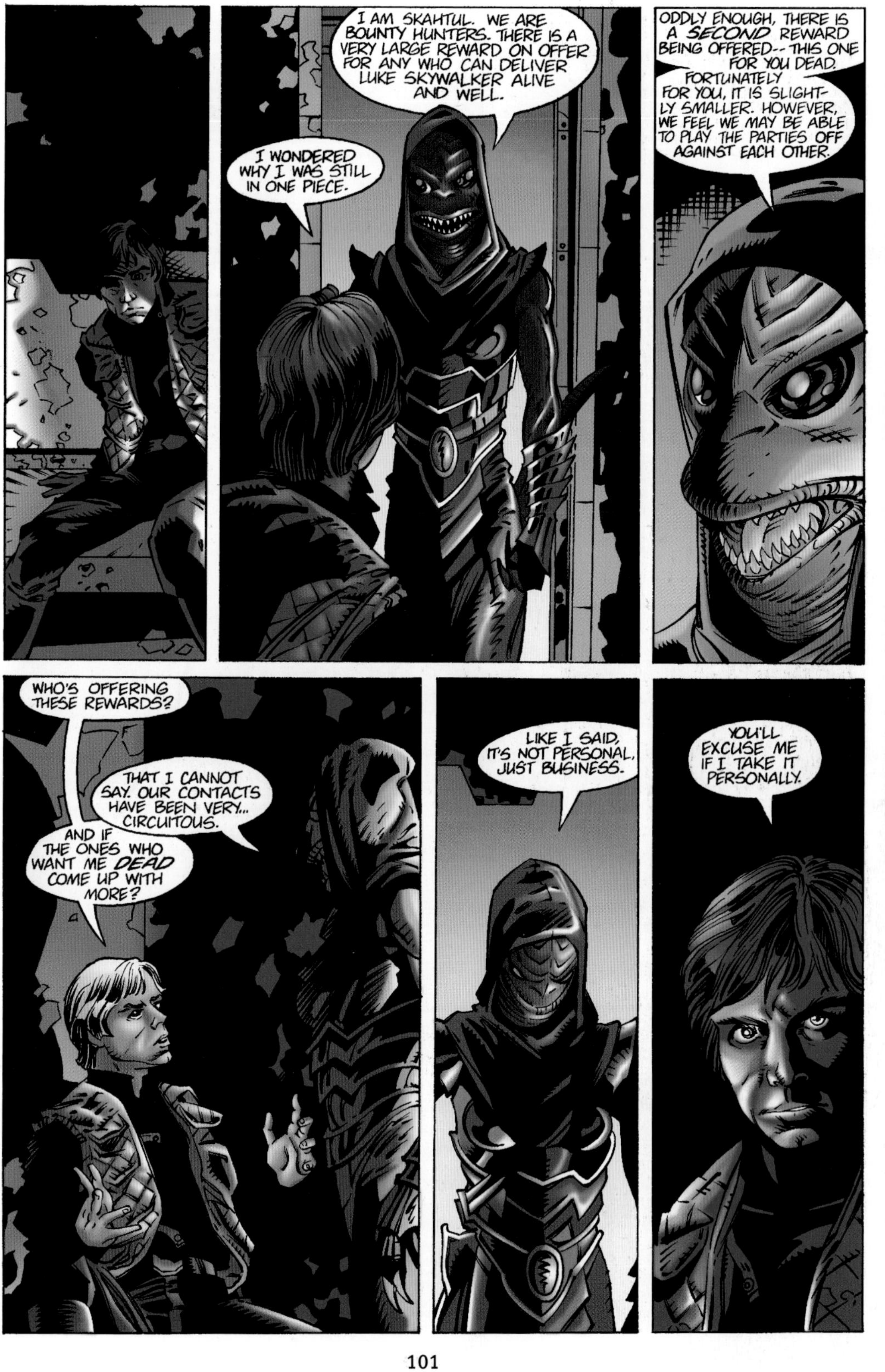
I AM SKAHTUL. WE ARE BOUNTY HUNTERS. THERE IS A VERY LARGE REWARD ON OFFER FOR ANY WHO CAN DELIVER LUKE SKYWALKER ALIVE AND WELL.
I WONDERED WHY I WAS STILL IN ONE PIECE.
ODDLY ENOUGH, THERE IS A SECOND REWARD BEING OFFERED-- THIS ONE FOR YOU DEAD.
FORTUNATELY FOR YOU, IT IS SLIGHTLY SMALLER. HOWEVER, WE FEEL WE MAY BE ABLE TO PLAY THE PARTIES OFF AGAINST EACH OTHER.
WHO'S OFFERING THESE REWARDS?
THAT I CANNOT SAY. OUR CONTACTS HAVE BEEN VERY... CIRCUITOUS.
AND IF THE ONES WHO WANT ME DEAD COME UP WITH MORE?
LIKE I SAID, IT'S NOT PERSONAL, JUST BUSINESS.
YOU'LL EXCUSE ME IF I TAKE IT PERSONALLY.

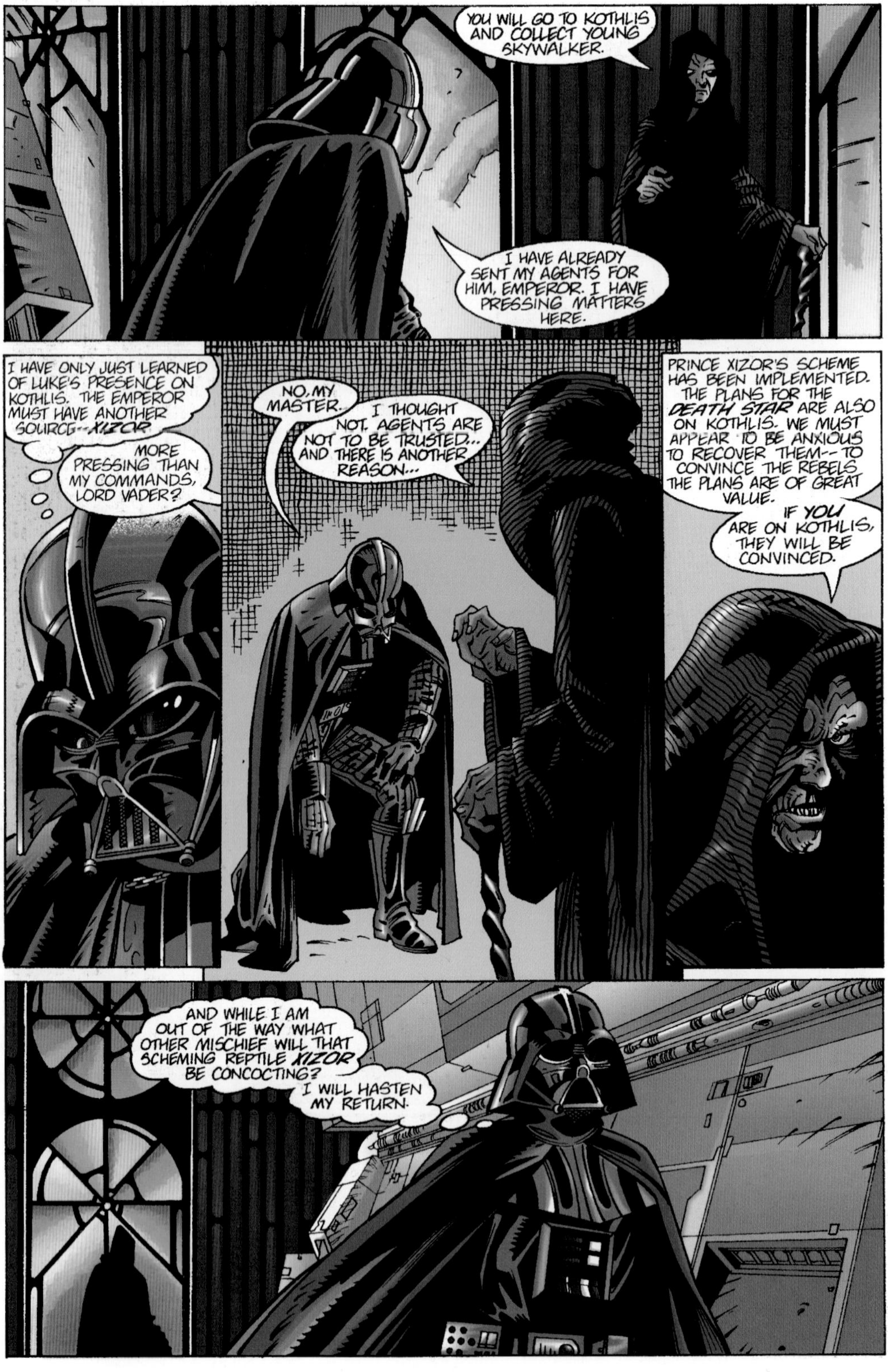
YOU WILL GO TO KOTHLIS AND COLLECT YOUNG SKYWALKER.
I HAVE ALREADY SENT MY AGENTS FOR HIM, EMPEROR. I HAVE PRESSING MATTERS HERE.
MORE PRESSING THAN MY COMMANDS, LORD VADER?
I HAVE ONLY JUST LEARNED OF LUKE'S PRESENCE ON KOTHLIS. THE EMPEROR MUST HAVE ANOTHER SOURCE--XIZOR.
NO, MY MASTER.
I THOUGHT NOT. AGENTS ARE NOT TO BE TRUSTED... AND THERE IS ANOTHER REASON...
PRINCE XIZOR'S SCHEME HAS BEEN IMPLEMENTED. THE PLANS FOR THE DEATH STAR ARE ALSO ON KOTHLIS. WE MUST APPEAR TO BE ANXIOUS TO RECOVER THEM-- TO CONVINCE THE REBELS THE PLANS ARE OF GREAT VALUE.
IF YOU ARE ON KOTHLIS, THEY WILL BE CONVINCED.
AND WHILE I AM OUT OF THE WAY WHAT OTHER MISCHIEF WILL THAT SCHEMING REPTILE XIZOR BE CONCOCTING?
I WILL HASTEN MY RETURN.

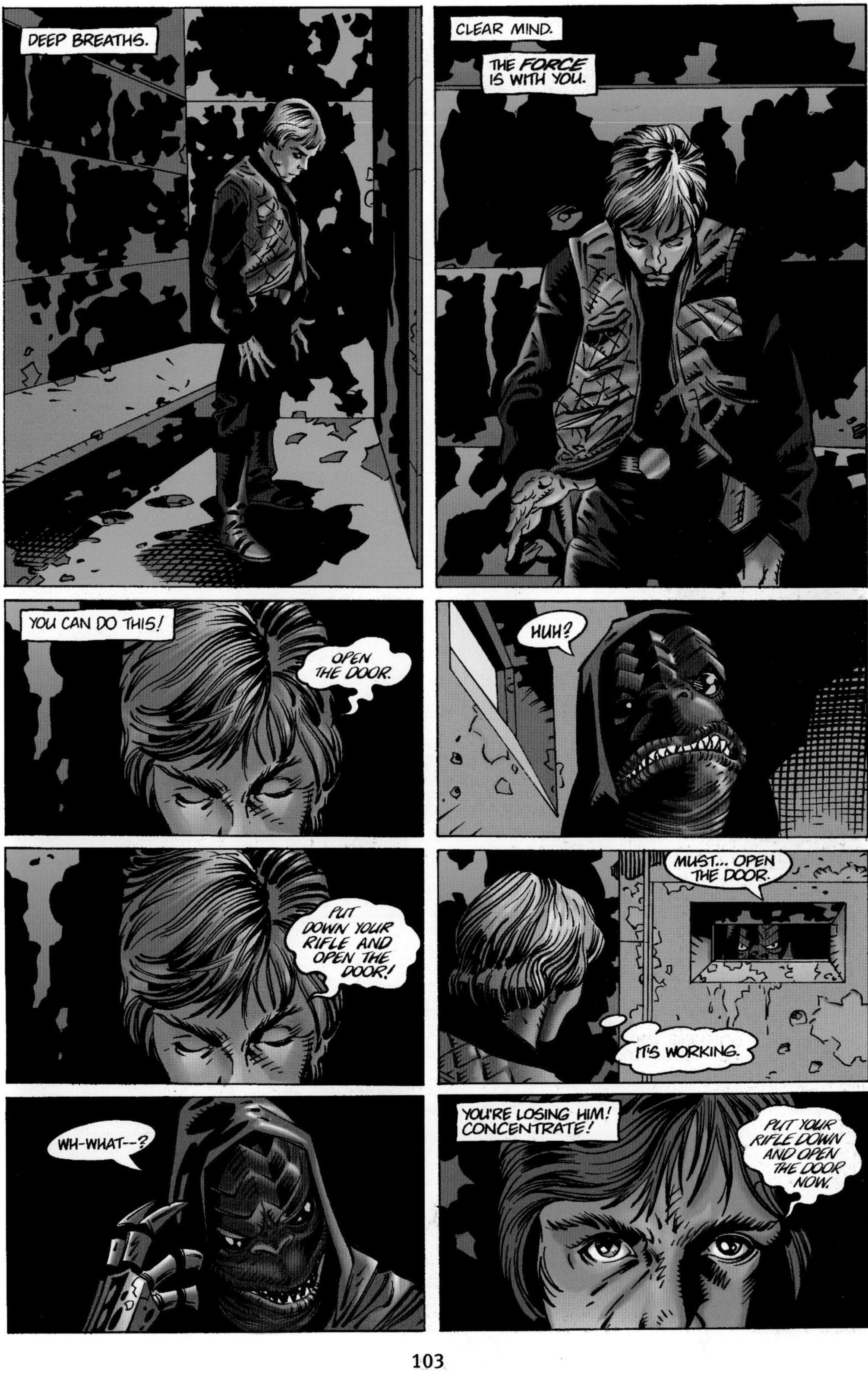
DEEP BREATHS.
CLEAR MIND.
THE FORCE IS WITH YOU.
YOU CAN DO THIS!
OPEN THE DOOR.
HUH?
PUT DOWN YOUR RIFLE AND OPEN THE DOOR!
MUST... OPEN THE DOOR.
IT'S WORKING.
WH-WHAT--?
YOU'RE LOSING HIM! CONCENTRATE!
PUT YOUR RIFLE DOWN AND OPEN THE DOOR NOW.

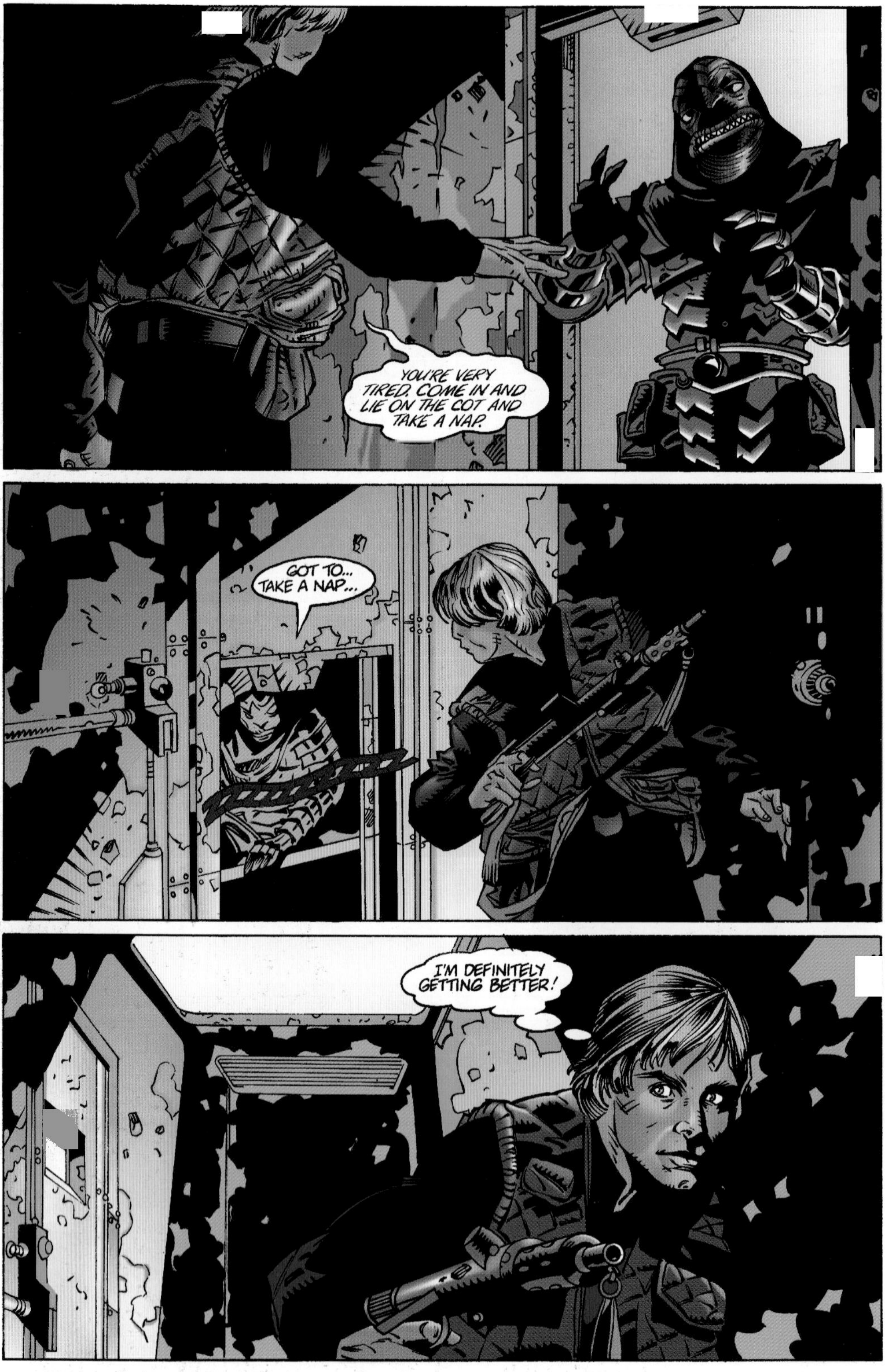
YOU'RE VERY TIRED. COME IN AND LIE ON THE COT AND TAKE A NAP.
GOT TO... TAKE A NAP...
I'M DEFINITELY GETTING BETTER!

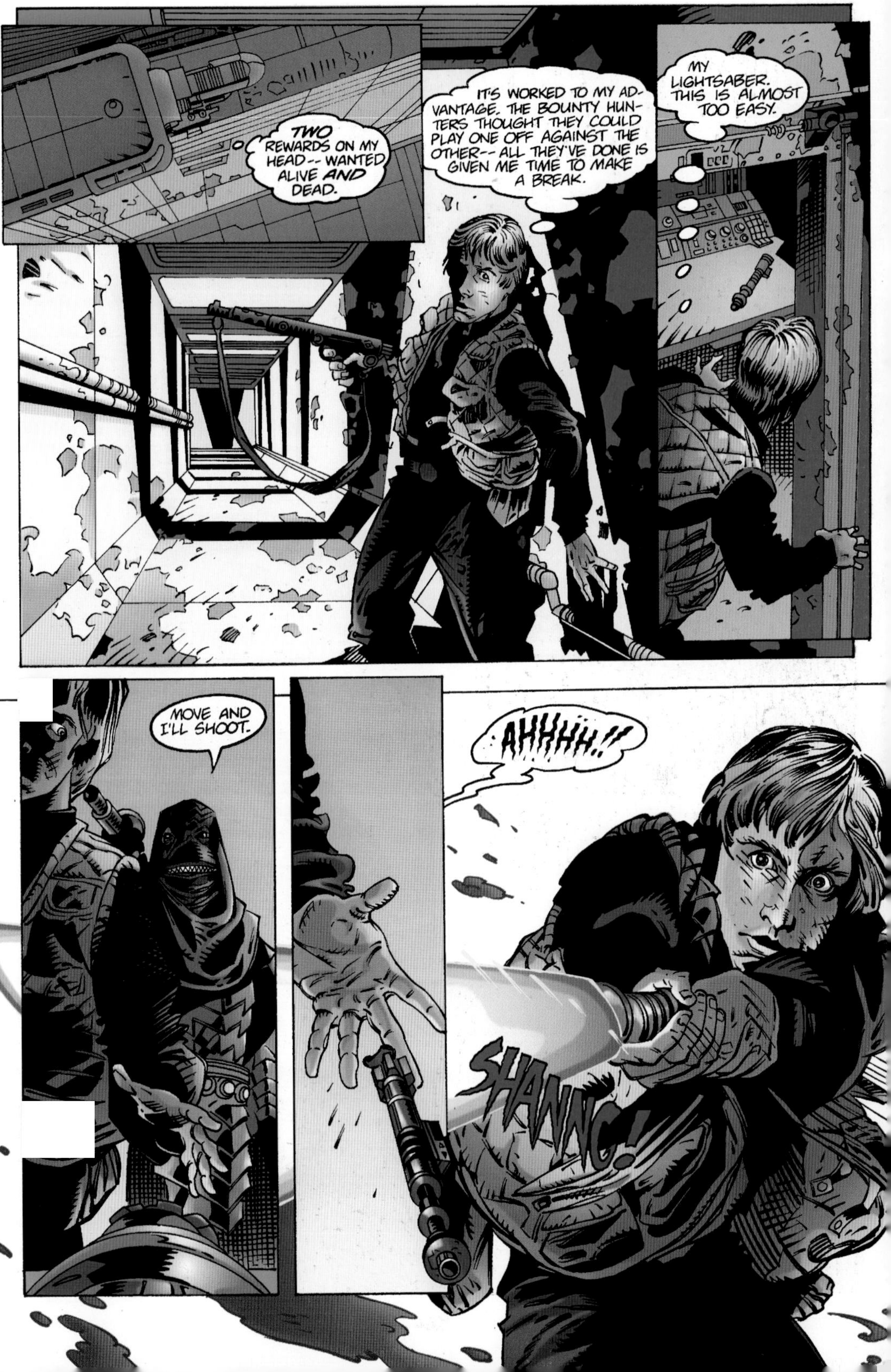
TWO REWARDS ON MY HEAD-- WANTED ALIVE AND DEAD.
IT'S WORKED TO MY ADVANTAGE. THE BOUNTY HUNTERS THOUGHT THEY COULD PLAY ONE OFF AGAINST THE OTHER-- ALL THEY'VE DONE IS GIVEN ME TIME TO MAKE A BREAK.
MY LIGHTSABER. THIS IS ALMOST TOO EASY.
MOVE AND I'LL SHOOT.
AHHHH!!
SHANNG!

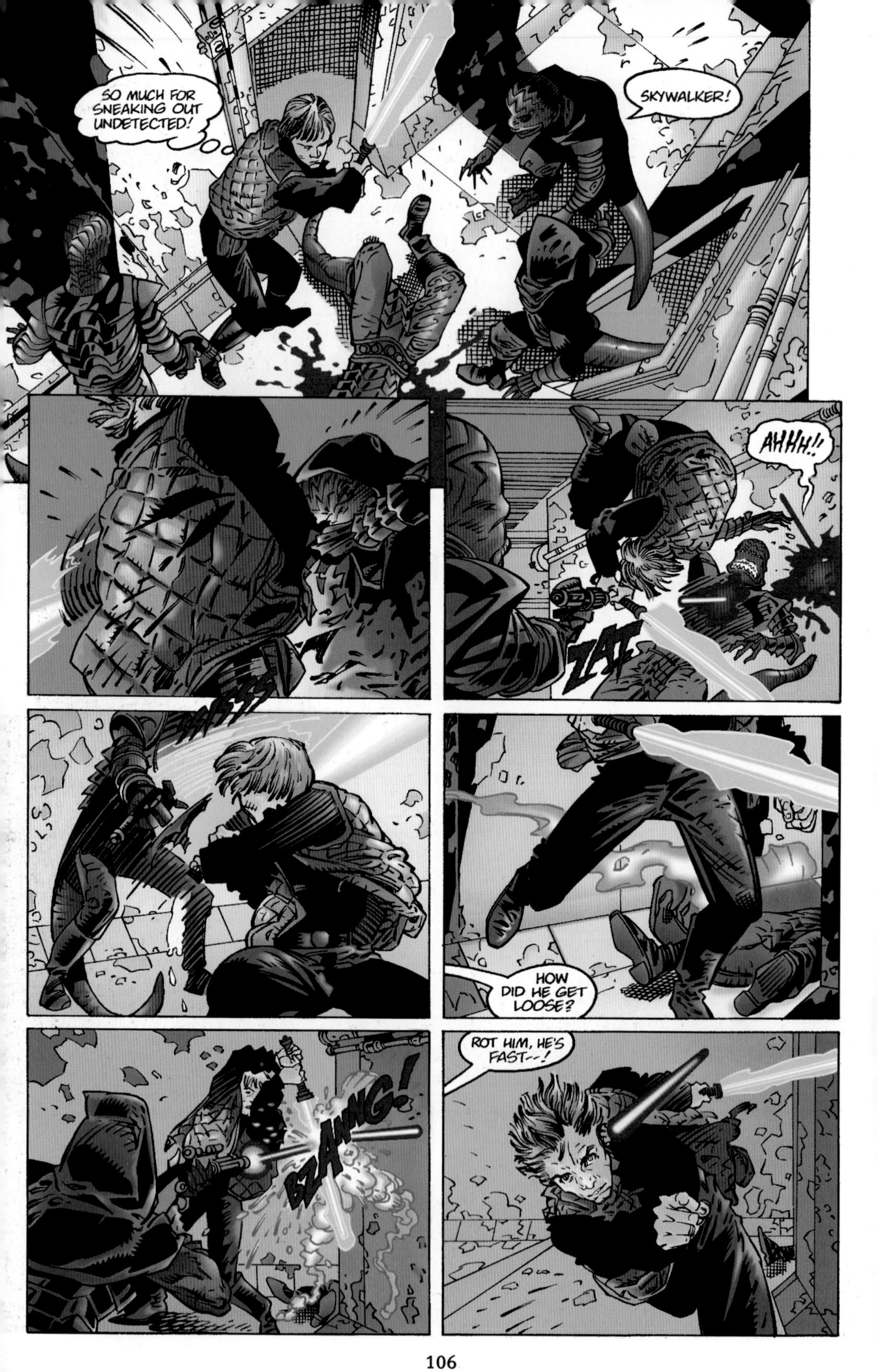
SO MUCH FOR SNEAKING OUT UNDETECTED!
SKYWALKER!
AHHH!!
ZAT
HOW DID HE GET LOOSE?
BZANNG!
ROT HIM, HE'S FAST--!

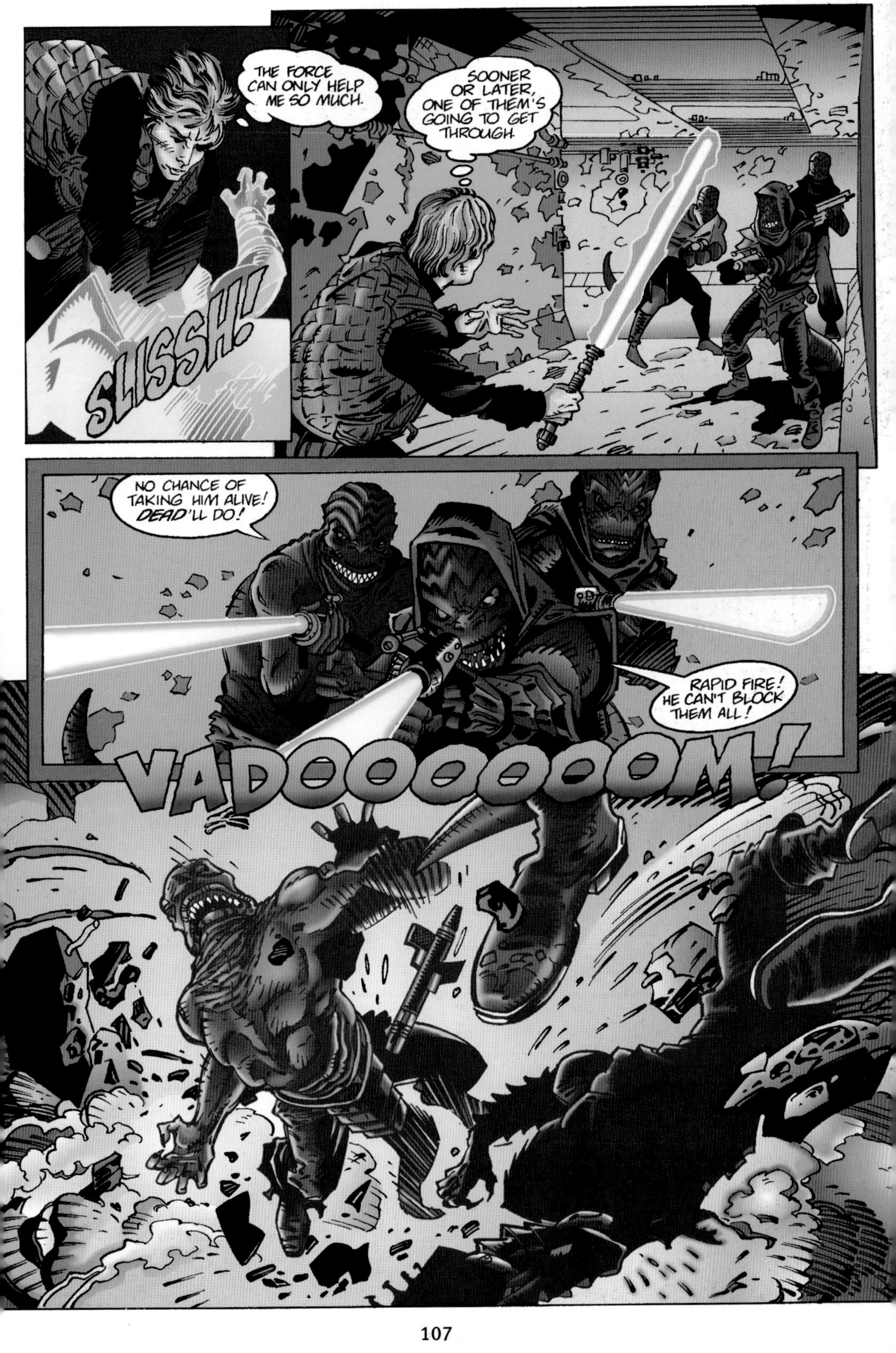
THE FORCE CAN ONLY HELP ME SO MUCH.
SOONER OR LATER, ONE OF THEM'S GOING TO GET THROUGH.
SLISSH!
NO CHANCE OF TAKING HIM ALIVE! DEAD'LL DO!
RAPID FIRE! HE CAN'T BLOCK THEM ALL!
VADOOOOOOOM!

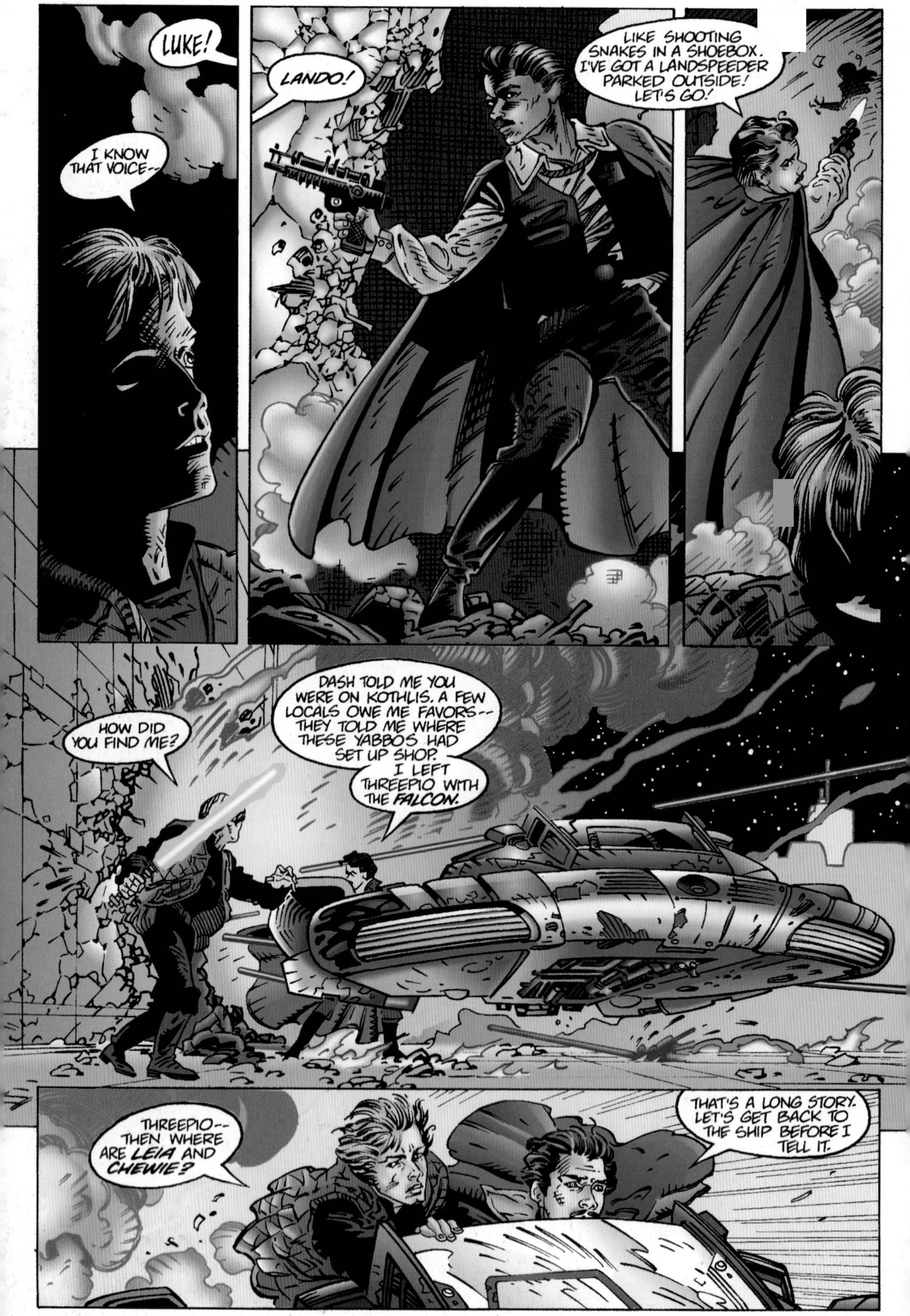
LUKE!
I KNOW THAT VOICE--
LANDO!
LIKE SHOOTING SNAKES IN A SHOEBOX. I'VE GOT A LANDSPEEDER PARKED OUTSIDE! LET'S GO!
HOW DID YOU FIND ME?
DASH TOLD ME YOU WERE ON KOTHLIS. A FEW LOCALS OWE ME FAVORS-- THEY TOLD ME WHERE THESE YABBOS HAD SET UP SHOP.
I LEFT THREEPIO WITH THE FALCON.
THREEPIO-- THEN WHERE ARE LEIA AND CHEWIE?
THAT'S A LONG STORY. LET'S GET BACK TO THE SHIP BEFORE I TELL IT.

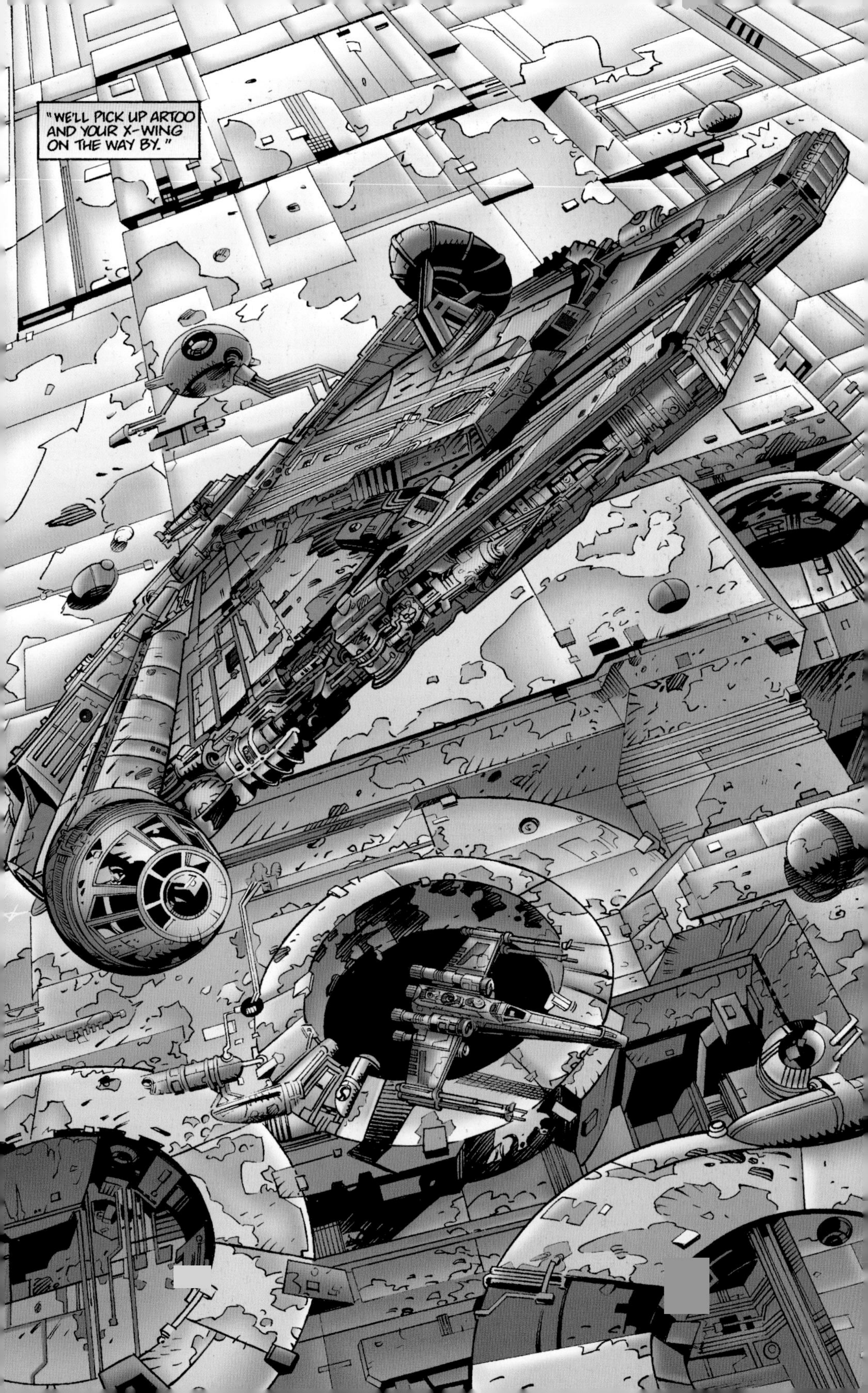
"WE'LL PICK UP ARTOO AND YOUR X-WING ON THE WAY BY."

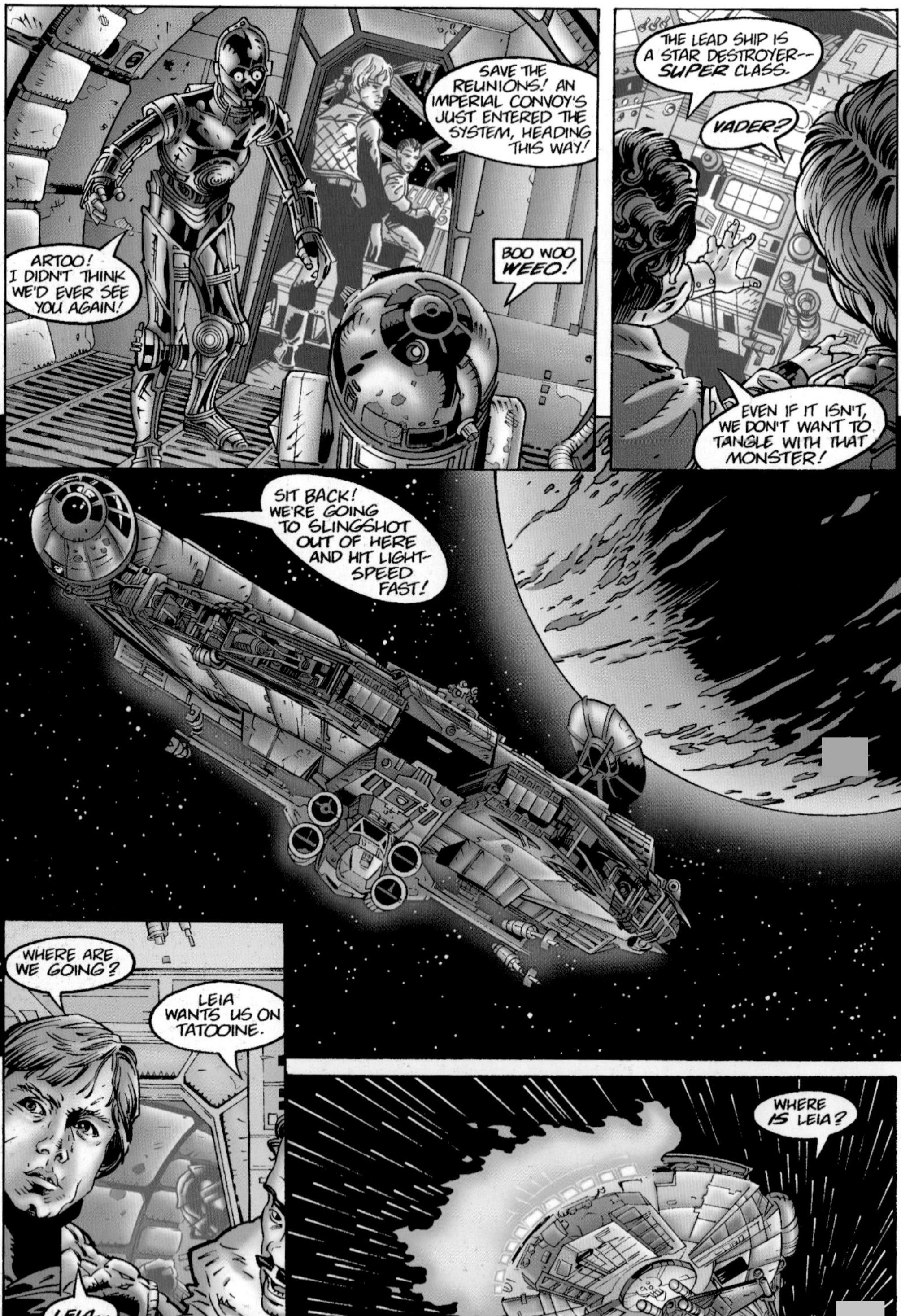
SAVE THE REUNIONS! AN IMPERIAL CONVOY'S JUST ENTERED THE SYSTEM, HEADING THIS WAY!
ARTOO! I DIDN'T THINK WE'D EVER SEE YOU AGAIN!
BOO WOO WEEO!
THE LEAD SHIP IS A STAR DESTROYER-- SUPER CLASS.
VADER?
EVEN IF IT ISN'T, WE DON'T WANT TO TANGLE WITH THAT MONSTER!
SIT BACK! WE'RE GOING TO SLINGSHOT OUT OF HERE AND HIT LIGHT-SPEED FAST!
WHERE ARE WE GOING?
LEIA WANTS US ON TATOOINE.
LEIA--
WHERE IS LEIA?

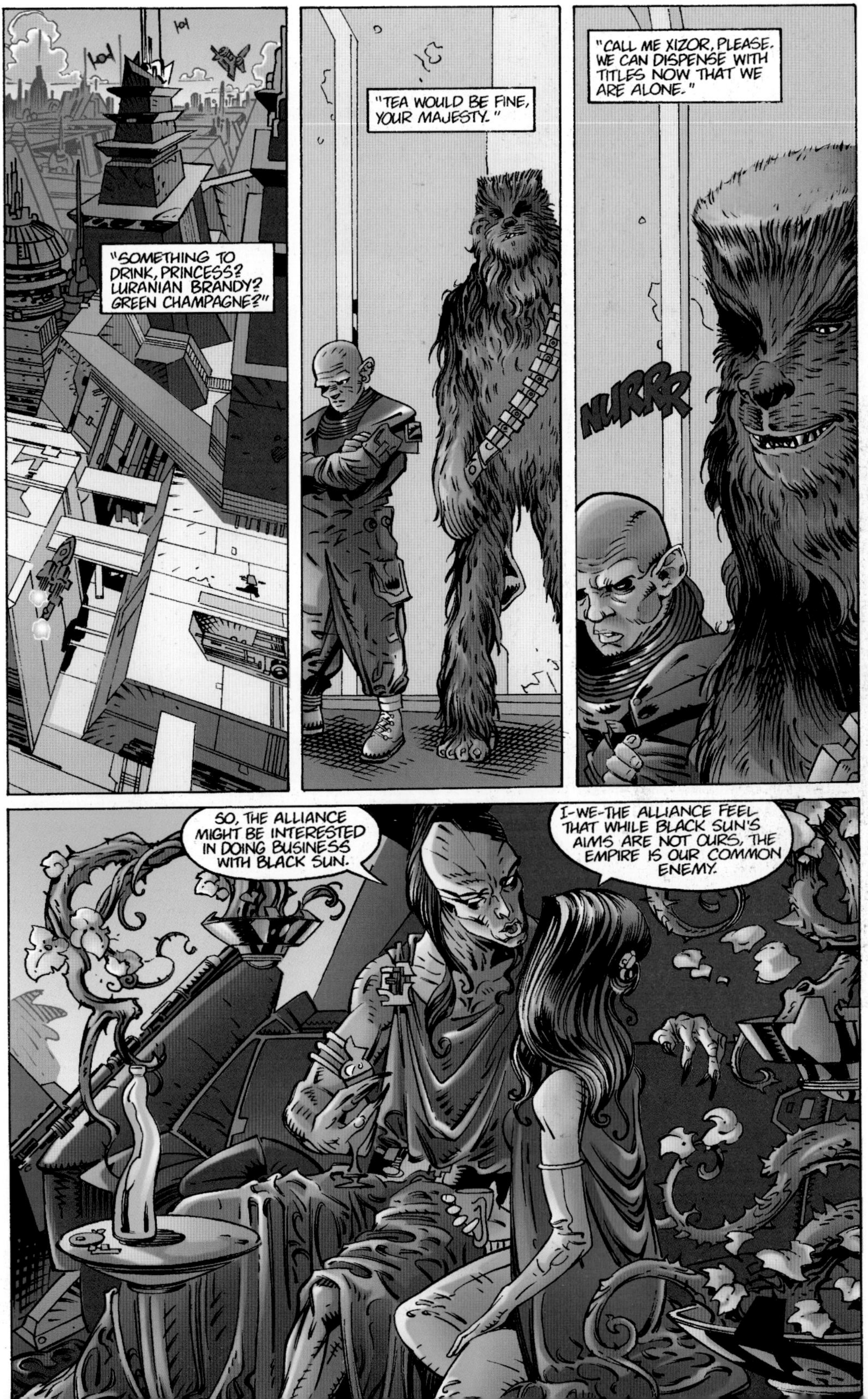
"SOMETHING TO DRINK, PRINCESS? LURANIAN BRANDY? GREEN CHAMPAGNE?"
"TEA WOULD BE FINE, YOUR MAJESTY."
"CALL ME XIZOR, PLEASE. WE CAN DISPENSE WITH TITLES NOW THAT WE ARE ALONE."
NURRR
SO, THE ALLIANCE MIGHT BE INTERESTED IN DOING BUSINESS WITH BLACK SUN.
I-WE-THE ALLIANCE FEEL THAT WHILE BLACK SUN'S AIMS ARE NOT OURS, THE EMPIRE IS OUR COMMON ENEMY.

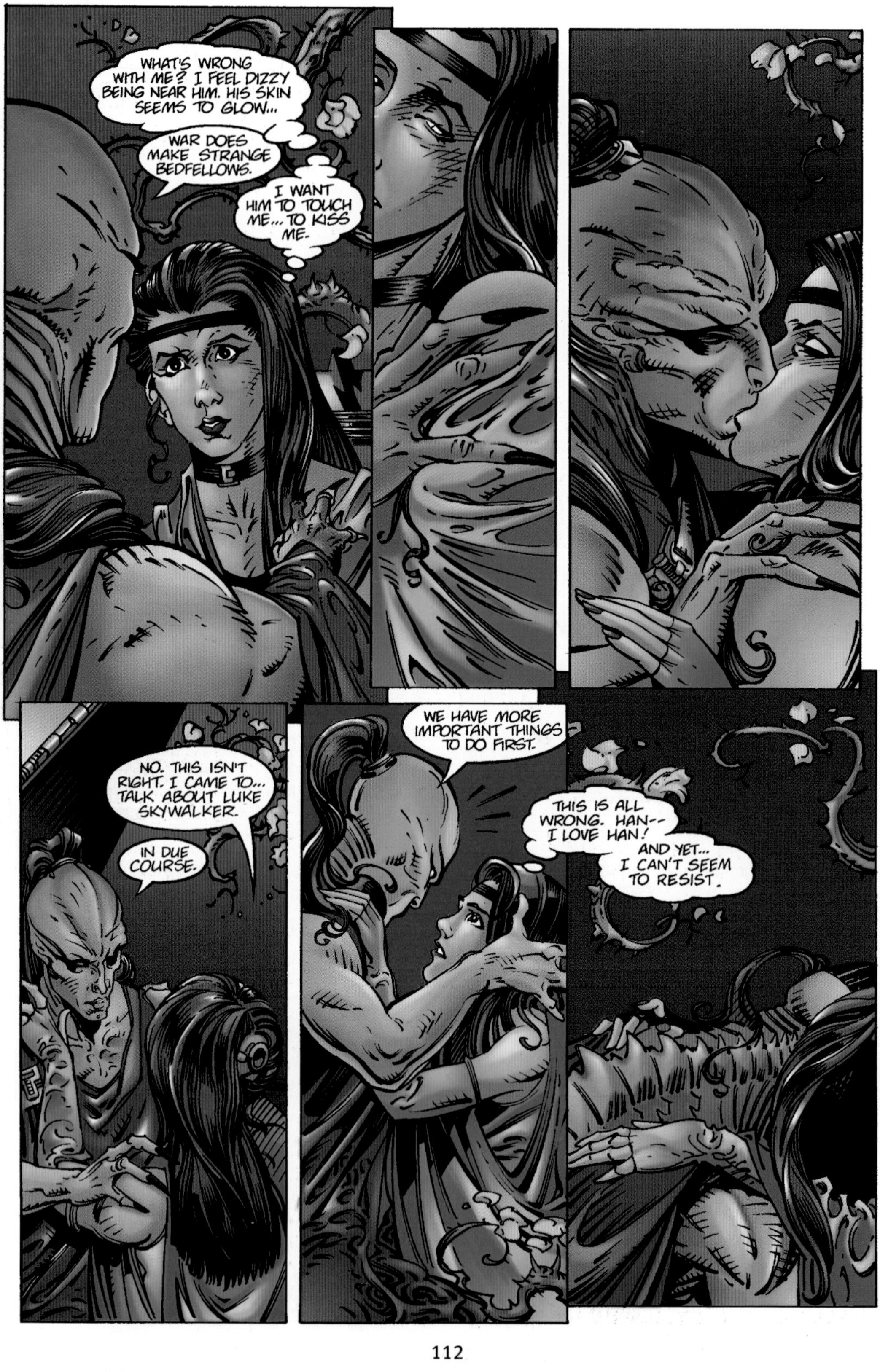
WHAT'S WRONG WITH ME? I FEEL DIZZY BEING NEAR HIM. HIS SKIN SEEMS TO GLOW...
WAR DOES MAKE STRANGE BEDFELLOWS.
I WANT HIM TO TOUCH ME... TO KISS ME.
NO. THIS ISN'T RIGHT. I CAME TO... TALK ABOUT LUKE SKYWALKER.
IN DUE COURSE.
WE HAVE MORE IMPORTANT THINGS TO DO FIRST.
THIS IS ALL WRONG. HAN-- I LOVE HAN!
AND YET... I CAN'T SEEM TO RESIST.

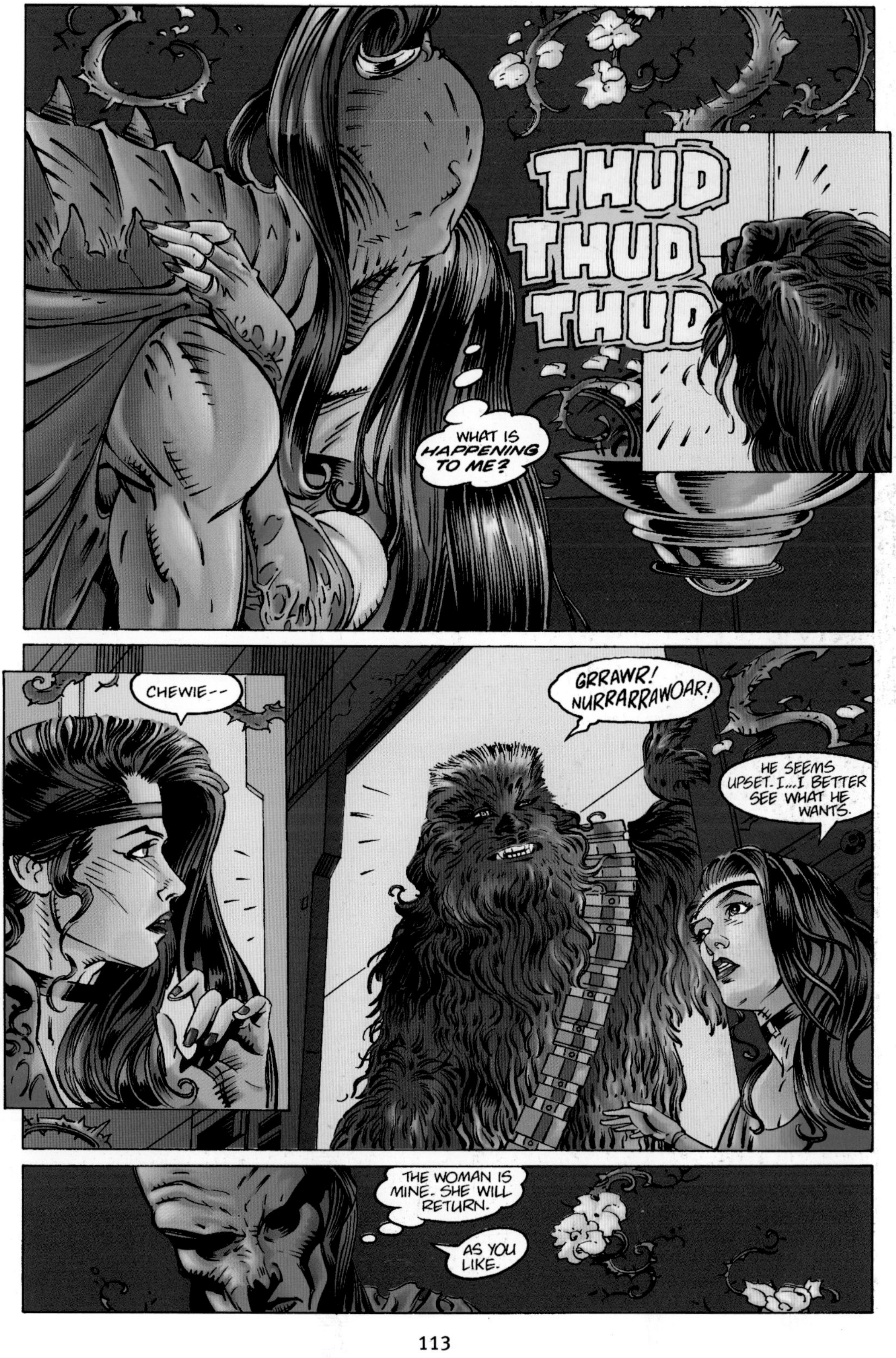
THUD
THUD
THUD
WHAT IS HAPPENING TO ME?
CHEWIE--
GRRAWR! NURRARRAWOAR!
HE SEEMS UPSET. I...I BETTER SEE WHAT HE WANTS.
THE WOMAN IS MINE. SHE WILL RETURN.
AS YOU LIKE.

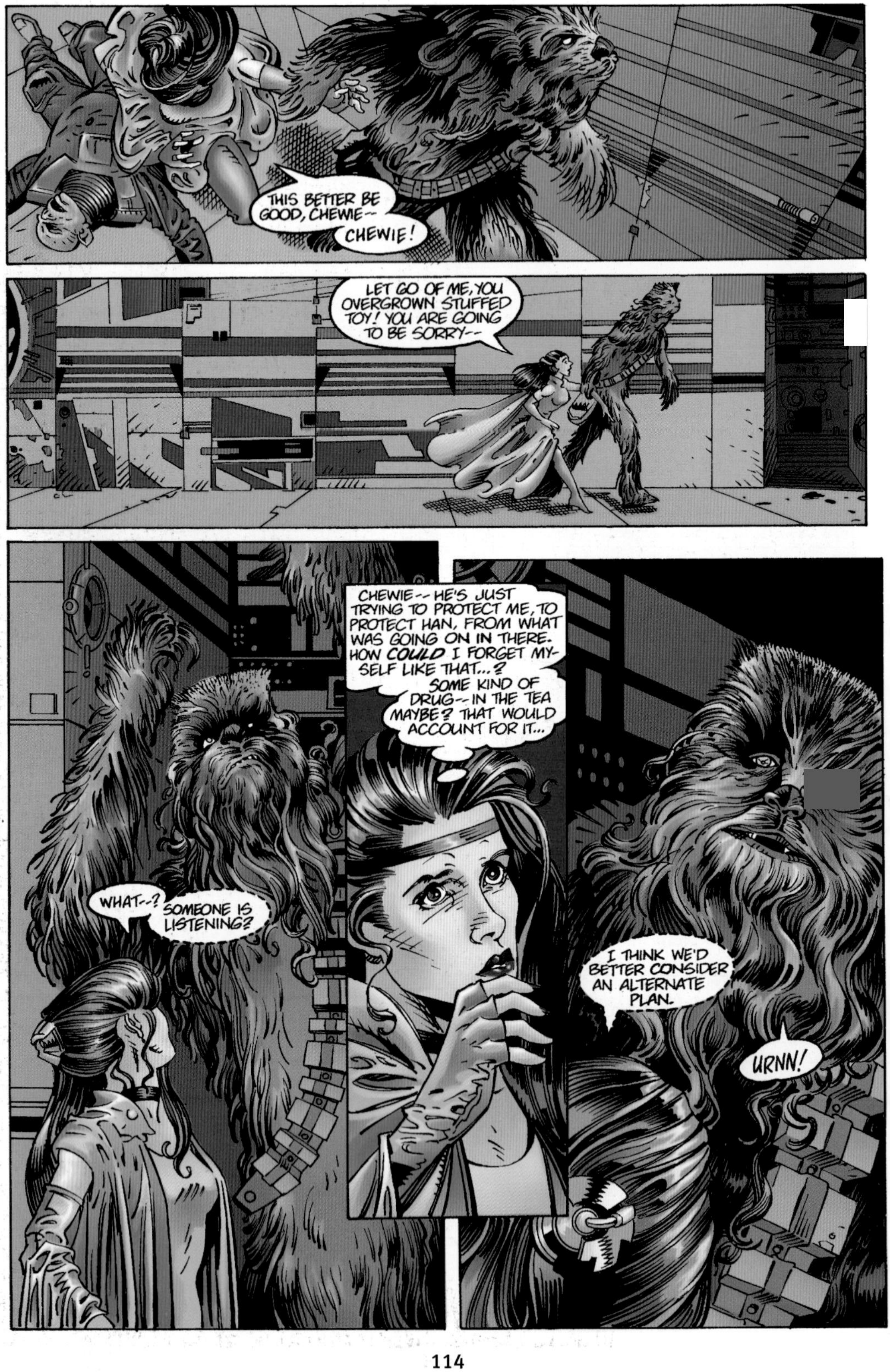

THIS BETTER BE GOOD, CHEWIE--
CHEWIE!
LET GO OF ME, YOU OVERGROWN STUFFED TOY! YOU ARE GOING TO BE SORRY--
CHEWIE--HE'S JUST TRYING TO PROTECT ME, TO PROTECT HAN, FROM WHAT WAS GOING ON IN THERE. HOW COULD I FORGET MYSELF LIKE THAT...?
SOME KIND OF DRUG--IN THE TEA MAYBE? THAT WOULD ACCOUNT FOR IT...
WHAT--?
SOMEONE IS LISTENING?
I THINK WE'D BETTER CONSIDER AN ALTERNATE PLAN.
URNN!

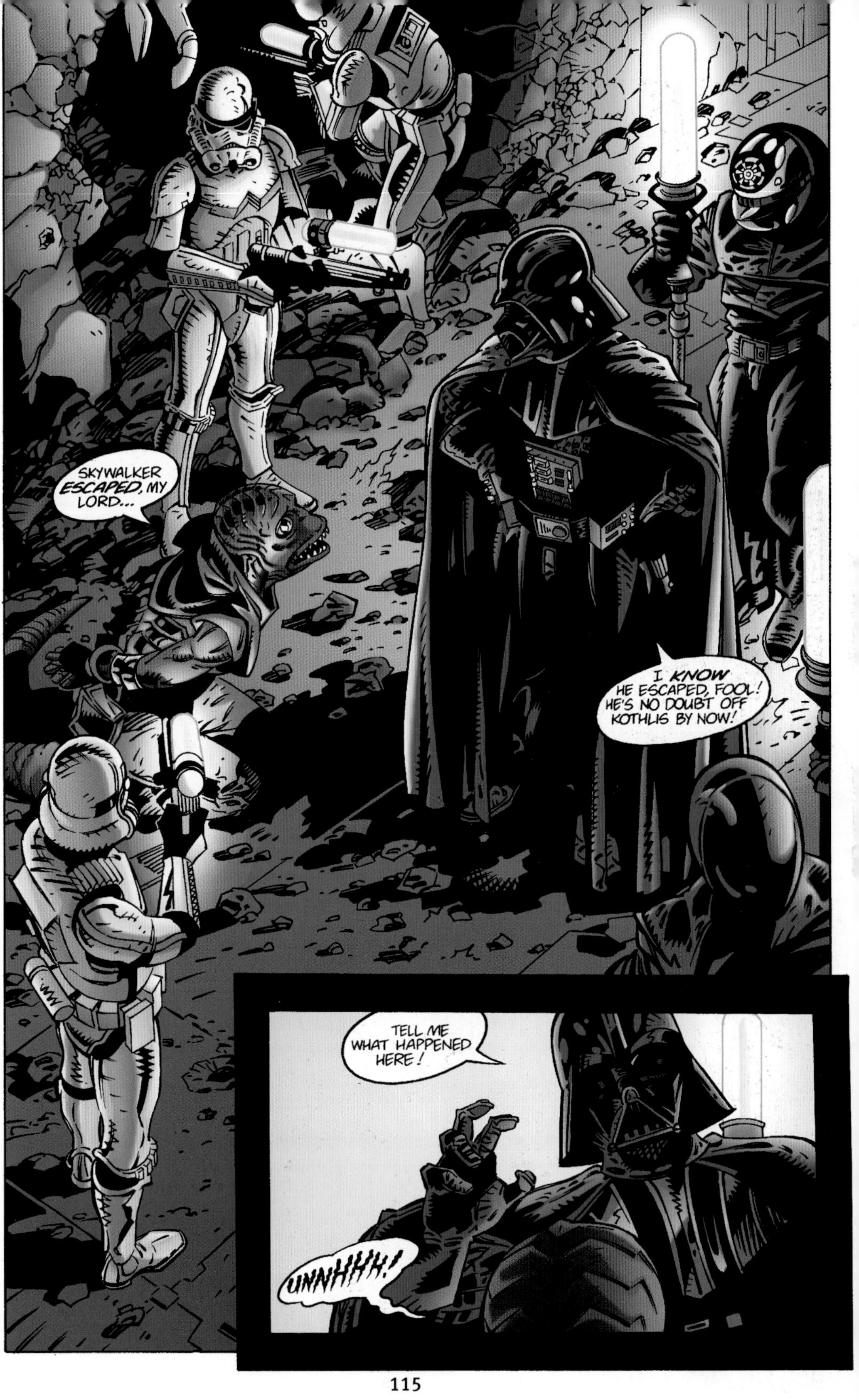
SKYWALKER ESCAPED, MY LORD...
I KNOW HE ESCAPED, FOOL! HE'S NO DOUBT OFF KOTHLIS BY NOW!
TELL ME WHAT HAPPENED HERE!
UNNHHH!

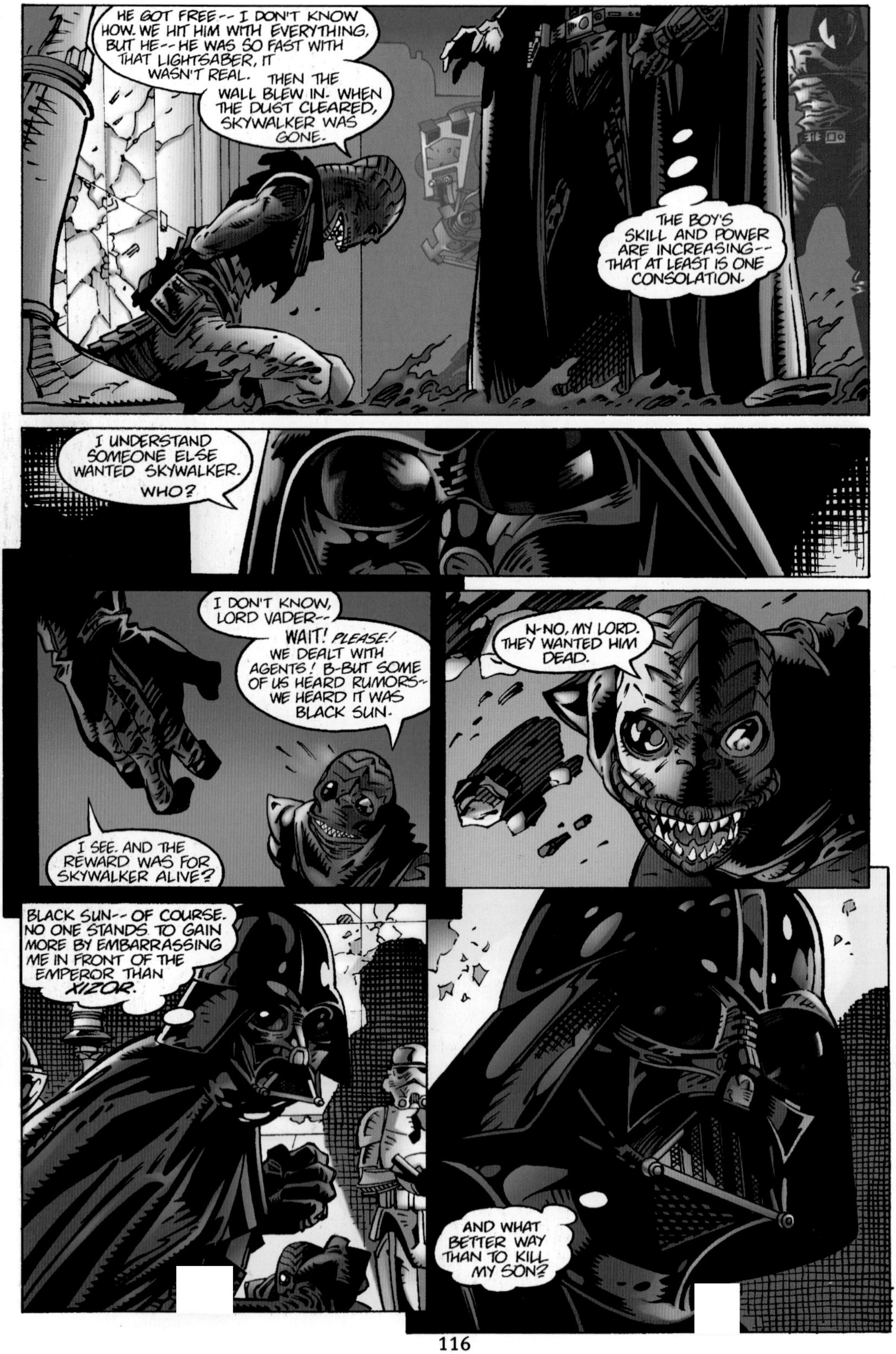
HE GOT FREE-- I DON'T KNOW HOW. WE HIT HIM WITH EVERYTHING, BUT HE--HE WAS SO FAST WITH THAT LIGHTSABER, IT WASN'T REAL.
THEN THE WALL BLEW IN. WHEN THE DUST CLEARED, SKYWALKER WAS GONE.
THE BOY'S SKILL AND POWER ARE INCREASING-- THAT AT LEAST IS ONE CONSOLATION.
I UNDERSTAND SOMEONE ELSE WANTED SKYWALKER.
WHO?
I DON'T KNOW, LORD VADER--
WAIT! PLEASE! WE DEALT WITH AGENTS! B-BUT SOME OF US HEARD RUMORS-- WE HEARD IT WAS BLACK SUN.
I SEE. AND THE REWARD WAS FOR SKYWALKER ALIVE?
N-NO, MY LORD. THEY WANTED HIM DEAD.
BLACK SUN-- OF COURSE. NO ONE STANDS TO GAIN MORE BY EMBARRASSING ME IN FRONT OF THE EMPEROR THAN XIZOR.
AND WHAT BETTER WAY THAN TO KILL MY SON?

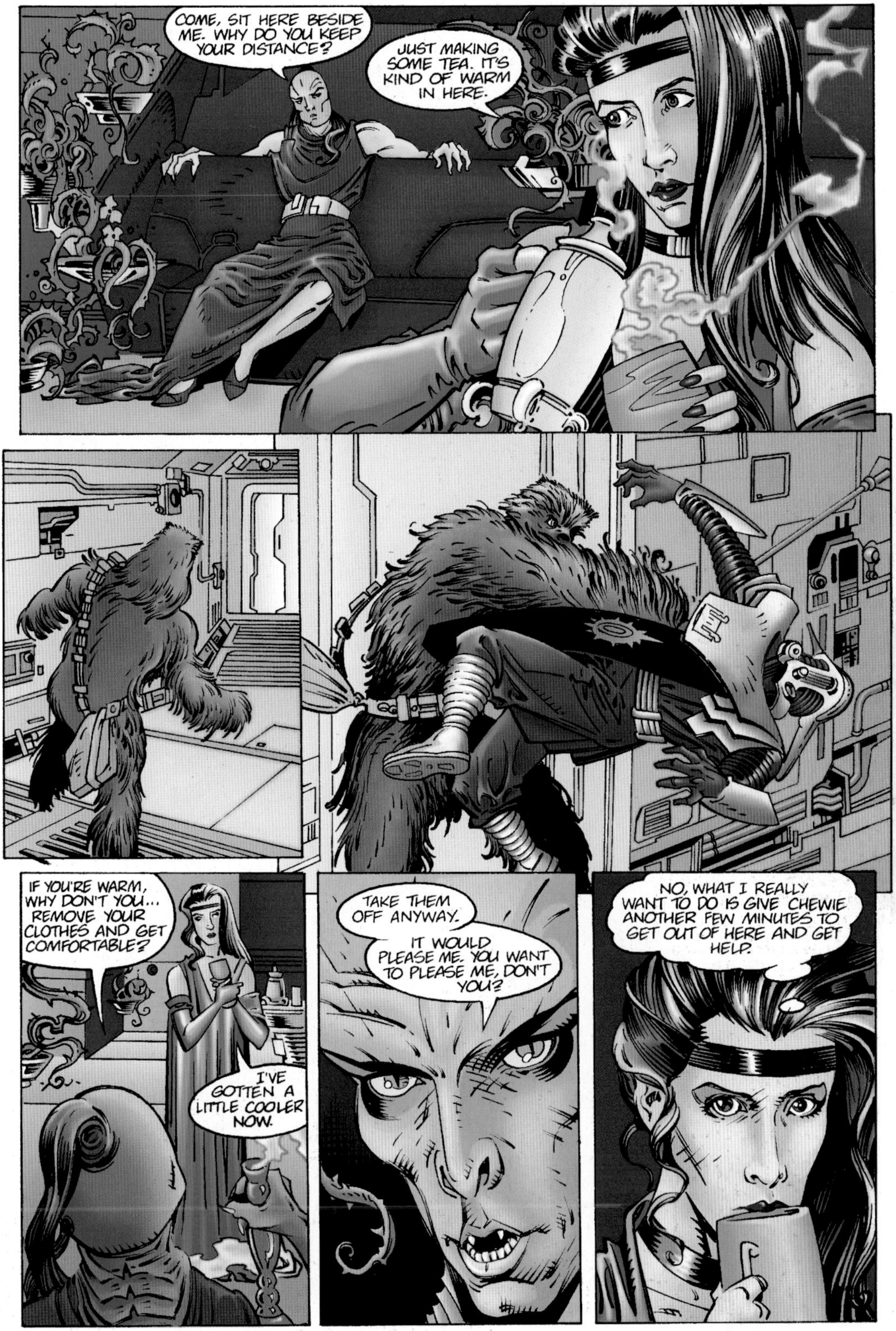
COME, SIT HERE BESIDE ME. WHY DO YOU KEEP YOUR DISTANCE?
JUST MAKING SOME TEA. IT'S KIND OF WARM IN HERE.
IF YOU'RE WARM, WHY DON'T YOU... REMOVE YOUR CLOTHES AND GET COMFORTABLE?
I'VE GOTTEN A LITTLE COOLER NOW.
TAKE THEM OFF ANYWAY.
IT WOULD PLEASE ME. YOU WANT TO PLEASE ME, DON'T YOU?
NO, WHAT I REALLY WANT TO DO IS GIVE CHEWIE ANOTHER FEW MINUTES TO GET OUT OF HERE AND GET HELP.

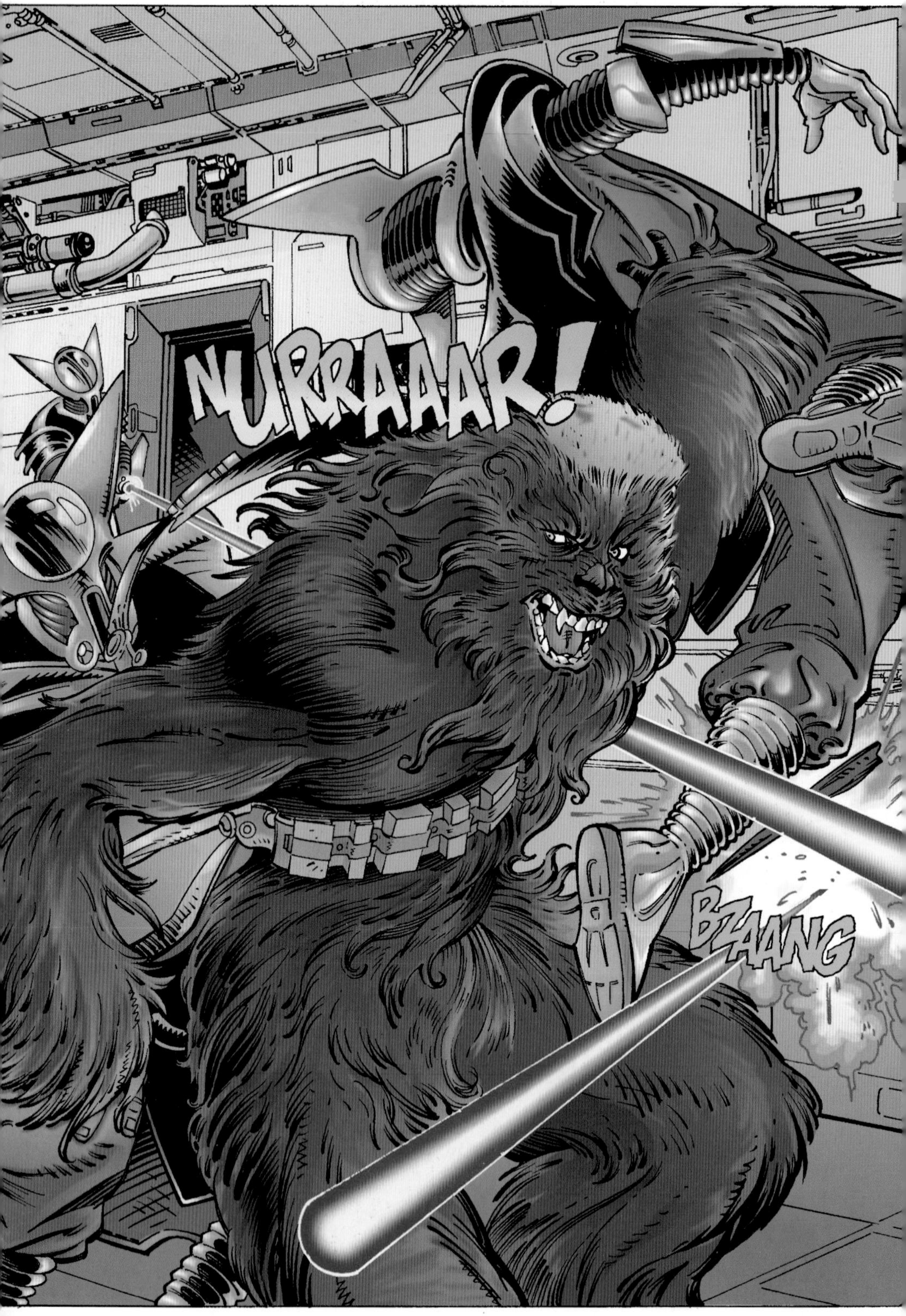
NURRAAAR!
BZAANG

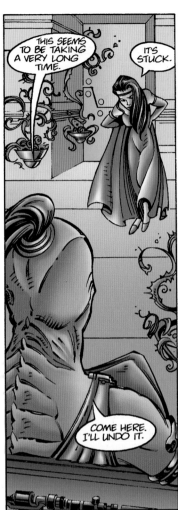

THIS SEEMS TO BE TAKING A VERY LONG TIME.

IT'S STUCK.

COME HERE. I'LL UNDO IT.

WAIT. THERE IT IS.

NOW THE REST OF IT.

I HOPE CHEWIE'S HAD LONG ENOUGH, BECAUSE THIS IS AS FAR AS I GO.

I DON'T THINK SO.

WHAT?

IT ISN'T PROPER TO REMOVE ONE'S CLOTHES IN FRONT OF A STRANGER.

YOU CANNOT REFUSE ME! NO FEMALE CAN!

I CAN FEEL IT WASHING OVER ME AGAIN--THE *DESIRE* FOR HIM.

THAT WAS NO DRUG IN MY TEA--IT WAS *HIM*. HE MUST GIVE OFF SOME POWERFUL CHEMICAL ATTRACTANTS.

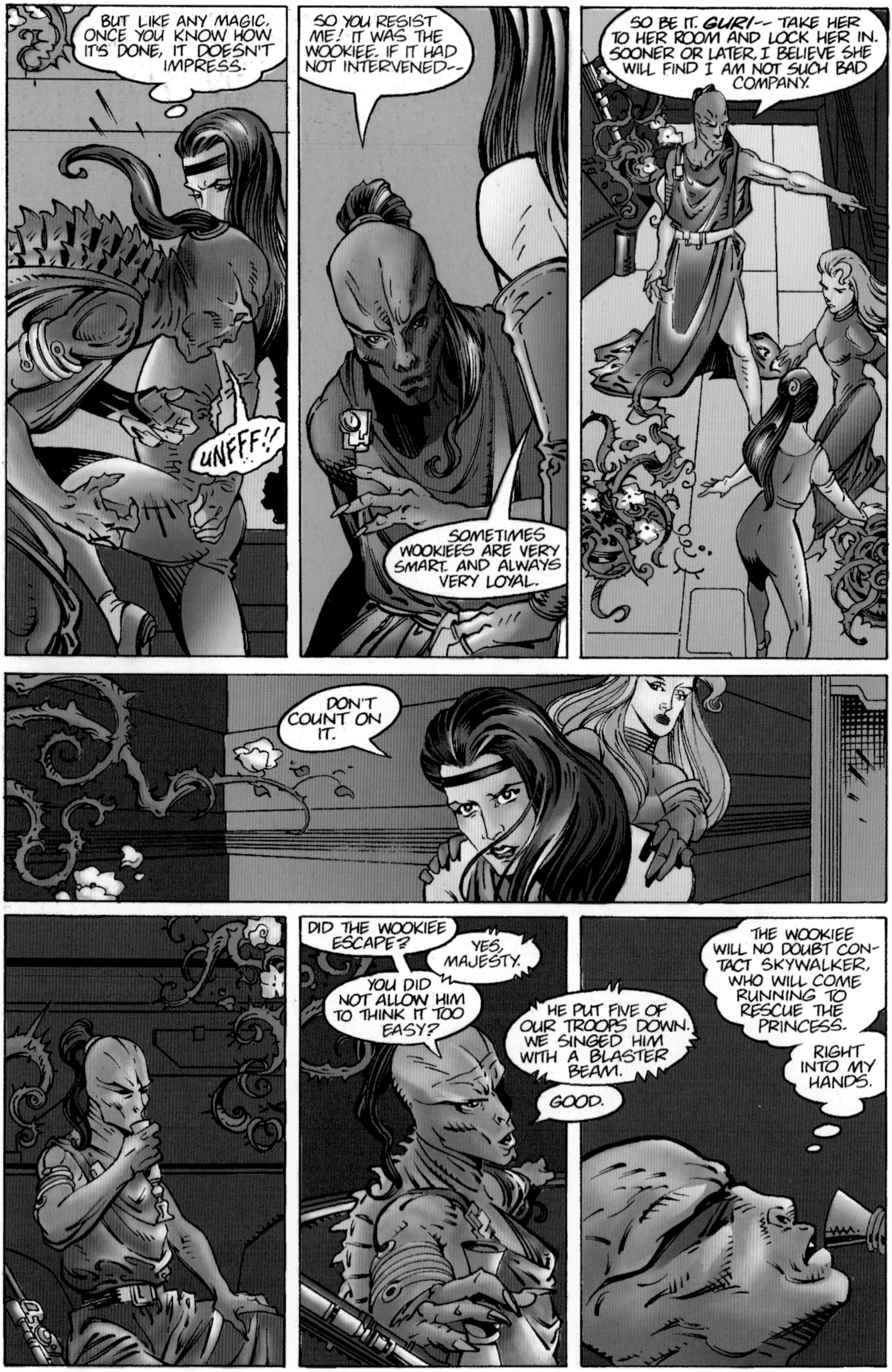
BUT LIKE ANY MAGIC, ONCE YOU KNOW HOW IT'S DONE, IT DOESN'T IMPRESS.
UNFFF!!
SO YOU RESIST ME! IT WAS THE WOOKIEE. IF IT HAD NOT INTERVENED--
SOMETIMES WOOKIEES ARE VERY SMART. AND ALWAYS VERY LOYAL.
SO BE IT. GURI-- TAKE HER TO HER ROOM AND LOCK HER IN. SOONER OR LATER, I BELIEVE SHE WILL FIND I AM NOT SUCH BAD COMPANY.
DON'T COUNT ON IT.
DID THE WOOKIEE ESCAPE?
YES, MAJESTY.
YOU DID NOT ALLOW HIM TO THINK IT TOO EASY?
HE PUT FIVE OF OUR TROOPS DOWN. WE SINGED HIM WITH A BLASTER BEAM.
GOOD.
THE WOOKIEE WILL NO DOUBT CONTACT SKYWALKER, WHO WILL COME RUNNING TO RESCUE THE PRINCESS.
RIGHT INTO MY HANDS.

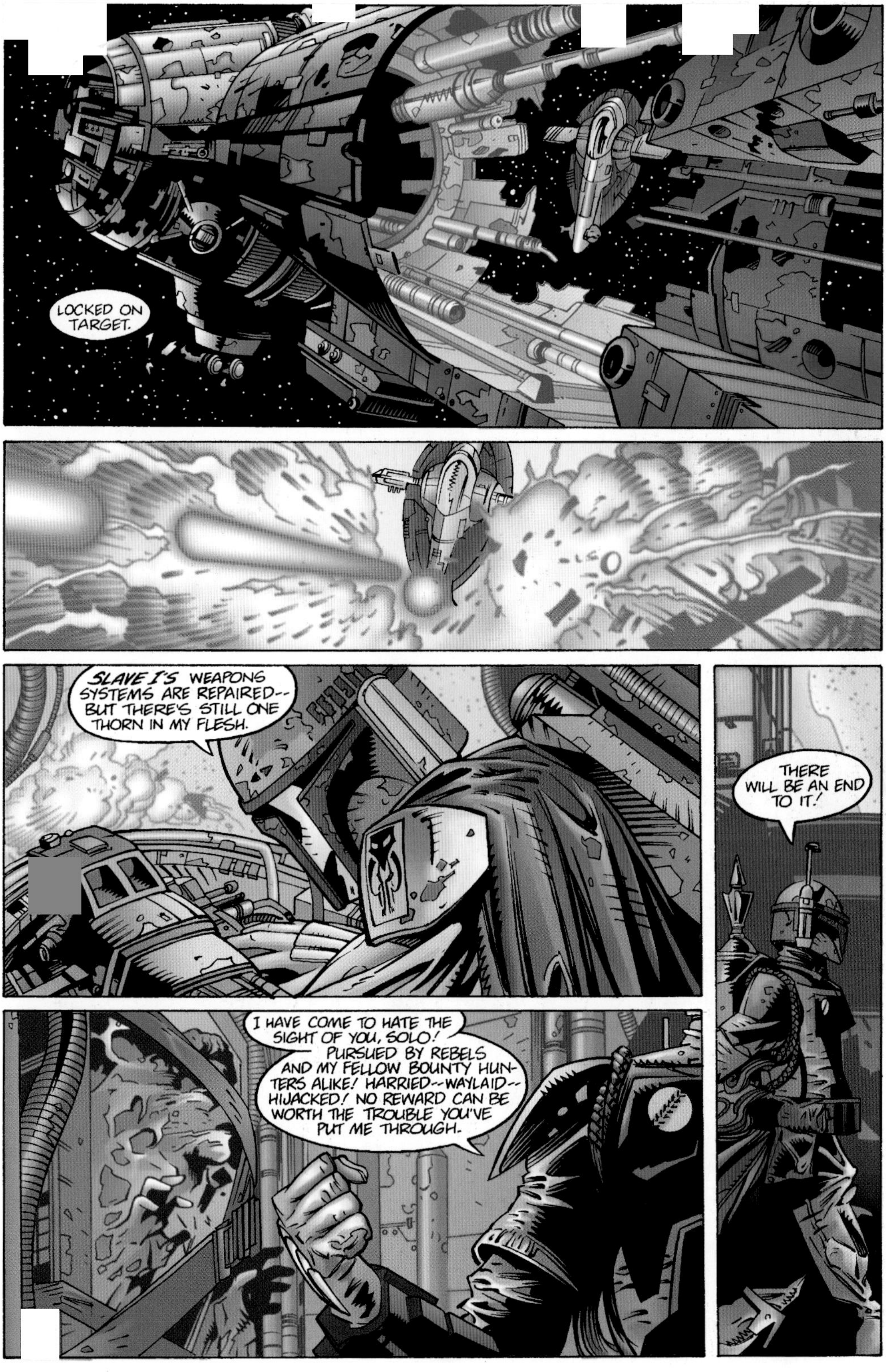
LOCKED ON TARGET.
SLAVE I'S WEAPONS SYSTEMS ARE REPAIRED-- BUT THERE'S STILL ONE THORN IN MY FLESH.
THERE WILL BE AN END TO IT!
I HAVE COME TO HATE THE SIGHT OF YOU, SOLO! PURSUED BY REBELS AND MY FELLOW BOUNTY HUNTERS ALIKE! HARRIED--WAYLAID--HIJACKED! NO REWARD CAN BE WORTH THE TROUBLE YOU'VE PUT ME THROUGH.

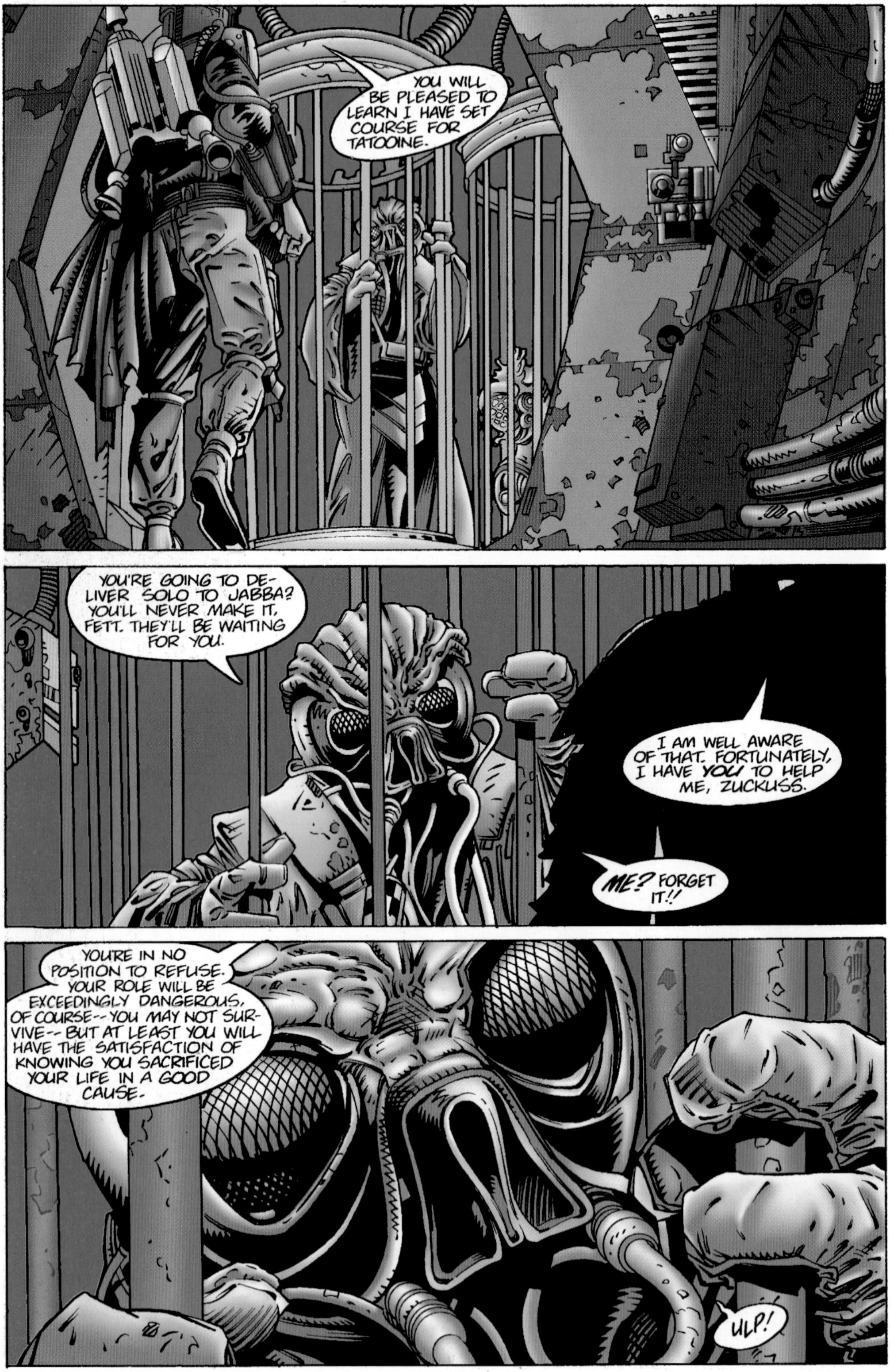
YOU WILL BE PLEASED TO LEARN I HAVE SET COURSE FOR TATOOINE.
YOU'RE GOING TO DE-LIVER SOLO TO JABBA? YOU'LL NEVER MAKE IT, FETT. THEY'LL BE WAITING FOR YOU.
I AM WELL AWARE OF THAT. FORTUNATELY, I HAVE *YOU* TO HELP ME, ZUCKUSS.
ME? FORGET IT!!
YOU'RE IN NO POSITION TO REFUSE. YOUR ROLE WILL BE EXCEEDINGLY DANGEROUS, OF COURSE-- YOU MAY NOT SUR-VIVE-- BUT AT LEAST YOU WILL HAVE THE SATISFACTION OF KNOWING YOU SACRIFICED YOUR LIFE IN A GOOD CAUSE.
ULP!

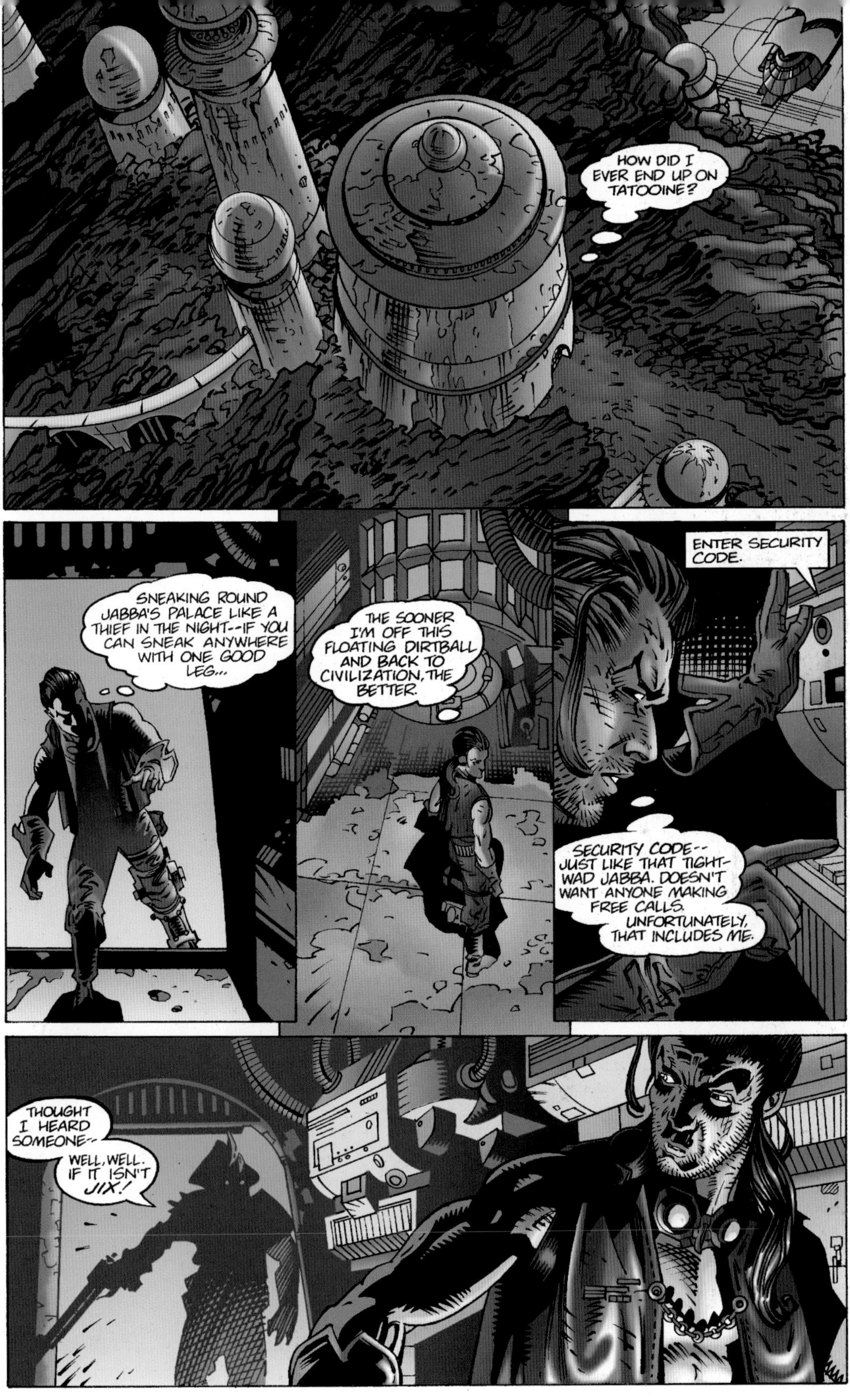
HOW DID I EVER END UP ON TATOOINE?
SNEAKING ROUND JABBA'S PALACE LIKE A THIEF IN THE NIGHT--IF YOU CAN SNEAK ANYWHERE WITH ONE GOOD LEG...
THE SOONER I'M OFF THIS FLOATING DIRTBALL AND BACK TO CIVILIZATION, THE BETTER.
ENTER SECURITY CODE.
SECURITY CODE--JUST LIKE THAT TIGHTWAD JABBA. DOESN'T WANT ANYONE MAKING FREE CALLS.
UNFORTUNATELY, THAT INCLUDES ME.
THOUGHT I HEARD SOMEONE--
WELL, WELL. IF IT ISN'T JIX!

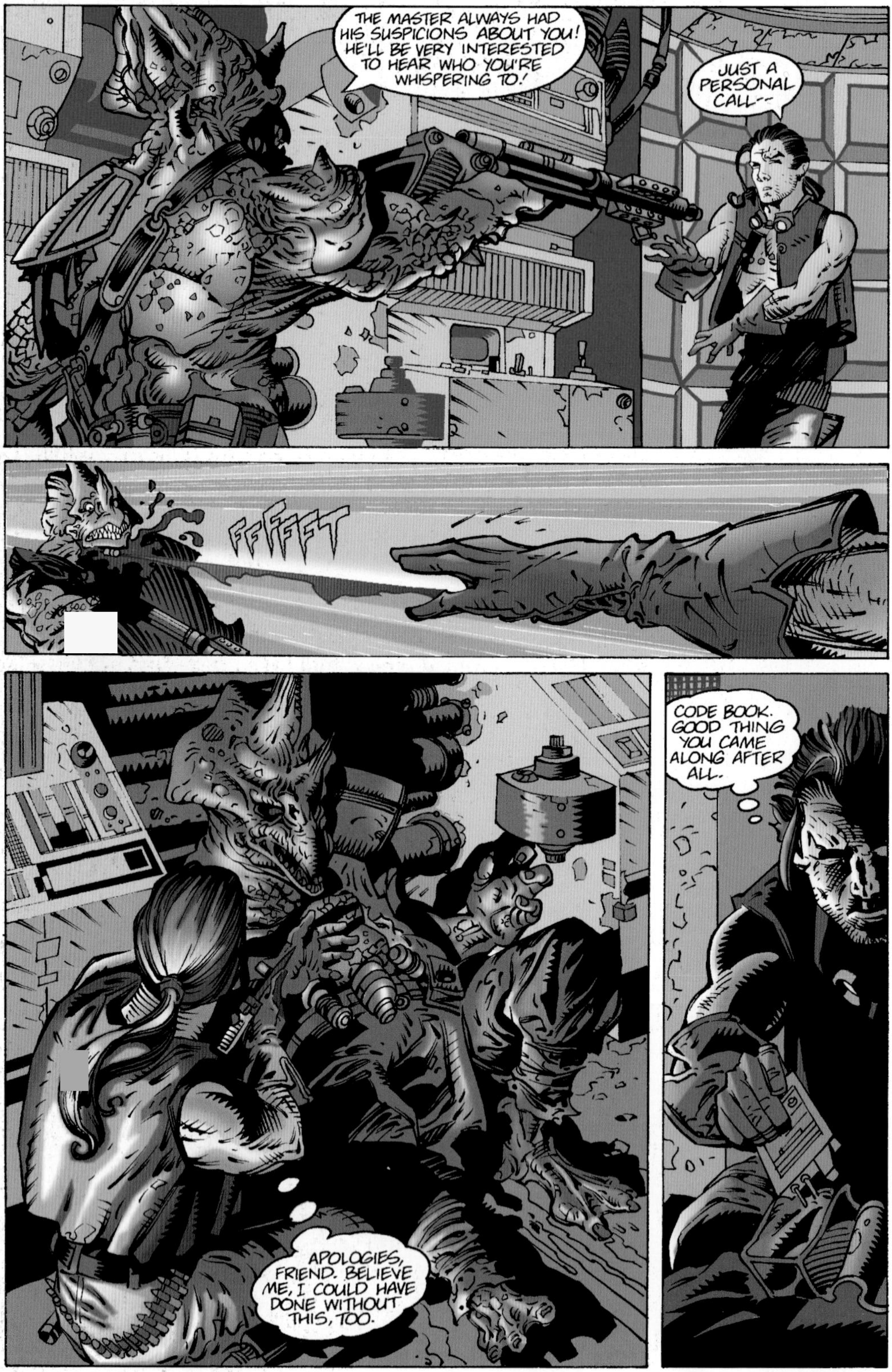
THE MASTER ALWAYS HAD HIS SUSPICIONS ABOUT YOU! HE'LL BE VERY INTERESTED TO HEAR WHO YOU'RE WHISPERING TO!
JUST A PERSONAL CALL--
FFFFFT
APOLOGIES, FRIEND. BELIEVE ME, I COULD HAVE DONE WITHOUT THIS, TOO.
CODE BOOK. GOOD THING YOU CAME ALONG AFTER ALL.

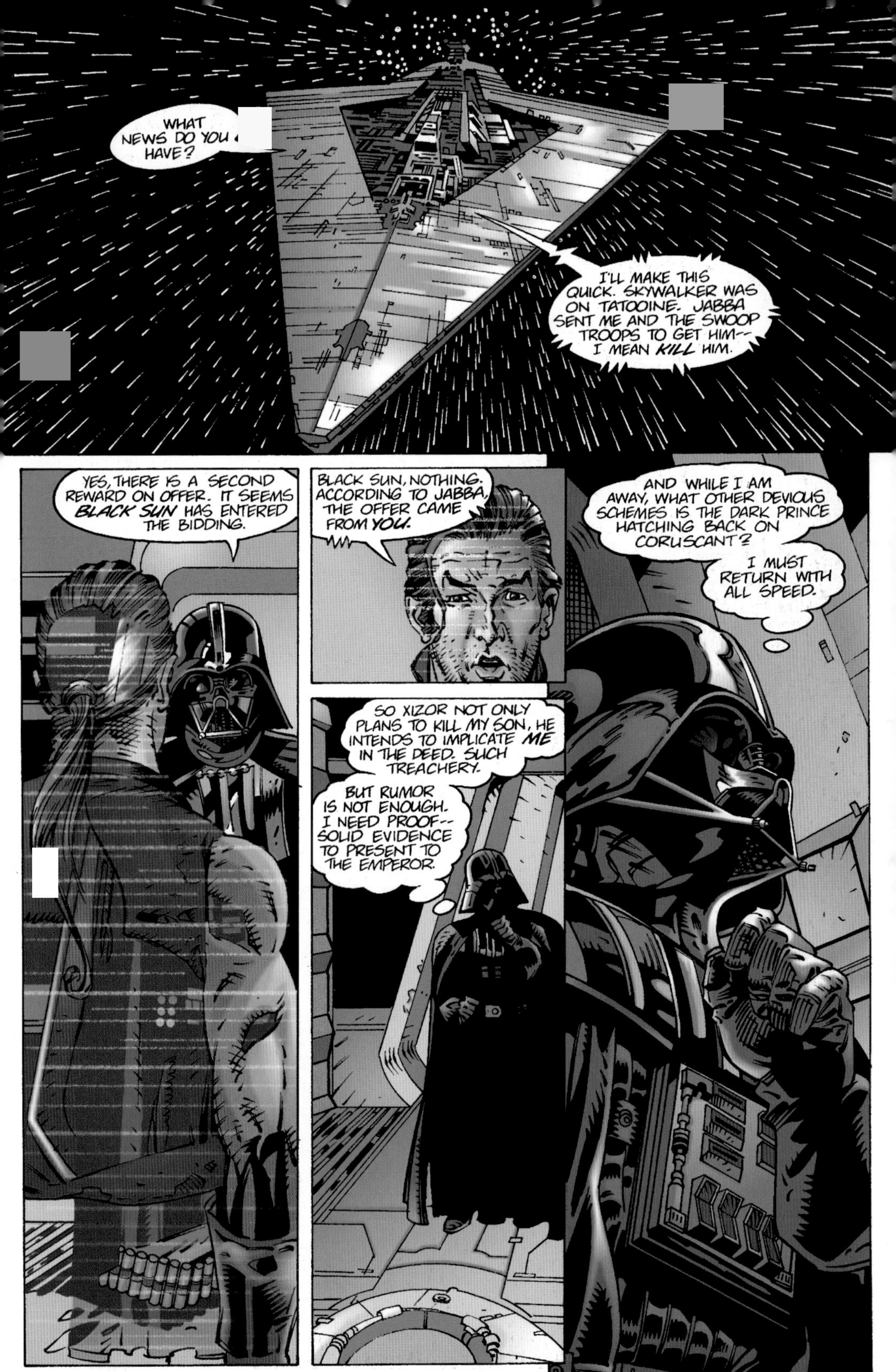
WHAT NEWS DO YOU HAVE?
I'LL MAKE THIS QUICK. SKYWALKER WAS ON TATOOINE. JABBA SENT ME AND THE SWOOP TROOPS TO GET HIM-- I MEAN KILL HIM.
YES, THERE IS A SECOND REWARD ON OFFER. IT SEEMS BLACK SUN HAS ENTERED THE BIDDING.
BLACK SUN, NOTHING. ACCORDING TO JABBA, THE OFFER CAME FROM YOU.
SO XIZOR NOT ONLY PLANS TO KILL MY SON, HE INTENDS TO IMPLICATE ME IN THE DEED. SUCH TREACHERY.
BUT RUMOR IS NOT ENOUGH. I NEED PROOF-- SOLID EVIDENCE TO PRESENT TO THE EMPEROR.
AND WHILE I AM AWAY, WHAT OTHER DEVIOUS SCHEMES IS THE DARK PRINCE HATCHING BACK ON CORUSCANT?
I MUST RETURN WITH ALL SPEED.

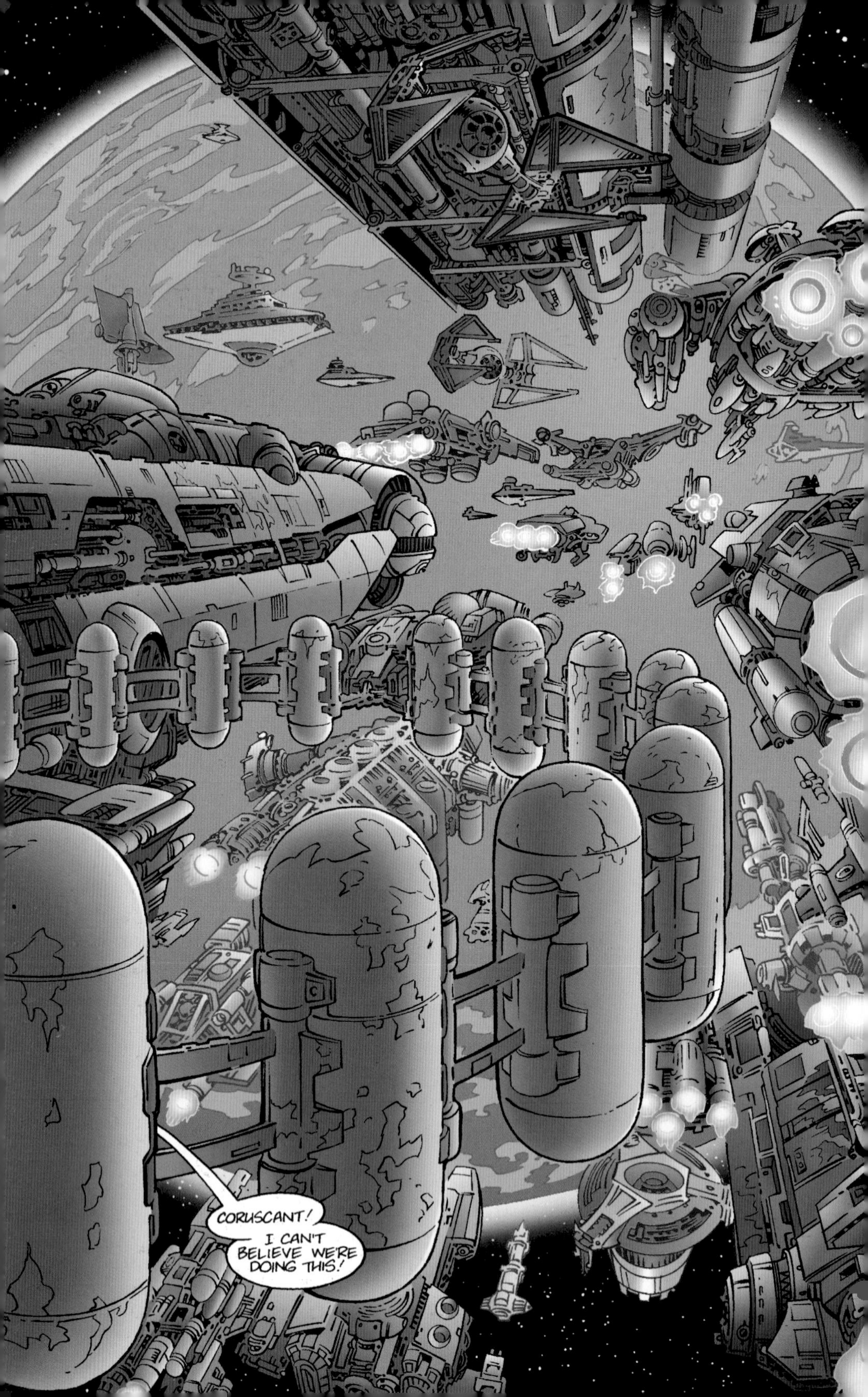
CORUSCANT! I CAN'T BELIEVE WE'RE DOING THIS!

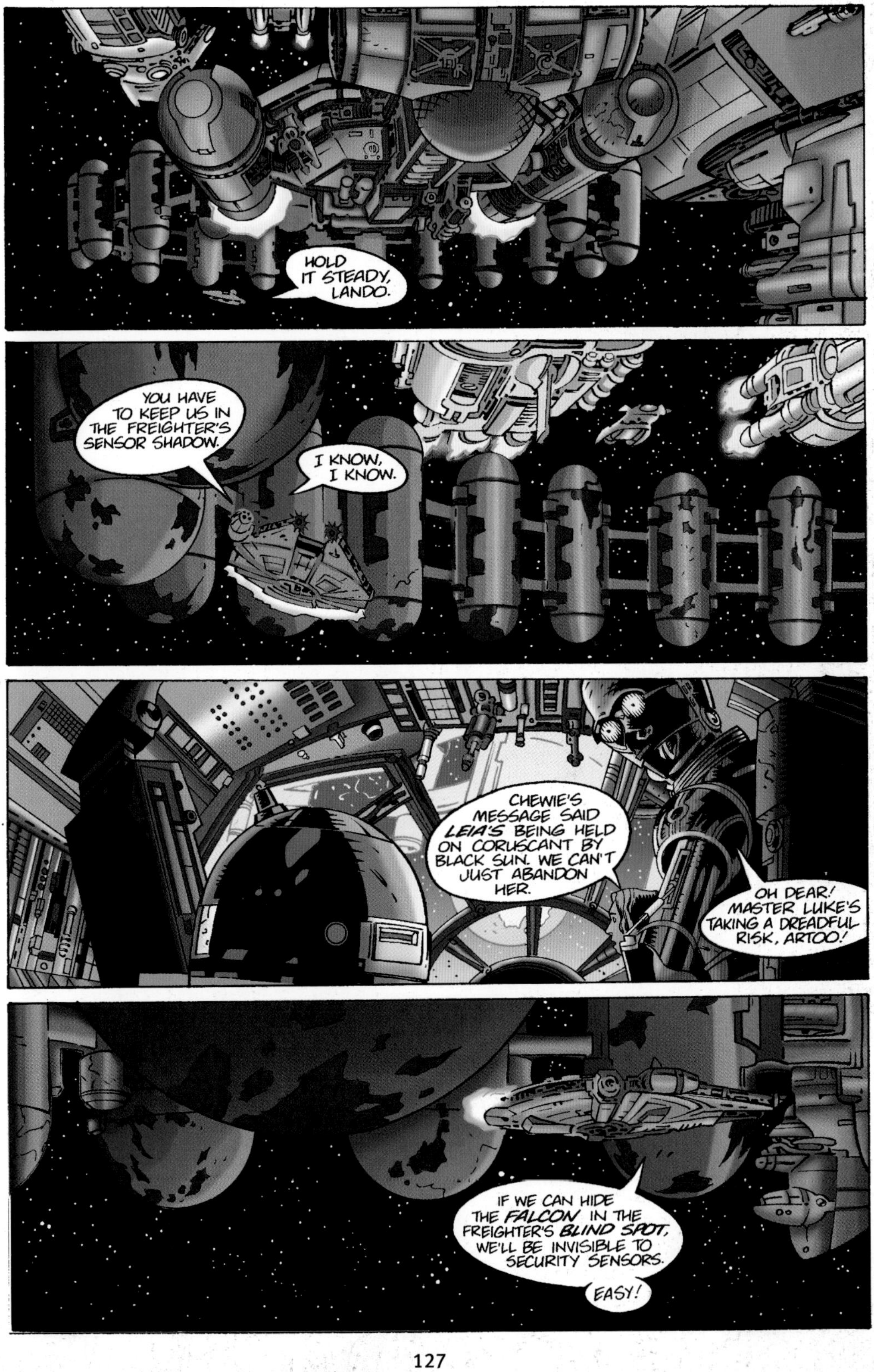
HOLD IT STEADY, LANDO.
YOU HAVE TO KEEP US IN THE FREIGHTER'S SENSOR SHADOW.
I KNOW, I KNOW.
CHEWIE'S MESSAGE SAID LEIA'S BEING HELD ON CORUSCANT BY BLACK SUN. WE CAN'T JUST ABANDON HER.
OH DEAR! MASTER LUKE'S TAKING A DREADFUL RISK, ARTOO!
IF WE CAN HIDE THE FALCON IN THE FREIGHTER'S BLIND SPOT, WE'LL BE INVISIBLE TO SECURITY SENSORS.
EASY!

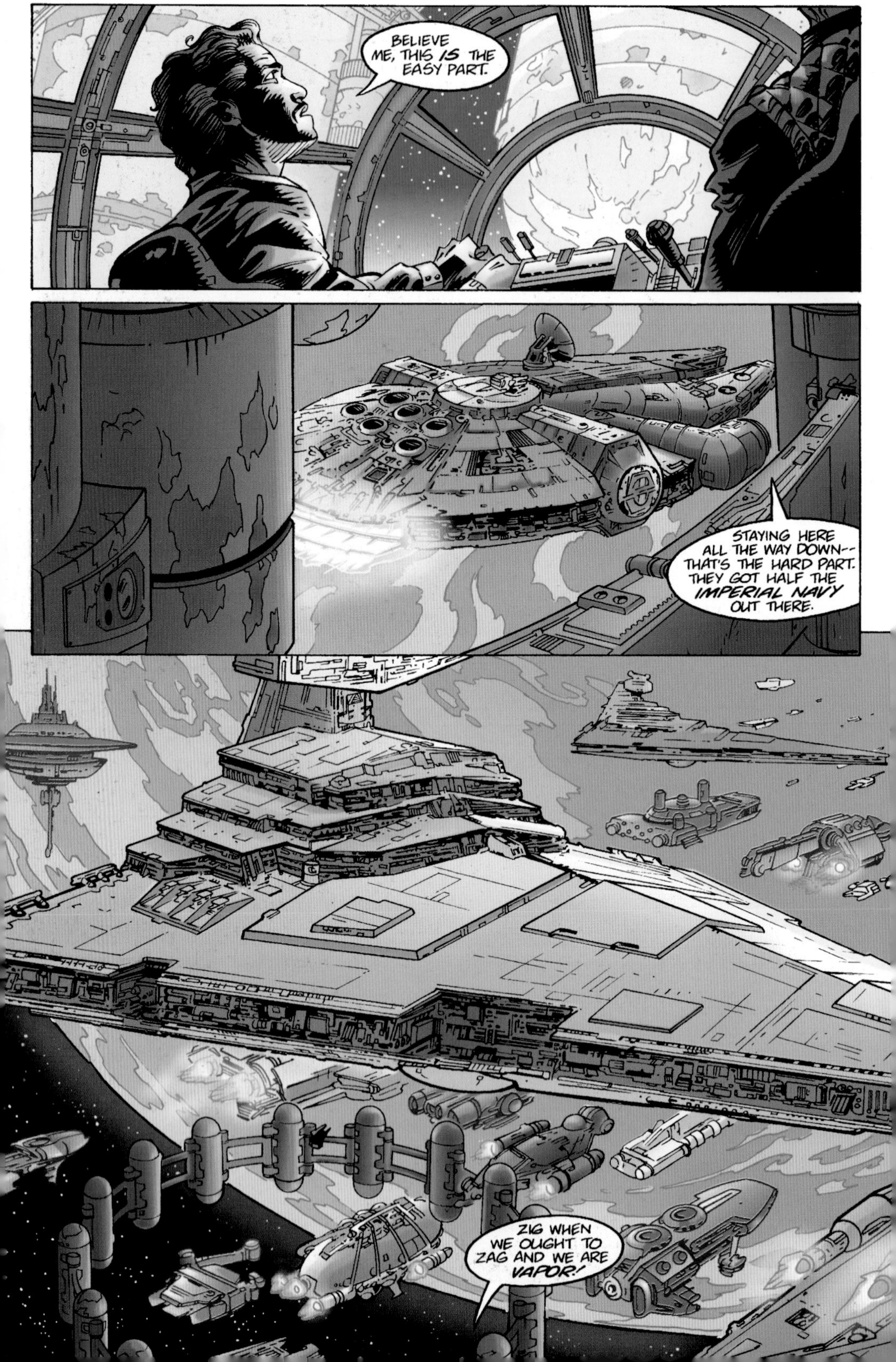
BELIEVE ME, THIS IS THE EASY PART.
STAYING HERE ALL THE WAY DOWN-- THAT'S THE HARD PART. THEY GOT HALF THE IMPERIAL NAVY OUT THERE.
ZIG WHEN WE OUGHT TO ZAG AND WE ARE VAPOR!

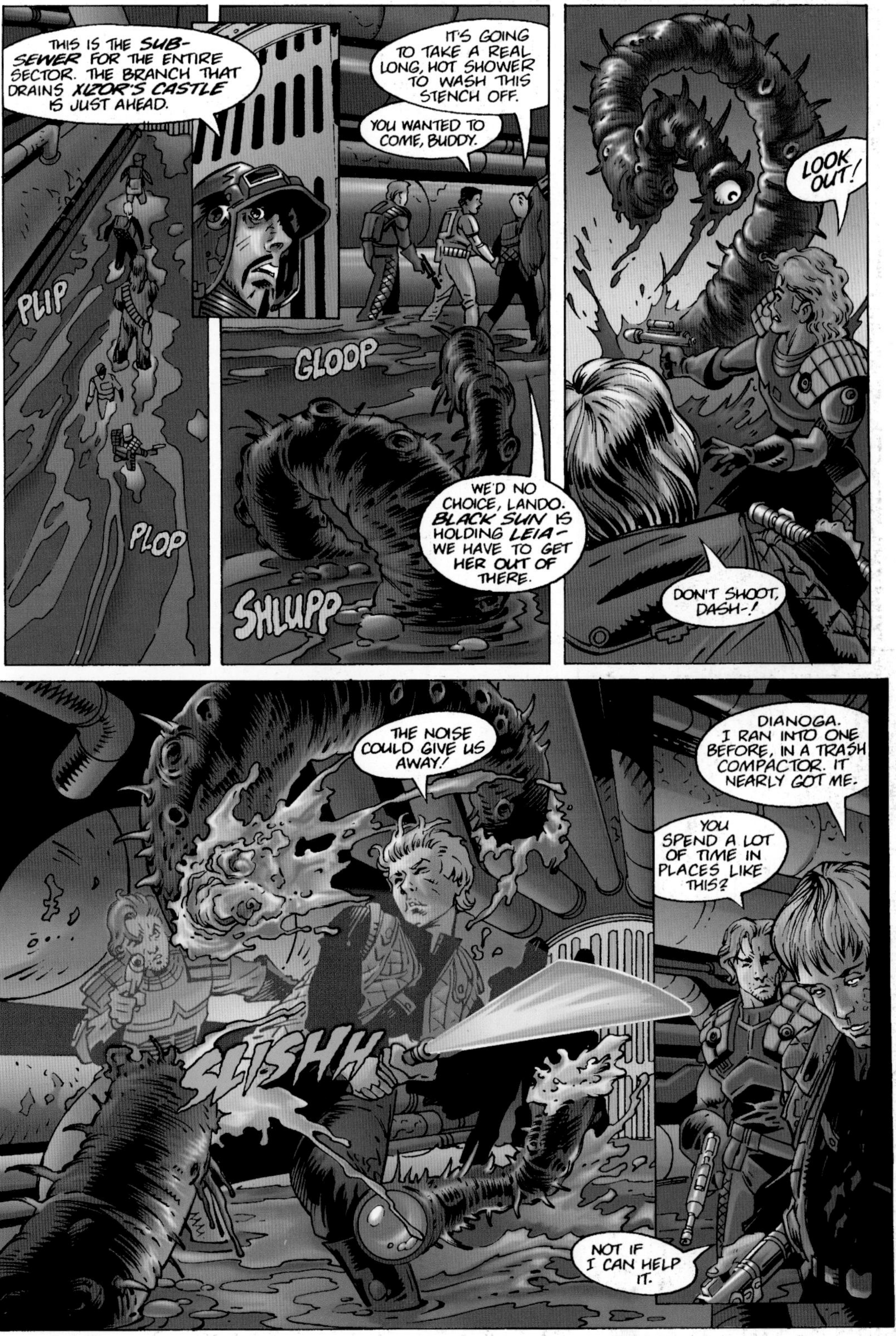
THIS IS THE SUB-SEWER FOR THE ENTIRE SECTOR. THE BRANCH THAT DRAINS XIZOR'S CASTLE IS JUST AHEAD.
PLIP
PLOP
IT'S GOING TO TAKE A REAL LONG, HOT SHOWER TO WASH THIS STENCH OFF.
YOU WANTED TO COME, BUDDY.
GLOOP
WE'D NO CHOICE, LANDO. BLACK SUN IS HOLDING LEIA-WE HAVE TO GET HER OUT OF THERE.
SHLUPP
LOOK OUT!
DON'T SHOOT, DASH-!
THE NOISE COULD GIVE US AWAY!
SLISHH
DIANOGA. I RAN INTO ONE BEFORE, IN A TRASH COMPACTOR. IT NEARLY GOT ME.
YOU SPEND A LOT OF TIME IN PLACES LIKE THIS?
NOT IF I CAN HELP IT.

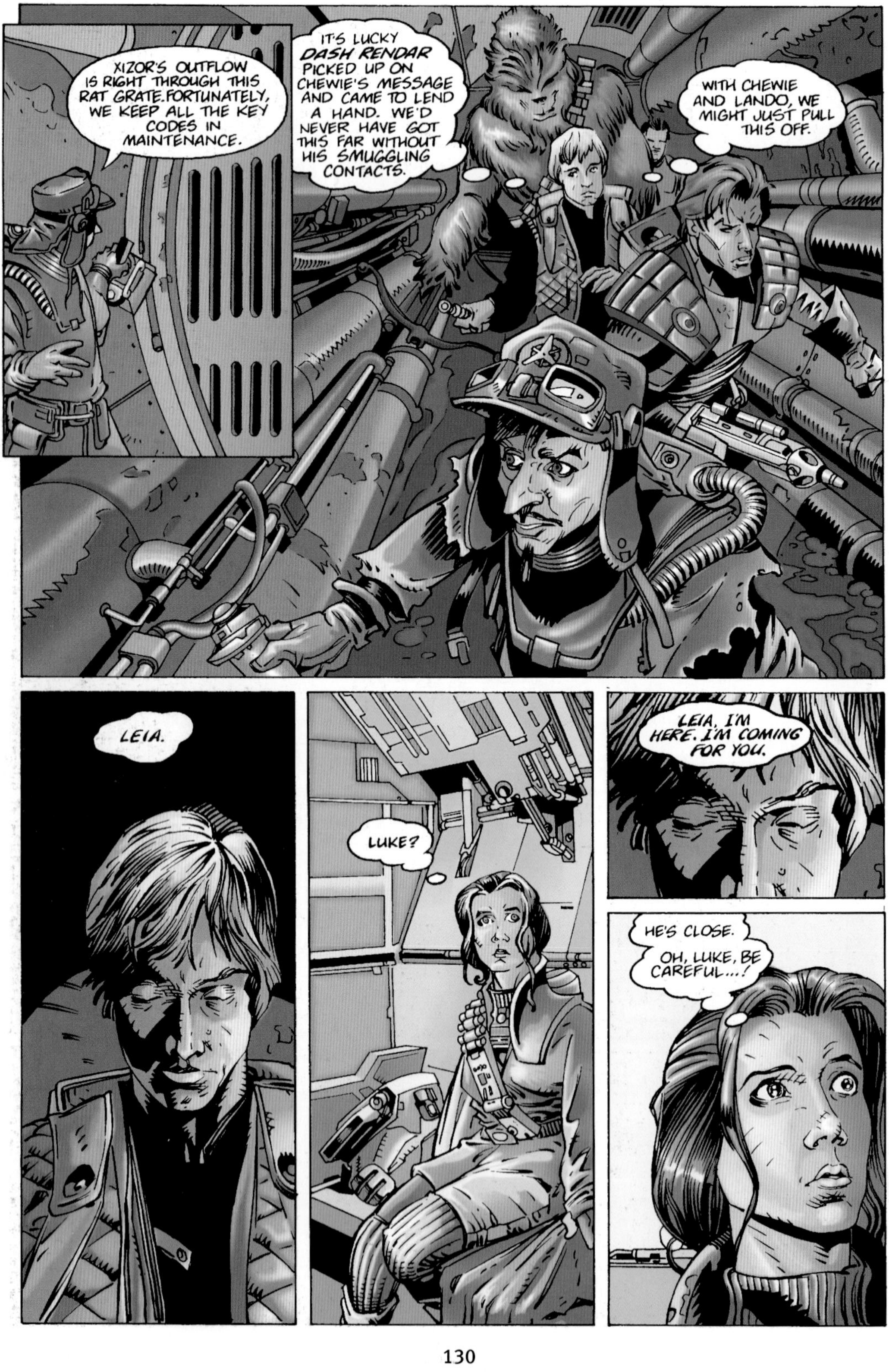
XIZOR'S OUTFLOW IS RIGHT THROUGH THIS RAT GRATE. FORTUNATELY, WE KEEP ALL THE KEY CODES IN MAINTENANCE.
IT'S LUCKY DASH RENDAR PICKED UP ON CHEWIE'S MESSAGE AND CAME TO LEND A HAND. WE'D NEVER HAVE GOT THIS FAR WITHOUT HIS SMUGGLING CONTACTS.
WITH CHEWIE AND LANDO, WE MIGHT JUST PULL THIS OFF.
LEIA.
LUKE?
LEIA, I'M HERE. I'M COMING FOR YOU.
HE'S CLOSE.
OH, LUKE, BE CAREFUL...!

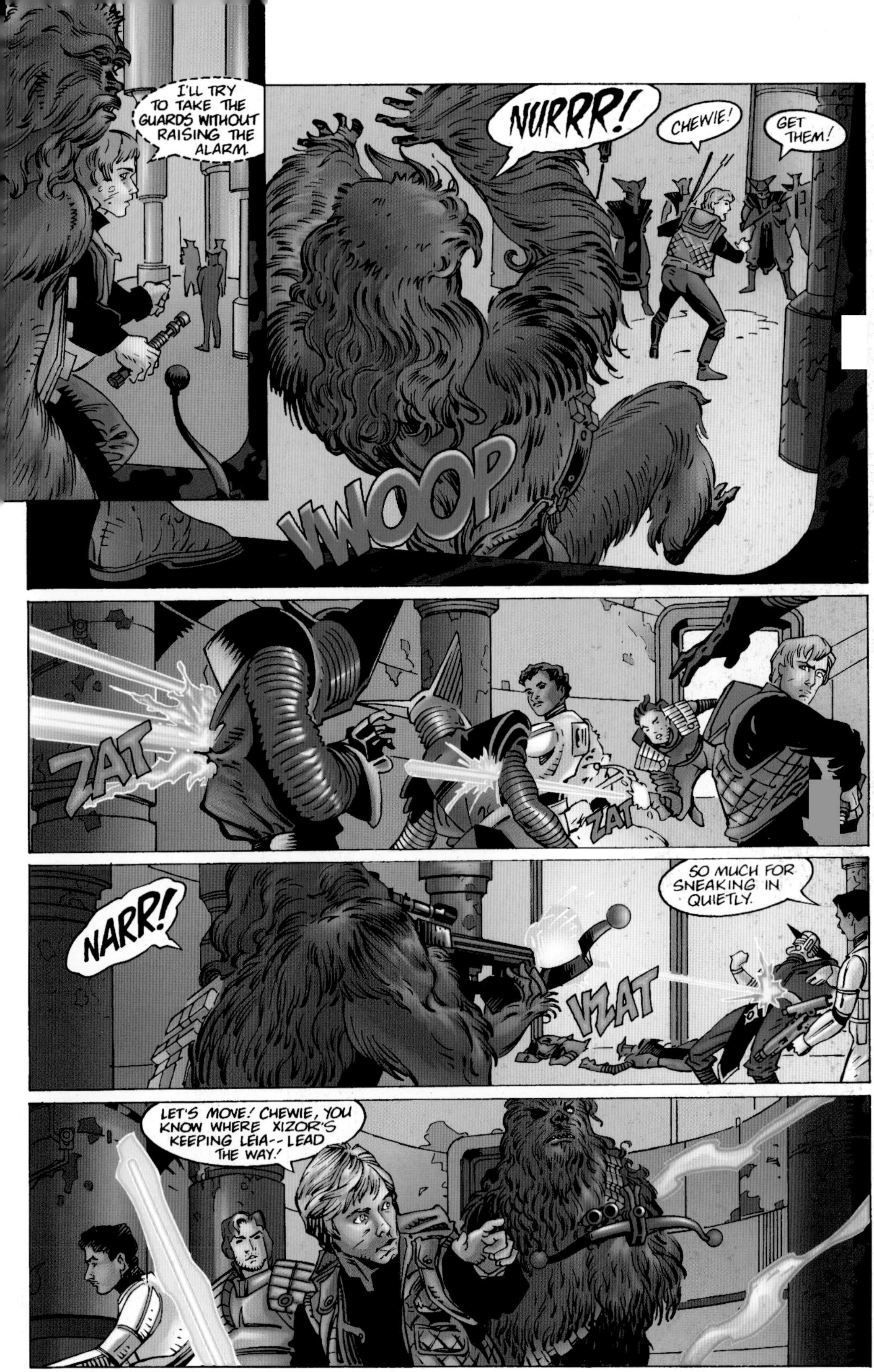

I'LL TRY TO TAKE THE GUARDS WITHOUT RAISING THE ALARM.
NURRR!
CHEWIE!
GET THEM!
VWOOP
ZAT
ZAT
NARR!
SO MUCH FOR SNEAKING IN QUIETLY.
VZAT
LET'S MOVE! CHEWIE, YOU KNOW WHERE XIZOR'S KEEPING LEIA-- LEAD THE WAY!

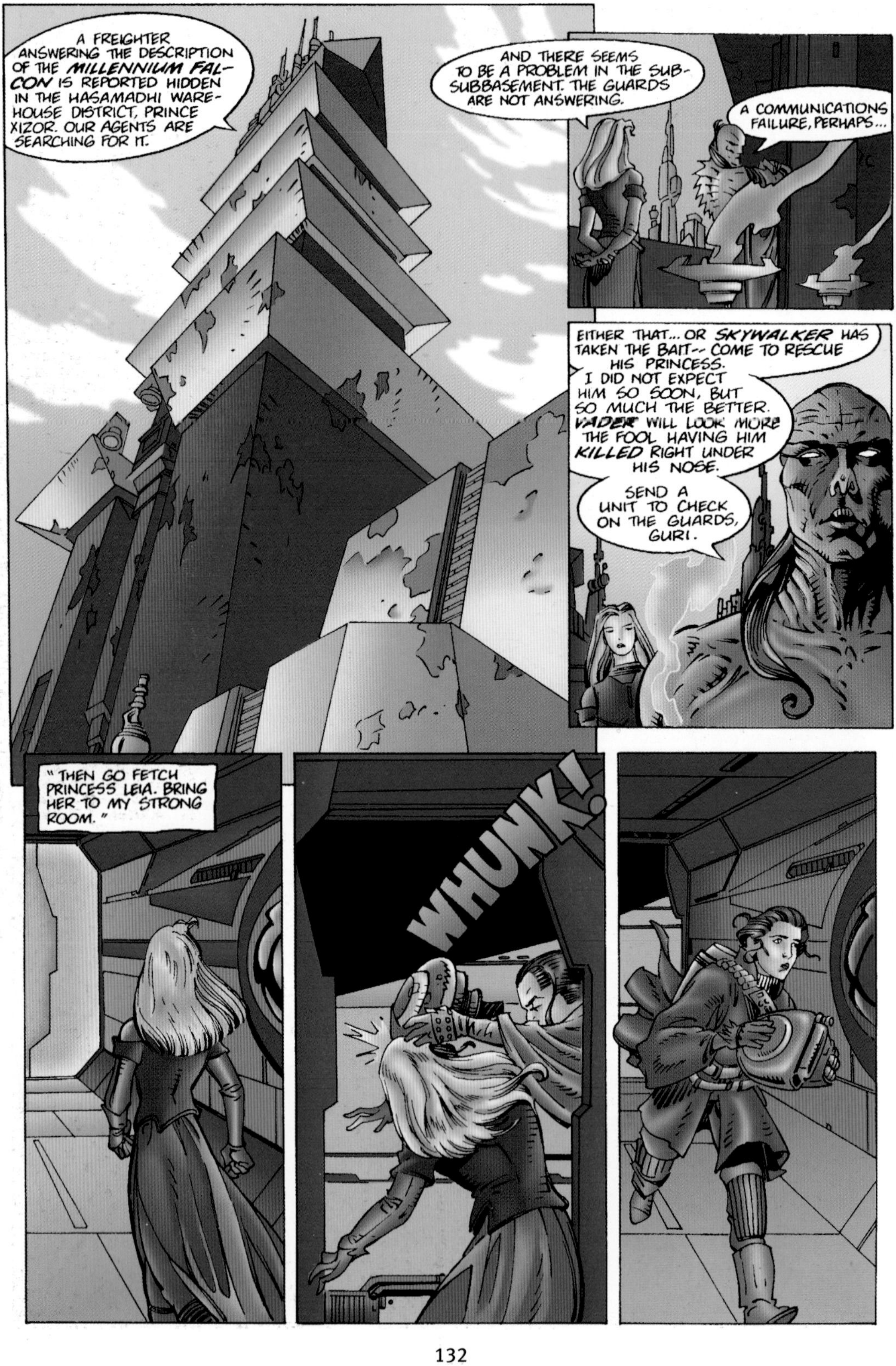
A FREIGHTER ANSWERING THE DESCRIPTION OF THE MILLENNIUM FALCON IS REPORTED HIDDEN IN THE HASAMADHI WAREHOUSE DISTRICT, PRINCE XIZOR. OUR AGENTS ARE SEARCHING FOR IT.
AND THERE SEEMS TO BE A PROBLEM IN THE SUB-SUBBASEMENT. THE GUARDS ARE NOT ANSWERING.
A COMMUNICATIONS FAILURE, PERHAPS...
EITHER THAT... OR SKYWALKER HAS TAKEN THE BAIT-- COME TO RESCUE HIS PRINCESS.
I DID NOT EXPECT HIM SO SOON, BUT SO MUCH THE BETTER. VADER WILL LOOK MORE THE FOOL HAVING HIM KILLED RIGHT UNDER HIS NOSE.
SEND A UNIT TO CHECK ON THE GUARDS, GURI.
"THEN GO FETCH PRINCESS LEIA. BRING HER TO MY STRONG ROOM."
WHUNK!

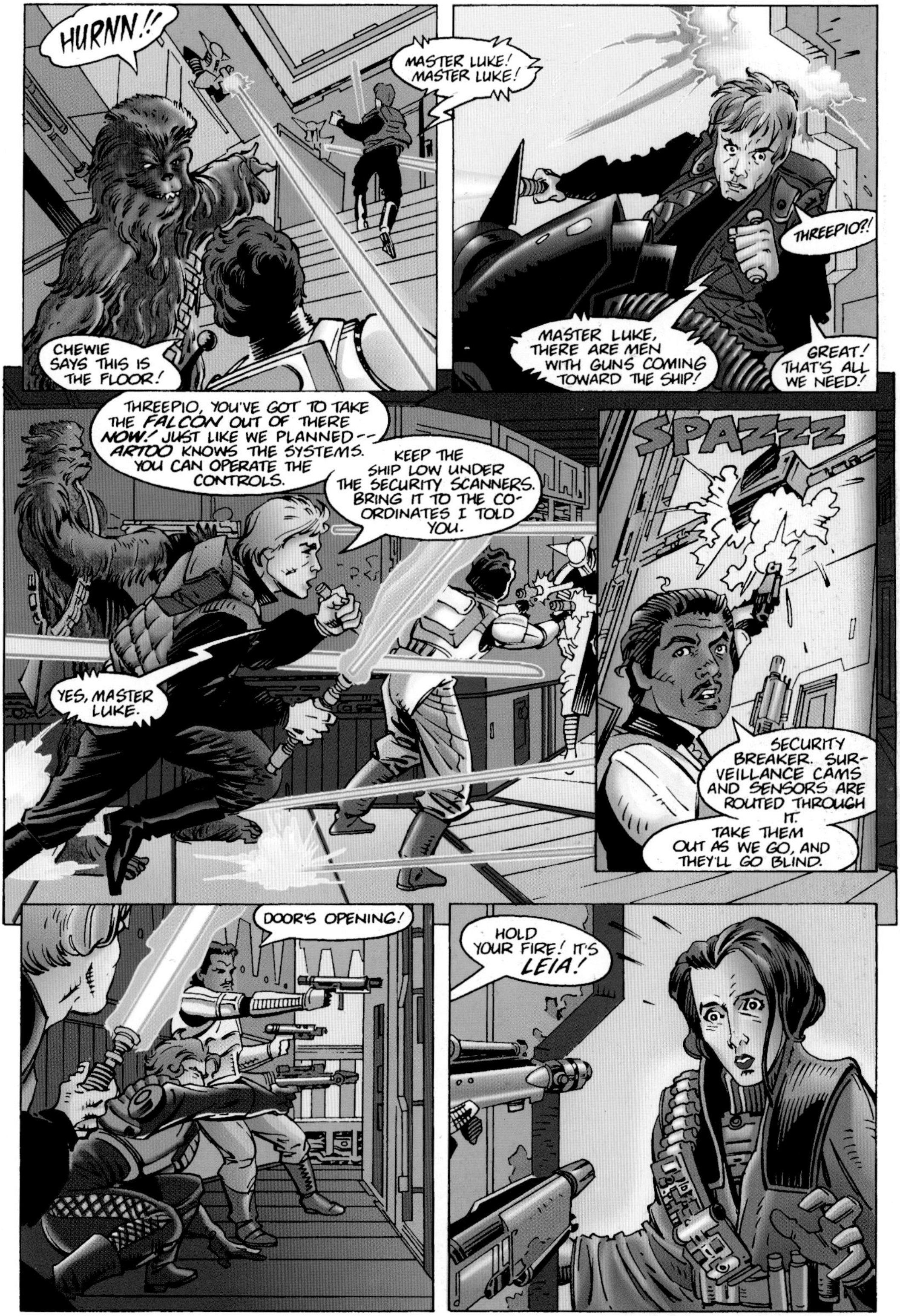
HURNN!!
MASTER LUKE! MASTER LUKE!
CHEWIE SAYS THIS IS THE FLOOR!
THREEPIO?!
MASTER LUKE, THERE ARE MEN WITH GUNS COMING TOWARD THE SHIP!
GREAT! THAT'S ALL WE NEED!
THREEPIO, YOU'VE GOT TO TAKE THE FALCON OUT OF THERE NOW! JUST LIKE WE PLANNED-- ARTOO KNOWS THE SYSTEMS. YOU CAN OPERATE THE CONTROLS.
KEEP THE SHIP LOW UNDER THE SECURITY SCANNERS. BRING IT TO THE CO-ORDINATES I TOLD YOU.
YES, MASTER LUKE.
SPAZZZ
SECURITY BREAKER. SUR-VEILLANCE CAMS AND SENSORS ARE ROUTED THROUGH IT.
TAKE THEM OUT AS WE GO, AND THEY'LL GO BLIND.
DOOR'S OPENING!
HOLD YOUR FIRE! IT'S LEIA!

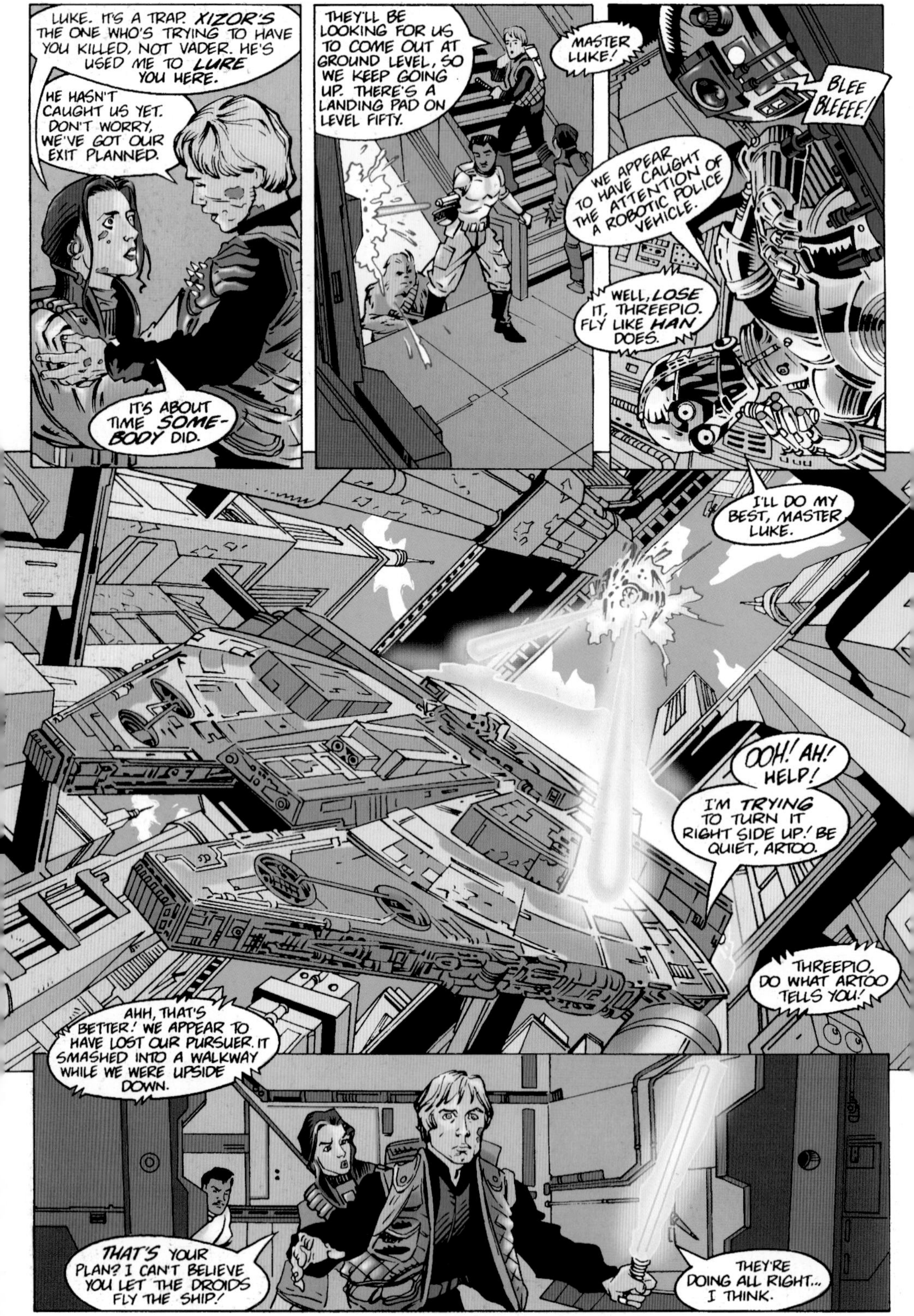

LUKE. IT'S A TRAP. XIZOR'S THE ONE WHO'S TRYING TO HAVE YOU KILLED, NOT VADER. HE'S USED ME TO LURE YOU HERE.
HE HASN'T CAUGHT US YET. DON'T WORRY, WE'VE GOT OUR EXIT PLANNED.
IT'S ABOUT TIME SOMEBODY DID.
THEY'LL BE LOOKING FOR US TO COME OUT AT GROUND LEVEL, SO WE KEEP GOING UP. THERE'S A LANDING PAD ON LEVEL FIFTY.
MASTER LUKE!
BLEE BLEEEE!
WE APPEAR TO HAVE CAUGHT THE ATTENTION OF A ROBOTIC POLICE VEHICLE.
WELL, LOSE IT, THREEPIO. FLY LIKE HAN DOES.
I'LL DO MY BEST, MASTER LUKE.
OOH! AH! HELP!
I'M TRYING TO TURN IT RIGHT SIDE UP! BE QUIET, ARTOO.
THREEPIO, DO WHAT ARTOO TELLS YOU!
AHH, THAT'S BETTER! WE APPEAR TO HAVE LOST OUR PURSUER. IT SMASHED INTO A WALKWAY WHILE WE WERE UPSIDE DOWN.
THAT'S YOUR PLAN? I CAN'T BELIEVE YOU LET THE DROIDS FLY THE SHIP!
THEY'RE DOING ALL RIGHT... I THINK.

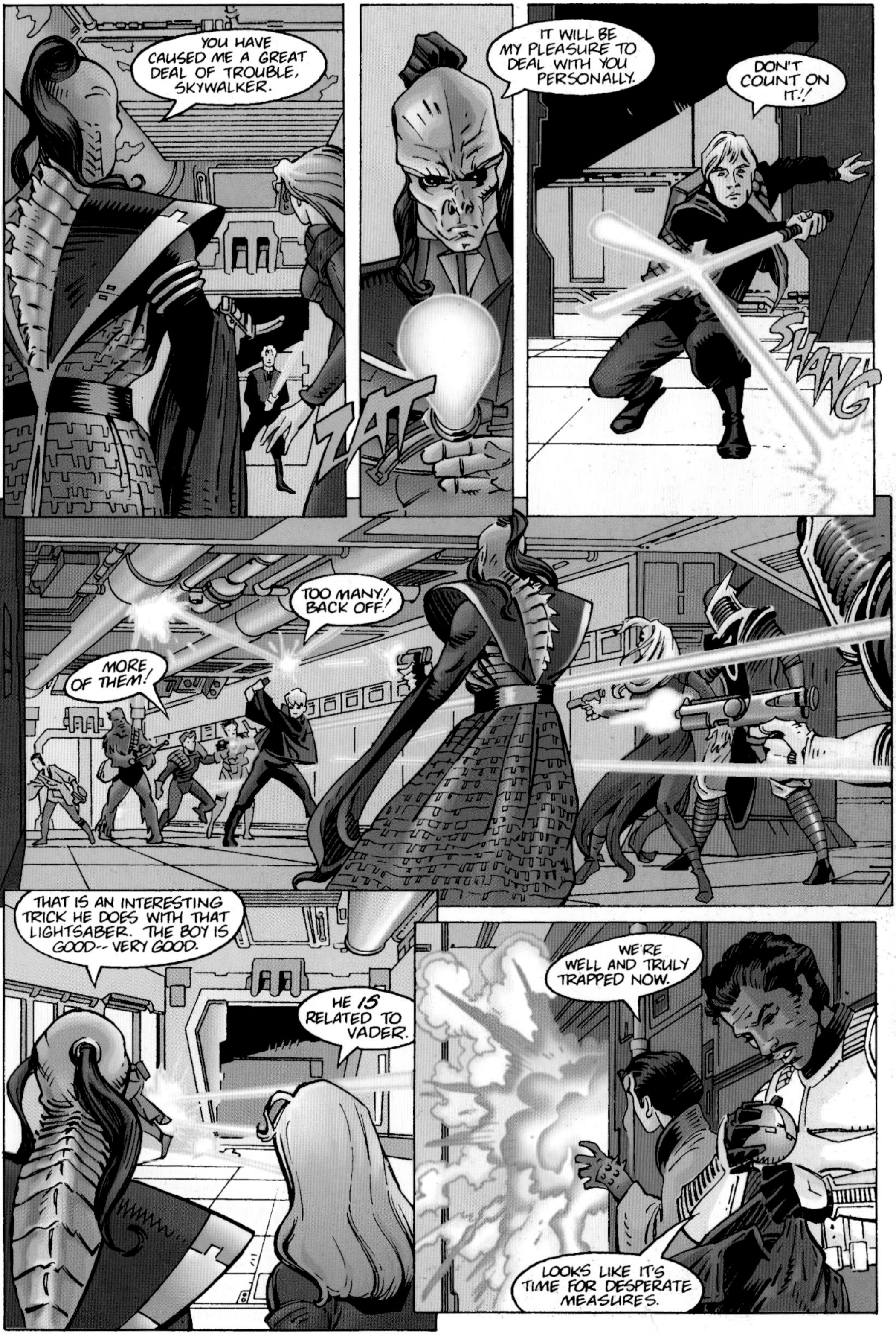
YOU HAVE CAUSED ME A GREAT DEAL OF TROUBLE, SKYWALKER.
IT WILL BE MY PLEASURE TO DEAL WITH YOU PERSONALLY.
ZAT
DON'T COUNT ON IT!!
SHANG
TOO MANY! BACK OFF!
MORE OF THEM!
THAT IS AN INTERESTING TRICK HE DOES WITH THAT LIGHTSABER. THE BOY IS GOOD-- VERY GOOD.
HE IS RELATED TO VADER.
WE'RE WELL AND TRULY TRAPPED NOW.
LOOKS LIKE IT'S TIME FOR DESPERATE MEASURES.

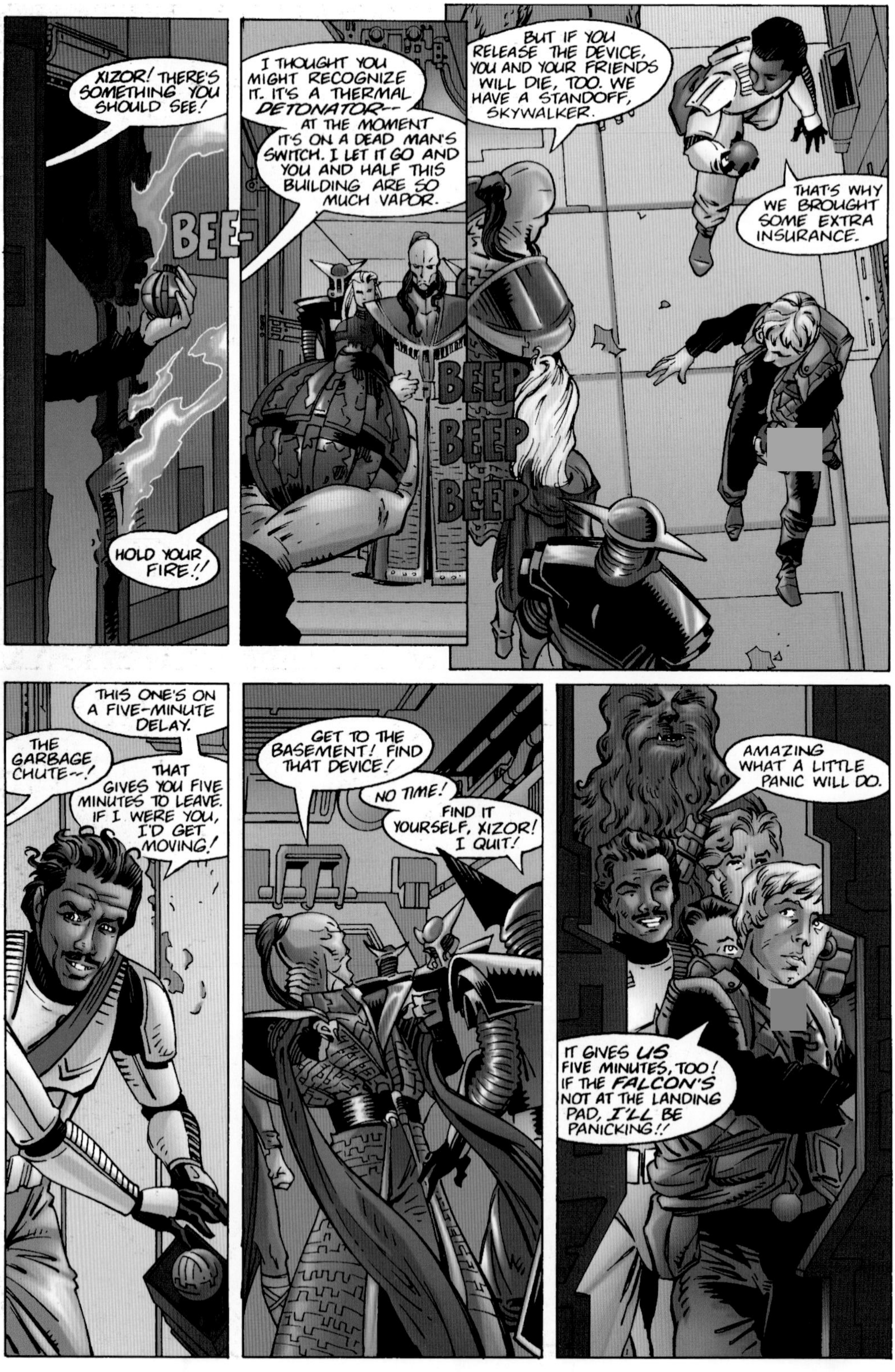
XIZOR! THERE'S SOMETHING YOU SHOULD SEE!
BEE-
HOLD YOUR FIRE!!
I THOUGHT YOU MIGHT RECOGNIZE IT. IT'S A THERMAL DETONATOR--
AT THE MOMENT IT'S ON A DEAD MAN'S SWITCH. I LET IT GO AND YOU AND HALF THIS BUILDING ARE SO MUCH VAPOR.
BEEP BEEP BEEP
BUT IF YOU RELEASE THE DEVICE, YOU AND YOUR FRIENDS WILL DIE, TOO. WE HAVE A STANDOFF, SKYWALKER.
THAT'S WHY WE BROUGHT SOME EXTRA INSURANCE.
THIS ONE'S ON A FIVE-MINUTE DELAY.
THE GARBAGE CHUTE--!
THAT GIVES YOU FIVE MINUTES TO LEAVE. IF I WERE YOU, I'D GET MOVING!
GET TO THE BASEMENT! FIND THAT DEVICE!
NO TIME!
FIND IT YOURSELF, XIZOR! I QUIT!
AMAZING WHAT A LITTLE PANIC WILL DO.
IT GIVES US FIVE MINUTES, TOO! IF THE FALCON'S NOT AT THE LANDING PAD, I'LL BE PANICKING!!

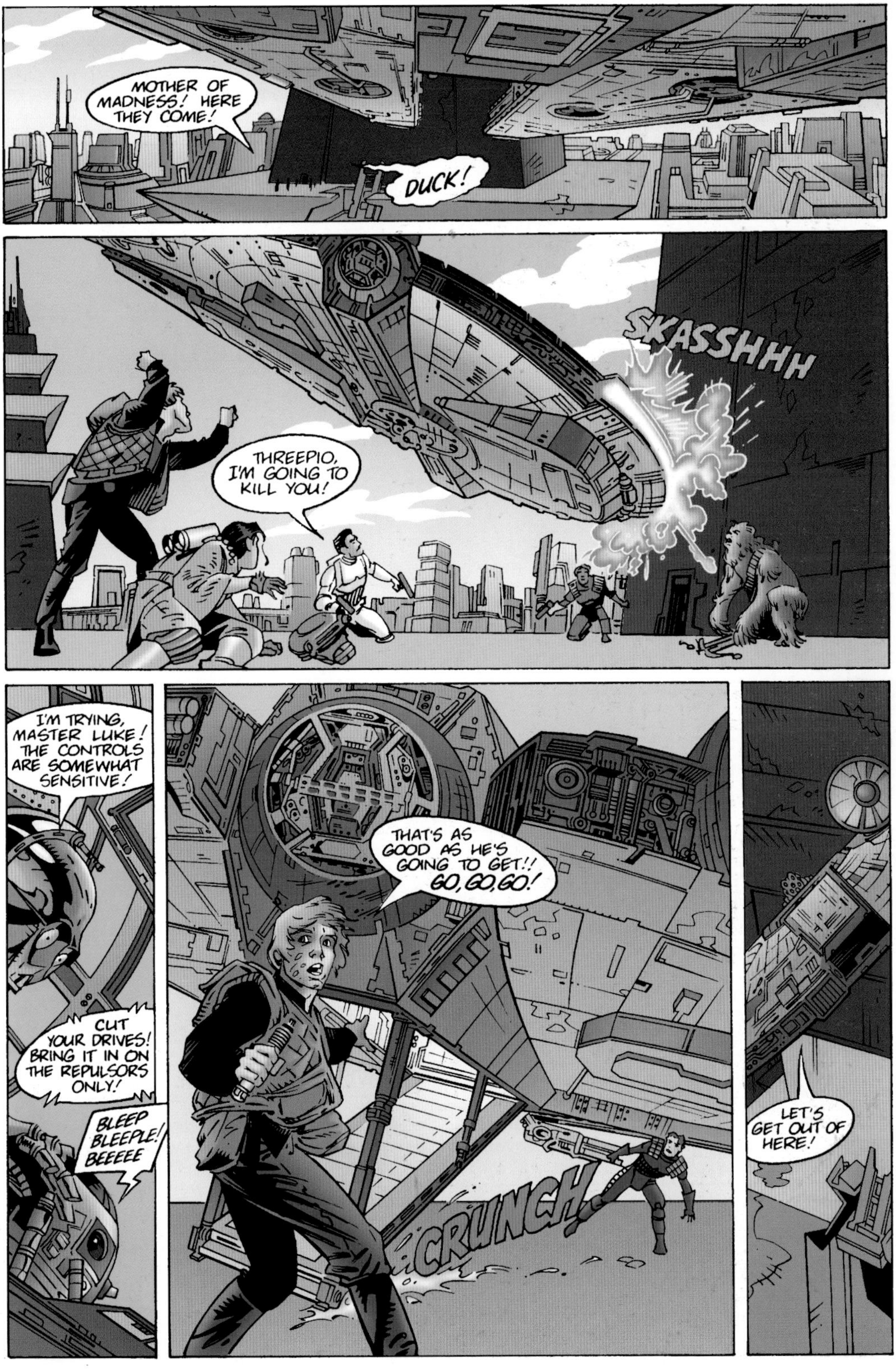
MOTHER OF MADNESS! HERE THEY COME!
DUCK!
SKASSHHH
THREEPIO, I'M GOING TO KILL YOU!
I'M TRYING, MASTER LUKE! THE CONTROLS ARE SOMEWHAT SENSITIVE!
CUT YOUR DRIVES! BRING IT IN ON THE REPULSORS ONLY!
BLEEP BLEEPLE! BEEEEE
THAT'S AS GOOD AS HE'S GOING TO GET!! GO, GO, GO!
CRUNCH
LET'S GET OUT OF HERE!

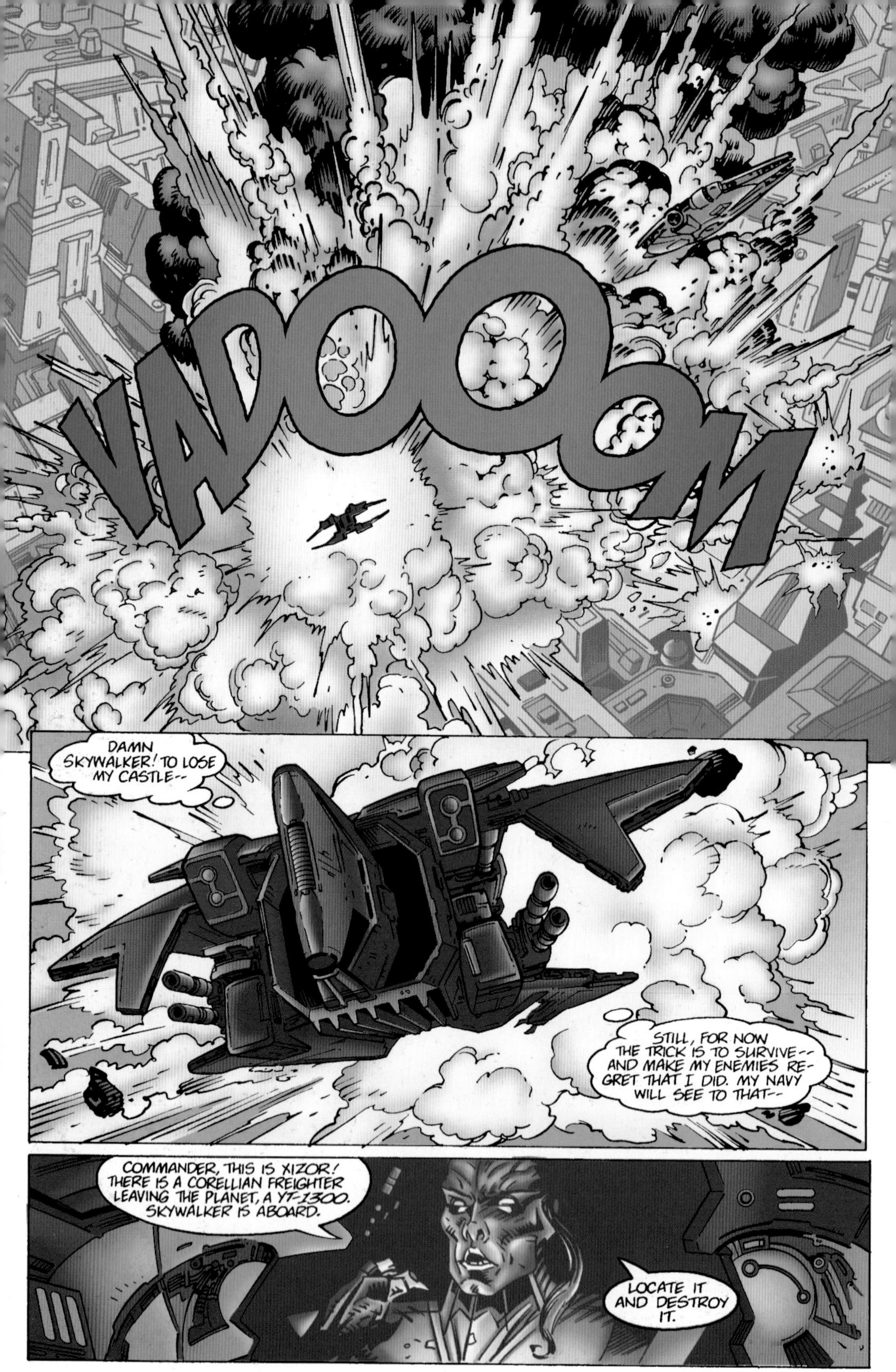
VADOOM
DAMN SKYWALKER! TO LOSE MY CASTLE--
STILL, FOR NOW THE TRICK IS TO SURVIVE--AND MAKE MY ENEMIES REGRET THAT I DID. MY NAVY WILL SEE TO THAT--
COMMANDER, THIS IS XIZOR! THERE IS A CORELLIAN FREIGHTER LEAVING THE PLANET, A YT-1300. SKYWALKER IS ABOARD.
LOCATE IT AND DESTROY IT.

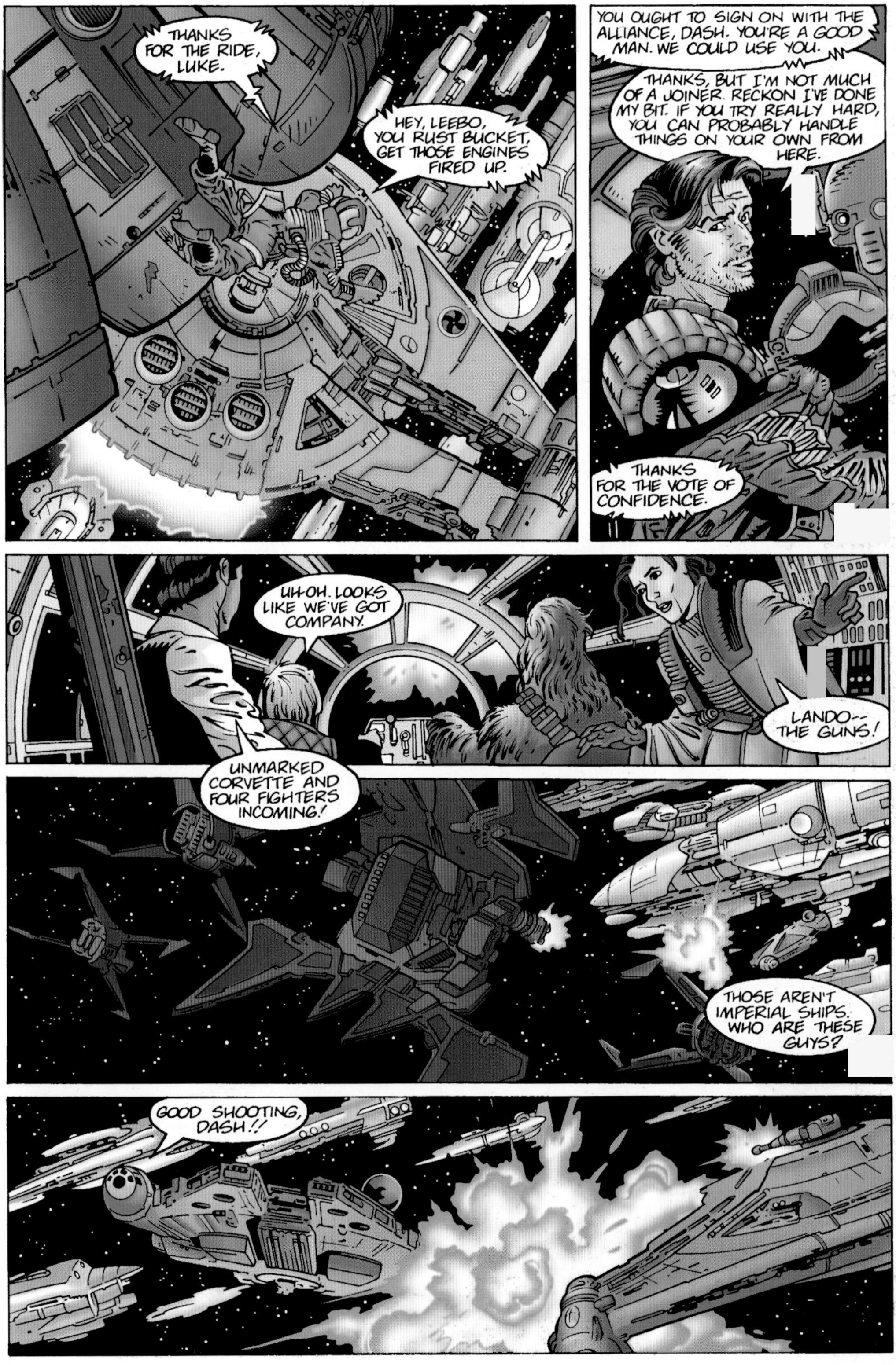
THANKS FOR THE RIDE, LUKE.
HEY, LEEBO, YOU RUST BUCKET, GET THOSE ENGINES FIRED UP.
YOU OUGHT TO SIGN ON WITH THE ALLIANCE, DASH. YOU'RE A GOOD MAN. WE COULD USE YOU.
THANKS, BUT I'M NOT MUCH OF A JOINER. RECKON I'VE DONE MY BIT. IF YOU TRY REALLY HARD, YOU CAN PROBABLY HANDLE THINGS ON YOUR OWN FROM HERE.
THANKS FOR THE VOTE OF CONFIDENCE.
UH-OH. LOOKS LIKE WE'VE GOT COMPANY.
LANDO-- THE GUNS!
UNMARKED CORVETTE AND FOUR FIGHTERS INCOMING!
THOSE AREN'T IMPERIAL SHIPS. WHO ARE THESE GUYS?
GOOD SHOOTING, DASH!!

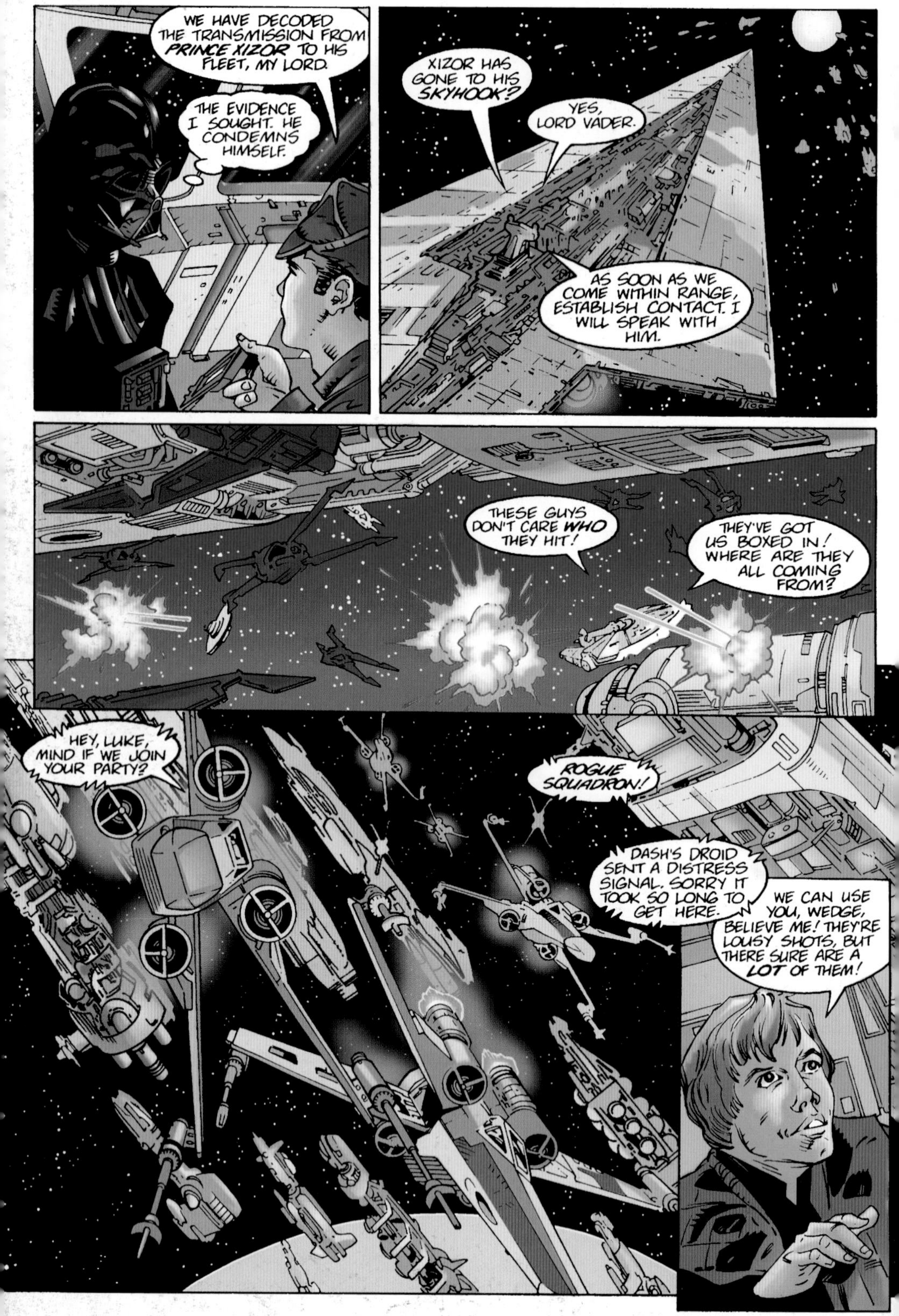
WE HAVE DECODED THE TRANSMISSION FROM PRINCE XIZOR TO HIS FLEET, MY LORD.
THE EVIDENCE I SOUGHT. HE CONDEMNS HIMSELF.
XIZOR HAS GONE TO HIS SKYHOOK?
YES, LORD VADER.
AS SOON AS WE COME WITHIN RANGE, ESTABLISH CONTACT. I WILL SPEAK WITH HIM.
THESE GUYS DON'T CARE WHO THEY HIT!
THEY'VE GOT US BOXED IN! WHERE ARE THEY ALL COMING FROM?
HEY, LUKE, MIND IF WE JOIN YOUR PARTY?
ROGUE SQUADRON!
DASH'S DROID SENT A DISTRESS SIGNAL. SORRY IT TOOK SO LONG TO GET HERE.
WE CAN USE YOU, WEDGE, BELIEVE ME! THEY'RE LOUSY SHOTS, BUT THERE SURE ARE A LOT OF THEM!

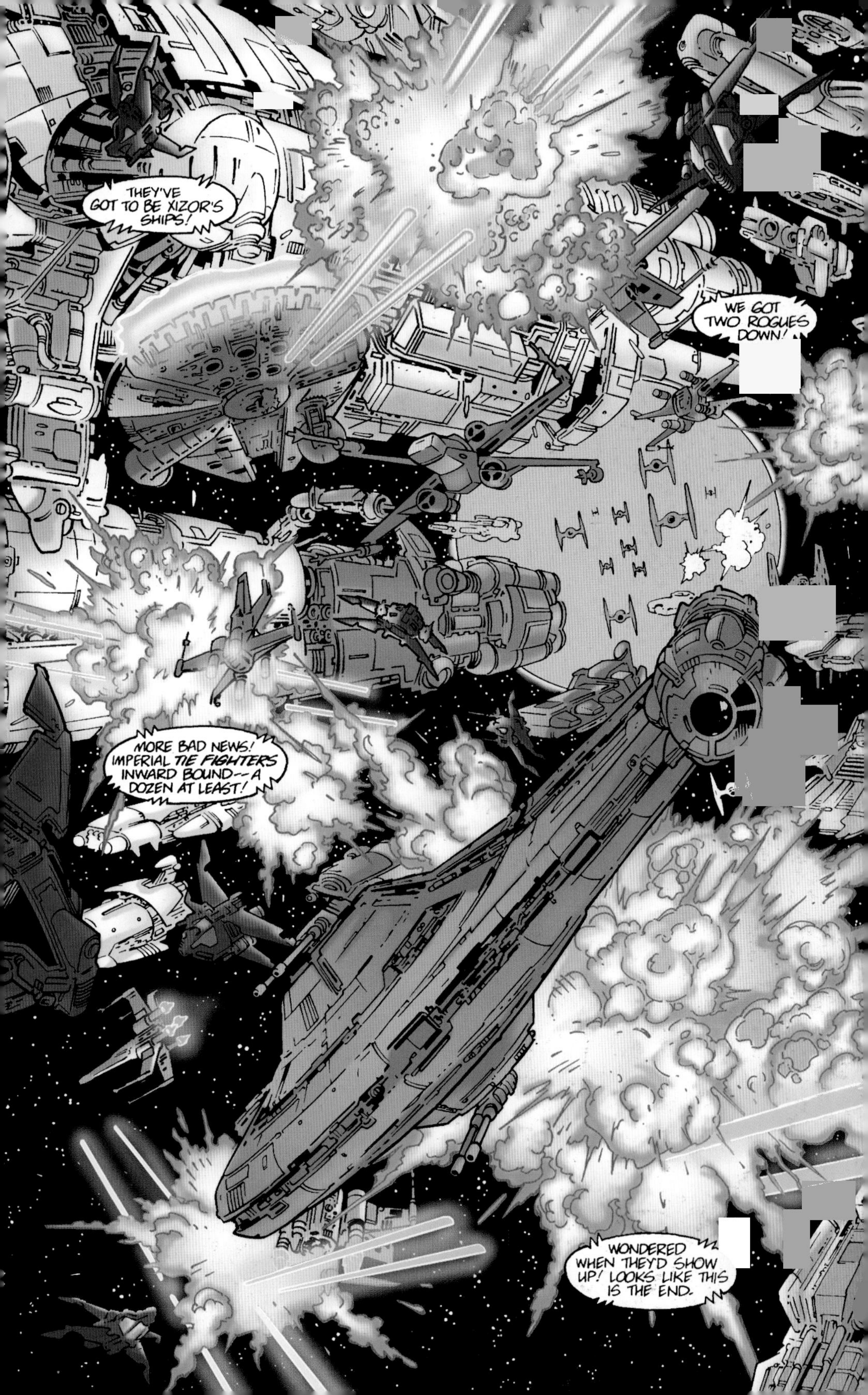
THEY'VE GOT TO BE XIZOR'S SHIPS!
WE GOT TWO ROGUES DOWN!
MORE BAD NEWS! IMPERIAL *TIE FIGHTERS* INWARD BOUND-- A DOZEN AT LEAST!
WONDERED WHEN THEY'D SHOW UP! LOOKS LIKE THIS IS THE END.

THEY'RE FIRING ON OUR ATTACKERS...!

LORD VADER! WHY IS THE IMPERIAL NAVY ATTACKING MY SHIPS?

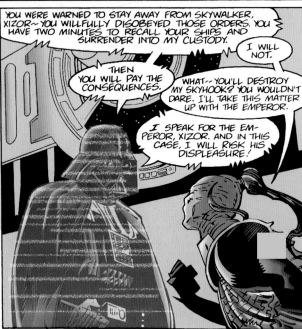

YOU WERE WARNED TO STAY AWAY FROM SKYWALKER, XIZOR-- YOU WILLFULLY DISOBEYED THOSE ORDERS. YOU HAVE TWO MINUTES TO RECALL YOUR SHIPS AND SURRENDER INTO MY CUSTODY.

I WILL NOT.

THEN YOU WILL PAY THE CONSEQUENCES.

WHAT-- YOU'LL DESTROY MY SKYHOOK? YOU WOULDN'T DARE. I'LL TAKE THIS MATTER UP WITH THE EMPEROR.

I SPEAK FOR THE EMPEROR, XIZOR. AND IN THIS CASE, I WILL RISK HIS DISPLEASURE!

TWO MINUTES HAVE ELAPSED, MY LORD-- HIS FLEET IS BEING OBLITERATED, BUT STILL PRINCE XIZOR REMAINS SILENT...!

CARRY OUT MY ORDERS, COMMANDER.

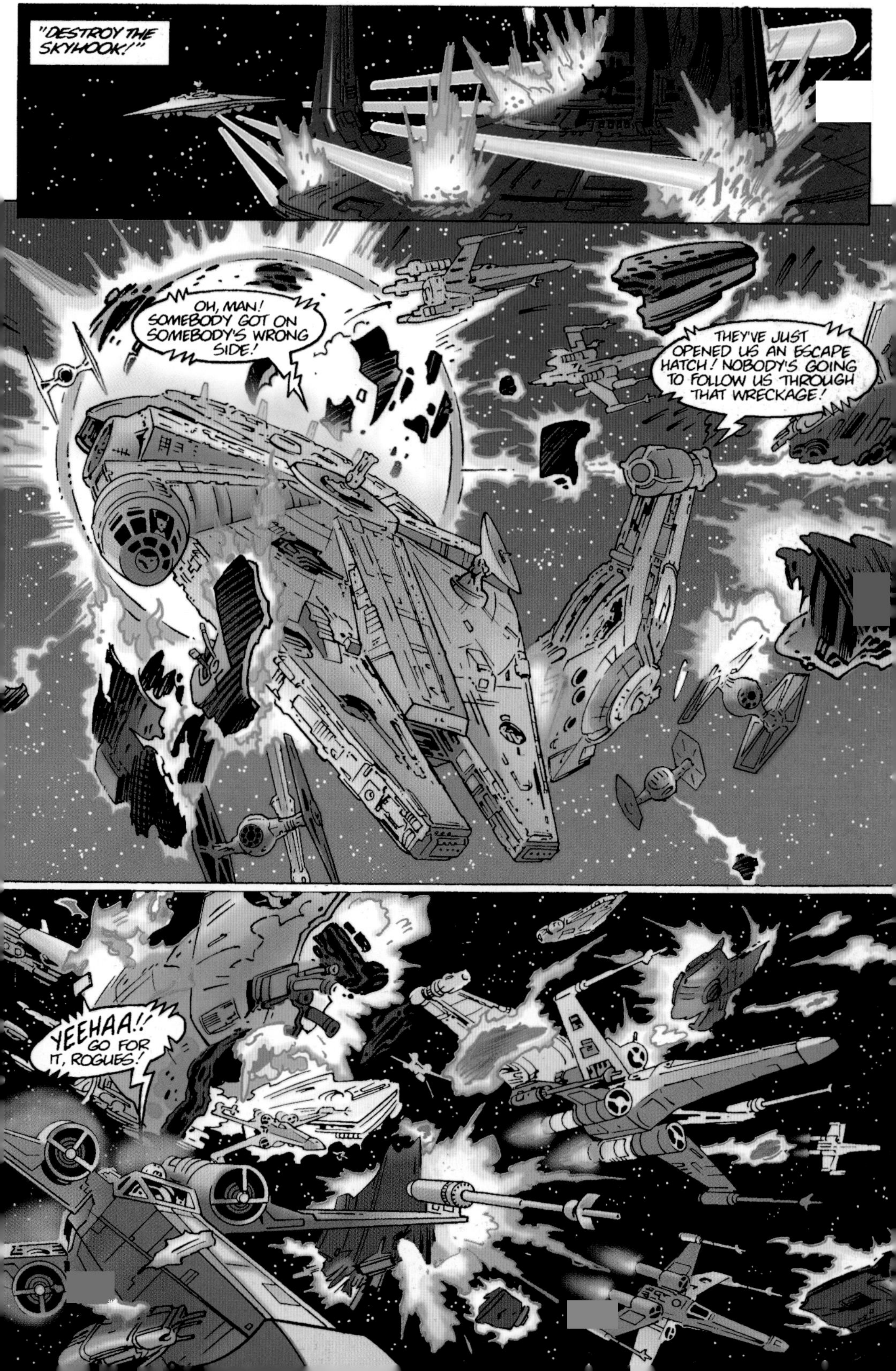
"DESTROY THE SKYHOOK!"
OH, MAN! SOMEBODY GOT ON SOMEBODY'S WRONG SIDE!
THEY'VE JUST OPENED US AN ESCAPE HATCH! NOBODY'S GOING TO FOLLOW US THROUGH THAT WRECKAGE!
YEEHAA!! GO FOR IT, ROGUES!

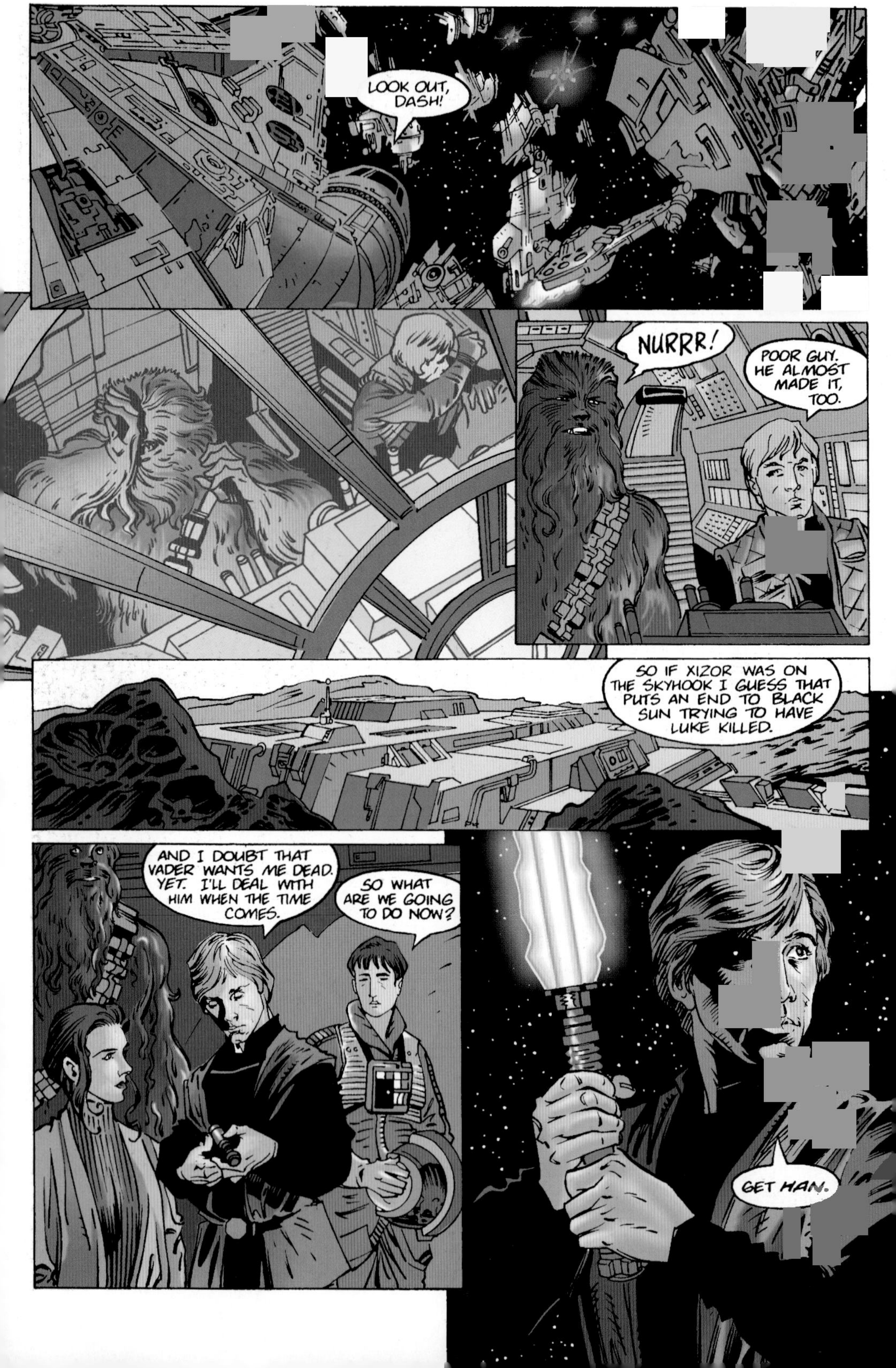
LOOK OUT, DASH!
NURRR!
POOR GUY. HE ALMOST MADE IT, TOO.
SO IF XIZOR WAS ON THE SKYHOOK I GUESS THAT PUTS AN END TO BLACK SUN TRYING TO HAVE LUKE KILLED.
AND I DOUBT THAT VADER WANTS ME DEAD. YET. I'LL DEAL WITH HIM WHEN THE TIME COMES.
SO WHAT ARE WE GOING TO DO NOW?
GET HAN.

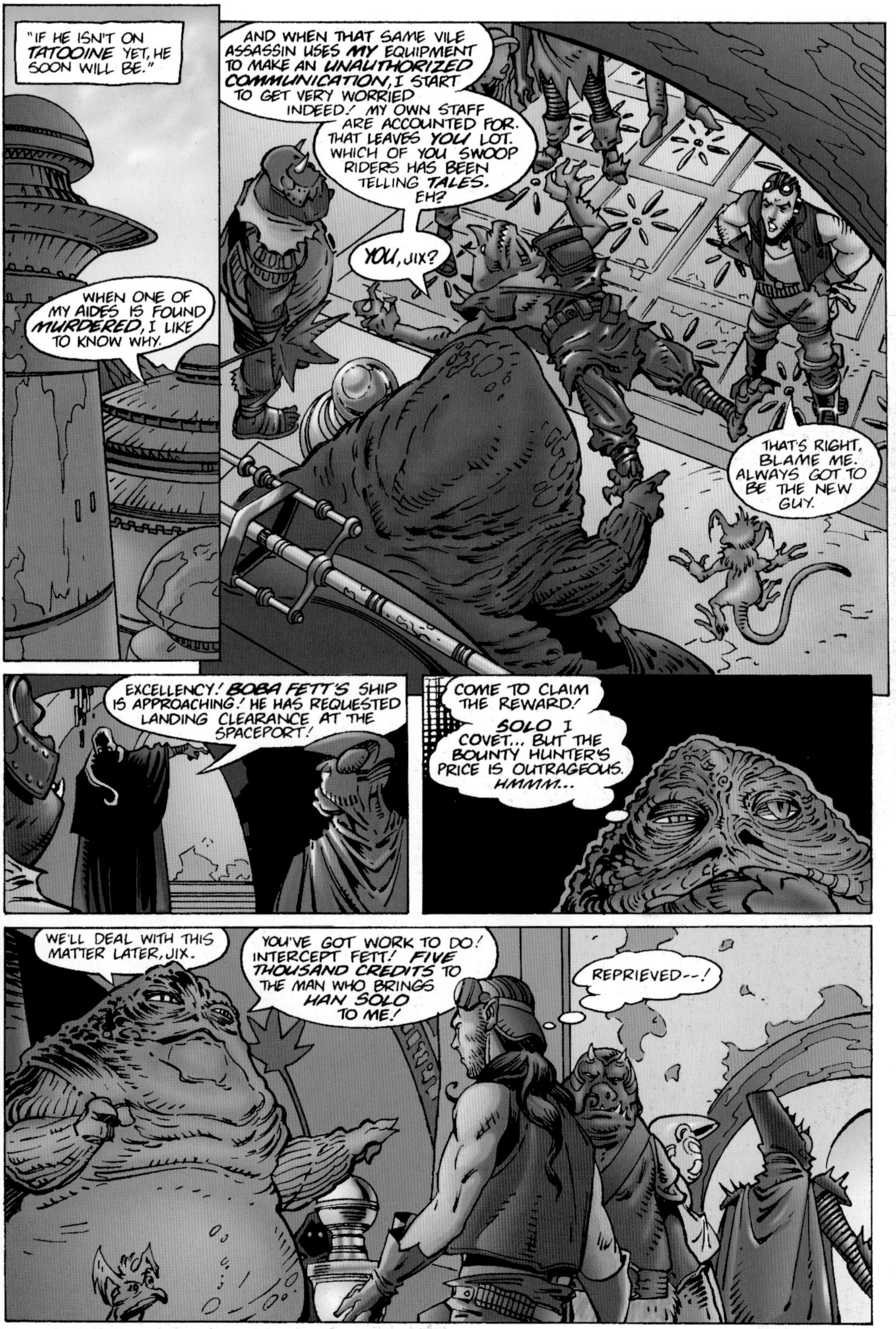
"IF HE ISN'T ON TATOOINE YET, HE SOON WILL BE."
WHEN ONE OF MY AIDES IS FOUND MURDERED, I LIKE TO KNOW WHY.
AND WHEN THAT SAME VILE ASSASSIN USES MY EQUIPMENT TO MAKE AN UNAUTHORIZED COMMUNICATION, I START TO GET VERY WORRIED INDEED! MY OWN STAFF ARE ACCOUNTED FOR. THAT LEAVES YOU LOT. WHICH OF YOU SWOOP RIDERS HAS BEEN TELLING TALES, EH?
YOU, JIX?
THAT'S RIGHT, BLAME ME. ALWAYS GOT TO BE THE NEW GUY.
EXCELLENCY! BOBA FETT'S SHIP IS APPROACHING! HE HAS REQUESTED LANDING CLEARANCE AT THE SPACEPORT!
COME TO CLAIM THE REWARD!
SOLO I COVET... BUT THE BOUNTY HUNTER'S PRICE IS OUTRAGEOUS. HMMM...
WE'LL DEAL WITH THIS MATTER LATER, JIX.
YOU'VE GOT WORK TO DO! INTERCEPT FETT! FIVE THOUSAND CREDITS TO THE MAN WHO BRINGS HAN SOLO TO ME!
REPRIEVED--!

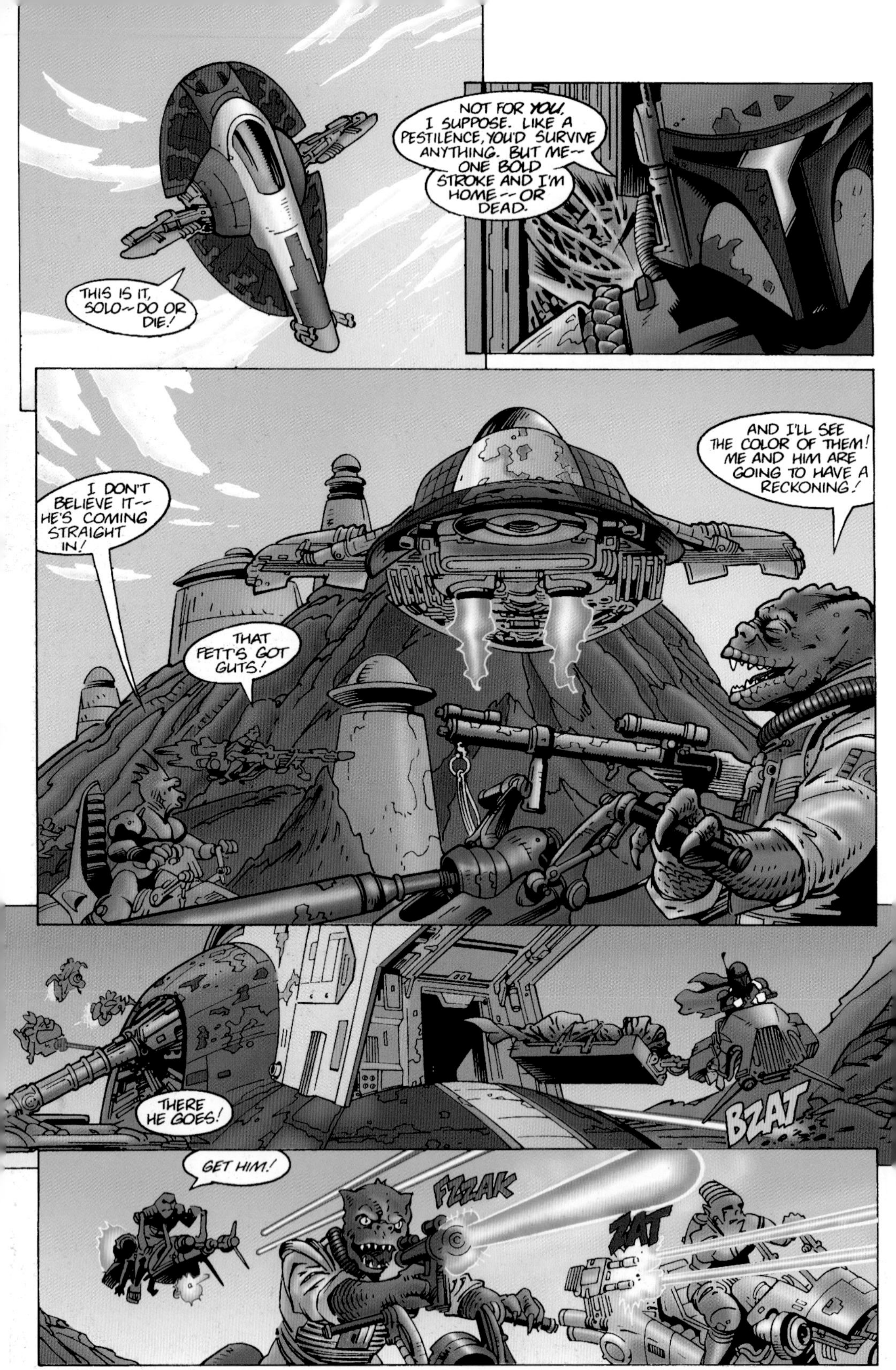
THIS IS IT, SOLO--DO OR DIE!
NOT FOR YOU, I SUPPOSE. LIKE A PESTILENCE, YOU'D SURVIVE ANYTHING. BUT ME-- ONE BOLD STROKE AND I'M HOME--OR DEAD.
I DON'T BELIEVE IT-- HE'S COMING STRAIGHT IN!
THAT FETT'S GOT GUTS!
AND I'LL SEE THE COLOR OF THEM! ME AND HIM ARE GOING TO HAVE A RECKONING!
THERE HE GOES!
BZAT
GET HIM!
FZZZAK
ZAT

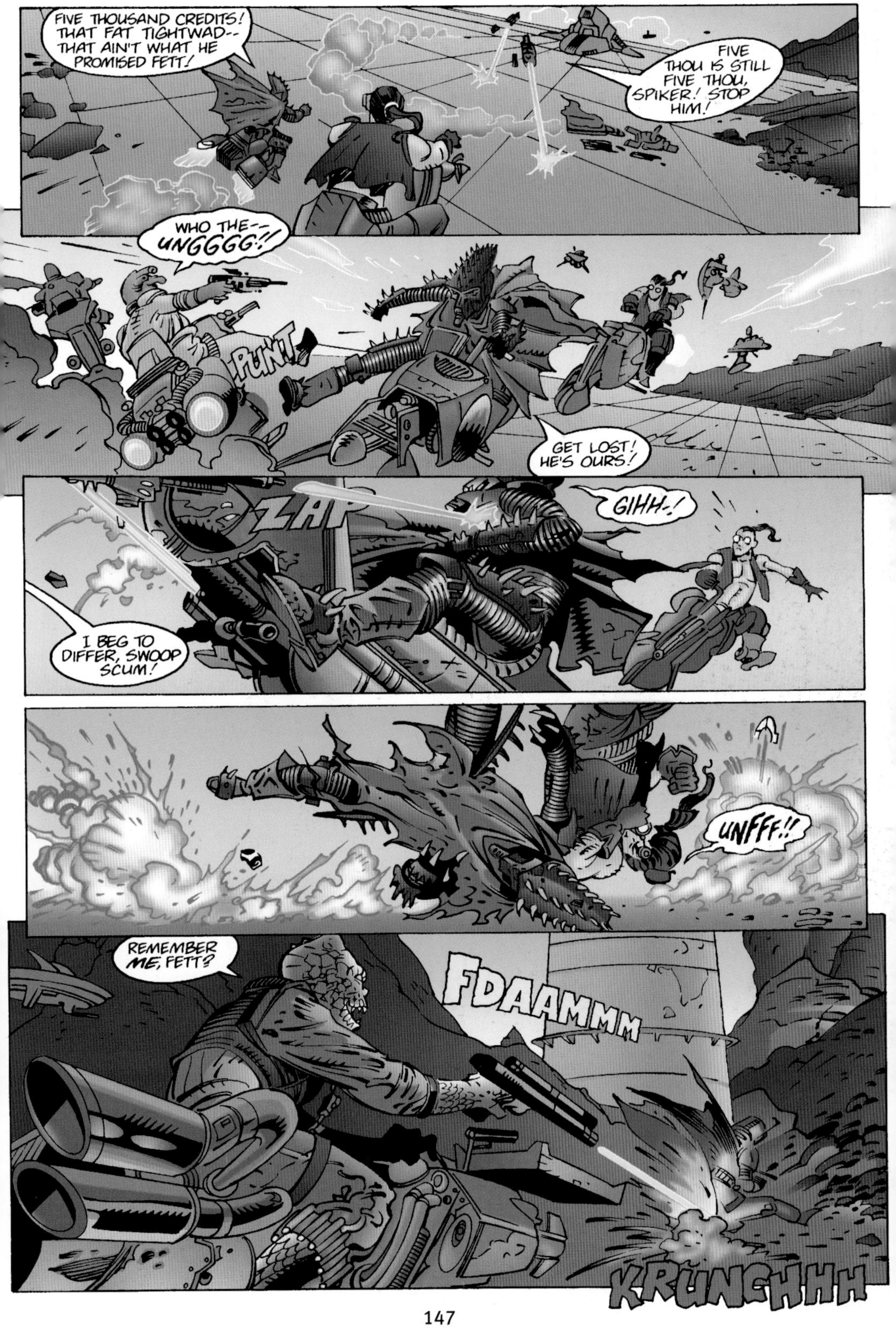
FIVE THOUSAND CREDITS! THAT FAT TIGHTWAD-- THAT AIN'T WHAT HE PROMISED FETT!
FIVE THOU IS STILL FIVE THOU, SPIKER! STOP HIM!
WHO THE-- UNGGGG!!
PUNT
GET LOST! HE'S OURS!
ZAP
GIHH-!
I BEG TO DIFFER, SWOOP SCUM!
UNFFF!!
REMEMBER ME, FETT?
FDAAMMM
KRUNCHHH

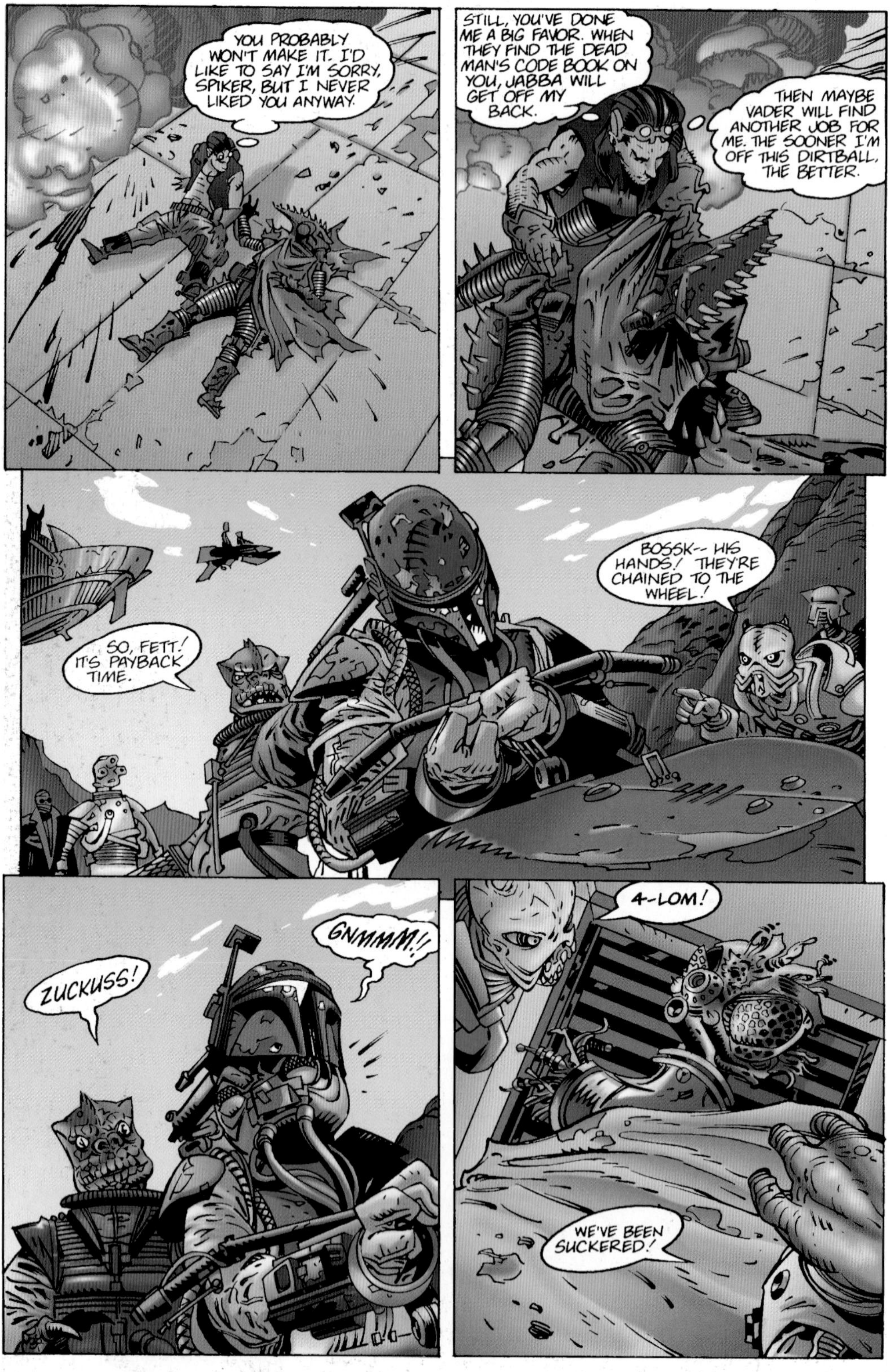
YOU PROBABLY WON'T MAKE IT. I'D LIKE TO SAY I'M SORRY, SPIKER, BUT I NEVER LIKED YOU ANYWAY.
STILL, YOU'VE DONE ME A BIG FAVOR. WHEN THEY FIND THE DEAD MAN'S CODE BOOK ON YOU, JABBA WILL GET OFF MY BACK.
THEN MAYBE VADER WILL FIND ANOTHER JOB FOR ME. THE SOONER I'M OFF THIS DIRTBALL, THE BETTER.
SO, FETT! IT'S PAYBACK TIME.
BOSSK-- HIS HANDS! THEY'RE CHAINED TO THE WHEEL!
ZUCKUSS!
GNMMM!!
4-LOM!
WE'VE BEEN SUCKERED!

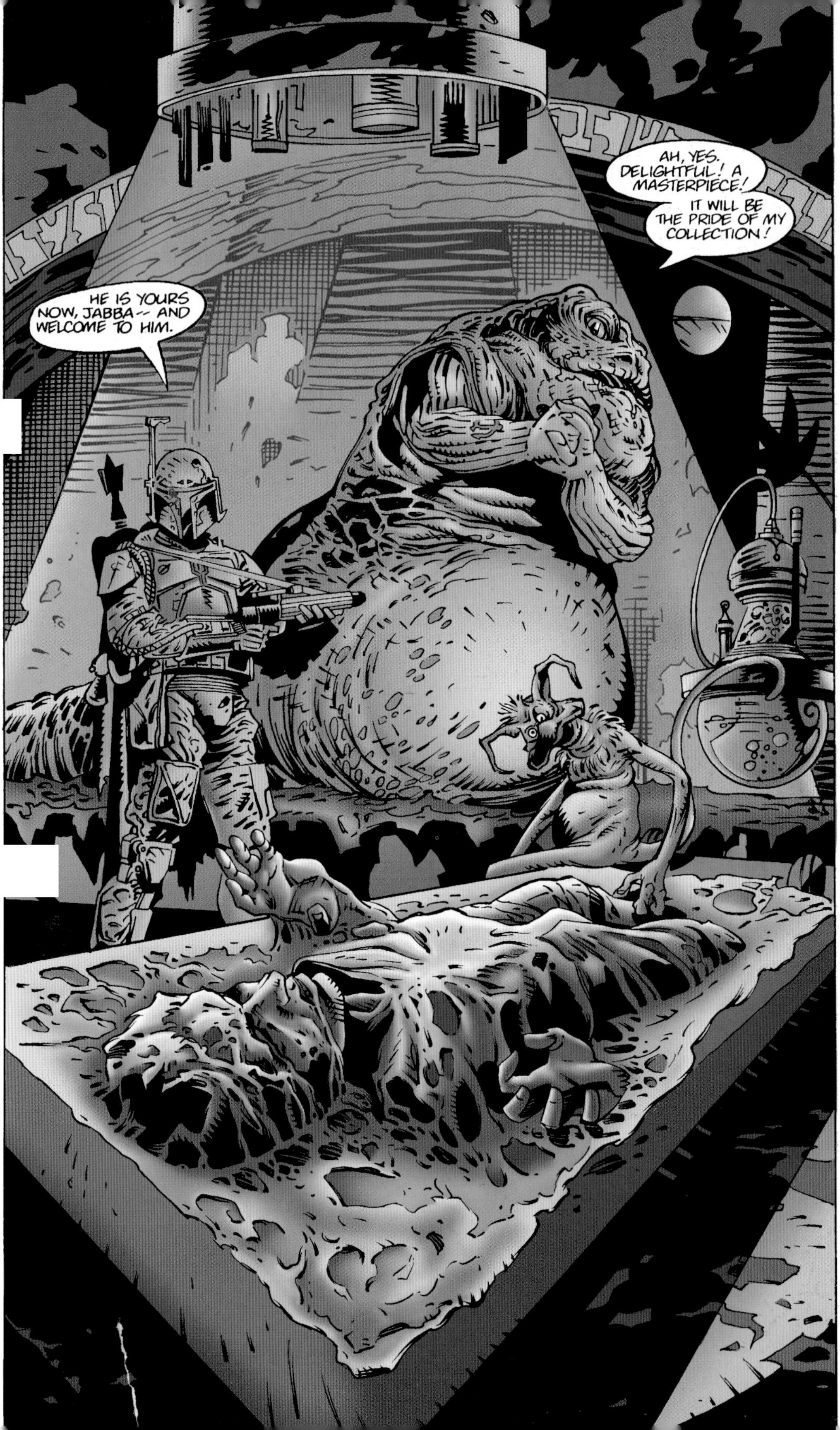
HE IS YOURS NOW, JABBA-- AND WELCOME TO HIM.
AH, YES. DELIGHTFUL! A MASTERPIECE!
IT WILL BE THE PRIDE OF MY COLLECTION!

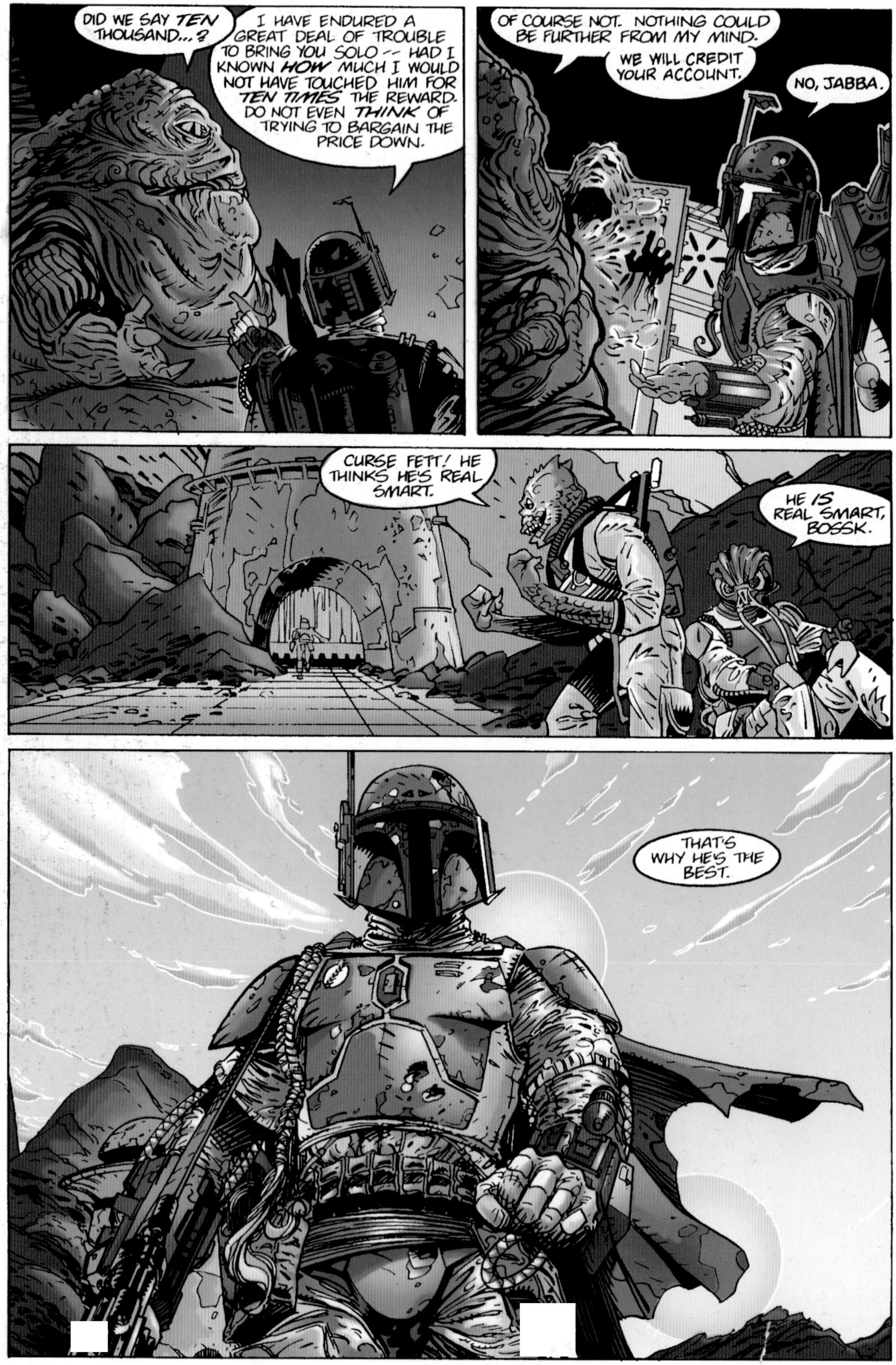
DID WE SAY TEN THOUSAND...?
I HAVE ENDURED A GREAT DEAL OF TROUBLE TO BRING YOU SOLO -- HAD I KNOWN HOW MUCH I WOULD NOT HAVE TOUCHED HIM FOR TEN TIMES THE REWARD. DO NOT EVEN THINK OF TRYING TO BARGAIN THE PRICE DOWN.
OF COURSE NOT. NOTHING COULD BE FURTHER FROM MY MIND.
WE WILL CREDIT YOUR ACCOUNT.
NO, JABBA.
CURSE FETT! HE THINKS HE'S REAL SMART.
HE IS REAL SMART, BOSSK.
THAT'S WHY HE'S THE BEST.

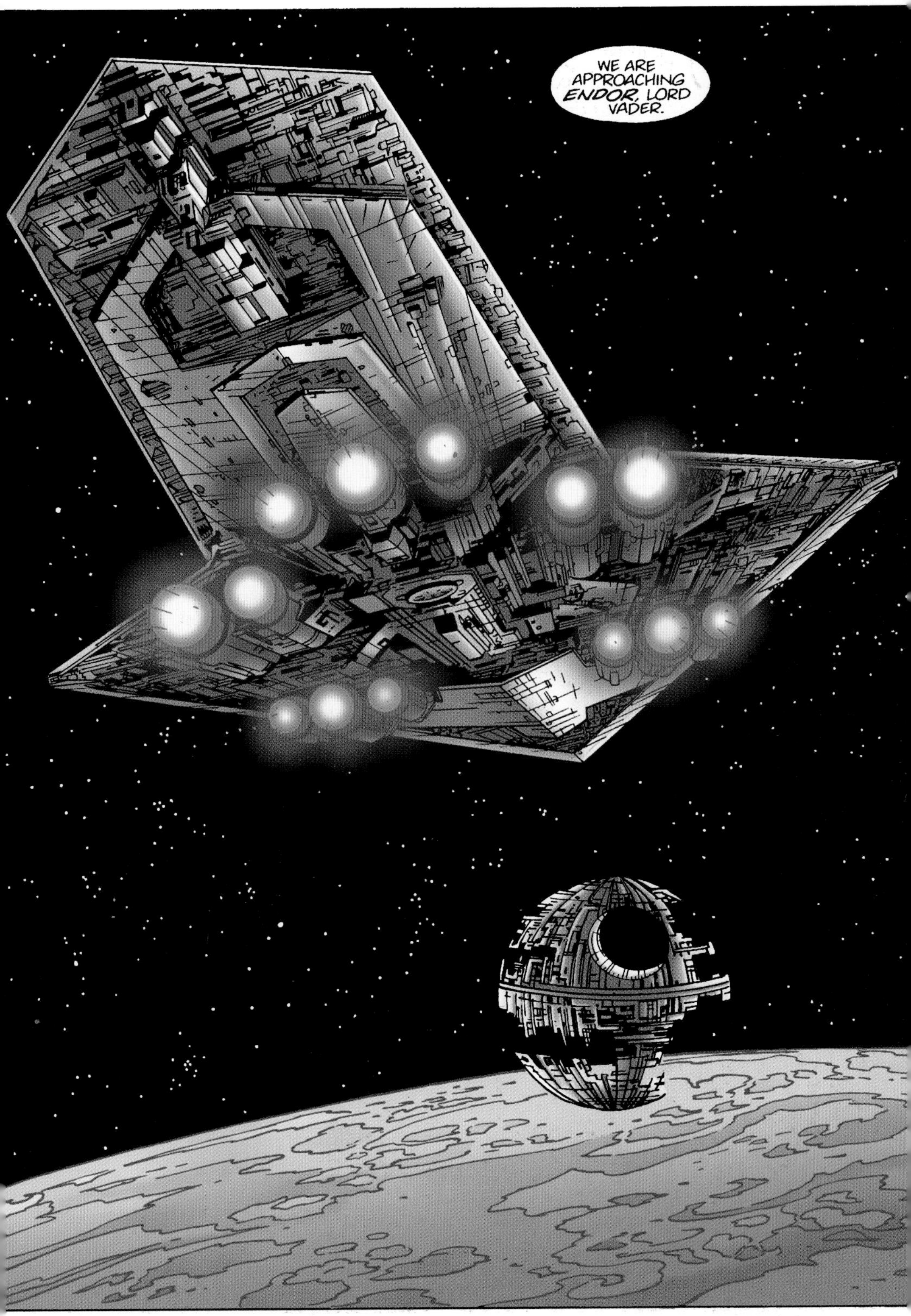
WE ARE APPROACHING ENDOR, LORD VADER.

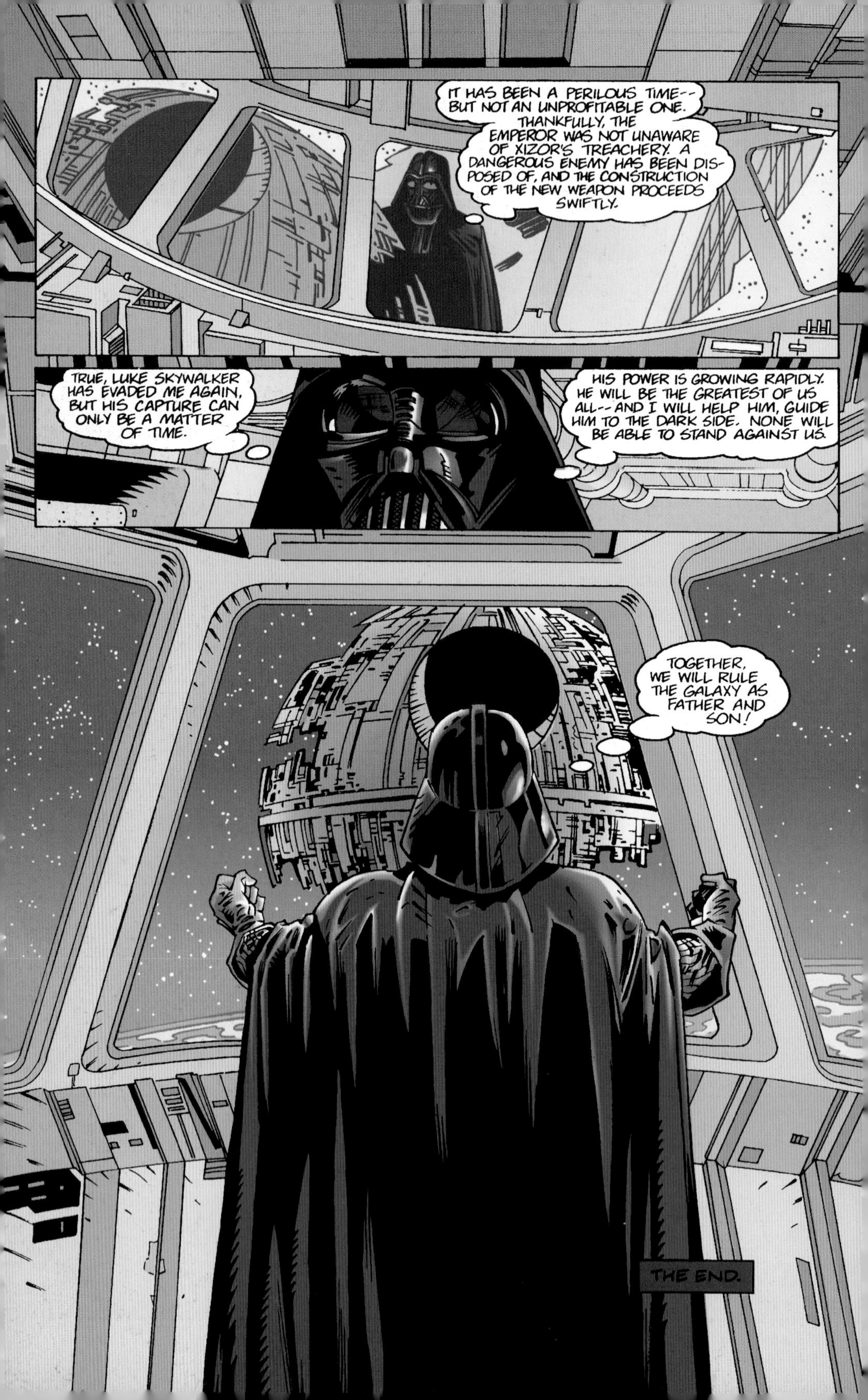
IT HAS BEEN A PERILOUS TIME-- BUT NOT AN UNPROFITABLE ONE. THANKFULLY, THE EMPEROR WAS NOT UNAWARE OF XIZOR'S TREACHERY. A DANGEROUS ENEMY HAS BEEN DISPOSED OF, AND THE CONSTRUCTION OF THE NEW WEAPON PROCEEDS SWIFTLY.
TRUE, LUKE SKYWALKER HAS EVADED ME AGAIN, BUT HIS CAPTURE CAN ONLY BE A MATTER OF TIME.
HIS POWER IS GROWING RAPIDLY. HE WILL BE THE GREATEST OF US ALL--AND I WILL HELP HIM, GUIDE HIM TO THE DARK SIDE. NONE WILL BE ABLE TO STAND AGAINST US.
TOGETHER, WE WILL RULE THE GALAXY AS FATHER AND SON!
THE END.

Mara Jade: By the Emperor's Hand | Illustration by Kilian Plunkett

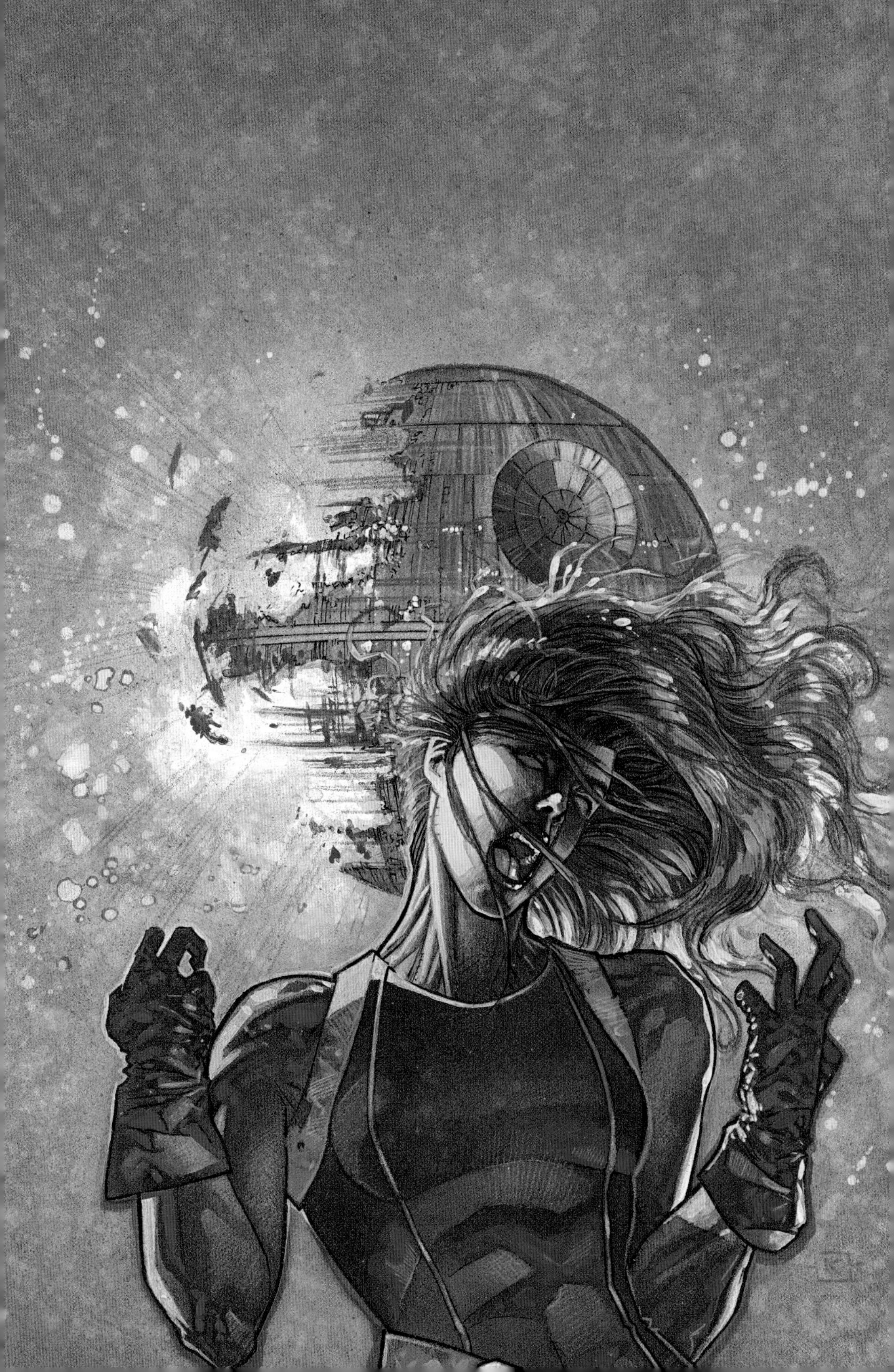

APPROXIMATELY FOUR YEARS AFTER THE BATTLE
OF YAVIN . . .

story by Timothy Zahn
script by Michael A. Stackpole
art by Carlos Ezquerra
color design by James Sinclair
color rendering by James Sinclair and Chris Chuckry
letters by Michael Taylor

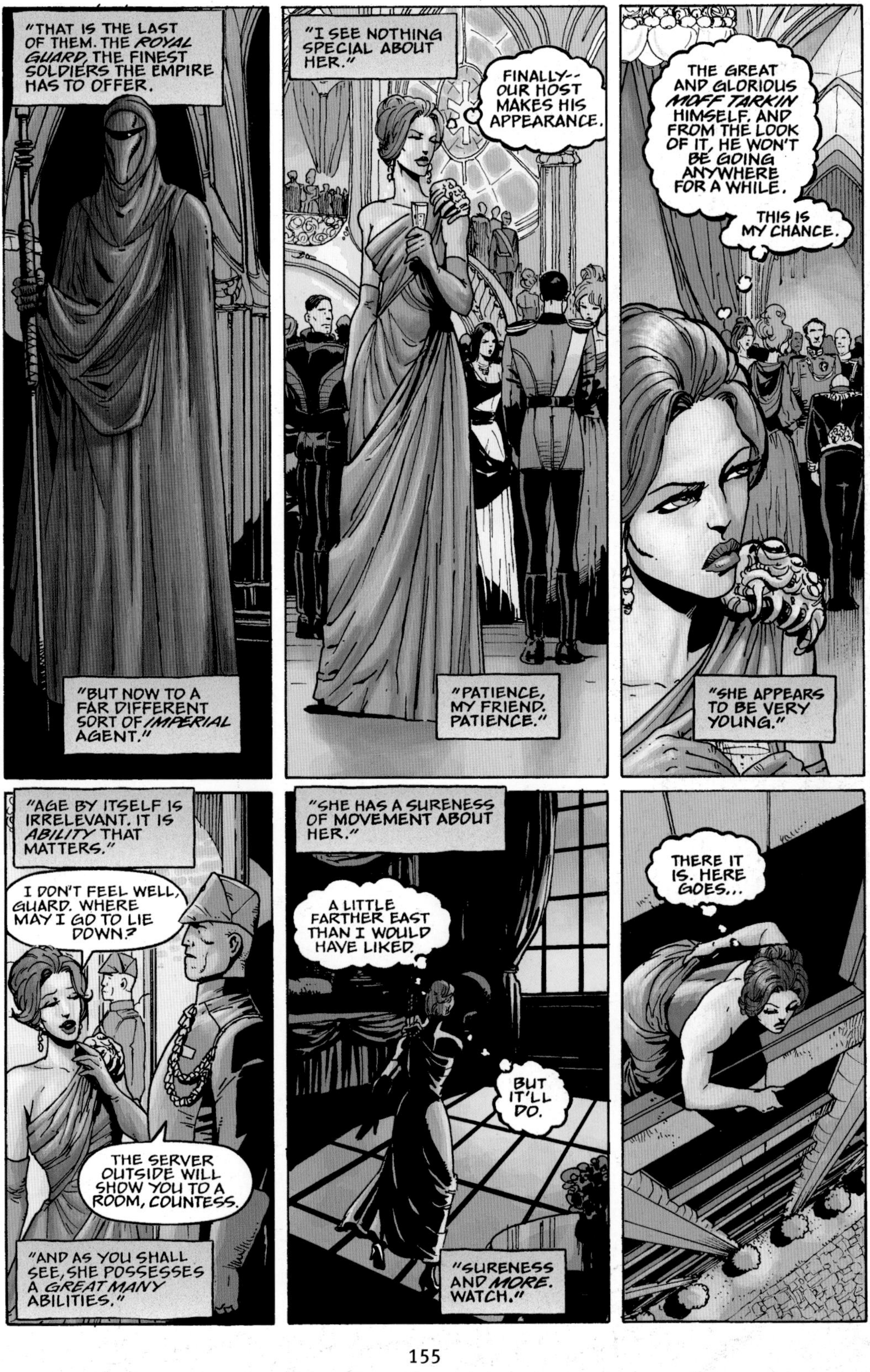
"THAT IS THE LAST OF THEM. THE ROYAL GUARD, THE FINEST SOLDIERS THE EMPIRE HAS TO OFFER.
"BUT NOW TO A FAR DIFFERENT SORT OF IMPERIAL AGENT."
"I SEE NOTHING SPECIAL ABOUT HER."
FINALLY-- OUR HOST MAKES HIS APPEARANCE.
"PATIENCE, MY FRIEND. PATIENCE."
THE GREAT AND GLORIOUS MOFF TARKIN HIMSELF. AND FROM THE LOOK OF IT, HE WON'T BE GOING ANYWHERE FOR A WHILE.
THIS IS MY CHANCE.
"SHE APPEARS TO BE VERY YOUNG."
"AGE BY ITSELF IS IRRELEVANT. IT IS ABILITY THAT MATTERS."
I DON'T FEEL WELL, GUARD. WHERE MAY I GO TO LIE DOWN?
THE SERVER OUTSIDE WILL SHOW YOU TO A ROOM, COUNTESS.
"AND AS YOU SHALL SEE, SHE POSSESSES A GREAT MANY ABILITIES."
"SHE HAS A SURENESS OF MOVEMENT ABOUT HER."
A LITTLE FARTHER EAST THAN I WOULD HAVE LIKED.
BUT IT'LL DO.
"SURENESS AND MORE. WATCH."
THERE IT IS. HERE GOES...

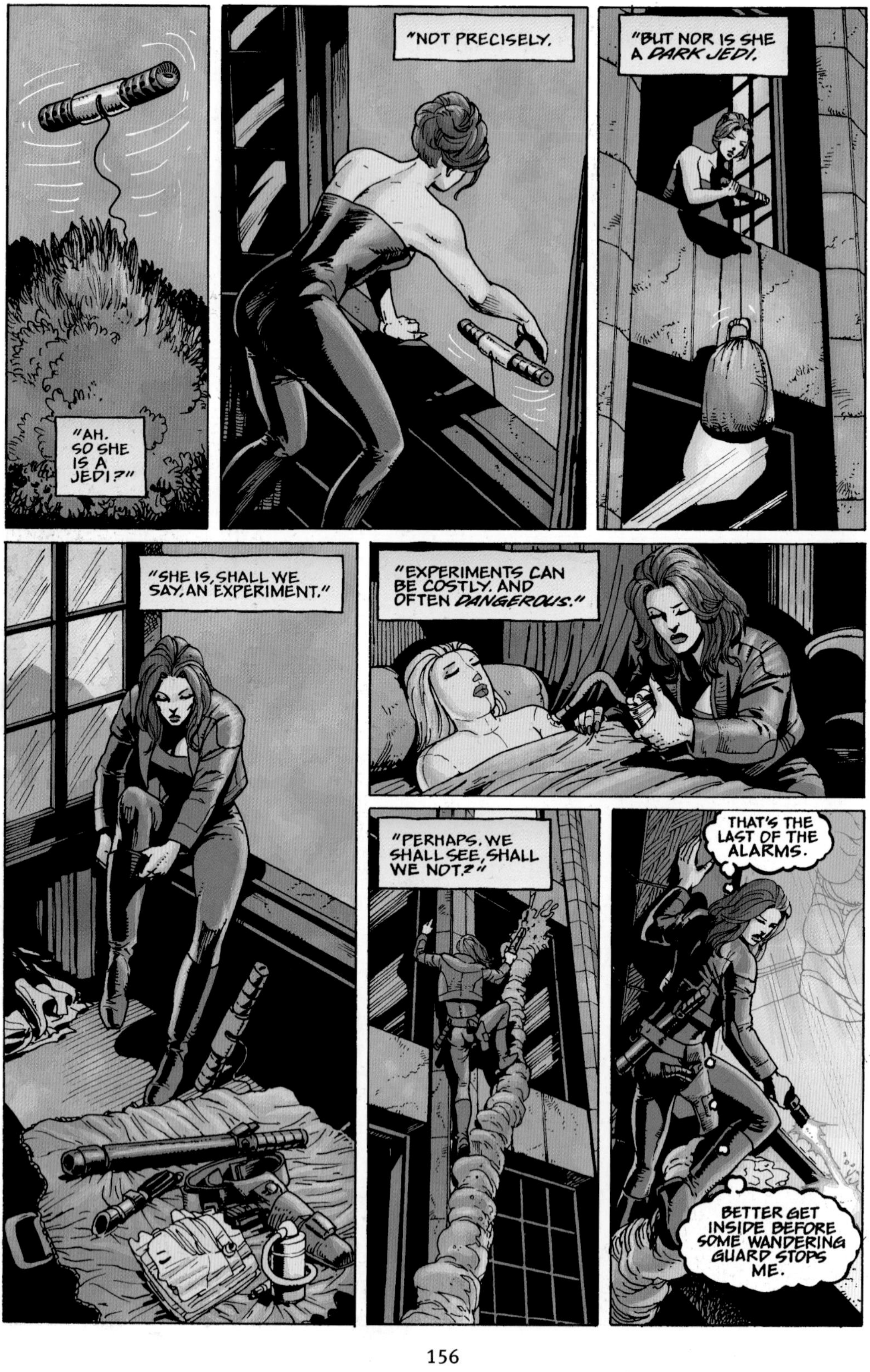
"AH. SO SHE IS A JEDI?"
"NOT PRECISELY.
"BUT NOR IS SHE A DARK JEDI.
"SHE IS, SHALL WE SAY, AN EXPERIMENT."
"EXPERIMENTS CAN BE COSTLY. AND OFTEN DANGEROUS."
"PERHAPS. WE SHALL SEE, SHALL WE NOT?"
THAT'S THE LAST OF THE ALARMS.
BETTER GET INSIDE BEFORE SOME WANDERING GUARD STOPS ME.

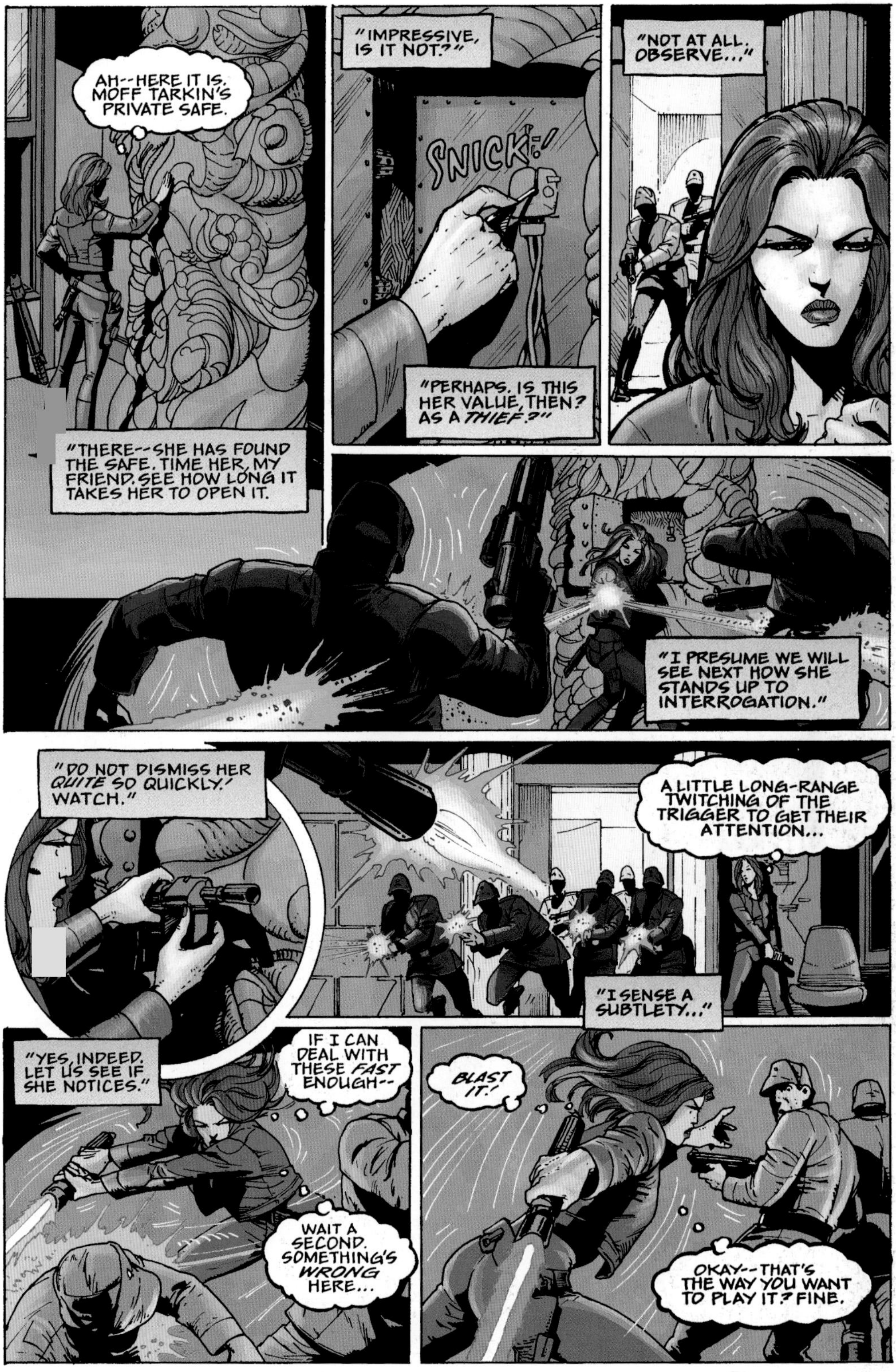
AH--HERE IT IS. MOFF TARKIN'S PRIVATE SAFE.
"THERE--SHE HAS FOUND THE SAFE. TIME HER, MY FRIEND. SEE HOW LONG IT TAKES HER TO OPEN IT.
"IMPRESSIVE, IS IT NOT?"
SNICK!
"PERHAPS. IS THIS HER VALUE, THEN? AS A *THIEF?*"
"NOT AT ALL. OBSERVE..."
"I PRESUME WE WILL SEE NEXT HOW SHE STANDS UP TO INTERROGATION."
"DO NOT DISMISS HER *QUITE* SO QUICKLY! WATCH."
A LITTLE LONG-RANGE TWITCHING OF THE TRIGGER TO GET THEIR ATTENTION...
"I SENSE A SUBTLETY..."
"YES, INDEED. LET US SEE IF SHE NOTICES."
IF I CAN DEAL WITH THESE *FAST* ENOUGH--
WAIT A SECOND. SOMETHING'S *WRONG* HERE...
BLAST IT!
OKAY--THAT'S THE WAY YOU WANT TO PLAY IT? FINE.

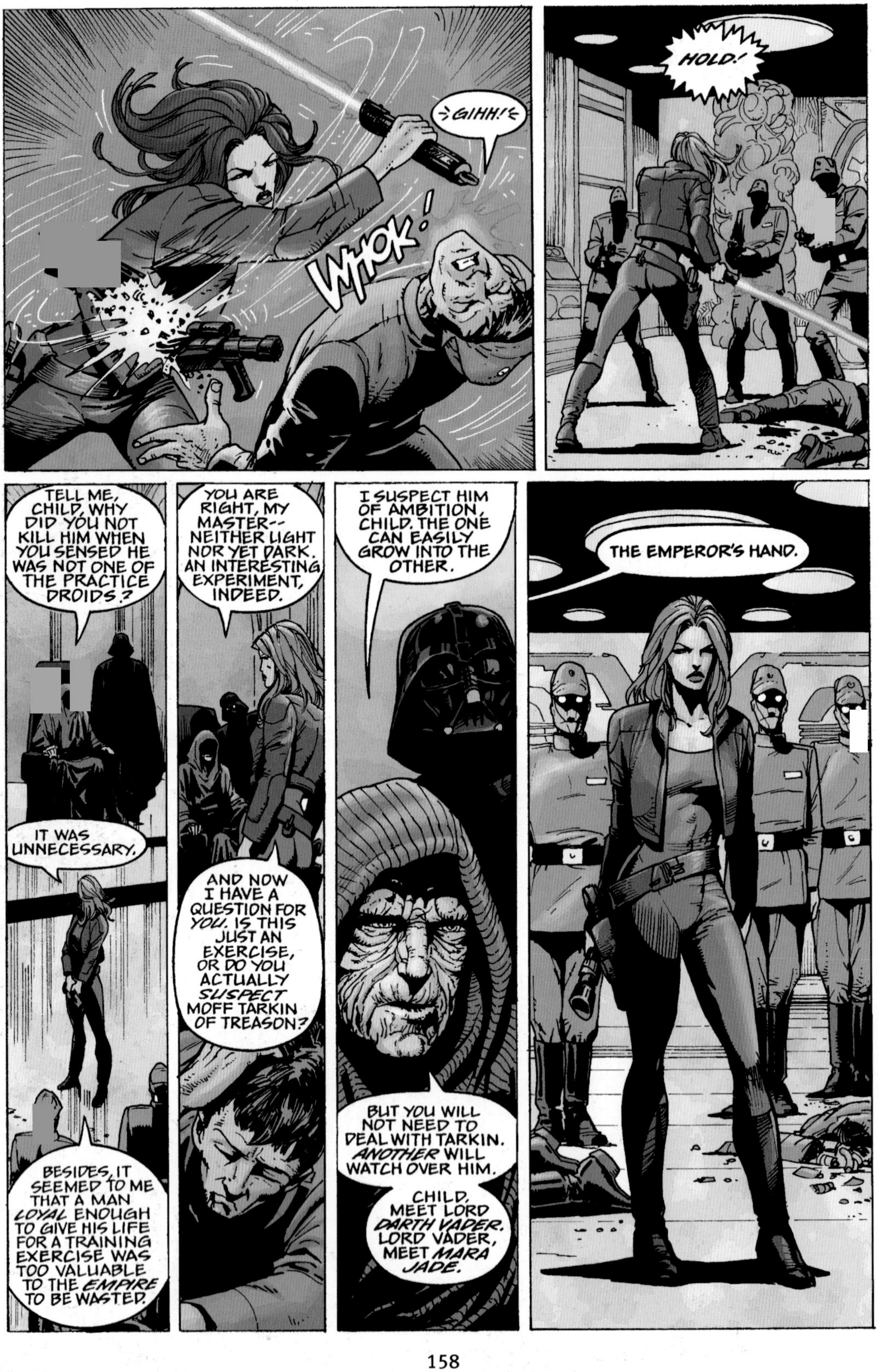
GIHH!
WHOK!
HOLD!
TELL ME, CHILD, WHY DID YOU NOT KILL HIM WHEN YOU SENSED HE WAS NOT ONE OF THE PRACTICE DROIDS?
IT WAS UNNECESSARY.
BESIDES, IT SEEMED TO ME THAT A MAN LOYAL ENOUGH TO GIVE HIS LIFE FOR A TRAINING EXERCISE WAS TOO VALUABLE TO THE EMPIRE TO BE WASTED.
YOU ARE RIGHT, MY MASTER-- NEITHER LIGHT NOR YET DARK. AN INTERESTING EXPERIMENT, INDEED.
AND NOW I HAVE A QUESTION FOR YOU. IS THIS JUST AN EXERCISE, OR DO YOU ACTUALLY SUSPECT MOFF TARKIN OF TREASON?
I SUSPECT HIM OF AMBITION, CHILD. THE ONE CAN EASILY GROW INTO THE OTHER.
BUT YOU WILL NOT NEED TO DEAL WITH TARKIN. ANOTHER WILL WATCH OVER HIM.
CHILD, MEET LORD DARTH VADER. LORD VADER, MEET MARA JADE.
THE EMPEROR'S HAND.

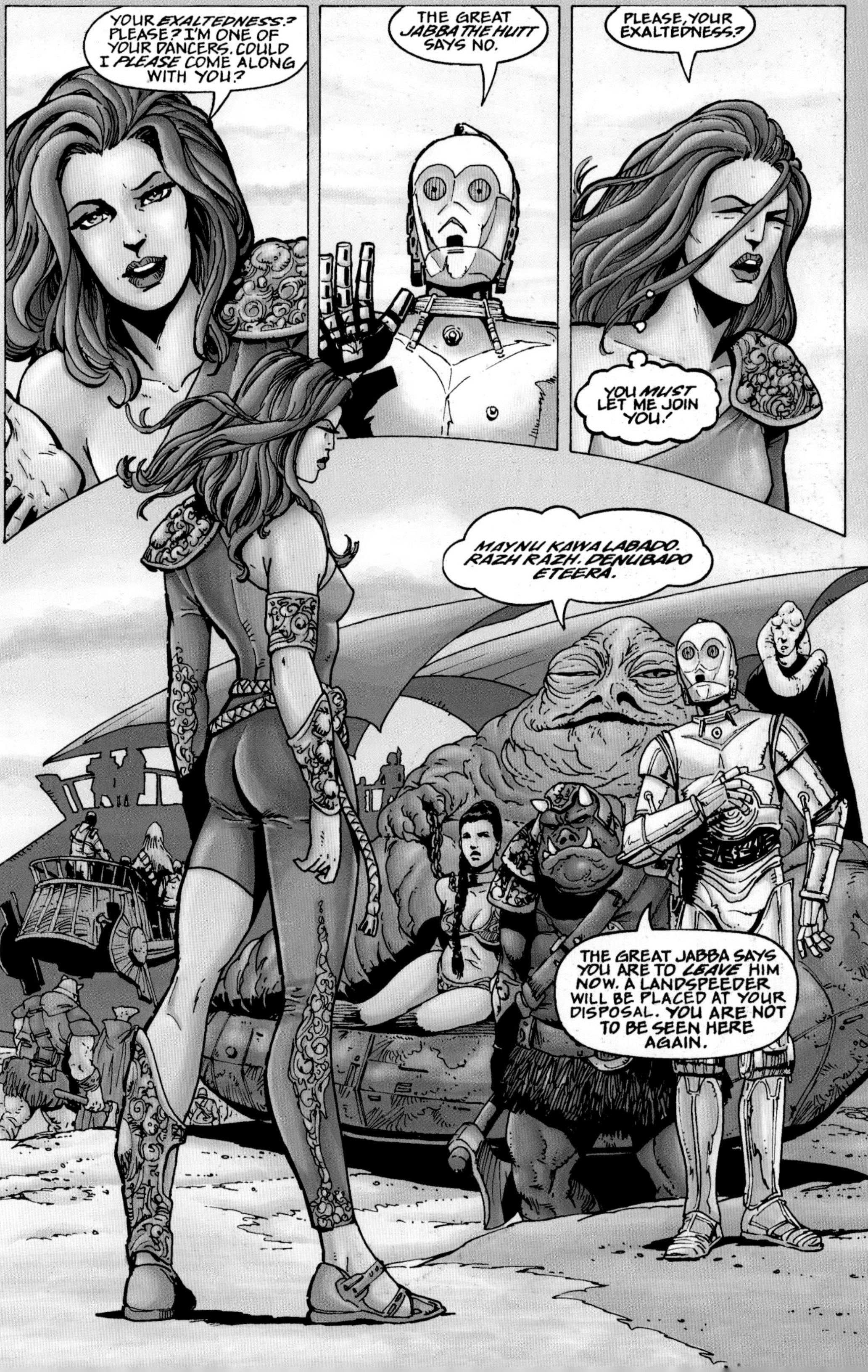
YOUR *EXALTEDNESS*? PLEASE? I'M ONE OF YOUR DANCERS. COULD I *PLEASE* COME ALONG WITH YOU?
THE GREAT *JABBA THE HUTT* SAYS NO.
PLEASE, YOUR EXALTEDNESS?
YOU *MUST* LET ME JOIN YOU!
MAYNU KAWA LABADO. RAZH RAZH. DENUBADO ETEERA.
THE GREAT JABBA SAYS YOU ARE TO *LEAVE* HIM NOW. A LANDSPEEDER WILL BE PLACED AT YOUR DISPOSAL. YOU ARE NOT TO BE SEEN HERE AGAIN.

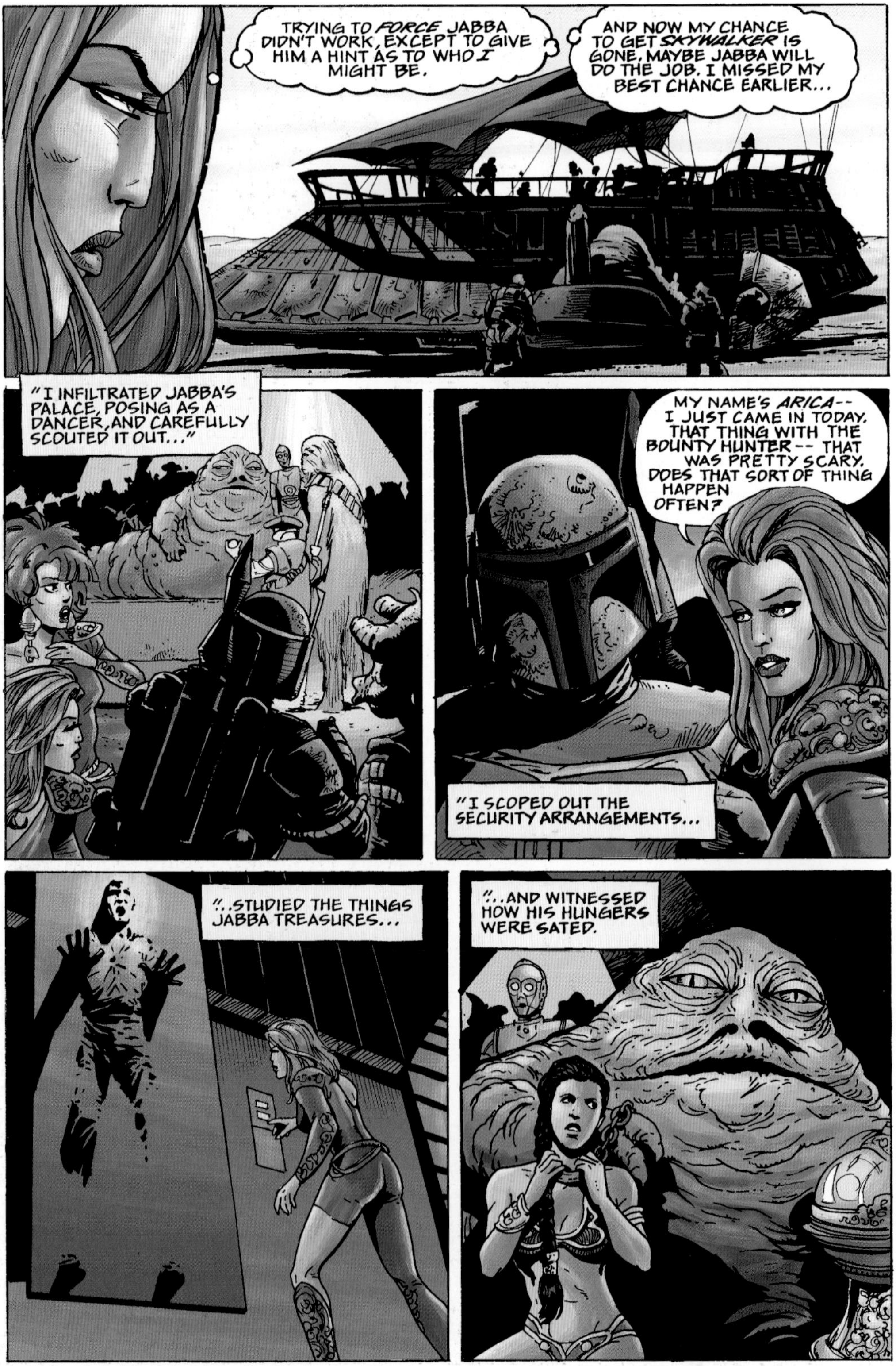
TRYING TO FORCE JABBA DIDN'T WORK, EXCEPT TO GIVE HIM A HINT AS TO WHO I MIGHT BE.
AND NOW MY CHANCE TO GET SKYWALKER IS GONE. MAYBE JABBA WILL DO THE JOB. I MISSED MY BEST CHANCE EARLIER...
"I INFILTRATED JABBA'S PALACE, POSING AS A DANCER, AND CAREFULLY SCOUTED IT OUT..."
MY NAME'S ARICA-- I JUST CAME IN TODAY. THAT THING WITH THE BOUNTY HUNTER-- THAT WAS PRETTY SCARY. DOES THAT SORT OF THING HAPPEN OFTEN?
"I SCOPED OUT THE SECURITY ARRANGEMENTS...
"...STUDIED THE THINGS JABBA TREASURES...
"...AND WITNESSED HOW HIS HUNGERS WERE SATED.

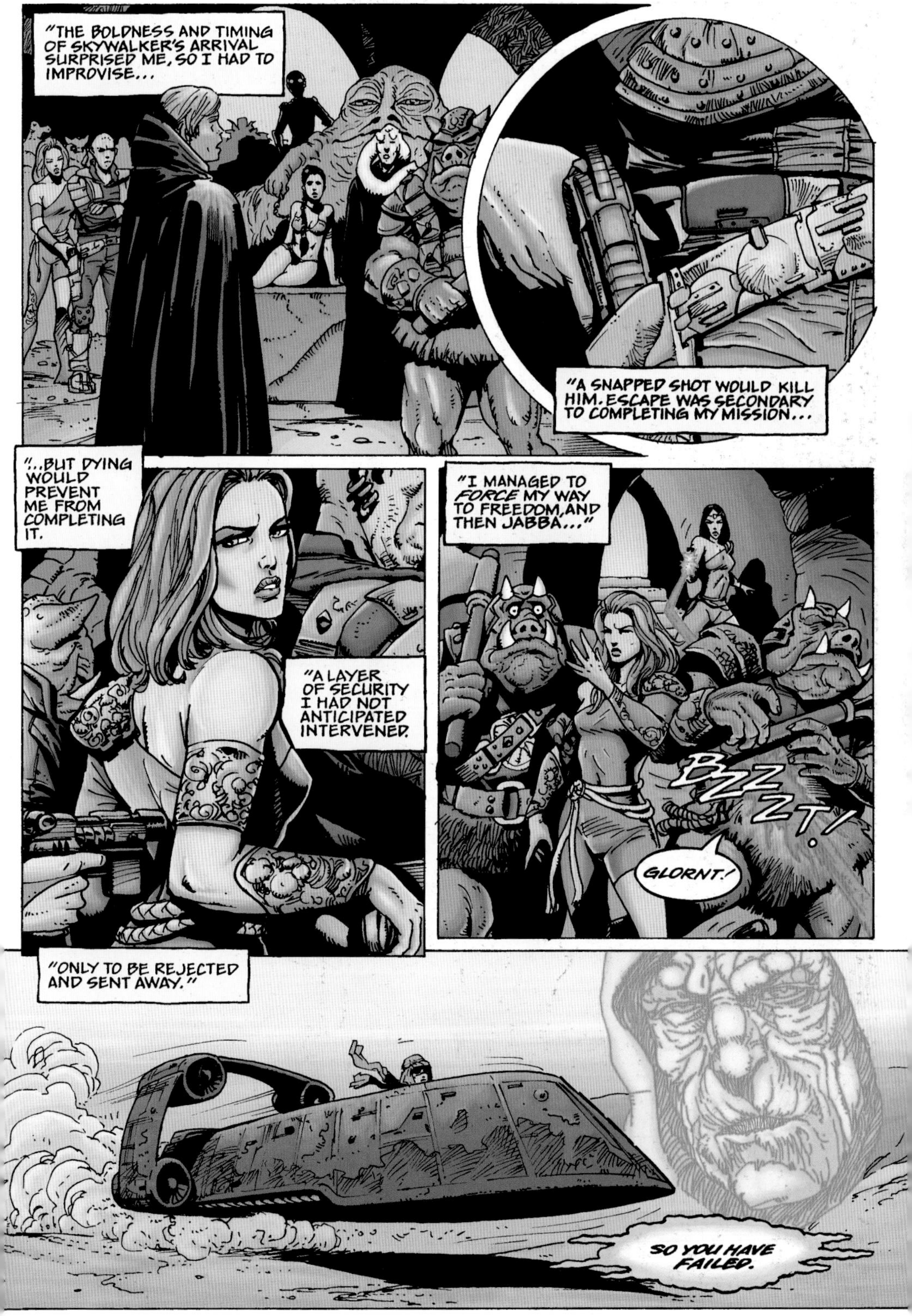
"THE BOLDNESS AND TIMING OF SKYWALKER'S ARRIVAL SURPRISED ME, SO I HAD TO IMPROVISE...
"A SNAPPED SHOT WOULD KILL HIM. ESCAPE WAS SECONDARY TO COMPLETING MY MISSION...
"...BUT DYING WOULD PREVENT ME FROM COMPLETING IT.
"A LAYER OF SECURITY I HAD NOT ANTICIPATED INTERVENED.
"I MANAGED TO *FORCE* MY WAY TO FREEDOM, AND THEN JABBA..."
BZZZZT!
GLORNT!
"ONLY TO BE REJECTED AND SENT AWAY."
SO YOU HAVE FAILED.

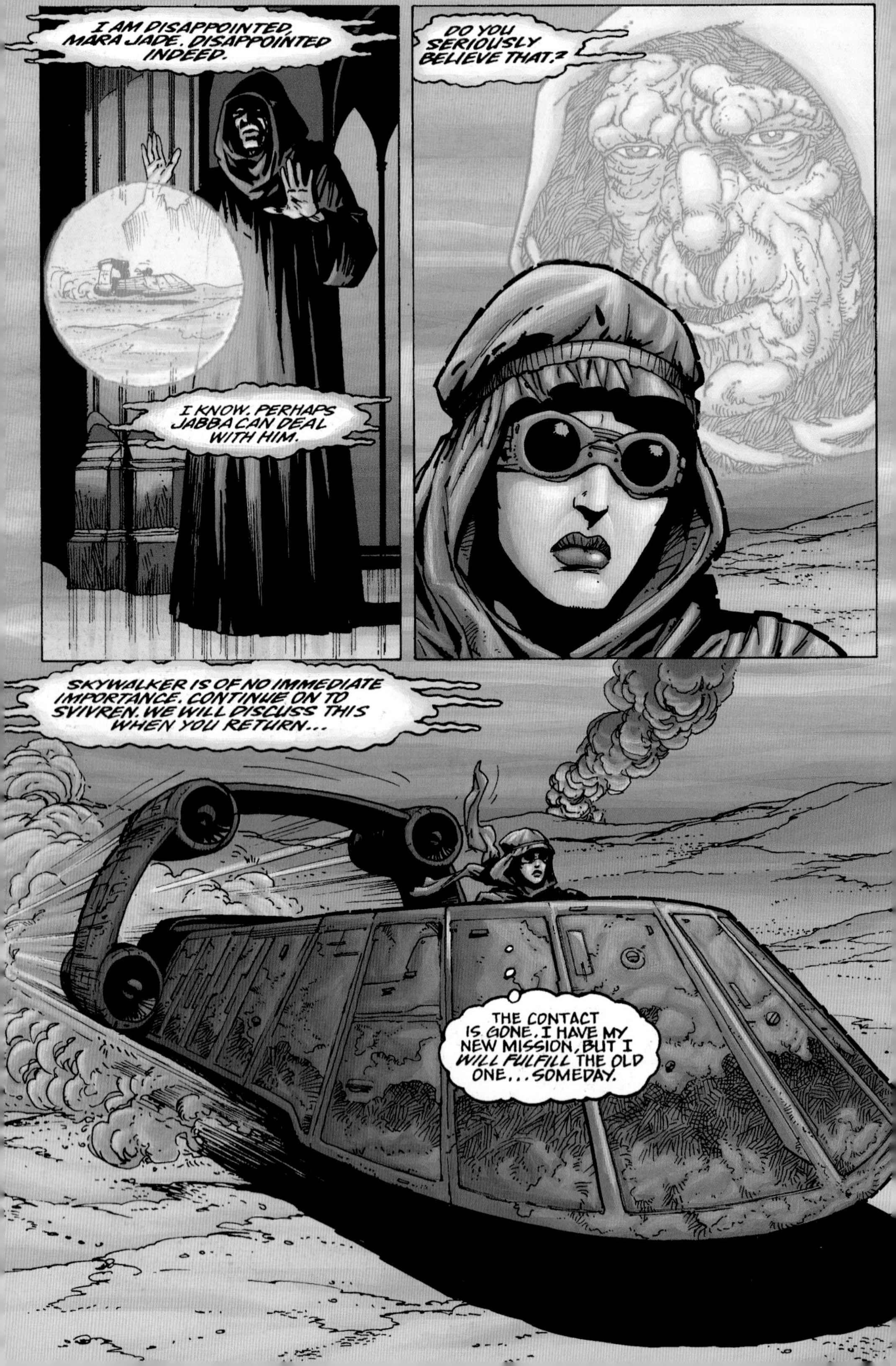
I AM DISAPPOINTED, MARA JADE. DISAPPOINTED INDEED.
DO YOU SERIOUSLY BELIEVE THAT?
I KNOW. PERHAPS JABBA CAN DEAL WITH HIM.
SKYWALKER IS OF NO IMMEDIATE IMPORTANCE. CONTINUE ON TO SVIVREN. WE WILL DISCUSS THIS WHEN YOU RETURN...
THE CONTACT IS GONE. I HAVE MY NEW MISSION, BUT I WILL FULFILL THE OLD ONE... SOMEDAY.

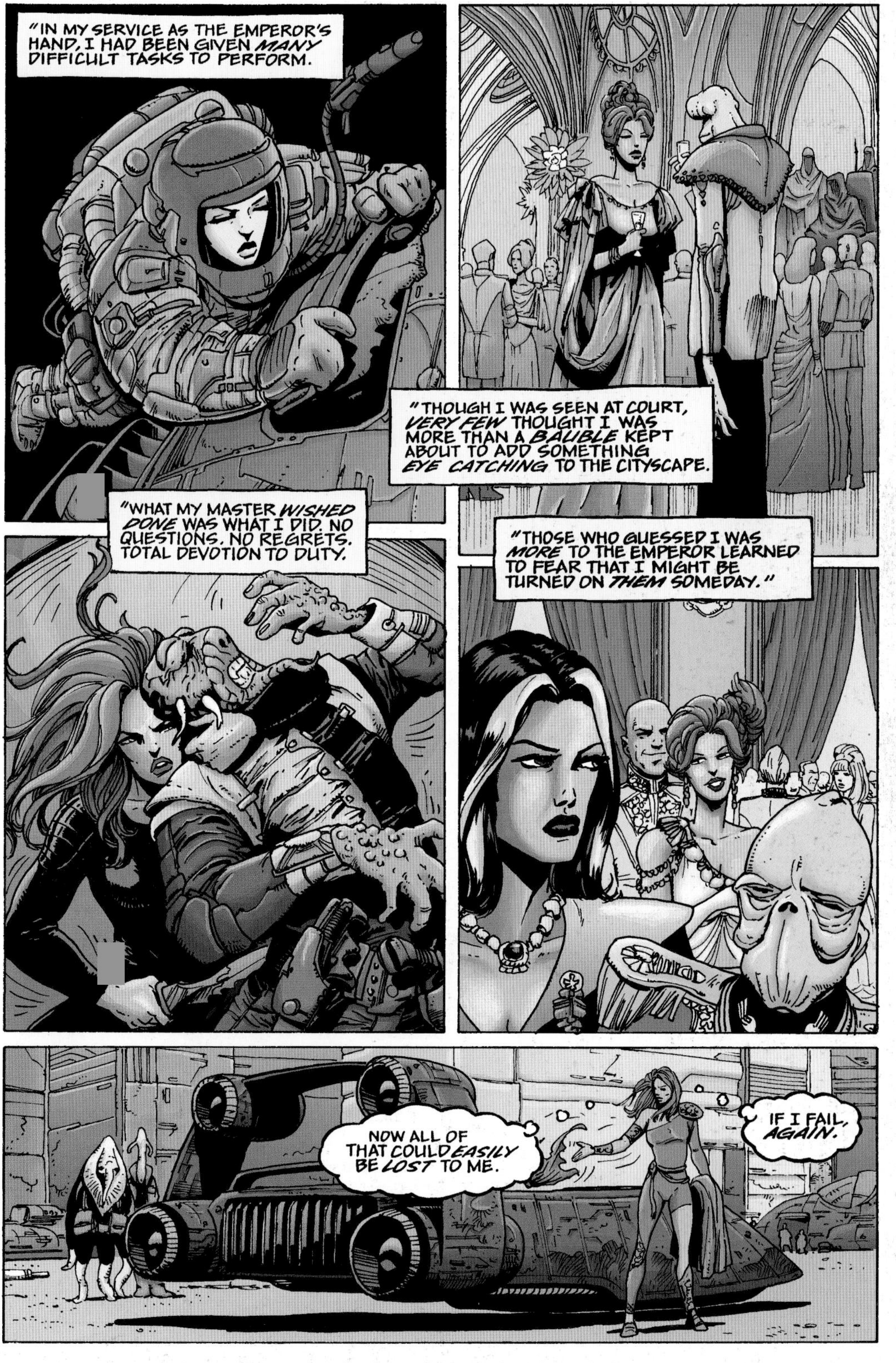

"IN MY SERVICE AS THE EMPEROR'S HAND, I HAD BEEN GIVEN MANY DIFFICULT TASKS TO PERFORM.
"THOUGH I WAS SEEN AT COURT, VERY FEW THOUGHT I WAS MORE THAN A BAUBLE KEPT ABOUT TO ADD SOMETHING EYE CATCHING TO THE CITYSCAPE.
"WHAT MY MASTER WISHED DONE WAS WHAT I DID. NO QUESTIONS. NO REGRETS. TOTAL DEVOTION TO DUTY.
"THOSE WHO GUESSED I WAS MORE TO THE EMPEROR LEARNED TO FEAR THAT I MIGHT BE TURNED ON THEM SOMEDAY."
NOW ALL OF THAT COULD EASILY BE LOST TO ME.
IF I FAIL, AGAIN.

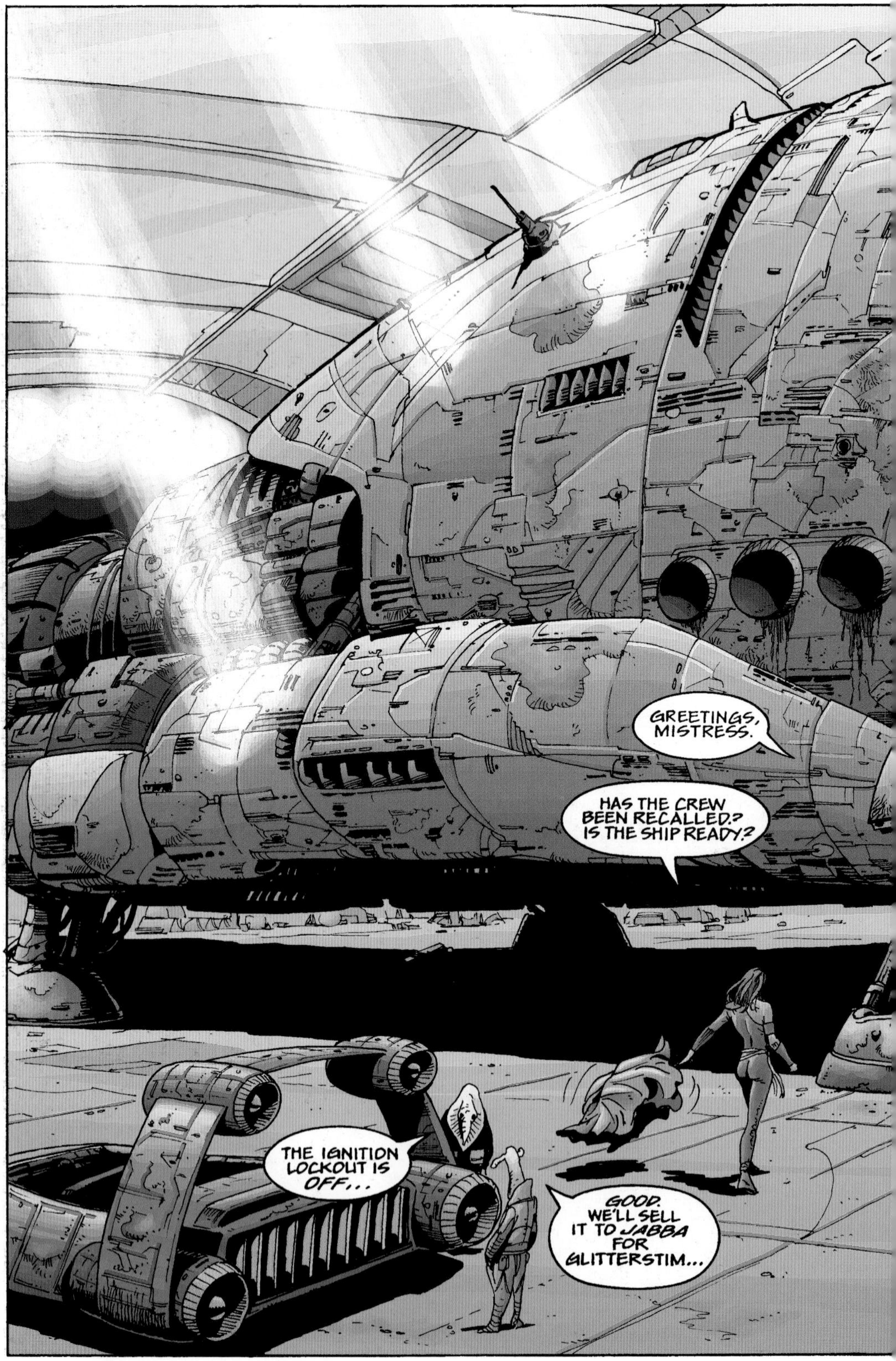
GREETINGS, MISTRESS.
HAS THE CREW BEEN RECALLED? IS THE SHIP READY?
THE IGNITION LOCKOUT IS OFF...
GOOD. WE'LL SELL IT TO JABBA FOR GLITTERSTIM...

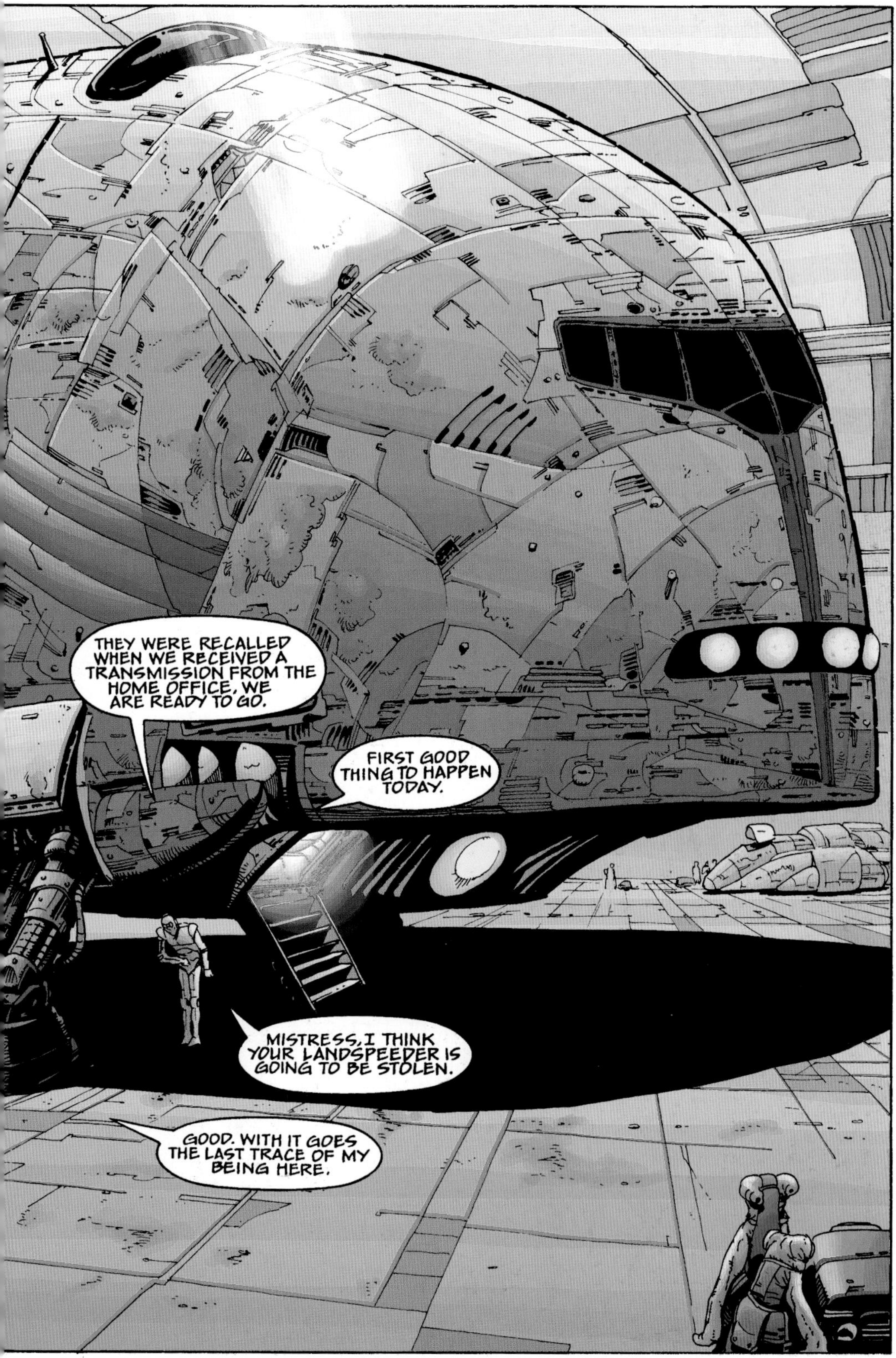
THEY WERE RECALLED WHEN WE RECEIVED A TRANSMISSION FROM THE HOME OFFICE, WE ARE READY TO GO.
FIRST GOOD THING TO HAPPEN TODAY.
MISTRESS, I THINK YOUR LANDSPEEDER IS GOING TO BE STOLEN.
GOOD. WITH IT GOES THE LAST TRACE OF MY BEING HERE.

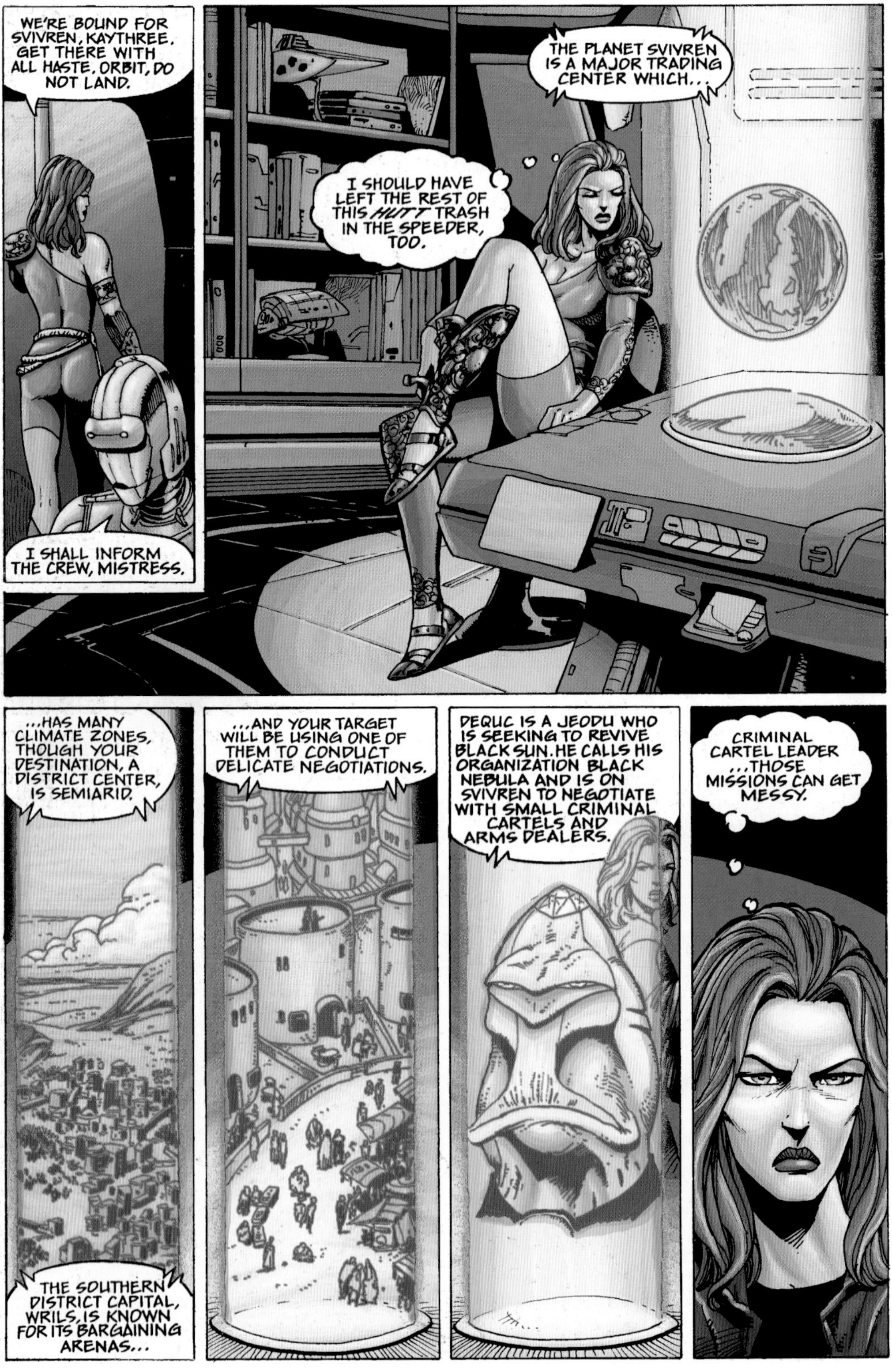

WE'RE BOUND FOR SVIVREN, KAYTHREE. GET THERE WITH ALL HASTE. ORBIT, DO NOT LAND.
I SHALL INFORM THE CREW, MISTRESS.
THE PLANET SVIVREN IS A MAJOR TRADING CENTER WHICH...
I SHOULD HAVE LEFT THE REST OF THIS *HUTT* TRASH IN THE SPEEDER, TOO.
...HAS MANY CLIMATE ZONES, THOUGH YOUR DESTINATION, A DISTRICT CENTER, IS SEMIARID.
THE SOUTHERN DISTRICT CAPITAL, WRILS, IS KNOWN FOR ITS BARGAINING ARENAS...
...AND YOUR TARGET WILL BE USING ONE OF THEM TO CONDUCT DELICATE NEGOTIATIONS.
DEQUC IS A JEODU WHO IS SEEKING TO REVIVE BLACK SUN. HE CALLS HIS ORGANIZATION BLACK NEBULA AND IS ON SVIVREN TO NEGOTIATE WITH SMALL CRIMINAL CARTELS AND ARMS DEALERS.
CRIMINAL CARTEL LEADER ...THOSE MISSIONS CAN GET MESSY.

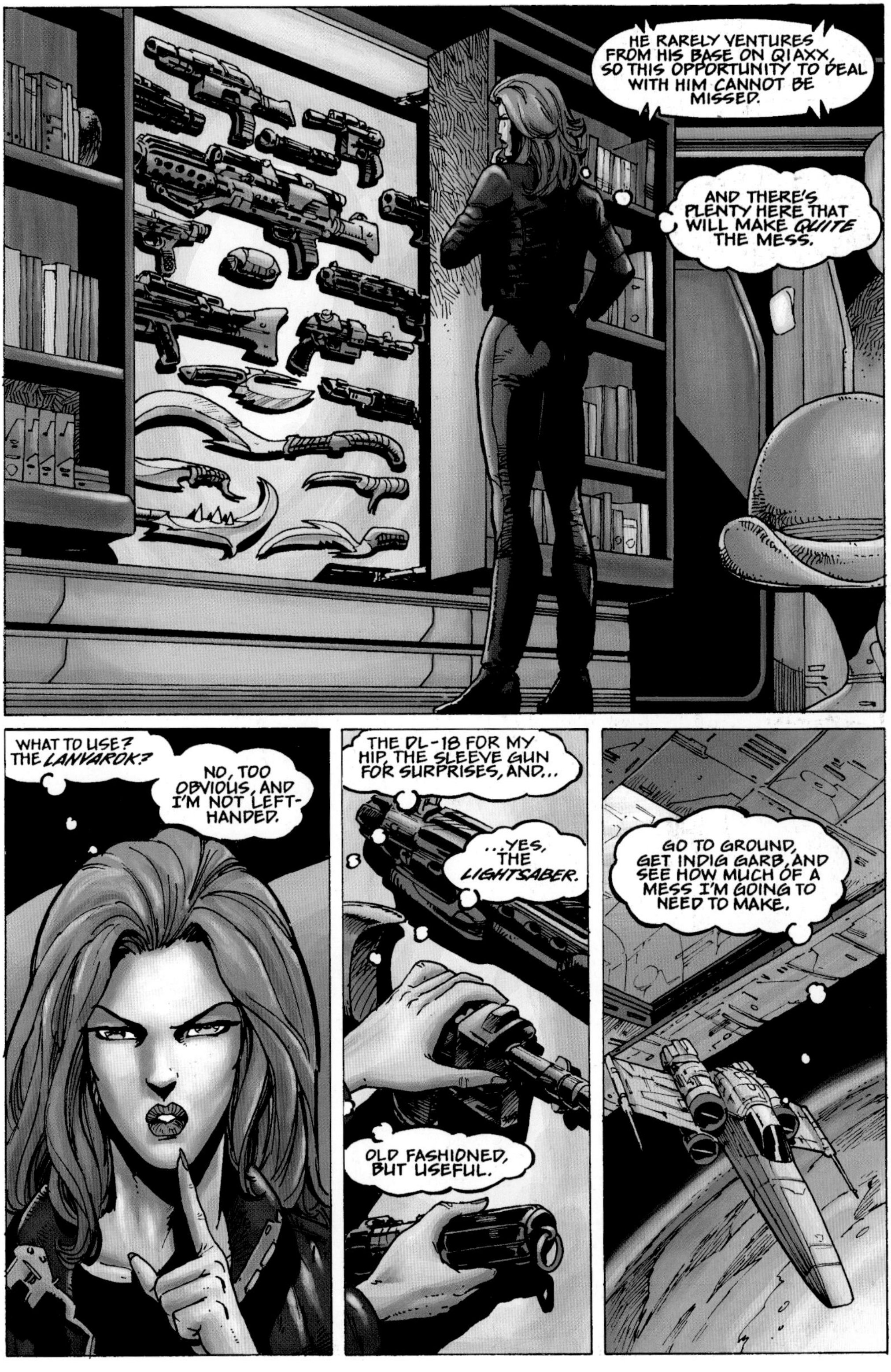
HE RARELY VENTURES FROM HIS BASE ON QIAXX, SO THIS OPPORTUNITY TO DEAL WITH HIM CANNOT BE MISSED.
AND THERE'S PLENTY HERE THAT WILL MAKE *QUITE* THE MESS.
WHAT TO USE? THE *LANVAROK?*
NO, TOO OBVIOUS, AND I'M NOT LEFT-HANDED.
THE DL-18 FOR MY HIP, THE SLEEVE GUN FOR SURPRISES, AND...
...YES, THE *LIGHTSABER.*
OLD FASHIONED, BUT USEFUL.
GO TO GROUND, GET INDIG GARB, AND SEE HOW MUCH OF A MESS I'M GOING TO NEED TO MAKE.

"INSERTION ONTO SVIVREN WENT UNNOTICED *AND* UNCHALLENGED."

NO HUTTS, NO JAWAS.

THIS IS *ALREADY* BETTER THAN TATOOINE.

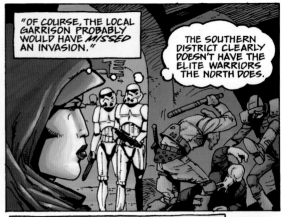

"OF COURSE, THE LOCAL GARRISON PROBABLY WOULD HAVE *MISSED* AN INVASION."

THE SOUTHERN DISTRICT CLEARLY DOESN'T HAVE THE ELITE WARRIORS THE NORTH DOES.

"THE BLACK NEBULA SOLDIERS APPEARED MORE ALERT.

"AND THEIR LEADER RATHER *BOLD*."

THERE HE IS.

DEQUC MEANS "WHITEHEAD" IN BASIC. AN OBVIOUS ALIAS... HE'S CLEARLY NOT AS COMMON AS THAT NAME IS AMONG THE JEODU.

"BUT DEQUC WASN'T THE *ONLY* ONE INCLINED TO BE BOLD."

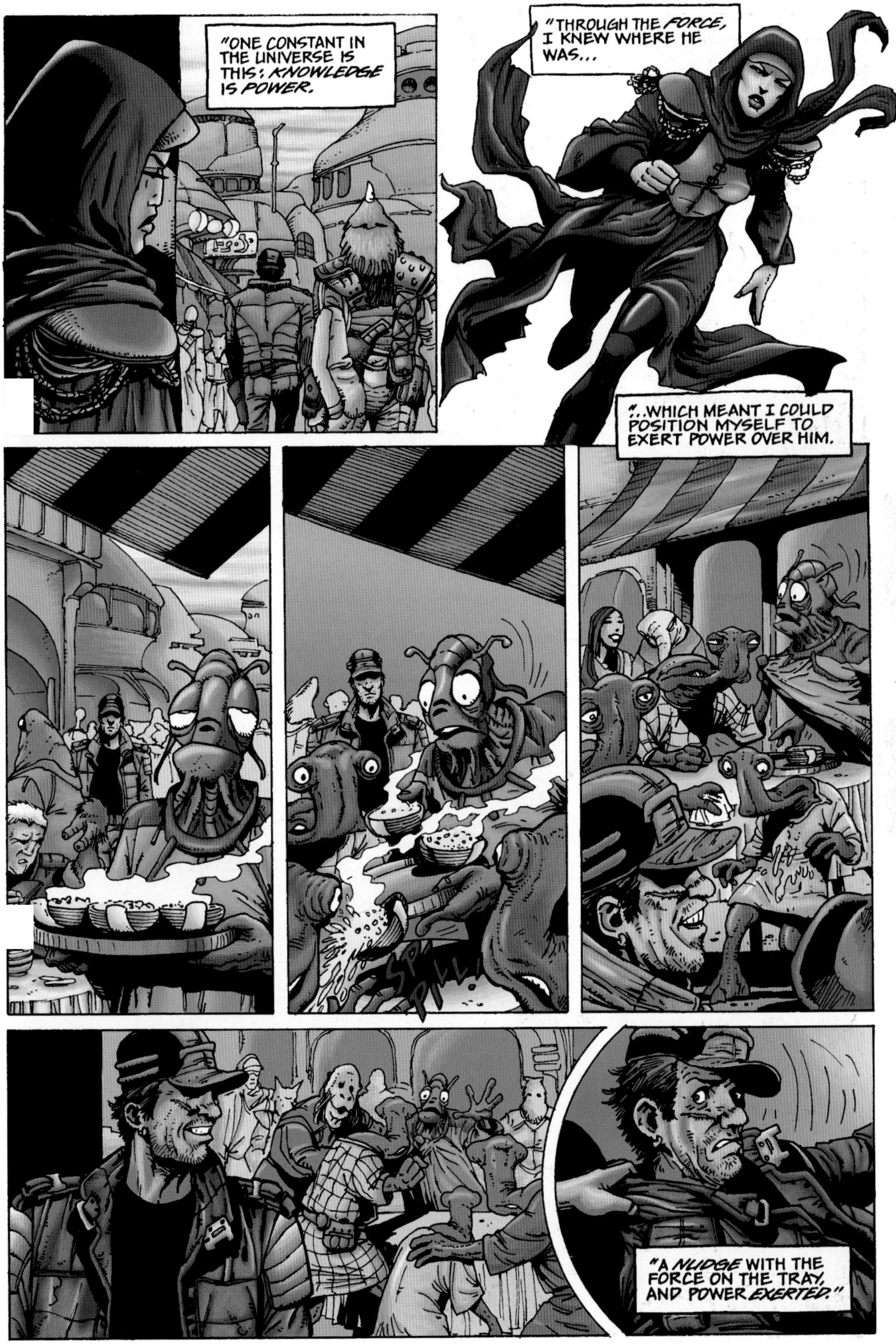
"ONE CONSTANT IN THE UNIVERSE IS THIS: *KNOWLEDGE* IS *POWER*.
"THROUGH THE *FORCE*, I KNEW WHERE HE WAS...
"...WHICH MEANT I COULD POSITION MYSELF TO EXERT POWER OVER HIM.
"A *NUDGE* WITH THE FORCE ON THE TRAY, AND POWER *EXERTED*."

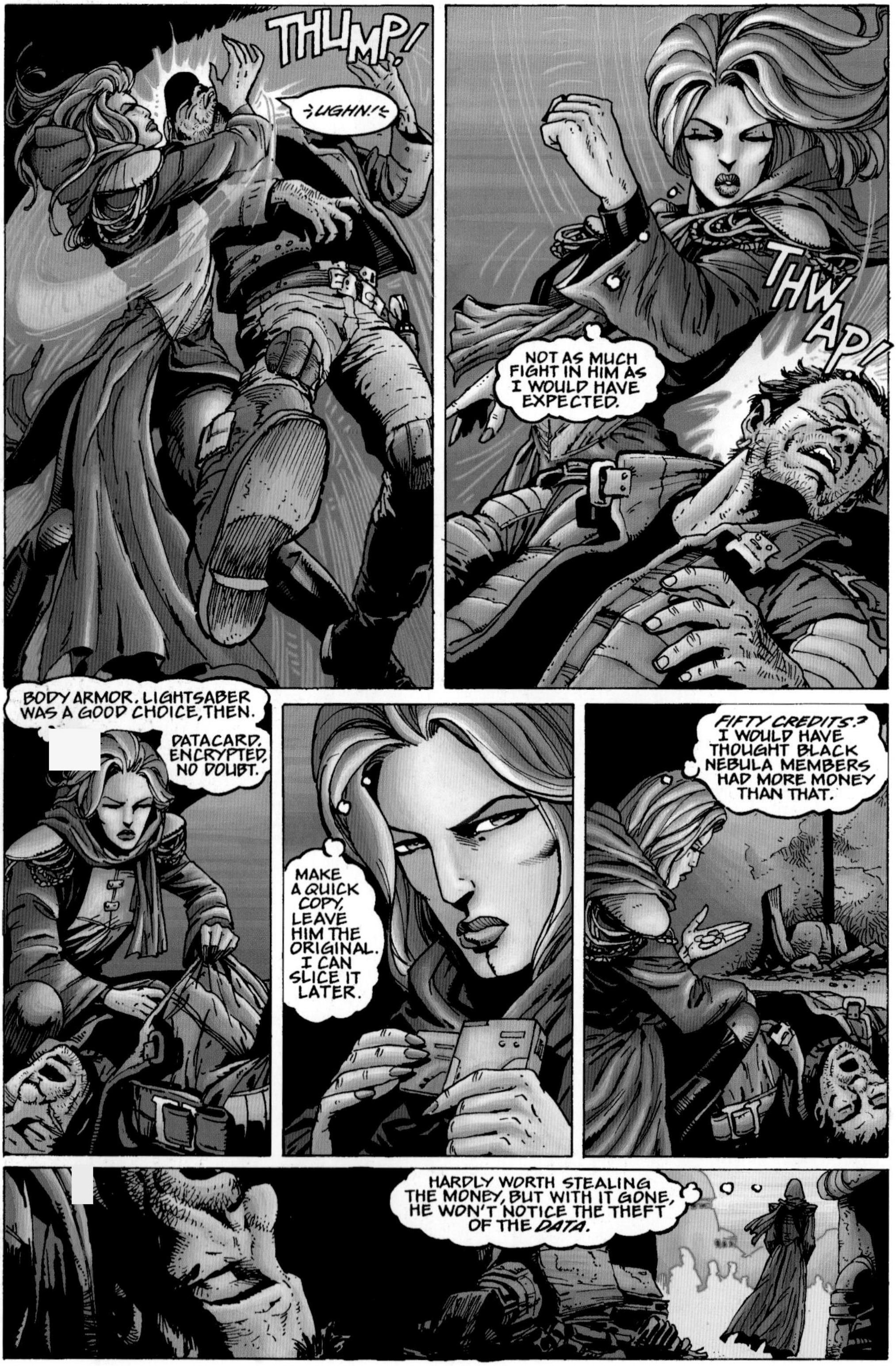
THUMP!
UGHN!
NOT AS MUCH FIGHT IN HIM AS I WOULD HAVE EXPECTED.
THWAP!
BODY ARMOR. LIGHTSABER WAS A GOOD CHOICE, THEN.
DATACARD. ENCRYPTED, NO DOUBT.
MAKE A QUICK COPY, LEAVE HIM THE ORIGINAL. I CAN SLICE IT LATER.
FIFTY CREDITS? I WOULD HAVE THOUGHT BLACK NEBULA MEMBERS HAD MORE MONEY THAN THAT.
HARDLY WORTH STEALING THE MONEY, BUT WITH IT GONE, HE WON'T NOTICE THE THEFT OF THE DATA.

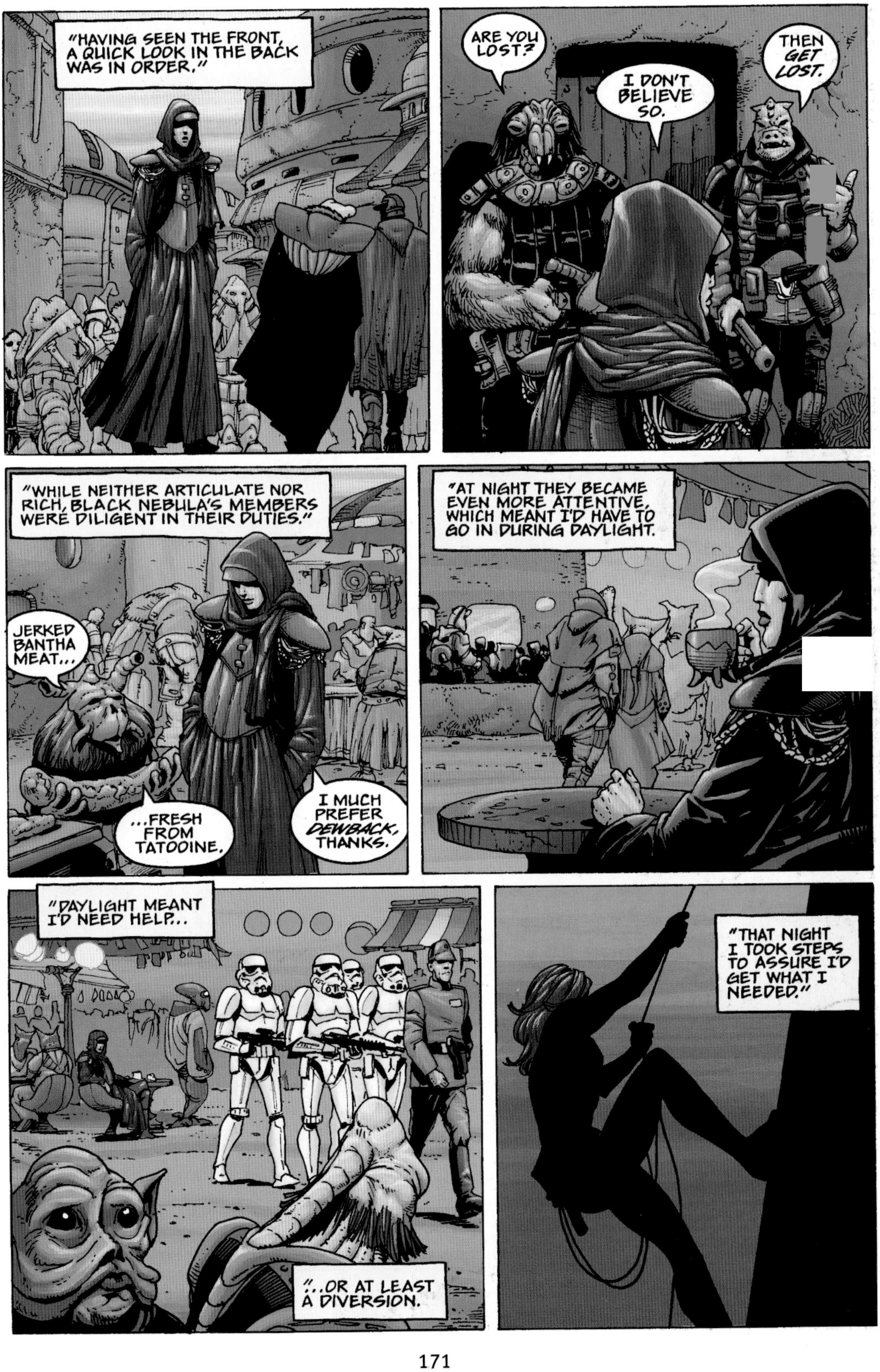
"HAVING SEEN THE FRONT, A QUICK LOOK IN THE BACK WAS IN ORDER."
ARE YOU LOST?
I DON'T BELIEVE SO.
THEN GET LOST.
"WHILE NEITHER ARTICULATE NOR RICH, BLACK NEBULA'S MEMBERS WERE DILIGENT IN THEIR DUTIES."
JERKED BANTHA MEAT...
...FRESH FROM TATOOINE.
I MUCH PREFER DEWBACK, THANKS.
"AT NIGHT THEY BECAME EVEN MORE ATTENTIVE, WHICH MEANT I'D HAVE TO GO IN DURING DAYLIGHT.
"DAYLIGHT MEANT I'D NEED HELP...
"...OR AT LEAST A DIVERSION.
"THAT NIGHT I TOOK STEPS TO ASSURE I'D GET WHAT I NEEDED."

GOOD MORNING. I'M HERE TO SEE GENERAL TOUNO.

YOU'RE NOT ON THE GENERAL'S SCHEDULE.

I KNOW. I'M GIVING YOU AN *AT3 DIRECTIVE.* I WANT TO SEE HIM.

NOW!

AT3 MEANS YOU RENDER ME ALL ASSISTANCE.

YOU CAN'T GO *IN* THERE.

SINCE I KNOW WHERE HE IS...

...YOU'VE DONE YOUR PART. *NEW ORDER.* SIT. SHUT UP. NOW.

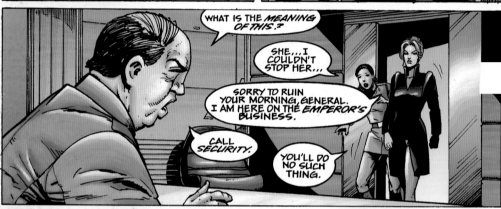

WHAT IS THE *MEANING OF THIS?*

SHE...I COULDN'T STOP HER...

SORRY TO RUIN YOUR MORNING, GENERAL. I AM HERE ON THE *EMPEROR'S BUSINESS.*

CALL SECURITY.

YOU'LL DO NO SUCH THING.

YOU DON'T GIVE THE ORDERS HERE.

AN AT3 DIRECTIVE INDICATES I *DO.* EVEN SOMEONE WHO RUNS AS SLOVENLY AN OUTFIT AS YOU HAVE HERE KNOWS WHAT THAT IS.

SLOVENLY? IF I HAD THE TROOPS THEY DO IN THE NORTH...

IF YOU WERE THE SORT OF LEADER THEY HAVE IN THE NORTH... ARE YOU READY TO AID ME?

YOU HAVE NO JURISDICTION OVER ME *OR* MY PEOPLE.

IN YOUR SAFE YOU HAVE A DATACARD SPELLING OUT YOUR DUTIES IN THIS SITUATION.

THERE IS NO SUCH THING IN MY SAFE.

NO.? CHECK.

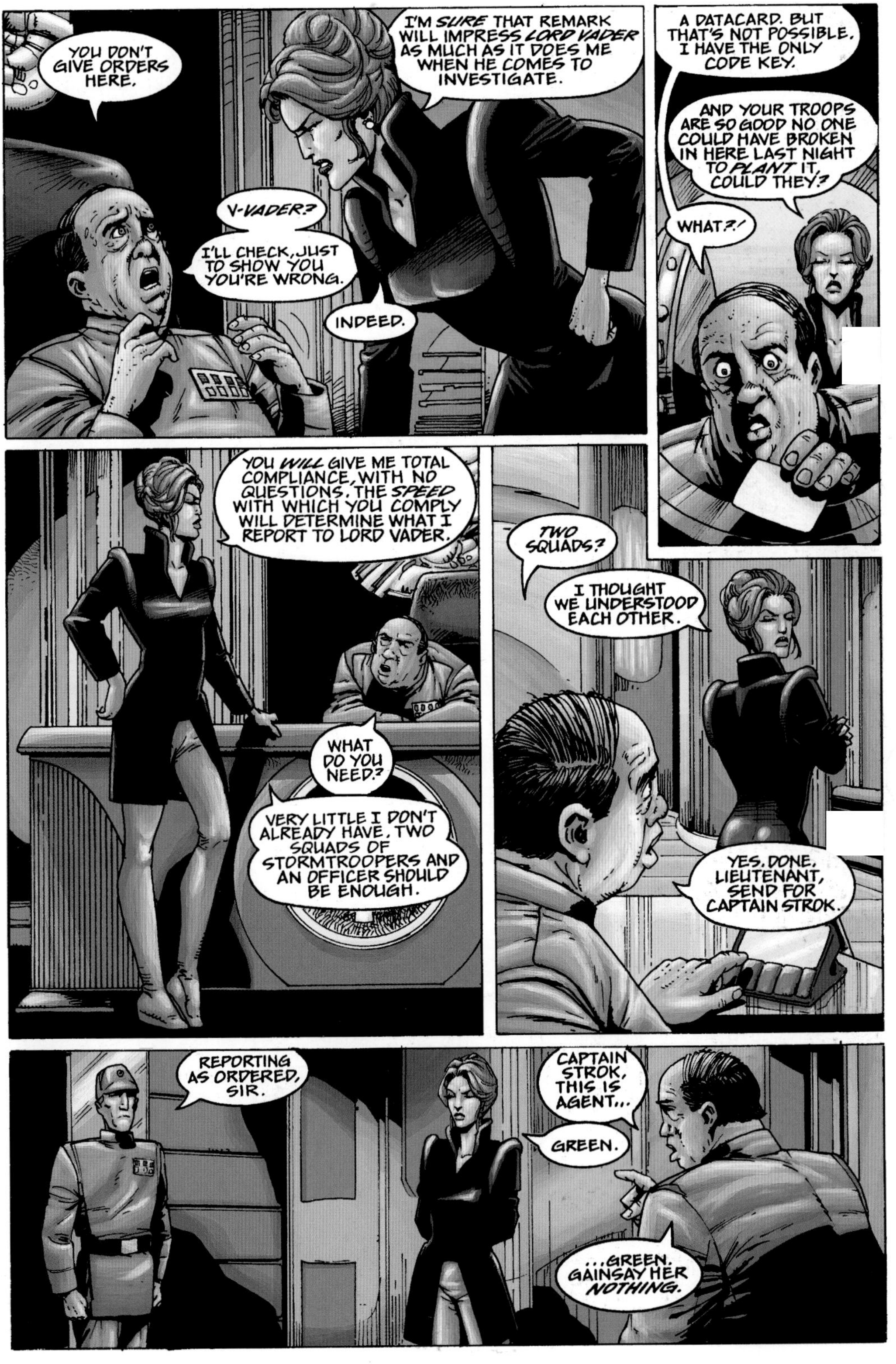
YOU DON'T GIVE ORDERS HERE.
I'M SURE THAT REMARK WILL IMPRESS LORD VADER AS MUCH AS IT DOES ME WHEN HE COMES TO INVESTIGATE.
V-VADER?
I'LL CHECK, JUST TO SHOW YOU YOU'RE WRONG.
INDEED.
A DATACARD. BUT THAT'S NOT POSSIBLE. I HAVE THE ONLY CODE KEY.
AND YOUR TROOPS ARE SO GOOD NO ONE COULD HAVE BROKEN IN HERE LAST NIGHT TO PLANT IT, COULD THEY?
WHAT?!
YOU WILL GIVE ME TOTAL COMPLIANCE, WITH NO QUESTIONS. THE SPEED WITH WHICH YOU COMPLY WILL DETERMINE WHAT I REPORT TO LORD VADER.
WHAT DO YOU NEED?
VERY LITTLE I DON'T ALREADY HAVE. TWO SQUADS OF STORMTROOPERS AND AN OFFICER SHOULD BE ENOUGH.
TWO SQUADS?
I THOUGHT WE UNDERSTOOD EACH OTHER.
YES. DONE. LIEUTENANT, SEND FOR CAPTAIN STROK.
REPORTING AS ORDERED, SIR.
CAPTAIN STROK, THIS IS AGENT...
GREEN.
...GREEN. GAINSAY HER NOTHING.

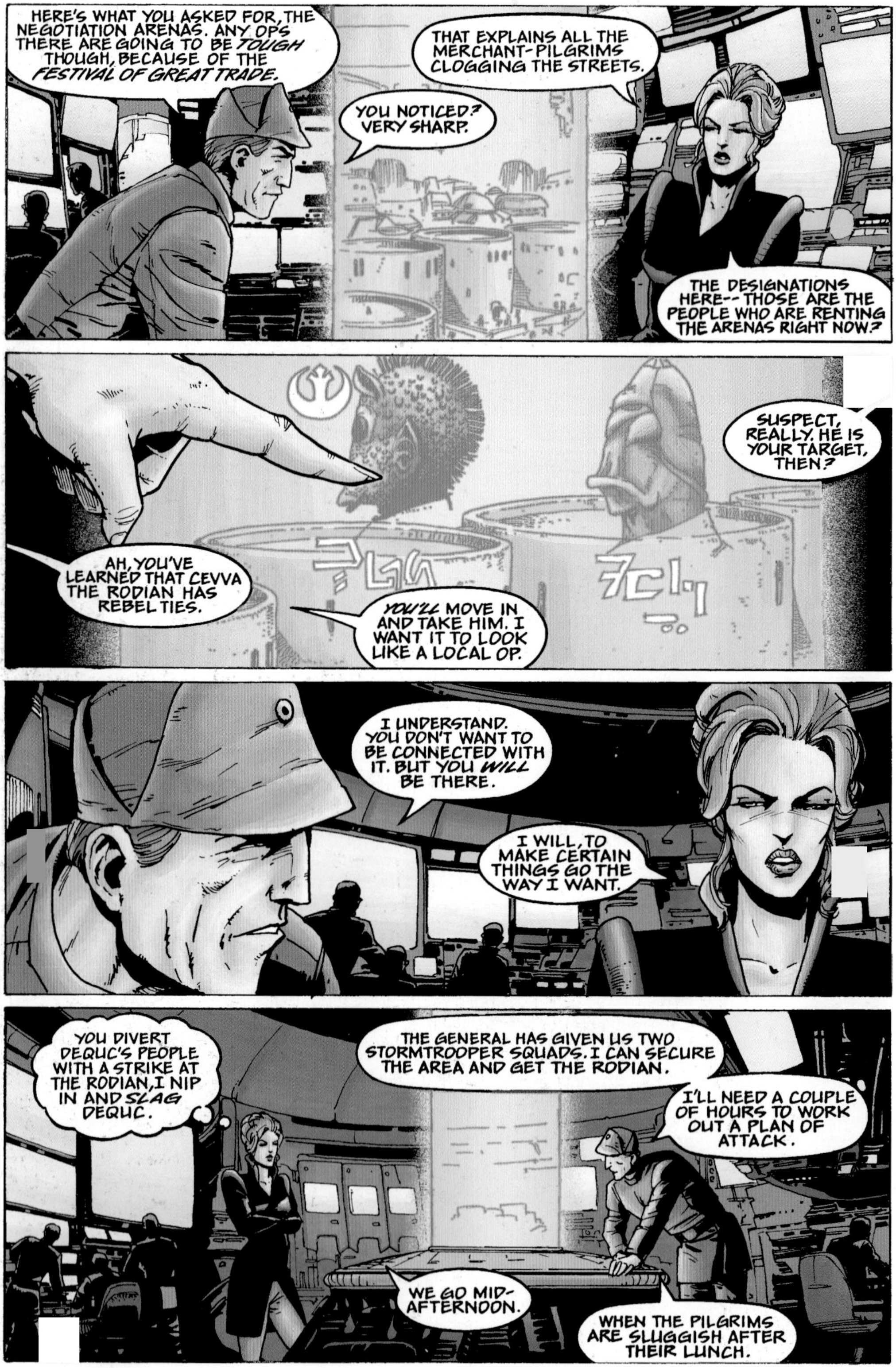
HERE'S WHAT YOU ASKED FOR, THE NEGOTIATION ARENAS. ANY OPS THERE ARE GOING TO BE *TOUGH* THOUGH, BECAUSE OF THE *FESTIVAL OF GREAT TRADE.*
THAT EXPLAINS ALL THE MERCHANT-PILGRIMS CLOGGING THE STREETS.
YOU NOTICED? VERY SHARP.
THE DESIGNATIONS HERE-- THOSE ARE THE PEOPLE WHO ARE RENTING THE ARENAS RIGHT NOW?
AH, YOU'VE LEARNED THAT CEVVA THE RODIAN HAS REBEL TIES.
SUSPECT, REALLY. HE IS YOUR TARGET, THEN?
YOU'LL MOVE IN AND TAKE HIM. I WANT IT TO LOOK LIKE A LOCAL OP.
I UNDERSTAND. YOU DON'T WANT TO BE CONNECTED WITH IT. BUT YOU *WILL* BE THERE.
I WILL, TO MAKE CERTAIN THINGS GO THE WAY I WANT.
YOU DIVERT DEQUC'S PEOPLE WITH A STRIKE AT THE RODIAN, I NIP IN AND *SLAG* DEQUC.
THE GENERAL HAS GIVEN US TWO STORMTROOPER SQUADS. I CAN SECURE THE AREA AND GET THE RODIAN.
I'LL NEED A COUPLE OF HOURS TO WORK OUT A PLAN OF ATTACK.
WE GO MID-AFTERNOON.
WHEN THE PILGRIMS ARE SLUGGISH AFTER THEIR LUNCH.

YOU DISAGREE?

NO, NOT AT ALL. NICE TO HEAR *PLANNING* FOR ONCE.

AS YOU'VE NOTICED, TOUNO ISN'T AN *ELITE LEADER*, AND DISCIPLINE AND MORALE *REFLECT* THAT HERE.

YOU'VE BEEN HERE WHAT, TWO DAYS, AND *ALREADY* KNOW MORE ABOUT THE INDIG CUSTOMS THAN TOUNO *EVER* WILL.

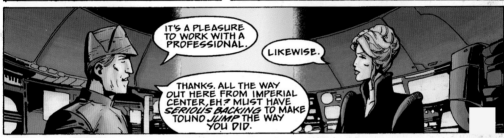

IT'S A PLEASURE TO WORK WITH A PROFESSIONAL.

LIKEWISE.

THANKS. ALL THE WAY OUT HERE FROM IMPERIAL CENTER, EH? MUST HAVE *SERIOUS BACKING* TO MAKE TOUNO *JUMP* THE WAY YOU DID.

SOMETHING LIKE THAT.

AND A WOMAN. YOU MUST BE GOOD AT WHAT YOU DO.

THERE'S NO *GOOD SPOT* TO SET UP A HEAVY-WEAPONS TEAM WITH THE *CROWDED COURTYARD* IN THE MIDDLE THERE.

TOUNO WOULD HAVE MISSED THAT, TOO. BLASTER CARBINES MOSTLY, I GUESS.

YOUR *PREVIOUS* EXPERIENCE POINTED THE PROBLEM OUT TO YOU, YES?

I HOPE YOU'RE BETTER AT ASSAULT PLANNING THAN YOU ARE AT *INTERROGATING* ME.

I, AH... WHAT? NO, YOU MISUNDERSTAND.

I UNDERSTAND.

TWO HOURS PAST NOON, AT THE ARENAS. I'LL SEE YOU THEN, CAPTAIN STROK.

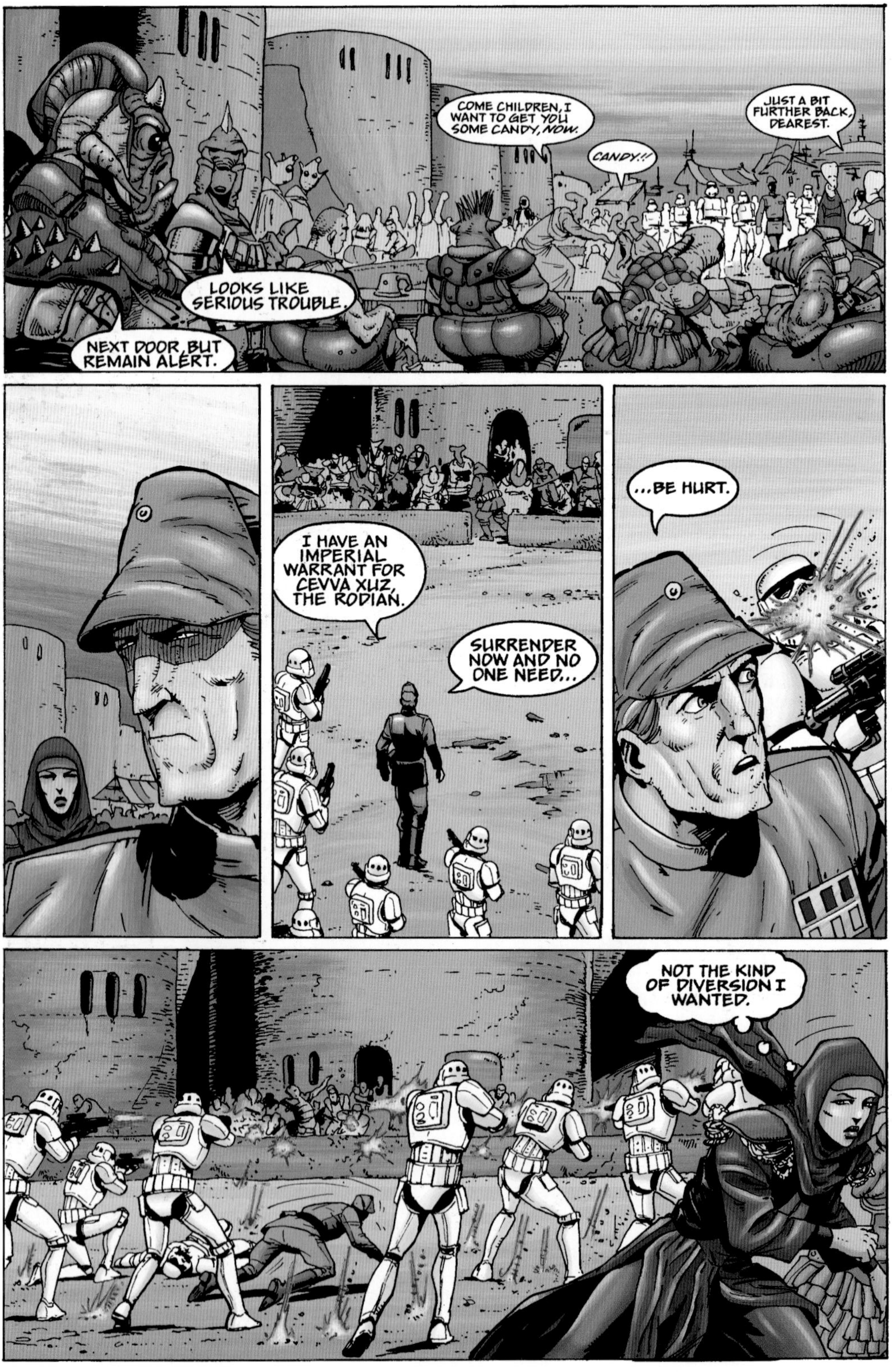
COME CHILDREN, I WANT TO GET YOU SOME CANDY, NOW.
CANDY!!
JUST A BIT FURTHER BACK, DEAREST.
LOOKS LIKE SERIOUS TROUBLE.
NEXT DOOR, BUT REMAIN ALERT.
I HAVE AN IMPERIAL WARRANT FOR CEVVA XUZ, THE RODIAN.
SURRENDER NOW AND NO ONE NEED...
...BE HURT.
NOT THE KIND OF DIVERSION I WANTED.

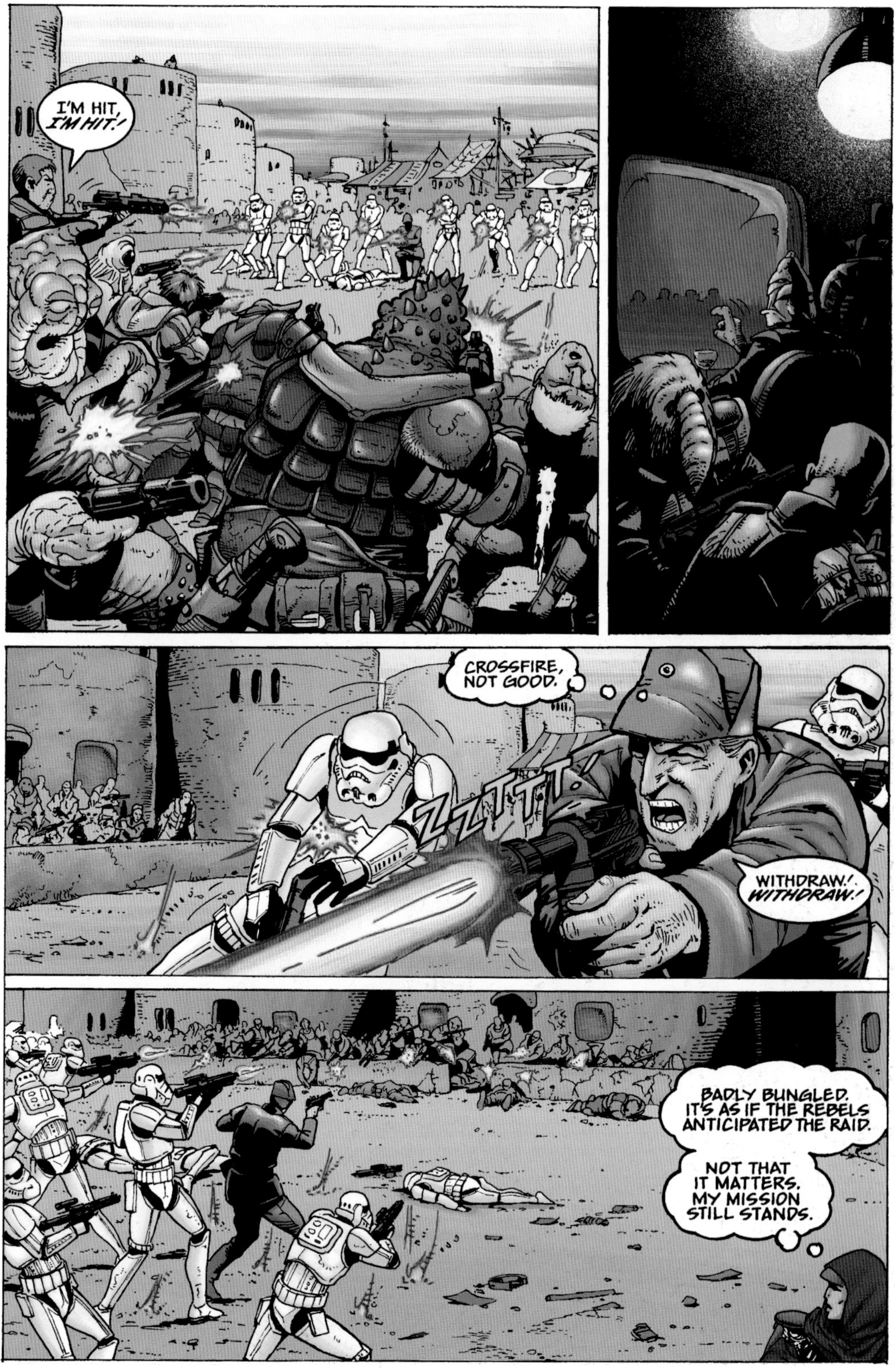
I'M HIT, I'M HIT!
CROSSFIRE, NOT GOOD.
ZZTTT!
WITHDRAW! WITHDRAW!
BADLY BUNGLED. IT'S AS IF THE REBELS ANTICIPATED THE RAID.
NOT THAT IT MATTERS. MY MISSION STILL STANDS.

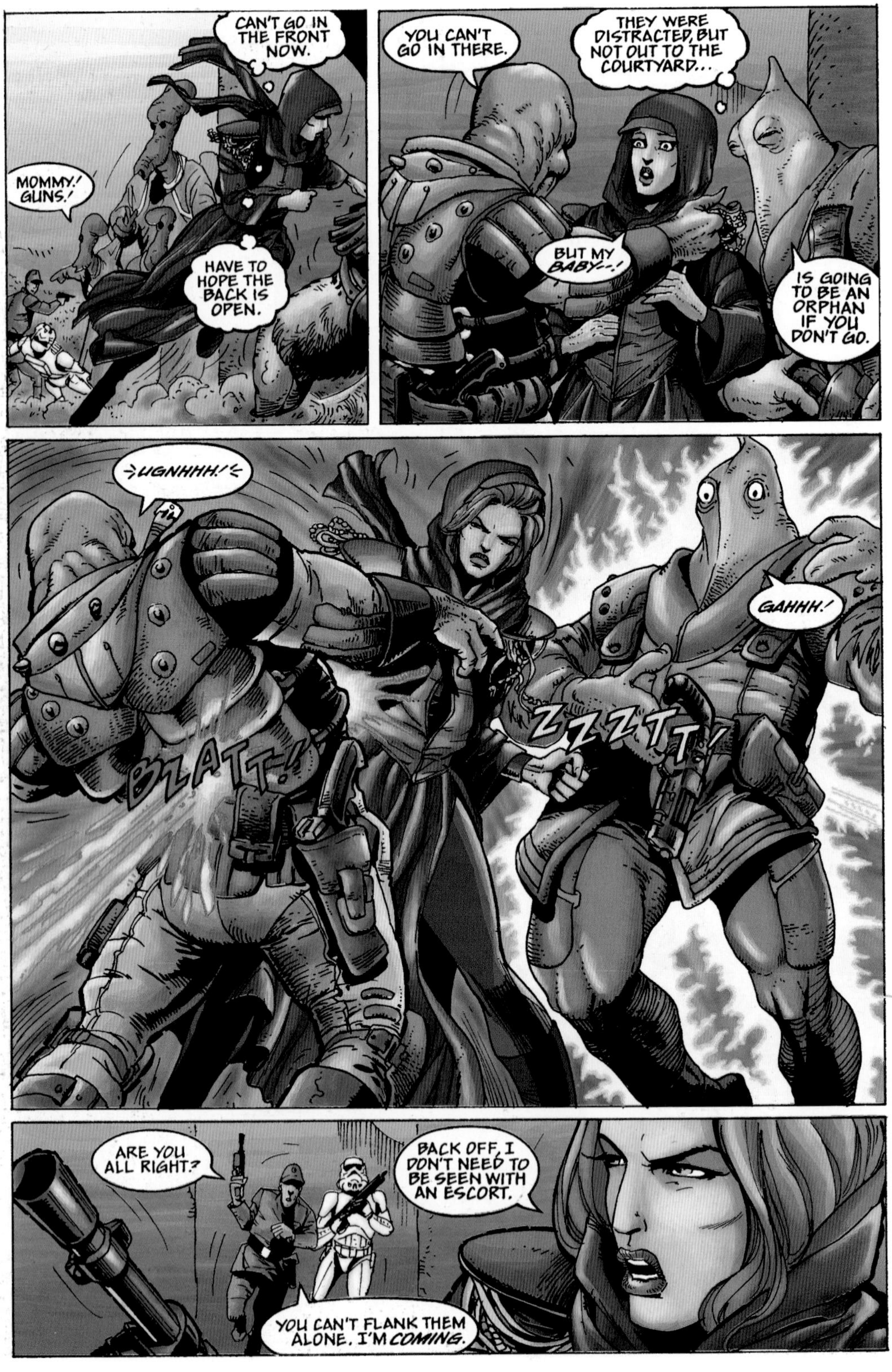
CAN'T GO IN THE FRONT NOW.
MOMMY! GUNS!
HAVE TO HOPE THE BACK IS OPEN.
YOU CAN'T GO IN THERE.
THEY WERE DISTRACTED, BUT NOT OUT TO THE COURTYARD...
BUT MY BABY--!
IS GOING TO BE AN ORPHAN IF YOU DON'T GO.
UGNHHH!
GAHHH!
BZATT!
ZZZTTT!
ARE YOU ALL RIGHT?
BACK OFF, I DON'T NEED TO BE SEEN WITH AN ESCORT.
YOU CAN'T FLANK THEM ALONE. I'M COMING.

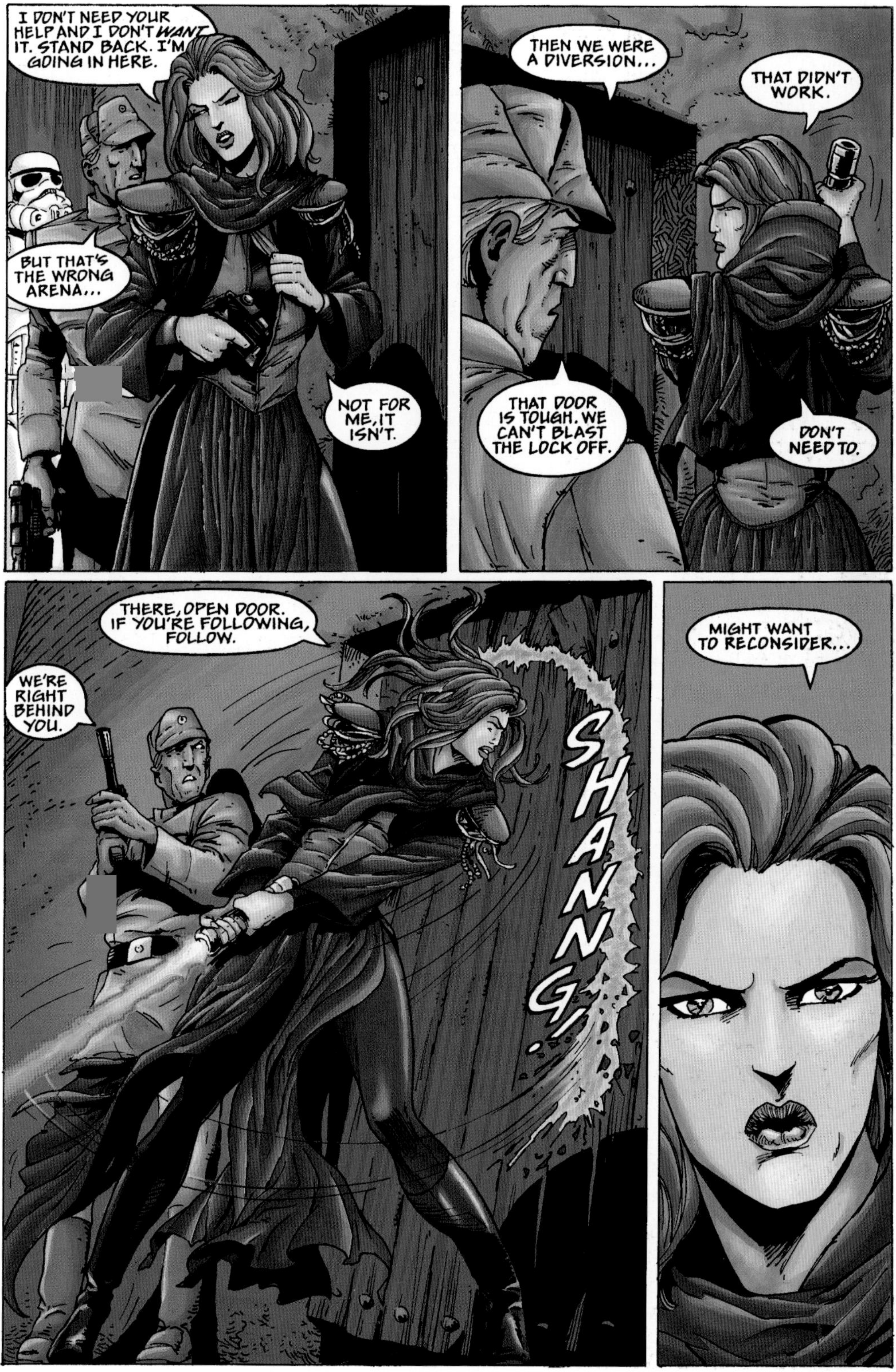
I DON'T NEED YOUR HELP AND I DON'T WANT IT. STAND BACK. I'M GOING IN HERE.
BUT THAT'S THE WRONG ARENA...
NOT FOR ME, IT ISN'T.
THEN WE WERE A DIVERSION...
THAT DIDN'T WORK.
THAT DOOR IS TOUGH. WE CAN'T BLAST THE LOCK OFF.
DON'T NEED TO.
THERE, OPEN DOOR. IF YOU'RE FOLLOWING, FOLLOW.
WE'RE RIGHT BEHIND YOU.
SHANNG!
MIGHT WANT TO RECONSIDER...

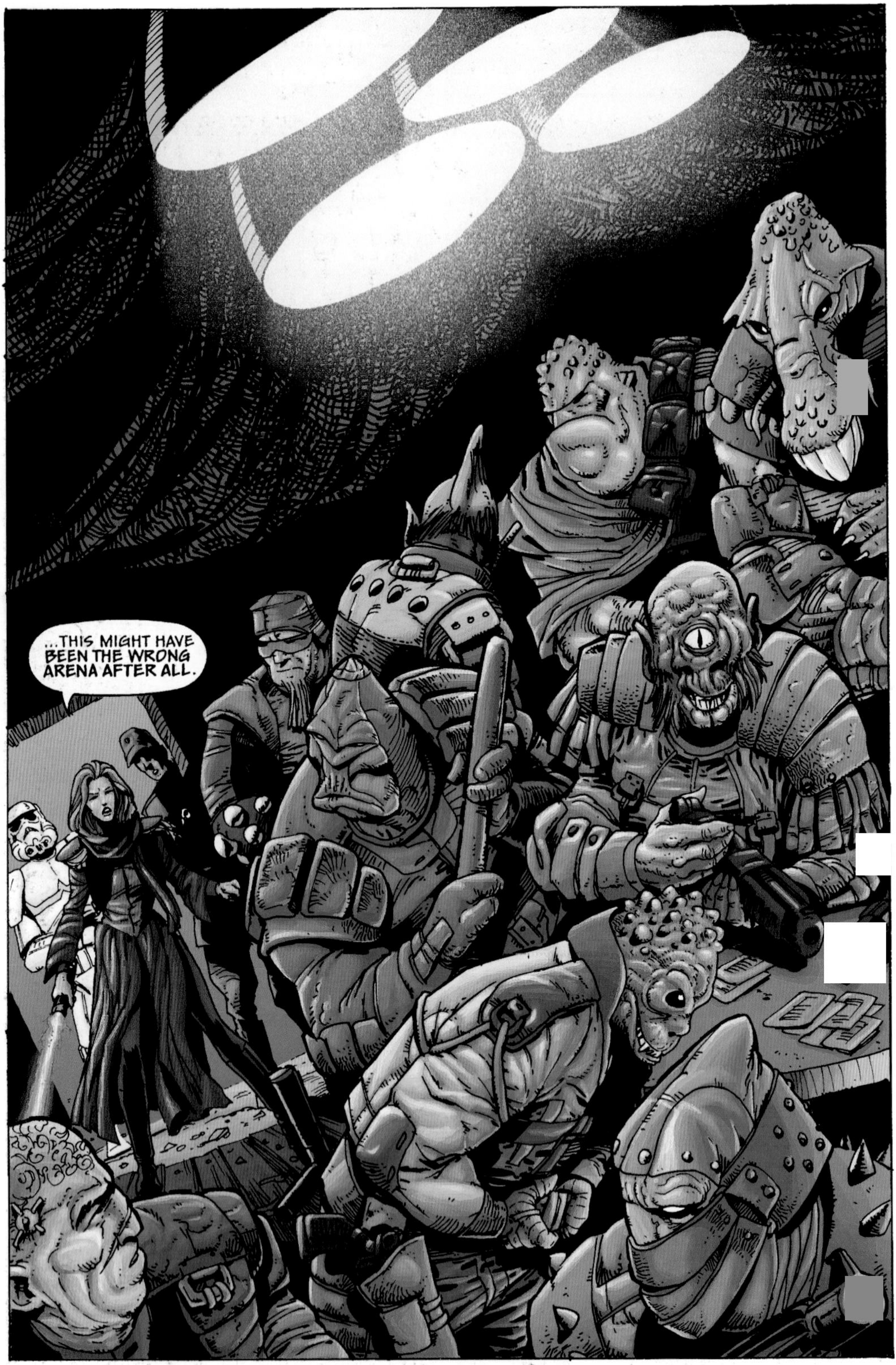
...THIS MIGHT HAVE BEEN THE WRONG ARENA AFTER ALL.

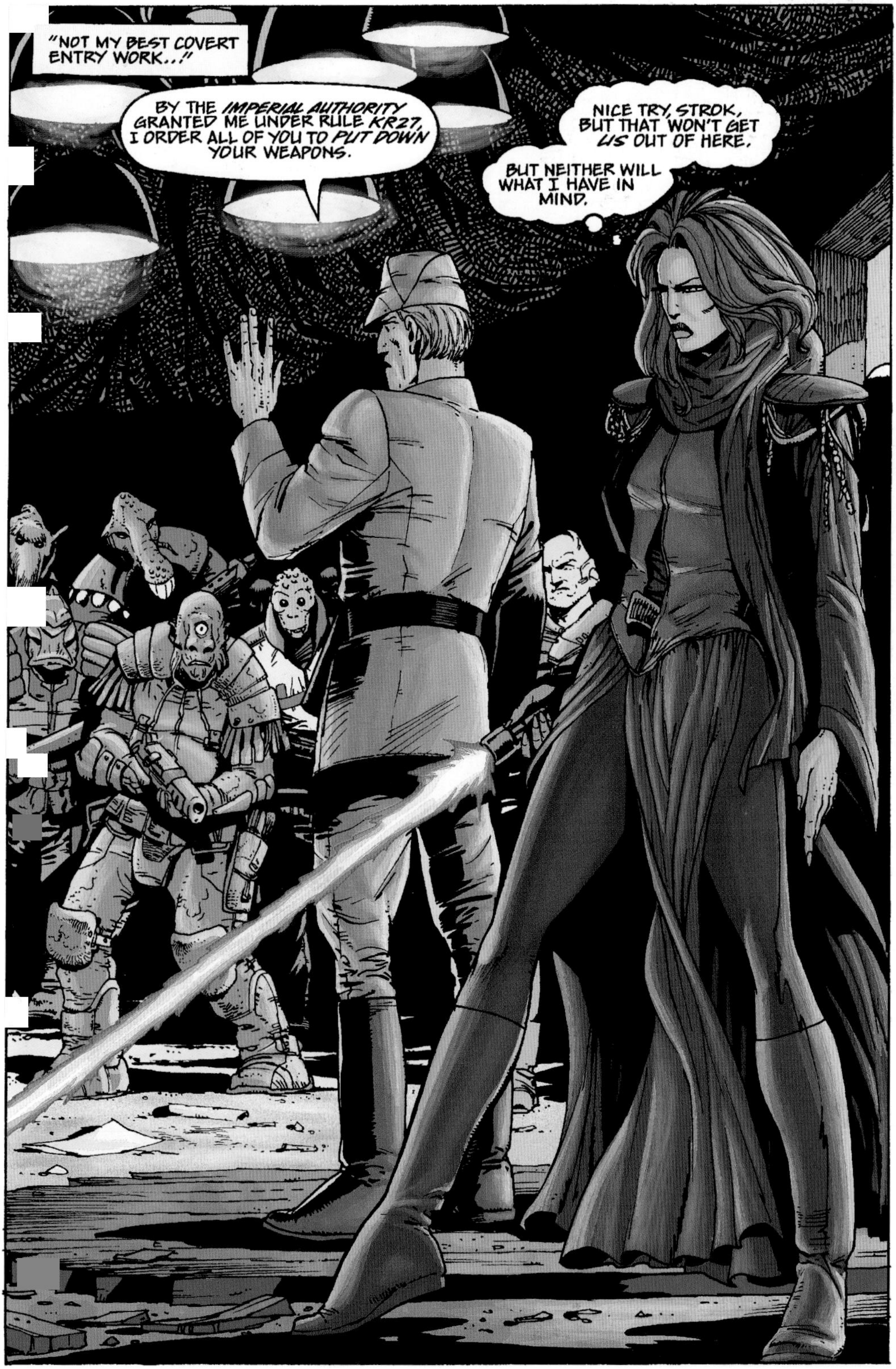
"NOT MY BEST COVERT ENTRY WORK..."
BY THE IMPERIAL AUTHORITY GRANTED ME UNDER RULE KR27, I ORDER ALL OF YOU TO PUT DOWN YOUR WEAPONS.
NICE TRY, STROK, BUT THAT WON'T GET US OUT OF HERE.
BUT NEITHER WILL WHAT I HAVE IN MIND.

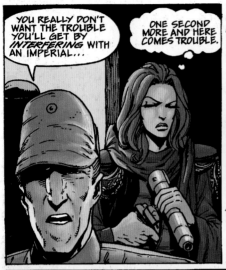

YOU REALLY DON'T WANT THE TROUBLE YOU'LL GET BY *INTERFERING* WITH AN IMPERIAL...

ONE SECOND MORE AND HERE COMES TROUBLE.

...OFFICER IN PURSUIT OF HIS

--WHAT?

YOU HAVE YOUR DUTY, I HAVE MINE.

SPRAO!

A PUSH FROM THE *FORCE* TO GET ME UP HERE...

SPRAO! VI'IP!

DISTRIBUTE MY WEIGHT AND THIS MESH WILL HOLD.

TSING! VI'IP! VI'IP!

WRONG PLACE, WRONG TIME FOR *YOU.*

≥OOOF!≤

THUMP

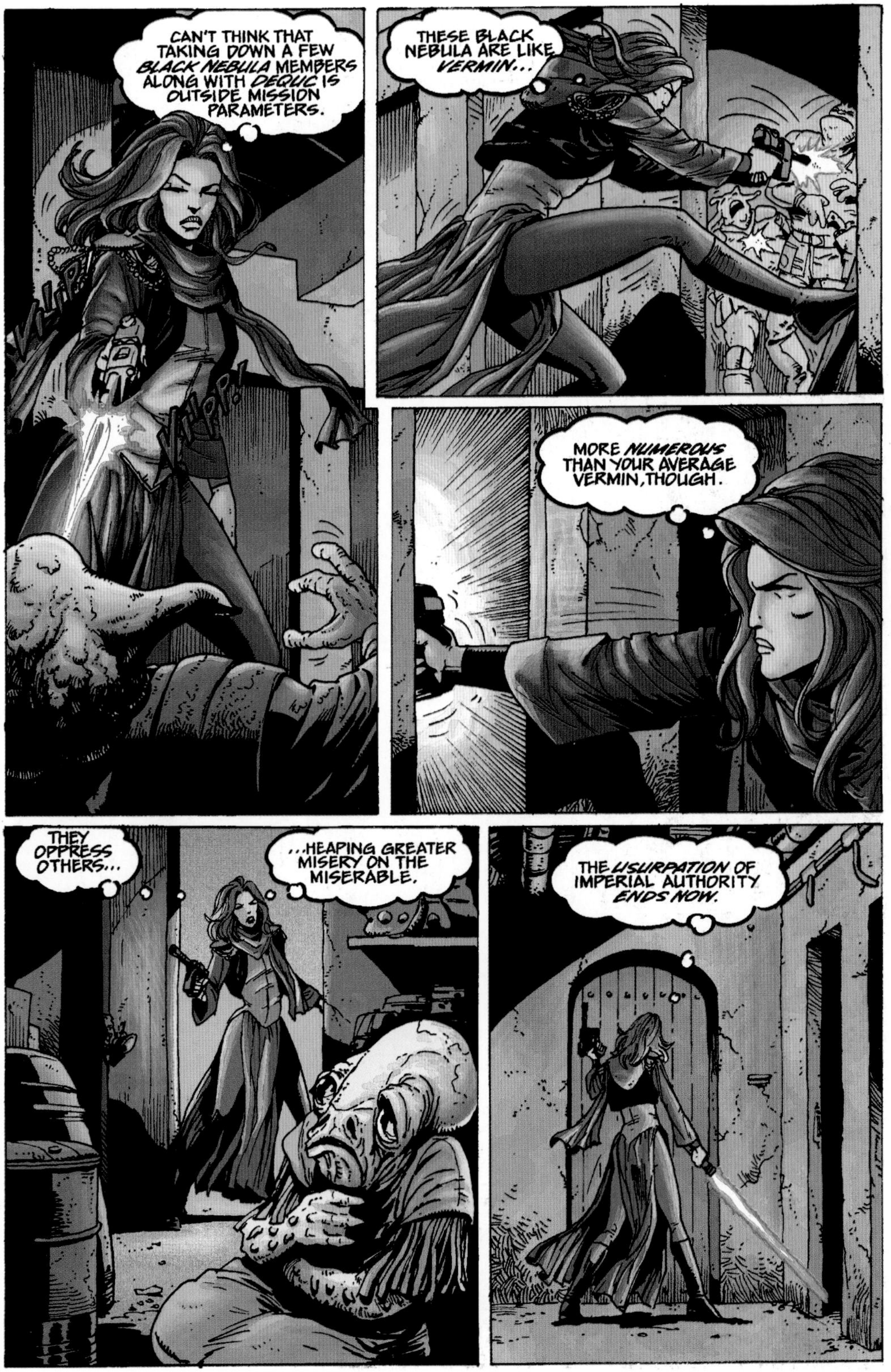
CAN'T THINK THAT TAKING DOWN A FEW BLACK NEBULA MEMBERS ALONG WITH DEQUC IS OUTSIDE MISSION PARAMETERS.
THESE BLACK NEBULA ARE LIKE VERMIN...
MORE NUMEROUS THAN YOUR AVERAGE VERMIN, THOUGH.
THEY OPPRESS OTHERS...
...HEAPING GREATER MISERY ON THE MISERABLE.
THE USURPATION OF IMPERIAL AUTHORITY ENDS NOW.

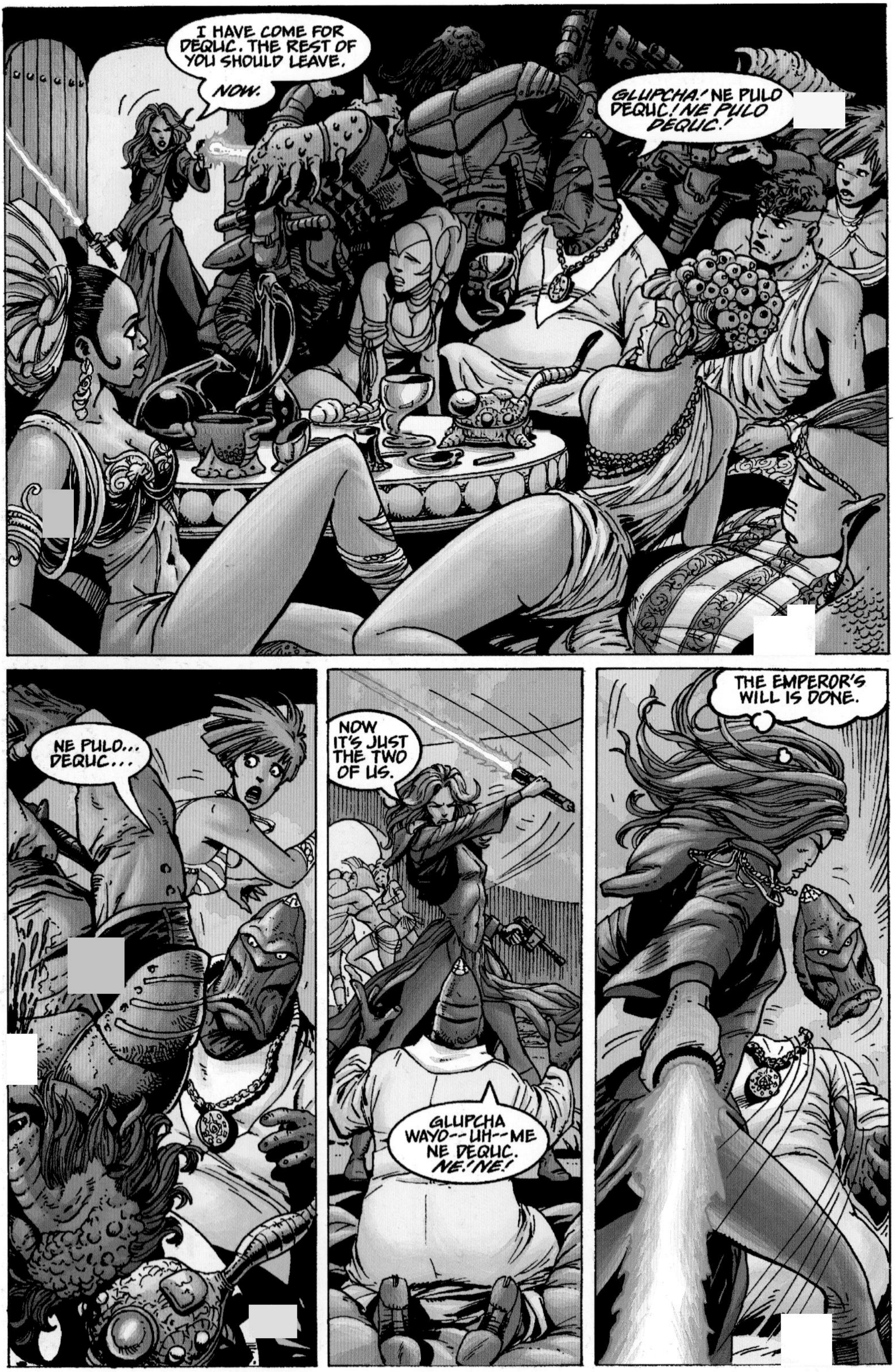
I HAVE COME FOR DEQUC. THE REST OF YOU SHOULD LEAVE.
NOW.
GLUPCHA! NE PULO DEQUC! NE PULO DEQUC!
NE PULO... DEQUC...
NOW IT'S JUST THE TWO OF US.
GLUPCHA WAYO--UH--ME NE DEQUC. NE! NE!
THE EMPEROR'S WILL IS DONE.

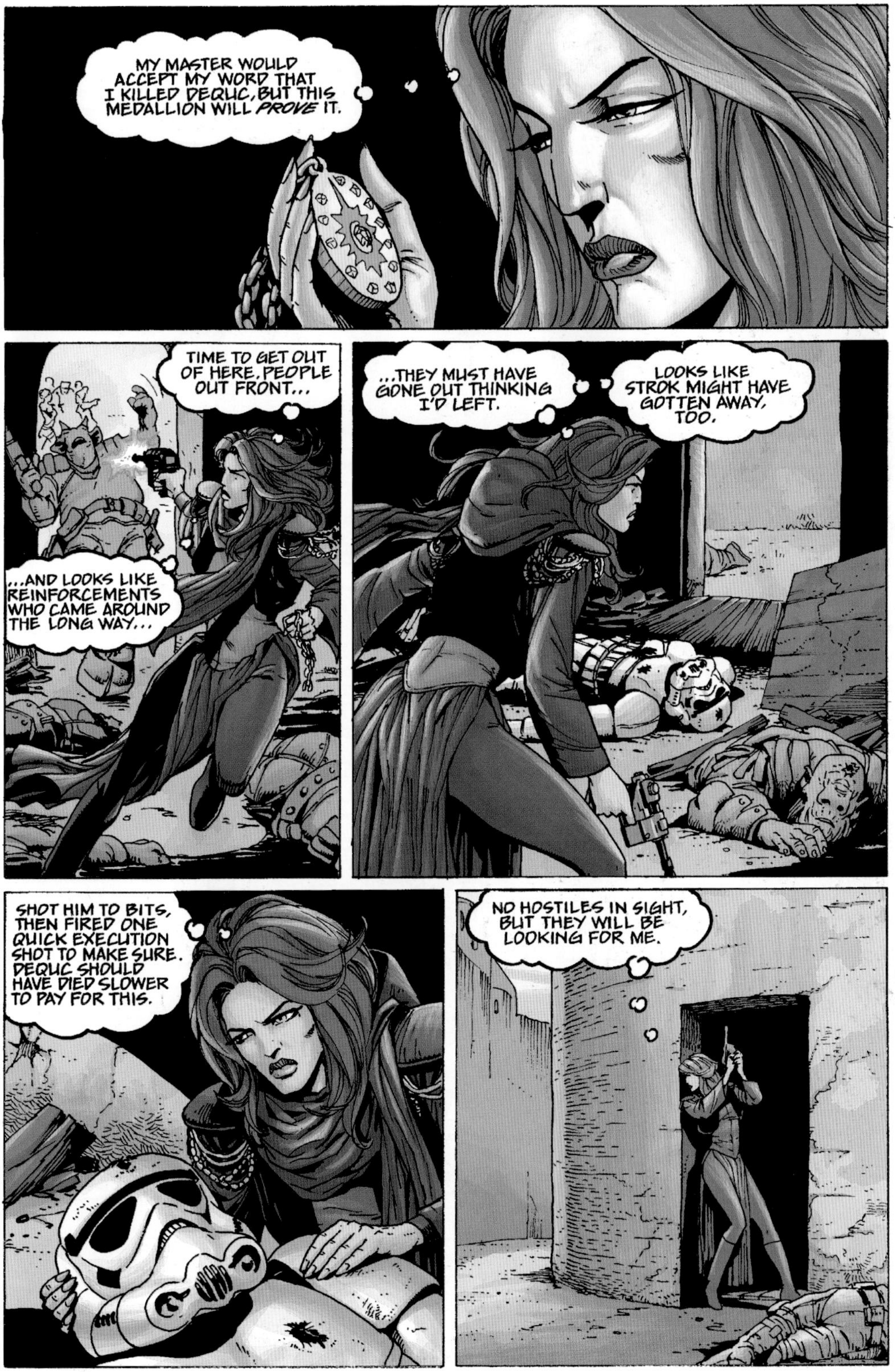
MY MASTER WOULD ACCEPT MY WORD THAT I KILLED DEQUC, BUT THIS MEDALLION WILL *PROVE* IT.
TIME TO GET OUT OF HERE, PEOPLE OUT FRONT...
...AND LOOKS LIKE REINFORCEMENTS WHO CAME AROUND THE LONG WAY...
...THEY MUST HAVE GONE OUT THINKING I'D LEFT.
LOOKS LIKE STROK MIGHT HAVE GOTTEN AWAY, TOO.
SHOT HIM TO BITS, THEN FIRED ONE QUICK EXECUTION SHOT TO MAKE SURE. DEQUC SHOULD HAVE DIED SLOWER TO PAY FOR THIS.
NO HOSTILES IN SIGHT, BUT THEY WILL BE LOOKING FOR ME.

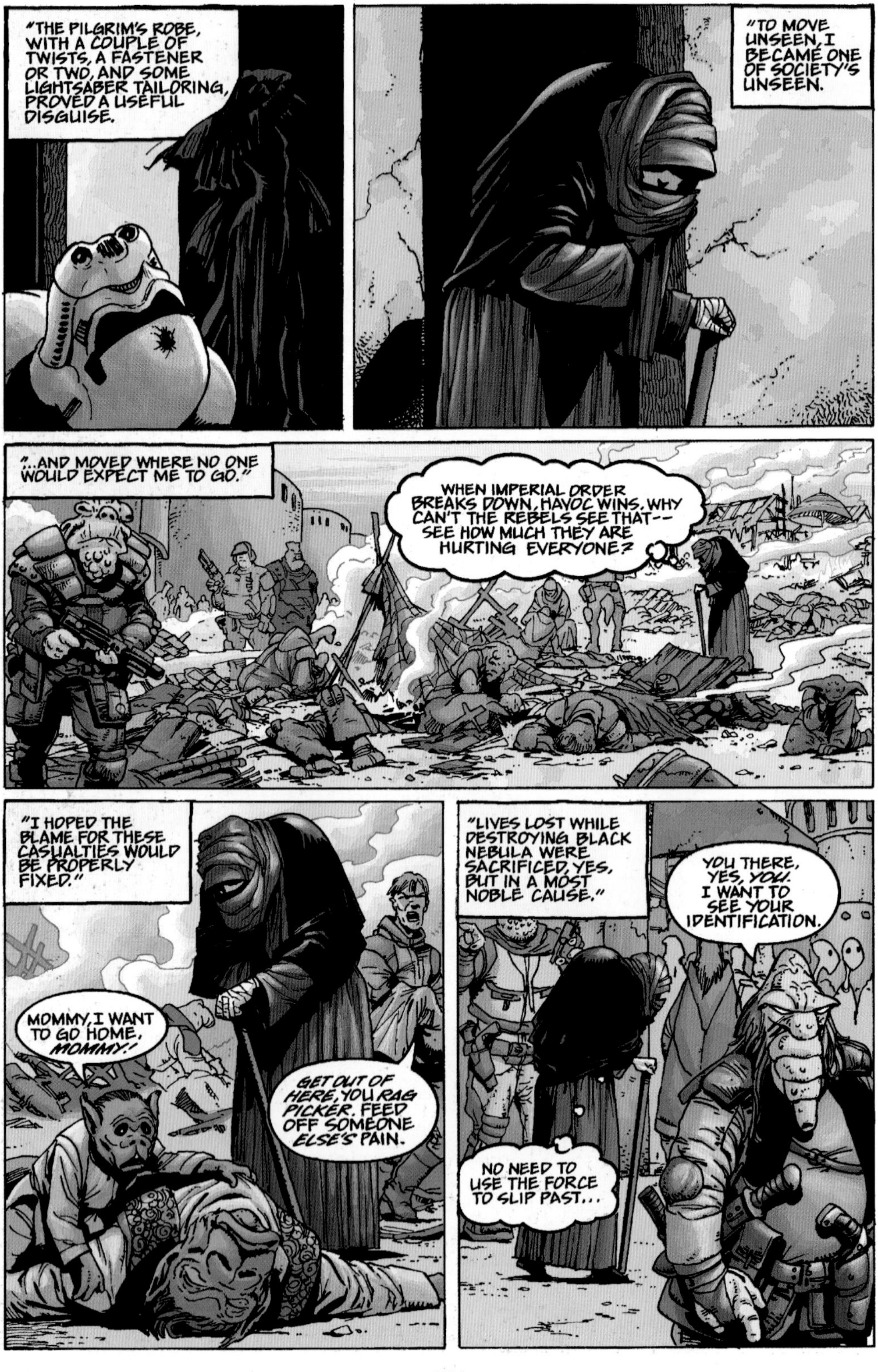

"THE PILGRIM'S ROBE, WITH A COUPLE OF TWISTS, A FASTENER OR TWO, AND SOME LIGHTSABER TAILORING, PROVED A USEFUL DISGUISE.
"TO MOVE UNSEEN, I BECAME ONE OF SOCIETY'S UNSEEN.
"...AND MOVED WHERE NO ONE WOULD EXPECT ME TO GO."
WHEN IMPERIAL ORDER BREAKS DOWN, HAVOC WINS. WHY CAN'T THE REBELS SEE THAT-- SEE HOW MUCH THEY ARE HURTING EVERYONE?
"I HOPED THE BLAME FOR THESE CASUALTIES WOULD BE PROPERLY FIXED."
MOMMY, I WANT TO GO HOME, *MOMMY!*
GET OUT OF HERE, YOU *RAG PICKER.* FEED OFF SOMEONE *ELSE'S* PAIN.
"LIVES LOST WHILE DESTROYING BLACK NEBULA WERE SACRIFICED, YES, BUT IN A MOST NOBLE CAUSE."
YOU THERE, YES, *YOU.* I WANT TO SEE YOUR IDENTIFICATION.
NO NEED TO USE THE FORCE TO SLIP PAST...

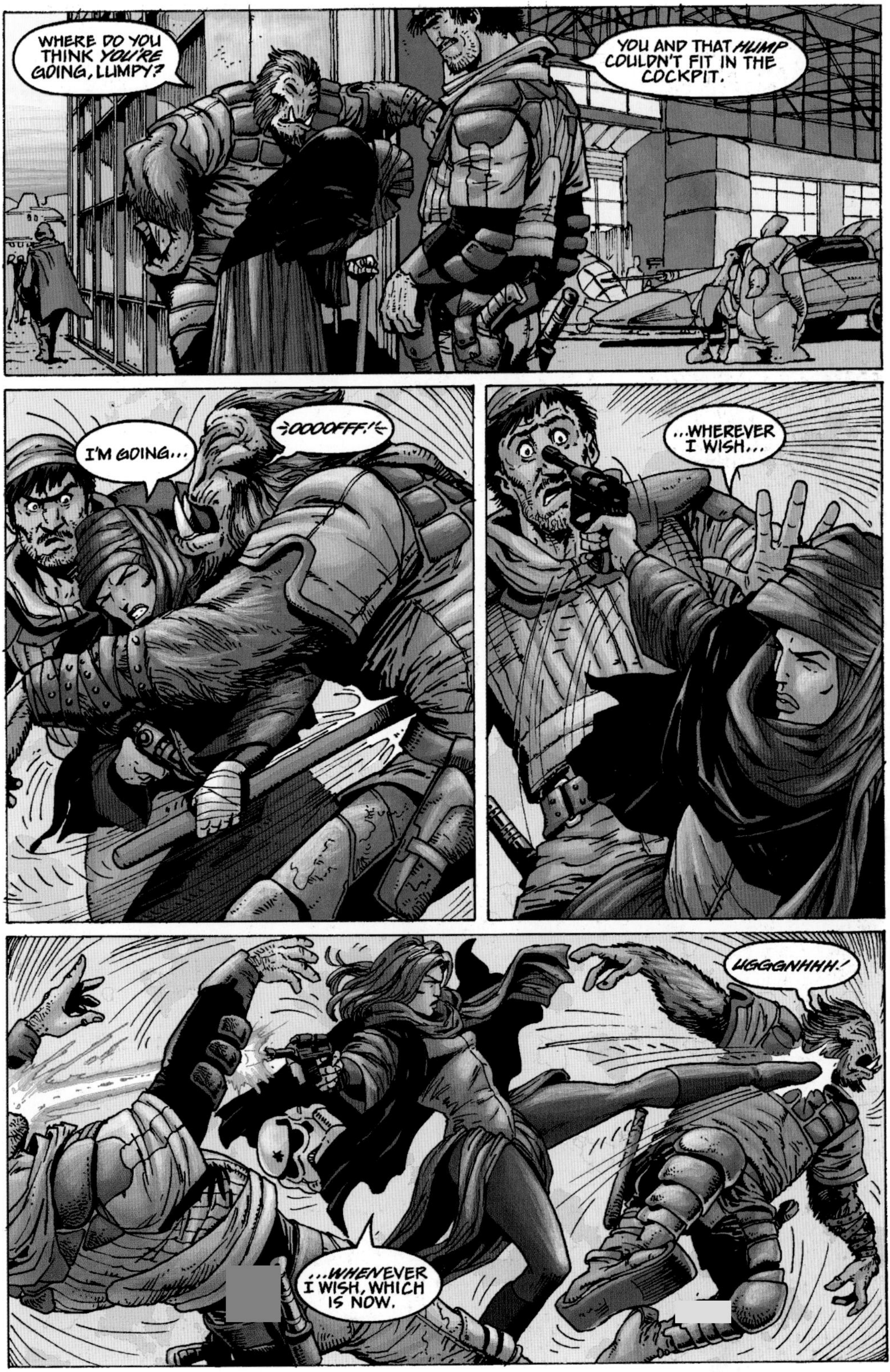
WHERE DO YOU THINK YOU'RE GOING, LUMPY?
YOU AND THAT HUMP COULDN'T FIT IN THE COCKPIT.
I'M GOING...
OOOOFFF!
...WHEREVER I WISH...
UGGGNHHH!
...WHENEVER I WISH, WHICH IS NOW.

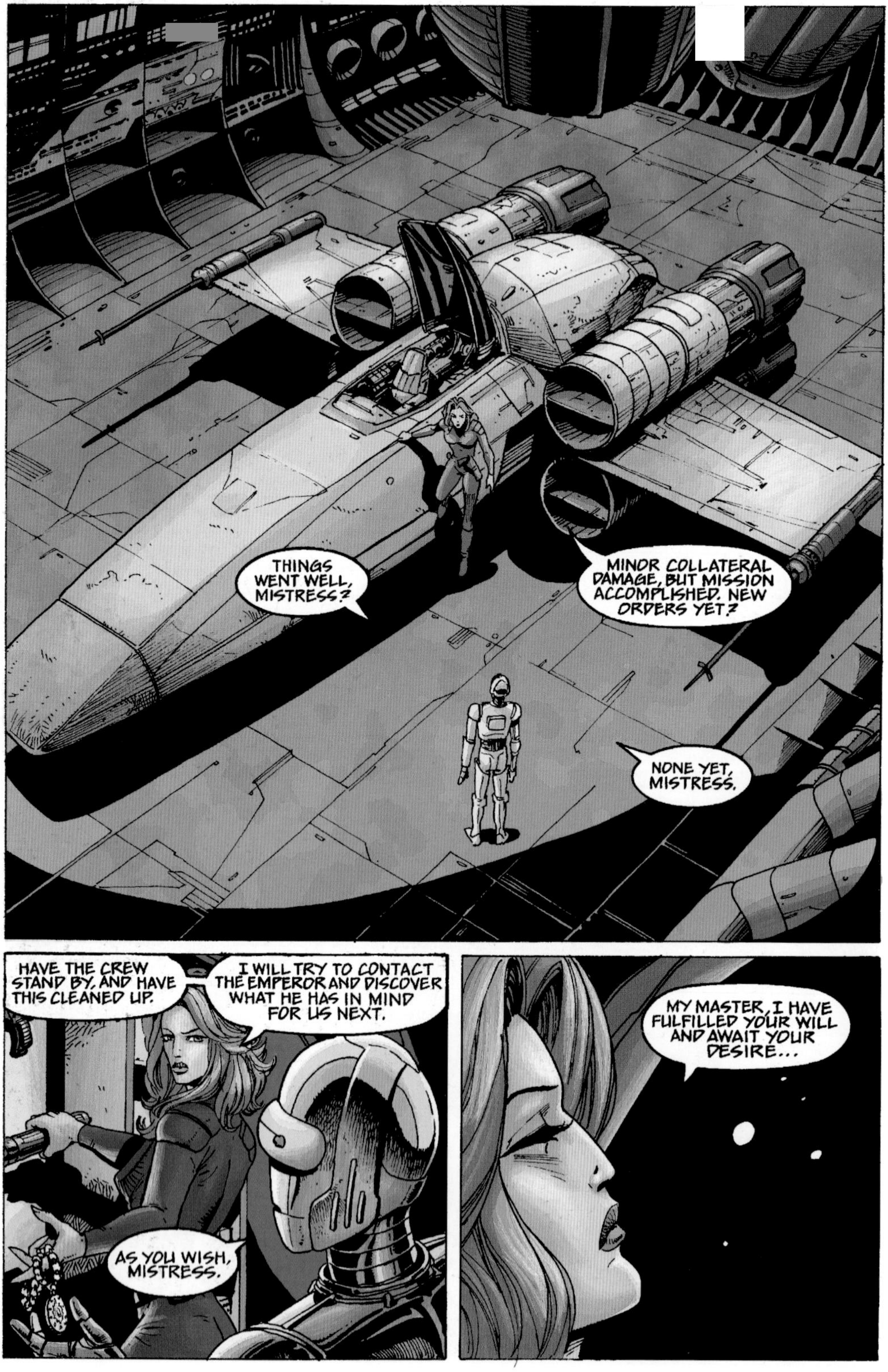
THINGS WENT WELL, MISTRESS?
MINOR COLLATERAL DAMAGE, BUT MISSION ACCOMPLISHED. NEW ORDERS YET?
NONE YET, MISTRESS.
HAVE THE CREW STAND BY, AND HAVE THIS CLEANED UP.
I WILL TRY TO CONTACT THE EMPEROR AND DISCOVER WHAT HE HAS IN MIND FOR US NEXT.
AS YOU WISH, MISTRESS.
MY MASTER, I HAVE FULFILLED YOUR WILL AND AWAIT YOUR DESIRE...

THE JEODU DEQUC IS DEAD? SO QUICKLY?

THE OPPORTUNITY PRESENTED ITSELF, EXALTED ONE.

AND YOU, *MY HAND* SNATCHED AWAY HIS LIFE.

SPLENDID.

IF YOU WISH, I COULD CONTINUE MY HUNT FOR SKYWALKER AND DESTROY HIM.

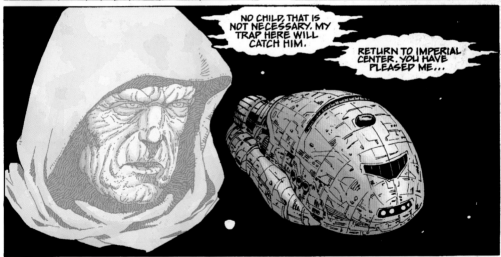

NO CHILD, THAT IS NOT NECESSARY. MY TRAP HERE WILL CATCH HIM.

RETURN TO IMPERIAL CENTER. YOU HAVE PLEASED ME...

...NOW I WOULD REWARD YOU BY REQUIRING YOU TO ENJOY YOURSELF...

ENJOY MYSELF?

AS MY MASTER WISHES...

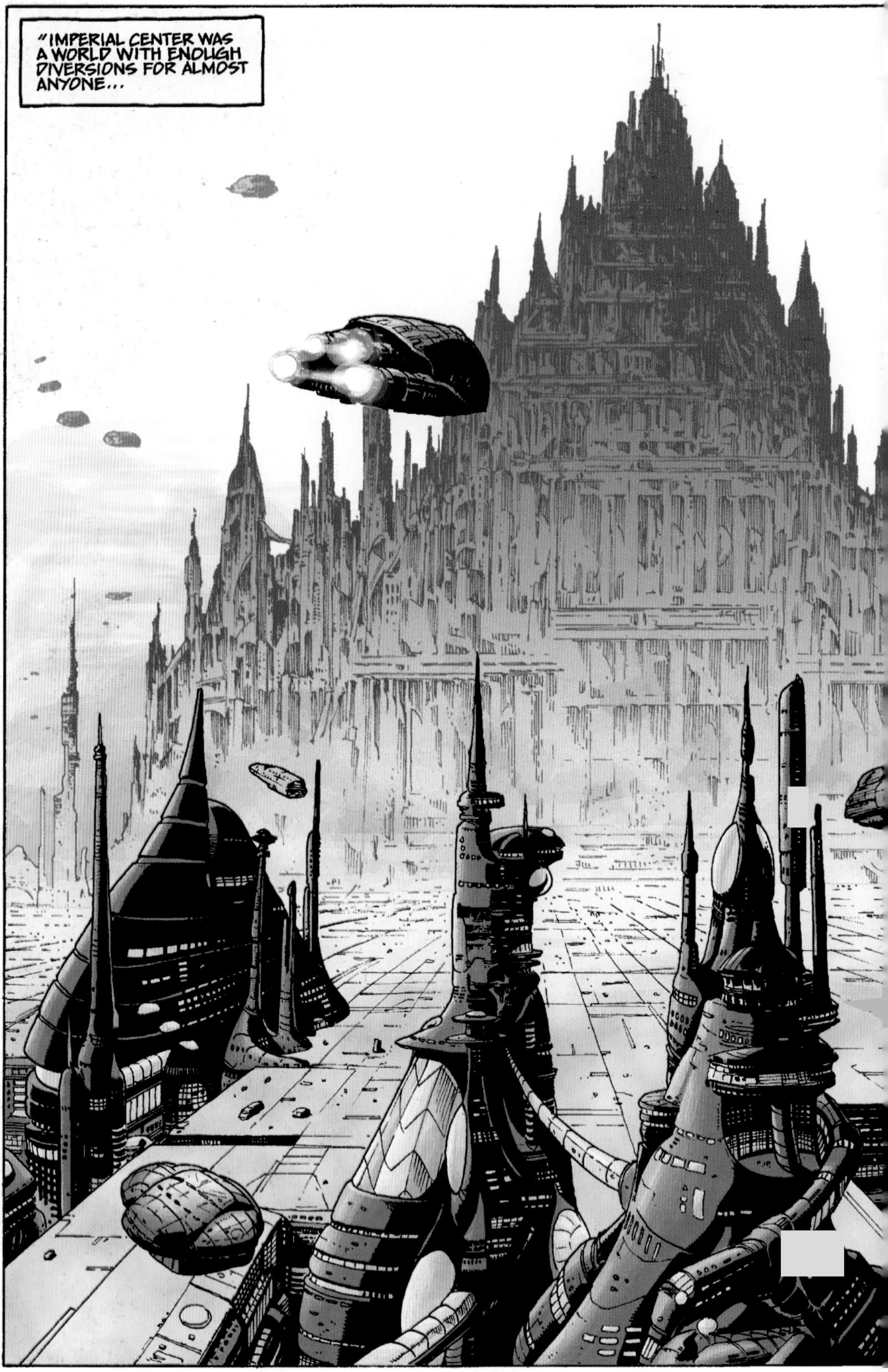
"IMPERIAL CENTER WAS A WORLD WITH ENOUGH DIVERSIONS FOR ALMOST ANYONE...

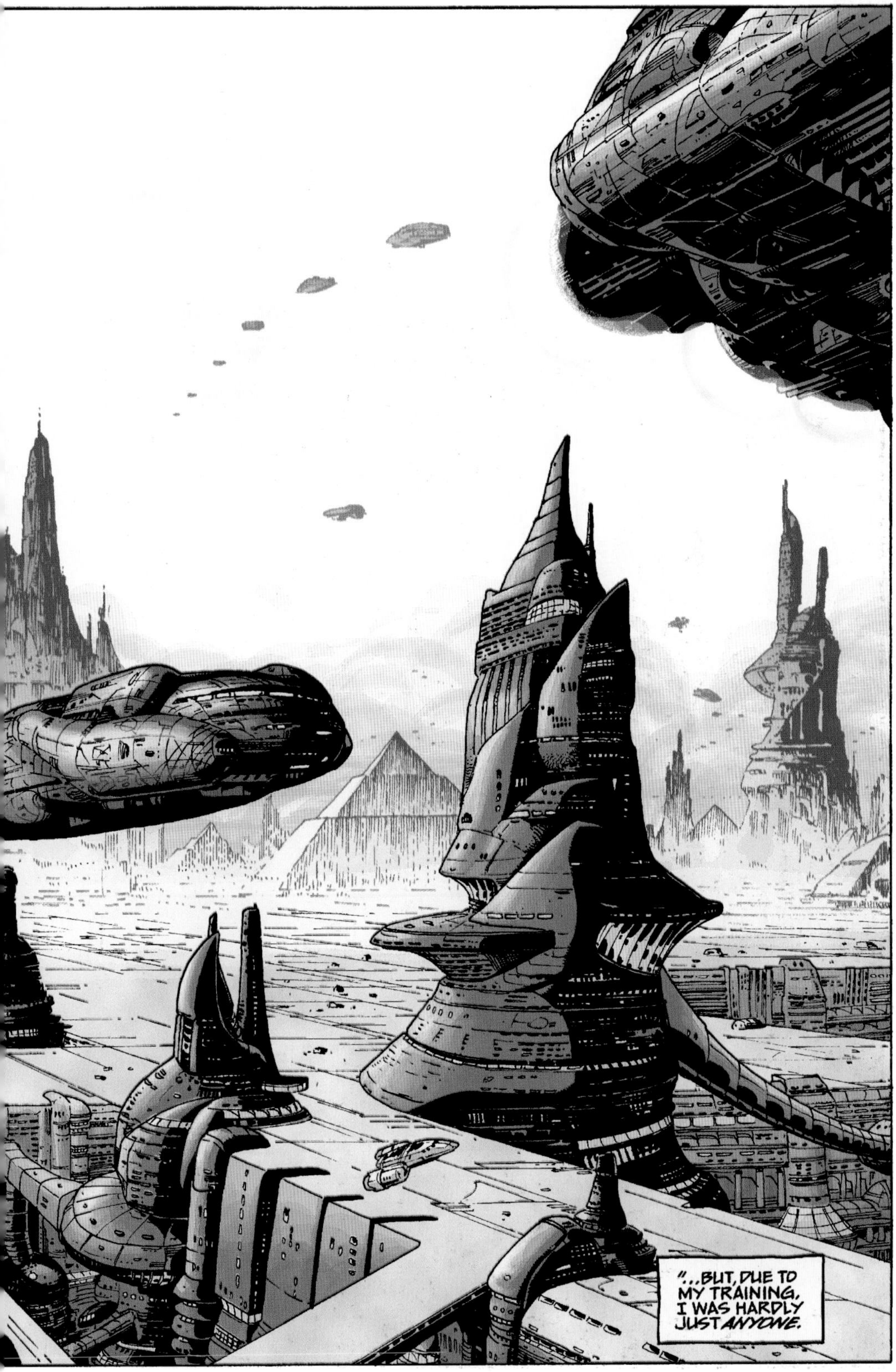
"...BUT, DUE TO MY TRAINING, I WAS HARDLY JUST ANYONE.

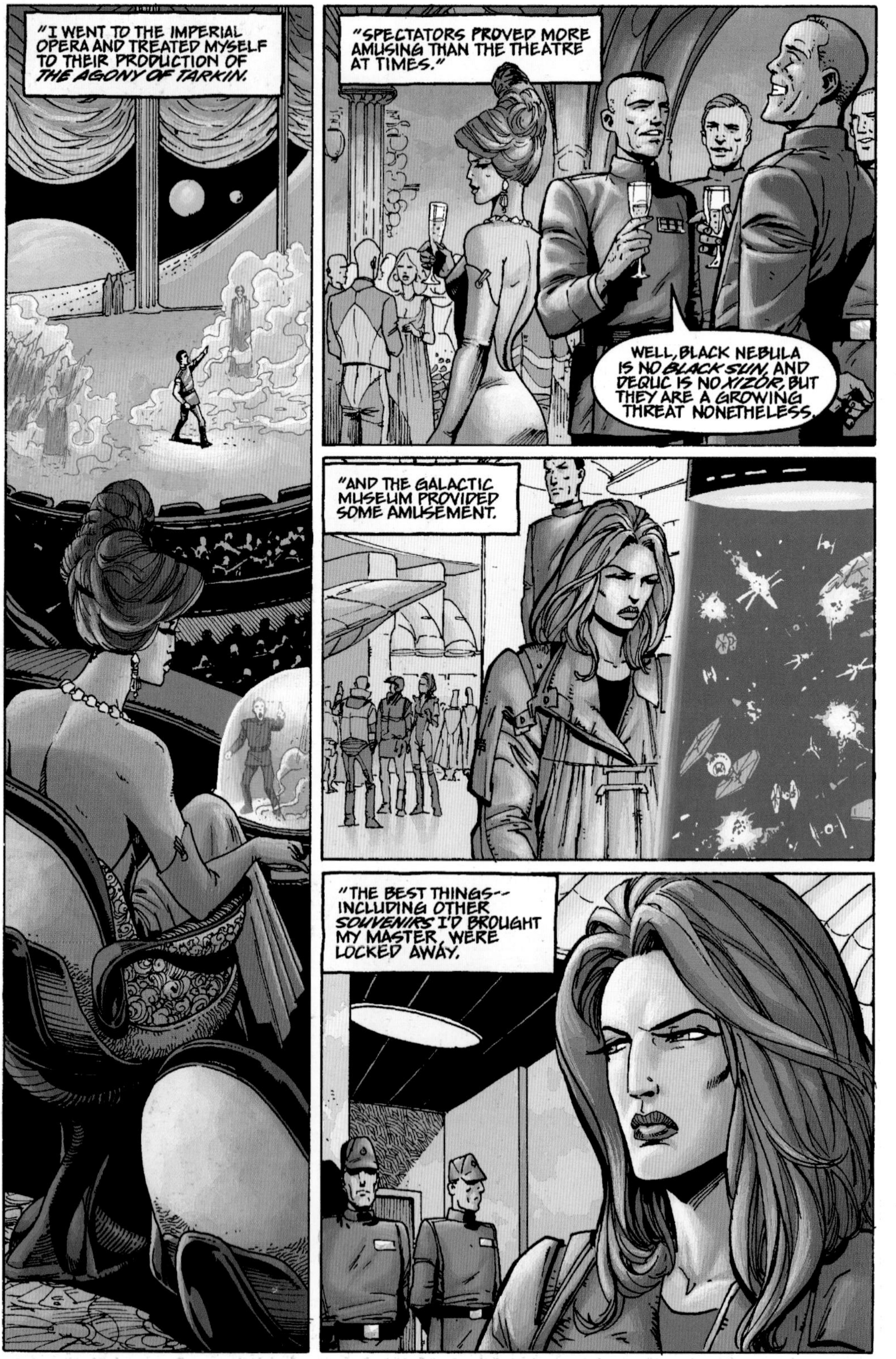
"I WENT TO THE IMPERIAL OPERA AND TREATED MYSELF TO THEIR PRODUCTION OF *THE AGONY OF TARKIN*.
"SPECTATORS PROVED MORE AMUSING THAN THE THEATRE AT TIMES."
WELL, BLACK NEBULA IS NO *BLACK SUN*, AND DEQUC IS NO *XIZOR*, BUT THEY ARE A GROWING THREAT NONETHELESS.
"AND THE GALACTIC MUSEUM PROVIDED SOME AMUSEMENT.
"THE BEST THINGS-- INCLUDING OTHER *SOUVENIRS* I'D BROUGHT MY MASTER, WERE LOCKED AWAY.

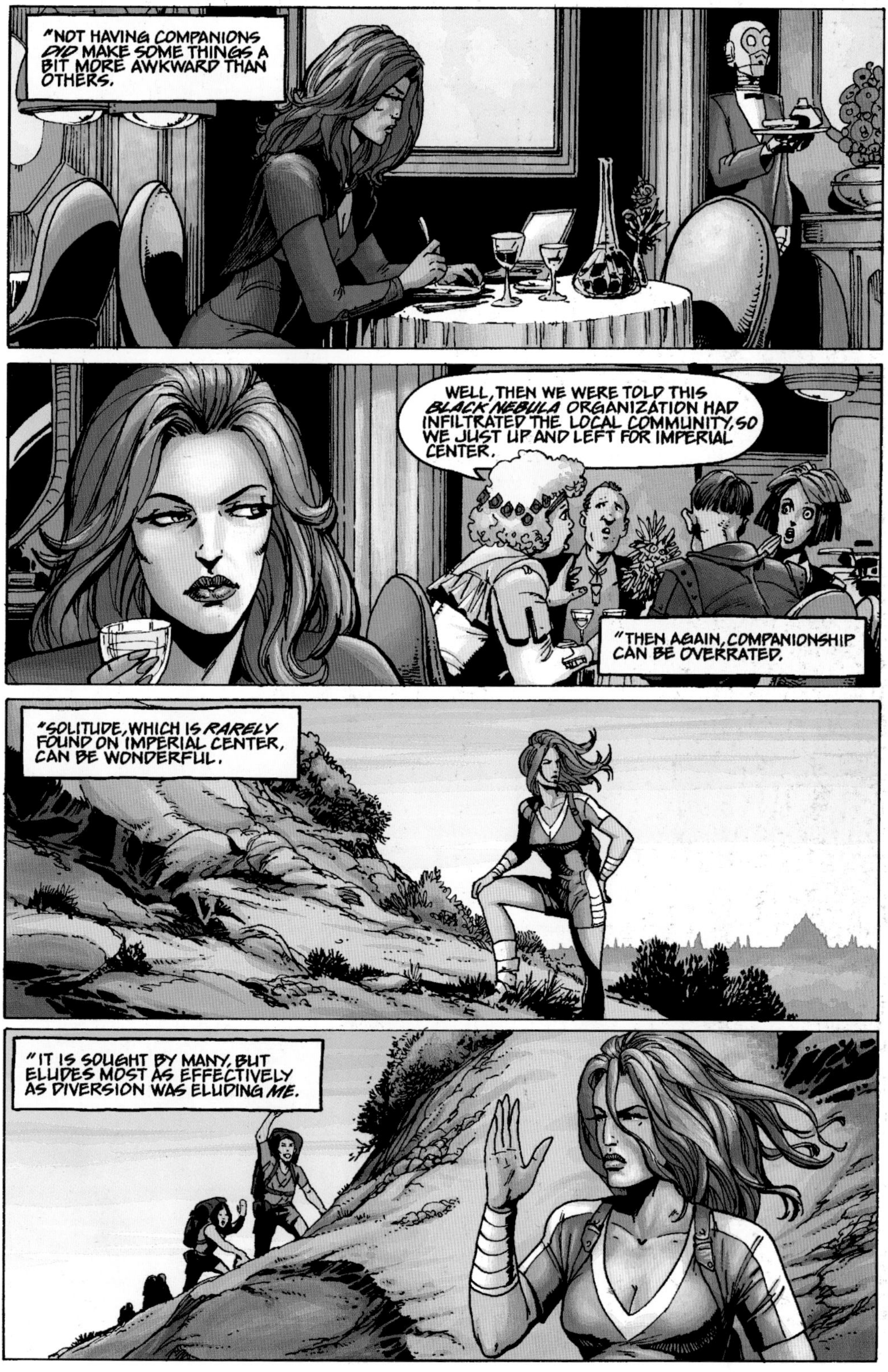
"NOT HAVING COMPANIONS *DID* MAKE SOME THINGS A BIT MORE AWKWARD THAN OTHERS.
WELL, THEN WE WERE TOLD THIS *BLACK NEBULA* ORGANIZATION HAD INFILTRATED THE LOCAL COMMUNITY, SO WE JUST UP AND LEFT FOR IMPERIAL CENTER.
"THEN AGAIN, COMPANIONSHIP CAN BE OVERRATED.
"SOLITUDE, WHICH IS *RARELY* FOUND ON IMPERIAL CENTER, CAN BE WONDERFUL.
"IT IS SOUGHT BY MANY, BUT ELUDES MOST AS EFFECTIVELY AS DIVERSION WAS ELUDING *ME*.

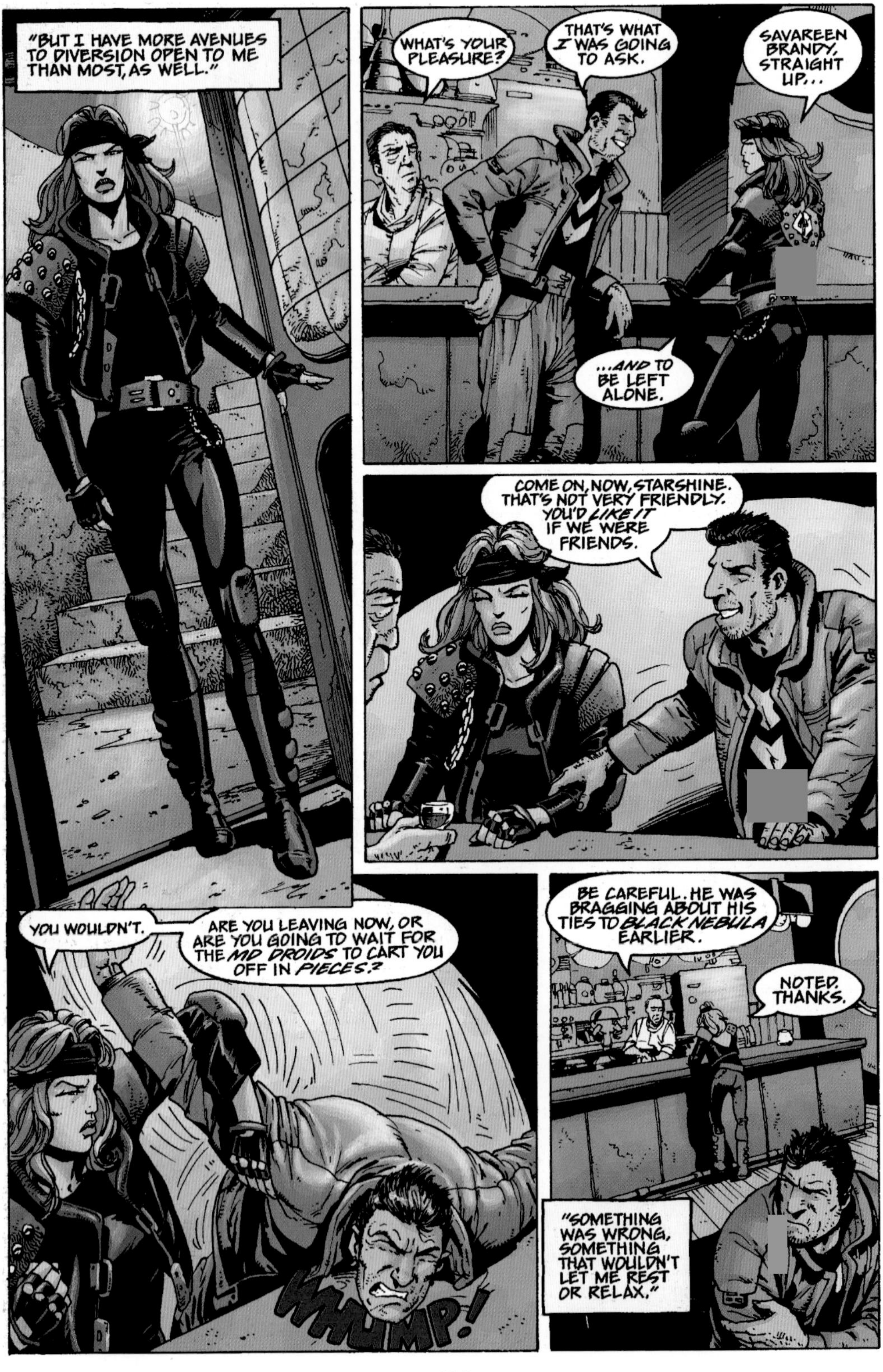
"BUT I HAVE MORE AVENUES TO DIVERSION OPEN TO ME THAN MOST, AS WELL."
WHAT'S YOUR PLEASURE?
THAT'S WHAT I WAS GOING TO ASK.
SAVAREEN BRANDY, STRAIGHT UP...
...AND TO BE LEFT ALONE.
COME ON, NOW, STARSHINE. THAT'S NOT VERY FRIENDLY. YOU'D LIKE IT IF WE WERE FRIENDS.
YOU WOULDN'T.
ARE YOU LEAVING NOW, OR ARE YOU GOING TO WAIT FOR THE MD DROIDS TO CART YOU OFF IN PIECES?
WHUMP!
BE CAREFUL. HE WAS BRAGGING ABOUT HIS TIES TO BLACK NEBULA EARLIER.
NOTED. THANKS.
"SOMETHING WAS WRONG, SOMETHING THAT WOULDN'T LET ME REST OR RELAX."

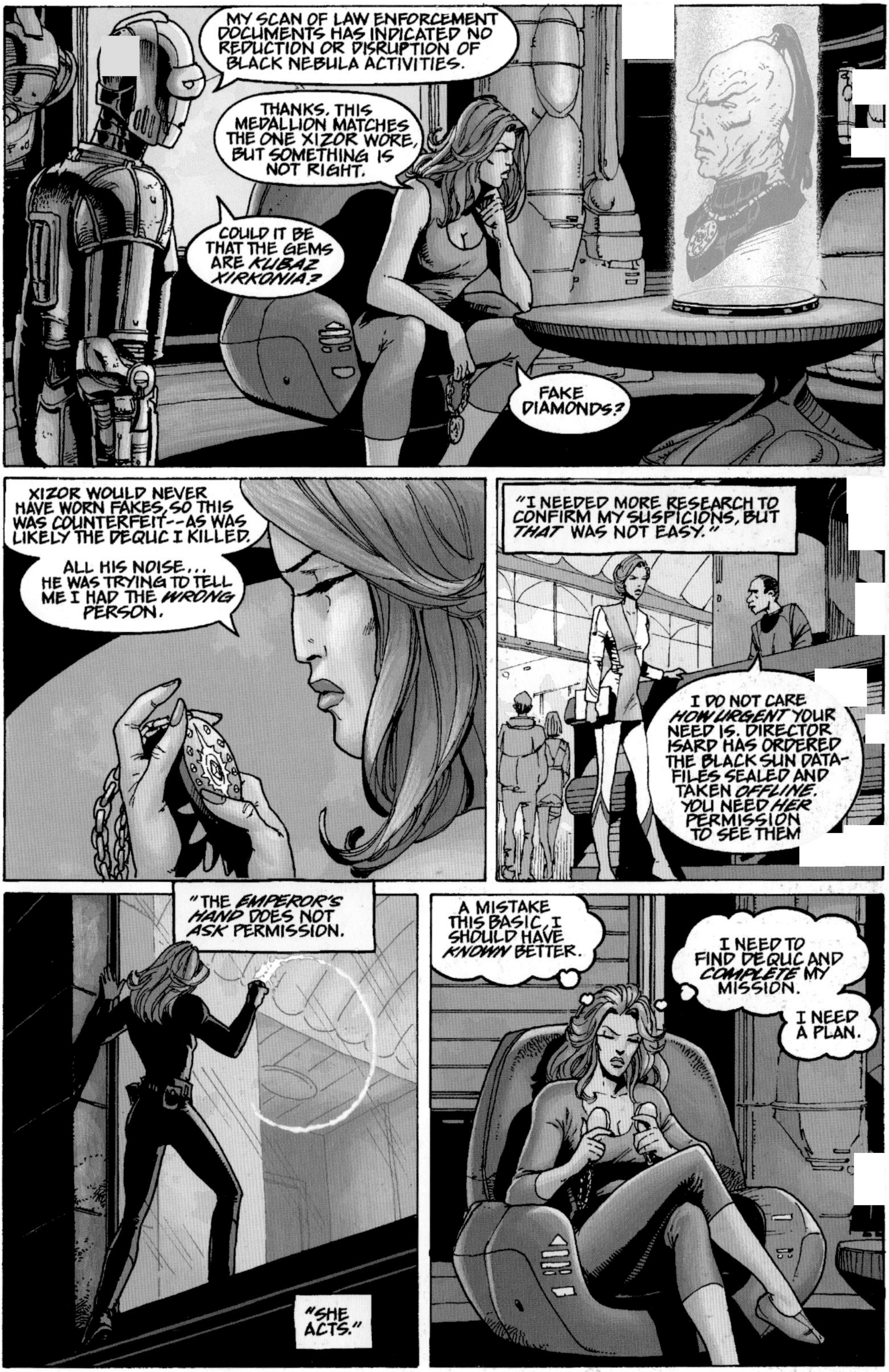
MY SCAN OF LAW ENFORCEMENT DOCUMENTS HAS INDICATED NO REDUCTION OR DISRUPTION OF BLACK NEBULA ACTIVITIES.
THANKS. THIS MEDALLION MATCHES THE ONE XIZOR WORE, BUT SOMETHING IS NOT RIGHT.
COULD IT BE THAT THE GEMS ARE *KUBAZ XIRKONIA?*
FAKE DIAMONDS?
XIZOR WOULD NEVER HAVE WORN FAKES, SO THIS WAS COUNTERFEIT--AS WAS LIKELY THE DEQUC I KILLED.
ALL HIS NOISE... HE WAS TRYING TO TELL ME I HAD THE *WRONG* PERSON.
"I NEEDED MORE RESEARCH TO CONFIRM MY SUSPICIONS, BUT *THAT* WAS NOT EASY."
I DO NOT CARE *HOW URGENT* YOUR NEED IS. DIRECTOR ISARD HAS ORDERED THE BLACK SUN DATA-FILES SEALED AND TAKEN *OFFLINE*. YOU NEED *HER* PERMISSION TO SEE THEM
"THE *EMPEROR'S HAND* DOES NOT *ASK* PERMISSION.
"SHE ACTS."
A MISTAKE THIS BASIC, I SHOULD HAVE *KNOWN* BETTER.
I NEED TO FIND DEQUC AND *COMPLETE* MY MISSION.
I NEED A PLAN.

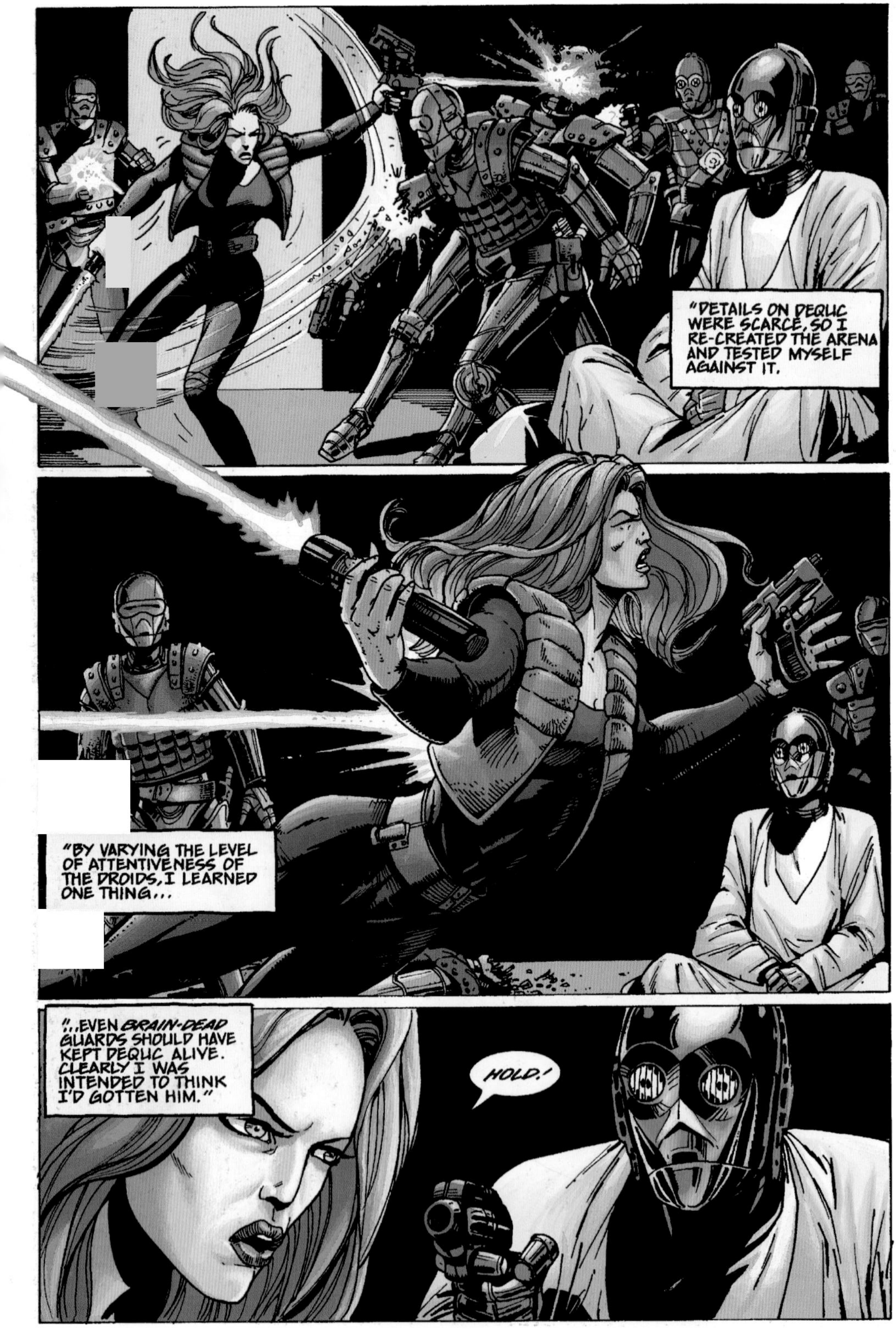
"DETAILS ON DEQUC WERE SCARCE, SO I RE-CREATED THE ARENA AND TESTED MYSELF AGAINST IT.
"BY VARYING THE LEVEL OF ATTENTIVENESS OF THE DROIDS, I LEARNED ONE THING...
"...EVEN BRAIN-DEAD GUARDS SHOULD HAVE KEPT DEQUC ALIVE. CLEARLY I WAS INTENDED TO THINK I'D GOTTEN HIM."
HOLD!

YOU RAN THE SCENARIO FIVE TIMES AND GOT DEQUC TWICE, ESCAPING ON ONE OF THOSE RUNS.

SO THE DECOY WAS IN PLACE TO FOIL AN ASSASSIN...

...BUT DID DEQUC *KNOW* IT WAS ME?

DOUBTFUL. AS A CRIMINAL CHIEFTAIN, HE LIKELY HAS OTHERS FRONT FOR HIM ON A REGULAR BASIS. HIS LAXITY SHOWS HE DOES NOT RESPECT HIS ENEMIES.

BUT NOW THE *EMPEROR* IS HIS ENEMY. HE WILL DIE FOR HIS LACK OF RESPECT.

I NEED YOU TO FIND ME ALL YOU CAN ON DEQUC. *ALL* THE FILES, NO MATTER *WHAT* YOU HAVE TO DO TO GET THEM.

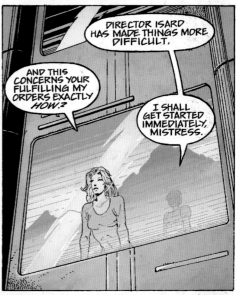

DIRECTOR ISARD HAS MADE THINGS MORE DIFFICULT.

AND THIS CONCERNS YOUR FULFILLING MY ORDERS EXACTLY *HOW?*

I SHALL GET STARTED IMMEDIATELY, MISTRESS.

"I HAD FAILED MY MASTER. I KNEW I WOULD ADMIT MY ERROR AND ACCEPT HIS DISPLEASURE, BUT I DIDN'T EXPECT CONTACT SO QUICKLY."

MARA JADE...

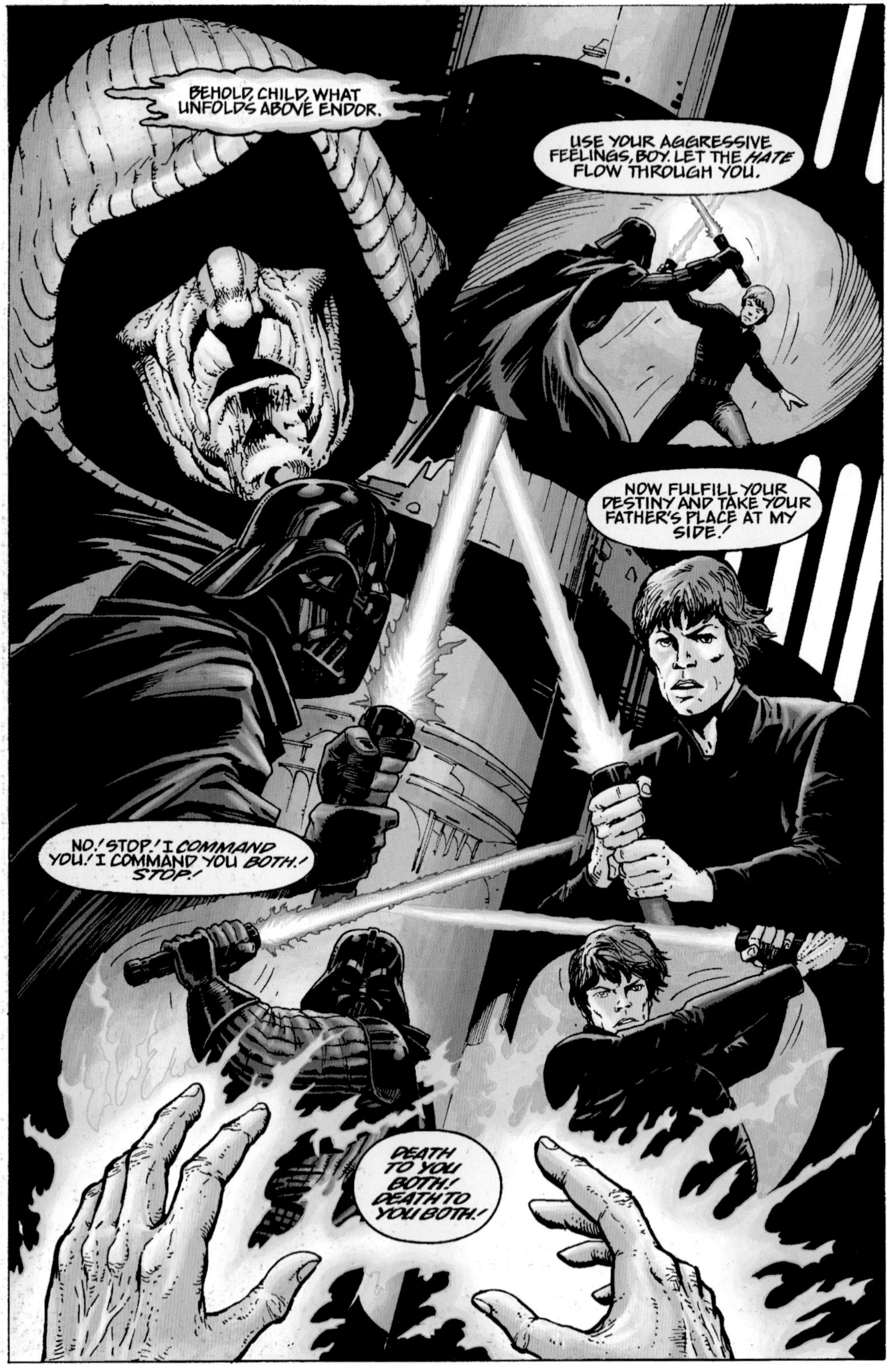
BEHOLD, CHILD, WHAT UNFOLDS ABOVE ENDOR.
USE YOUR AGGRESSIVE FEELINGS, BOY. LET THE *HATE* FLOW THROUGH YOU.
NOW FULFILL YOUR DESTINY AND TAKE YOUR FATHER'S PLACE AT MY SIDE!
NO! STOP! I *COMMAND* YOU! I COMMAND YOU *BOTH*! STOP!
DEATH TO YOU BOTH! DEATH TO YOU BOTH!

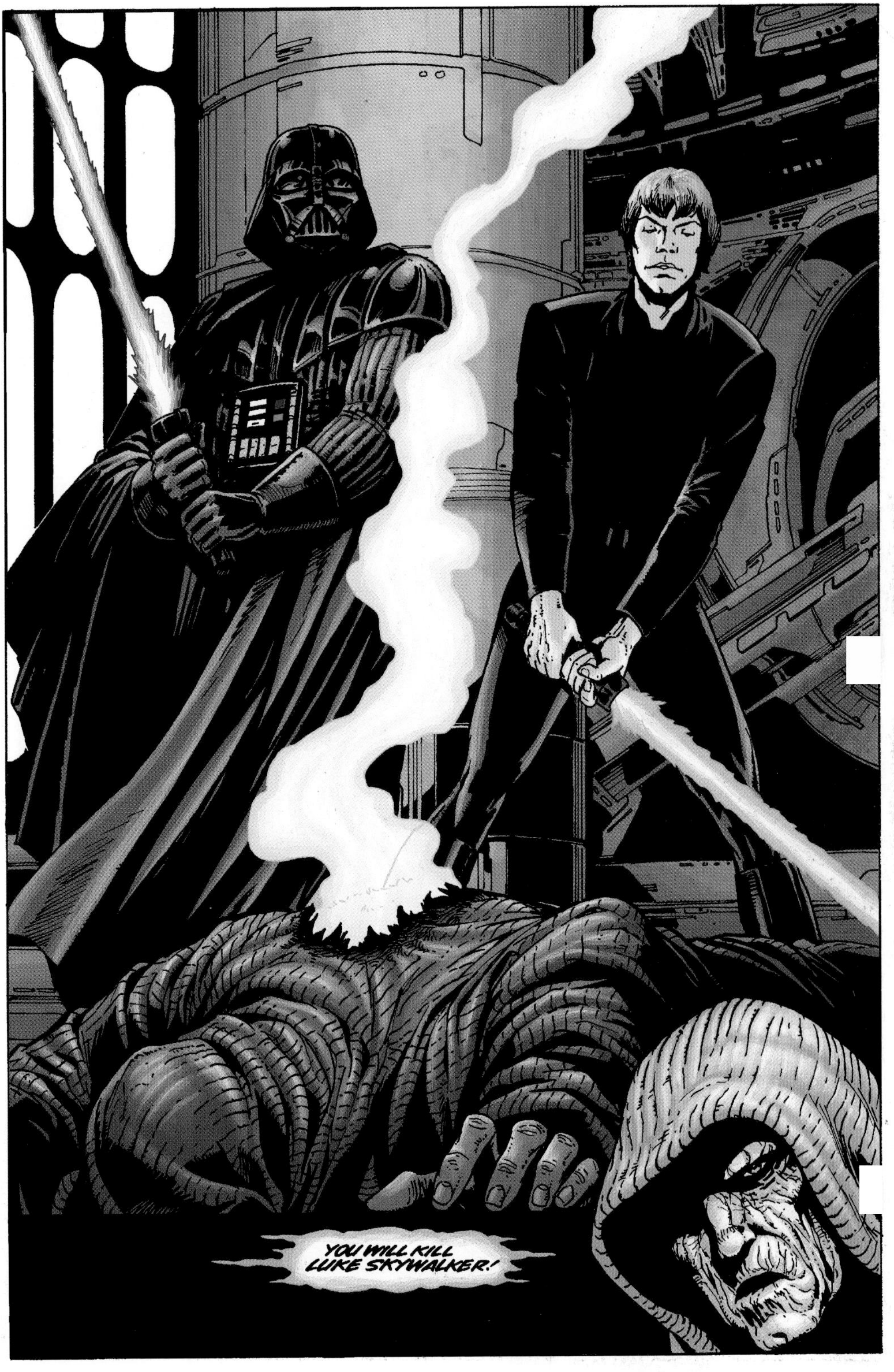
YOU WILL KILL LUKE SKYWALKER!

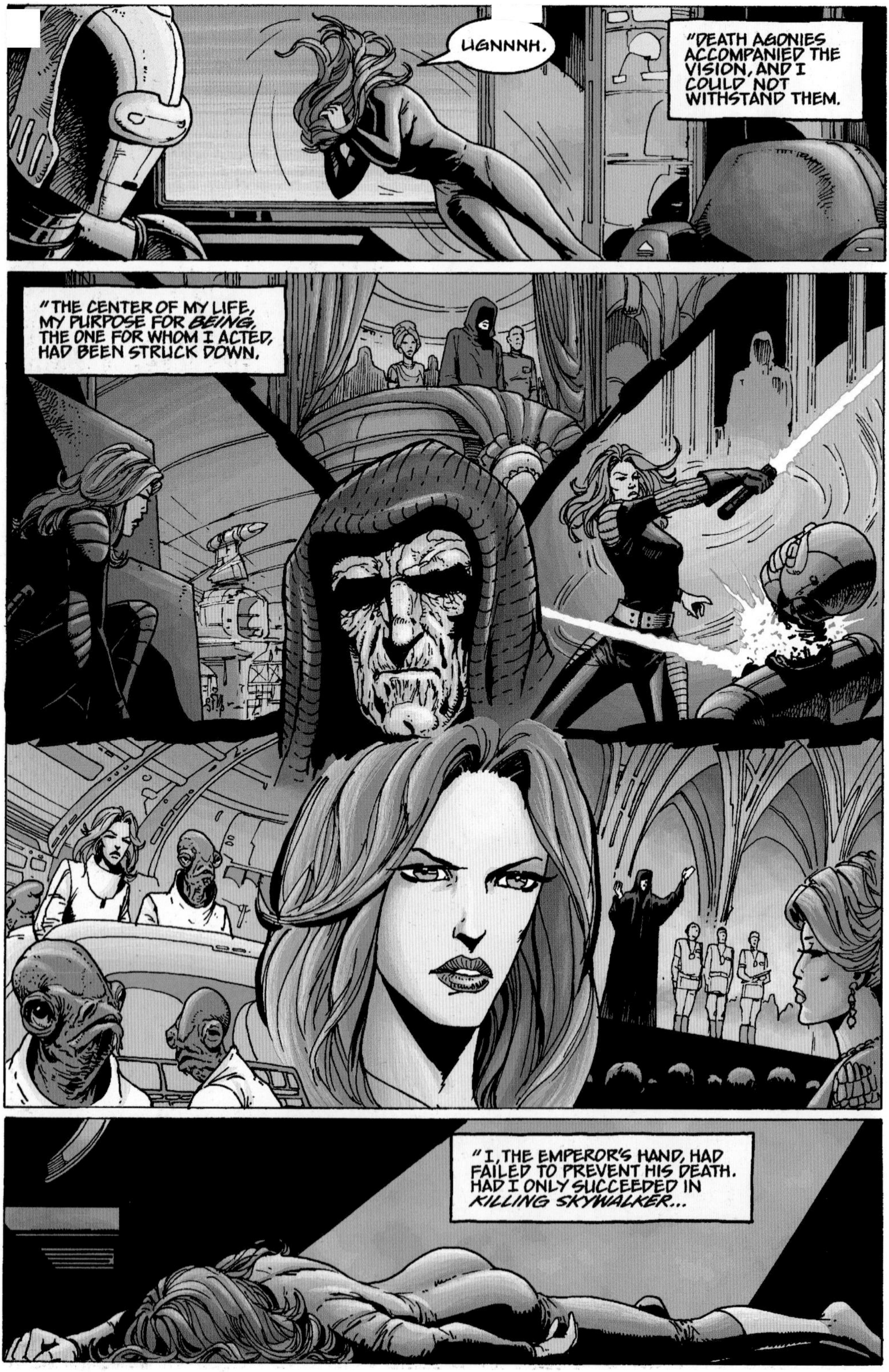
UGNNNH.
"DEATH AGONIES ACCOMPANIED THE VISION, AND I COULD NOT WITHSTAND THEM.
"THE CENTER OF MY LIFE, MY PURPOSE FOR *BEING*, THE ONE FOR WHOM I ACTED, HAD BEEN STRUCK DOWN.
"I, THE EMPEROR'S HAND, HAD FAILED TO PREVENT HIS DEATH. HAD I ONLY SUCCEEDED IN *KILLING SKYWALKER*...

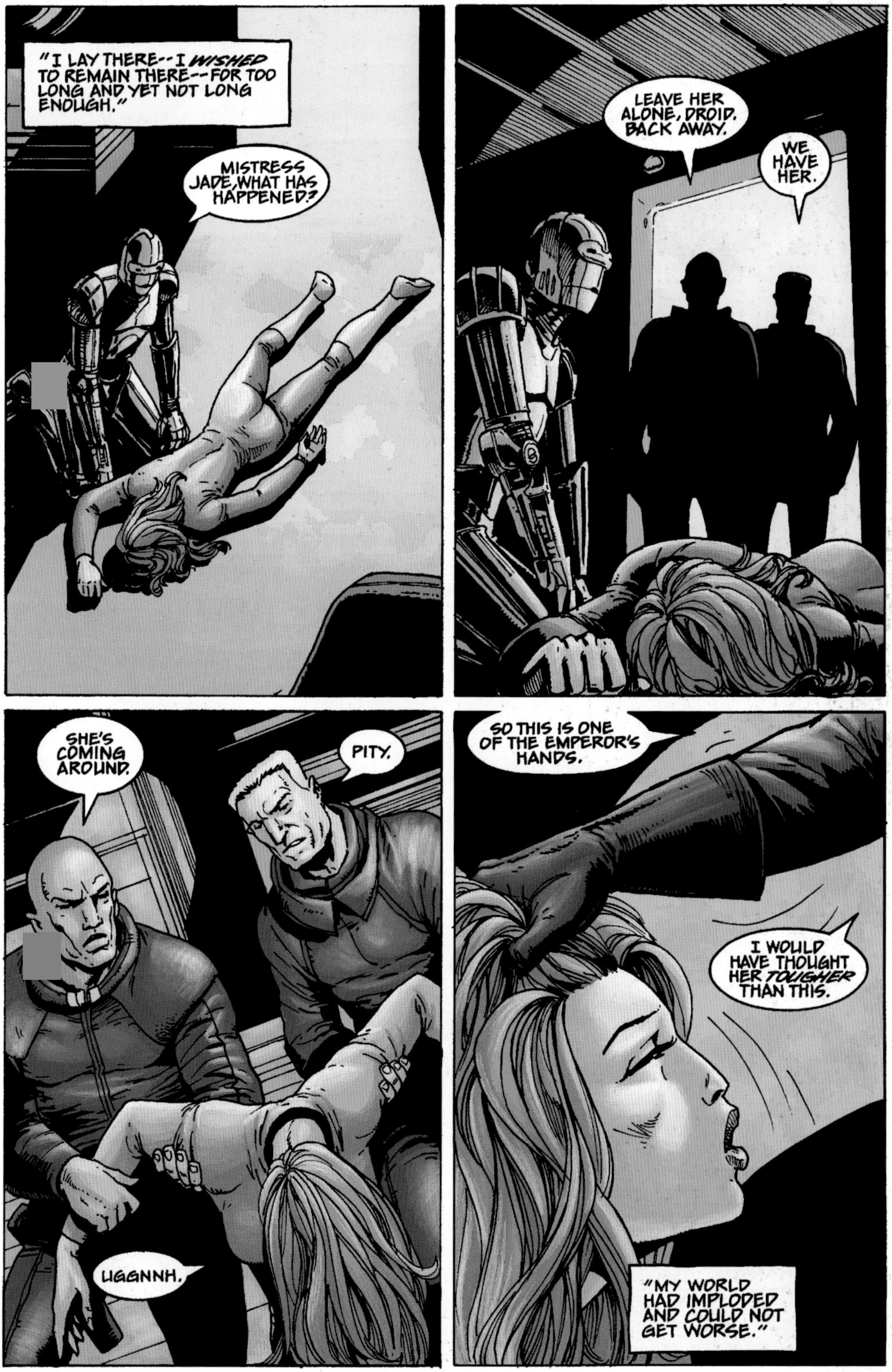
"I LAY THERE--I WISHED TO REMAIN THERE--FOR TOO LONG AND YET NOT LONG ENOUGH."
MISTRESS JADE, WHAT HAS HAPPENED?
LEAVE HER ALONE, DROID. BACK AWAY.
WE HAVE HER.
SHE'S COMING AROUND.
PITY.
UGGNNH.
SO THIS IS ONE OF THE EMPEROR'S HANDS.
I WOULD HAVE THOUGHT HER TOUGHER THAN THIS.
"MY WORLD HAD IMPLODED AND COULD NOT GET WORSE."

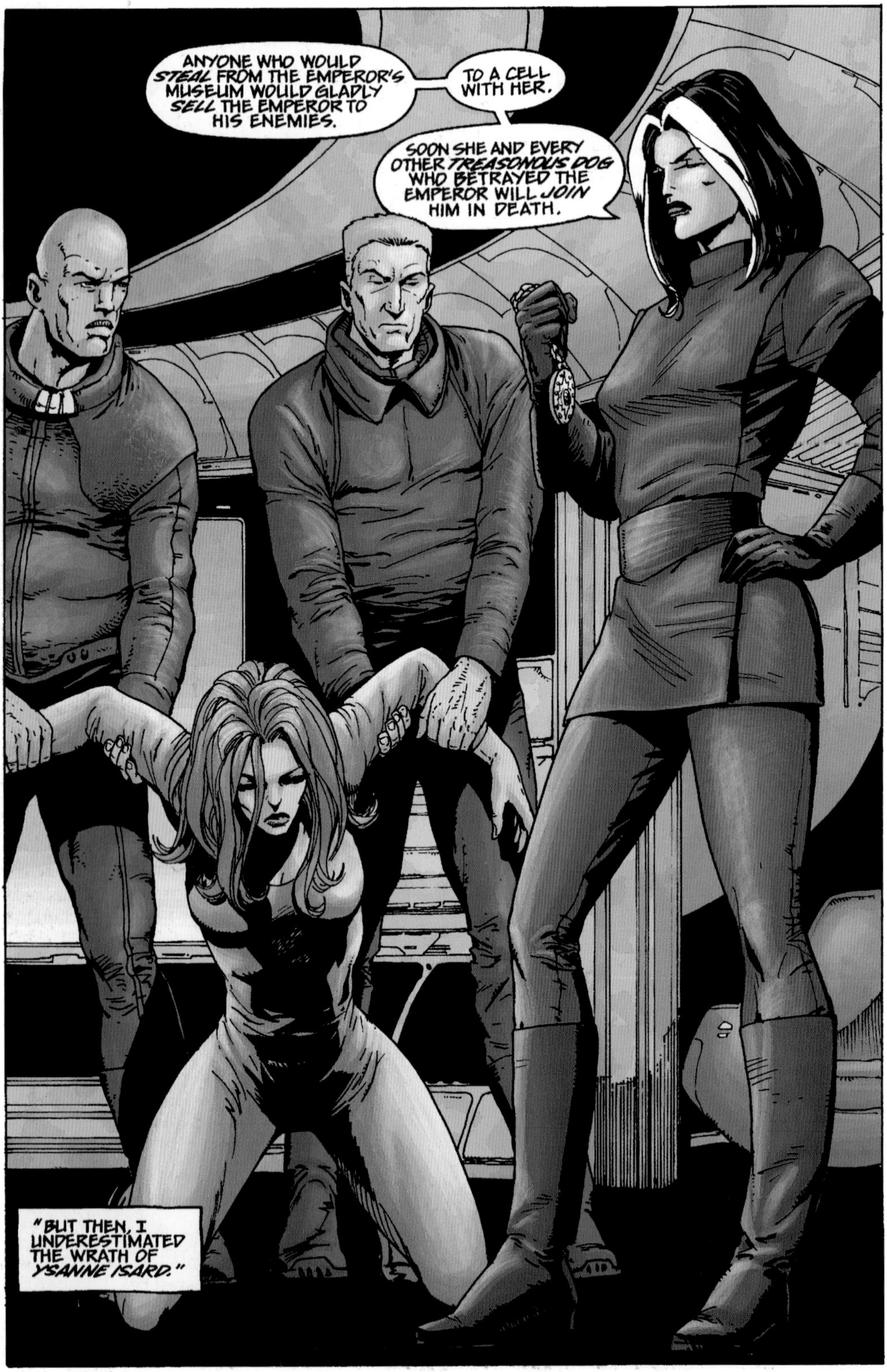

ANYONE WHO WOULD *STEAL* FROM THE EMPEROR'S MUSEUM WOULD GLADLY *SELL* THE EMPEROR TO HIS ENEMIES.
TO A CELL WITH HER.
SOON SHE AND EVERY OTHER *TREASONOUS DOG* WHO BETRAYED THE EMPEROR WILL *JOIN* HIM IN DEATH.
"BUT THEN, I UNDERESTIMATED THE WRATH OF *YSANNE ISARD.*"

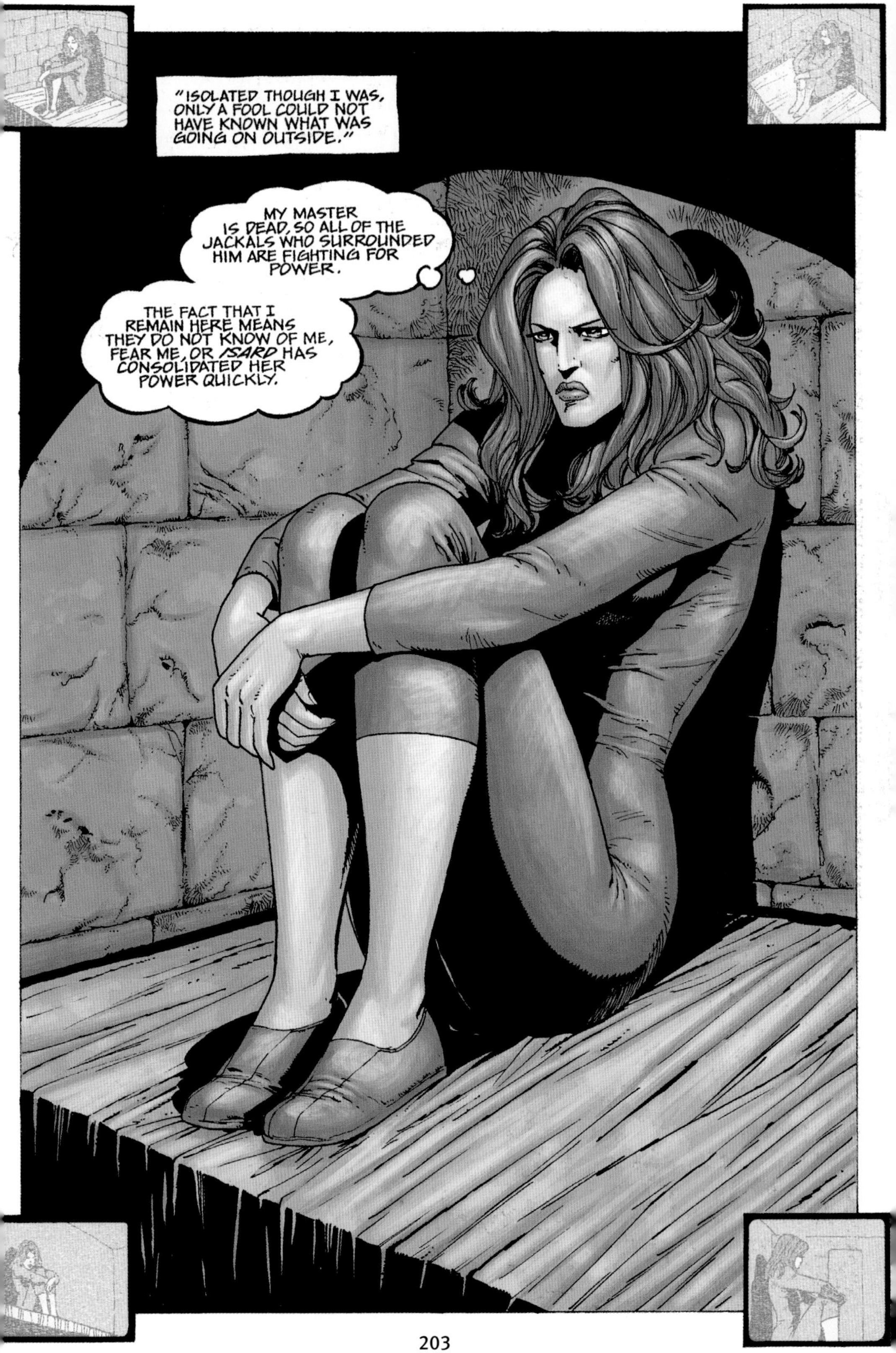
"ISOLATED THOUGH I WAS, ONLY A FOOL COULD NOT HAVE KNOWN WHAT WAS GOING ON OUTSIDE."
MY MASTER IS DEAD, SO ALL OF THE JACKALS WHO SURROUNDED HIM ARE FIGHTING FOR POWER.
THE FACT THAT I REMAIN HERE MEANS THEY DO NOT KNOW OF ME, FEAR ME, OR ISARD HAS CONSOLIDATED HER POWER QUICKLY.

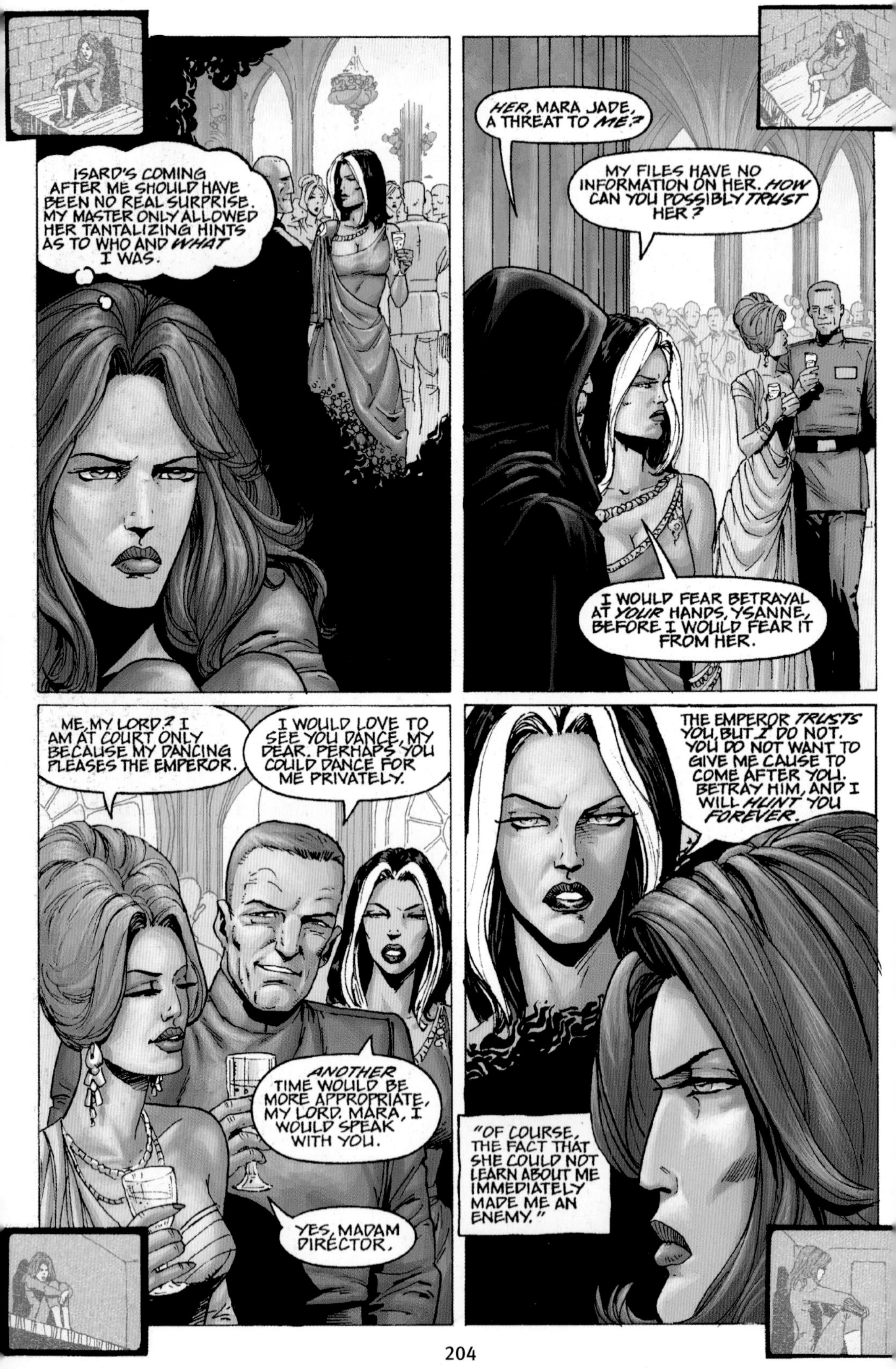
ISARD'S COMING AFTER ME SHOULD HAVE BEEN NO REAL SURPRISE. MY MASTER ONLY ALLOWED HER TANTALIZING HINTS AS TO WHO AND WHAT I WAS.
HER, MARA JADE, A THREAT TO ME?
MY FILES HAVE NO INFORMATION ON HER. HOW CAN YOU POSSIBLY TRUST HER?
I WOULD FEAR BETRAYAL AT YOUR HANDS, YSANNE, BEFORE I WOULD FEAR IT FROM HER.
ME, MY LORD? I AM AT COURT ONLY BECAUSE MY DANCING PLEASES THE EMPEROR.
I WOULD LOVE TO SEE YOU DANCE, MY DEAR. PERHAPS YOU COULD DANCE FOR ME PRIVATELY.
ANOTHER TIME WOULD BE MORE APPROPRIATE, MY LORD. MARA, I WOULD SPEAK WITH YOU.
YES, MADAM DIRECTOR.
THE EMPEROR TRUSTS YOU, BUT I DO NOT. YOU DO NOT WANT TO GIVE ME CAUSE TO COME AFTER YOU. BETRAY HIM, AND I WILL HUNT YOU FOREVER.
"OF COURSE, THE FACT THAT SHE COULD NOT LEARN ABOUT ME IMMEDIATELY MADE ME AN ENEMY."

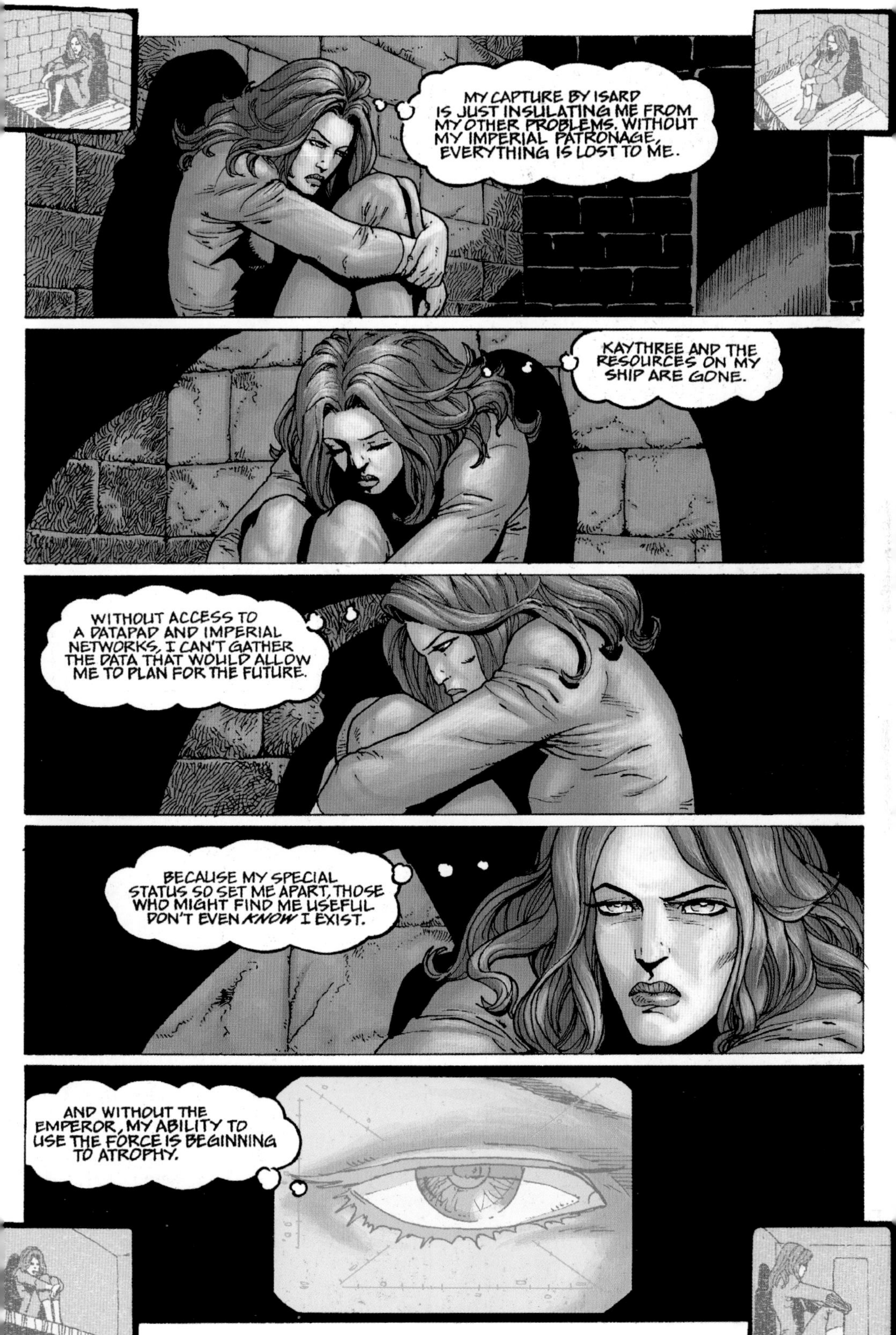
MY CAPTURE BY ISARD IS JUST INSULATING ME FROM MY OTHER PROBLEMS. WITHOUT MY IMPERIAL PATRONAGE, EVERYTHING IS LOST TO ME.
KAYTHREE AND THE RESOURCES ON MY SHIP ARE GONE.
WITHOUT ACCESS TO A DATAPAD AND IMPERIAL NETWORKS, I CAN'T GATHER THE DATA THAT WOULD ALLOW ME TO PLAN FOR THE FUTURE.
BECAUSE MY SPECIAL STATUS SO SET ME APART, THOSE WHO MIGHT FIND ME USEFUL DON'T EVEN *KNOW* I EXIST.
AND WITHOUT THE EMPEROR, MY ABILITY TO USE THE FORCE IS BEGINNING TO ATROPHY.

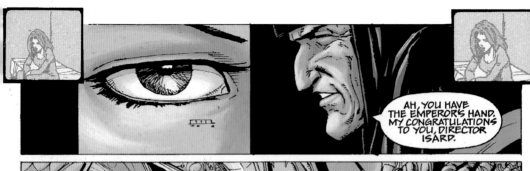

AH, YOU HAVE THE EMPEROR'S HAND. MY CONGRATULATIONS TO YOU, DIRECTOR ISARD.

THANK YOU, MY LORD. I KNEW GETTING HER UNDER CONTROL WAS IMPORTANT. THE EMPEROR SET *GREAT STORE* BY HER.

TRUE AND TRUER THAT I KNOW AS LITTLE ABOUT HER AS YOU DO. VEXING, ISN'T IT?

WHAT DO YOU KNOW?

I'LL TAKE THAT AS A YES.

SHE WAS HIS SPECIAL AGENT. TAKEN AS A YOUTH, THE EMPEROR TRAINED HER TO SERVE HIM. SHE DID, DILIGENTLY.

AS DID I.

TRUE, THOUGH YOU ARE NOT ADEPT AT THE *FORCE.* BLIND TO IT, AREN'T YOU?

YOUR POINT BEING?

DILIGENCE WAS NOT ALWAYS *ENOUGH* FOR OUR EMPEROR.

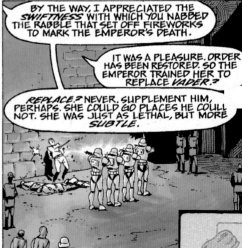

BY THE WAY, I APPRECIATED THE *SWIFTNESS* WITH WHICH YOU NABBED THE RABBLE THAT SET OFF FIREWORKS TO MARK THE EMPEROR'S DEATH.

IT WAS A PLEASURE. ORDER HAS BEEN RESTORED. SO THE EMPEROR TRAINED HER TO REPLACE *VADER?*

REPLACE? NEVER. SUPPLEMENT HIM, PERHAPS. SHE COULD GO PLACES HE COULD NOT. SHE WAS JUST AS LETHAL, BUT MORE *SUBTLE.*

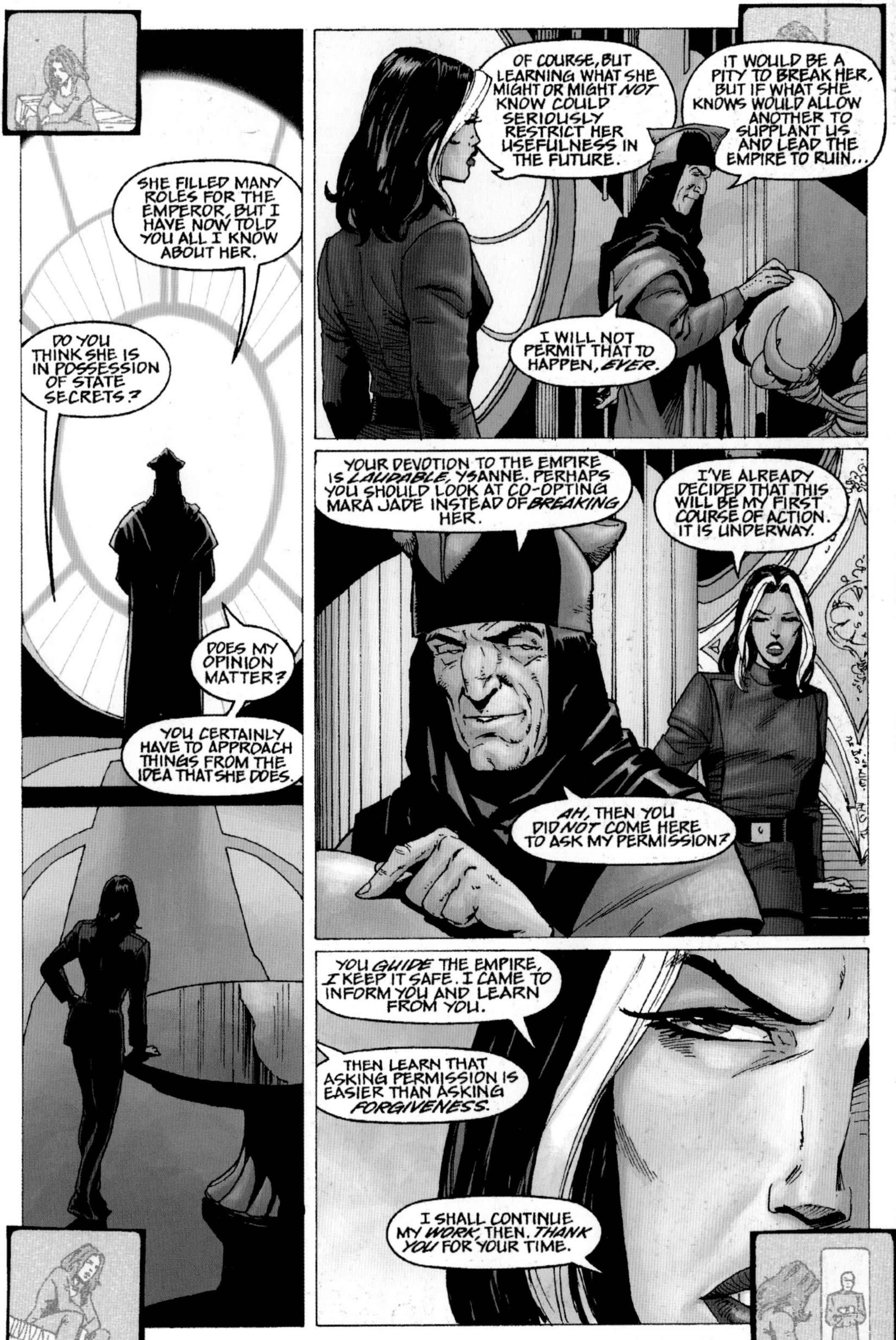
SHE FILLED MANY ROLES FOR THE EMPEROR, BUT I HAVE NOW TOLD YOU ALL I KNOW ABOUT HER.
DO YOU THINK SHE IS IN POSSESSION OF STATE SECRETS?
DOES MY OPINION MATTER?
YOU CERTAINLY HAVE TO APPROACH THINGS FROM THE IDEA THAT SHE DOES.
OF COURSE, BUT LEARNING WHAT SHE MIGHT OR MIGHT NOT KNOW COULD SERIOUSLY RESTRICT HER USEFULNESS IN THE FUTURE.
IT WOULD BE A PITY TO BREAK HER, BUT IF WHAT SHE KNOWS WOULD ALLOW ANOTHER TO SUPPLANT US AND LEAD THE EMPIRE TO RUIN...
I WILL NOT PERMIT THAT TO HAPPEN, EVER.
YOUR DEVOTION TO THE EMPIRE IS LAUDABLE, YSANNE. PERHAPS YOU SHOULD LOOK AT CO-OPTING MARA JADE INSTEAD OF BREAKING HER.
I'VE ALREADY DECIDED THAT THIS WILL BE MY FIRST COURSE OF ACTION. IT IS UNDERWAY.
AH, THEN YOU DID NOT COME HERE TO ASK MY PERMISSION?
YOU GUIDE THE EMPIRE, I KEEP IT SAFE. I CAME TO INFORM YOU AND LEARN FROM YOU.
THEN LEARN THAT ASKING PERMISSION IS EASIER THAN ASKING FORGIVENESS.
I SHALL CONTINUE MY WORK, THEN. THANK YOU FOR YOUR TIME.

THIS REALLY ISN'T THE SORT OF FARE YOU'RE USED TO AS THE *EMPEROR'S HAND.* BUT IT'S THE BEST I CAN GET YOU RIGHT NOW.

IT'S WARM AND SMELLS ABOUT RIGHT.

AND I APOLOGIZE FOR HAVING NO UTENSILS, BUT DIRECTOR *ISARD* THINKS YOU COULD MAKE ALMOST *ANYTHING* INTO A WEAPON.

ME? I'M JUST A DANCER AT COURT. I DON'T KNOW ANYTHING ABOUT WEAPONS.

I KNOW WHAT YOU'VE TOLD OTHERS IN THE PAST, BUT THAT WAS THE *PAST.* RIGHT NOW WE NEED TO THINK OF THE FUTURE, YOU AND I.

HOW SO?

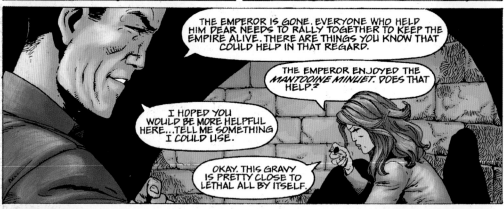

THE EMPEROR IS GONE. EVERYONE WHO HELD HIM DEAR NEEDS TO RALLY TOGETHER TO KEEP THE EMPIRE ALIVE. THERE ARE THINGS YOU KNOW THAT COULD HELP IN THAT REGARD.

THE EMPEROR ENJOYED THE *MANTOOINE MINUET.* DOES THAT HELP?

I HOPED YOU WOULD BE MORE HELPFUL HERE...TELL ME SOMETHING I COULD USE.

OKAY. THIS GRAVY IS PRETTY CLOSE TO LETHAL ALL BY ITSELF.

I HAD *HOPED* YOUR LOYALTY TO THE EMPEROR WOULD TRANSLATE TO HIS DREAM AND *KEEPING* IT *ALIVE.*

THERE IS LITTLE A DANCER CAN DO TO *SAVE* THE EMPIRE.

BUT THERE IS *MUCH* A DANCER CAN DO TO SAVE *HERSELF.* YOU ARE IN A VERY DIFFICULT POSITION.

YES, BALANCING THIS TRAY IS DIFFICULT. IF I HAD A TABLE...

I CAN ARRANGE A *NUMBER OF* THINGS TO MAKE YOUR LIFE MUCH *EASIER,* MARA JADE.

INCLUDING BETTER GRAVY?

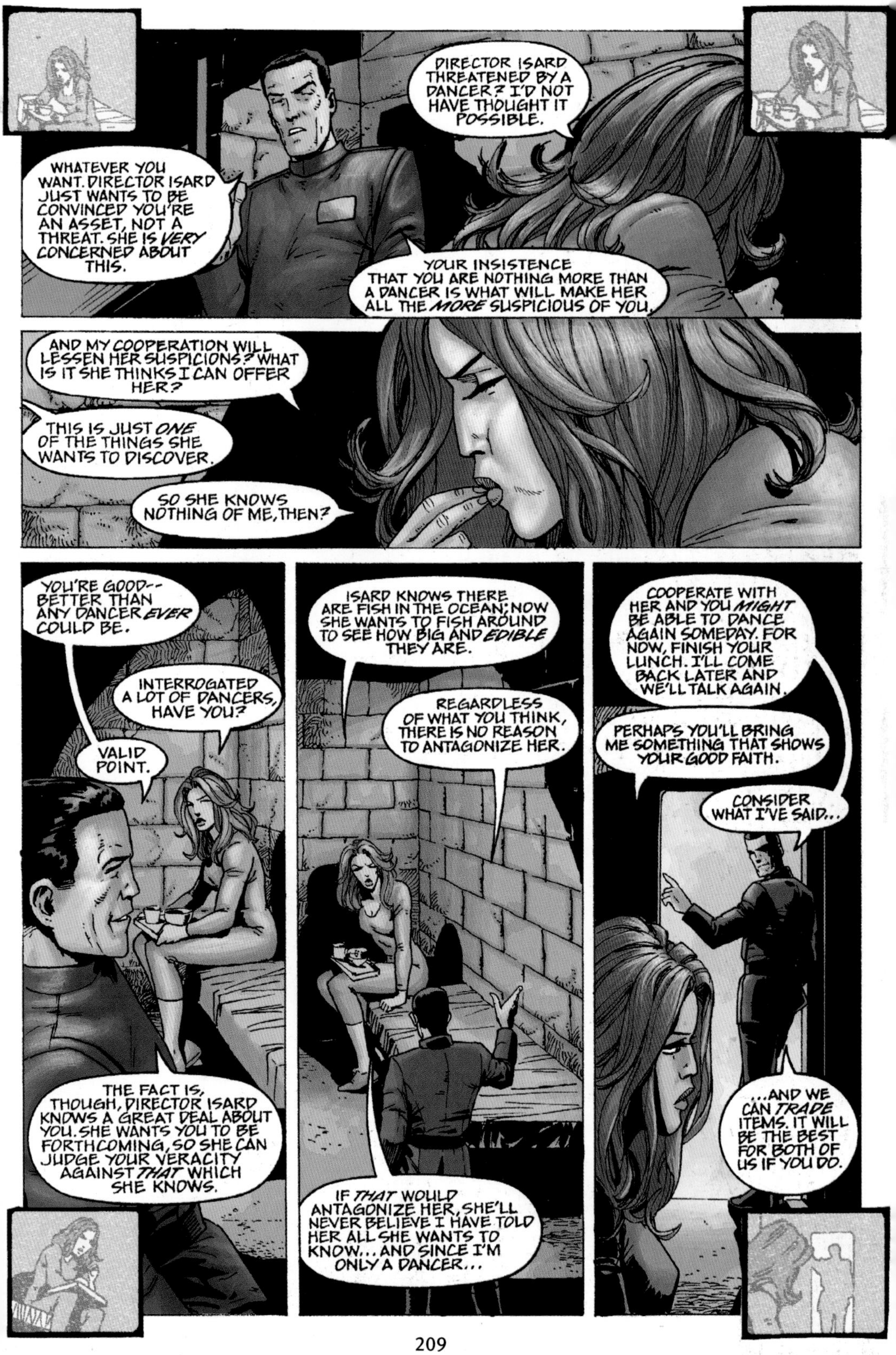
DIRECTOR ISARD THREATENED BY A DANCER? I'D NOT HAVE THOUGHT IT POSSIBLE.
WHATEVER YOU WANT. DIRECTOR ISARD JUST WANTS TO BE CONVINCED YOU'RE AN ASSET, NOT A THREAT. SHE IS VERY CONCERNED ABOUT THIS.
YOUR INSISTENCE THAT YOU ARE NOTHING MORE THAN A DANCER IS WHAT WILL MAKE HER ALL THE MORE SUSPICIOUS OF YOU.
AND MY COOPERATION WILL LESSEN HER SUSPICIONS? WHAT IS IT SHE THINKS I CAN OFFER HER?
THIS IS JUST ONE OF THE THINGS SHE WANTS TO DISCOVER.
SO SHE KNOWS NOTHING OF ME, THEN?
YOU'RE GOOD-- BETTER THAN ANY DANCER EVER COULD BE.
INTERROGATED A LOT OF DANCERS, HAVE YOU?
VALID POINT.
THE FACT IS, THOUGH, DIRECTOR ISARD KNOWS A GREAT DEAL ABOUT YOU. SHE WANTS YOU TO BE FORTHCOMING, SO SHE CAN JUDGE YOUR VERACITY AGAINST THAT WHICH SHE KNOWS.
ISARD KNOWS THERE ARE FISH IN THE OCEAN; NOW SHE WANTS TO FISH AROUND TO SEE HOW BIG AND EDIBLE THEY ARE.
REGARDLESS OF WHAT YOU THINK, THERE IS NO REASON TO ANTAGONIZE HER.
IF THAT WOULD ANTAGONIZE HER, SHE'LL NEVER BELIEVE I HAVE TOLD HER ALL SHE WANTS TO KNOW... AND SINCE I'M ONLY A DANCER...
COOPERATE WITH HER AND YOU MIGHT BE ABLE TO DANCE AGAIN SOMEDAY. FOR NOW, FINISH YOUR LUNCH. I'LL COME BACK LATER AND WE'LL TALK AGAIN.
PERHAPS YOU'LL BRING ME SOMETHING THAT SHOWS YOUR GOOD FAITH.
CONSIDER WHAT I'VE SAID...
...AND WE CAN TRADE ITEMS. IT WILL BE THE BEST FOR BOTH OF US IF YOU DO.

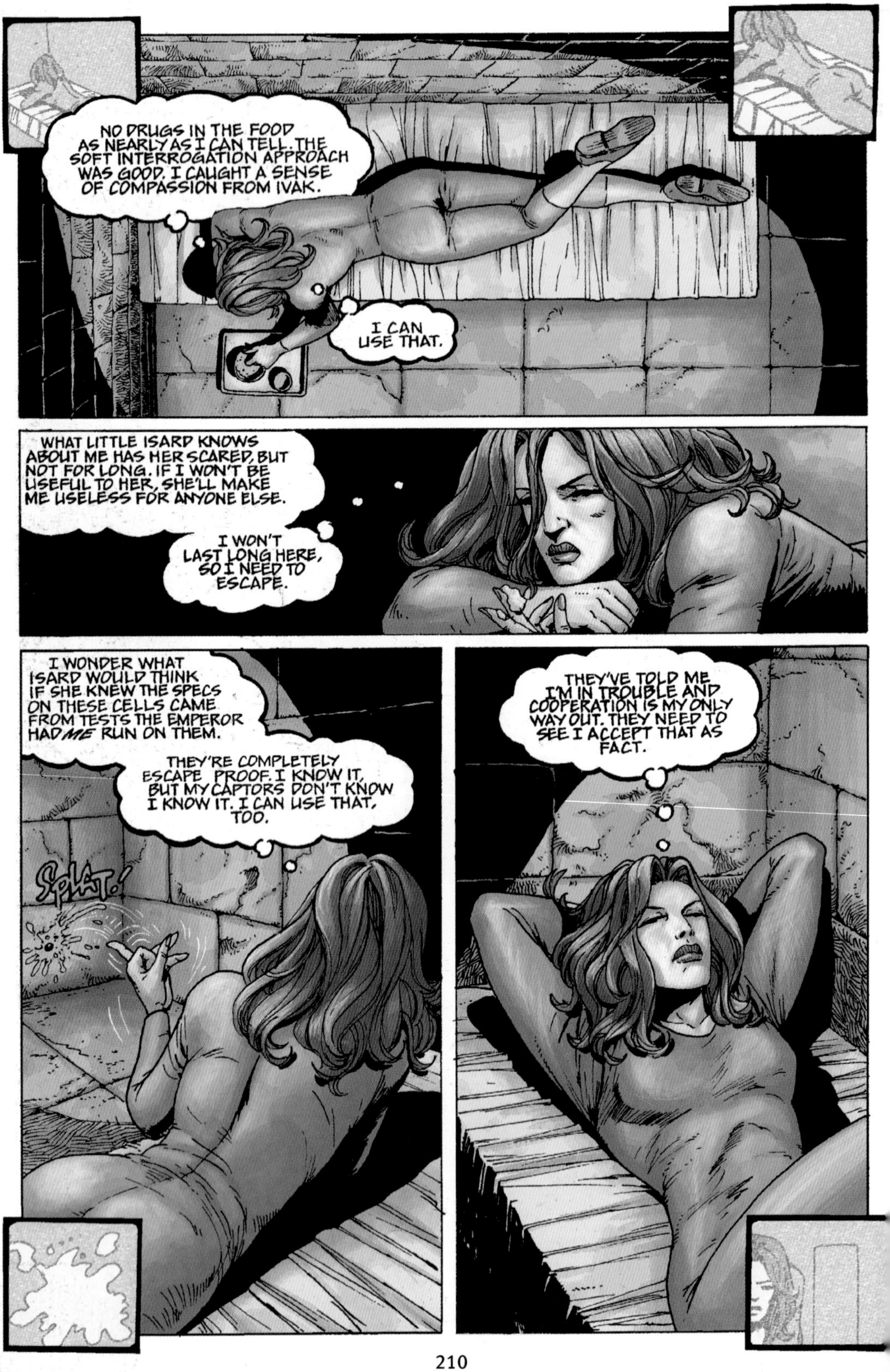
NO DRUGS IN THE FOOD AS NEARLY AS I CAN TELL. THE SOFT INTERROGATION APPROACH WAS GOOD. I CAUGHT A SENSE OF COMPASSION FROM IVAK.
I CAN USE THAT.
WHAT LITTLE ISARD KNOWS ABOUT ME HAS HER SCARED, BUT NOT FOR LONG. IF I WON'T BE USEFUL TO HER, SHE'LL MAKE ME USELESS FOR ANYONE ELSE.
I WON'T LAST LONG HERE, SO I NEED TO ESCAPE.
I WONDER WHAT ISARD WOULD THINK IF SHE KNEW THE SPECS ON THESE CELLS CAME FROM TESTS THE EMPEROR HAD *ME* RUN ON THEM.
THEY'RE COMPLETELY ESCAPE PROOF. I KNOW IT, BUT MY CAPTORS DON'T KNOW I KNOW IT. I CAN USE THAT, TOO.
SPLAT!
THEY'VE TOLD ME I'M IN TROUBLE AND COOPERATION IS MY ONLY WAY OUT. THEY NEED TO SEE I ACCEPT THAT AS FACT.

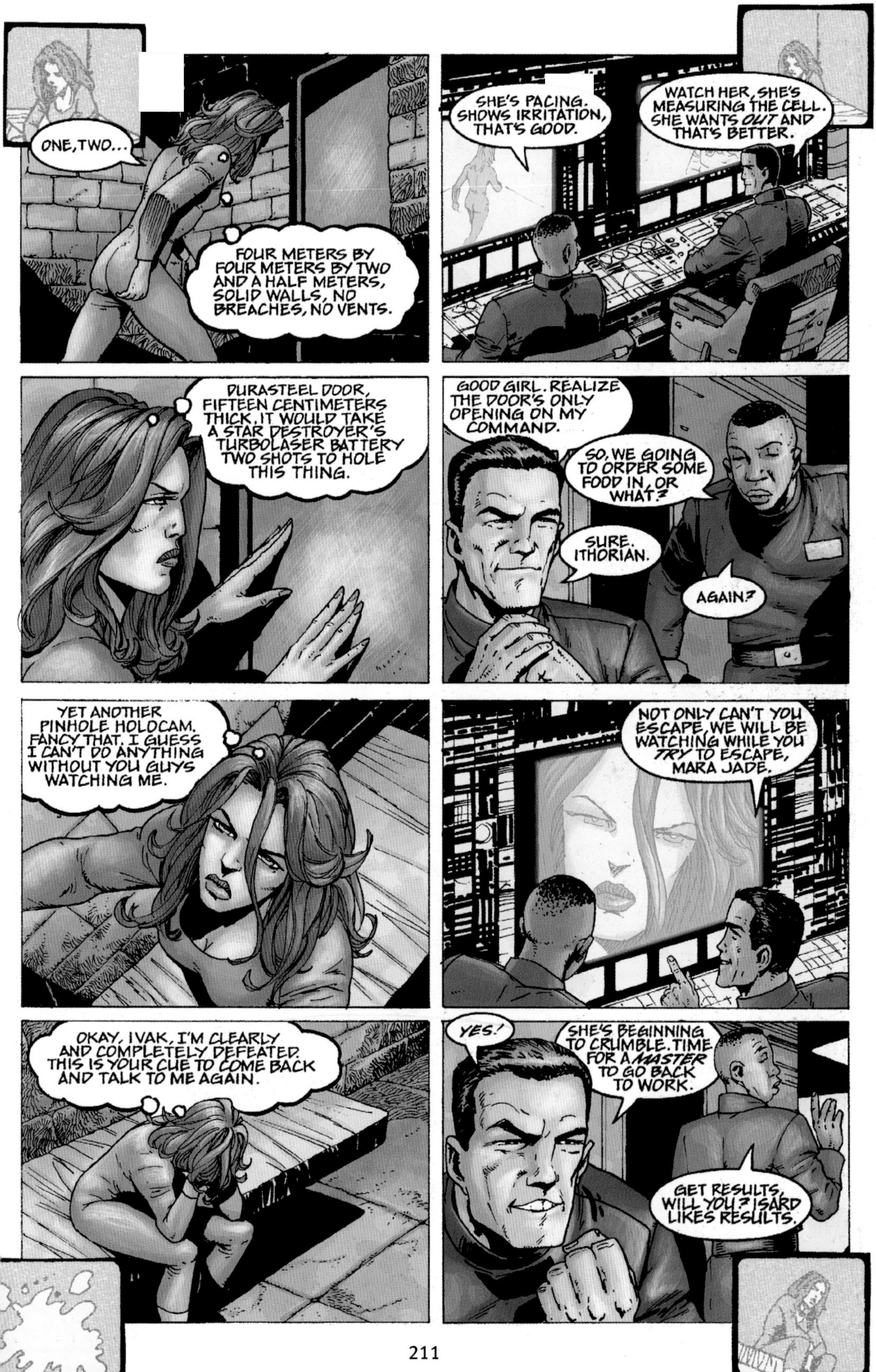
ONE, TWO...
FOUR METERS BY FOUR METERS BY TWO AND A HALF METERS, SOLID WALLS, NO BREACHES, NO VENTS.
SHE'S PACING. SHOWS IRRITATION, THAT'S GOOD.
WATCH HER, SHE'S MEASURING THE CELL. SHE WANTS OUT AND THAT'S BETTER.
DURASTEEL DOOR, FIFTEEN CENTIMETERS THICK. IT WOULD TAKE A STAR DESTROYER'S TURBOLASER BATTERY TWO SHOTS TO HOLE THIS THING.
GOOD GIRL. REALIZE THE DOOR'S ONLY OPENING ON MY COMMAND.
SO, WE GOING TO ORDER SOME FOOD IN, OR WHAT?
SURE. ITHORIAN.
AGAIN?
YET ANOTHER PINHOLE HOLOCAM. FANCY THAT. I GUESS I CAN'T DO ANYTHING WITHOUT YOU GUYS WATCHING ME.
NOT ONLY CAN'T YOU ESCAPE, WE WILL BE WATCHING WHILE YOU TRY TO ESCAPE, MARA JADE.
OKAY, IVAK, I'M CLEARLY AND COMPLETELY DEFEATED. THIS IS YOUR CUE TO COME BACK AND TALK TO ME AGAIN.
YES!
SHE'S BEGINNING TO CRUMBLE. TIME FOR A MASTER TO GO BACK TO WORK.
GET RESULTS, WILL YOU? ISARD LIKES RESULTS.

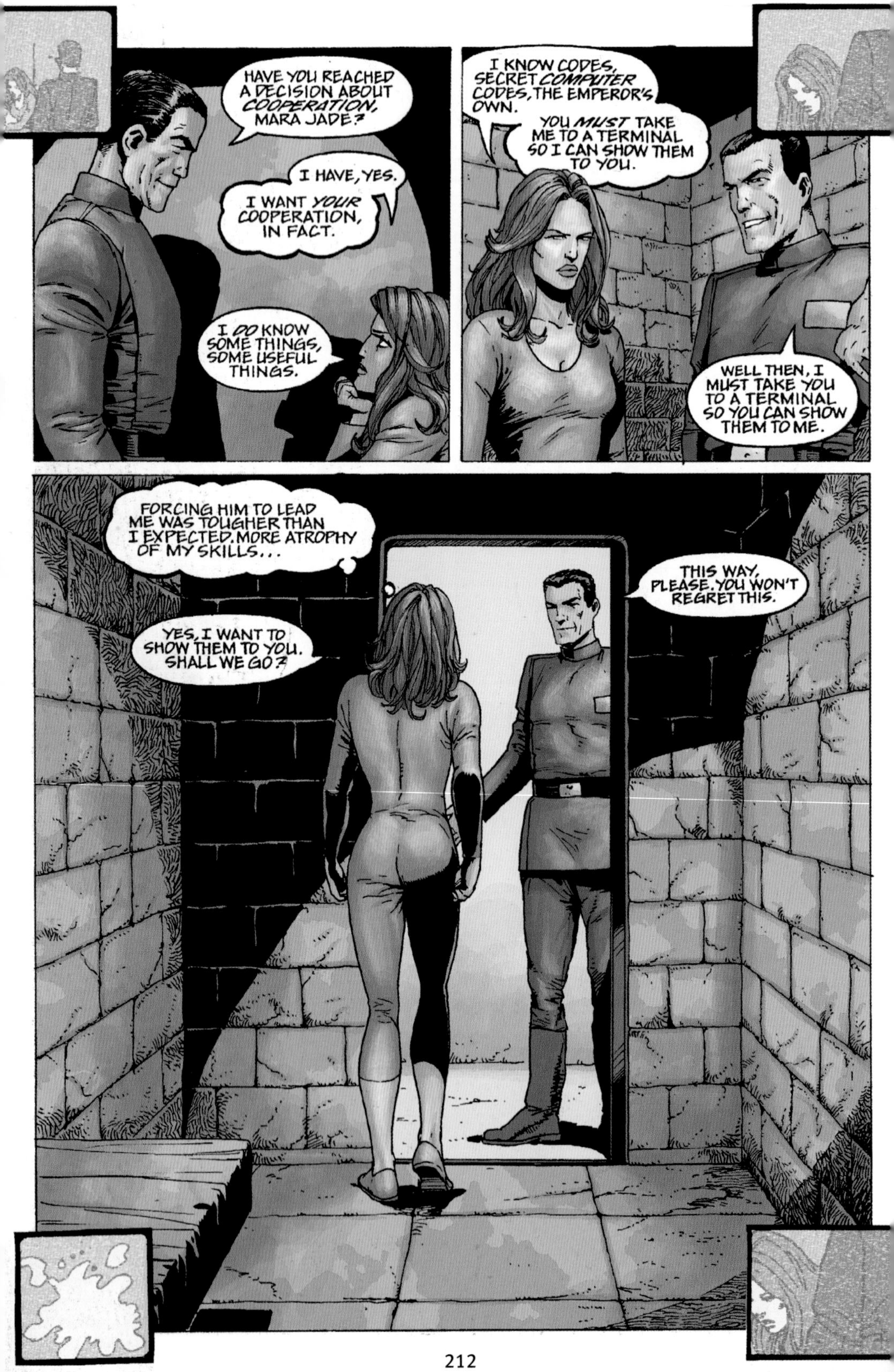
HAVE YOU REACHED A DECISION ABOUT COOPERATION, MARA JADE?
I HAVE, YES.
I WANT YOUR COOPERATION, IN FACT.
I DO KNOW SOME THINGS, SOME USEFUL THINGS.
I KNOW CODES, SECRET COMPUTER CODES, THE EMPEROR'S OWN.
YOU MUST TAKE ME TO A TERMINAL SO I CAN SHOW THEM TO YOU.
WELL THEN, I MUST TAKE YOU TO A TERMINAL SO YOU CAN SHOW THEM TO ME.
FORCING HIM TO LEAD ME WAS TOUGHER THAN I EXPECTED. MORE ATROPHY OF MY SKILLS...
YES, I WANT TO SHOW THEM TO YOU. SHALL WE GO?
THIS WAY, PLEASE. YOU WON'T REGRET THIS.

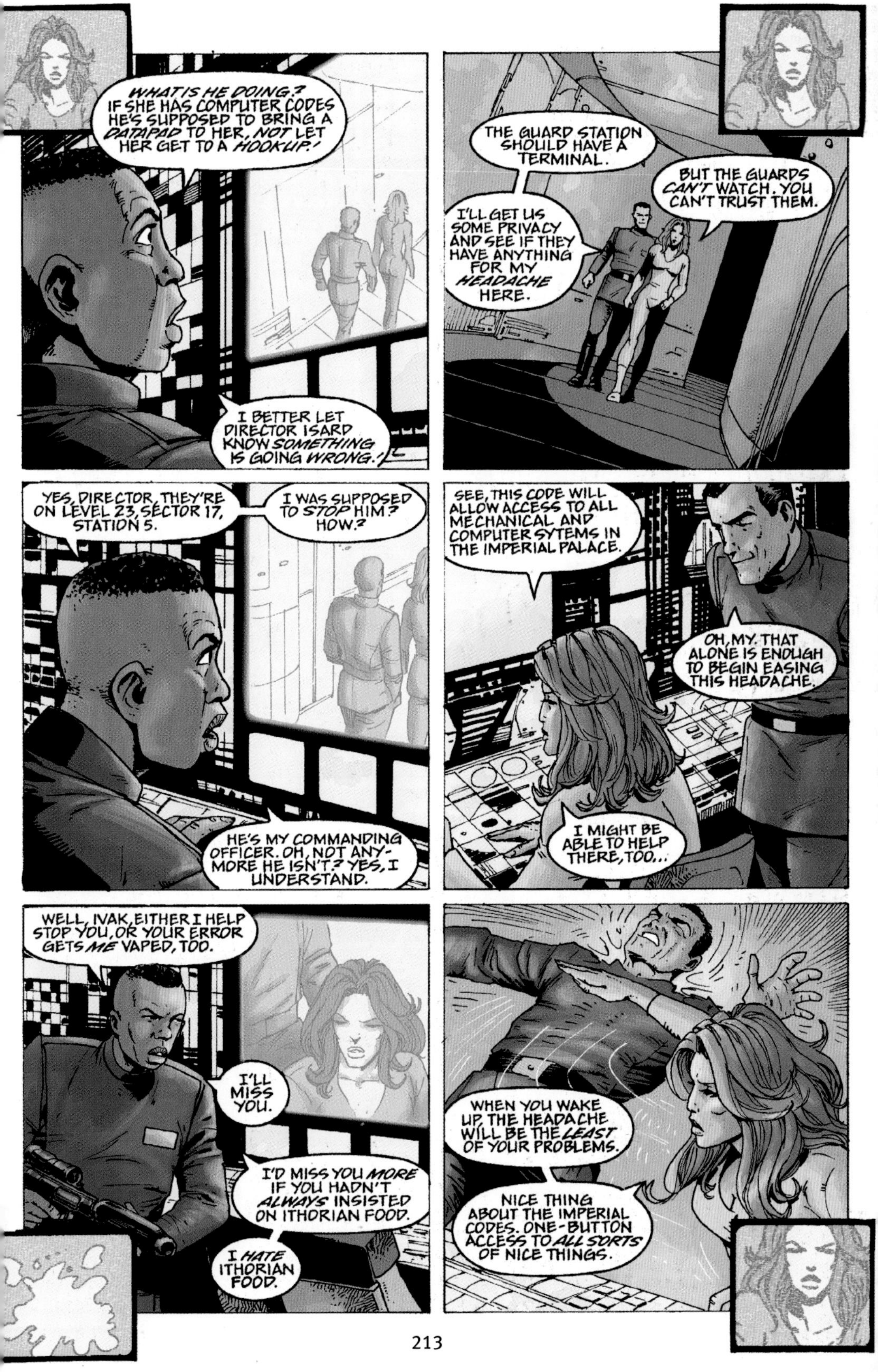
WHAT IS HE DOING? IF SHE HAS COMPUTER CODES HE'S SUPPOSED TO BRING A DATAPAD TO HER, NOT LET HER GET TO A HOOKUP!
I BETTER LET DIRECTOR ISARD KNOW SOMETHING IS GOING WRONG.!
THE GUARD STATION SHOULD HAVE A TERMINAL.
I'LL GET US SOME PRIVACY AND SEE IF THEY HAVE ANYTHING FOR MY HEADACHE HERE.
BUT THE GUARDS CAN'T WATCH. YOU CAN'T TRUST THEM.
YES, DIRECTOR, THEY'RE ON LEVEL 23, SECTOR 17, STATION 5.
I WAS SUPPOSED TO STOP HIM? HOW?
HE'S MY COMMANDING OFFICER. OH, NOT ANYMORE HE ISN'T? YES, I UNDERSTAND.
SEE, THIS CODE WILL ALLOW ACCESS TO ALL MECHANICAL AND COMPUTER SYTEMS IN THE IMPERIAL PALACE.
OH, MY. THAT ALONE IS ENOUGH TO BEGIN EASING THIS HEADACHE.
I MIGHT BE ABLE TO HELP THERE, TOO...
WELL, IVAK, EITHER I HELP STOP YOU, OR YOUR ERROR GETS ME VAPED, TOO.
I'LL MISS YOU.
I'D MISS YOU MORE IF YOU HADN'T ALWAYS INSISTED ON ITHORIAN FOOD.
I HATE ITHORIAN FOOD.
WHEN YOU WAKE UP, THE HEADACHE WILL BE THE LEAST OF YOUR PROBLEMS.
NICE THING ABOUT THE IMPERIAL CODES. ONE-BUTTON ACCESS TO ALL SORTS OF NICE THINGS.

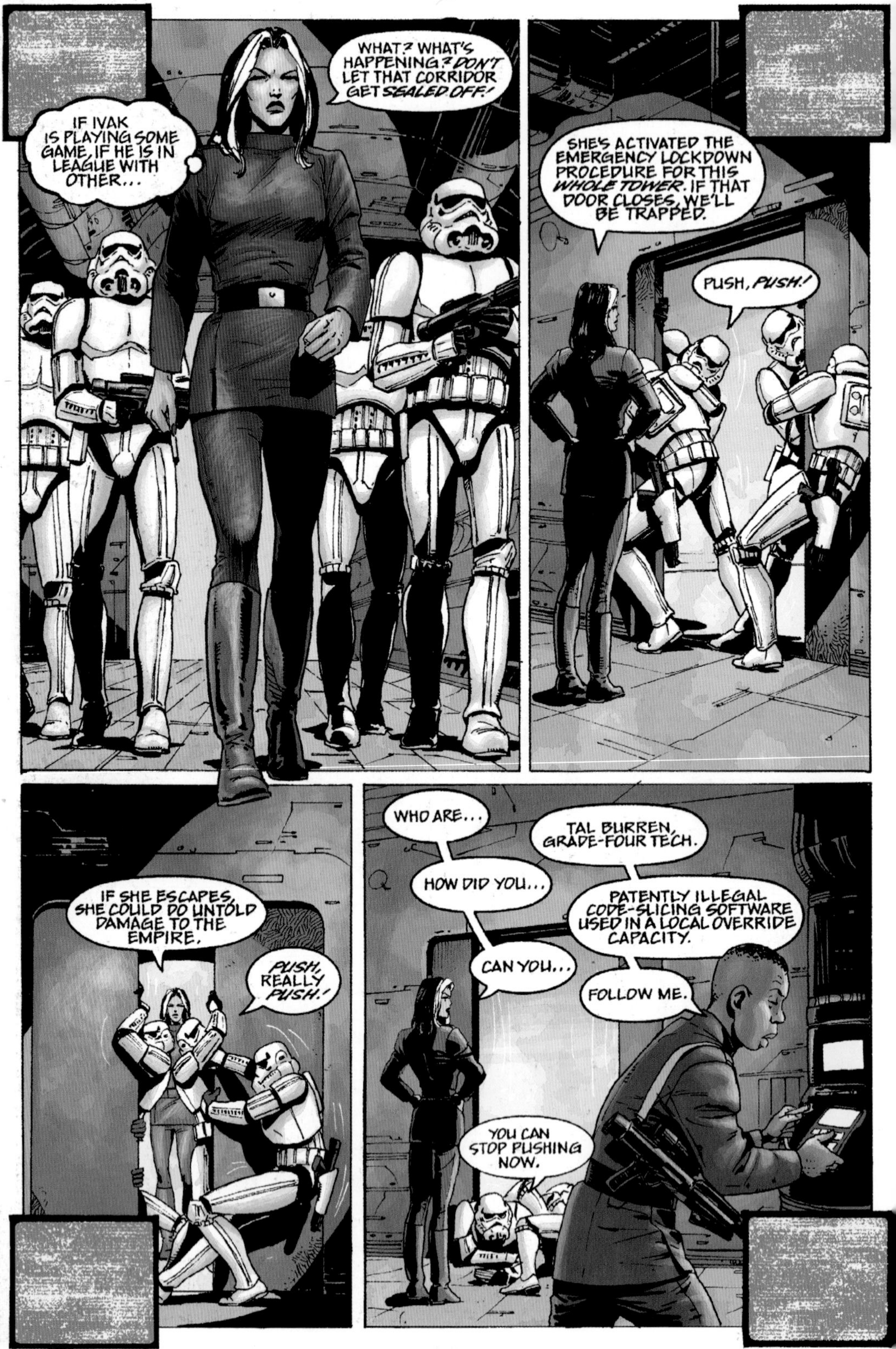
IF IVAK IS PLAYING SOME GAME, IF HE IS IN LEAGUE WITH OTHER...
WHAT? WHAT'S HAPPENING? DON'T LET THAT CORRIDOR GET SEALED OFF!
SHE'S ACTIVATED THE EMERGENCY LOCKDOWN PROCEDURE FOR THIS WHOLE TOWER. IF THAT DOOR CLOSES, WE'LL BE TRAPPED.
PUSH, PUSH!
IF SHE ESCAPES, SHE COULD DO UNTOLD DAMAGE TO THE EMPIRE.
PUSH, REALLY PUSH!
WHO ARE...
TAL BURREN, GRADE-FOUR TECH.
HOW DID YOU...
PATENTLY ILLEGAL CODE-SLICING SOFTWARE USED IN A LOCAL OVERRIDE CAPACITY.
CAN YOU...
FOLLOW ME.
YOU CAN STOP PUSHING NOW.

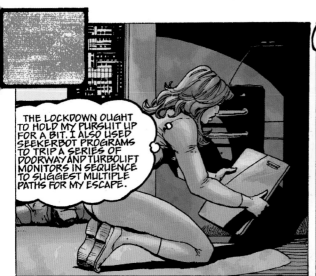

THE LOCKDOWN OUGHT TO HOLD MY PURSUIT UP FOR A BIT. I ALSO USED SEEKERBOT PROGRAMS TO TRIP A SERIES OF DOORWAY AND TURBOLIFT MONITORS IN SEQUENCE TO SUGGEST MULTIPLE PATHS FOR MY ESCAPE.

ISARD MIGHT KNOW ABOUT SOME OF THE SECRET PASSAGES IN THE PALACE HERE...

...BUT I DOUBT SHE KNOWS ABOUT *ALL* OF THEM.

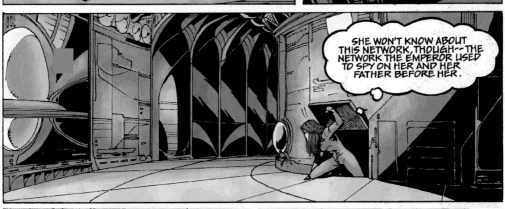

SHE WON'T KNOW ABOUT THIS NETWORK, THOUGH-- THE NETWORK THE EMPEROR USED TO SPY ON HER AND HER FATHER BEFORE HER.

ISARD WILL TAKE MY ESCAPE AS A PERSONAL AFFRONT, SO DISAPPEARING FROM IMPERIAL CENTER, OR INTO ITS DEPTHS, OFFER THE ONLY WAYS AWAY FROM HER.

OR I *COULD* KILL HER...

NO. ISARD IS AFTER ME BECAUSE SHE BELIEVES I CAN HURT THE EMPIRE. KILL HER AND THE REBELS WILL SUCCEED ALL THAT MUCH FASTER. I DON'T WANT THAT.

HERE'S THE TOWER WITH AN OVERLAY OF ACCESS POINTS TRIPPED SINCE THE LOCKDOWN. SHE'S *EVERYWHERE.*

DATA PHANTOMS. CROSSCHECK THE DOORS THAT HAVE BEEN TRIPPED WITH UPDATES TO THE MAINTENANCE FILES INDICATING OPENINGS AND CLOSINGS.

IT'LL TAKE JUST A MINUTE.

MAKE IT *THIRTY SECONDS* AND YOU'RE A GRADE-FIVE TECH.

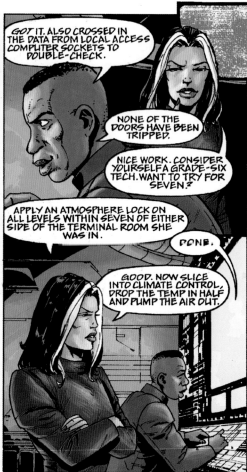

GOT IT. ALSO CROSSED IN THE DATA FROM LOCAL ACCESS COMPUTER SOCKETS TO DOUBLE-CHECK.

NONE OF THE DOORS HAVE BEEN TRIPPED.

NICE WORK. CONSIDER YOURSELF A GRADE-SIX TECH. WANT TO TRY FOR SEVEN?

APPLY AN ATMOSPHERE LOCK ON ALL LEVELS WITHIN SEVEN OF EITHER SIDE OF THE TERMINAL ROOM SHE WAS IN.

DONE.

GOOD. NOW SLICE INTO CLIMATE CONTROL, DROP THE TEMP IN HALF AND PUMP THE AIR OUT.

I CAN, IF YOU WISH, LOCK OUT ALL THE CELLS SO WE DON'T KILL THE PRISONERS.

REASONABLE IDEA. DO IT.

AND IF I THIN THE ATMOSPHERE I CAN KNOCK PEOPLE OUT WITHOUT SUFFOCATING THEM.

AND YOUR SUPERVISOR'S LAST EVALUATION SUGGESTED YOU'D NEVER MAKE GRADE-EIGHT. PROCEED.

ATMOSPHERE IS CONSISTENT WITH BEING ON TOP OF A 7,000 METER PEAK, MADAM DIRECTOR. MOVING WILL BE TORTURE.

SPLENDID. WE CAN USE FIREFIGHTERS' SUPPLEMENTAL OXYGEN SYSTEMS TO GET US TO THE TERMINAL ROOM.

I'LL CODE US SOME PASSES TO GIVE US ACCESS. THE SUPPLIES ARE JUST DOWN THE HALL.

ARE YOU NORMALLY THIS RESOURCEFUL, TAL BURREN...

...OR DID YOU *KNOW* I HAD AN OPENING FOR A GRADE-TEN TECH ON MY PERSONAL STAFF?

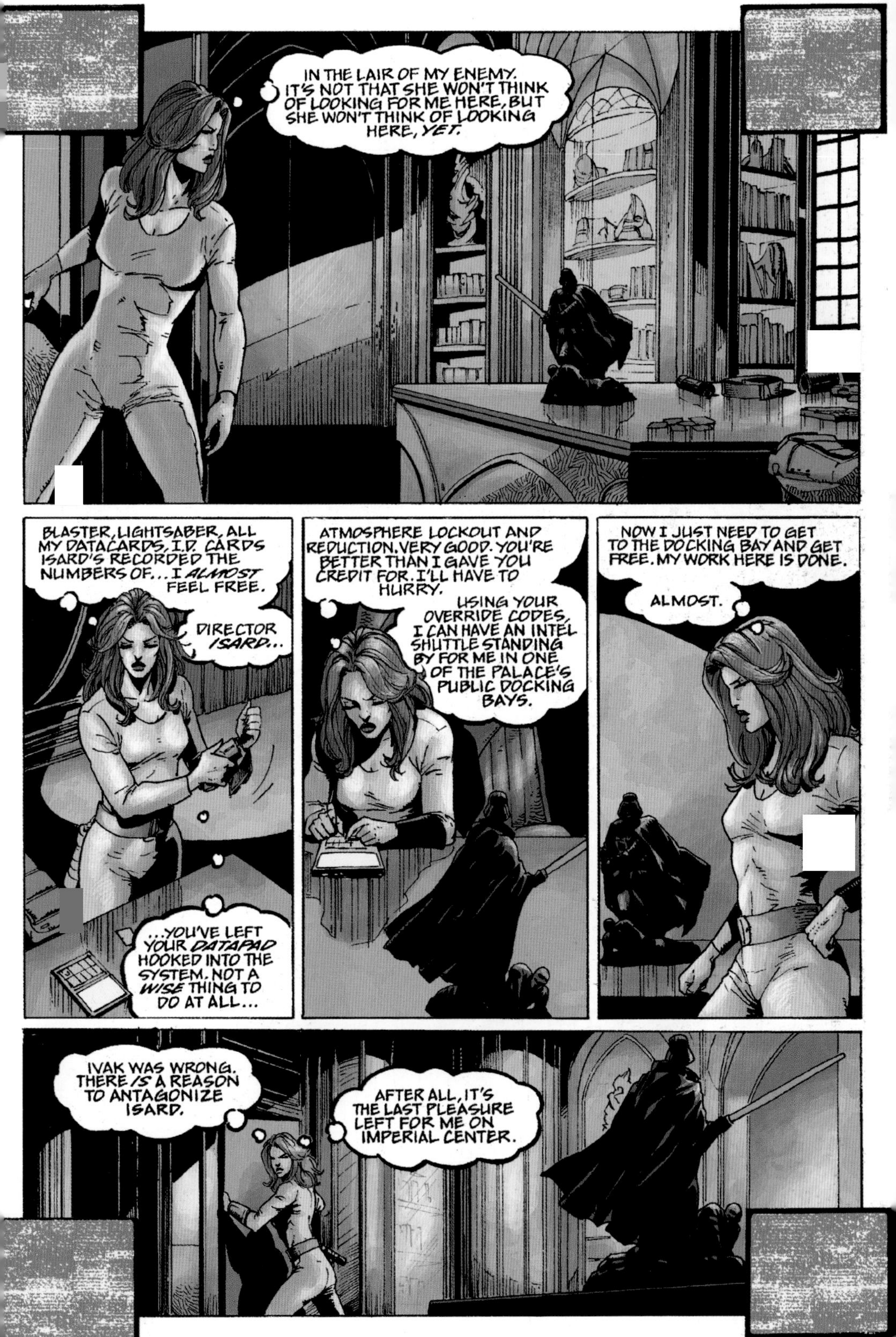

IN THE LAIR OF MY ENEMY. IT'S NOT THAT SHE WON'T THINK OF LOOKING FOR ME HERE, BUT SHE WON'T THINK OF LOOKING HERE, YET.
BLASTER, LIGHTSABER, ALL MY DATACARDS, I.D. CARDS ISARD'S RECORDED THE NUMBERS OF... I ALMOST FEEL FREE.
DIRECTOR ISARD...
...YOU'VE LEFT YOUR DATAPAD HOOKED INTO THE SYSTEM. NOT A WISE THING TO DO AT ALL...
ATMOSPHERE LOCKOUT AND REDUCTION. VERY GOOD. YOU'RE BETTER THAN I GAVE YOU CREDIT FOR. I'LL HAVE TO HURRY.
USING YOUR OVERRIDE CODES, I CAN HAVE AN INTEL SHUTTLE STANDING BY FOR ME IN ONE OF THE PALACE'S PUBLIC DOCKING BAYS.
NOW I JUST NEED TO GET TO THE DOCKING BAY AND GET FREE. MY WORK HERE IS DONE.
ALMOST.
IVAK WAS WRONG. THERE IS A REASON TO ANTAGONIZE ISARD.
AFTER ALL, IT'S THE LAST PLEASURE LEFT FOR ME ON IMPERIAL CENTER.

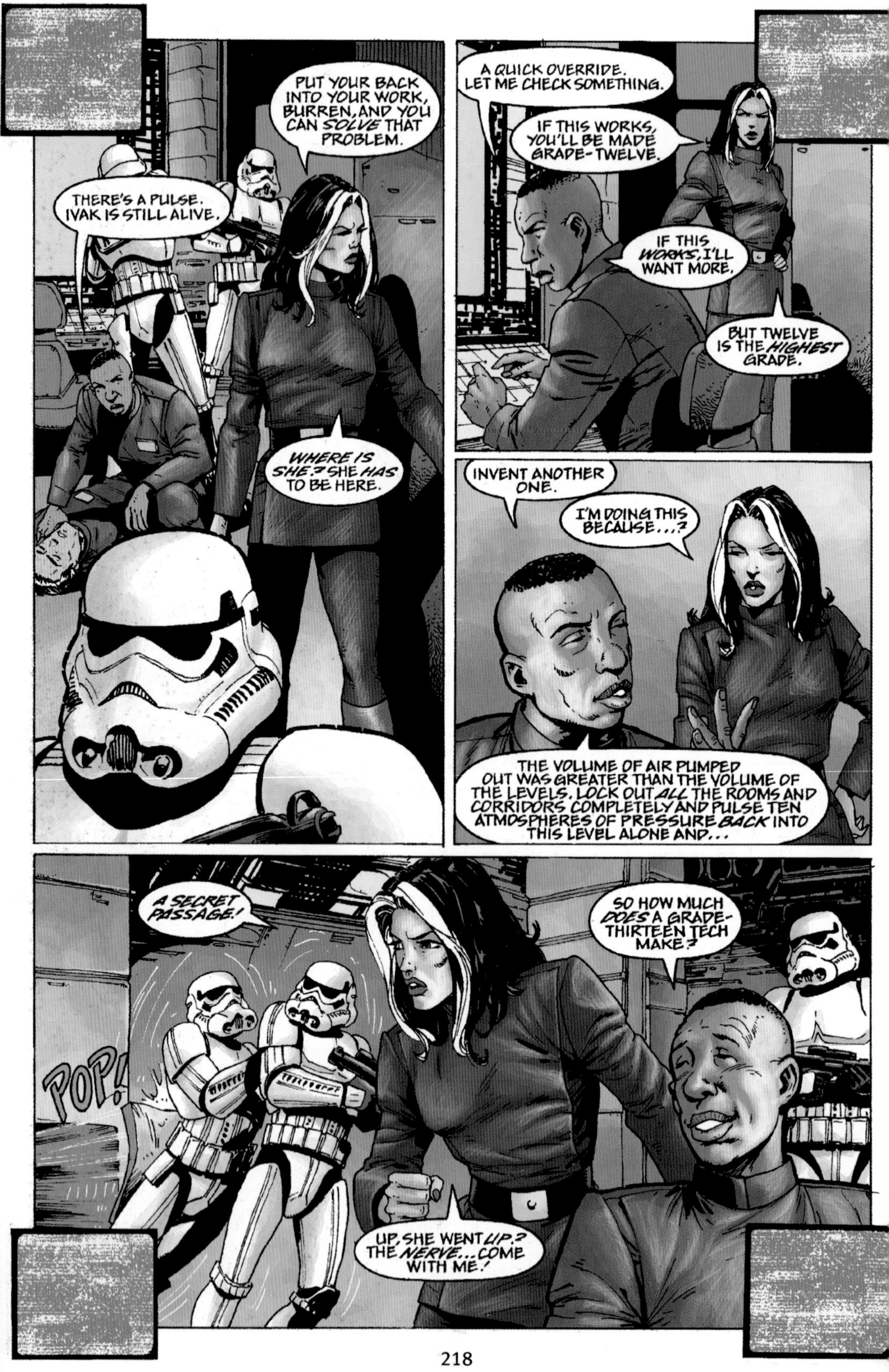
PUT YOUR BACK INTO YOUR WORK, BURREN, AND YOU CAN SOLVE THAT PROBLEM.
THERE'S A PULSE. IVAK IS STILL ALIVE.
WHERE IS SHE? SHE HAS TO BE HERE.
A QUICK OVERRIDE. LET ME CHECK SOMETHING.
IF THIS WORKS, YOU'LL BE MADE GRADE-TWELVE.
IF THIS WORKS, I'LL WANT MORE.
BUT TWELVE IS THE HIGHEST GRADE.
INVENT ANOTHER ONE.
I'M DOING THIS BECAUSE...?
THE VOLUME OF AIR PUMPED OUT WAS GREATER THAN THE VOLUME OF THE LEVELS. LOCK OUT ALL THE ROOMS AND CORRIDORS COMPLETELY AND PULSE TEN ATMOSPHERES OF PRESSURE BACK INTO THIS LEVEL ALONE AND...
A SECRET PASSAGE!
POP!
UP, SHE WENT UP? THE NERVE... COME WITH ME!
SO HOW MUCH DOES A GRADE-THIRTEEN TECH MAKE?

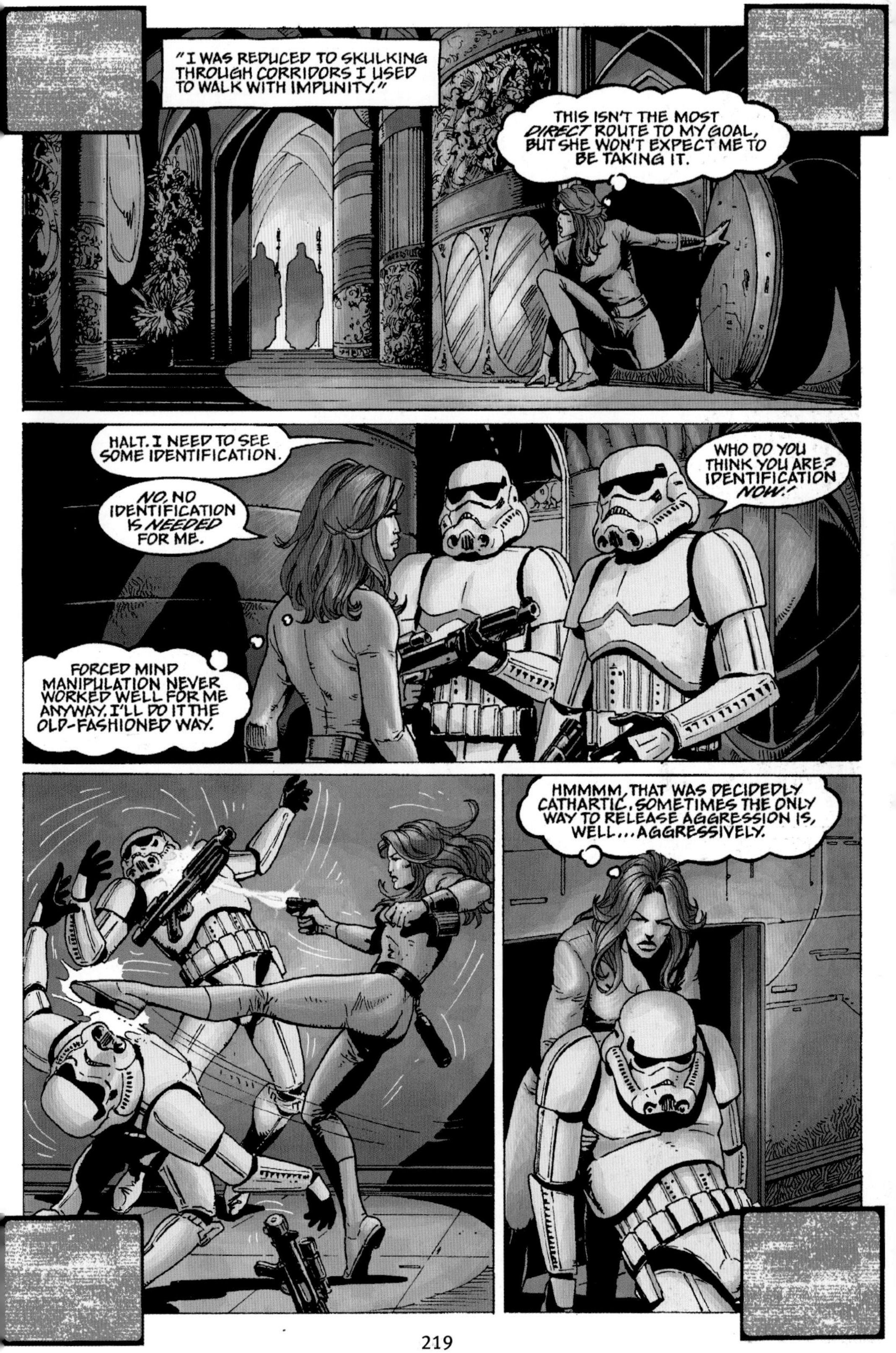
"I WAS REDUCED TO SKULKING THROUGH CORRIDORS I USED TO WALK WITH IMPUNITY."
THIS ISN'T THE MOST *DIRECT* ROUTE TO MY GOAL, BUT SHE WON'T EXPECT ME TO BE TAKING IT.
HALT. I NEED TO SEE SOME IDENTIFICATION.
NO. NO IDENTIFICATION IS *NEEDED* FOR ME.
WHO DO YOU THINK YOU ARE? IDENTIFICATION *NOW!*
FORCED MIND MANIPULATION NEVER WORKED WELL FOR ME ANYWAY. I'LL DO IT THE OLD-FASHIONED WAY.
HMMMM, THAT WAS DECIDEDLY CATHARTIC. SOMETIMES THE ONLY WAY TO RELEASE AGGRESSION IS, WELL... AGGRESSIVELY.

SHE WAS HERE. IN MY OFFICE. HERE, AND NOT LONG AGO.

DATAPAD IS ON, AND IT HAS LEVEL ALPHA-SUPERNOVA CLEARANCE. YOU LEFT IT ON, I TAKE IT? NASTY SECURITY BREACH.

TECH GRADES ALSO GO *DOWN*, BURREN.

SO WILL SHE. SHE ORDERED AN INTEL SHUTTLE TO DOCKING BAY 54, THIS TOWER.

I'LL ORDER ALL TRAFFIC INTO AND OUT OF THAT BAY *FROZEN*. WE WILL *HAVE* HER.

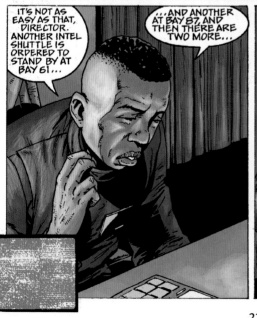

IT'S NOT AS EASY AS THAT, DIRECTOR. ANOTHER INTEL SHUTTLE IS ORDERED TO STAND BY AT BAY 61...

...AND ANOTHER AT BAY 87, AND THEN THERE ARE TWO MORE...

THIS IS SIMPLY *TOO MUCH*. MY OFFICE, MY CODES...

AND ANOTHER ONE...

SHUT UP, FOOL! FIND THE SHUTTLE *LOKVAR*, MY PERSONAL SHUTTLE. SEND PEOPLE TO COVER THE OTHERS...

...BUT WE WILL GO TO THE *LOKVAR*.

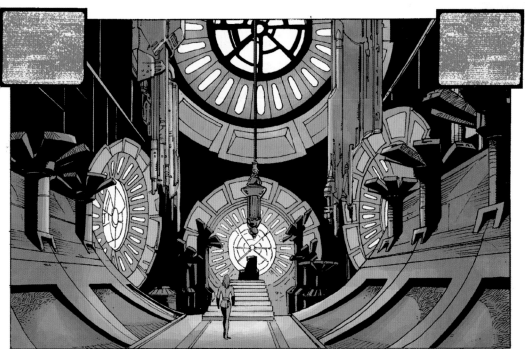

ALL I EVER WANTED WAS TO SERVE THE MAN FOR WHOM THIS THRONE WAS CREATED. IF I HAD DONE *MORE*, DONE *BETTER*, HE WOULD BE HERE STILL.

NOW I HAVE TO DO WHAT I CAN TO *GUARANTEE* THAT I WILL *LIVE* WITH THE *CONSEQUENCES* OF MY *FAILURE*.

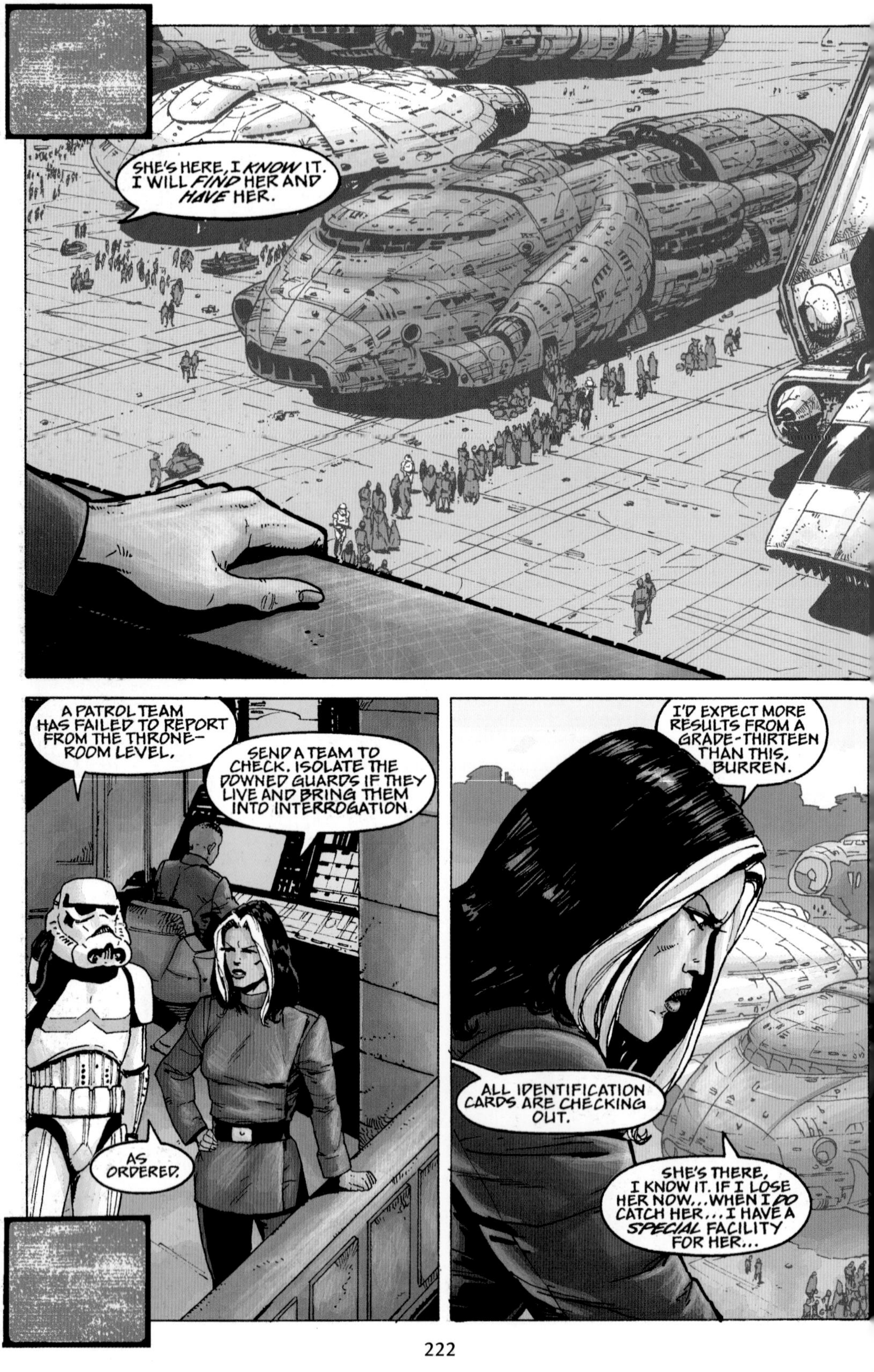
SHE'S HERE, I *KNOW* IT. I WILL *FIND* HER AND *HAVE* HER.
A PATROL TEAM HAS FAILED TO REPORT FROM THE THRONE-ROOM LEVEL.
SEND A TEAM TO CHECK. ISOLATE THE DOWNED GUARDS IF THEY LIVE AND BRING THEM INTO INTERROGATION.
AS ORDERED.
I'D EXPECT MORE RESULTS FROM A GRADE-THIRTEEN THAN THIS, BURREN.
ALL IDENTIFICATION CARDS ARE CHECKING OUT.
SHE'S THERE, I KNOW IT. IF I LOSE HER NOW... WHEN I *DO* CATCH HER... I HAVE A *SPECIAL* FACILITY FOR HER...

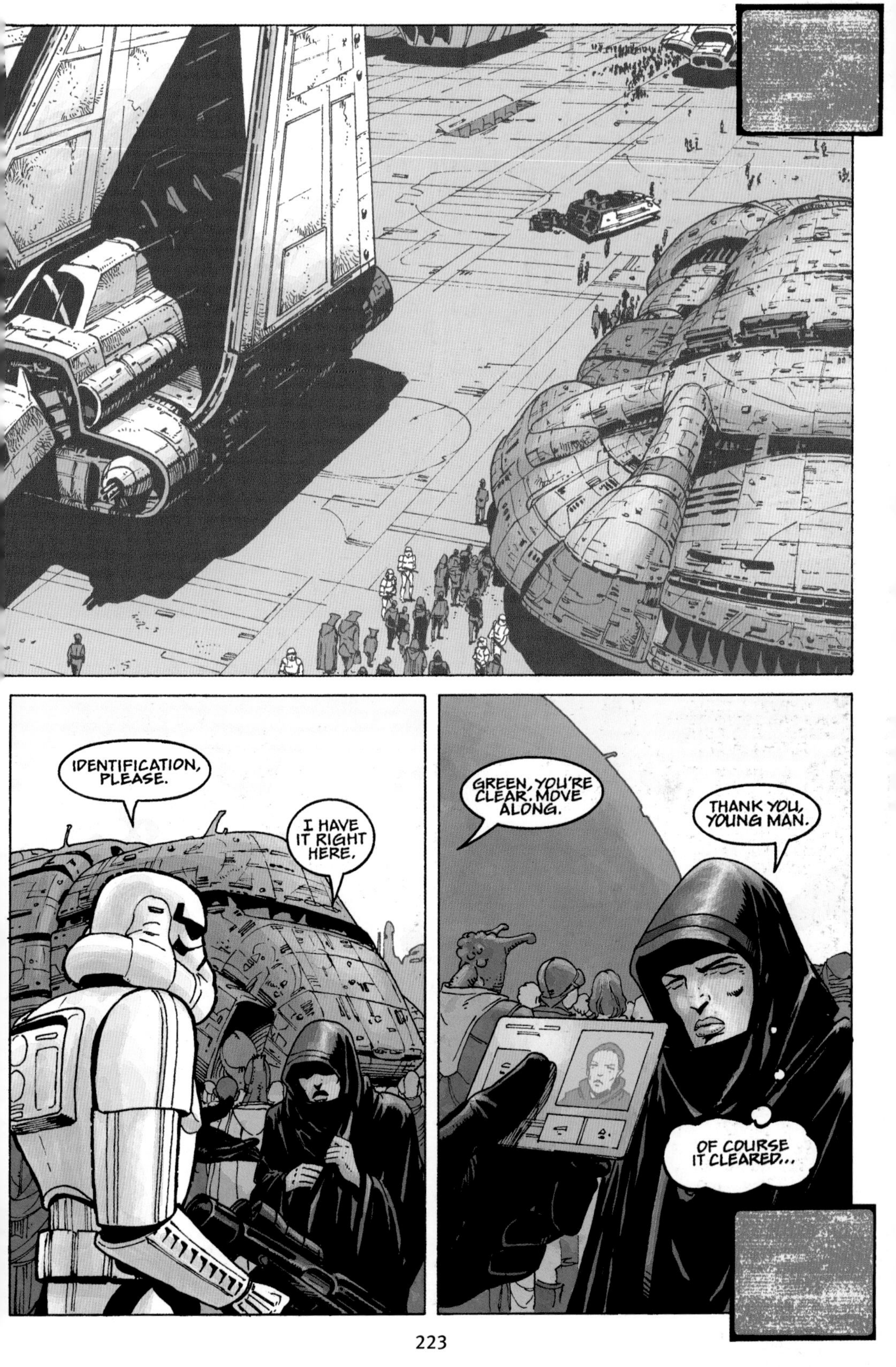
IDENTIFICATION, PLEASE.
I HAVE IT RIGHT HERE.
GREEN, YOU'RE CLEAR. MOVE ALONG.
THANK YOU, YOUNG MAN.
OF COURSE IT CLEARED...

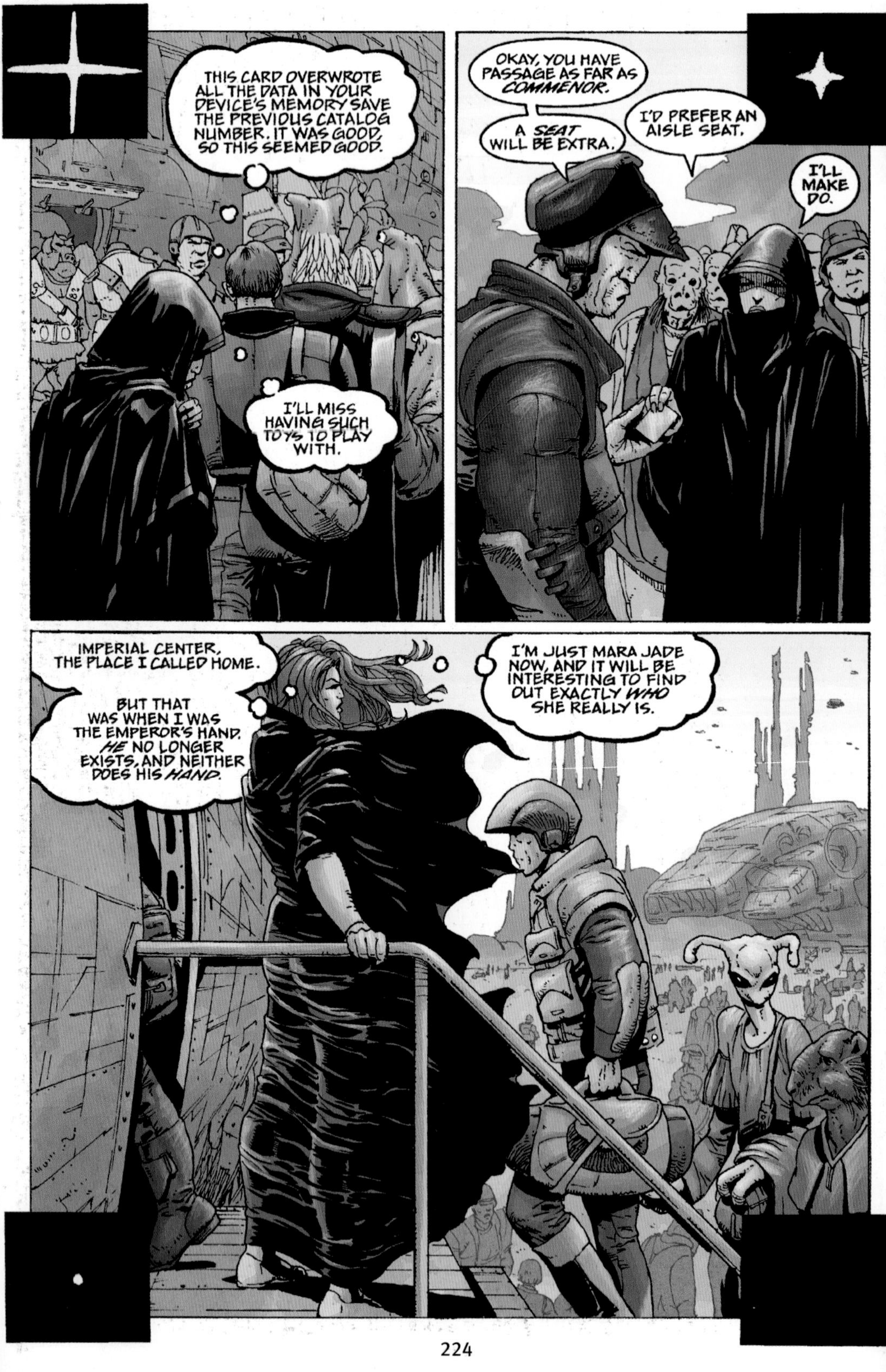
THIS CARD OVERWROTE ALL THE DATA IN YOUR DEVICE'S MEMORY SAVE THE PREVIOUS CATALOG NUMBER. IT WAS GOOD, SO THIS SEEMED GOOD.
I'LL MISS HAVING SUCH TOYS TO PLAY WITH.
OKAY, YOU HAVE PASSAGE AS FAR AS COMMENOR.
A SEAT WILL BE EXTRA.
I'D PREFER AN AISLE SEAT.
I'LL MAKE DO.
IMPERIAL CENTER, THE PLACE I CALLED HOME.
BUT THAT WAS WHEN I WAS THE EMPEROR'S HAND. HE NO LONGER EXISTS, AND NEITHER DOES HIS HAND.
I'M JUST MARA JADE NOW, AND IT WILL BE INTERESTING TO FIND OUT EXACTLY WHO SHE REALLY IS.

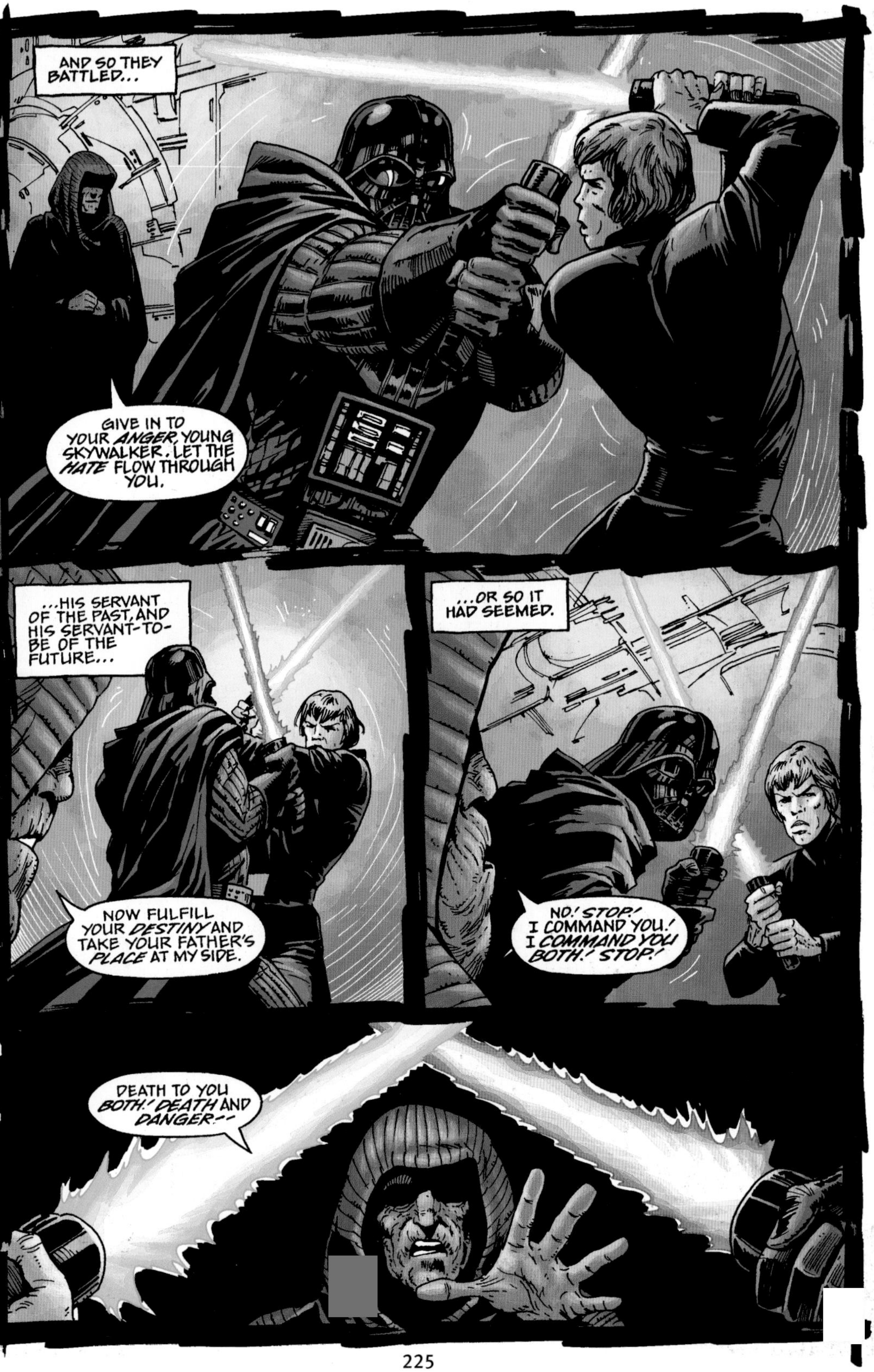
AND SO THEY BATTLED...
GIVE IN TO YOUR *ANGER*, YOUNG SKYWALKER. LET THE *HATE* FLOW THROUGH YOU.
...HIS SERVANT OF THE PAST, AND HIS SERVANT-TO-BE OF THE FUTURE...
NOW FULFILL YOUR *DESTINY* AND TAKE YOUR FATHER'S *PLACE* AT MY SIDE.
...OR SO IT HAD SEEMED.
NO! *STOP!* I COMMAND YOU! I *COMMAND YOU BOTH! STOP!*
DEATH TO YOU *BOTH! DEATH* AND *DANGER--*

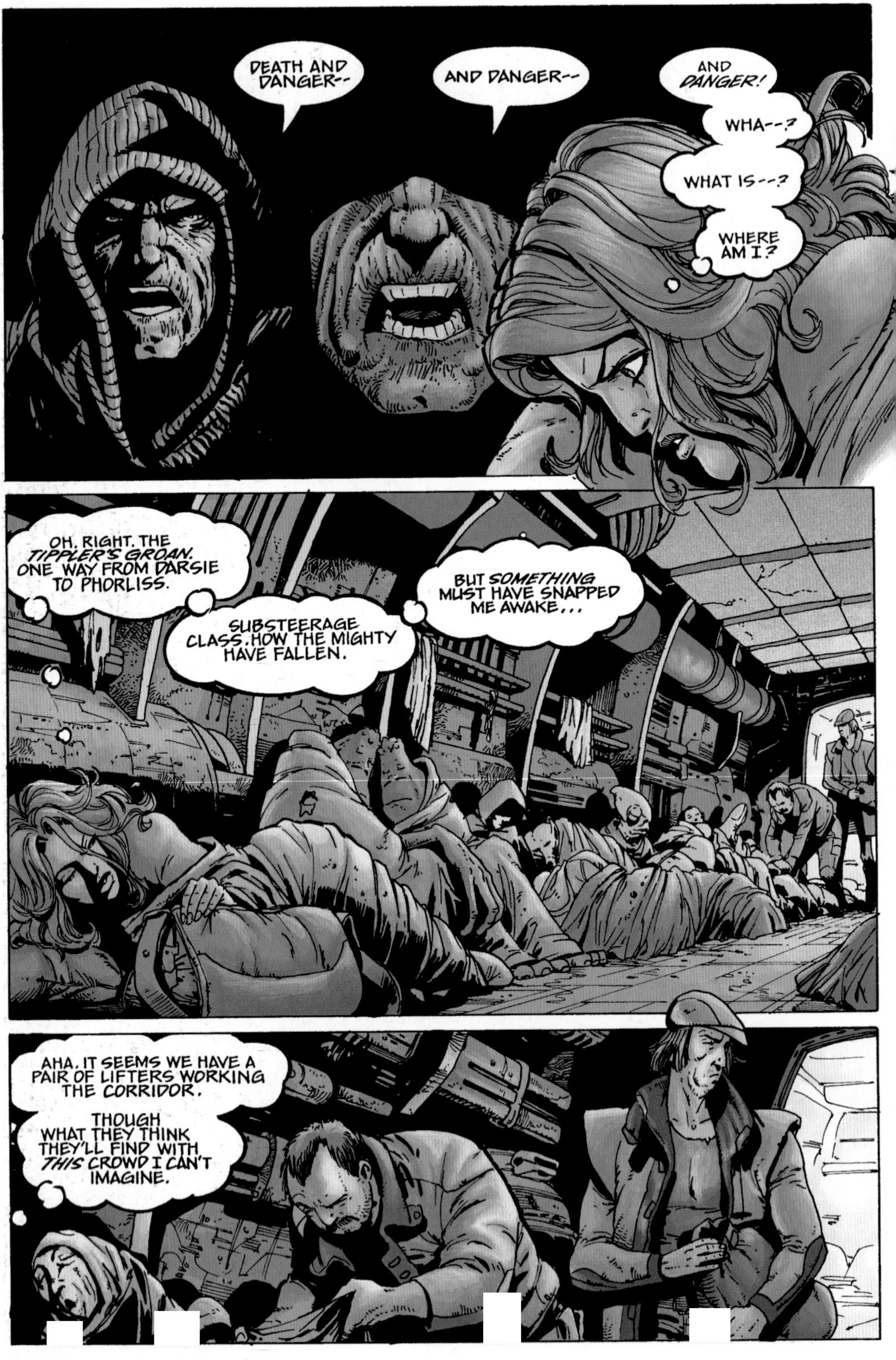
DEATH AND DANGER--
AND DANGER--
AND *DANGER!*
WHA--?
WHAT IS--?
WHERE AM I?
OH, RIGHT. THE *TIPPLER'S GROAN.* ONE WAY FROM DARSIE TO PHORLISS.
SUBSTEERAGE CLASS. HOW THE MIGHTY HAVE FALLEN.
BUT *SOMETHING* MUST HAVE SNAPPED ME AWAKE...
AHA. IT SEEMS WE HAVE A PAIR OF LIFTERS WORKING THE CORRIDOR.
THOUGH WHAT THEY THINK THEY'LL FIND WITH *THIS* CROWD I CAN'T IMAGINE.

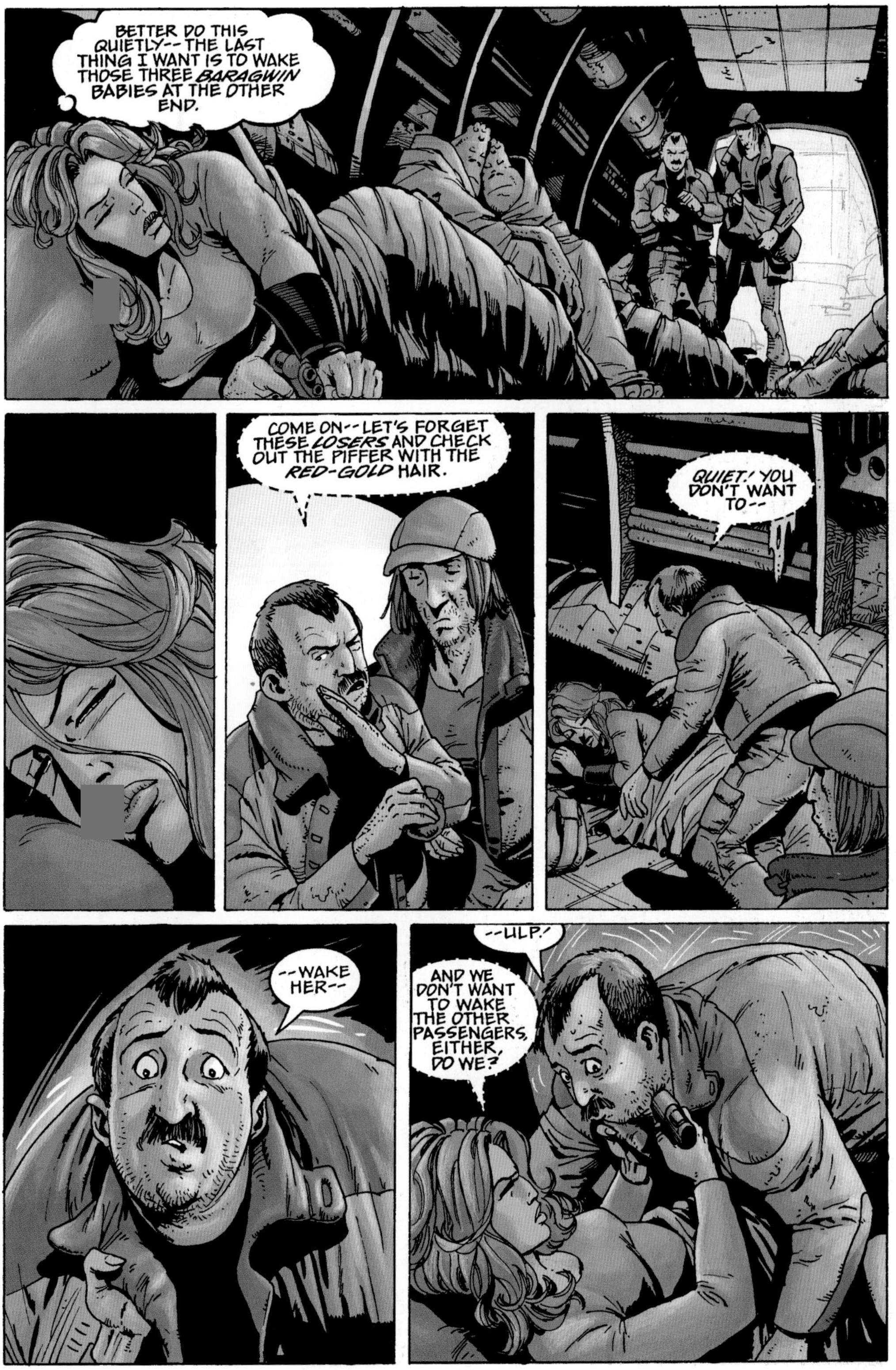
BETTER DO THIS QUIETLY-- THE LAST THING I WANT IS TO WAKE THOSE THREE BARAGWIN BABIES AT THE OTHER END.
COME ON--LET'S FORGET THESE LOSERS AND CHECK OUT THE PIFFER WITH THE RED-GOLD HAIR.
QUIET! YOU DON'T WANT TO--
--WAKE HER--
--ULP!
AND WE DON'T WANT TO WAKE THE OTHER PASSENGERS, EITHER, DO WE?

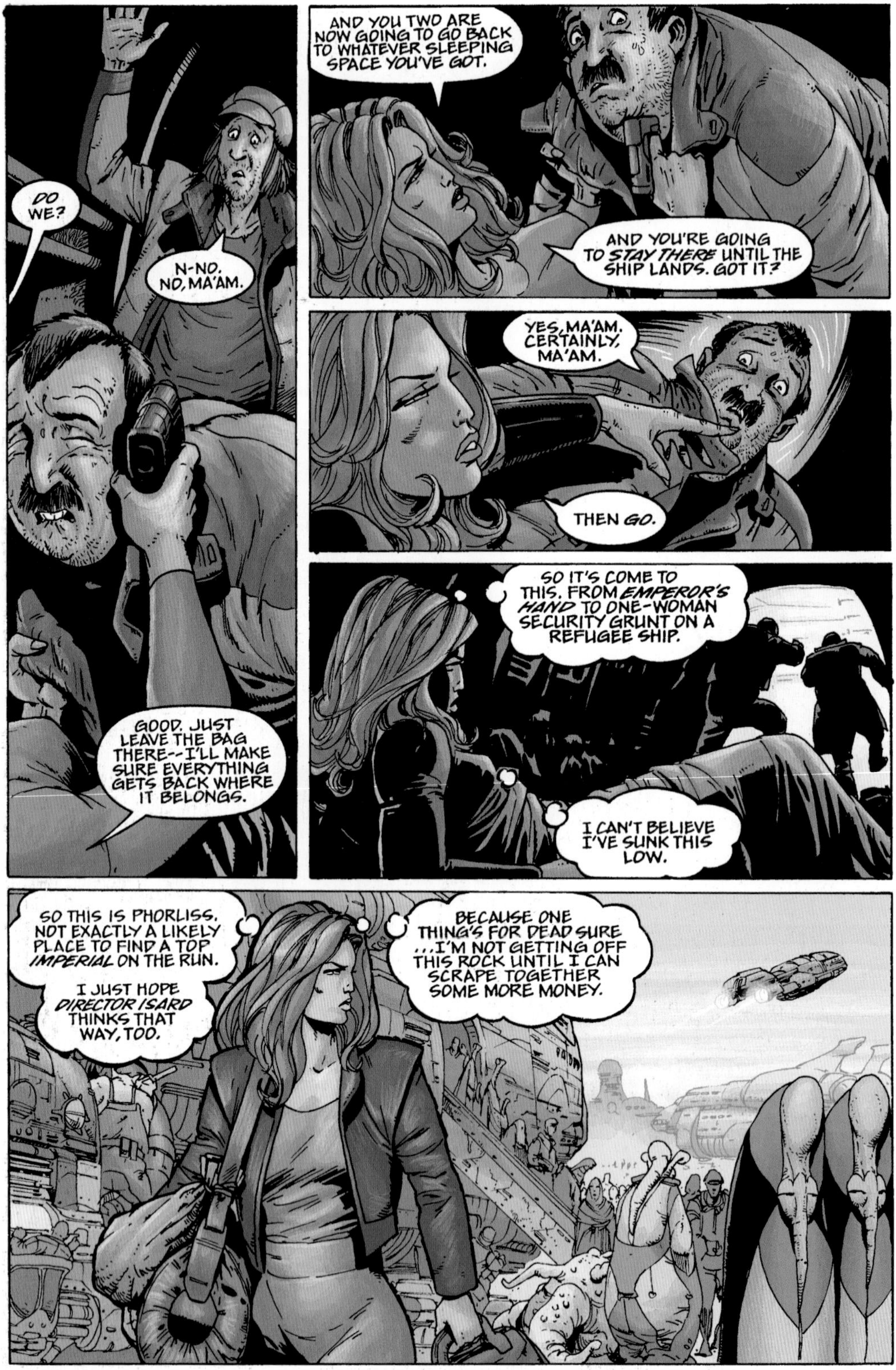
DO WE?
N-NO. NO, MA'AM.
GOOD. JUST LEAVE THE BAG THERE--I'LL MAKE SURE EVERYTHING GETS BACK WHERE IT BELONGS.
AND YOU TWO ARE NOW GOING TO GO BACK TO WHATEVER SLEEPING SPACE YOU'VE GOT.
AND YOU'RE GOING TO STAY THERE UNTIL THE SHIP LANDS. GOT IT?
YES, MA'AM. CERTAINLY, MA'AM.
THEN GO.
SO IT'S COME TO THIS. FROM EMPEROR'S HAND TO ONE-WOMAN SECURITY GRUNT ON A REFUGEE SHIP.
I CAN'T BELIEVE I'VE SUNK THIS LOW.
SO THIS IS PHORLISS. NOT EXACTLY A LIKELY PLACE TO FIND A TOP IMPERIAL ON THE RUN.
I JUST HOPE DIRECTOR ISARD THINKS THAT WAY, TOO.
BECAUSE ONE THING'S FOR DEAD SURE ...I'M NOT GETTING OFF THIS ROCK UNTIL I CAN SCRAPE TOGETHER SOME MORE MONEY.

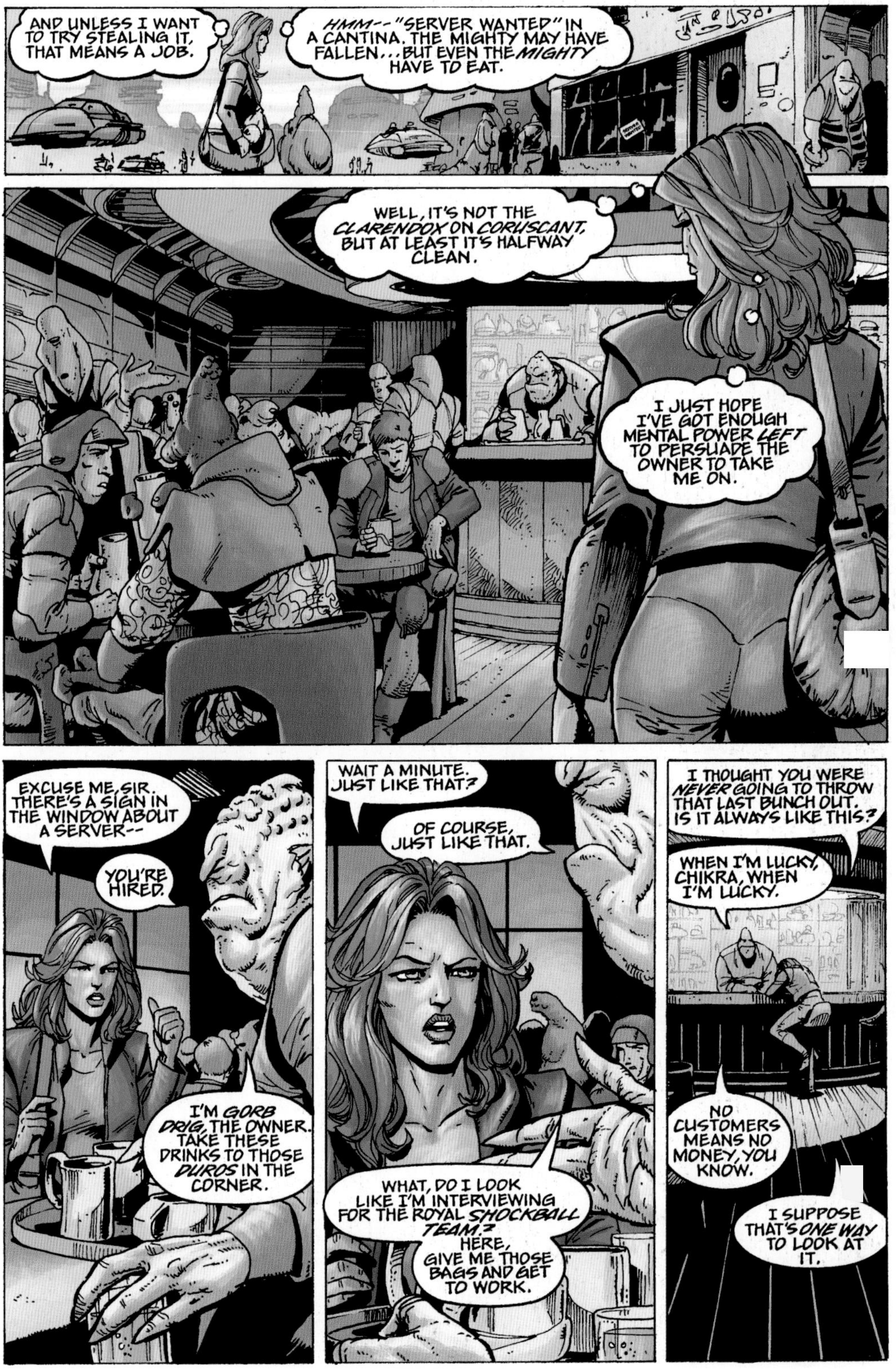
AND UNLESS I WANT TO TRY STEALING IT, THAT MEANS A JOB.
HMM-- "SERVER WANTED" IN A CANTINA. THE MIGHTY MAY HAVE FALLEN... BUT EVEN THE MIGHTY HAVE TO EAT.
WELL, IT'S NOT THE CLARENDOX ON CORUSCANT, BUT AT LEAST IT'S HALFWAY CLEAN.
I JUST HOPE I'VE GOT ENOUGH MENTAL POWER LEFT TO PERSUADE THE OWNER TO TAKE ME ON.
EXCUSE ME, SIR. THERE'S A SIGN IN THE WINDOW ABOUT A SERVER--
YOU'RE HIRED.
I'M GORB DRIG, THE OWNER. TAKE THESE DRINKS TO THOSE DUROS IN THE CORNER.
WAIT A MINUTE. JUST LIKE THAT?
OF COURSE, JUST LIKE THAT.
WHAT, DO I LOOK LIKE I'M INTERVIEWING FOR THE ROYAL SHOCKBALL TEAM?
HERE, GIVE ME THOSE BAGS AND GET TO WORK.
I THOUGHT YOU WERE NEVER GOING TO THROW THAT LAST BUNCH OUT. IS IT ALWAYS LIKE THIS?
WHEN I'M LUCKY, CHIKRA, WHEN I'M LUCKY.
NO CUSTOMERS MEANS NO MONEY, YOU KNOW.
I SUPPOSE THAT'S ONE WAY TO LOOK AT IT.

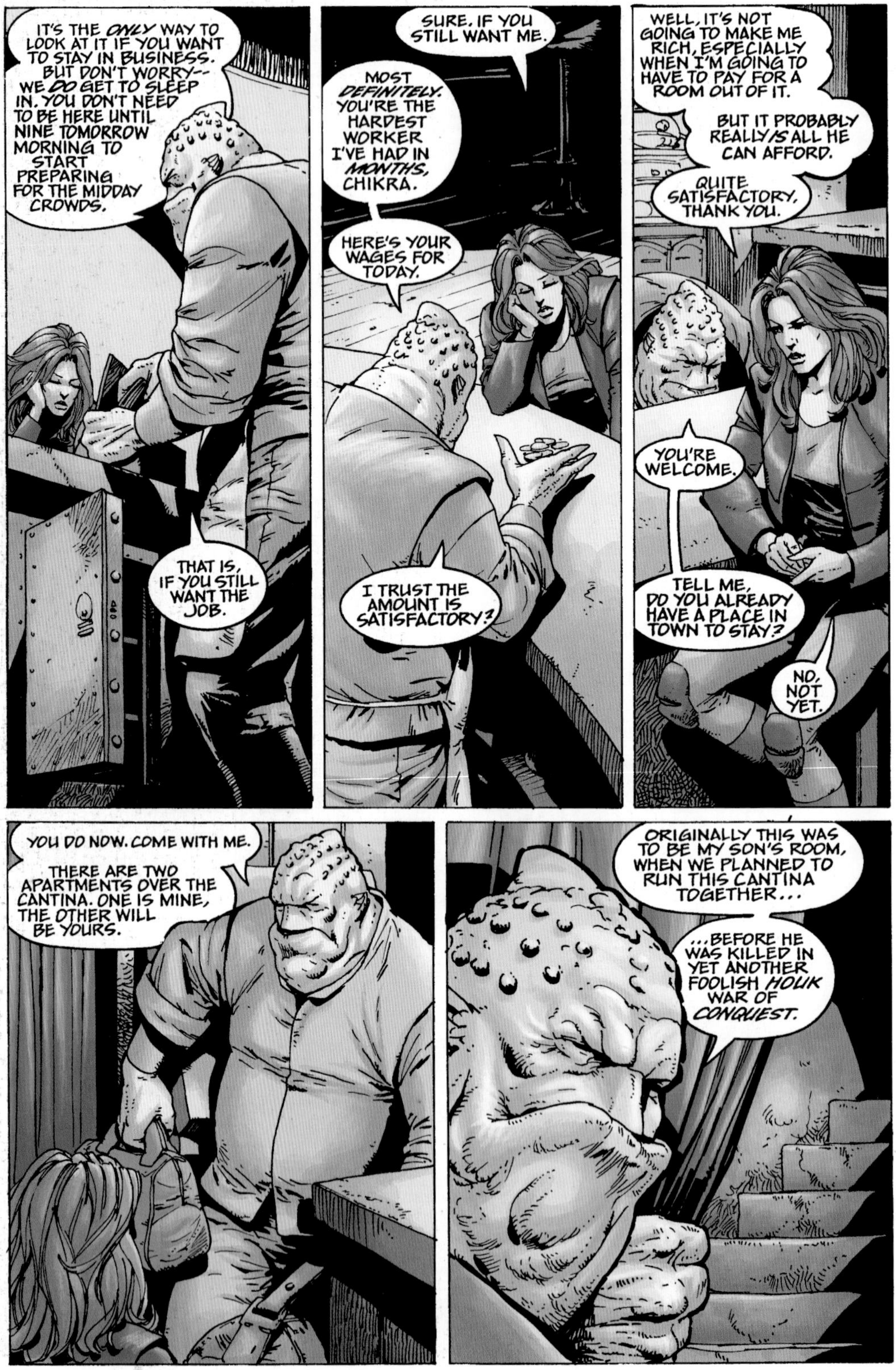
IT'S THE ONLY WAY TO LOOK AT IT IF YOU WANT TO STAY IN BUSINESS.
BUT DON'T WORRY-- WE DO GET TO SLEEP IN. YOU DON'T NEED TO BE HERE UNTIL NINE TOMORROW MORNING TO START PREPARING FOR THE MIDDAY CROWDS.
THAT IS, IF YOU STILL WANT THE JOB.
SURE. IF YOU STILL WANT ME.
MOST DEFINITELY. YOU'RE THE HARDEST WORKER I'VE HAD IN MONTHS, CHIKRA.
HERE'S YOUR WAGES FOR TODAY.
I TRUST THE AMOUNT IS SATISFACTORY?
WELL, IT'S NOT GOING TO MAKE ME RICH, ESPECIALLY WHEN I'M GOING TO HAVE TO PAY FOR A ROOM OUT OF IT.
BUT IT PROBABLY REALLY IS ALL HE CAN AFFORD.
QUITE SATISFACTORY, THANK YOU.
YOU'RE WELCOME.
TELL ME, DO YOU ALREADY HAVE A PLACE IN TOWN TO STAY?
NO, NOT YET.
YOU DO NOW. COME WITH ME.
THERE ARE TWO APARTMENTS OVER THE CANTINA. ONE IS MINE, THE OTHER WILL BE YOURS.
ORIGINALLY THIS WAS TO BE MY SON'S ROOM, WHEN WE PLANNED TO RUN THIS CANTINA TOGETHER...
...BEFORE HE WAS KILLED IN YET ANOTHER FOOLISH HOUK WAR OF CONQUEST.

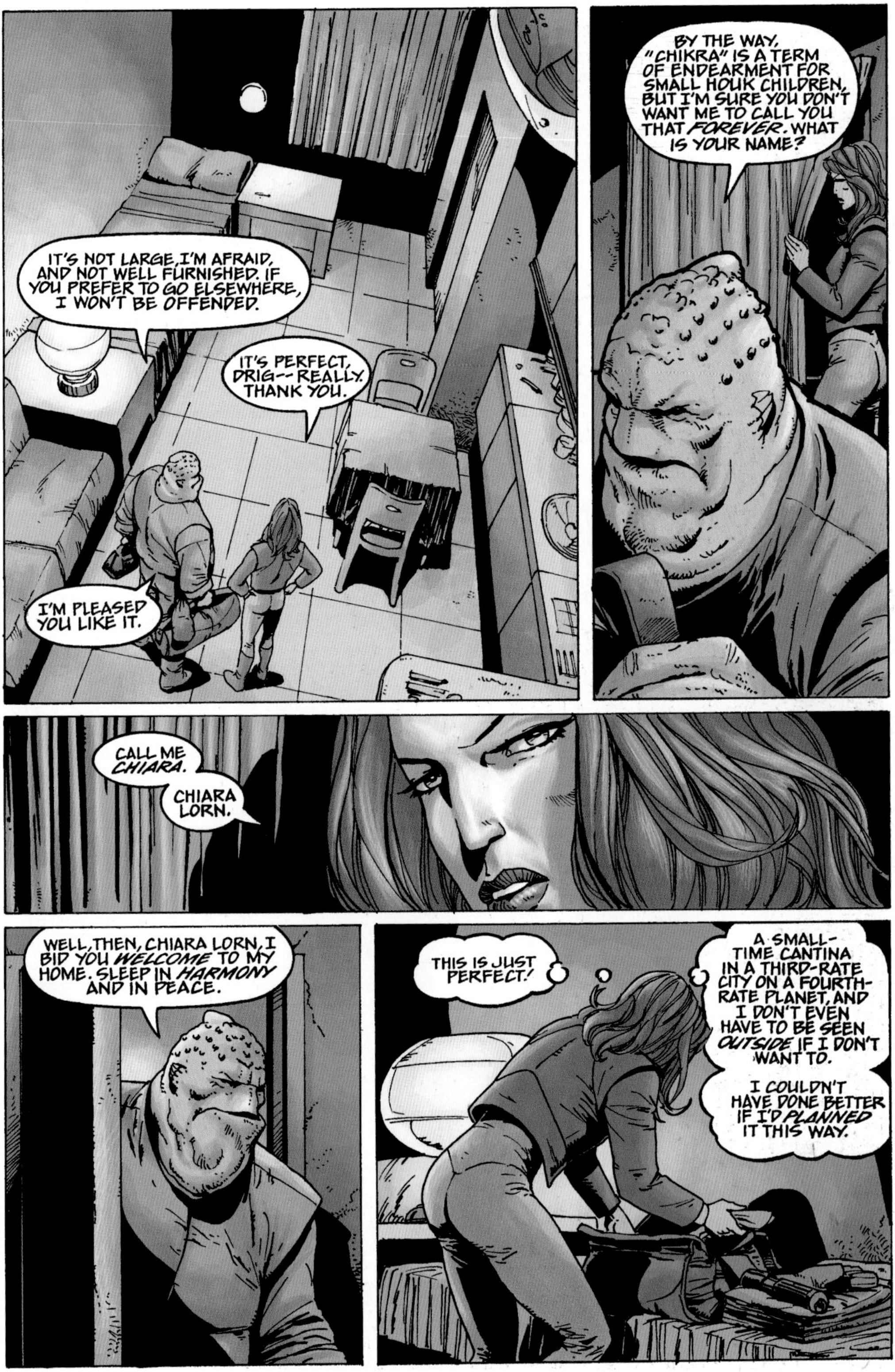

IT'S NOT LARGE, I'M AFRAID, AND NOT WELL FURNISHED. IF YOU PREFER TO GO ELSEWHERE, I WON'T BE OFFENDED.
IT'S PERFECT, DRIG--REALLY. THANK YOU.
I'M PLEASED YOU LIKE IT.
BY THE WAY, "CHIKRA" IS A TERM OF ENDEARMENT FOR SMALL HOUK CHILDREN, BUT I'M SURE YOU DON'T WANT ME TO CALL YOU THAT FOREVER. WHAT IS YOUR NAME?
CALL ME CHIARA.
CHIARA LORN.
WELL, THEN, CHIARA LORN, I BID YOU WELCOME TO MY HOME. SLEEP IN HARMONY AND IN PEACE.
THIS IS JUST PERFECT!
A SMALL-TIME CANTINA IN A THIRD-RATE CITY ON A FOURTH-RATE PLANET, AND I DON'T EVEN HAVE TO BE SEEN OUTSIDE IF I DON'T WANT TO.
I COULDN'T HAVE DONE BETTER IF I'D PLANNED IT THIS WAY.

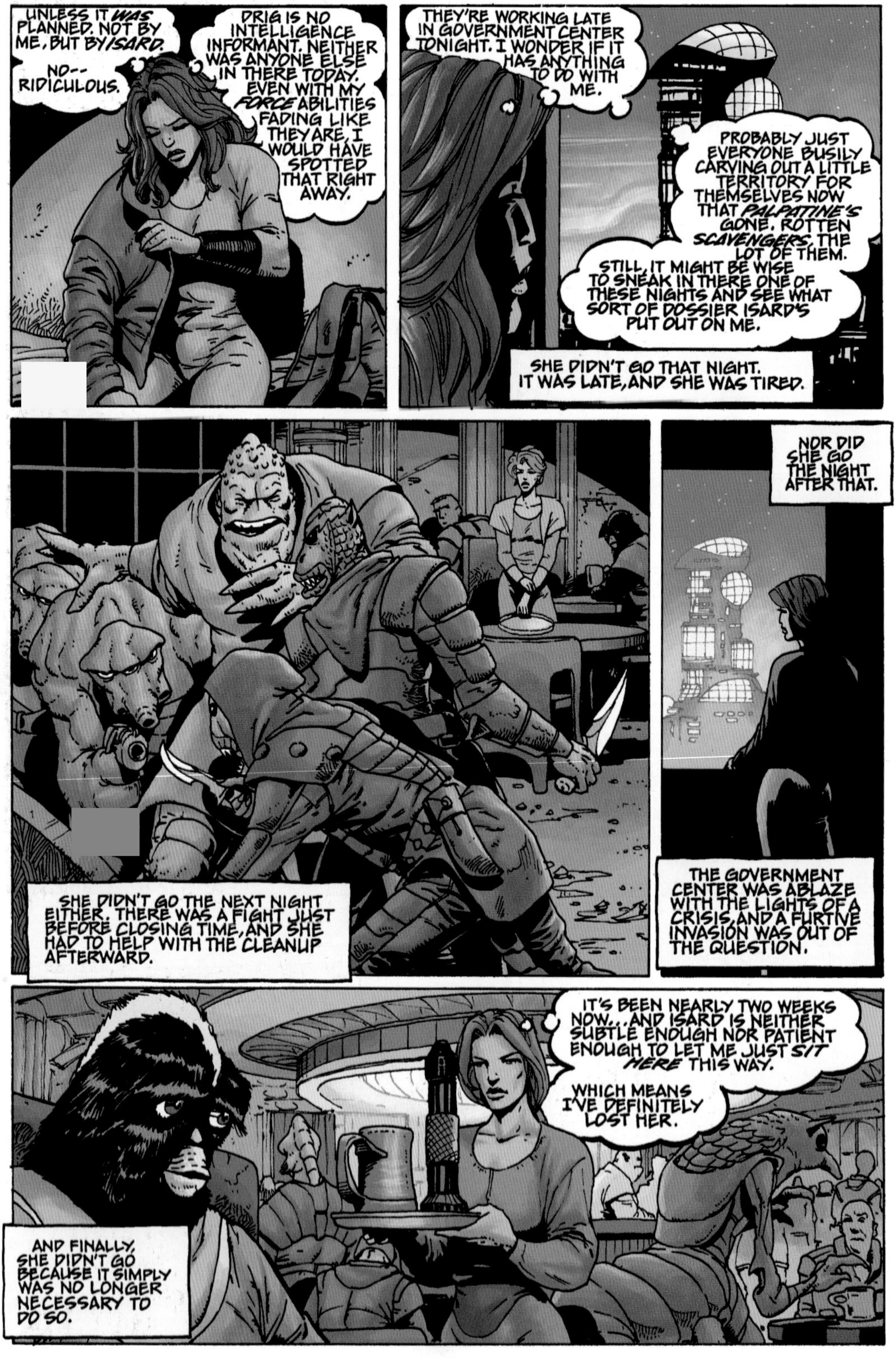

UNLESS IT WAS PLANNED. NOT BY ME, BUT BY ISARD.
NO-- RIDICULOUS.
DRIG IS NO INTELLIGENCE INFORMANT. NEITHER WAS ANYONE ELSE IN THERE TODAY. EVEN WITH MY FORCE ABILITIES FADING LIKE THEY ARE, I WOULD HAVE SPOTTED THAT RIGHT AWAY.
THEY'RE WORKING LATE IN GOVERNMENT CENTER TONIGHT. I WONDER IF IT HAS ANYTHING TO DO WITH ME.
PROBABLY JUST EVERYONE BUSILY CARVING OUT A LITTLE TERRITORY FOR THEMSELVES NOW THAT PALPATINE'S GONE. ROTTEN SCAVENGERS, THE LOT OF THEM.
STILL, IT MIGHT BE WISE TO SNEAK IN THERE ONE OF THESE NIGHTS AND SEE WHAT SORT OF DOSSIER ISARD'S PUT OUT ON ME.
SHE DIDN'T GO THAT NIGHT. IT WAS LATE, AND SHE WAS TIRED.
SHE DIDN'T GO THE NEXT NIGHT EITHER. THERE WAS A FIGHT JUST BEFORE CLOSING TIME, AND SHE HAD TO HELP WITH THE CLEANUP AFTERWARD.
NOR DID SHE GO THE NIGHT AFTER THAT.
THE GOVERNMENT CENTER WAS ABLAZE WITH THE LIGHTS OF A CRISIS, AND A FURTIVE INVASION WAS OUT OF THE QUESTION.
AND FINALLY, SHE DIDN'T GO BECAUSE IT SIMPLY WAS NO LONGER NECESSARY TO DO SO.
IT'S BEEN NEARLY TWO WEEKS NOW... AND ISARD IS NEITHER SUBTLE ENOUGH NOR PATIENT ENOUGH TO LET ME JUST SIT HERE THIS WAY.
WHICH MEANS I'VE DEFINITELY LOST HER.

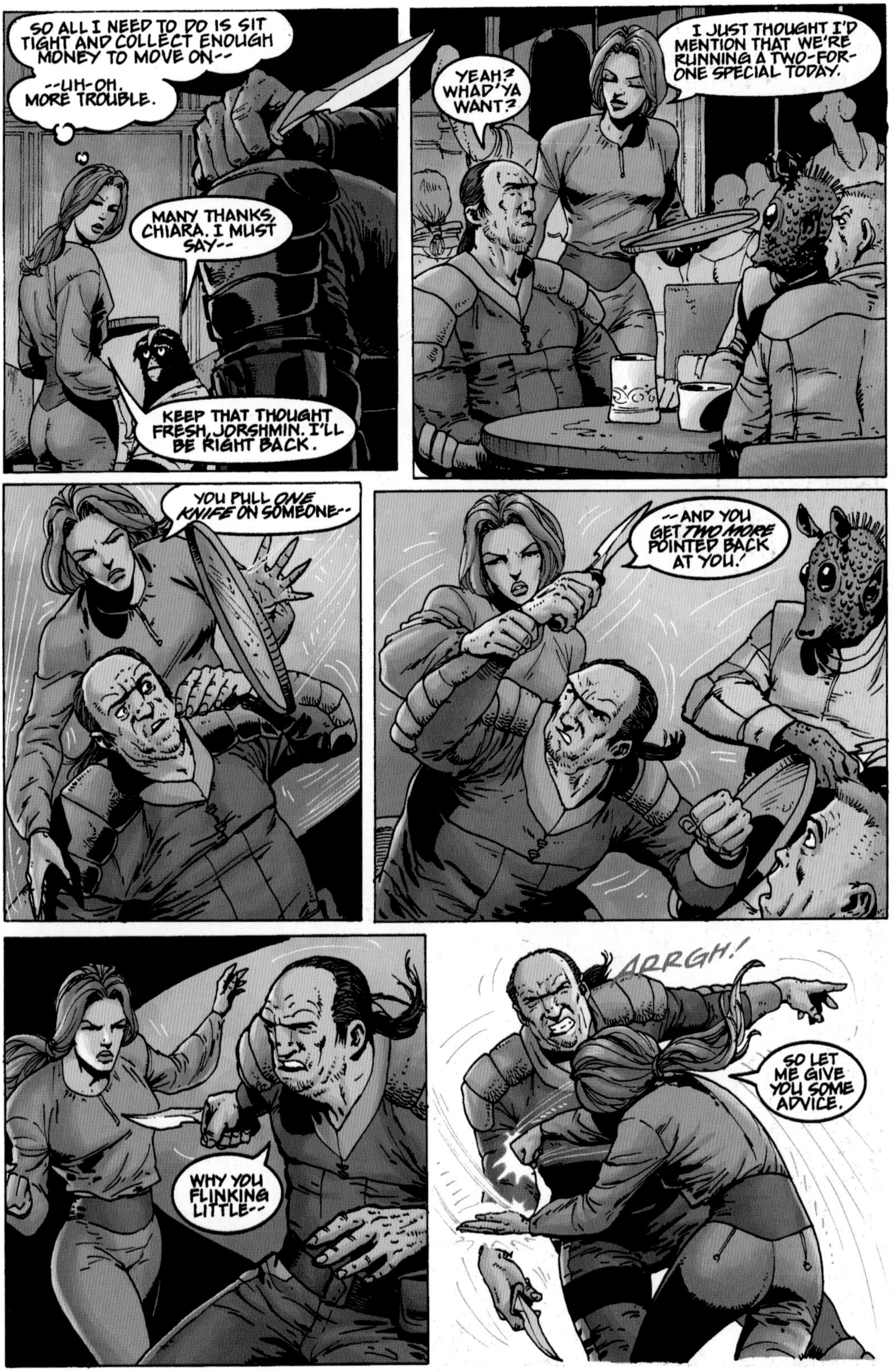
SO ALL I NEED TO DO IS SIT TIGHT AND COLLECT ENOUGH MONEY TO MOVE ON--
--UH-OH. MORE TROUBLE.
MANY THANKS, CHIARA. I MUST SAY--
KEEP THAT THOUGHT FRESH, JORSHMIN. I'LL BE RIGHT BACK.
YEAH? WHAD'YA WANT?
I JUST THOUGHT I'D MENTION THAT WE'RE RUNNING A TWO-FOR-ONE SPECIAL TODAY.
YOU PULL ONE KNIFE ON SOMEONE--
--AND YOU GET TWO MORE POINTED BACK AT YOU!
WHY YOU FLINKING LITTLE--
ARRGH!
SO LET ME GIVE YOU SOME ADVICE.

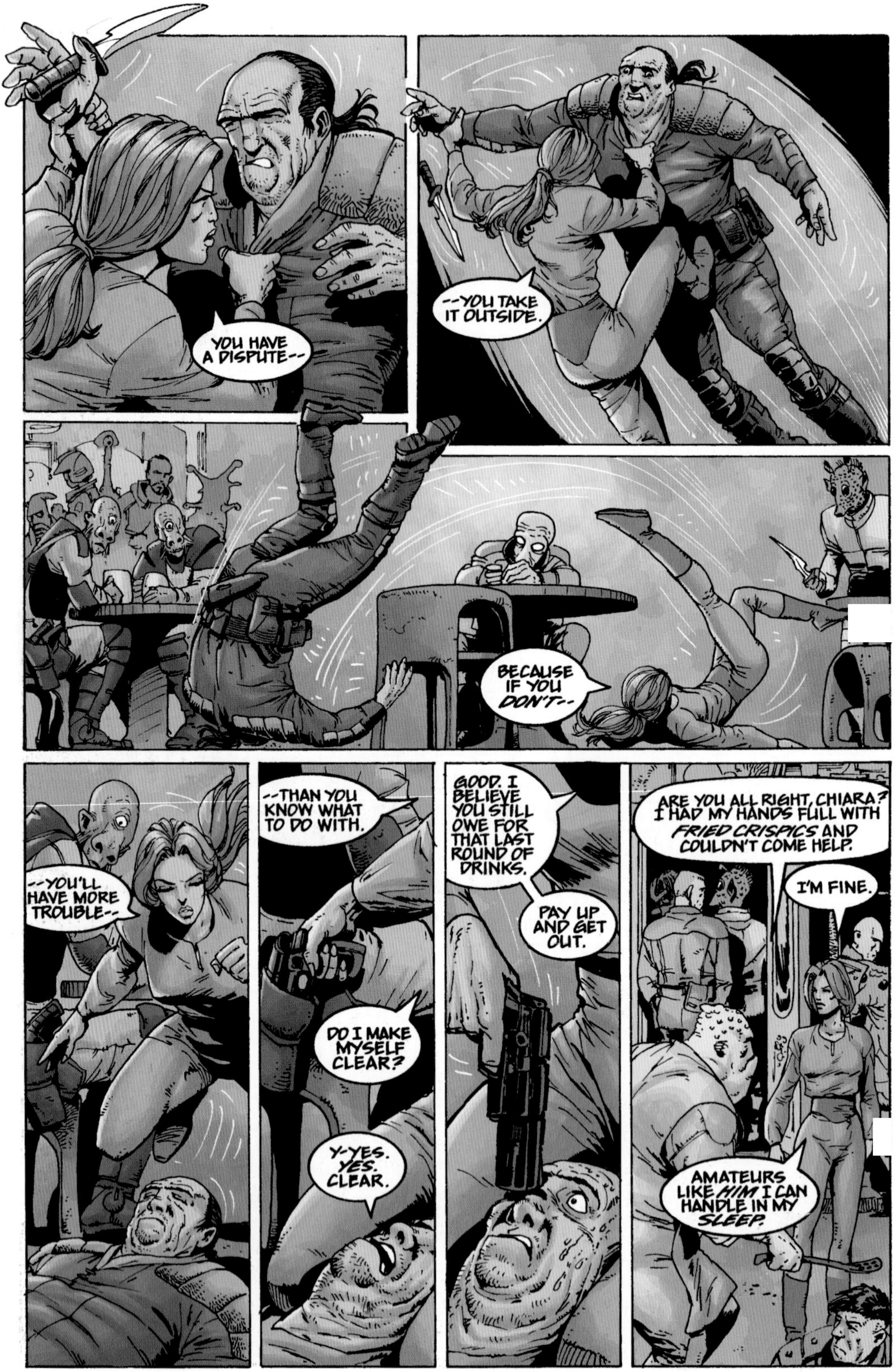
YOU HAVE A DISPUTE--
--YOU TAKE IT OUTSIDE.
BECAUSE IF YOU DON'T--
--YOU'LL HAVE MORE TROUBLE--
--THAN YOU KNOW WHAT TO DO WITH.
DO I MAKE MYSELF CLEAR?
Y-YES. YES. CLEAR.
GOOD. I BELIEVE YOU STILL OWE FOR THAT LAST ROUND OF DRINKS.
PAY UP AND GET OUT.
ARE YOU ALL RIGHT, CHIARA? I HAD MY HANDS FULL WITH FRIED CRISPICS AND COULDN'T COME HELP.
I'M FINE.
AMATEURS LIKE HIM I CAN HANDLE IN MY SLEEP.

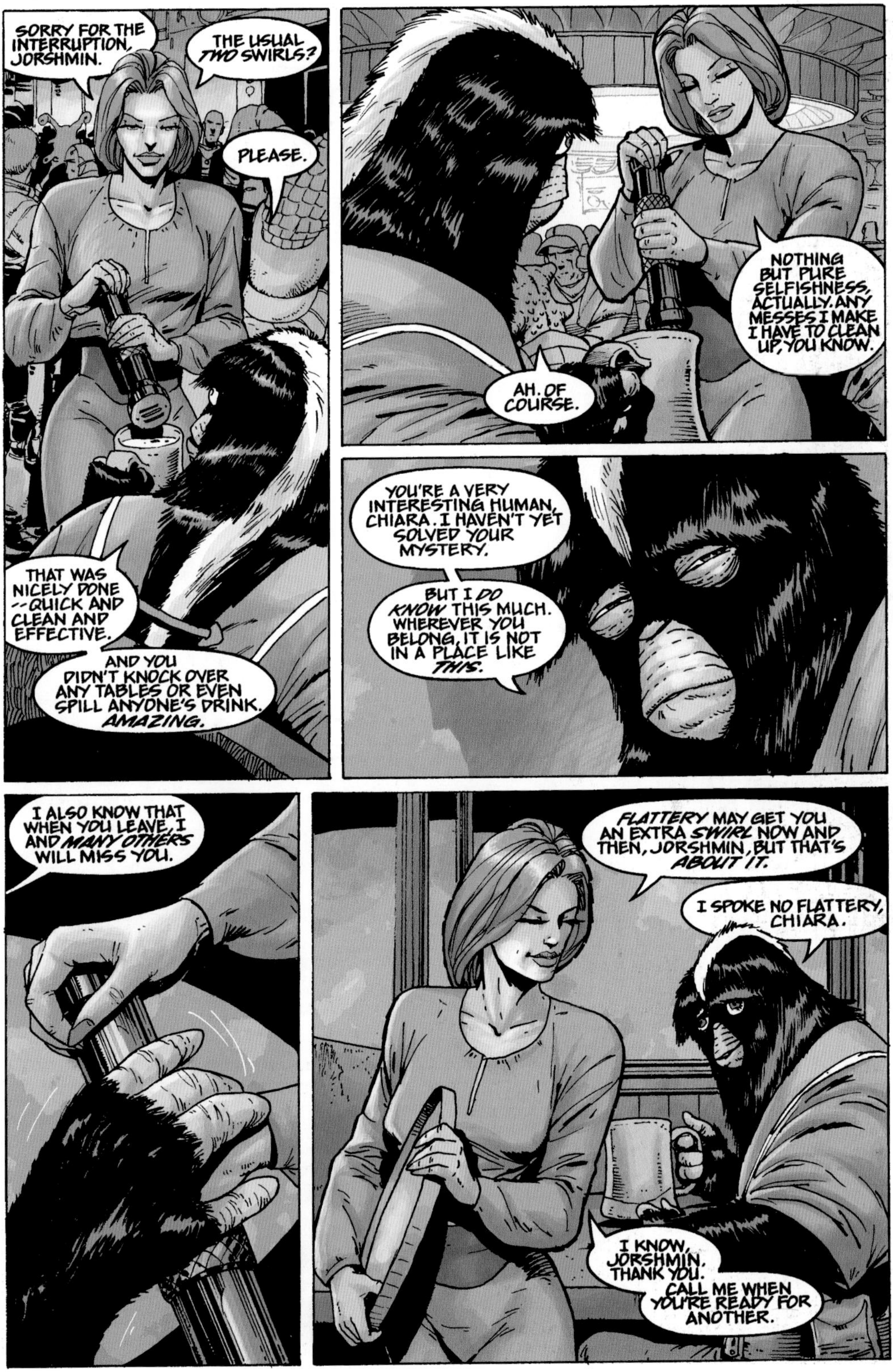
SORRY FOR THE INTERRUPTION, JORSHMIN.
THE USUAL *TWO* SWIRLS?
PLEASE.
NOTHING BUT PURE SELFISHNESS, ACTUALLY. ANY MESSES I MAKE I HAVE TO CLEAN UP, YOU KNOW.
AH. OF COURSE.
THAT WAS NICELY DONE --QUICK AND CLEAN AND EFFECTIVE.
AND YOU DIDN'T KNOCK OVER ANY TABLES OR EVEN SPILL ANYONE'S DRINK. *AMAZING.*
YOU'RE A VERY INTERESTING HUMAN, CHIARA. I HAVEN'T YET SOLVED YOUR MYSTERY.
BUT I *DO KNOW* THIS MUCH. WHEREVER YOU BELONG, IT IS NOT IN A PLACE LIKE *THIS.*
I ALSO KNOW THAT WHEN YOU LEAVE, I AND *MANY OTHERS* WILL MISS YOU.
FLATTERY MAY GET YOU AN EXTRA *SWIRL* NOW AND THEN, JORSHMIN, BUT THAT'S *ABOUT IT.*
I SPOKE NO FLATTERY, CHIARA.
I KNOW, JORSHMIN. THANK YOU.
CALL ME WHEN YOU'RE READY FOR ANOTHER.

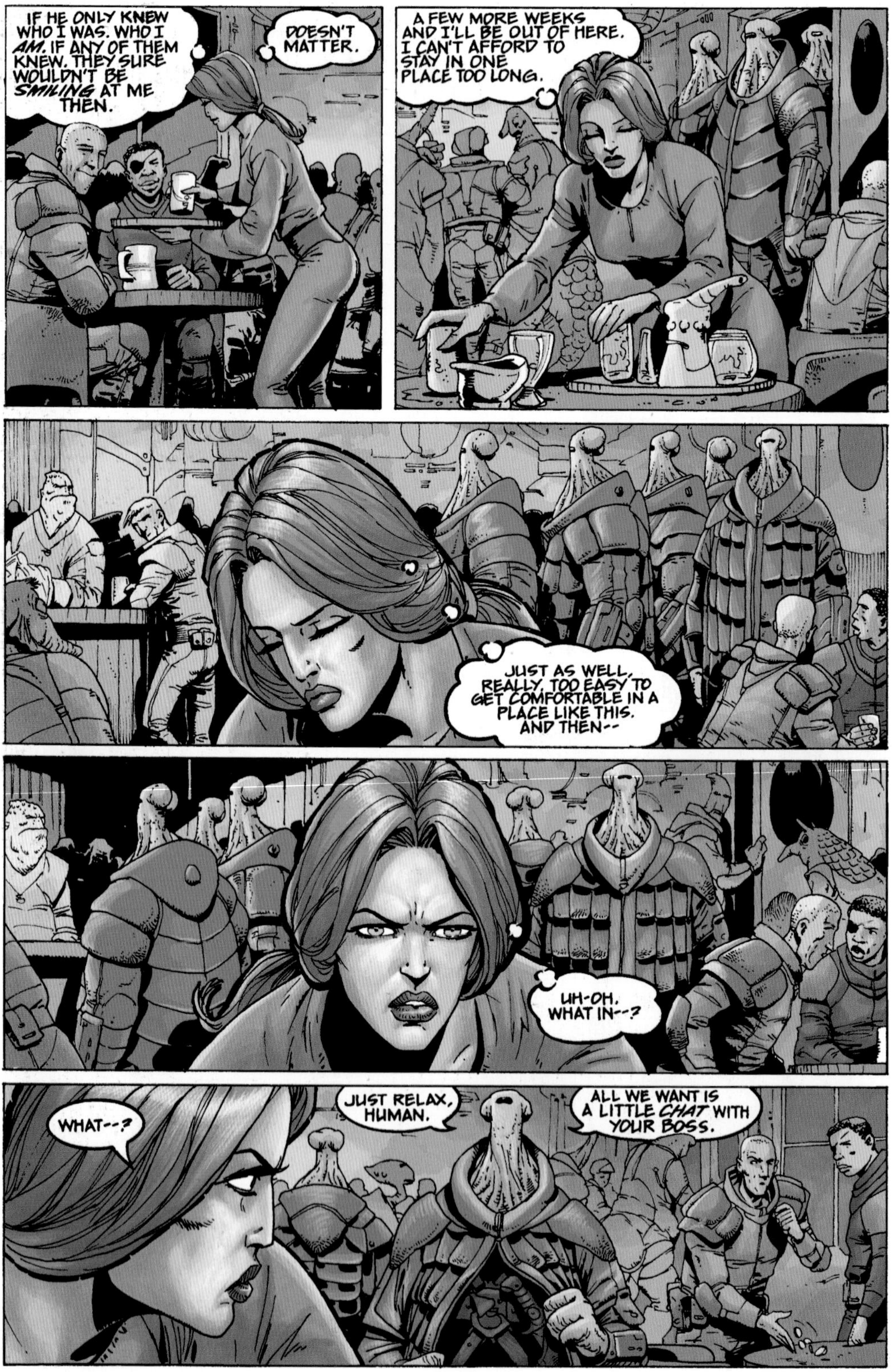
IF HE ONLY KNEW WHO I WAS. WHO I AM. IF ANY OF THEM KNEW. THEY SURE WOULDN'T BE SMILING AT ME THEN.
DOESN'T MATTER.
A FEW MORE WEEKS AND I'LL BE OUT OF HERE. I CAN'T AFFORD TO STAY IN ONE PLACE TOO LONG.
JUST AS WELL, REALLY. TOO EASY TO GET COMFORTABLE IN A PLACE LIKE THIS. AND THEN--
UH-OH. WHAT IN--?
WHAT--?
JUST RELAX, HUMAN.
ALL WE WANT IS A LITTLE CHAT WITH YOUR BOSS.

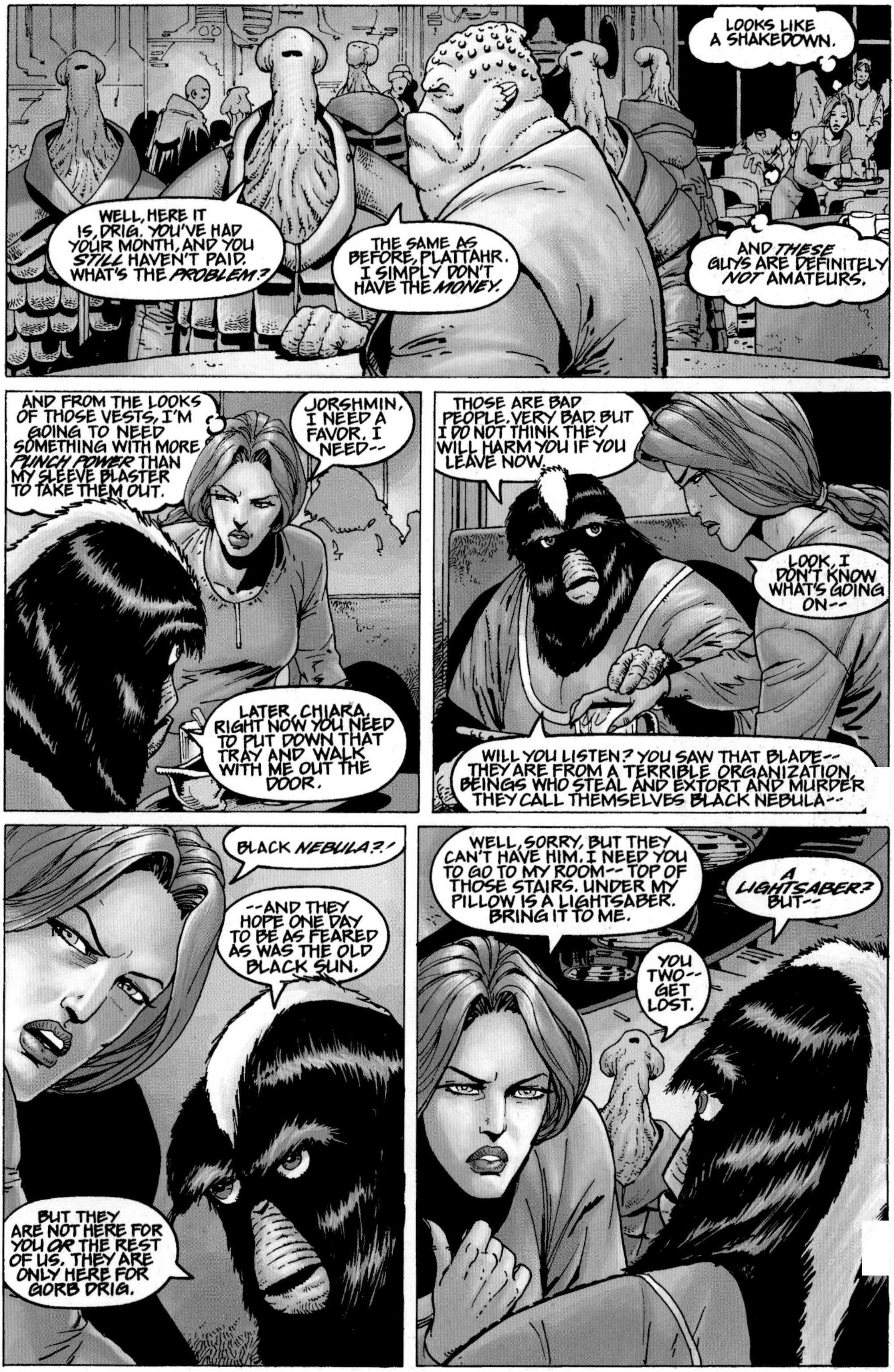
LOOKS LIKE A SHAKEDOWN.
WELL, HERE IT IS, DRIG. YOU'VE HAD YOUR MONTH, AND YOU STILL HAVEN'T PAID. WHAT'S THE PROBLEM?
THE SAME AS BEFORE, PLATTAHR. I SIMPLY DON'T HAVE THE MONEY.
AND THESE GUYS ARE DEFINITELY NOT AMATEURS.
AND FROM THE LOOKS OF THOSE VESTS, I'M GOING TO NEED SOMETHING WITH MORE PUNCH POWER THAN MY SLEEVE BLASTER TO TAKE THEM OUT.
JORSHMIN, I NEED A FAVOR. I NEED--
LATER, CHIARA. RIGHT NOW YOU NEED TO PUT DOWN THAT TRAY AND WALK WITH ME OUT THE DOOR.
THOSE ARE BAD PEOPLE. VERY BAD. BUT I DO NOT THINK THEY WILL HARM YOU IF YOU LEAVE NOW.
LOOK, I DON'T KNOW WHAT'S GOING ON--
WILL YOU LISTEN? YOU SAW THAT BLADE-- THEY ARE FROM A TERRIBLE ORGANIZATION. BEINGS WHO STEAL AND EXTORT AND MURDER. THEY CALL THEMSELVES BLACK NEBULA--
BLACK NEBULA?!
--AND THEY HOPE ONE DAY TO BE AS FEARED AS WAS THE OLD BLACK SUN.
BUT THEY ARE NOT HERE FOR YOU OR THE REST OF US. THEY ARE ONLY HERE FOR GORB DRIG.
WELL, SORRY, BUT THEY CAN'T HAVE HIM. I NEED YOU TO GO TO MY ROOM-- TOP OF THOSE STAIRS. UNDER MY PILLOW IS A LIGHTSABER. BRING IT TO ME.
A LIGHTSABER? BUT--
YOU TWO-- GET LOST.

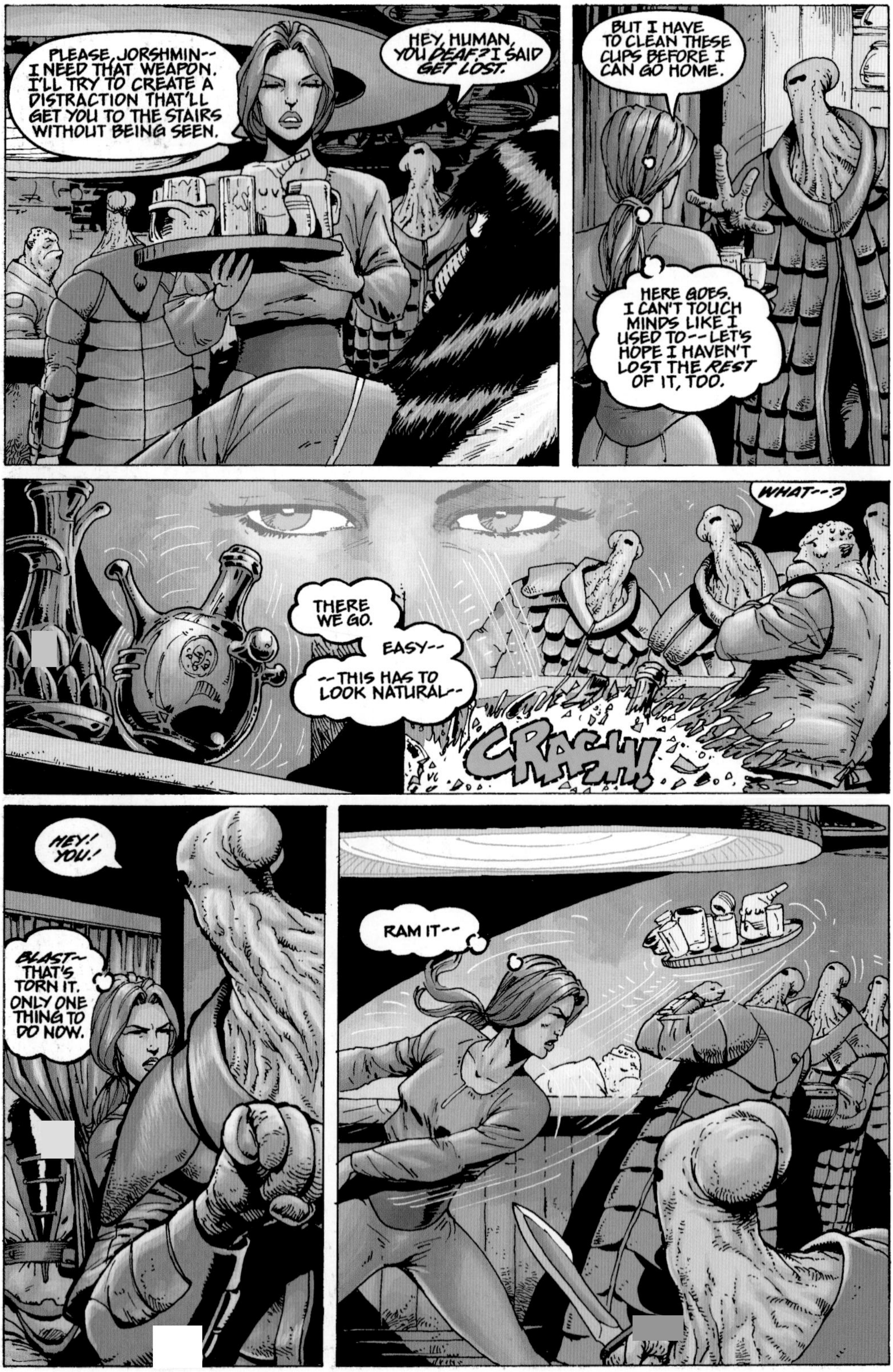
PLEASE, JORSHMIN-- I NEED THAT WEAPON. I'LL TRY TO CREATE A DISTRACTION THAT'LL GET YOU TO THE STAIRS WITHOUT BEING SEEN.
HEY, HUMAN, YOU DEAF? I SAID GET LOST.
BUT I HAVE TO CLEAN THESE CUPS BEFORE I CAN GO HOME.
HERE GOES. I CAN'T TOUCH MINDS LIKE I USED TO--LET'S HOPE I HAVEN'T LOST THE REST OF IT, TOO.
WHAT--?
THERE WE GO.
EASY--
--THIS HAS TO LOOK NATURAL--
CRASH!
HEY! YOU!
BLAST-- THAT'S TORN IT. ONLY ONE THING TO DO NOW.
RAM IT--

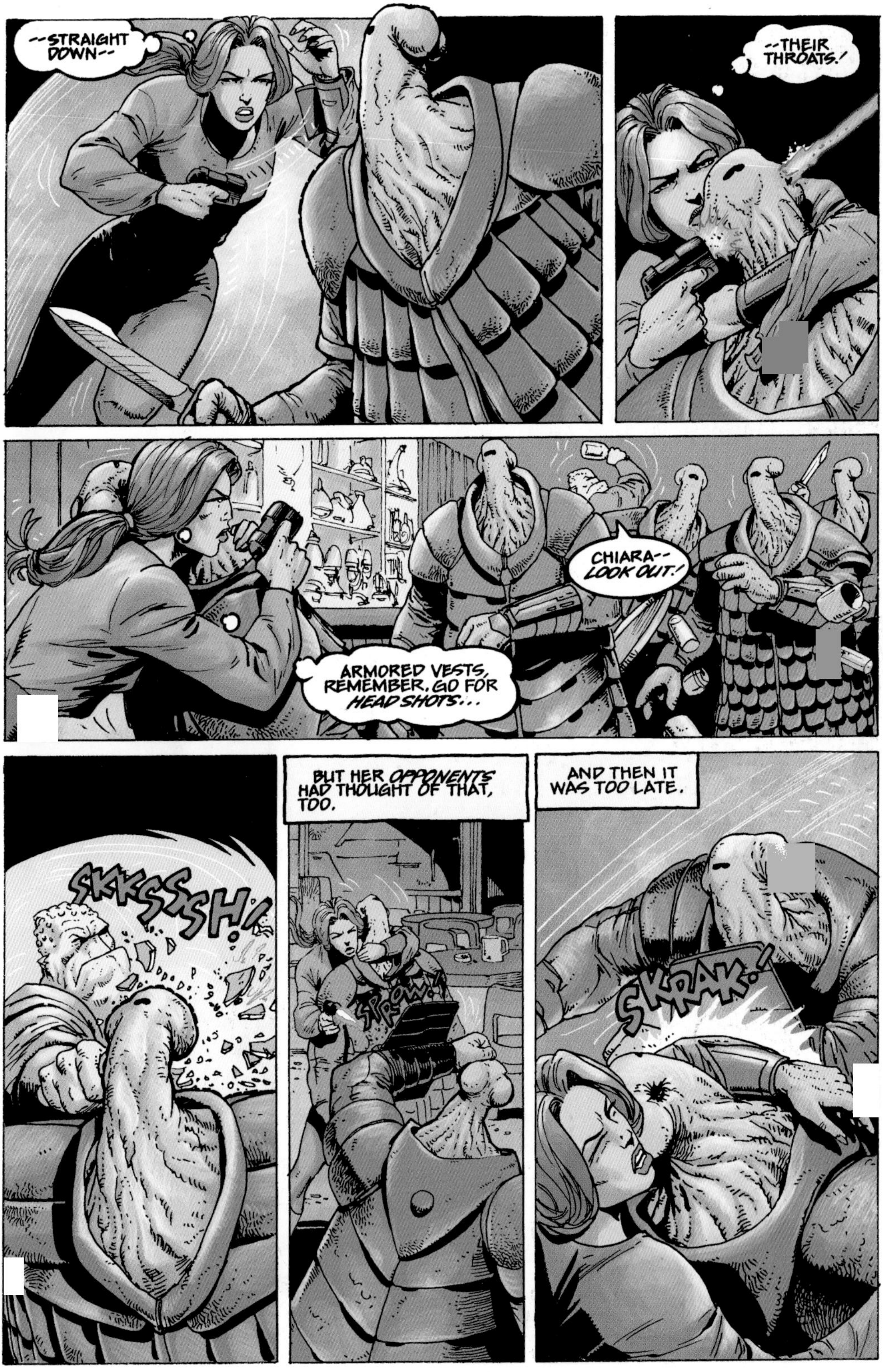
--STRAIGHT DOWN--
--THEIR THROATS!
CHIARA-- LOOK OUT!
ARMORED VESTS, REMEMBER. GO FOR HEAD SHOTS...
SKKSSSSH!
BUT HER OPPONENTS HAD THOUGHT OF THAT, TOO.
AND THEN IT WAS TOO LATE.
SKRAK!

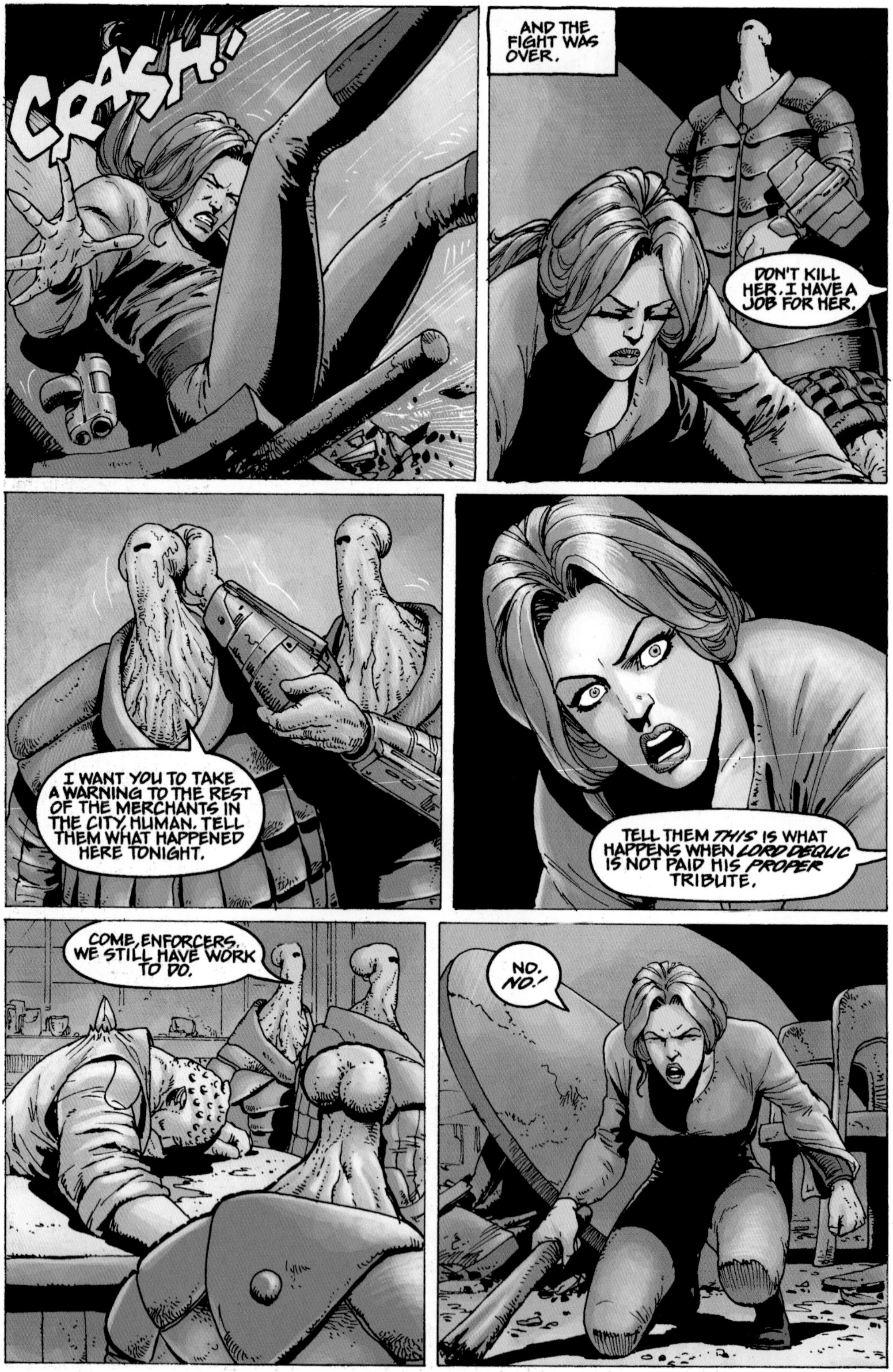
CRASH!
AND THE FIGHT WAS OVER.
DON'T KILL HER. I HAVE A JOB FOR HER.
I WANT YOU TO TAKE A WARNING TO THE REST OF THE MERCHANTS IN THE CITY, HUMAN. TELL THEM WHAT HAPPENED HERE TONIGHT.
TELL THEM *THIS* IS WHAT HAPPENS WHEN *LORD DEQUC* IS NOT PAID HIS *PROPER* TRIBUTE.
COME, ENFORCERS. WE STILL HAVE WORK TO DO.
NO. *NO!*

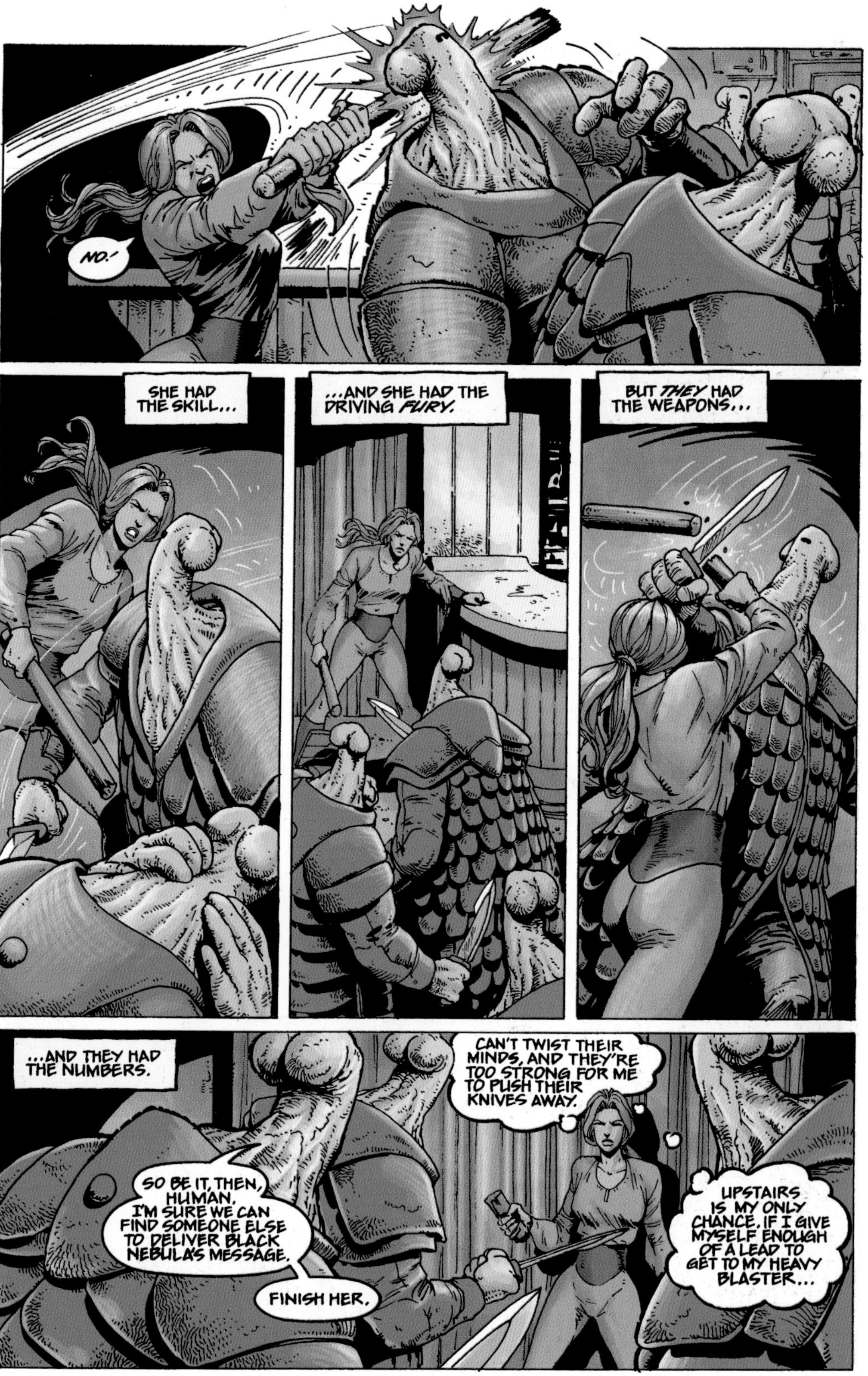
NO!
SHE HAD THE SKILL...
...AND SHE HAD THE DRIVING FURY.
BUT THEY HAD THE WEAPONS...
...AND THEY HAD THE NUMBERS.
CAN'T TWIST THEIR MINDS, AND THEY'RE TOO STRONG FOR ME TO PUSH THEIR KNIVES AWAY.
SO BE IT, THEN, HUMAN. I'M SURE WE CAN FIND SOMEONE ELSE TO DELIVER BLACK NEBULA'S MESSAGE.
FINISH HER.
UPSTAIRS IS MY ONLY CHANCE, IF I GIVE MYSELF ENOUGH OF A LEAD TO GET TO MY HEAVY BLASTER...

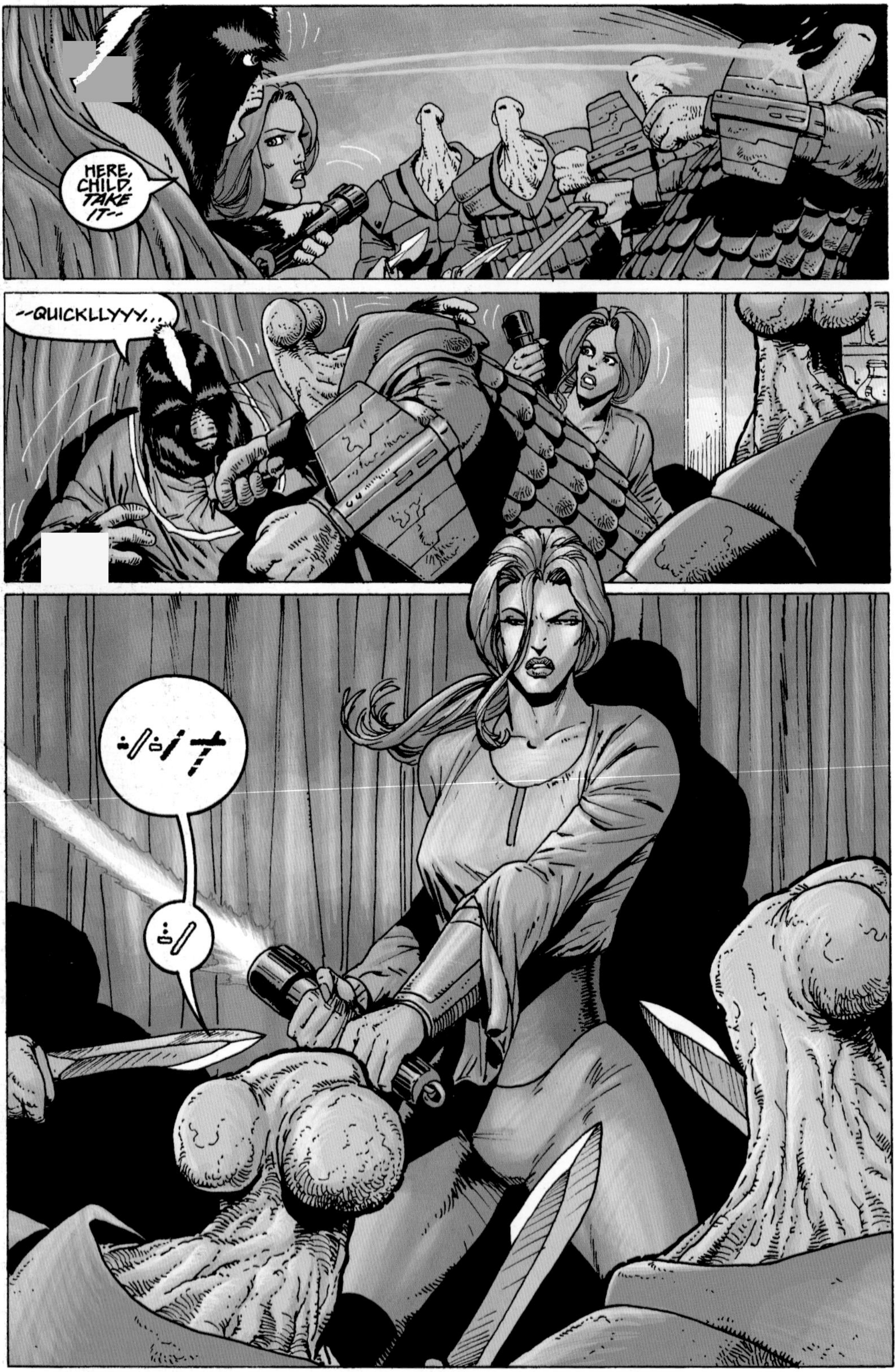
HERE, CHILD, TAKE IT--
--QUICKLLYYY...

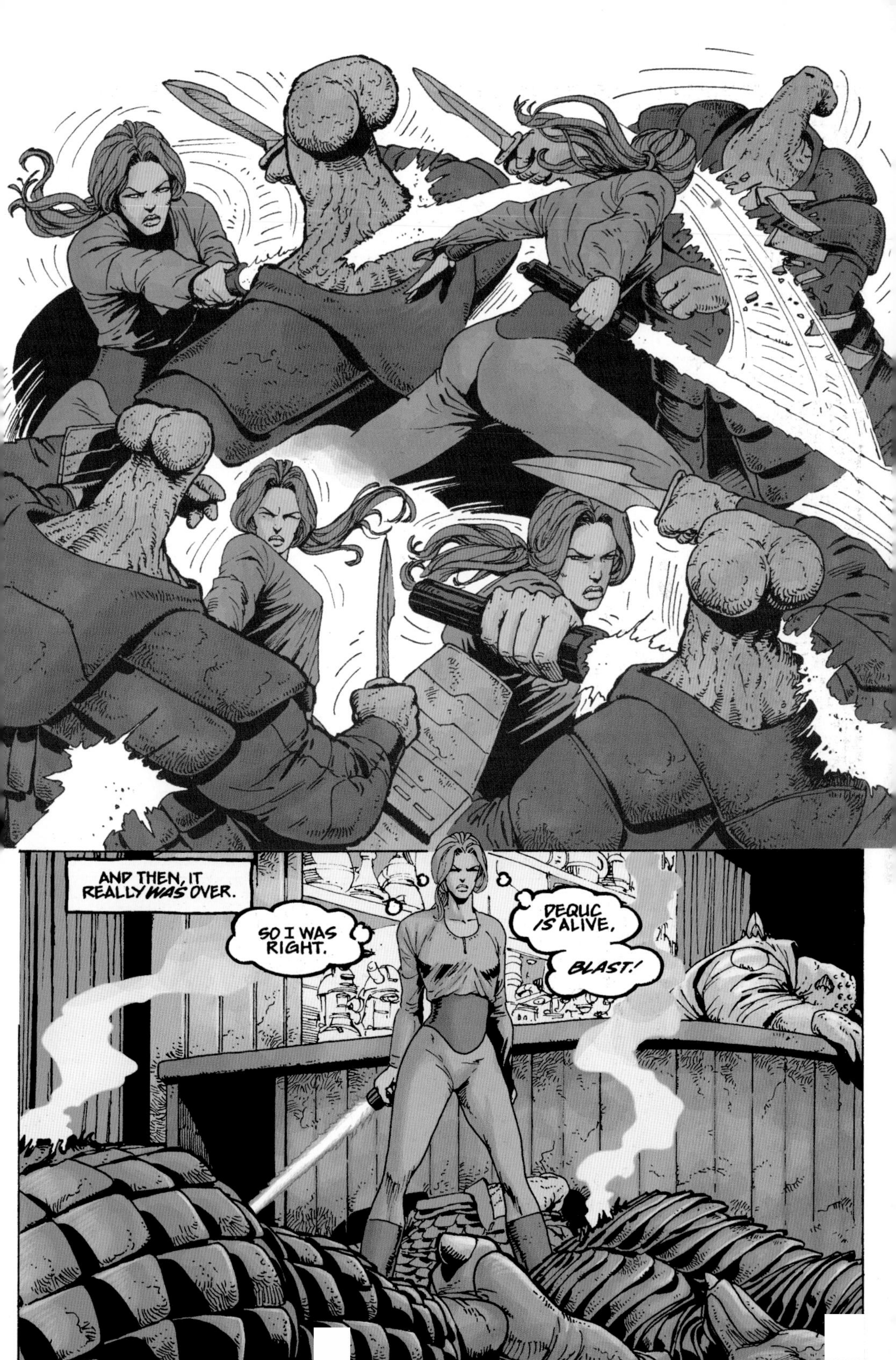
AND THEN, IT REALLY WAS OVER.
SO I WAS RIGHT.
DEQUC IS ALIVE,
BLAST!

AND THIS IS MY FAULT. ALL MY FAULT.

IF I'D DONE MY JOB RIGHT BACK ON *SVIVREN...*

BUT IT'S NO GOOD MOANING ABOUT THAT NOW. I HAVE TO GET OUT OF HERE.

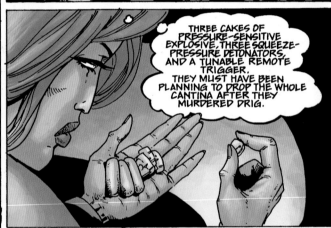

THREE CAKES OF PRESSURE-SENSITIVE EXPLOSIVE, THREE SQUEEZE-PRESSURE DETONATORS, AND A TUNABLE REMOTE TRIGGER. THEY MUST HAVE BEEN PLANNING TO DROP THE WHOLE CANTINA AFTER THEY MURDERED DRIG.

JUST AS WELL I NEVER REALLY *CONNECTED* WHEN I WAS SWINGING THAT TABLE LEG AROUND.

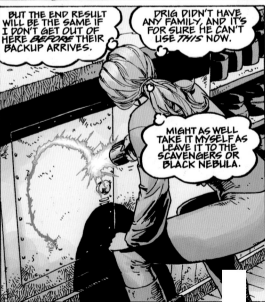

BUT THE END RESULT WILL BE THE SAME IF I DON'T GET OUT OF HERE *BEFORE* THEIR BACKUP ARRIVES.

DRIG DIDN'T HAVE ANY FAMILY, AND IT'S FOR SURE HE CAN'T USE *THIS* NOW.

MIGHT AS WELL TAKE IT MYSELF AS LEAVE IT TO THE SCAVENGERS OR BLACK NEBULA.

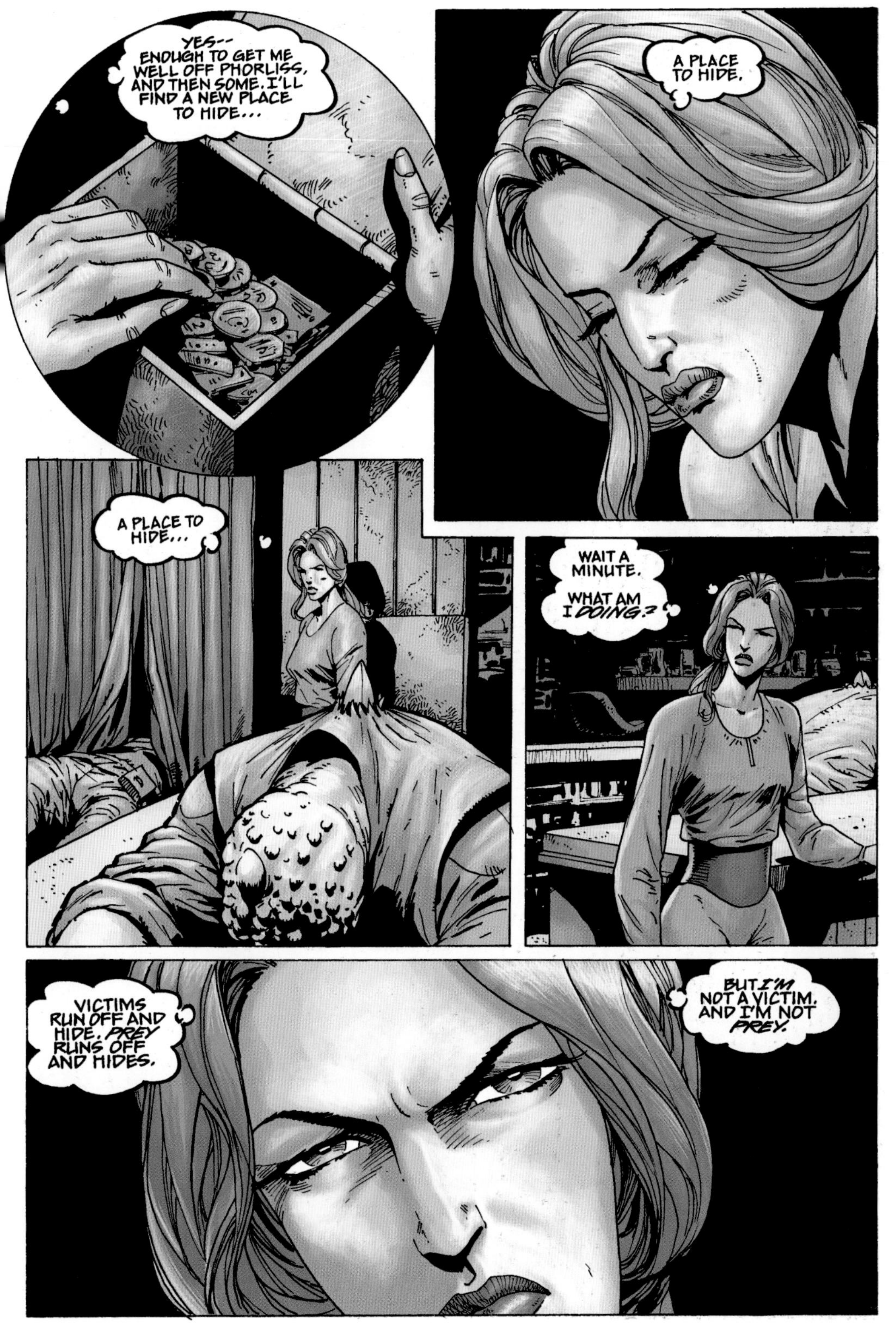
YES-- ENOUGH TO GET ME WELL OFF PHORLISS, AND THEN SOME. I'LL FIND A NEW PLACE TO HIDE...
A PLACE TO HIDE.
A PLACE TO HIDE...
WAIT A MINUTE.
WHAT AM I DOING?
VICTIMS RUN OFF AND HIDE. PREY RUNS OFF AND HIDES.
BUT I'M NOT A VICTIM. AND I'M NOT PREY.

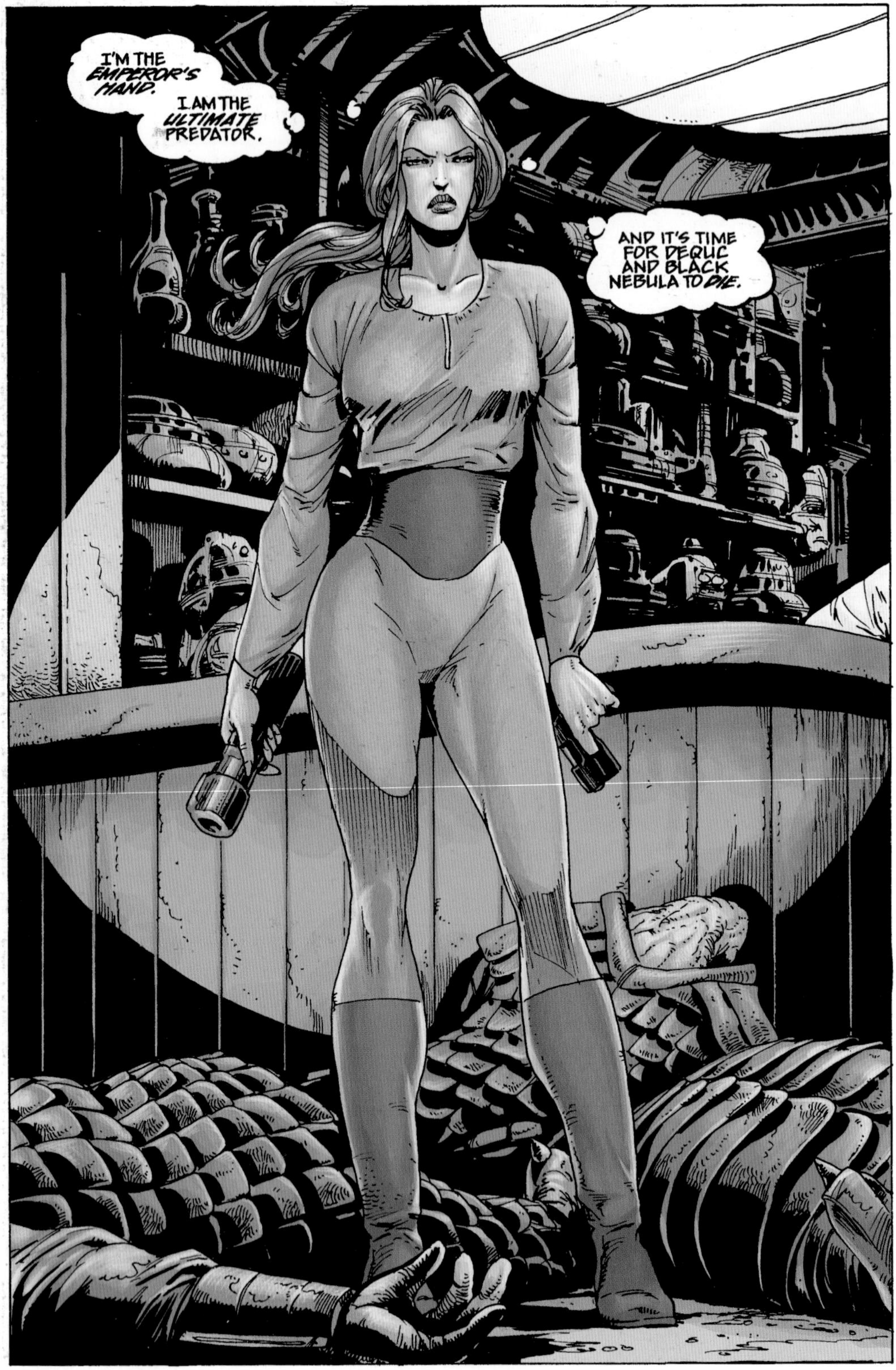
I'M THE EMPEROR'S HAND.
I AM THE ULTIMATE PREDATOR.
AND IT'S TIME FOR DEQUC AND BLACK NEBULA TO DIE.

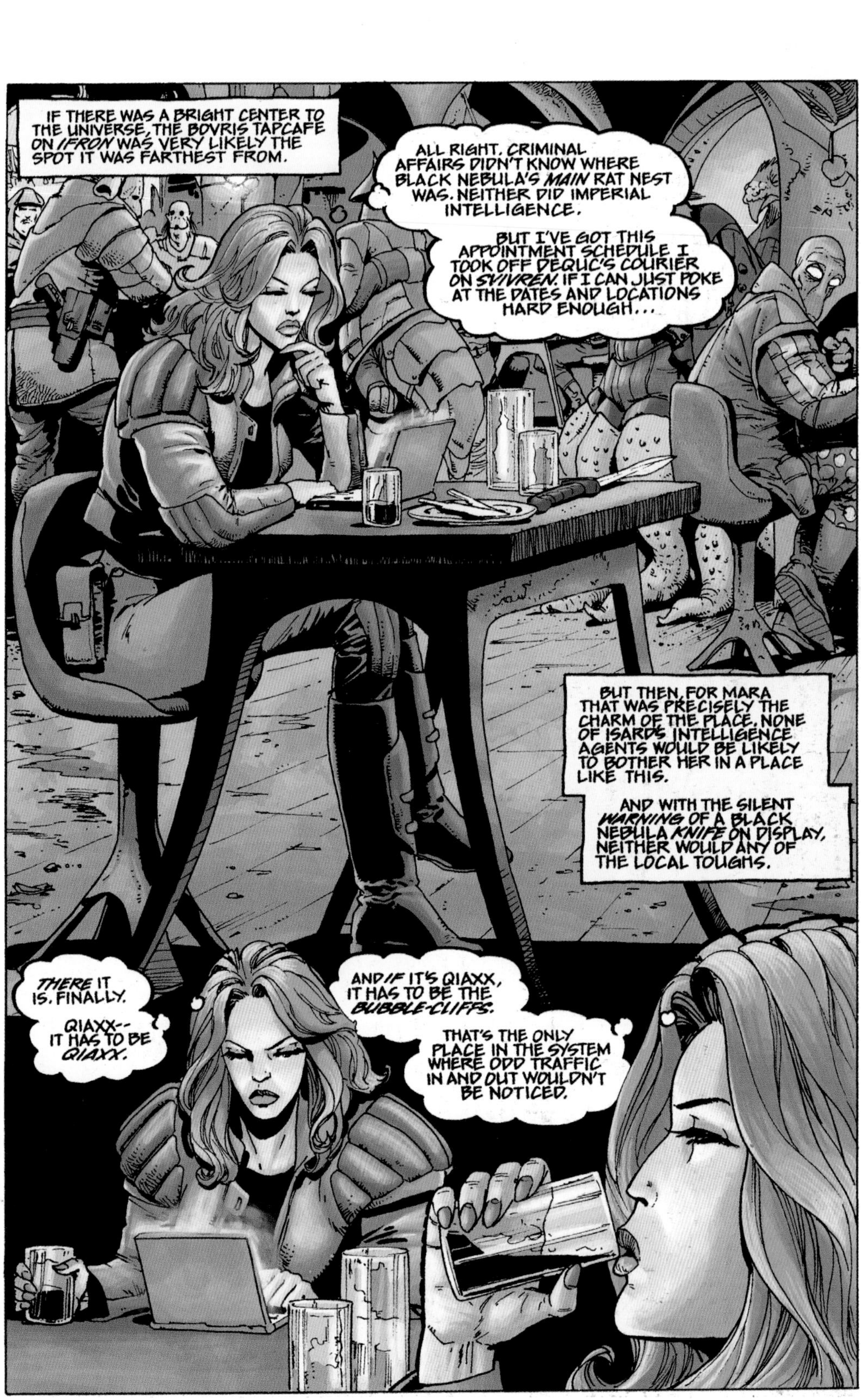
IF THERE WAS A BRIGHT CENTER TO THE UNIVERSE, THE BOVRIS TAPCAFE ON *IFRON* WAS VERY LIKELY THE SPOT IT WAS FARTHEST FROM.
ALL RIGHT. CRIMINAL AFFAIRS DIDN'T KNOW WHERE BLACK NEBULA'S *MAIN* RAT NEST WAS. NEITHER DID IMPERIAL INTELLIGENCE.
BUT I'VE GOT THIS APPOINTMENT SCHEDULE I TOOK OFF DEQUC'S COURIER ON *SVIVREN*. IF I CAN JUST POKE AT THE DATES AND LOCATIONS HARD ENOUGH...
BUT THEN, FOR MARA THAT WAS PRECISELY THE CHARM OF THE PLACE. NONE OF ISARD'S INTELLIGENCE AGENTS WOULD BE LIKELY TO BOTHER HER IN A PLACE LIKE THIS.
AND WITH THE SILENT *WARNING* OF A BLACK NEBULA *KNIFE* ON DISPLAY, NEITHER WOULD ANY OF THE LOCAL TOUGHS.
THERE IT IS. FINALLY.
QIAXX-- IT HAS TO BE *QIAXX*.
AND *IF* IT'S QIAXX, IT HAS TO BE THE *BUBBLE-CLIFFS*.
THAT'S THE ONLY PLACE IN THE SYSTEM WHERE ODD TRAFFIC IN AND OUT WOULDN'T BE NOTICED.

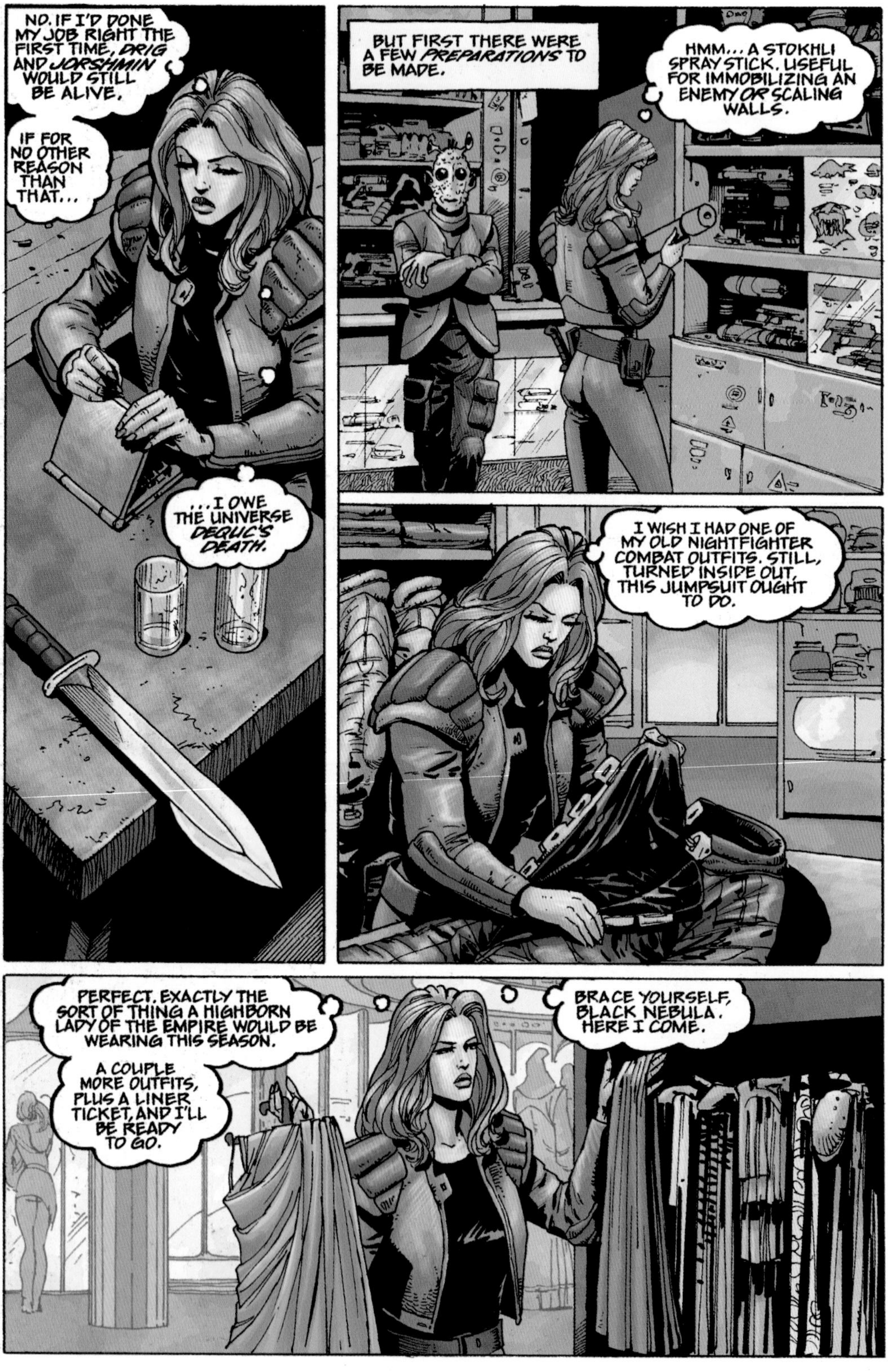
NO. IF I'D DONE MY JOB RIGHT THE FIRST TIME, *DRIG* AND *JORSHMIN* WOULD STILL BE ALIVE.
IF FOR NO OTHER REASON THAN THAT...
...I OWE THE UNIVERSE *DEQUC'S DEATH.*
BUT FIRST THERE WERE A FEW *PREPARATIONS* TO BE MADE.
HMM... A STOKHLI SPRAY STICK. USEFUL FOR IMMOBILIZING AN ENEMY *OR* SCALING WALLS.
I WISH I HAD ONE OF MY OLD NIGHTFIGHTER COMBAT OUTFITS. STILL, TURNED INSIDE OUT, THIS JUMPSUIT OUGHT TO DO.
PERFECT. EXACTLY THE SORT OF THING A HIGHBORN LADY OF THE EMPIRE WOULD BE WEARING THIS SEASON.
A COUPLE MORE OUTFITS, PLUS A LINER TICKET, AND I'LL BE READY TO GO.
BRACE YOURSELF, BLACK NEBULA. HERE I COME.

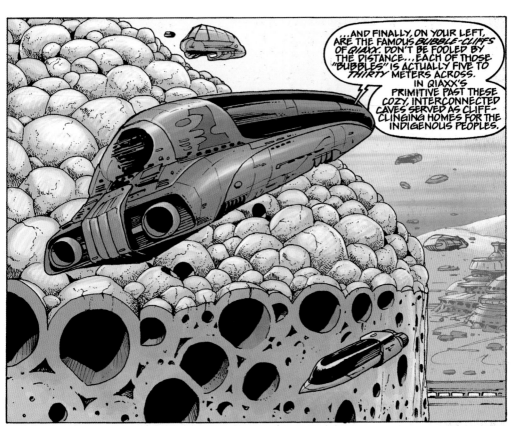

...AND FINALLY, ON YOUR LEFT, ARE THE FAMOUS *BUBBLE-CLIFFS* OF *QIAXX*. DON'T BE FOOLED BY THE DISTANCE...EACH OF THOSE "BUBBLES" IS ACTUALLY FIVE TO *THIRTY* METERS ACROSS.

IN QIAXX'S PRIMITIVE PAST THESE COZY, INTERCONNECTED CAVES SERVED AS CLIFF-CLINGING HOMES FOR THE INDIGENOUS PEOPLES.

NOW, MANY OF THE OLD DWELLINGS HAVE BEEN RESTORED FOR HISTORICAL PURPOSES, AND THERE ARE DAILY AIRSPEEDER TOURS TO THEM.

TOURS WHICH PROVIDE *IDEAL* COVER FOR BLACK NEBULA'S OWN FLIGHTS. THIS IS THE PLACE, ALL RIGHT.

NOW ALL I HAVE TO DO IS FIND A WAY IN.

REAL PEOPLE INSTEAD OF DROIDS. THIS *IS* AN UPSCALE PLACE. GOOD THING I SPRANG FOR THE FANCY CLOTHING.

YOU'RE IN ROOM 427, BARONESS, I TRUST YOU WILL *ENJOY* YOUR STAY HERE. THE RESTAURANTS AND CASINO ARE OPEN DAWN TO DAWN FOR YOUR CONVENIENCE. THE TOURS OF THE FAMOUS BUBBLE-CLIFFS ARE ALSO *HIGHLY RECOMMENDED.*

THANK YOU.

CASINO, EH? THIS HAS POSSIBILITIES.

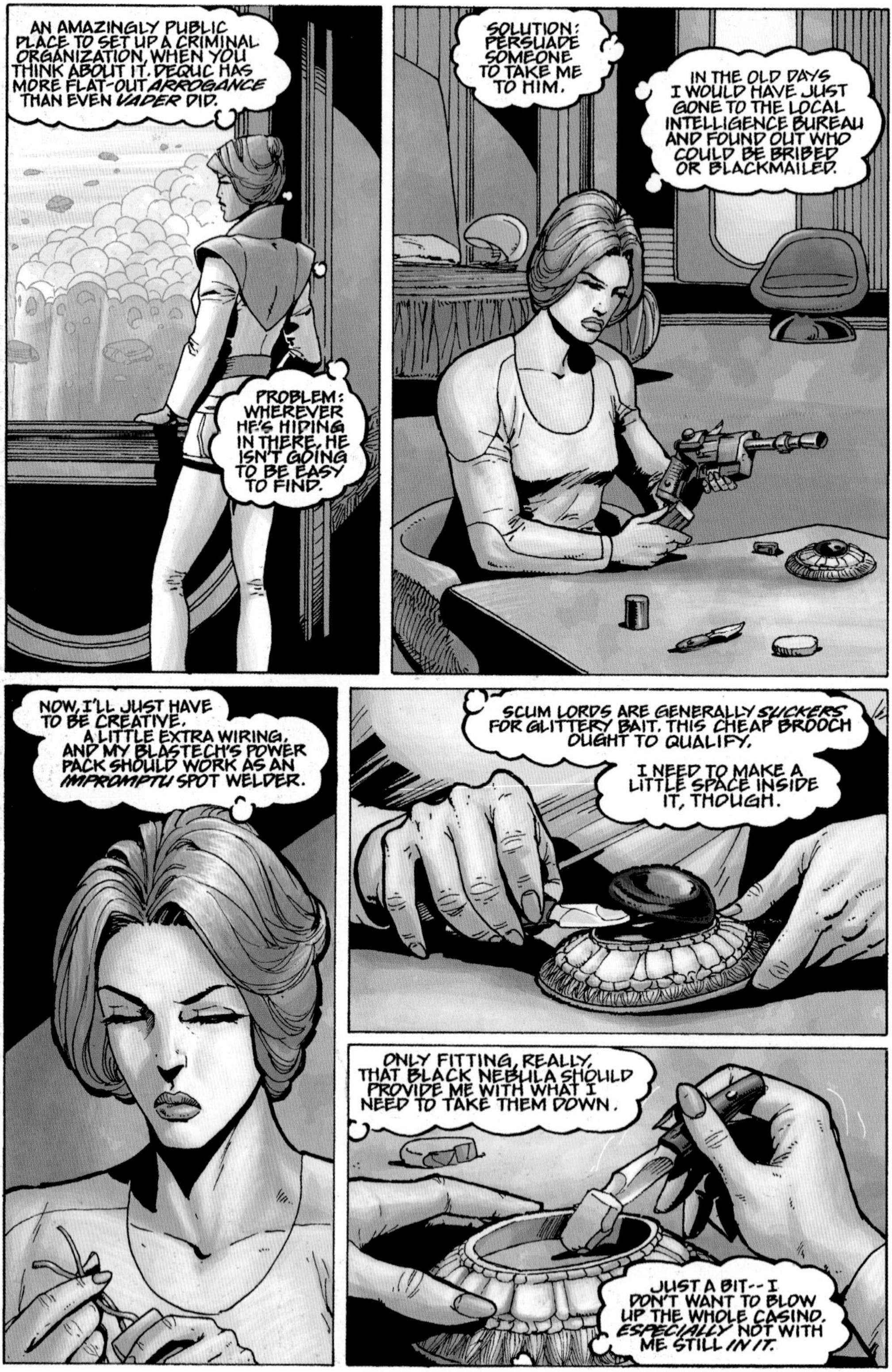
AN AMAZINGLY PUBLIC PLACE TO SET UP A CRIMINAL ORGANIZATION, WHEN YOU THINK ABOUT IT. DEQUC HAS MORE FLAT-OUT *ARROGANCE* THAN EVEN *VADER* DID.
PROBLEM: WHEREVER HE'S HIDING IN THERE, HE ISN'T GOING TO BE EASY TO FIND.
SOLUTION: PERSUADE SOMEONE TO TAKE ME TO HIM.
IN THE OLD DAYS I WOULD HAVE JUST GONE TO THE LOCAL INTELLIGENCE BUREAU AND FOUND OUT WHO COULD BE BRIBED OR BLACKMAILED.
NOW, I'LL JUST HAVE TO BE CREATIVE. A LITTLE EXTRA WIRING, AND MY BLASTECH'S POWER PACK SHOULD WORK AS AN *IMPROMPTU* SPOT WELDER.
SCUM LORDS ARE GENERALLY *SUCKERS* FOR GLITTERY BAIT. THIS CHEAP BROOCH OUGHT TO QUALIFY.
I NEED TO MAKE A LITTLE SPACE INSIDE IT, THOUGH.
ONLY FITTING, REALLY, THAT BLACK NEBULA SHOULD PROVIDE ME WITH WHAT I NEED TO TAKE THEM DOWN.
JUST A BIT-- I DON'T WANT TO BLOW UP THE WHOLE CASINO. *ESPECIALLY* NOT WITH ME STILL *IN IT.*

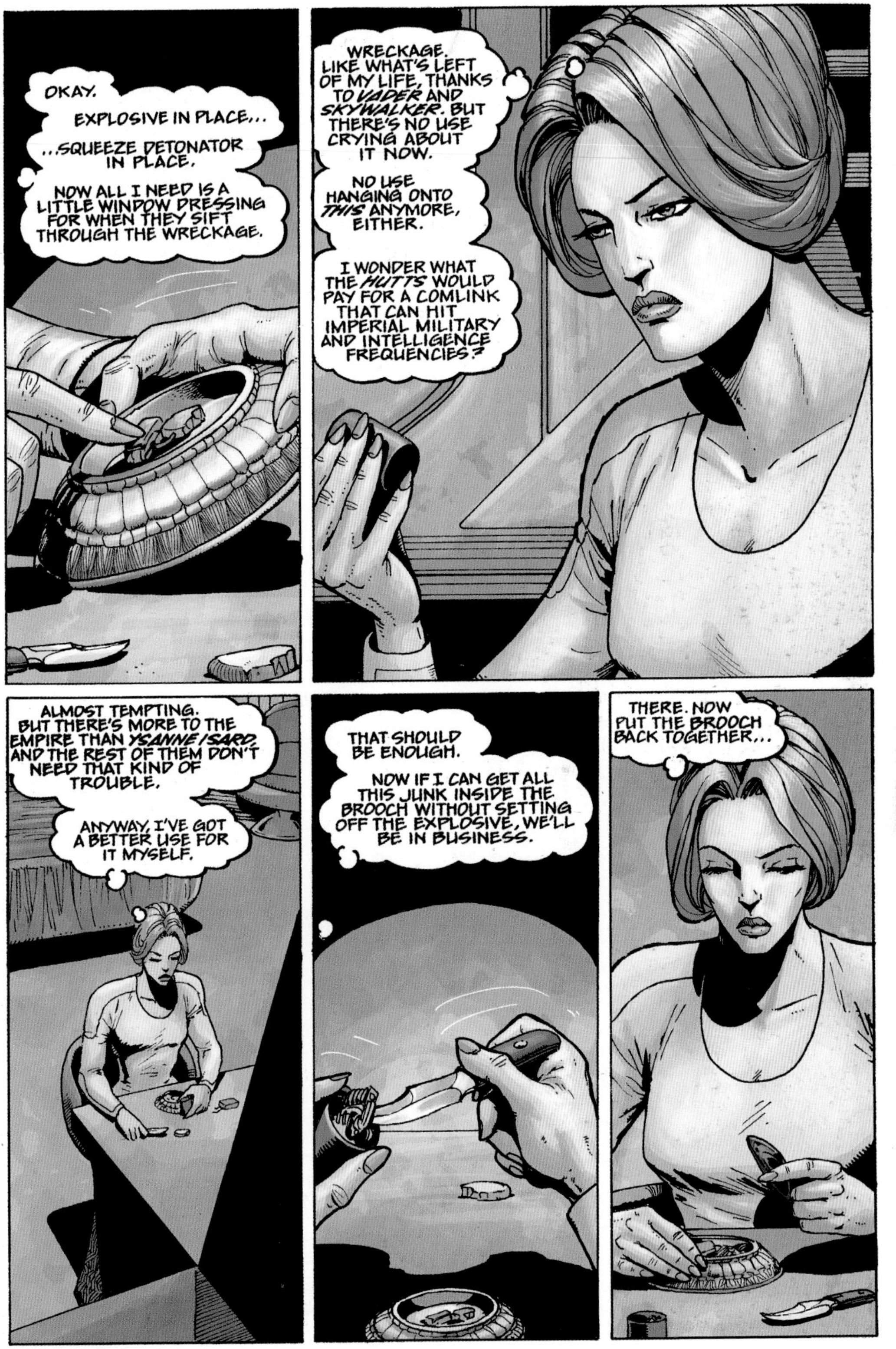
OKAY.
EXPLOSIVE IN PLACE,...
...SQUEEZE DETONATOR IN PLACE.
NOW ALL I NEED IS A LITTLE WINDOW DRESSING FOR WHEN THEY SIFT THROUGH THE WRECKAGE.
WRECKAGE. LIKE WHAT'S LEFT OF MY LIFE, THANKS TO VADER AND SKYWALKER. BUT THERE'S NO USE CRYING ABOUT IT NOW.
NO USE HANGING ONTO THIS ANYMORE, EITHER.
I WONDER WHAT THE HUTTS WOULD PAY FOR A COMLINK THAT CAN HIT IMPERIAL MILITARY AND INTELLIGENCE FREQUENCIES?
ALMOST TEMPTING. BUT THERE'S MORE TO THE EMPIRE THAN YSANNE ISARD, AND THE REST OF THEM DON'T NEED THAT KIND OF TROUBLE.
ANYWAY, I'VE GOT A BETTER USE FOR IT MYSELF.
THAT SHOULD BE ENOUGH.
NOW IF I CAN GET ALL THIS JUNK INSIDE THE BROOCH WITHOUT SETTING OFF THE EXPLOSIVE, WE'LL BE IN BUSINESS.
THERE. NOW PUT THE BROOCH BACK TOGETHER...

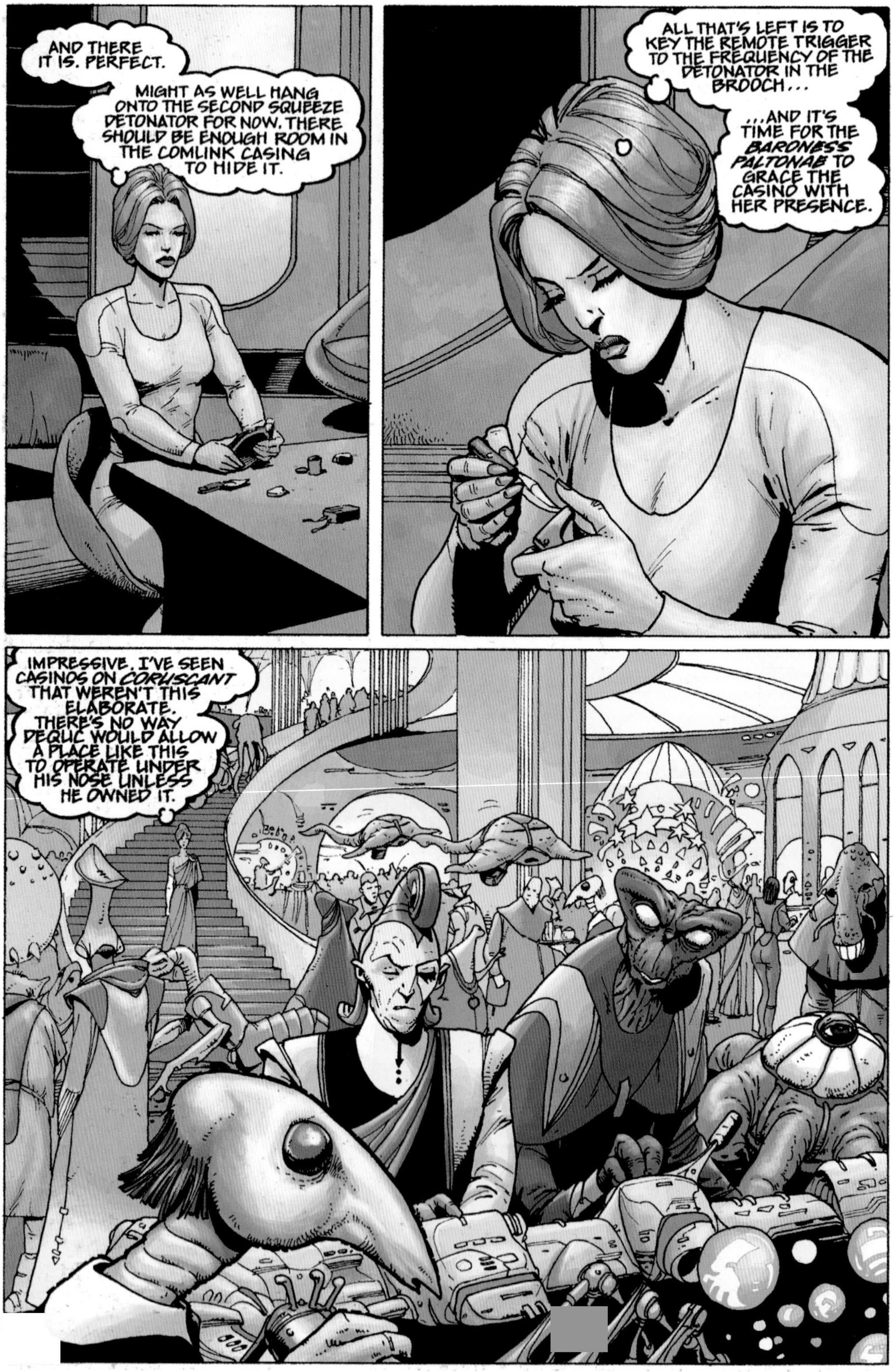
AND THERE IT IS. PERFECT.
MIGHT AS WELL HANG ONTO THE SECOND SQUEEZE DETONATOR FOR NOW. THERE SHOULD BE ENOUGH ROOM IN THE COMLINK CASING TO HIDE IT.
ALL THAT'S LEFT IS TO KEY THE REMOTE TRIGGER TO THE FREQUENCY OF THE DETONATOR IN THE BROOCH...
...AND IT'S TIME FOR THE BARONESS PALTONAB TO GRACE THE CASINO WITH HER PRESENCE.
IMPRESSIVE. I'VE SEEN CASINOS ON CORUSCANT THAT WEREN'T THIS ELABORATE. THERE'S NO WAY DEQUC WOULD ALLOW A PLACE LIKE THIS TO OPERATE UNDER HIS NOSE UNLESS HE OWNED IT.

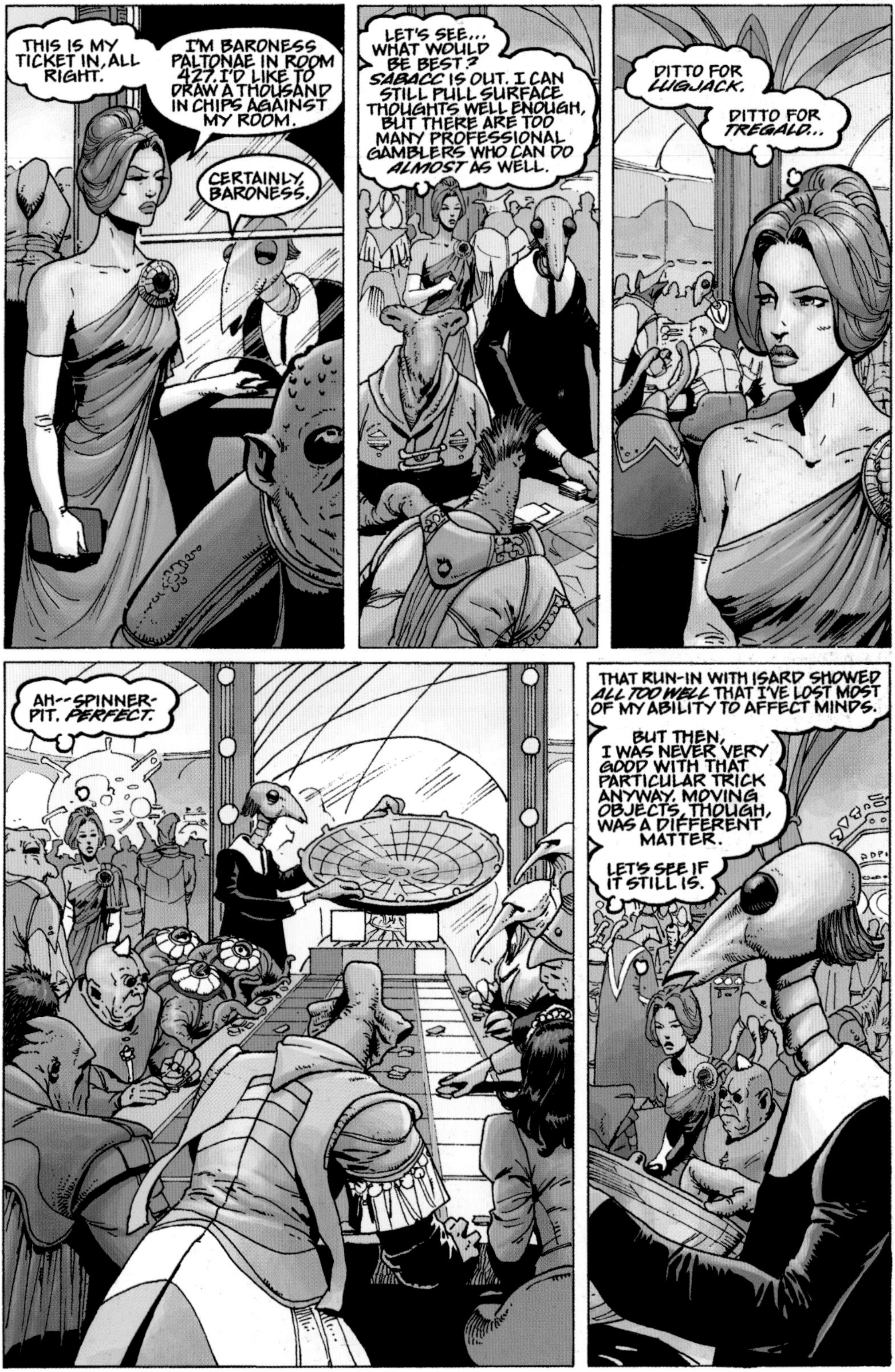
THIS IS MY TICKET IN, ALL RIGHT.
I'M BARONESS PALTONAE IN ROOM 427. I'D LIKE TO DRAW A THOUSAND IN CHIPS AGAINST MY ROOM.
CERTAINLY, BARONESS.
LET'S SEE... WHAT WOULD BE BEST? SABACC IS OUT. I CAN STILL PULL SURFACE THOUGHTS WELL ENOUGH, BUT THERE ARE TOO MANY PROFESSIONAL GAMBLERS WHO CAN DO ALMOST AS WELL.
DITTO FOR LUGJACK.
DITTO FOR TREGALD...
AH--SPINNER-PIT. PERFECT.
THAT RUN-IN WITH ISARD SHOWED ALL TOO WELL THAT I'VE LOST MOST OF MY ABILITY TO AFFECT MINDS.
BUT THEN, I WAS NEVER VERY GOOD WITH THAT PARTICULAR TRICK ANYWAY. MOVING OBJECTS, THOUGH, WAS A DIFFERENT MATTER.
LET'S SEE IF IT STILL IS.

NO FURTHER BETS, PLEASE.

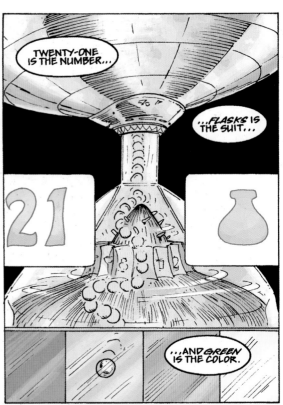

TWENTY-ONE IS THE NUMBER...

...FLASKS IS THE SUIT...

21

...AND *GREEN* IS THE COLOR.

LORD ALLIC PAYS TWENTY-ONE, FLASKS, AND *GREEN*. THANK YOU, GENTLEBEINGS.

YES. IT STILL WORKS.

FOR AN HOUR SHE WORKED THE TABLE...

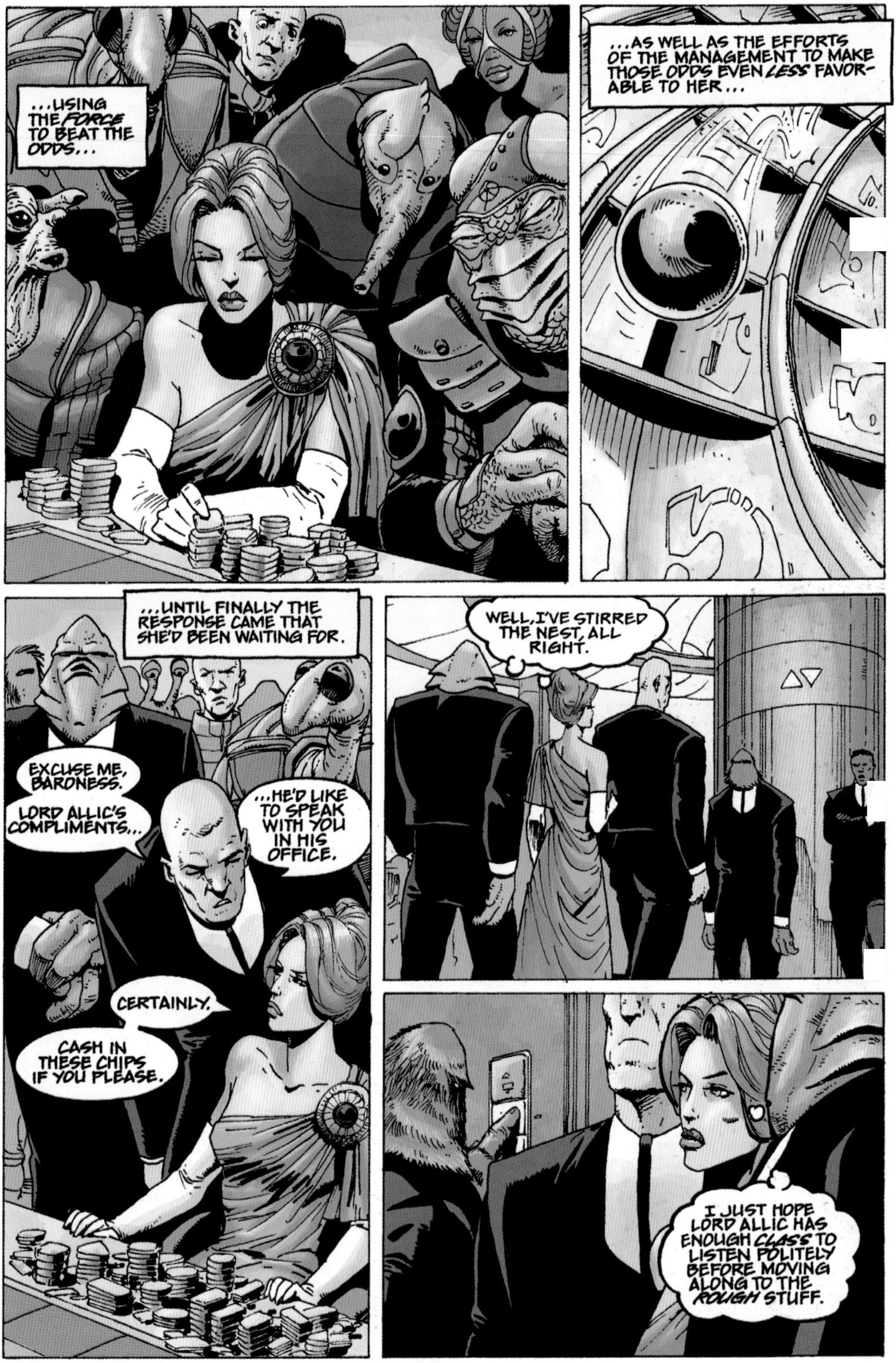
...USING THE FORCE TO BEAT THE ODDS...
...AS WELL AS THE EFFORTS OF THE MANAGEMENT TO MAKE THOSE ODDS EVEN LESS FAVORABLE TO HER...
...UNTIL FINALLY THE RESPONSE CAME THAT SHE'D BEEN WAITING FOR.
EXCUSE ME, BARONESS.
LORD ALLIC'S COMPLIMENTS...
...HE'D LIKE TO SPEAK WITH YOU IN HIS OFFICE.
CERTAINLY.
CASH IN THESE CHIPS IF YOU PLEASE.
WELL, I'VE STIRRED THE NEST, ALL RIGHT.
I JUST HOPE LORD ALLIC HAS ENOUGH CLASS TO LISTEN POLITELY BEFORE MOVING ALONG TO THE ROUGH STUFF.

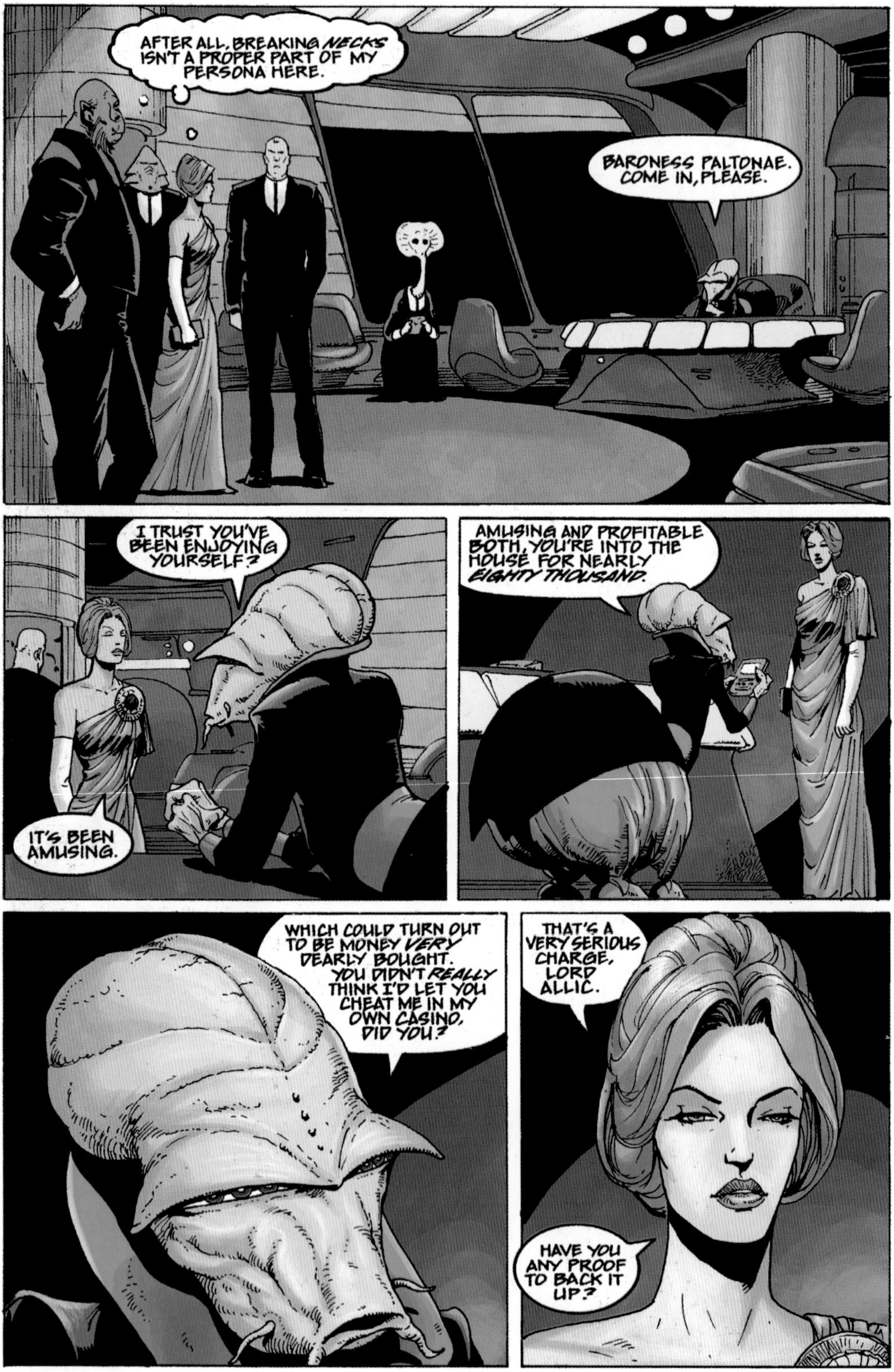
AFTER ALL, BREAKING NECKS ISN'T A PROPER PART OF MY PERSONA HERE.
BARONESS PALTONAE. COME IN, PLEASE.
I TRUST YOU'VE BEEN ENJOYING YOURSELF?
IT'S BEEN AMUSING.
AMUSING AND PROFITABLE BOTH, YOU'RE INTO THE HOUSE FOR NEARLY EIGHTY THOUSAND.
WHICH COULD TURN OUT TO BE MONEY VERY DEARLY BOUGHT. YOU DIDN'T REALLY THINK I'D LET YOU CHEAT ME IN MY OWN CASINO, DID YOU?
THAT'S A VERY SERIOUS CHARGE, LORD ALLIC.
HAVE YOU ANY PROOF TO BACK IT UP?

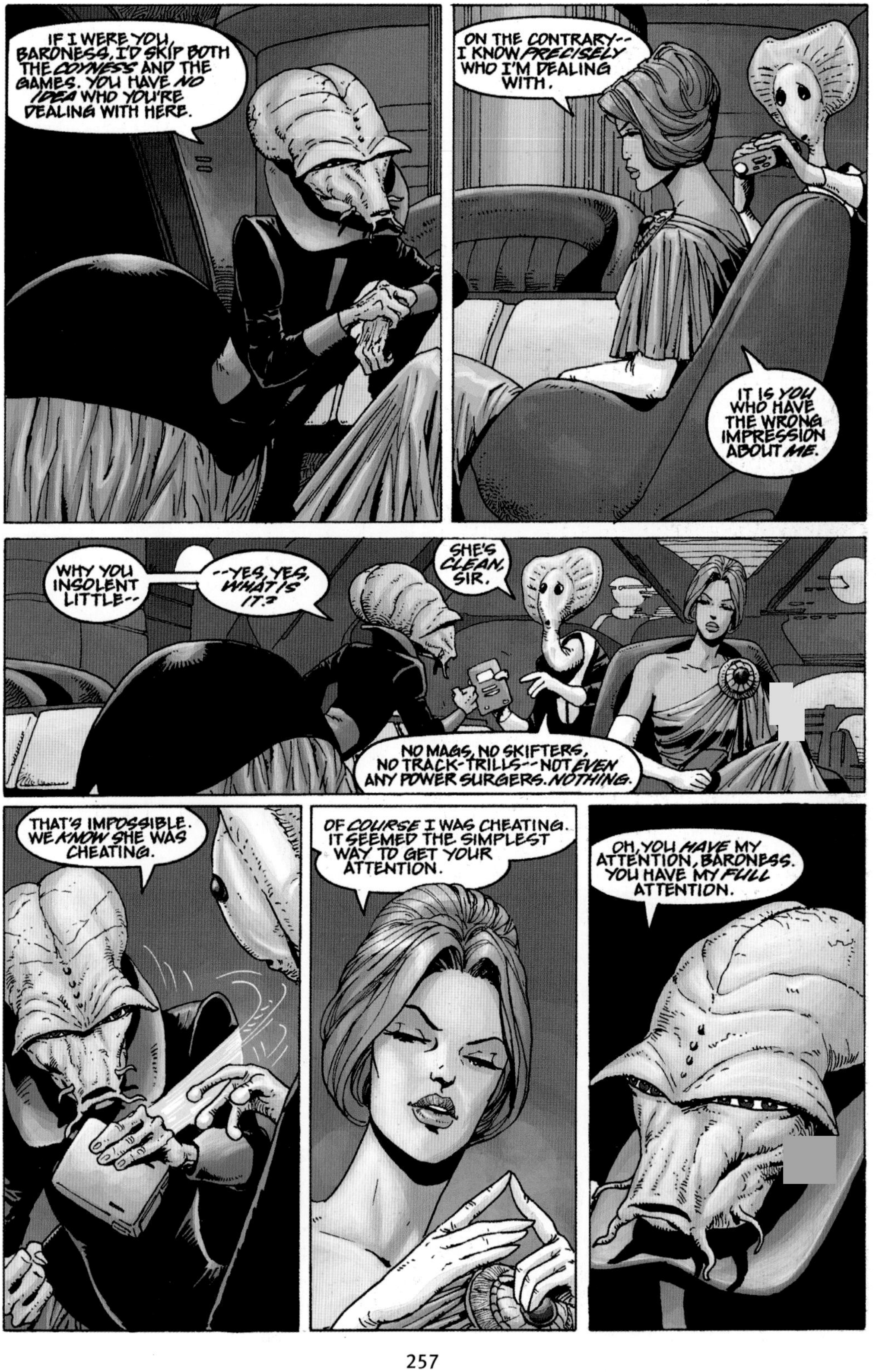
IF I WERE YOU, BARONESS, I'D SKIP BOTH THE COYNESS AND THE GAMES. YOU HAVE NO IDEA WHO YOU'RE DEALING WITH HERE.
ON THE CONTRARY-- I KNOW PRECISELY WHO I'M DEALING WITH.
IT IS YOU WHO HAVE THE WRONG IMPRESSION ABOUT ME.
WHY YOU INSOLENT LITTLE--
--YES, YES, WHAT IS IT?
SHE'S CLEAN, SIR.
NO MAGS, NO SKIFTERS, NO TRACK-TRILLS--NOT EVEN ANY POWER SURGERS. NOTHING.
THAT'S IMPOSSIBLE. WE KNOW SHE WAS CHEATING.
OF COURSE I WAS CHEATING. IT SEEMED THE SIMPLEST WAY TO GET YOUR ATTENTION.
OH, YOU HAVE MY ATTENTION, BARONESS. YOU HAVE MY FULL ATTENTION.

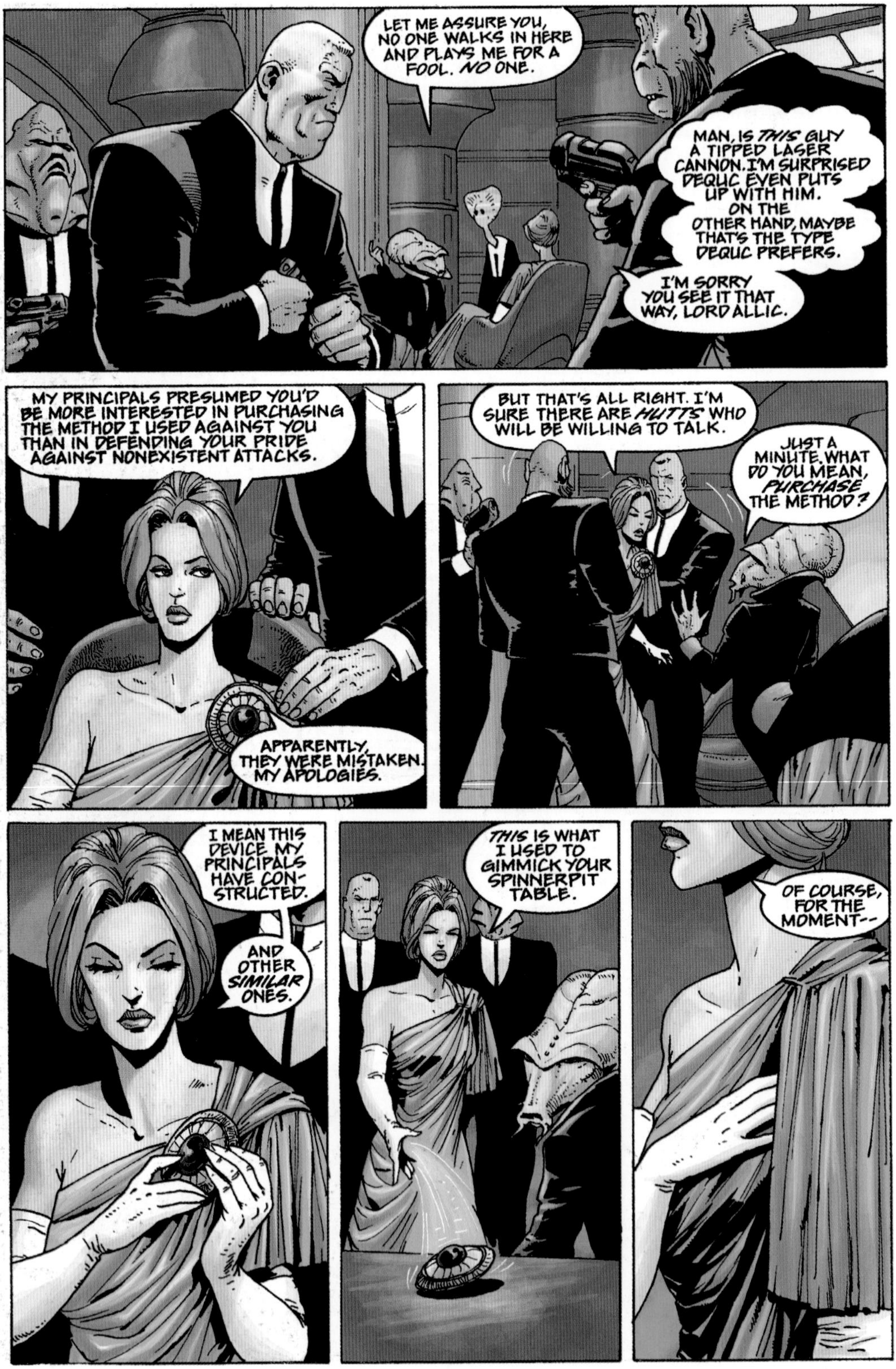
LET ME ASSURE YOU, NO ONE WALKS IN HERE AND PLAYS ME FOR A FOOL. NO ONE.
MAN, IS THIS GUY A TIPPED LASER CANNON. I'M SURPRISED DEQUC EVEN PUTS UP WITH HIM.
ON THE OTHER HAND, MAYBE THAT'S THE TYPE DEQUC PREFERS.
I'M SORRY YOU SEE IT THAT WAY, LORD ALLIC.
MY PRINCIPALS PRESUMED YOU'D BE MORE INTERESTED IN PURCHASING THE METHOD I USED AGAINST YOU THAN IN DEFENDING YOUR PRIDE AGAINST NONEXISTENT ATTACKS.
APPARENTLY, THEY WERE MISTAKEN. MY APOLOGIES.
BUT THAT'S ALL RIGHT. I'M SURE THERE ARE HUTTS WHO WILL BE WILLING TO TALK.
JUST A MINUTE. WHAT DO YOU MEAN, PURCHASE THE METHOD?
I MEAN THIS DEVICE MY PRINCIPALS HAVE CONSTRUCTED.
AND OTHER SIMILAR ONES.
THIS IS WHAT I USED TO GIMMICK YOUR SPINNERPIT TABLE.
OF COURSE, FOR THE MOMENT--

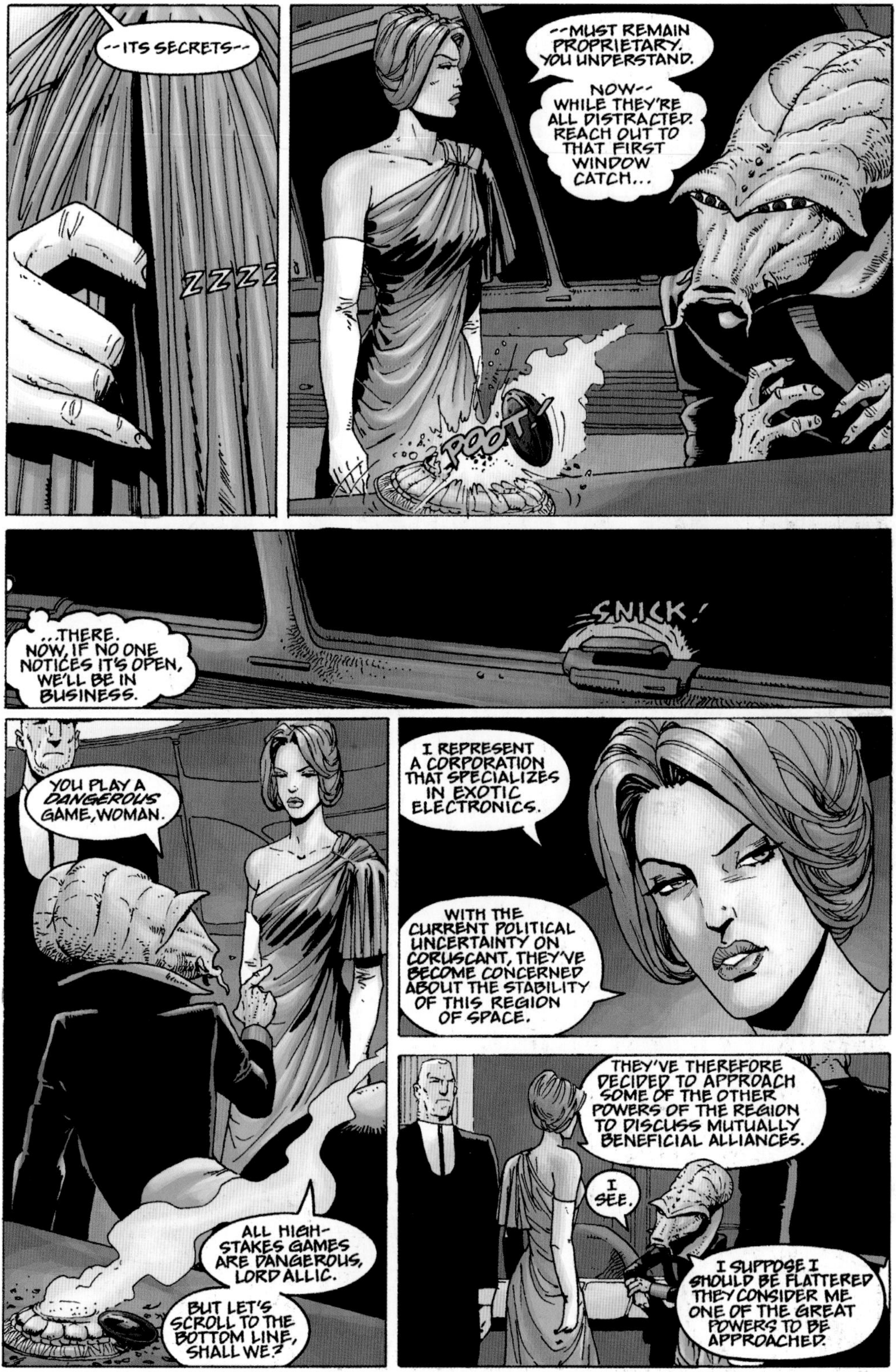
--ITS SECRETS--
ZZZZ
--MUST REMAIN PROPRIETARY. YOU UNDERSTAND.
NOW-- WHILE THEY'RE ALL DISTRACTED. REACH OUT TO THAT FIRST WINDOW CATCH...
POOT!
...THERE. NOW, IF NO ONE NOTICES IT'S OPEN, WE'LL BE IN BUSINESS.
SNICK!
YOU PLAY A DANGEROUS GAME, WOMAN.
ALL HIGH-STAKES GAMES ARE DANGEROUS, LORD ALLIC.
BUT LET'S SCROLL TO THE BOTTOM LINE, SHALL WE?
I REPRESENT A CORPORATION THAT SPECIALIZES IN EXOTIC ELECTRONICS.
WITH THE CURRENT POLITICAL UNCERTAINTY ON CORUSCANT, THEY'VE BECOME CONCERNED ABOUT THE STABILITY OF THIS REGION OF SPACE.
THEY'VE THEREFORE DECIDED TO APPROACH SOME OF THE OTHER POWERS OF THE REGION TO DISCUSS MUTUALLY BENEFICIAL ALLIANCES.
I SEE.
I SUPPOSE I SHOULD BE FLATTERED THEY CONSIDER ME ONE OF THE GREAT POWERS TO BE APPROACHED.

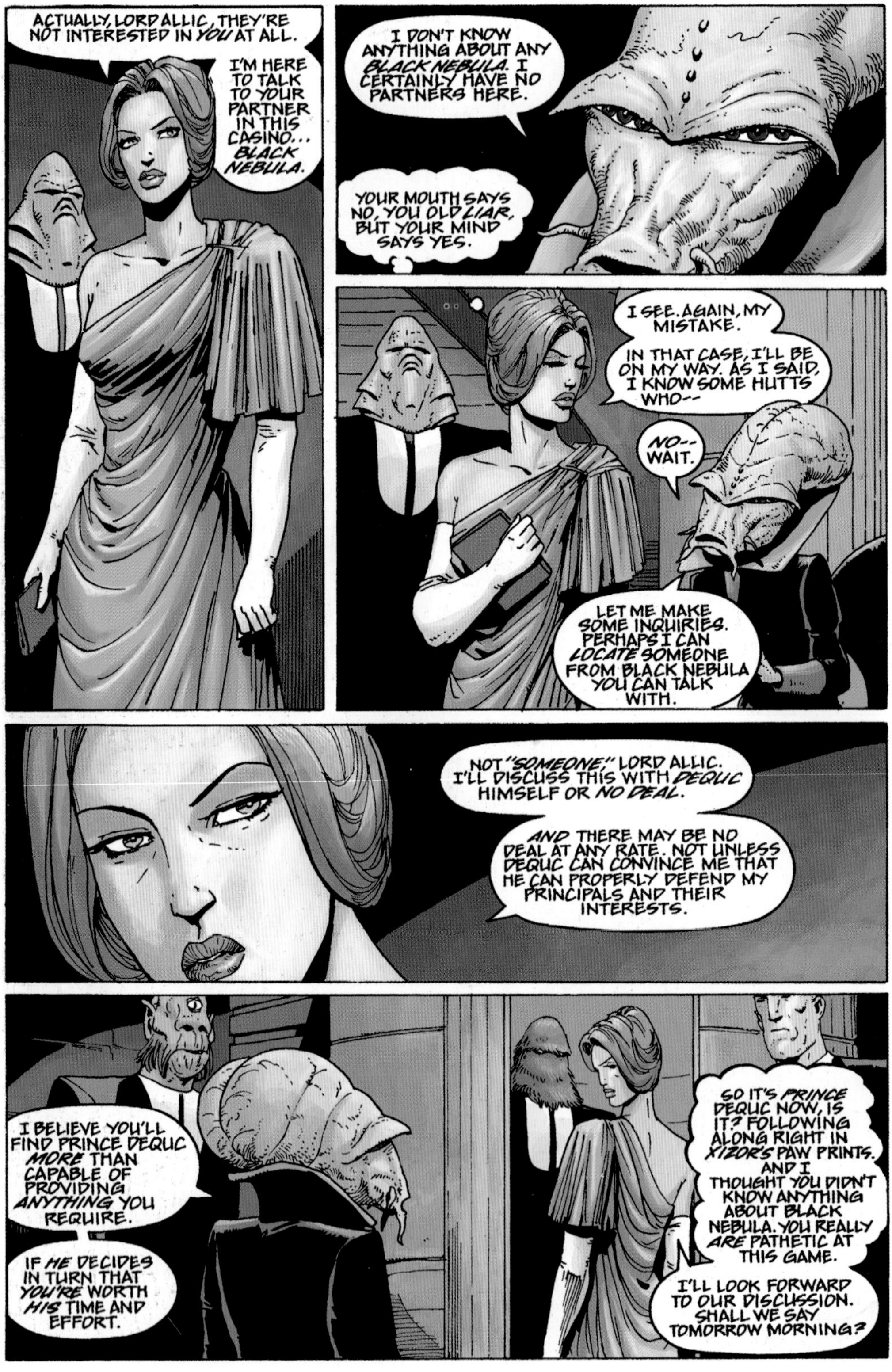
ACTUALLY, LORD ALLIC, THEY'RE NOT INTERESTED IN YOU AT ALL.
I'M HERE TO TALK TO YOUR PARTNER IN THIS CASINO... BLACK NEBULA.
I DON'T KNOW ANYTHING ABOUT ANY BLACK NEBULA. I CERTAINLY HAVE NO PARTNERS HERE.
YOUR MOUTH SAYS NO, YOU OLD LIAR, BUT YOUR MIND SAYS YES.
I SEE. AGAIN, MY MISTAKE.
IN THAT CASE, I'LL BE ON MY WAY. AS I SAID, I KNOW SOME HUTTS WHO--
NO-- WAIT.
LET ME MAKE SOME INQUIRIES. PERHAPS I CAN LOCATE SOMEONE FROM BLACK NEBULA YOU CAN TALK WITH.
NOT "SOMEONE," LORD ALLIC. I'LL DISCUSS THIS WITH DEQUC HIMSELF OR NO DEAL.
AND THERE MAY BE NO DEAL AT ANY RATE. NOT UNLESS DEQUC CAN CONVINCE ME THAT HE CAN PROPERLY DEFEND MY PRINCIPALS AND THEIR INTERESTS.
I BELIEVE YOU'LL FIND PRINCE DEQUC MORE THAN CAPABLE OF PROVIDING ANYTHING YOU REQUIRE.
IF HE DECIDES IN TURN THAT YOU'RE WORTH HIS TIME AND EFFORT.
SO IT'S PRINCE DEQUC NOW, IS IT? FOLLOWING ALONG RIGHT IN XIZOR'S PAW PRINTS.
AND I THOUGHT YOU DIDN'T KNOW ANYTHING ABOUT BLACK NEBULA. YOU REALLY ARE PATHETIC AT THIS GAME.
I'LL LOOK FORWARD TO OUR DISCUSSION. SHALL WE SAY TOMORROW MORNING?

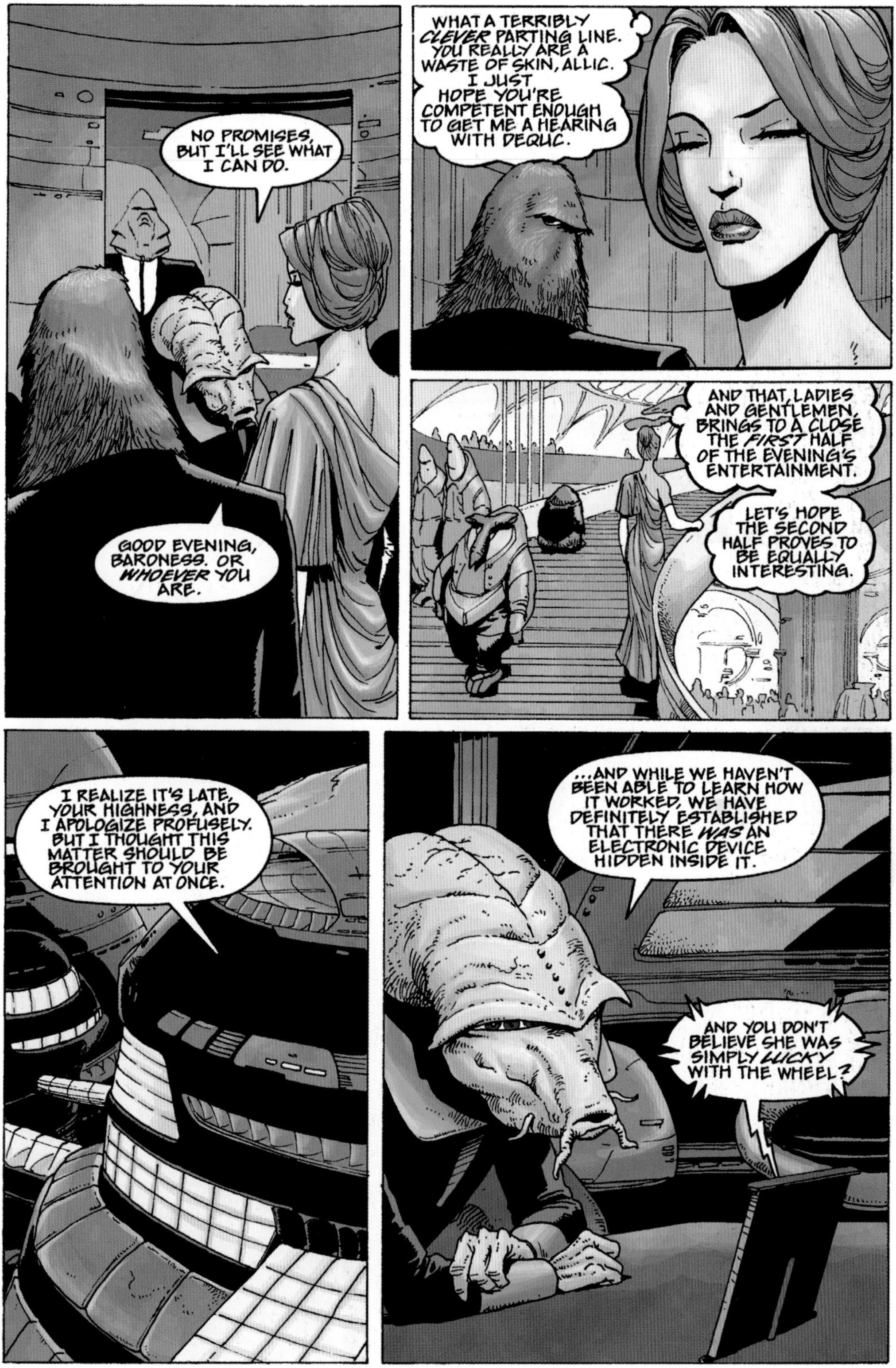
NO PROMISES, BUT I'LL SEE WHAT I CAN DO.
GOOD EVENING, BARONESS. OR *WHOEVER* YOU ARE.
WHAT A TERRIBLY *CLEVER* PARTING LINE. YOU REALLY ARE A WASTE OF SKIN, ALLIC. I JUST HOPE YOU'RE COMPETENT ENOUGH TO GET ME A HEARING WITH DEQUC.
AND THAT, LADIES AND GENTLEMEN, BRINGS TO A CLOSE THE *FIRST* HALF OF THE EVENING'S ENTERTAINMENT.
LET'S HOPE THE SECOND HALF PROVES TO BE EQUALLY INTERESTING.
I REALIZE IT'S LATE, YOUR HIGHNESS, AND I APOLOGIZE PROFUSELY. BUT I THOUGHT THIS MATTER SHOULD BE BROUGHT TO YOUR ATTENTION AT ONCE.
...AND WHILE WE HAVEN'T BEEN ABLE TO LEARN HOW IT WORKED, WE HAVE DEFINITELY ESTABLISHED THAT THERE *WAS* AN ELECTRONIC DEVICE HIDDEN INSIDE IT.
AND YOU DON'T BELIEVE SHE WAS SIMPLY *LUCKY* WITH THE WHEEL?

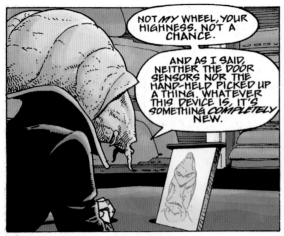

NOT *MY* WHEEL, YOUR HIGHNESS. NOT A CHANCE.

AND AS I SAID, NEITHER THE DOOR SENSORS NOR THE HAND-HELD PICKED UP A THING. WHATEVER THIS DEVICE IS, IT'S SOMETHING *COMPLETELY* NEW.

HMM. THESE PEOPLE MAY INDEED BE WORTH A CLOSER LOOK.

COME ON, DEQUC...

...SAY YOU'LL BE RIGHT OVER TO LOOK AT THE BROOCH. SAY YOU'LL BE RIGHT OVER TO LOOK AT THE BROOCH.

BUT FIRST I WANT A CLOSER LOOK AT WHAT'S LEFT OF HER DEVICE. COLLECT THE PIECES AND BRING THEM TO ME AT ONCE. IF I DECIDE I'M INTERESTED, I'LL ACCEPT HER SUGGESTION OF A MORNING MEETING.

YES, YOUR HIGHNESS.

I'LL BE THERE IN THIRTY MINUTES.

MARPRE, GET THE ASTRAL READY. YOU TWO-- GET THOSE PIECES TOGETHER.

AH, WELL. TOO BAD. BUT I SUPPOSE THAT WOULD HAVE BEEN TOO EASY. STILL, I WOULD HATE TO HAVE GOTTEN ALL DRESSED UP FOR NOTHING.

I WONDER IF ALLIC WOULD MIND HAVING A PASSENGER ALONG?

NO, OF COURSE HE WOULDN'T. PARTICULARLY IF HE DOESN'T *KNOW* ABOUT IT.

NICE AND QUIET. NO NEED TO WAKE ANY OF THE GUARDS.

UH-OH-- THAT SOUNDS LIKE MARPRE AND THE TURBOLIFT NOW. BETTER HURRY.

NO SIGN OF WEAPONS OR FIGHTER PROTECTION. THAT COULD BE HANDY IF I WIND UP HAVING TO MAKE A *FAST* EXIT.

NO GUARDS, NO SURVEILLANCE CAMS, NO SENSOR PLATES.

DEQUC IS REALLY PLAYING IT CASUAL HERE. THOUGH COME TO THINK OF IT, HE MAY NOT HAVE MUCH CHOICE.

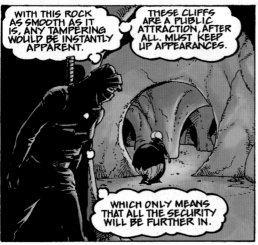

WITH THIS ROCK AS SMOOTH AS IT IS, ANY TAMPERING WOULD BE INSTANTLY APPARENT.

THESE CLIFFS ARE A PUBLIC ATTRACTION, AFTER ALL. MUST KEEP UP APPEARANCES.

WHICH ONLY MEANS THAT ALL THE SECURITY WILL BE FURTHER IN.

AND TEN CHAMBERS LATER, SHE FOUND IT.

WELL, WELL. I GUESS DEQUC'S SECURITY ISN'T SO *LAX* AFTER ALL.

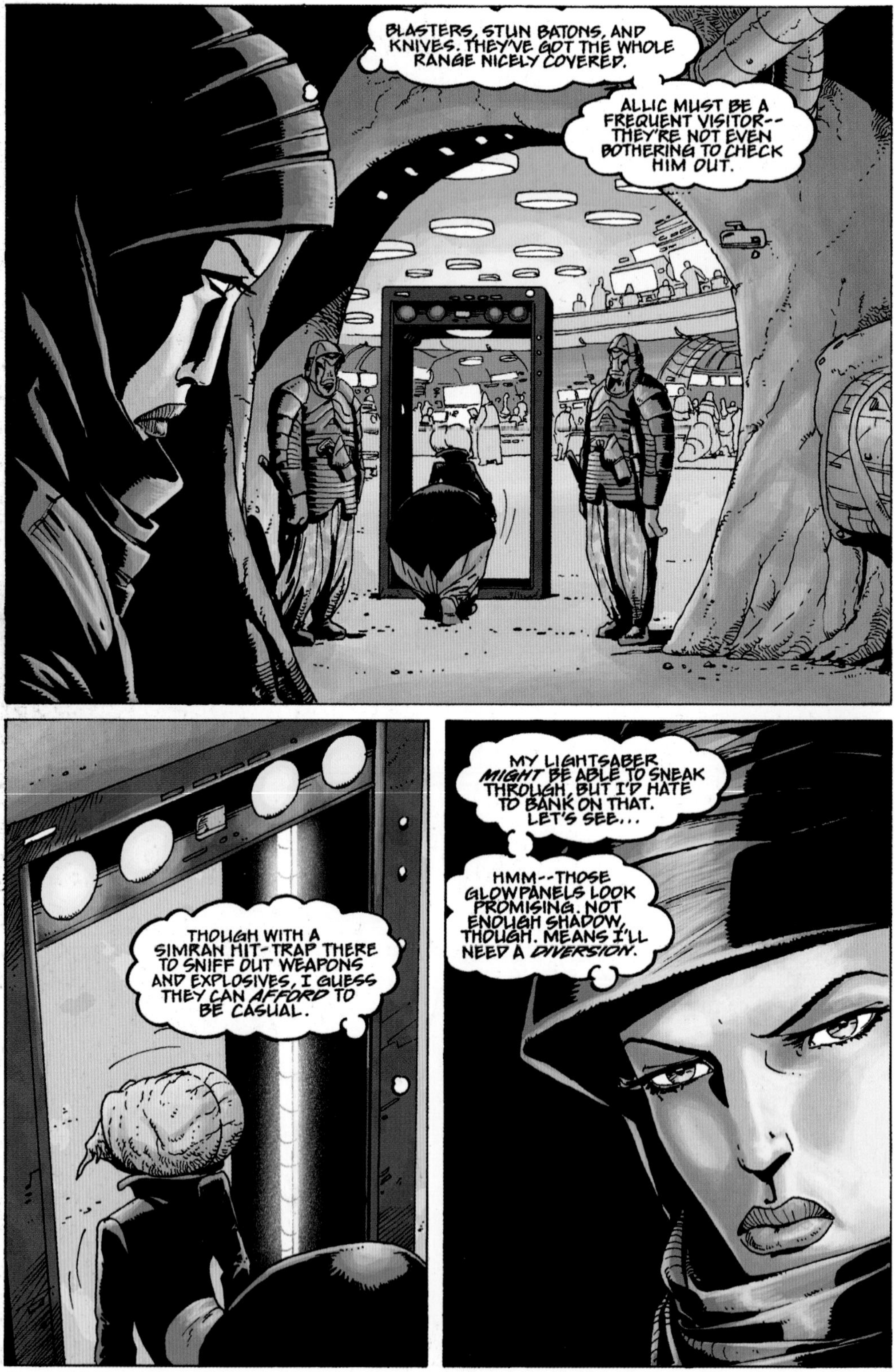
BLASTERS, STUN BATONS, AND KNIVES. THEY'VE GOT THE WHOLE RANGE NICELY COVERED.
ALLIC MUST BE A FREQUENT VISITOR--THEY'RE NOT EVEN BOTHERING TO CHECK HIM OUT.
THOUGH WITH A SIMRAN HIT-TRAP THERE TO SNIFF OUT WEAPONS AND EXPLOSIVES, I GUESS THEY CAN *AFFORD* TO BE CASUAL.
MY LIGHTSABER *MIGHT* BE ABLE TO SNEAK THROUGH, BUT I'D HATE TO BANK ON THAT. LET'S SEE...
HMM--THOSE GLOWPANELS LOOK PROMISING. NOT ENOUGH SHADOW, THOUGH. MEANS I'LL NEED A *DIVERSION*.

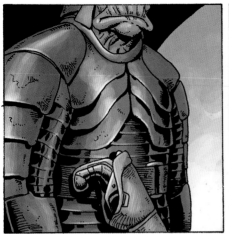

A LITTLE UNSUBTLE-- IN FACT, DOWNRIGHT *CRUDE.* BUT CRUDE USUALLY WORKS WITH THIS KIND OF LOWLIFE.

I'VE SEEN ENOUGH FOR NOW. BETTER GET BACK TO THE ASTRAL AND WAIT FOR ALLIC.

I JUST HOPE HIS TALK WITH DEQUC DOESN'T TAKE ALL NIGHT. TOMORROW'S GOING TO BE A BUSY DAY, AND IT'D BE NICE TO GET A LITTLE SLEEP FIRST.

GOOD MORNING, LORD ALLIC. I TRUST YOU HAVE NEWS?

I DO INDEED, BARONESS. PRINCE DEQUC HAS AGREED TO SEE YOU AT HIS HEADQUARTERS. THIS IS FITCH, AN ASSOCIATE OF HIS WHO WILL ESCORT YOU IN.

GOOD MORNING, BARONESS. PRINCE DEQUC WAS MOST INTRIGUED BY LORD ALLIC'S DESCRIPTION OF YOUR ACTIVITIES LAST EVENING.

MAY I ASSUME YOU'LL BE PREPARED TO DUPLICATE THE DEMONSTRATION?

NOT THAT ONE SPECIFICALLY, BUT I'VE BROUGHT OTHERS. *ALL* EQUALLY INTRIGUING, I ASSURE YOU. MY PRINCIPALS BELIEVE *VARIETY* IS MORE IMPRESSIVE THAN MERE REPETITION.

IT'S CLEAN, FITCH. NOTHING DANGEROUS.

NOTHING *USEFUL,* EITHER. JUST A BUNCH OF JUNK.

AH, BUT THAT'S THE QUESTION, TRAFF, ISN'T IT? THIS WAY, BARONESS-- OUR AIRSPEEDER'S WAITING ON THE ROOF.

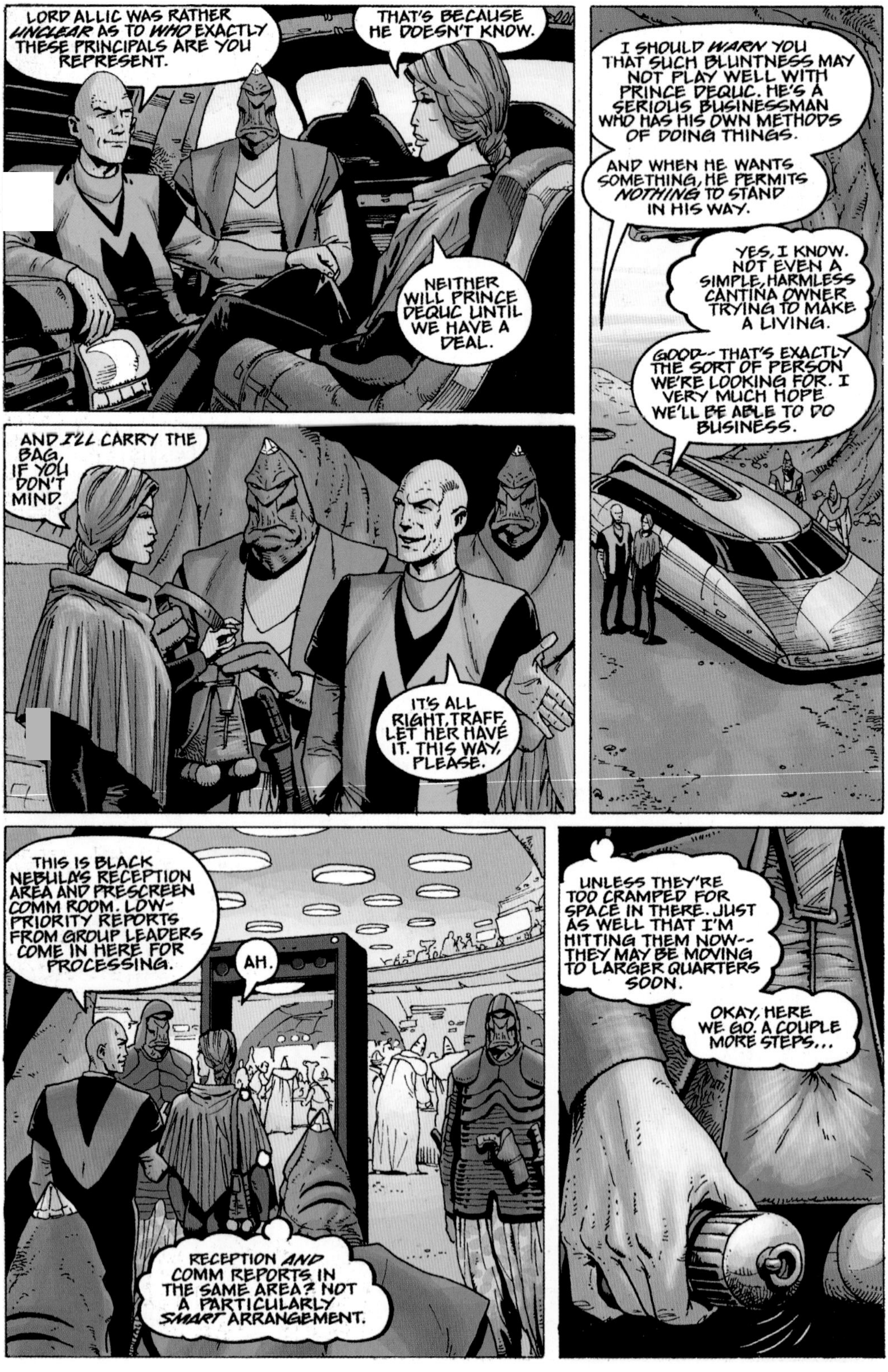
LORD ALLIC WAS RATHER UNCLEAR AS TO WHO EXACTLY THESE PRINCIPALS ARE YOU REPRESENT.
THAT'S BECAUSE HE DOESN'T KNOW.
NEITHER WILL PRINCE DEQUC UNTIL WE HAVE A DEAL.
I SHOULD WARN YOU THAT SUCH BLUNTNESS MAY NOT PLAY WELL WITH PRINCE DEQUC. HE'S A SERIOUS BUSINESSMAN WHO HAS HIS OWN METHODS OF DOING THINGS.
AND WHEN HE WANTS SOMETHING, HE PERMITS NOTHING TO STAND IN HIS WAY.
YES, I KNOW. NOT EVEN A SIMPLE, HARMLESS CANTINA OWNER TRYING TO MAKE A LIVING.
GOOD-- THAT'S EXACTLY THE SORT OF PERSON WE'RE LOOKING FOR. I VERY MUCH HOPE WE'LL BE ABLE TO DO BUSINESS.
AND I'LL CARRY THE BAG, IF YOU DON'T MIND.
IT'S ALL RIGHT, TRAFF. LET HER HAVE IT. THIS WAY, PLEASE.
THIS IS BLACK NEBULA'S RECEPTION AREA AND PRESCREEN COMM ROOM. LOW-PRIORITY REPORTS FROM GROUP LEADERS COME IN HERE FOR PROCESSING.
AH.
RECEPTION AND COMM REPORTS IN THE SAME AREA? NOT A PARTICULARLY SMART ARRANGEMENT.
UNLESS THEY'RE TOO CRAMPED FOR SPACE IN THERE. JUST AS WELL THAT I'M HITTING THEM NOW-- THEY MAY BE MOVING TO LARGER QUARTERS SOON.
OKAY, HERE WE GO. A COUPLE MORE STEPS...

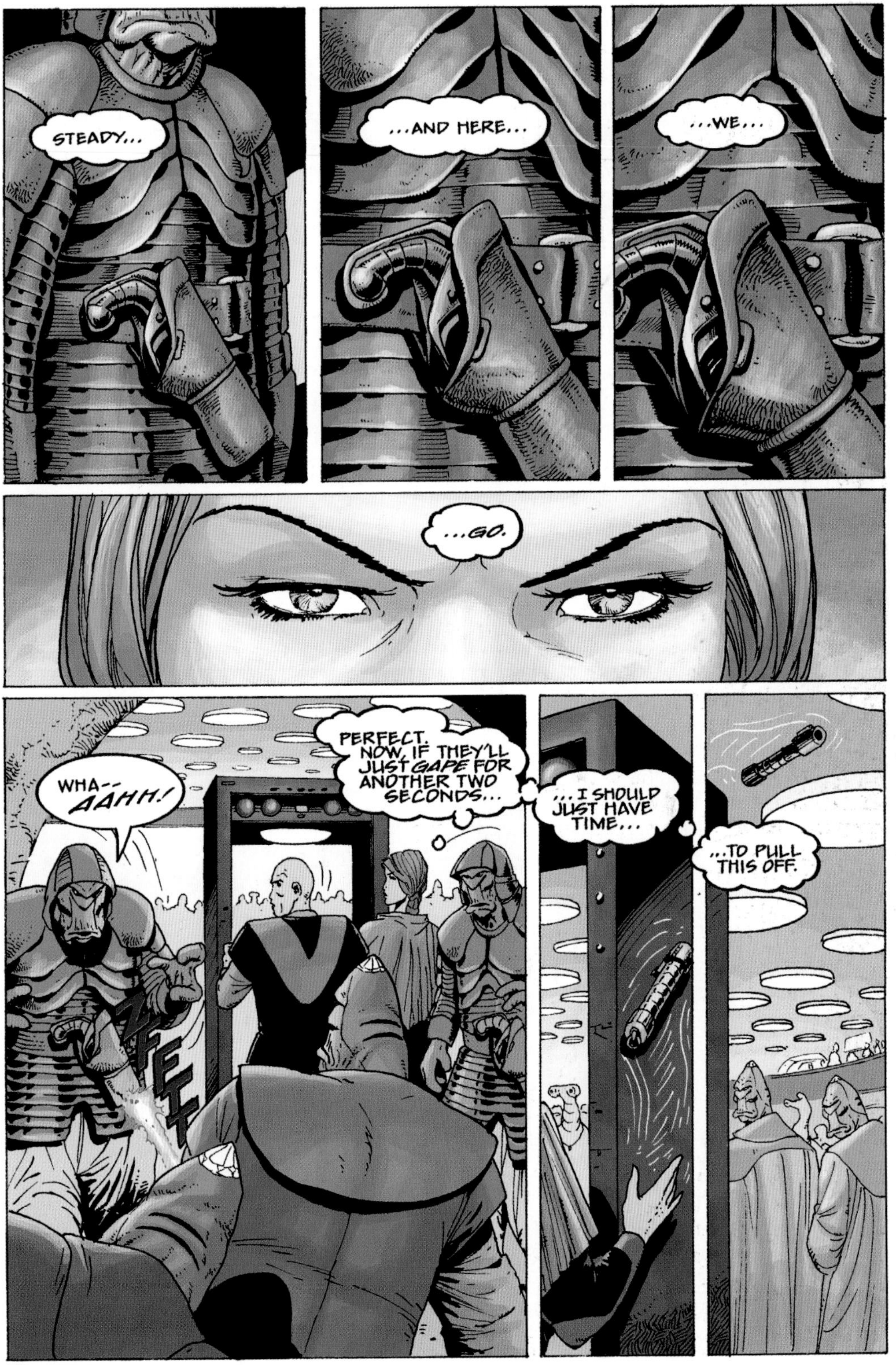
STEADY...
...AND HERE...
...WE...
...GO.
WHA--
AAHH!
PERFECT. NOW, IF THEY'LL JUST GAPE FOR ANOTHER TWO SECONDS...
ZFFFT
...I SHOULD JUST HAVE TIME...
...TO PULL THIS OFF.

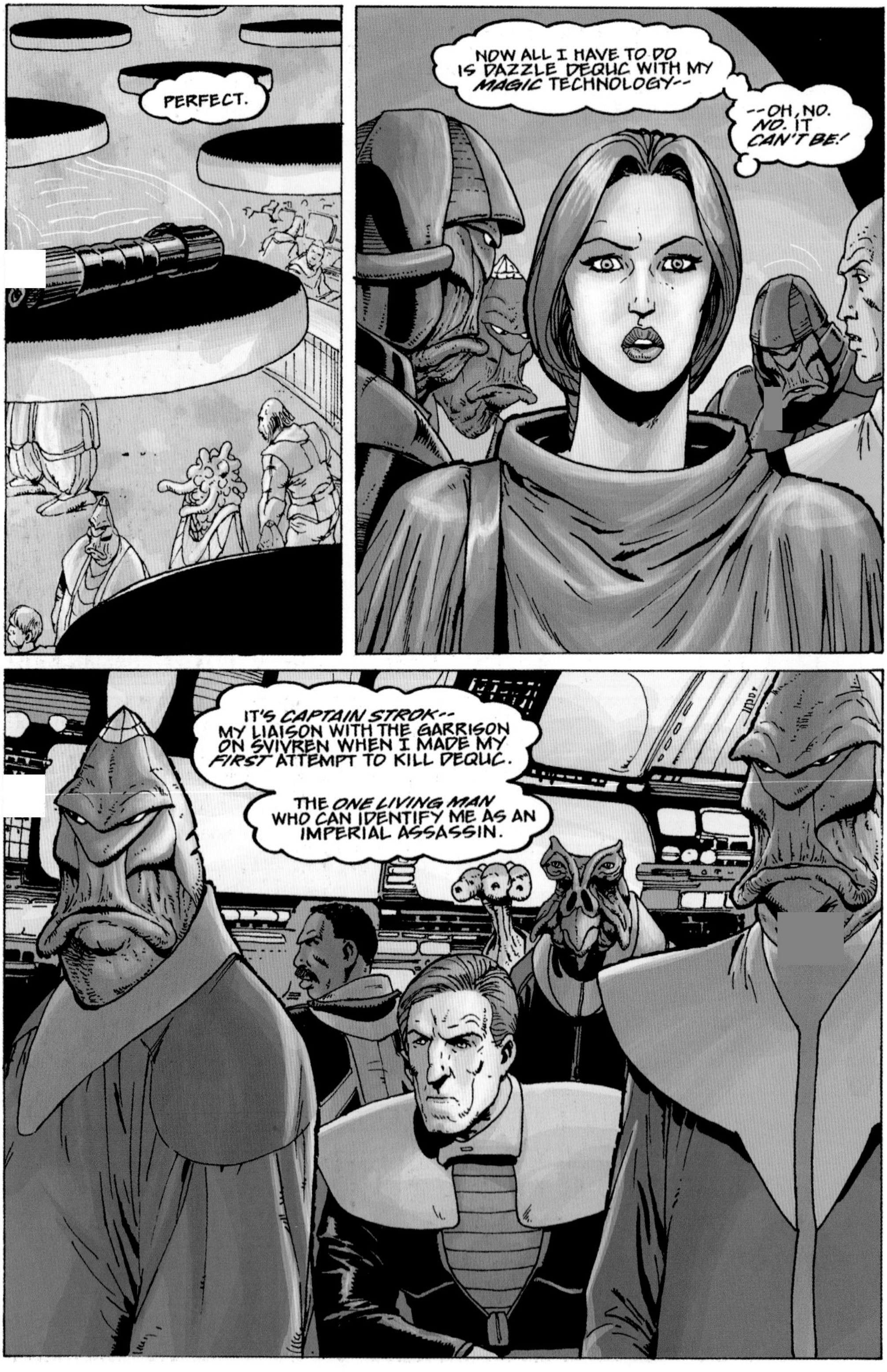
PERFECT.
NOW ALL I HAVE TO DO IS DAZZLE DEQUC WITH MY *MAGIC* TECHNOLOGY--
--OH, NO. *NO.* IT *CAN'T BE!*
IT'S *CAPTAIN STROK*-- MY LIAISON WITH THE GARRISON ON SVIVREN WHEN I MADE MY *FIRST* ATTEMPT TO KILL DEQUC.
THE *ONE LIVING MAN* WHO CAN IDENTIFY ME AS AN IMPERIAL ASSASSIN.

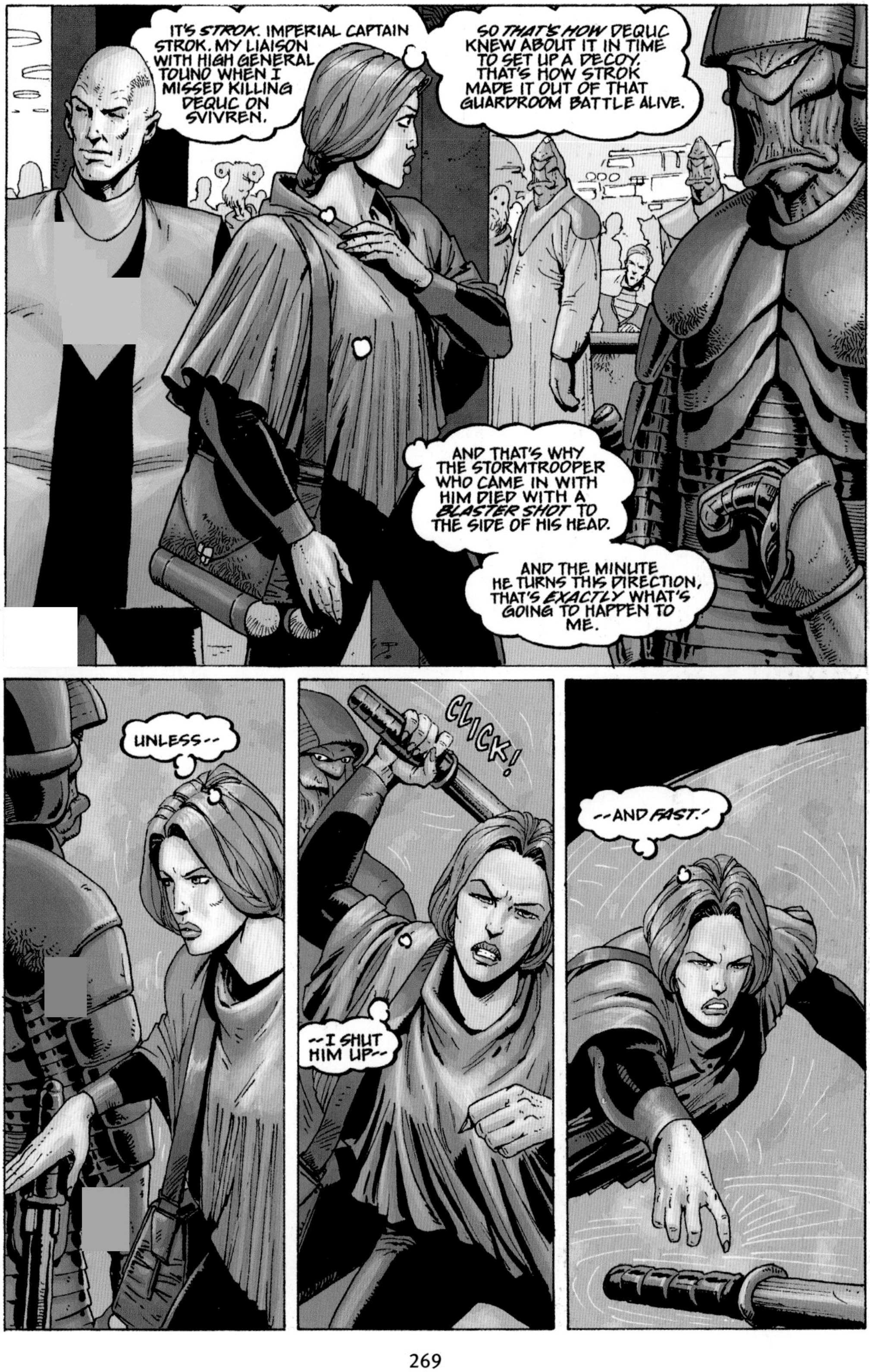
IT'S STROK. IMPERIAL CAPTAIN STROK. MY LIAISON WITH HIGH GENERAL TOUNO WHEN I MISSED KILLING DEQUC ON SVIVREN.
SO THAT'S HOW DEQUC KNEW ABOUT IT IN TIME TO SET UP A DECOY. THAT'S HOW STROK MADE IT OUT OF THAT GUARDROOM BATTLE ALIVE.
AND THAT'S WHY THE STORMTROOPER WHO CAME IN WITH HIM DIED WITH A BLASTER SHOT TO THE SIDE OF HIS HEAD.
AND THE MINUTE HE TURNS THIS DIRECTION, THAT'S EXACTLY WHAT'S GOING TO HAPPEN TO ME.
UNLESS--
CLICK!
--I SHUT HIM UP--
--AND FAST!

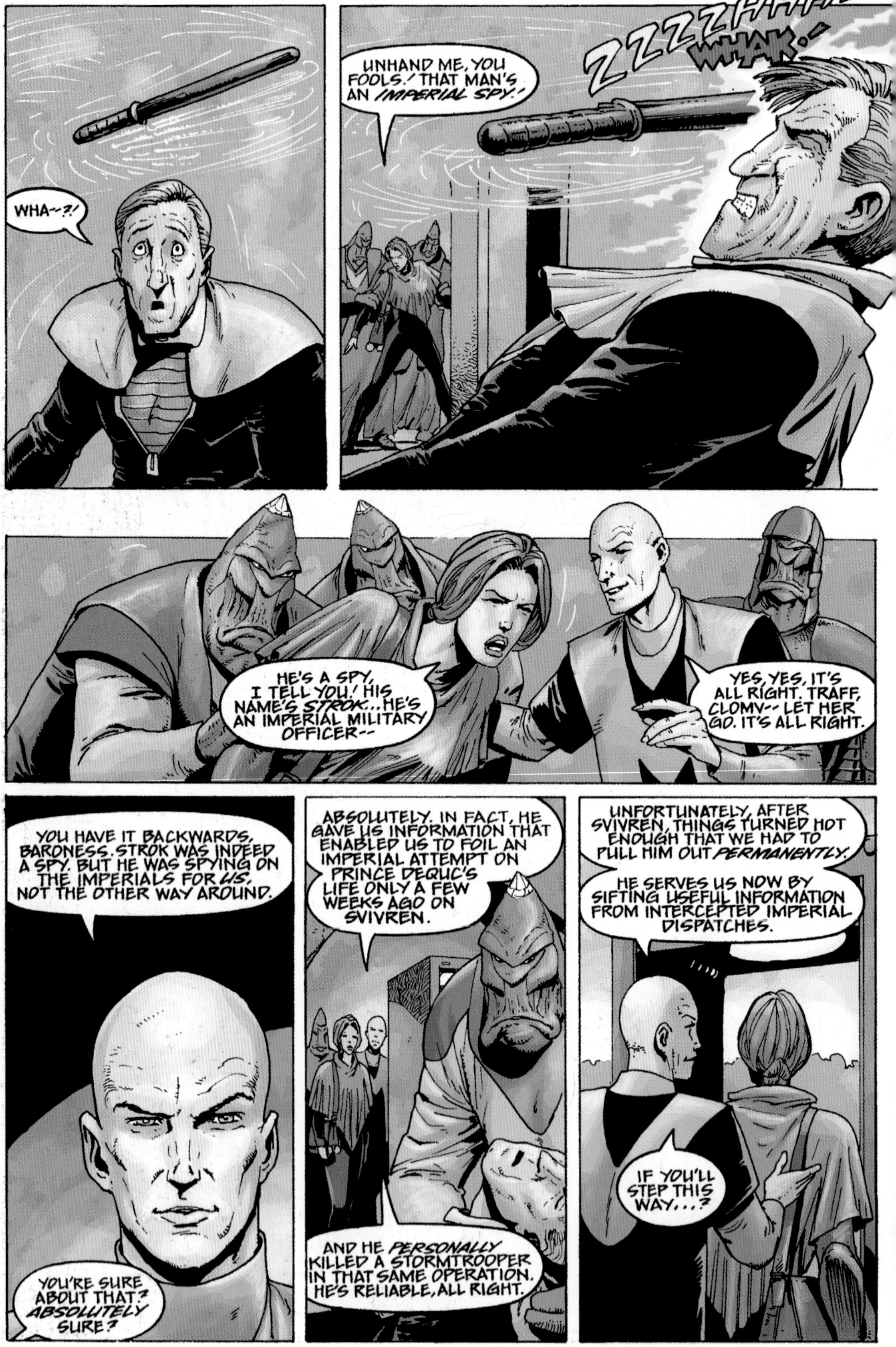
WHA--?!
UNHAND ME, YOU FOOLS! THAT MAN'S AN IMPERIAL SPY!
ZZZZZHHHH-
WHAK!
HE'S A SPY, I TELL YOU! HIS NAME'S STROK...HE'S AN IMPERIAL MILITARY OFFICER--
YES, YES, IT'S ALL RIGHT. TRAFF, CLOMV-- LET HER GO. IT'S ALL RIGHT.
YOU HAVE IT BACKWARDS, BARONESS. STROK WAS INDEED A SPY. BUT HE WAS SPYING ON THE IMPERIALS FOR US, NOT THE OTHER WAY AROUND.
YOU'RE SURE ABOUT THAT? ABSOLUTELY SURE?
ABSOLUTELY. IN FACT, HE GAVE US INFORMATION THAT ENABLED US TO FOIL AN IMPERIAL ATTEMPT ON PRINCE DEQUC'S LIFE ONLY A FEW WEEKS AGO ON SVIVREN.
AND HE PERSONALLY KILLED A STORMTROOPER IN THAT SAME OPERATION. HE'S RELIABLE, ALL RIGHT.
UNFORTUNATELY, AFTER SVIVREN, THINGS TURNED HOT ENOUGH THAT WE HAD TO PULL HIM OUT PERMANENTLY.
HE SERVES US NOW BY SIFTING USEFUL INFORMATION FROM INTERCEPTED IMPERIAL DISPATCHES.
IF YOU'LL STEP THIS WAY...?

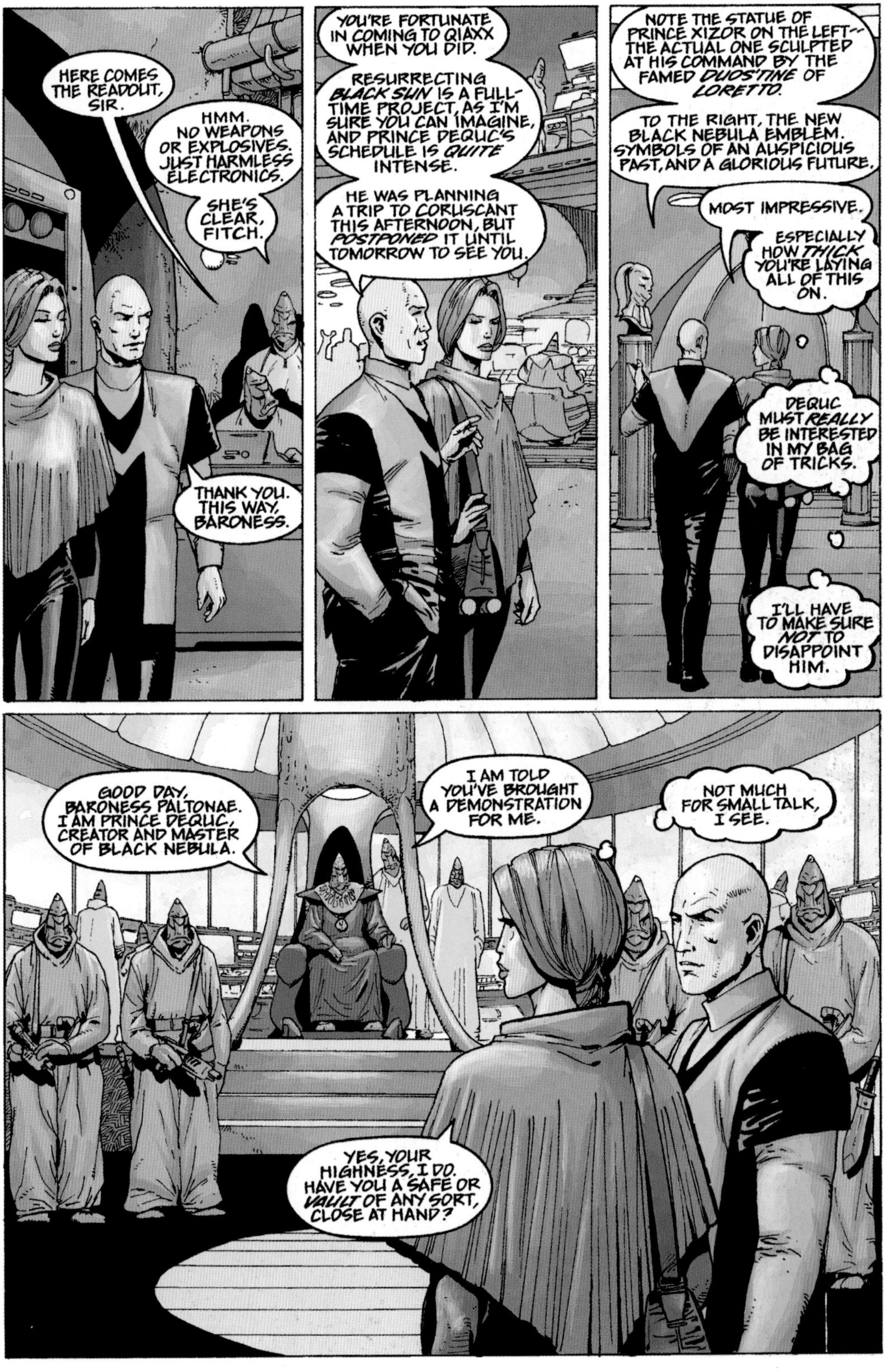
HERE COMES THE READOUT, SIR.
HMM. NO WEAPONS OR EXPLOSIVES. JUST HARMLESS ELECTRONICS.
SHE'S CLEAR, FITCH.
THANK YOU. THIS WAY, BARONESS.
YOU'RE FORTUNATE IN COMING TO QIAXX WHEN YOU DID.
RESURRECTING BLACK SUN IS A FULL-TIME PROJECT, AS I'M SURE YOU CAN IMAGINE, AND PRINCE DEQUC'S SCHEDULE IS QUITE INTENSE.
HE WAS PLANNING A TRIP TO CORUSCANT THIS AFTERNOON, BUT POSTPONED IT UNTIL TOMORROW TO SEE YOU.
NOTE THE STATUE OF PRINCE XIZOR ON THE LEFT-- THE ACTUAL ONE SCULPTED AT HIS COMMAND BY THE FAMED DUOS'TINE OF LORETTO.
TO THE RIGHT, THE NEW BLACK NEBULA EMBLEM. SYMBOLS OF AN AUSPICIOUS PAST, AND A GLORIOUS FUTURE.
MOST IMPRESSIVE.
ESPECIALLY HOW THICK YOU'RE LAYING ALL OF THIS ON.
DEQUC MUST REALLY BE INTERESTED IN MY BAG OF TRICKS.
I'LL HAVE TO MAKE SURE NOT TO DISAPPOINT HIM.
GOOD DAY, BARONESS PALTONAE. I AM PRINCE DEQUC, CREATOR AND MASTER OF BLACK NEBULA.
I AM TOLD YOU'VE BROUGHT A DEMONSTRATION FOR ME.
NOT MUCH FOR SMALL TALK, I SEE.
YES, YOUR HIGHNESS, I DO. HAVE YOU A SAFE OR VAULT OF ANY SORT, CLOSE AT HAND?

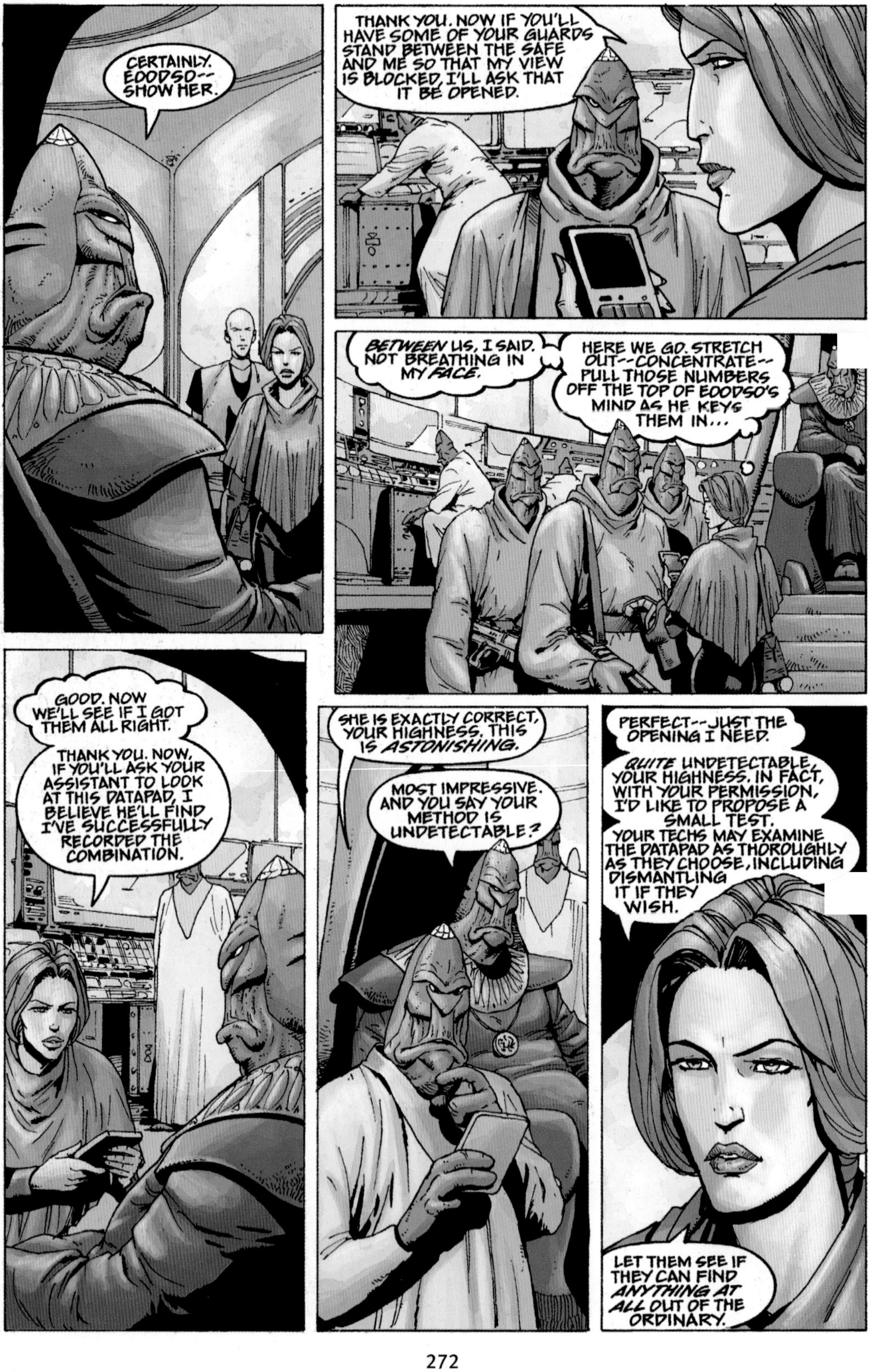
CERTAINLY. EOODSO-- SHOW HER.
THANK YOU. NOW IF YOU'LL HAVE SOME OF YOUR GUARDS STAND BETWEEN THE SAFE AND ME SO THAT MY VIEW IS BLOCKED, I'LL ASK THAT IT BE OPENED.
BETWEEN US, I SAID. NOT BREATHING IN MY FACE.
HERE WE GO. STRETCH OUT--CONCENTRATE--PULL THOSE NUMBERS OFF THE TOP OF EOODSO'S MIND AS HE KEYS THEM IN...
GOOD. NOW WE'LL SEE IF I GOT THEM ALL RIGHT.
THANK YOU. NOW, IF YOU'LL ASK YOUR ASSISTANT TO LOOK AT THIS DATAPAD, I BELIEVE HE'LL FIND I'VE SUCCESSFULLY RECORDED THE COMBINATION.
SHE IS EXACTLY CORRECT, YOUR HIGHNESS. THIS IS ASTONISHING.
MOST IMPRESSIVE. AND YOU SAY YOUR METHOD IS UNDETECTABLE?
PERFECT--JUST THE OPENING I NEED.
QUITE UNDETECTABLE, YOUR HIGHNESS. IN FACT, WITH YOUR PERMISSION, I'D LIKE TO PROPOSE A SMALL TEST.
YOUR TECHS MAY EXAMINE THE DATAPAD AS THOROUGHLY AS THEY CHOOSE, INCLUDING DISMANTLING IT IF THEY WISH.
LET THEM SEE IF THEY CAN FIND ANYTHING AT ALL OUT OF THE ORDINARY.

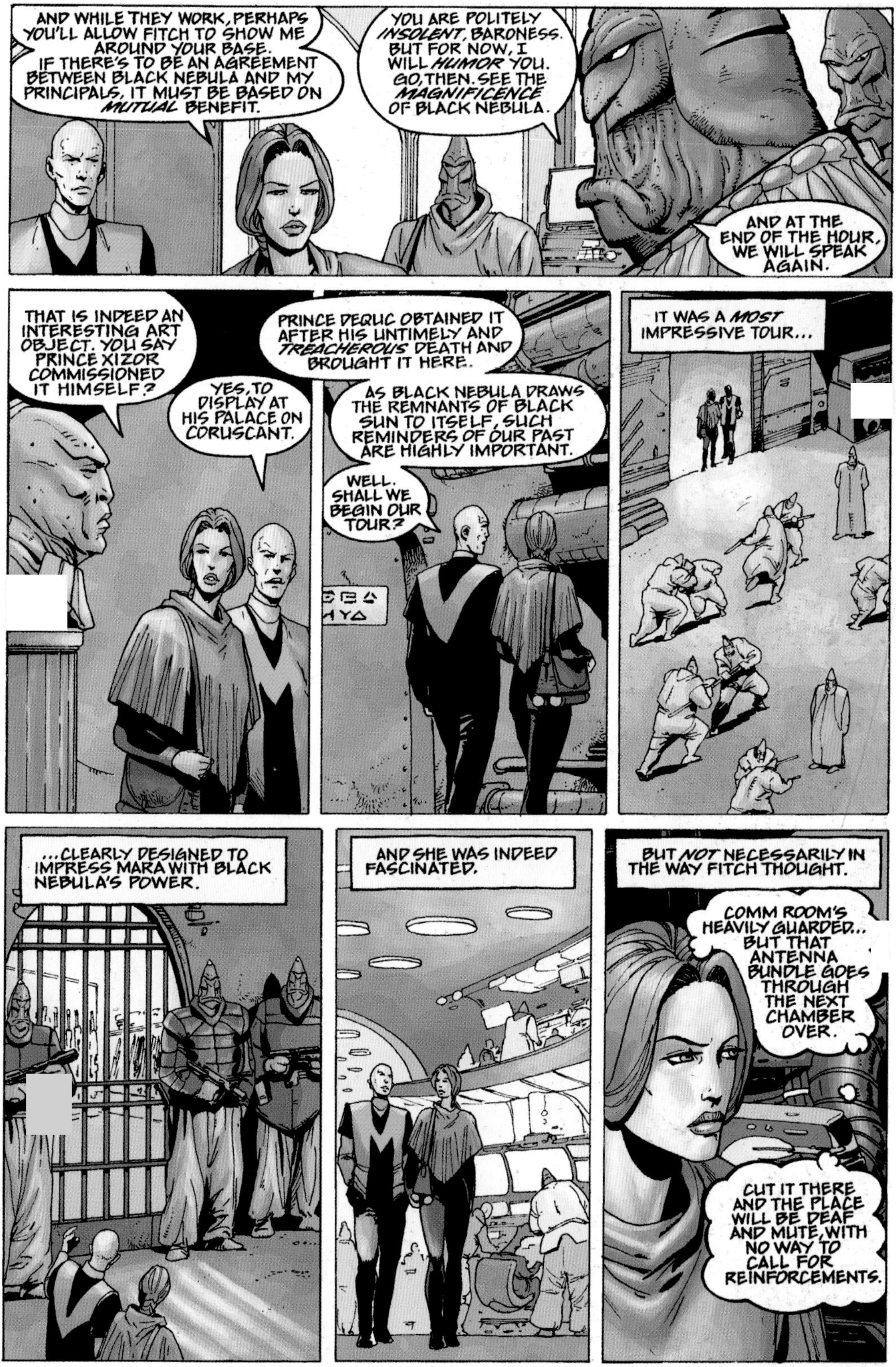
AND WHILE THEY WORK, PERHAPS YOU'LL ALLOW FITCH TO SHOW ME AROUND YOUR BASE. IF THERE'S TO BE AN AGREEMENT BETWEEN BLACK NEBULA AND MY PRINCIPALS, IT MUST BE BASED ON MUTUAL BENEFIT.
YOU ARE POLITELY INSOLENT, BARONESS. BUT FOR NOW, I WILL HUMOR YOU. GO, THEN. SEE THE MAGNIFICENCE OF BLACK NEBULA.
AND AT THE END OF THE HOUR, WE WILL SPEAK AGAIN.
THAT IS INDEED AN INTERESTING ART OBJECT. YOU SAY PRINCE XIZOR COMMISSIONED IT HIMSELF?
YES, TO DISPLAY AT HIS PALACE ON CORUSCANT.
PRINCE DEQUC OBTAINED IT AFTER HIS UNTIMELY AND TREACHEROUS DEATH AND BROUGHT IT HERE.
AS BLACK NEBULA DRAWS THE REMNANTS OF BLACK SUN TO ITSELF, SUCH REMINDERS OF OUR PAST ARE HIGHLY IMPORTANT.
WELL. SHALL WE BEGIN OUR TOUR?
IT WAS A MOST IMPRESSIVE TOUR...
...CLEARLY DESIGNED TO IMPRESS MARA WITH BLACK NEBULA'S POWER.
AND SHE WAS INDEED FASCINATED.
BUT NOT NECESSARILY IN THE WAY FITCH THOUGHT.
COMM ROOM'S HEAVILY GUARDED... BUT THAT ANTENNA BUNDLE GOES THROUGH THE NEXT CHAMBER OVER.
CUT IT THERE AND THE PLACE WILL BE DEAF AND MUTE, WITH NO WAY TO CALL FOR REINFORCEMENTS.

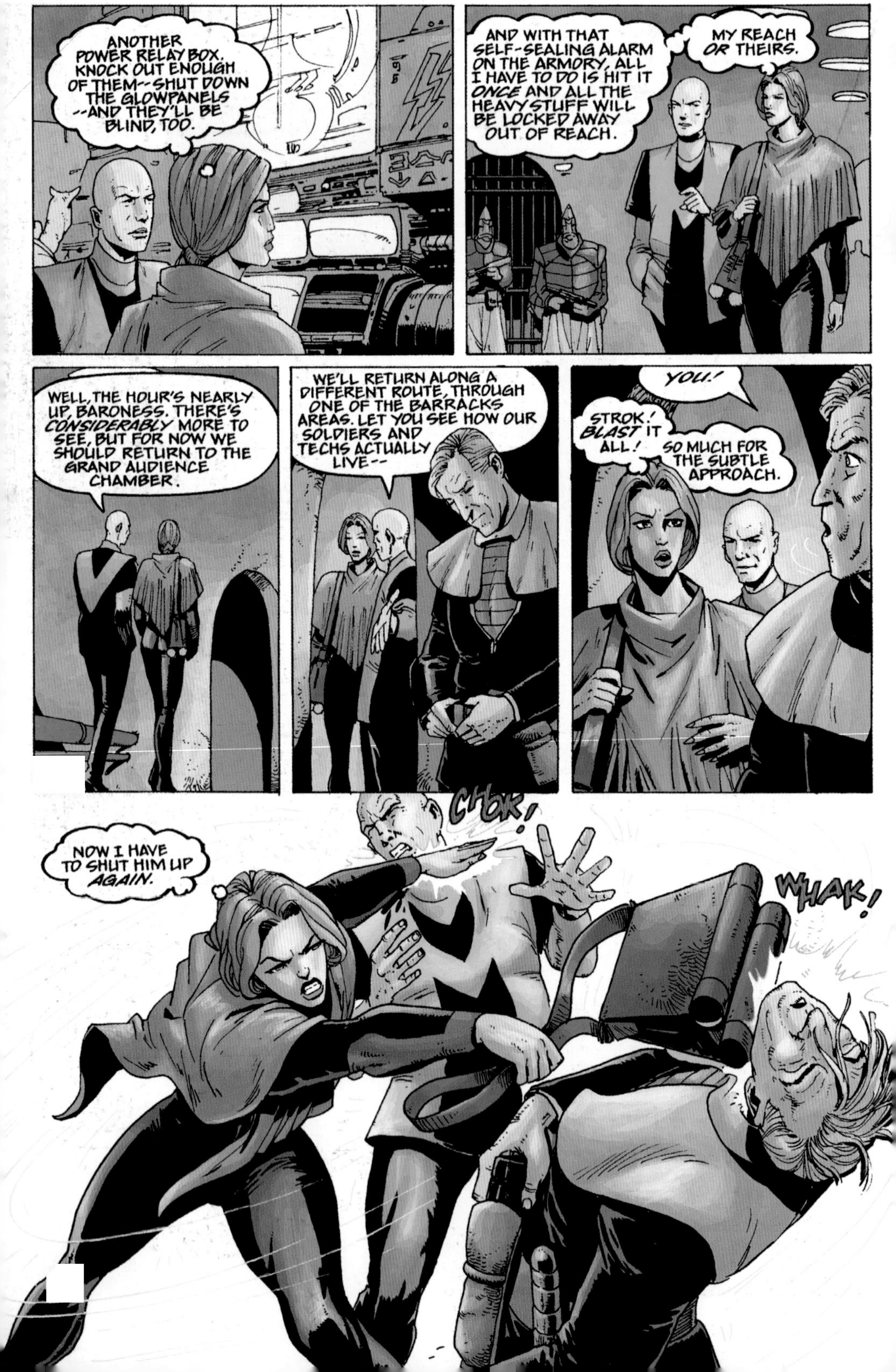
ANOTHER POWER RELAY BOX. KNOCK OUT ENOUGH OF THEM--SHUT DOWN THE GLOWPANELS --AND THEY'LL BE BLIND, TOO.
AND WITH THAT SELF-SEALING ALARM ON THE ARMORY, ALL I HAVE TO DO IS HIT IT ONCE AND ALL THE HEAVY STUFF WILL BE LOCKED AWAY OUT OF REACH.
MY REACH OR THEIRS.
WELL, THE HOUR'S NEARLY UP, BARONESS. THERE'S CONSIDERABLY MORE TO SEE, BUT FOR NOW WE SHOULD RETURN TO THE GRAND AUDIENCE CHAMBER.
WE'LL RETURN ALONG A DIFFERENT ROUTE, THROUGH ONE OF THE BARRACKS AREAS. LET YOU SEE HOW OUR SOLDIERS AND TECHS ACTUALLY LIVE--
YOU!
STROK! BLAST IT ALL!
SO MUCH FOR THE SUBTLE APPROACH.
CHOK!
NOW I HAVE TO SHUT HIM UP AGAIN.
WHAK!

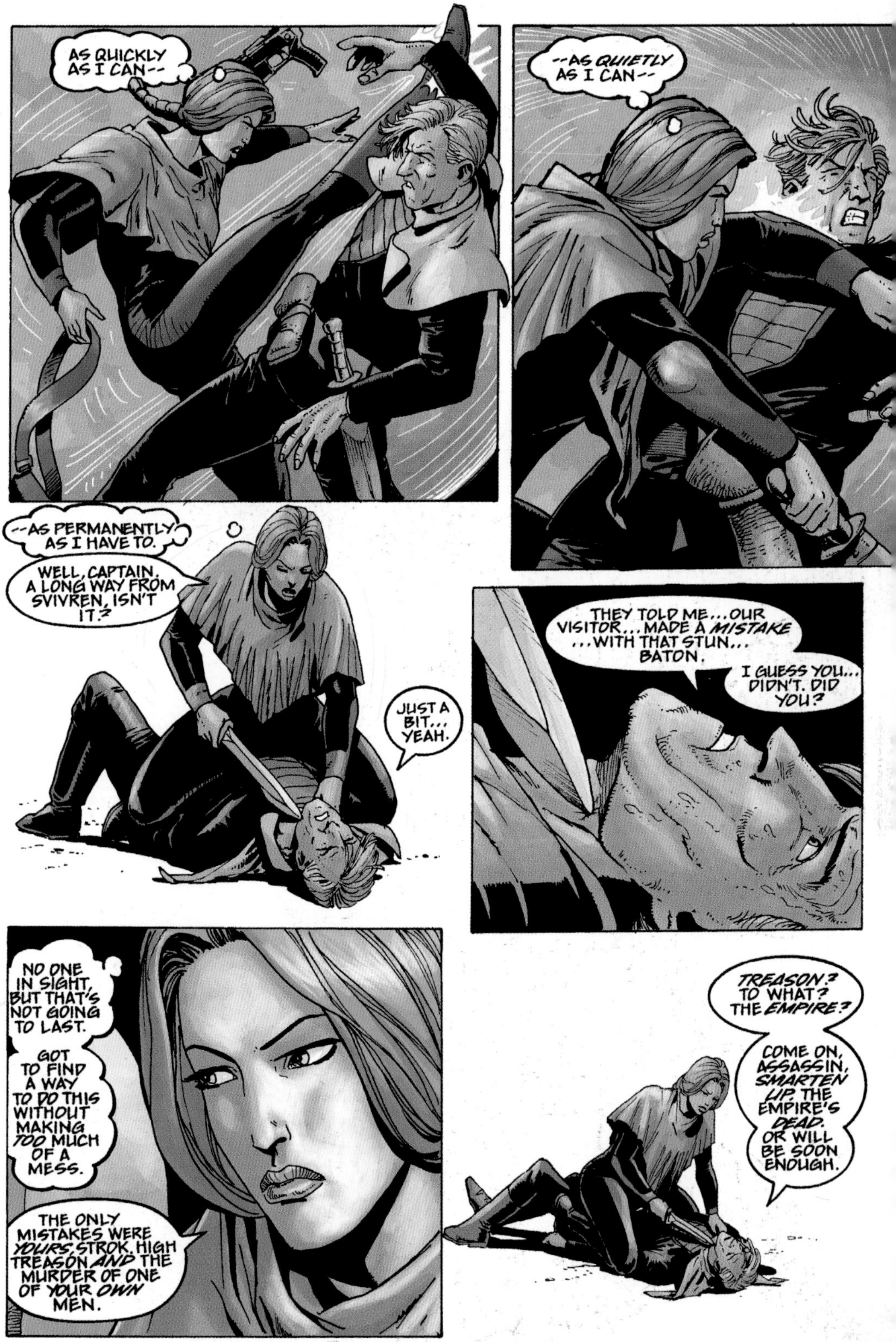
AS QUICKLY AS I CAN--
--AS QUIETLY AS I CAN--
--AS PERMANENTLY AS I HAVE TO.
WELL, CAPTAIN. A LONG WAY FROM SVIVREN, ISN'T IT?
JUST A BIT... YEAH.
THEY TOLD ME... OUR VISITOR... MADE A MISTAKE ... WITH THAT STUN... BATON.
I GUESS YOU... DIDN'T. DID YOU?
NO ONE IN SIGHT, BUT THAT'S NOT GOING TO LAST.
GOT TO FIND A WAY TO DO THIS WITHOUT MAKING TOO MUCH OF A MESS.
THE ONLY MISTAKES WERE YOURS, STROK. HIGH TREASON AND THE MURDER OF ONE OF YOUR OWN MEN.
TREASON? TO WHAT? THE EMPIRE?
COME ON, ASSASSIN, SMARTEN UP. THE EMPIRE'S DEAD. OR WILL BE SOON ENOUGH.

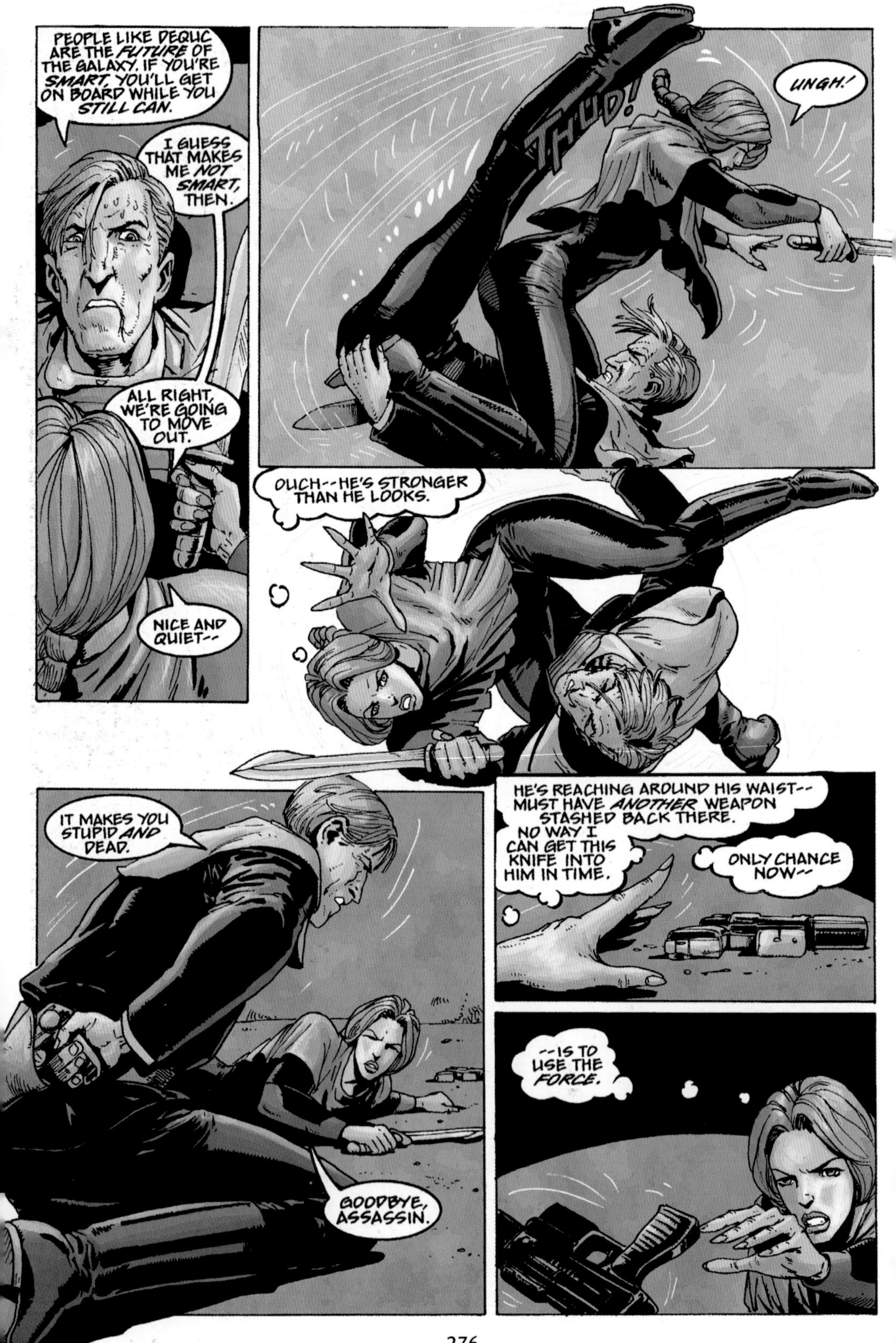
PEOPLE LIKE DEQUC ARE THE FUTURE OF THE GALAXY. IF YOU'RE SMART, YOU'LL GET ON BOARD WHILE YOU STILL CAN.
I GUESS THAT MAKES ME NOT SMART, THEN.
ALL RIGHT, WE'RE GOING TO MOVE OUT.
NICE AND QUIET--
THUD!
UNGH!
OUCH--HE'S STRONGER THAN HE LOOKS.
IT MAKES YOU STUPID AND DEAD.
GOODBYE, ASSASSIN.
HE'S REACHING AROUND HIS WAIST--MUST HAVE ANOTHER WEAPON STASHED BACK THERE.
NO WAY I CAN GET THIS KNIFE INTO HIM IN TIME.
ONLY CHANCE NOW--
--IS TO USE THE FORCE.

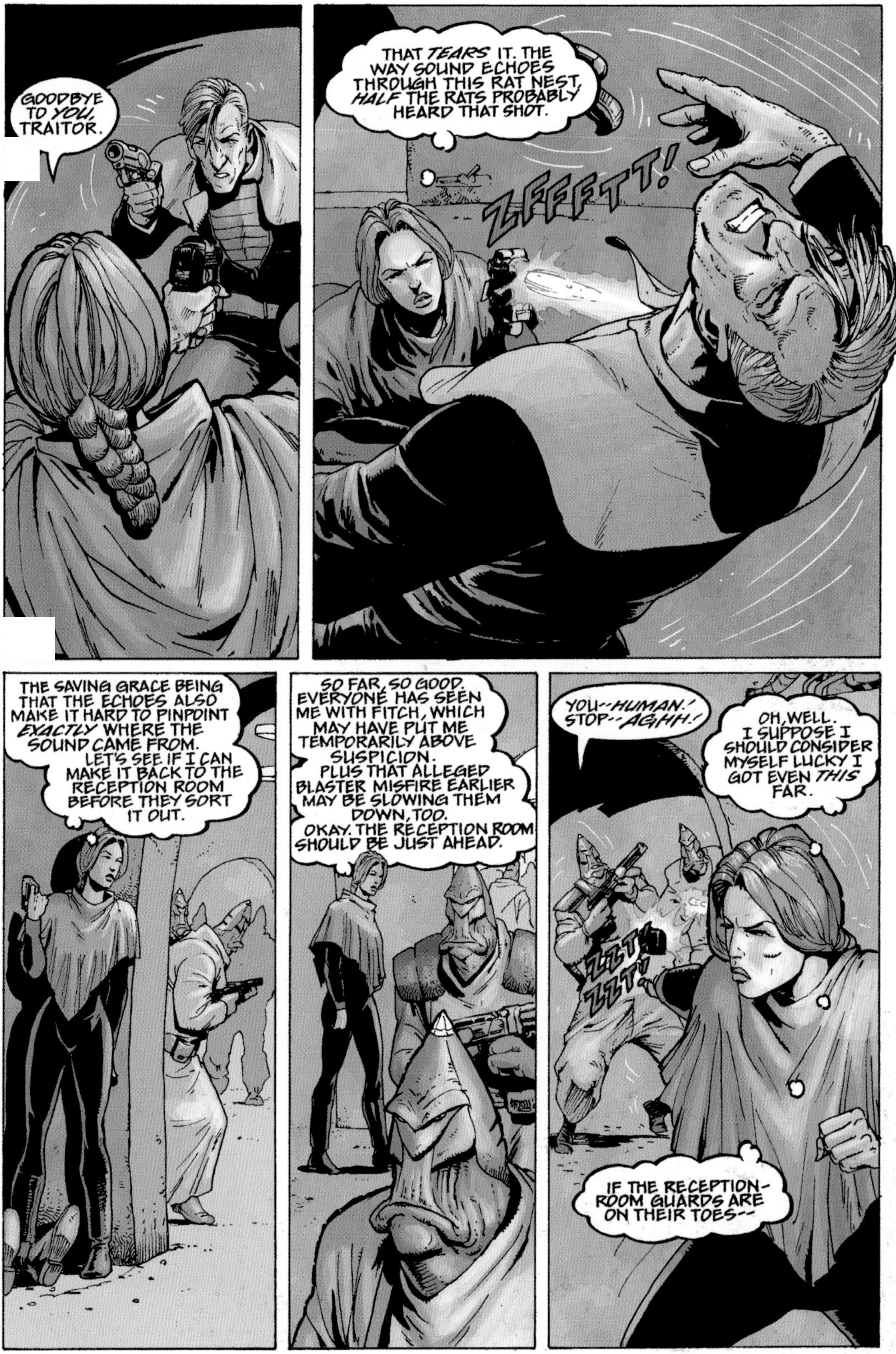
GOODBYE TO YOU, TRAITOR.
THAT TEARS IT. THE WAY SOUND ECHOES THROUGH THIS RAT NEST, HALF THE RATS PROBABLY HEARD THAT SHOT.
ZFFFTT!
THE SAVING GRACE BEING THAT THE ECHOES ALSO MAKE IT HARD TO PINPOINT EXACTLY WHERE THE SOUND CAME FROM.
LET'S SEE IF I CAN MAKE IT BACK TO THE RECEPTION ROOM BEFORE THEY SORT IT OUT.
SO FAR, SO GOOD. EVERYONE HAS SEEN ME WITH FITCH, WHICH MAY HAVE PUT ME TEMPORARILY ABOVE SUSPICION.
PLUS THAT ALLEGED BLASTER MISFIRE EARLIER MAY BE SLOWING THEM DOWN, TOO.
OKAY. THE RECEPTION ROOM SHOULD BE JUST AHEAD.
YOU--HUMAN! STOP--AGHH!
OH, WELL. I SUPPOSE I SHOULD CONSIDER MYSELF LUCKY I GOT EVEN THIS FAR.
ZZZT! ZZZT!
IF THE RECEPTION-ROOM GUARDS ARE ON THEIR TOES--

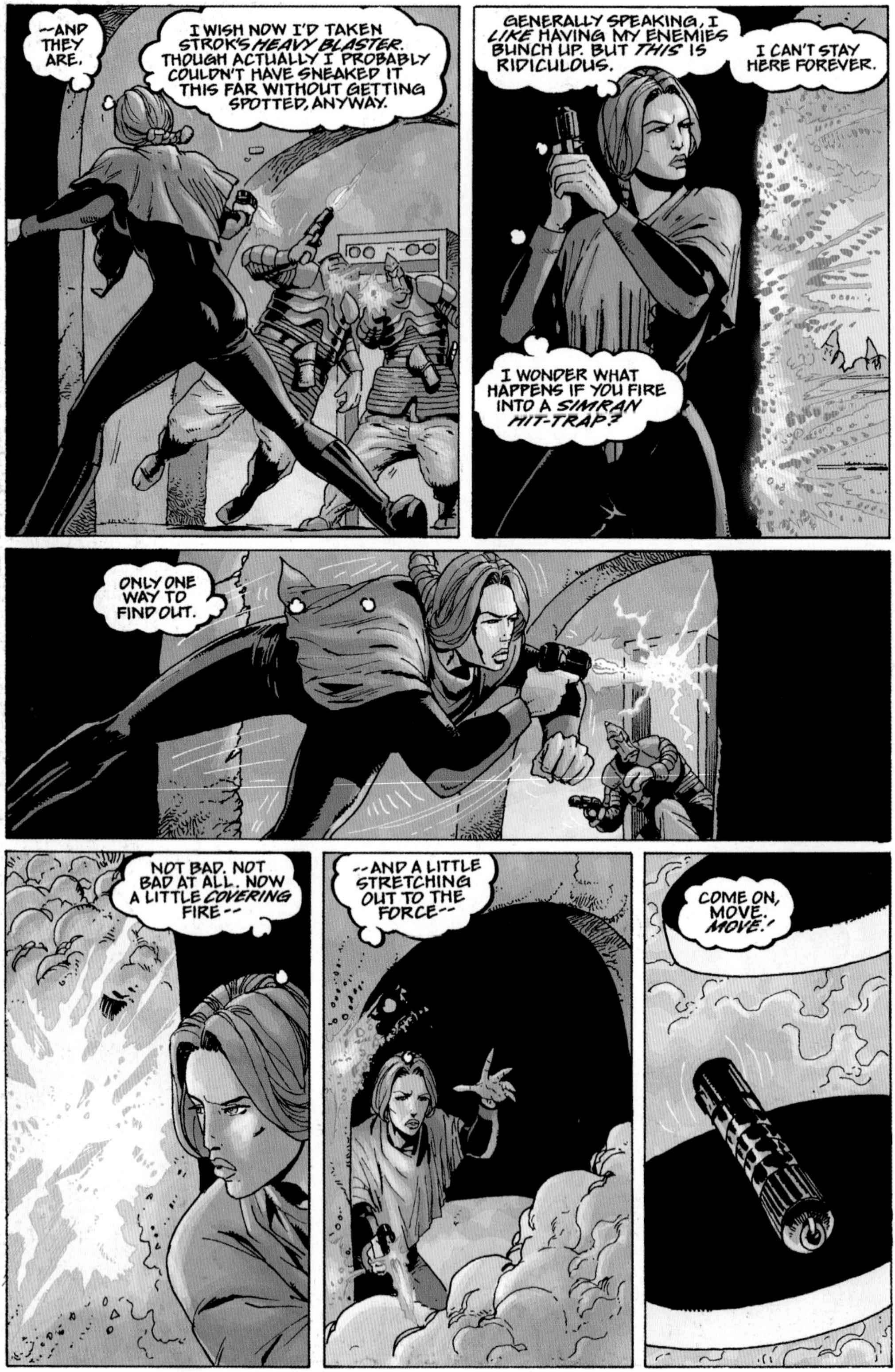
--AND THEY ARE.
I WISH NOW I'D TAKEN STROK'S *HEAVY BLASTER.* THOUGH ACTUALLY I PROBABLY COULDN'T HAVE SNEAKED IT THIS FAR WITHOUT GETTING SPOTTED, ANYWAY.
GENERALLY SPEAKING, I *LIKE* HAVING MY ENEMIES BUNCH UP. BUT *THIS* IS RIDICULOUS.
I CAN'T STAY HERE FOREVER.
I WONDER WHAT HAPPENS IF YOU FIRE INTO A *SIMRAN HIT-TRAP?*
ONLY ONE WAY TO FIND OUT.
NOT BAD. NOT BAD AT ALL. NOW A LITTLE *COVERING* FIRE--
--AND A LITTLE STRETCHING OUT TO THE FORCE--
COME ON, MOVE. *MOVE!*

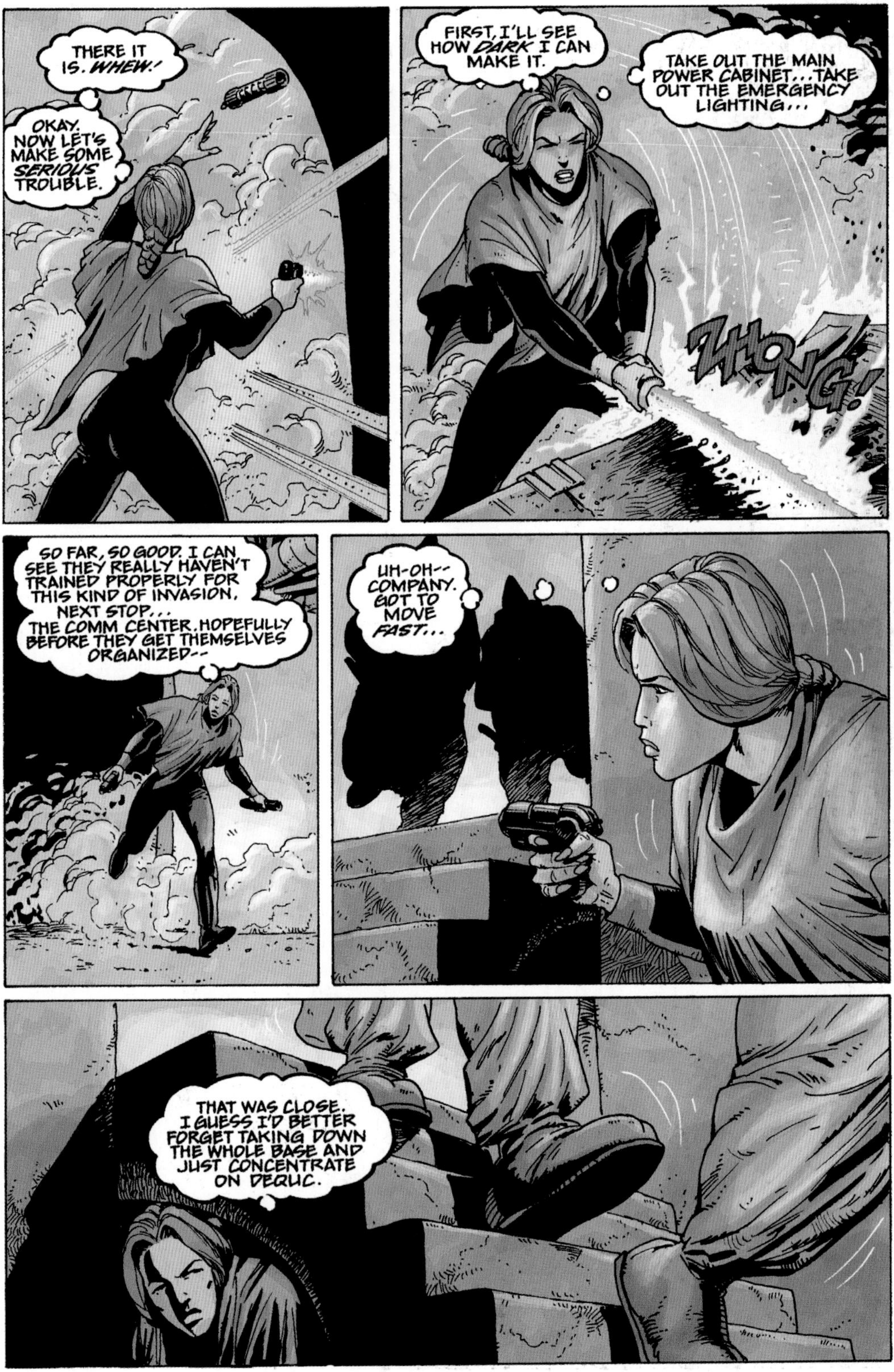
THERE IT IS. WHEW!
OKAY. NOW LET'S MAKE SOME SERIOUS TROUBLE.
FIRST, I'LL SEE HOW DARK I CAN MAKE IT.
TAKE OUT THE MAIN POWER CABINET... TAKE OUT THE EMERGENCY LIGHTING...
ZHONG!
SO FAR, SO GOOD. I CAN SEE THEY REALLY HAVEN'T TRAINED PROPERLY FOR THIS KIND OF INVASION. NEXT STOP... THE COMM CENTER, HOPEFULLY BEFORE THEY GET THEMSELVES ORGANIZED--
UH-OH-- COMPANY. GOT TO MOVE FAST...
THAT WAS CLOSE. I GUESS I'D BETTER FORGET TAKING DOWN THE WHOLE BASE AND JUST CONCENTRATE ON DEQUC.

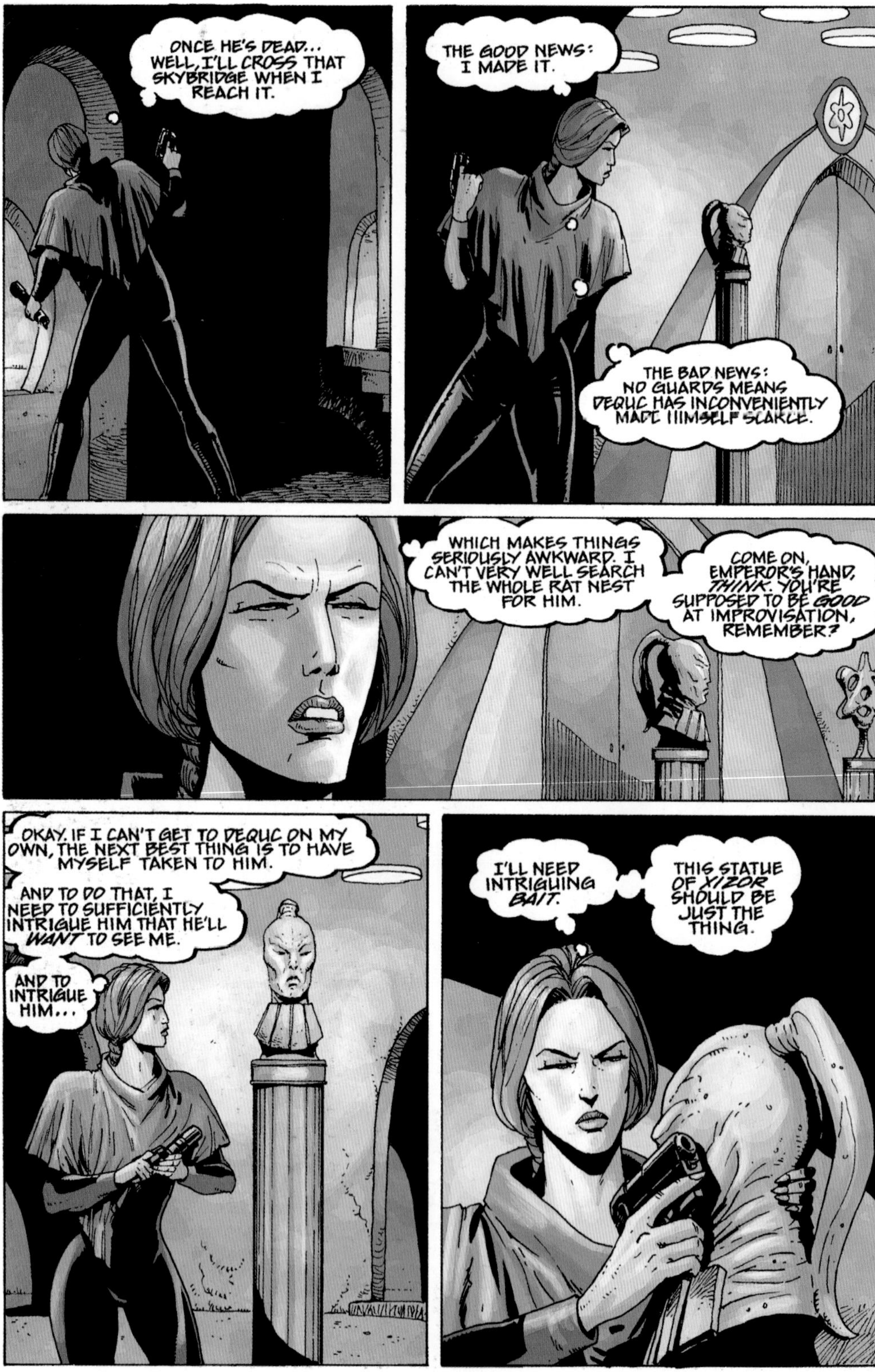
ONCE HE'S DEAD... WELL, I'LL CROSS THAT SKYBRIDGE WHEN I REACH IT.
THE GOOD NEWS: I MADE IT.
THE BAD NEWS: NO GUARDS MEANS DEQUC HAS INCONVENIENTLY MADE HIMSELF SCARCE.
WHICH MAKES THINGS SERIOUSLY AWKWARD. I CAN'T VERY WELL SEARCH THE WHOLE RAT NEST FOR HIM.
COME ON, EMPEROR'S HAND, THINK. YOU'RE SUPPOSED TO BE GOOD AT IMPROVISATION, REMEMBER?
OKAY. IF I CAN'T GET TO DEQUC ON MY OWN, THE NEXT BEST THING IS TO HAVE MYSELF TAKEN TO HIM.
AND TO DO THAT, I NEED TO SUFFICIENTLY INTRIGUE HIM THAT HE'LL WANT TO SEE ME.
AND TO INTRIGUE HIM...
I'LL NEED INTRIGUING BAIT.
THIS STATUE OF XIZOR SHOULD BE JUST THE THING.

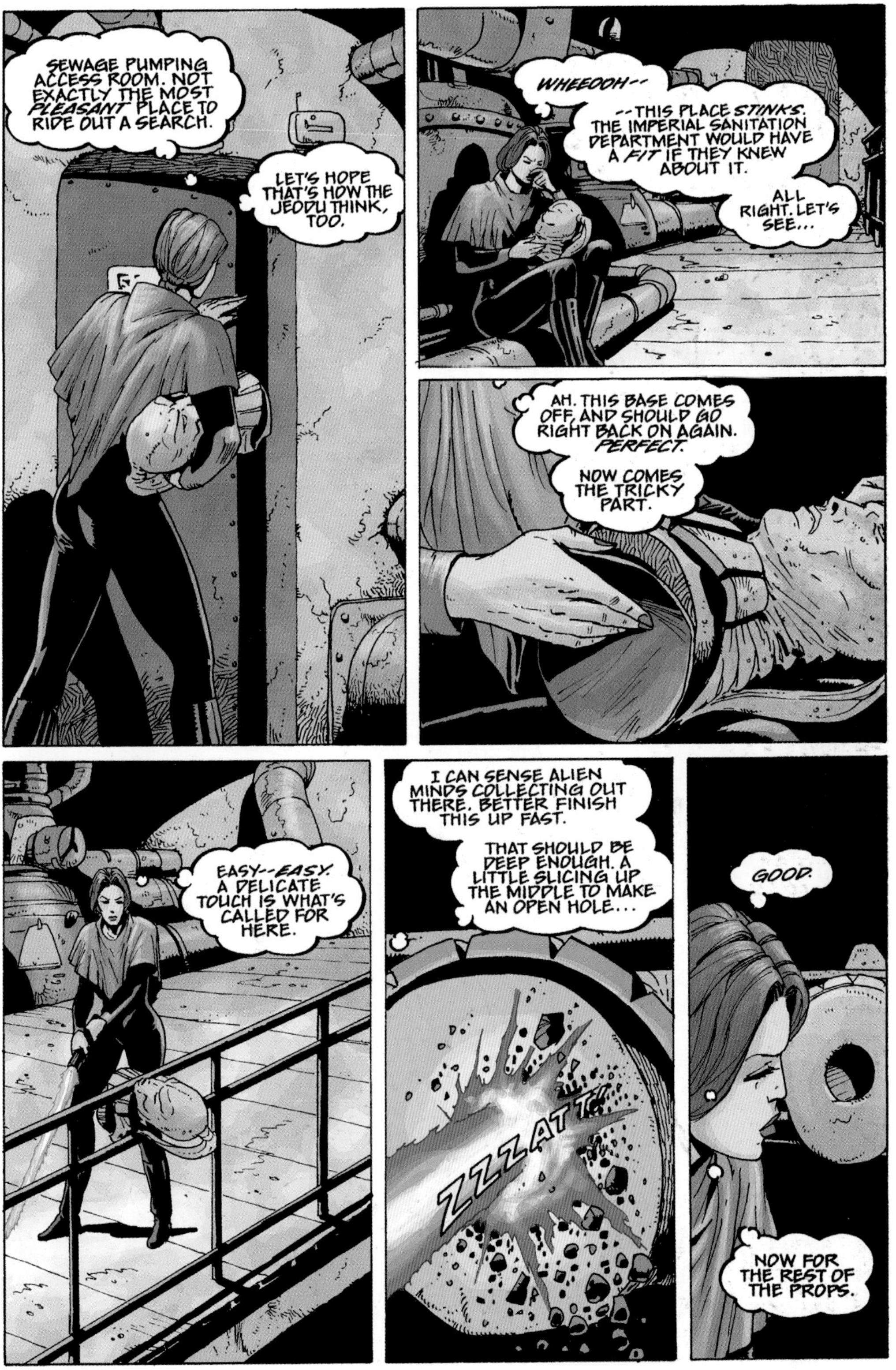
SEWAGE PUMPING ACCESS ROOM. NOT EXACTLY THE MOST *PLEASANT* PLACE TO RIDE OUT A SEARCH.
LET'S HOPE THAT'S HOW THE JEODU THINK, TOO.
WHEEOOH--
--THIS PLACE *STINKS*. THE IMPERIAL SANITATION DEPARTMENT WOULD HAVE A *FIT* IF THEY KNEW ABOUT IT.
ALL RIGHT. LET'S SEE...
AH. THIS BASE COMES OFF, AND SHOULD GO RIGHT BACK ON AGAIN. *PERFECT.*
NOW COMES THE TRICKY PART.
EASY--*EASY.* A DELICATE TOUCH IS WHAT'S CALLED FOR HERE.
I CAN SENSE ALIEN MINDS COLLECTING OUT THERE. BETTER FINISH THIS UP FAST.
THAT SHOULD BE DEEP ENOUGH. A LITTLE SLICING UP THE MIDDLE TO MAKE AN OPEN HOLE...
ZZZATT!
GOOD.
NOW FOR THE REST OF THE PROPS.

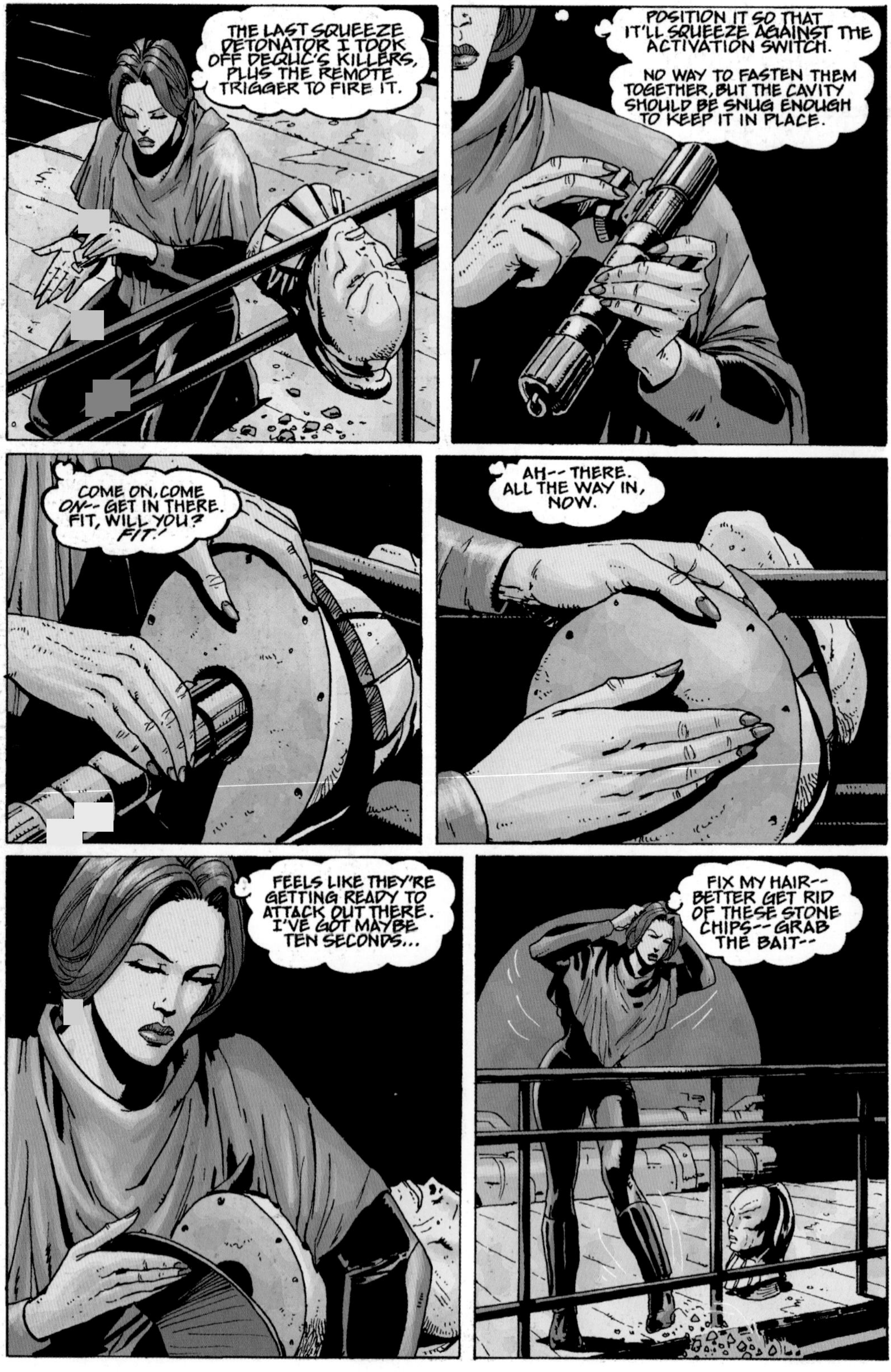
THE LAST SQUEEZE DETONATOR I TOOK OFF DEQUC'S KILLERS, PLUS THE REMOTE TRIGGER TO FIRE IT.
POSITION IT SO THAT IT'LL SQUEEZE AGAINST THE ACTIVATION SWITCH.
NO WAY TO FASTEN THEM TOGETHER, BUT THE CAVITY SHOULD BE SNUG ENOUGH TO KEEP IT IN PLACE.
COME ON, COME ON-- GET IN THERE. FIT, WILL YOU? FIT!
AH-- THERE. ALL THE WAY IN, NOW.
FEELS LIKE THEY'RE GETTING READY TO ATTACK OUT THERE. I'VE GOT MAYBE TEN SECONDS...
FIX MY HAIR-- BETTER GET RID OF THESE STONE CHIPS-- GRAB THE BAIT--

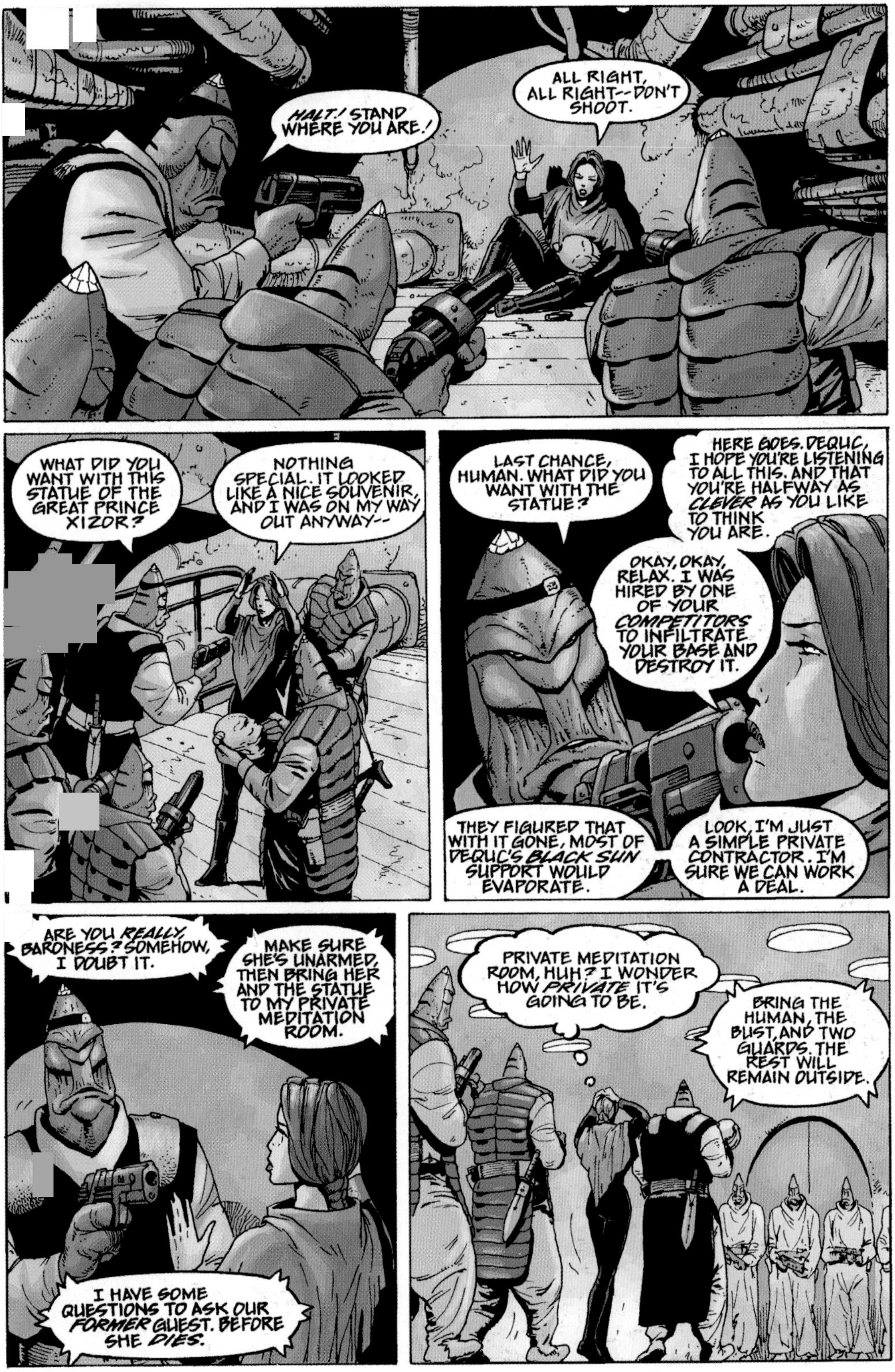
HALT! STAND WHERE YOU ARE!
ALL RIGHT, ALL RIGHT--DON'T SHOOT.
WHAT DID YOU WANT WITH THIS STATUE OF THE GREAT PRINCE XIZOR?
NOTHING SPECIAL. IT LOOKED LIKE A NICE SOUVENIR, AND I WAS ON MY WAY OUT ANYWAY--
LAST CHANCE, HUMAN. WHAT DID YOU WANT WITH THE STATUE?
HERE GOES. DEQUC, I HOPE YOU'RE LISTENING TO ALL THIS. AND THAT YOU'RE HALFWAY AS CLEVER AS YOU LIKE TO THINK YOU ARE.
OKAY, OKAY, RELAX. I WAS HIRED BY ONE OF YOUR COMPETITORS TO INFILTRATE YOUR BASE AND DESTROY IT.
THEY FIGURED THAT WITH IT GONE, MOST OF DEQUC'S BLACK SUN SUPPORT WOULD EVAPORATE.
LOOK, I'M JUST A SIMPLE PRIVATE CONTRACTOR. I'M SURE WE CAN WORK A DEAL.
ARE YOU REALLY, BARONESS? SOMEHOW, I DOUBT IT.
MAKE SURE SHE'S UNARMED, THEN BRING HER AND THE STATUE TO MY PRIVATE MEDITATION ROOM.
I HAVE SOME QUESTIONS TO ASK OUR FORMER GUEST. BEFORE SHE DIES.
PRIVATE MEDITATION ROOM, HUH? I WONDER HOW PRIVATE IT'S GOING TO BE.
BRING THE HUMAN, THE BUST, AND TWO GUARDS. THE REST WILL REMAIN OUTSIDE.

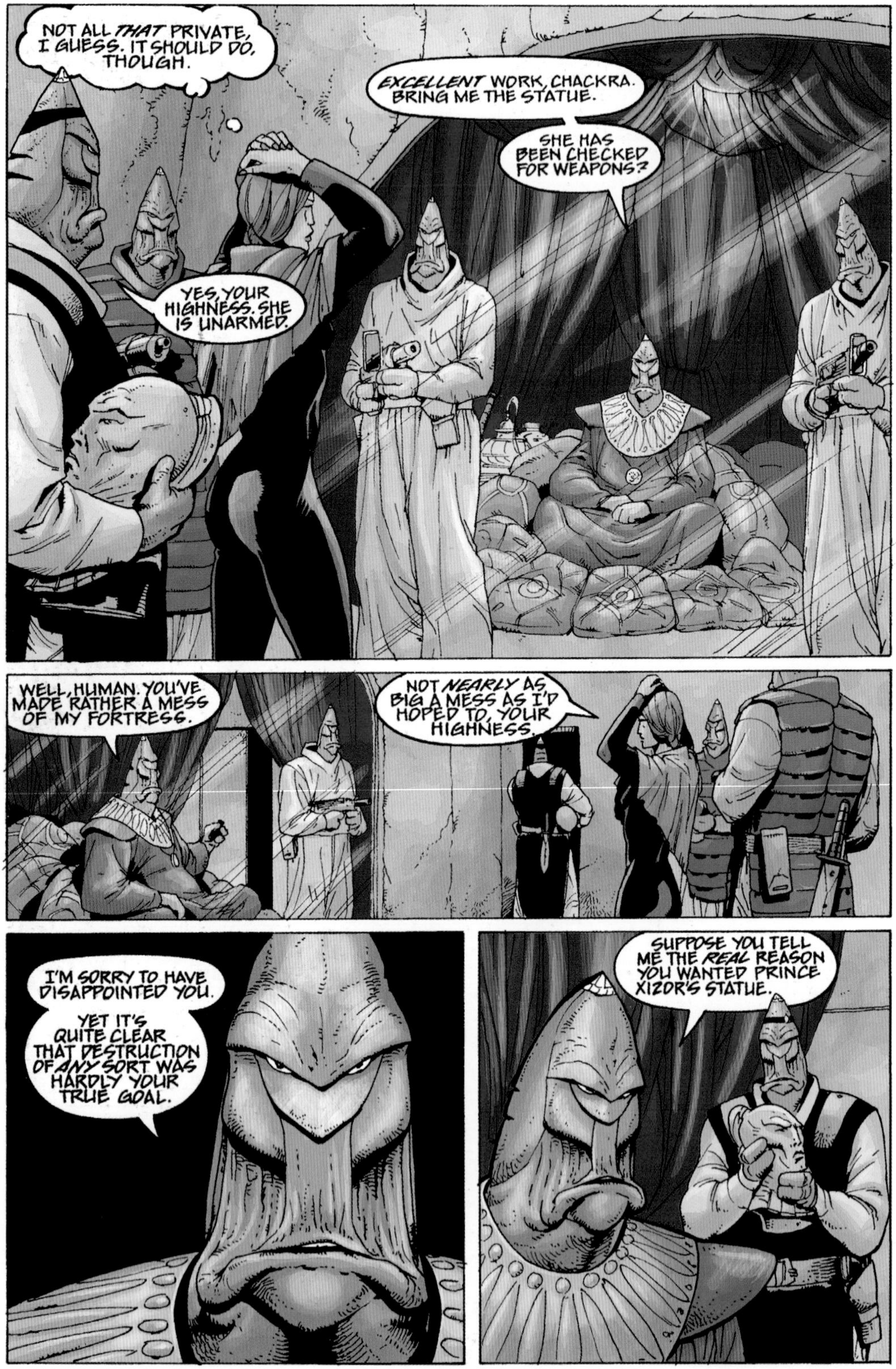
NOT ALL *THAT* PRIVATE, I GUESS. IT SHOULD DO, THOUGH.
EXCELLENT WORK, CHACKRA. BRING ME THE STATUE.
SHE HAS BEEN CHECKED FOR WEAPONS?
YES, YOUR HIGHNESS. SHE IS UNARMED.
WELL, HUMAN. YOU'VE MADE RATHER A MESS OF MY FORTRESS.
NOT *NEARLY* AS BIG A MESS AS I'D HOPED TO, YOUR HIGHNESS.
I'M SORRY TO HAVE DISAPPOINTED YOU.
YET IT'S QUITE CLEAR THAT DESTRUCTION OF *ANY* SORT WAS HARDLY YOUR TRUE GOAL.
SUPPOSE YOU TELL ME THE *REAL* REASON YOU WANTED PRINCE XIZOR'S STATUE.

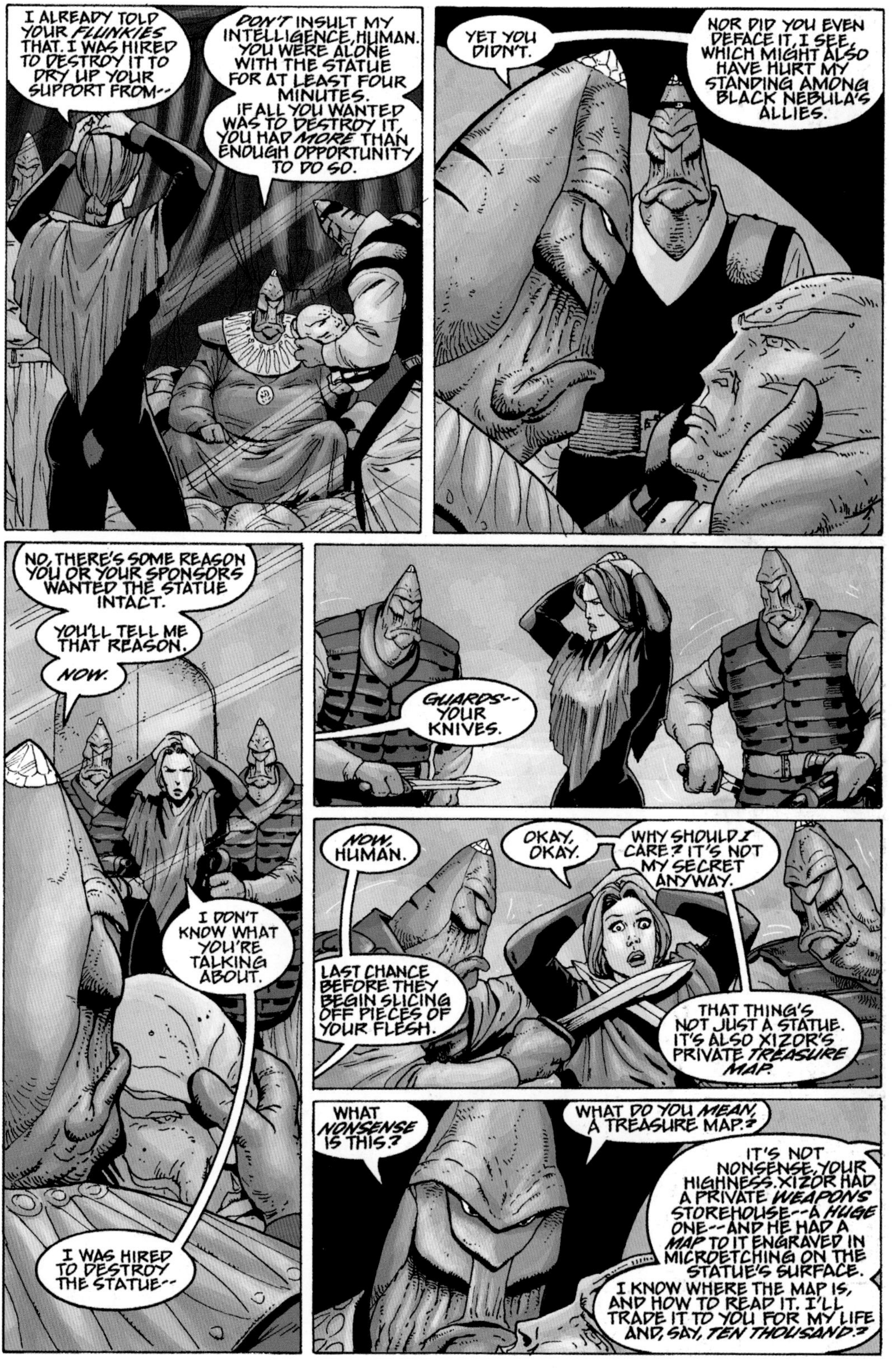
I ALREADY TOLD YOUR *FLUNKIES* THAT. I WAS HIRED TO DESTROY IT TO DRY UP YOUR SUPPORT FROM--
DON'T INSULT MY INTELLIGENCE, HUMAN. YOU WERE ALONE WITH THE STATUE FOR AT LEAST FOUR MINUTES.
IF ALL YOU WANTED WAS TO DESTROY IT, YOU HAD *MORE* THAN ENOUGH OPPORTUNITY TO DO SO.
YET YOU DIDN'T.
NOR DID YOU EVEN DEFACE IT, I SEE, WHICH MIGHT ALSO HAVE HURT MY STANDING AMONG BLACK NEBULA'S ALLIES.
NO, THERE'S SOME REASON YOU OR YOUR SPONSORS WANTED THE STATUE INTACT.
YOU'LL TELL ME THAT REASON.
NOW.
I DON'T KNOW WHAT YOU'RE TALKING ABOUT.
I WAS HIRED TO DESTROY THE STATUE--
GUARDS-- YOUR KNIVES.
NOW, HUMAN.
LAST CHANCE BEFORE THEY BEGIN SLICING OFF PIECES OF YOUR FLESH.
OKAY, OKAY.
WHY SHOULD *I* CARE?! IT'S NOT MY SECRET ANYWAY.
THAT THING'S NOT JUST A STATUE. IT'S ALSO XIZOR'S PRIVATE *TREASURE MAP.*
WHAT *NONSENSE* IS THIS?
WHAT DO YOU *MEAN,* A TREASURE MAP?!
IT'S NOT NONSENSE, YOUR HIGHNESS. XIZOR HAD A PRIVATE *WEAPONS* STOREHOUSE--A *HUGE* ONE--AND HE HAD A *MAP* TO IT ENGRAVED IN MICROETCHING ON THE STATUE'S SURFACE.
I KNOW WHERE THE MAP IS, AND HOW TO READ IT. I'LL TRADE IT TO YOU FOR MY LIFE AND, SAY, *TEN THOUSAND?!*

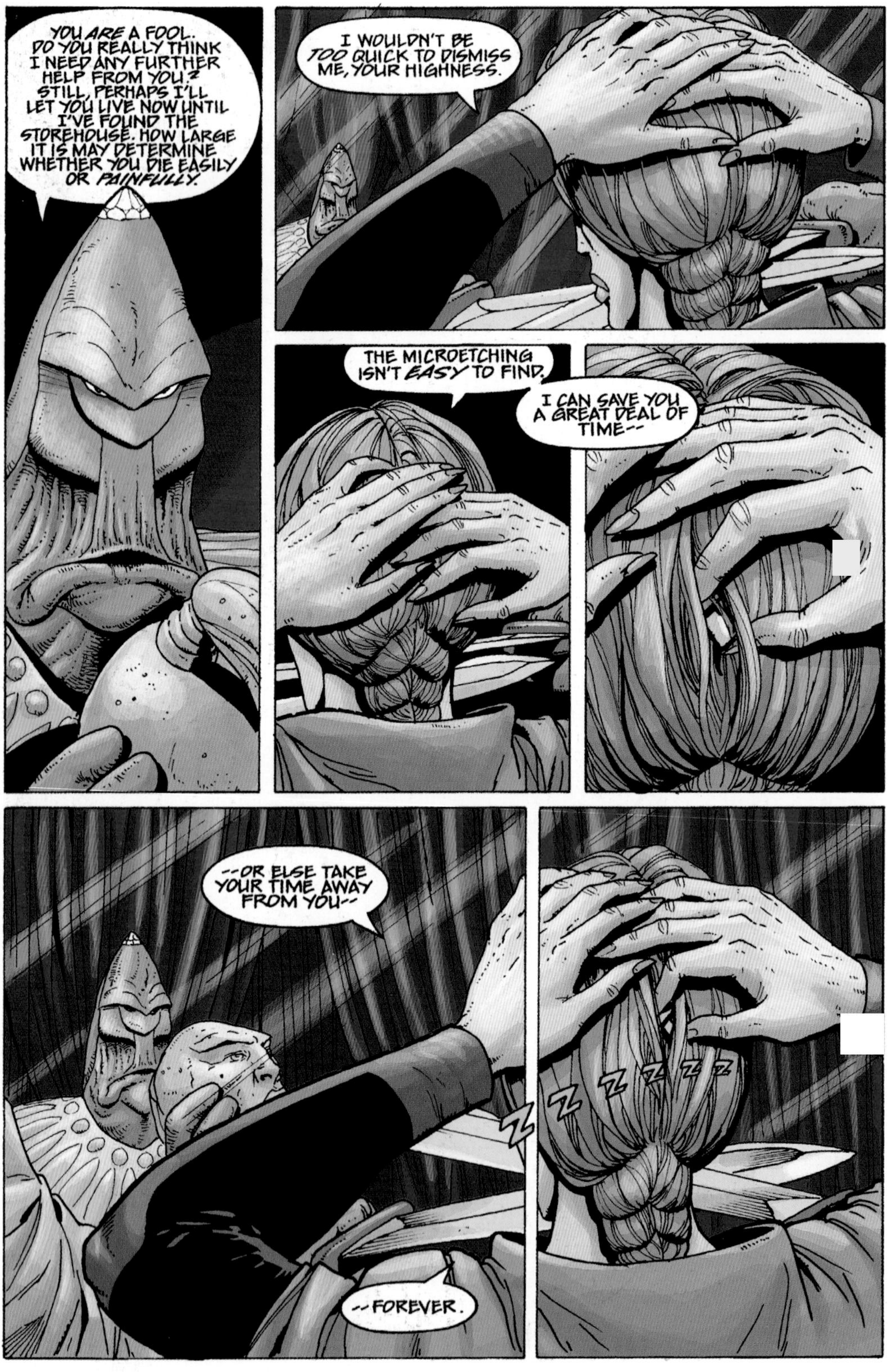
YOU ARE A FOOL. DO YOU REALLY THINK I NEED ANY FURTHER HELP FROM YOU? STILL, PERHAPS I'LL LET YOU LIVE NOW UNTIL I'VE FOUND THE STOREHOUSE. HOW LARGE IT IS MAY DETERMINE WHETHER YOU DIE EASILY OR PAINFULLY.
I WOULDN'T BE TOO QUICK TO DISMISS ME, YOUR HIGHNESS.
THE MICROETCHING ISN'T EASY TO FIND.
I CAN SAVE YOU A GREAT DEAL OF TIME--
--OR ELSE TAKE YOUR TIME AWAY FROM YOU--
--FOREVER.
Z Z Z Z Z Z

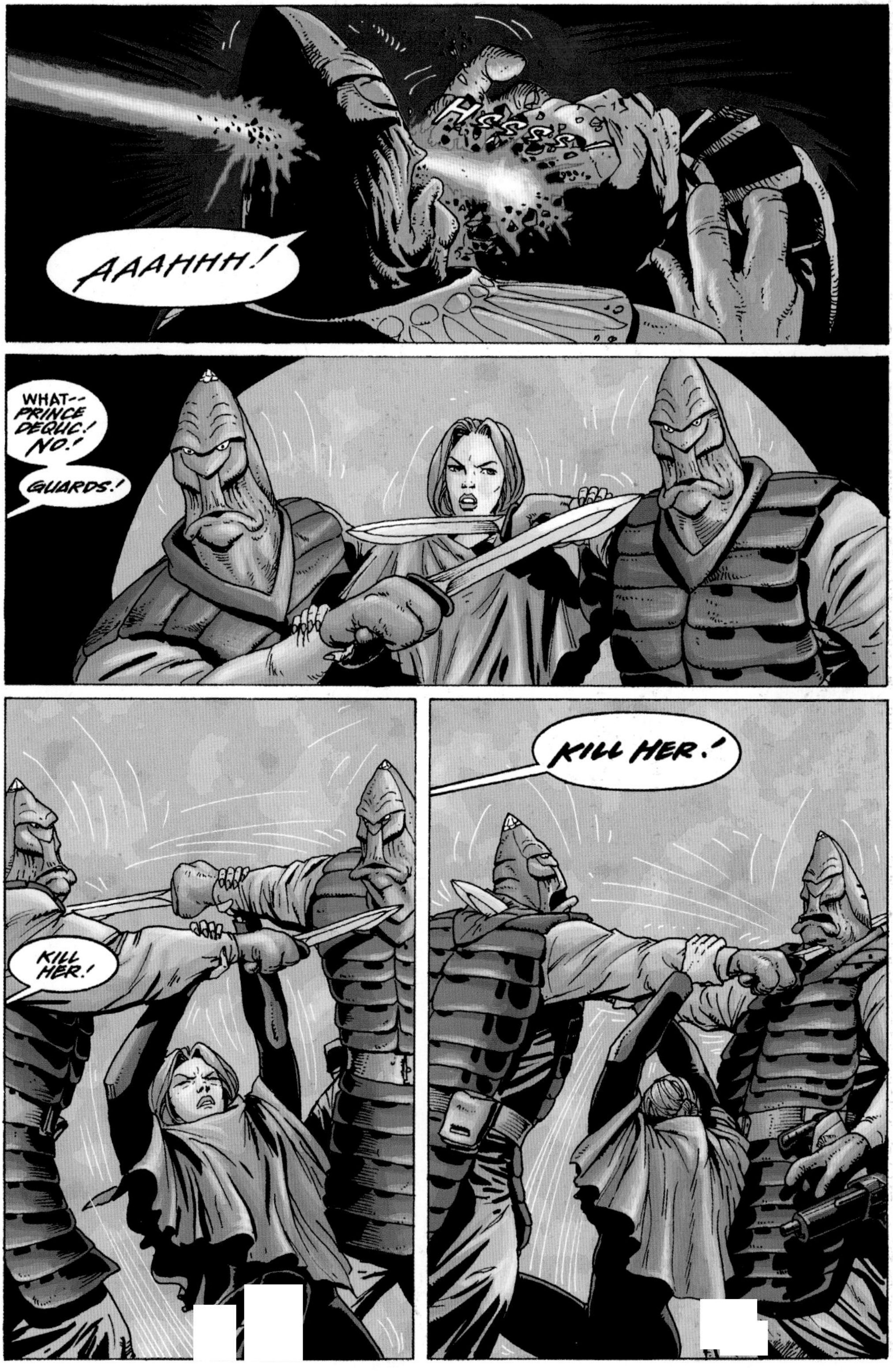
HSSSS—
AAAHHH!
WHAT--
PRINCE DEQUC! NO!
GUARDS!
KILL HER!
KILL HER!

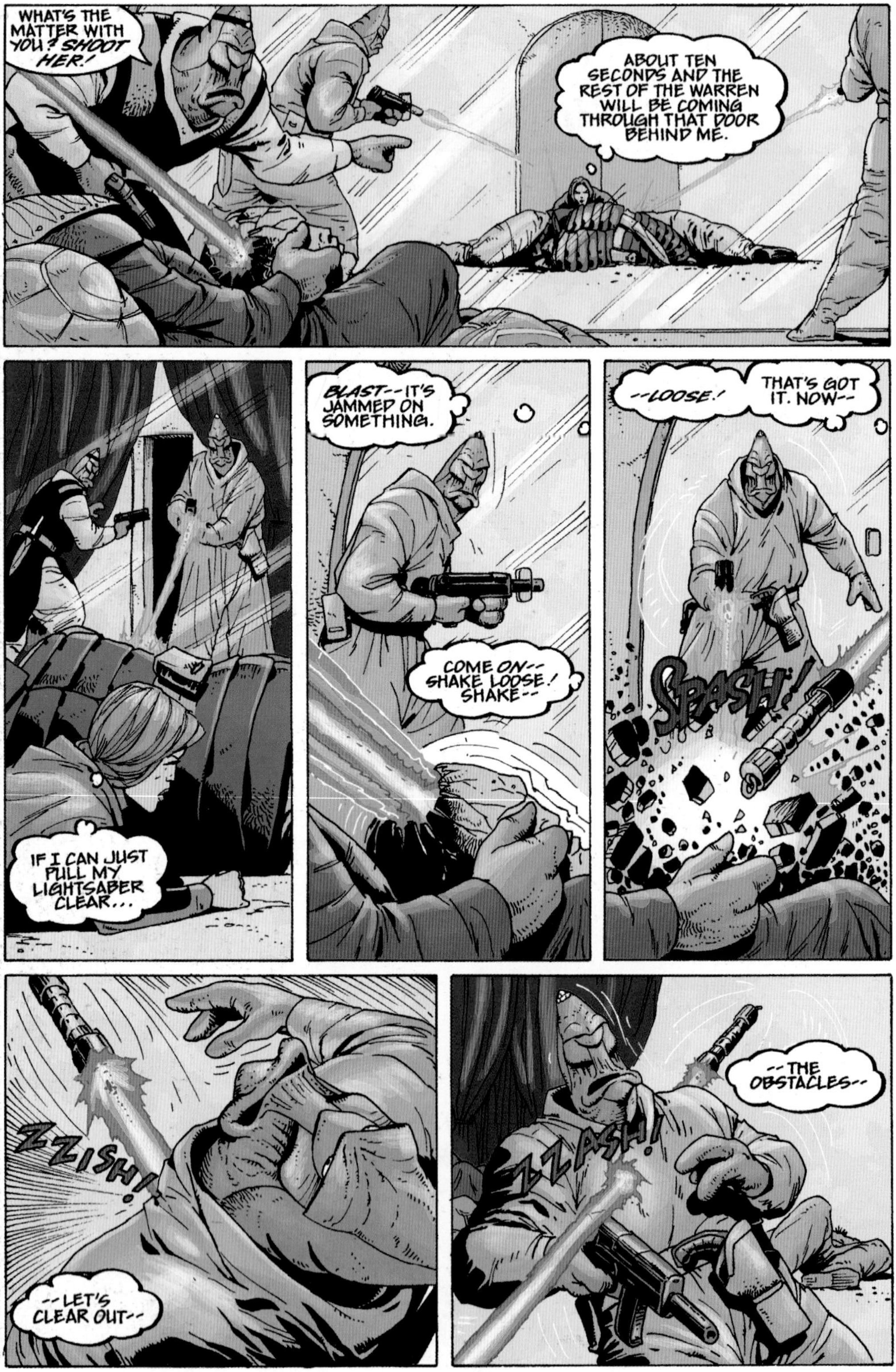
WHAT'S THE MATTER WITH YOU? SHOOT HER!
ABOUT TEN SECONDS AND THE REST OF THE WARREN WILL BE COMING THROUGH THAT DOOR BEHIND ME.
IF I CAN JUST PULL MY LIGHTSABER CLEAR...
BLAST--IT'S JAMMED ON SOMETHING.
COME ON--SHAKE LOOSE! SHAKE--
THAT'S GOT IT. NOW--
--LOOSE!
SPASH!
ZZISH!
--LET'S CLEAR OUT--
ZZASH!
--THE OBSTACLES--

--AND HOPE THAT DEQUC WAS AS PARANOID AS THE TYPICAL WOULD-BE GALACTIC SCUM LORD.

COME ON, DEQUC. BE A TYPICAL PARANOID--

KSSSSH!

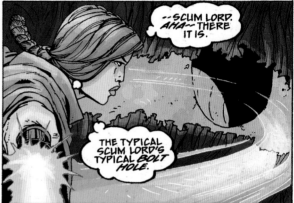

--SCUM LORD. *AHA--* THERE IT IS.

THE TYPICAL SCUM LORD'S TYPICAL *BOLT HOLE.*

HOPEFULLY, WAITING FOR ME AT THE FAR END--

--WILL BE SOME KIND OF TRANSPORT.

AND AS I SEEM TO HAVE OVERSTAYED MY WELCOME, I DON'T THINK IT WOULD BE WISE TO LINGER OVER MY GOODBYES.

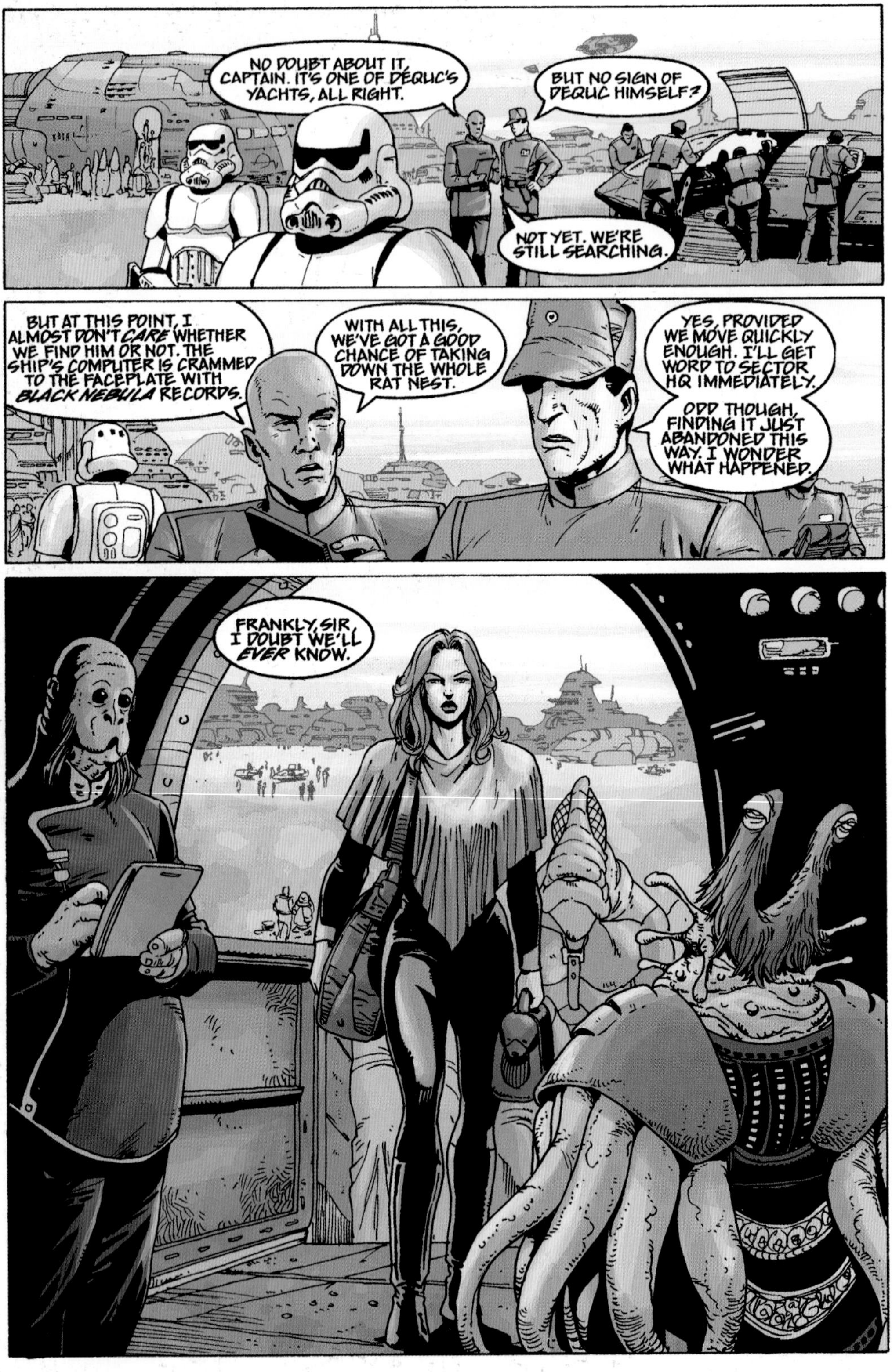
NO DOUBT ABOUT IT, CAPTAIN. IT'S ONE OF DEQUC'S YACHTS, ALL RIGHT.
BUT NO SIGN OF DEQUC HIMSELF?
NOT YET. WE'RE STILL SEARCHING.
BUT AT THIS POINT, I ALMOST DON'T *CARE* WHETHER WE FIND HIM OR NOT. THE SHIP'S COMPUTER IS CRAMMED TO THE FACEPLATE WITH *BLACK NEBULA* RECORDS.
WITH ALL THIS, WE'VE GOT A GOOD CHANCE OF TAKING DOWN THE WHOLE RAT NEST.
YES, PROVIDED WE MOVE QUICKLY ENOUGH. I'LL GET WORD TO SECTOR HQ IMMEDIATELY.
ODD THOUGH, FINDING IT JUST ABANDONED THIS WAY. I WONDER WHAT HAPPENED.
FRANKLY, SIR, I DOUBT WE'LL *EVER* KNOW.

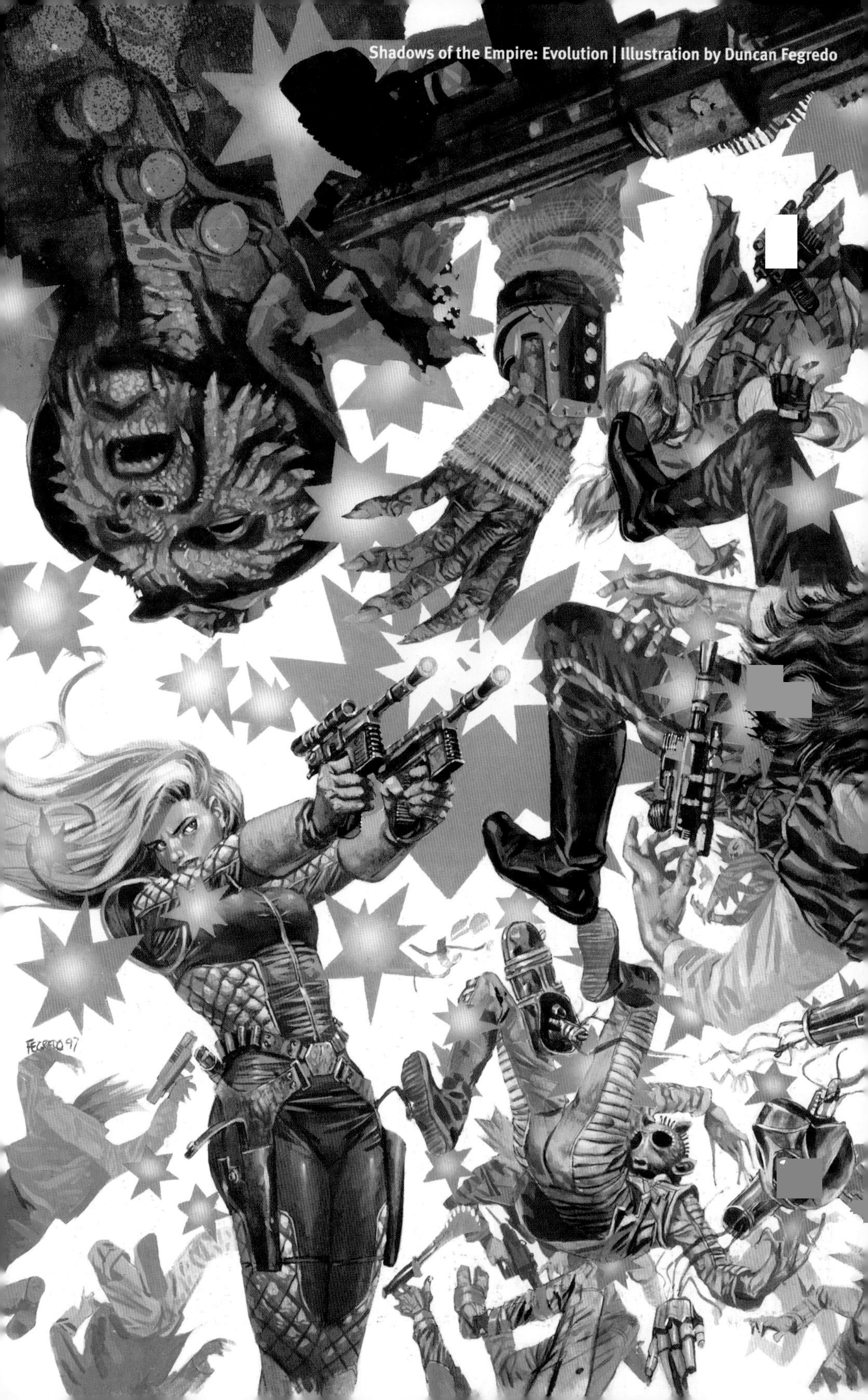
FEGREDO 97

Shadows of the Empire: Evolution | Illustration by Duncan Fegredo

APPROXIMATELY FOUR AND A HALF YEARS AFTER
THE BATTLE OF YAVIN . . .

script by Steve Perry
pencils by Ron Randall
inks by Tom Simmons and Ron Randall
colors by David Nestelle
letters by Steve Dutro

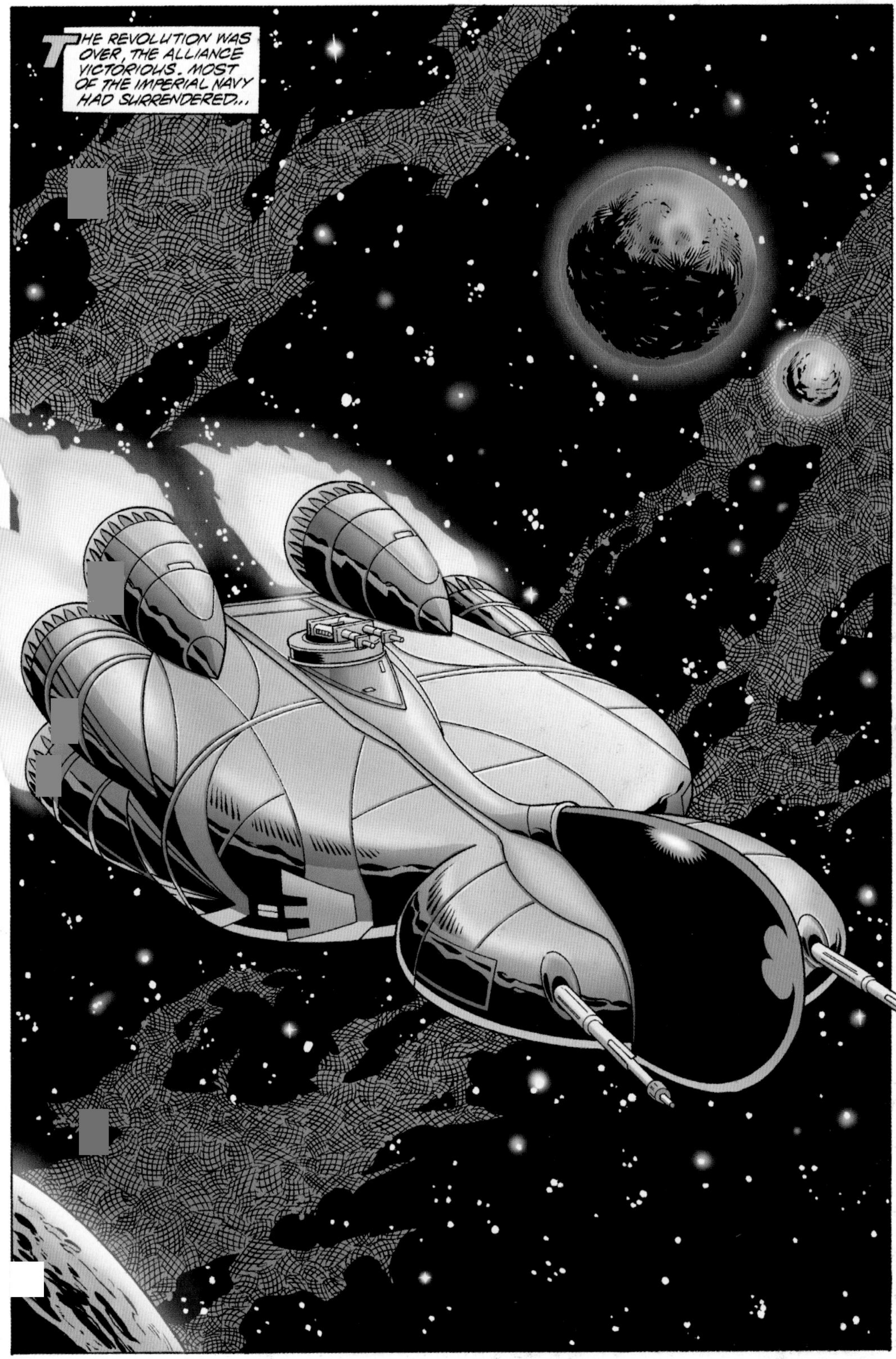
THE REVOLUTION WAS OVER, THE ALLIANCE VICTORIOUS. MOST OF THE IMPERIAL NAVY HAD SURRENDERED...

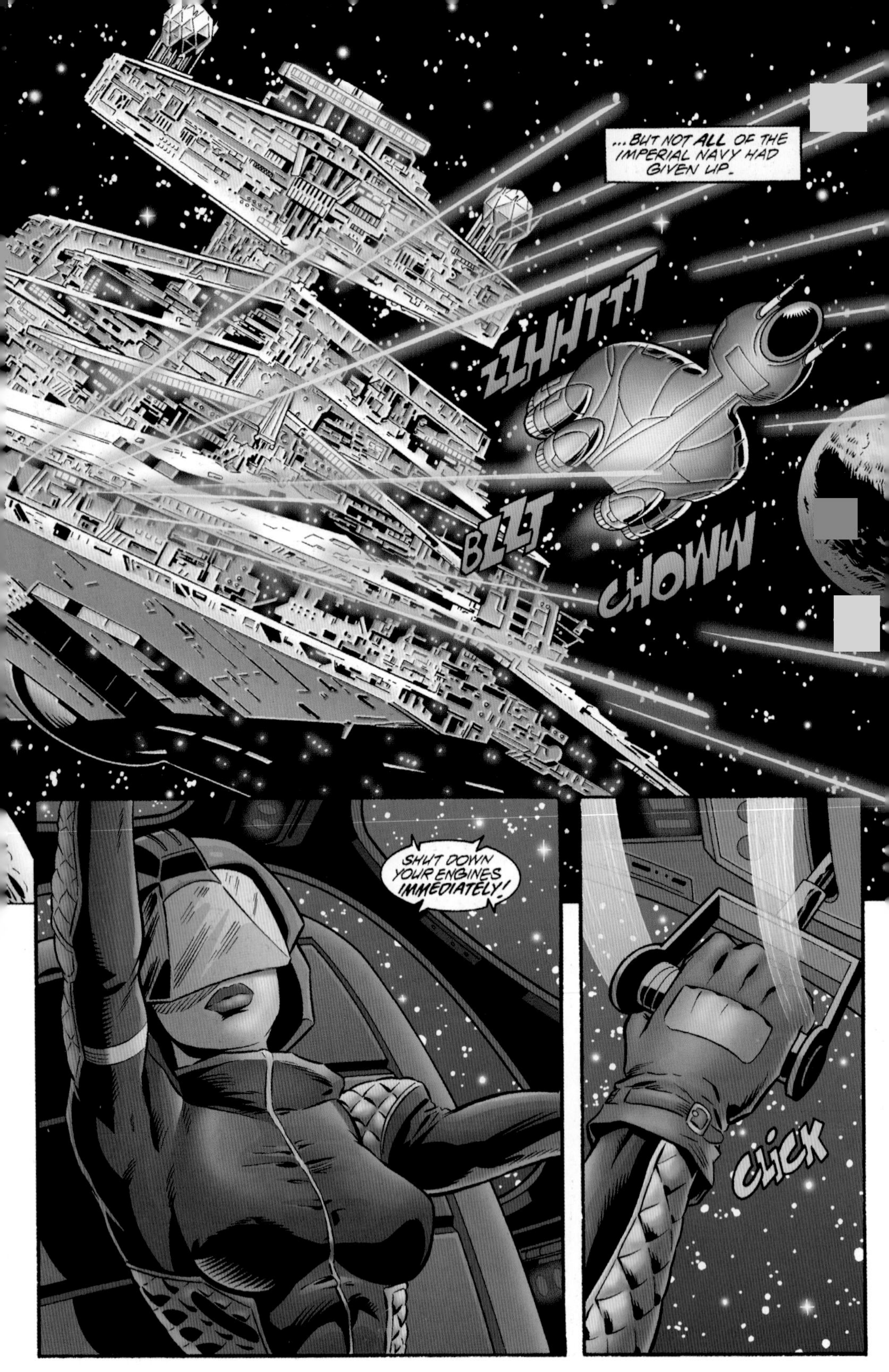
...BUT NOT ALL OF THE IMPERIAL NAVY HAD GIVEN UP.
ZZHHTTT
BZZT
CHOWW
SHUT DOWN YOUR ENGINES IMMEDIATELY!
CLICK

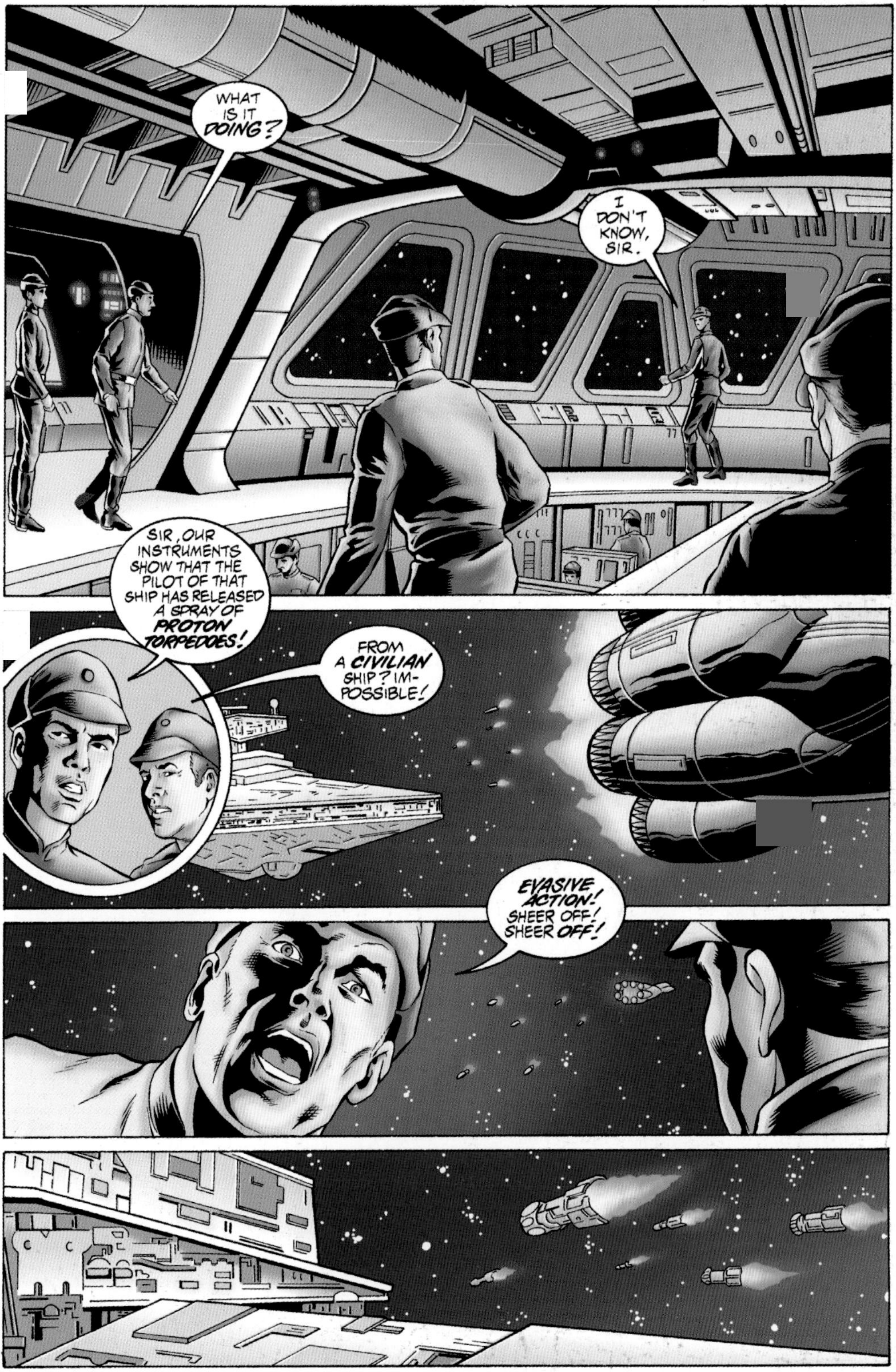
WHAT IS IT DOING?
I DON'T KNOW, SIR.
SIR, OUR INSTRUMENTS SHOW THAT THE PILOT OF THAT SHIP HAS RELEASED A SPRAY OF PROTON TORPEDOES!
FROM A CIVILIAN SHIP? IM-POSSIBLE!
EVASIVE ACTION! SHEER OFF! SHEER OFF!

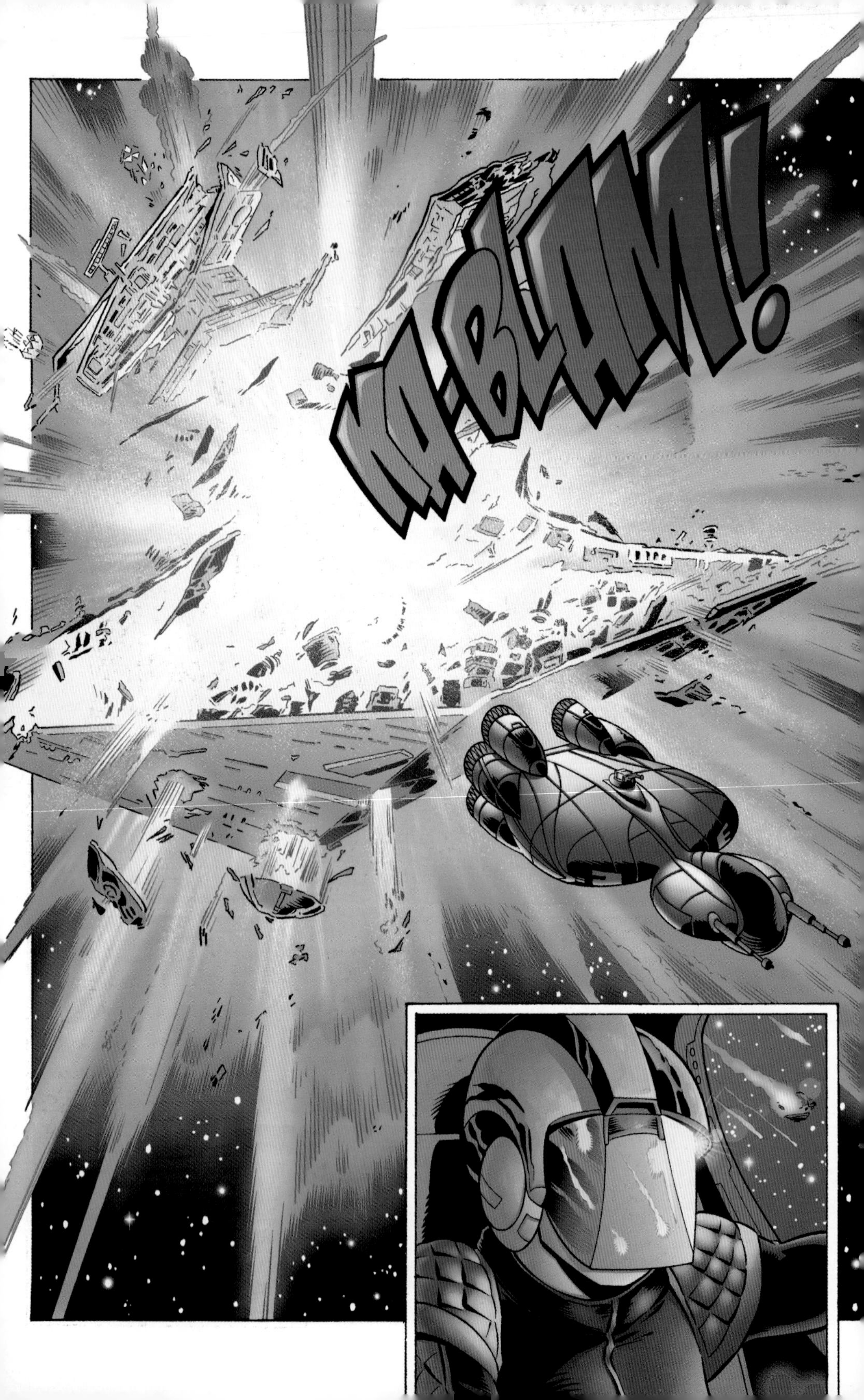
KA-BLAMM!

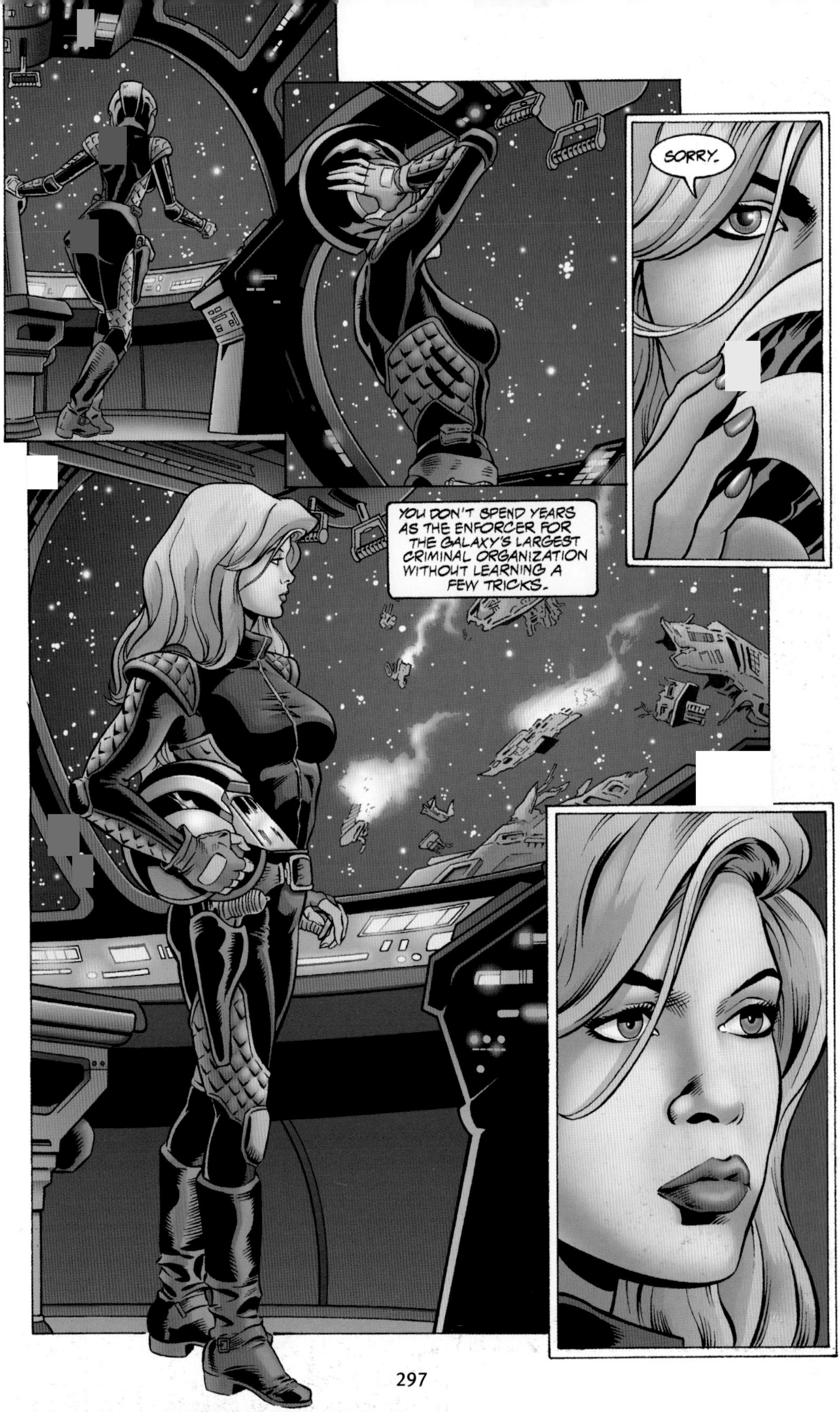
SORRY.
YOU DON'T SPEND YEARS AS THE ENFORCER FOR THE GALAXY'S LARGEST CRIMINAL ORGANIZATION WITHOUT LEARNING A FEW TRICKS.

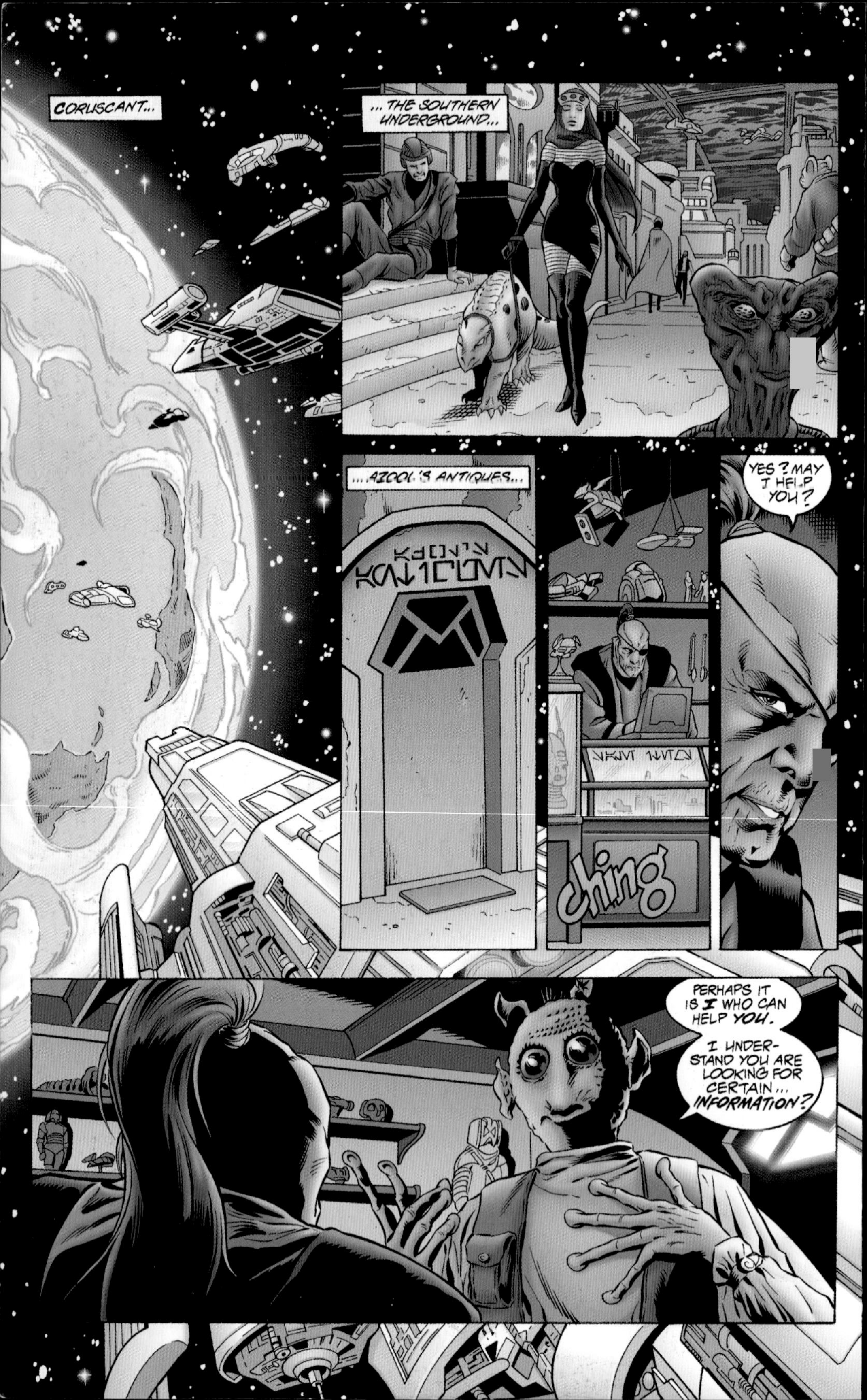
CORUSCANT...
...THE SOUTHERN UNDERGROUND...
...AZOOL'S ANTIQUES...
ching
YES? MAY I HELP YOU?
PERHAPS IT IS I WHO CAN HELP YOU.
I UNDERSTAND YOU ARE LOOKING FOR CERTAIN... INFORMATION?

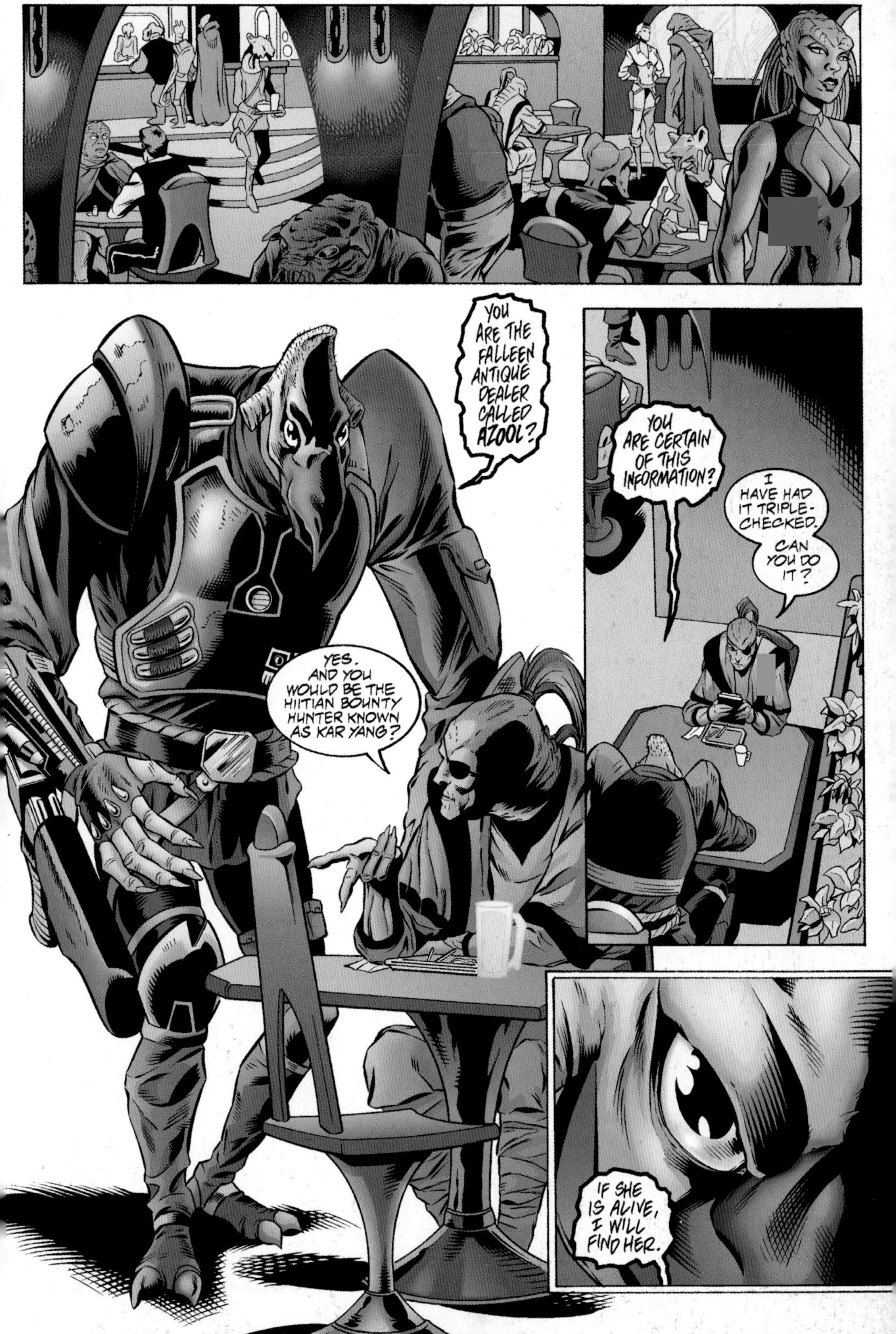
YOU ARE THE FALLEEN ANTIQUE DEALER CALLED AZOOL?
YES. AND YOU WOULD BE THE HIITIAN BOUNTY HUNTER KNOWN AS KAR YANG?
YOU ARE CERTAIN OF THIS INFORMATION?
I HAVE HAD IT TRIPLE-CHECKED.
CAN YOU DO IT?
IF SHE IS ALIVE, I WILL FIND HER.

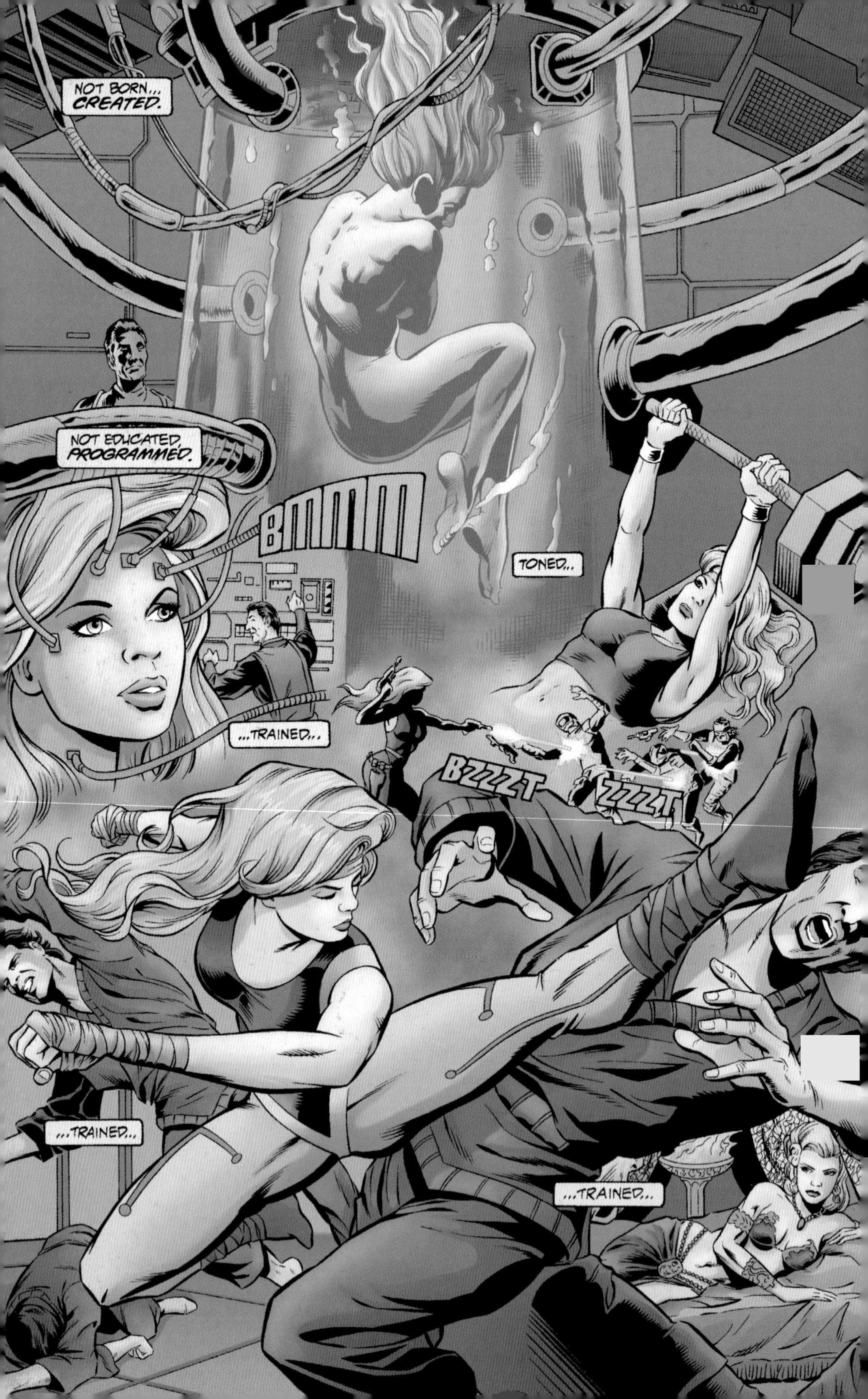
NOT BORN...
CREATED.
NOT EDUCATED,
PROGRAMMED.
BMMM
TONED...
...TRAINED...
BZZZT
ZZZZT
...TRAINED...
...TRAINED...

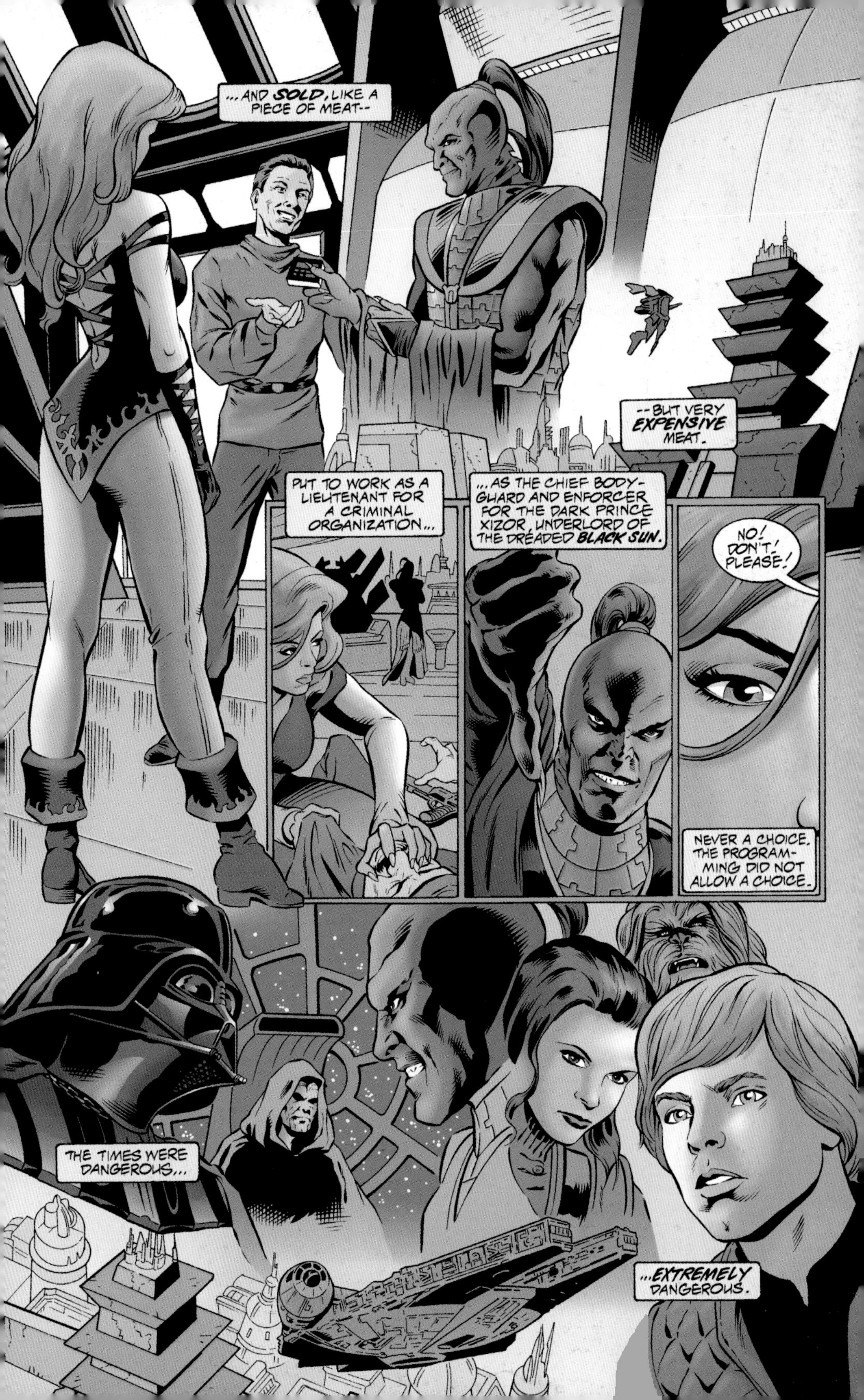
...AND SOLD, LIKE A PIECE OF MEAT--
--BUT VERY EXPENSIVE MEAT.
PUT TO WORK AS A LIEUTENANT FOR A CRIMINAL ORGANIZATION...
...AS THE CHIEF BODY-GUARD AND ENFORCER FOR THE DARK PRINCE XIZOR, UNDERLORD OF THE DREADED BLACK SUN.
NO! DON'T! PLEASE!
NEVER A CHOICE. THE PROGRAM-MING DID NOT ALLOW A CHOICE.
THE TIMES WERE DANGEROUS...
...EXTREMELY DANGEROUS.

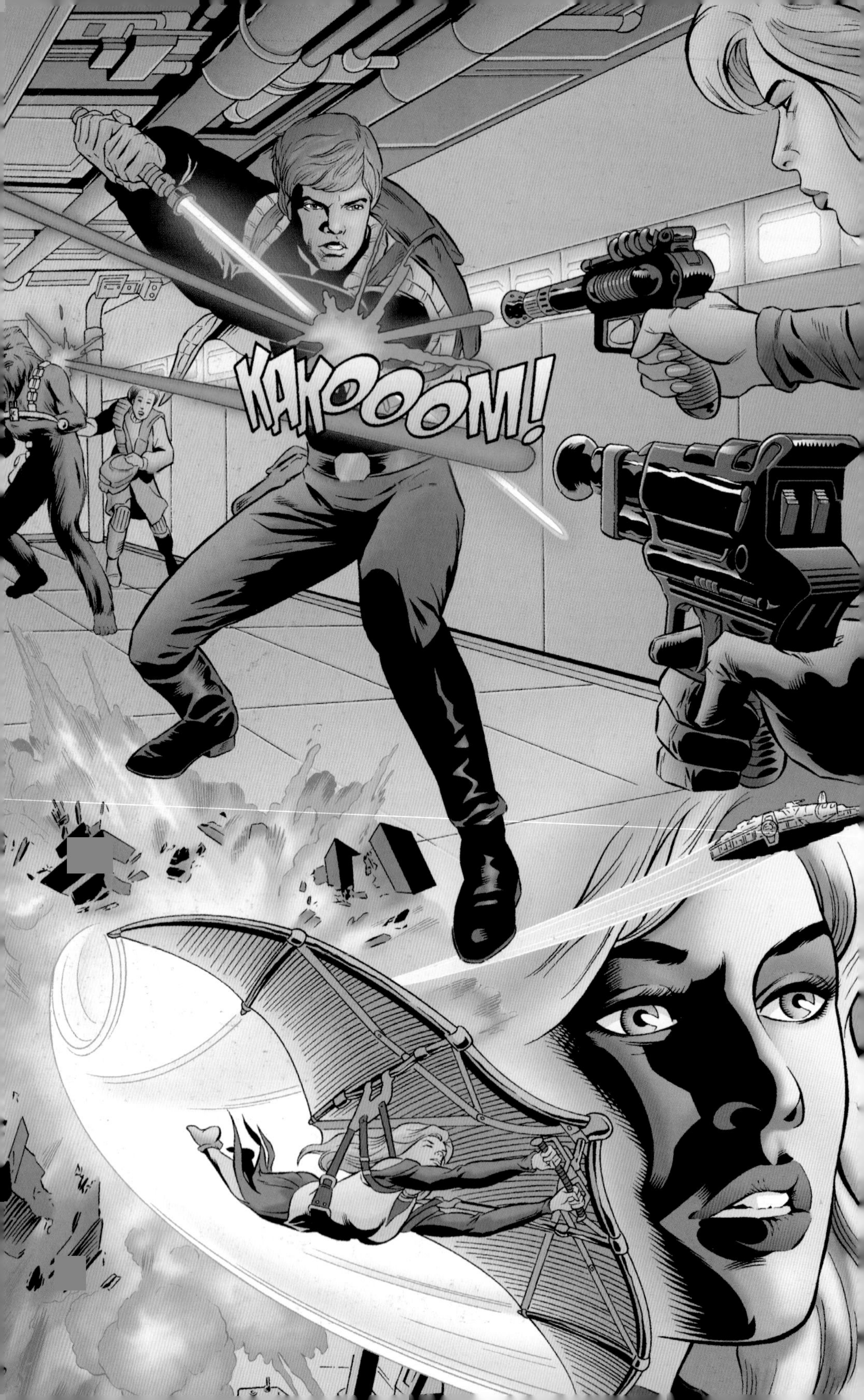
KAKOOOM!

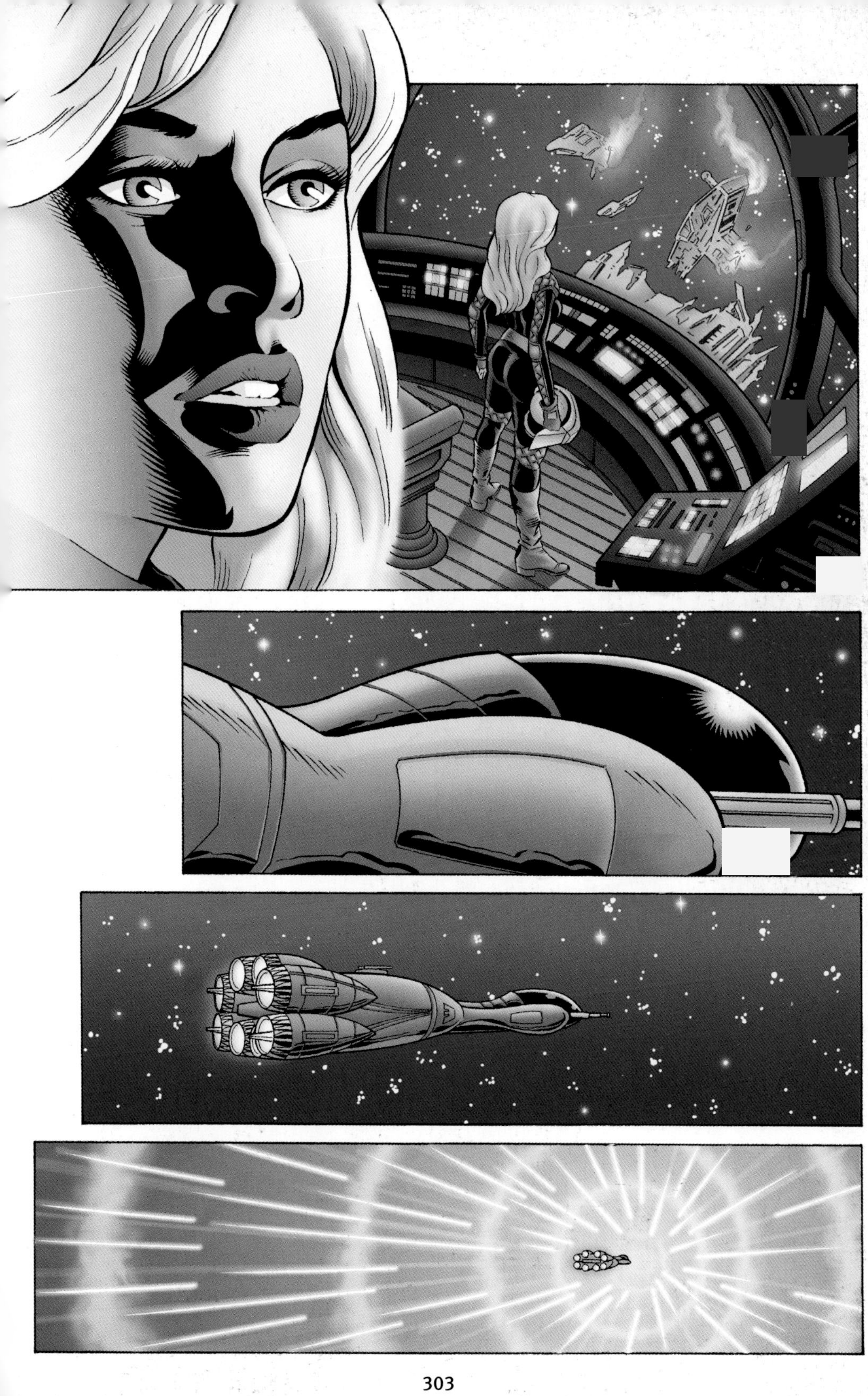

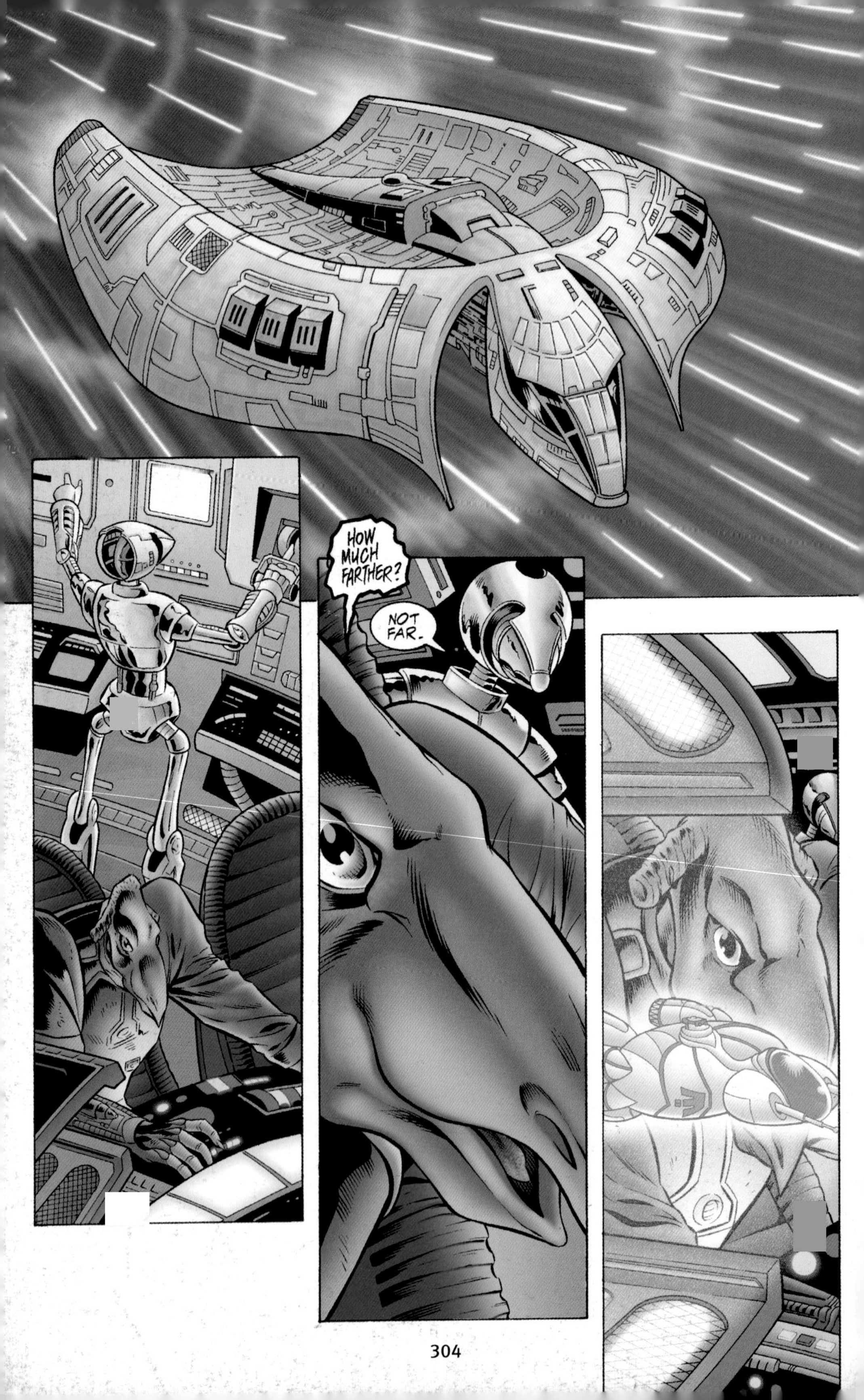
HOW MUCH FARTHER?
NOT FAR.

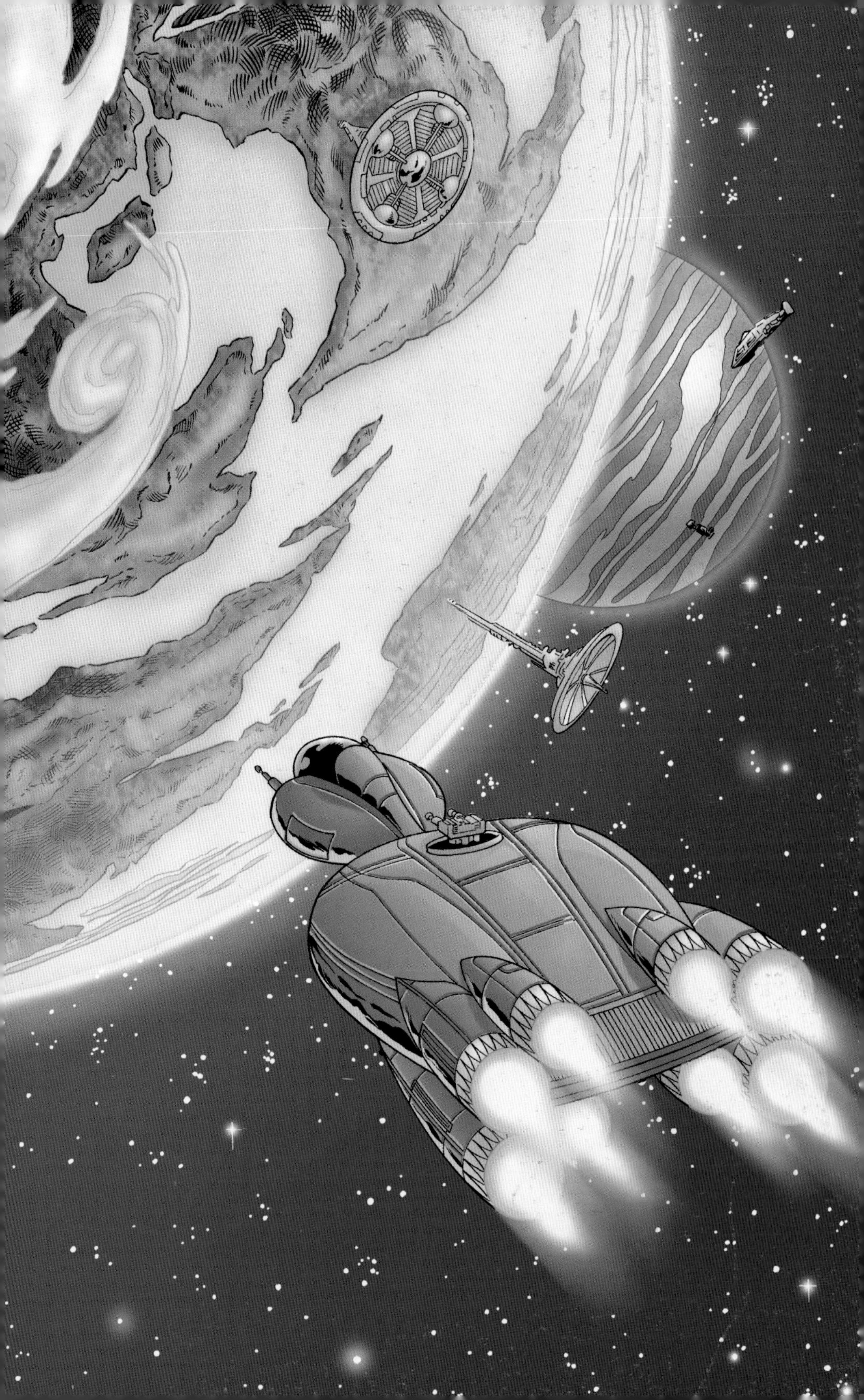

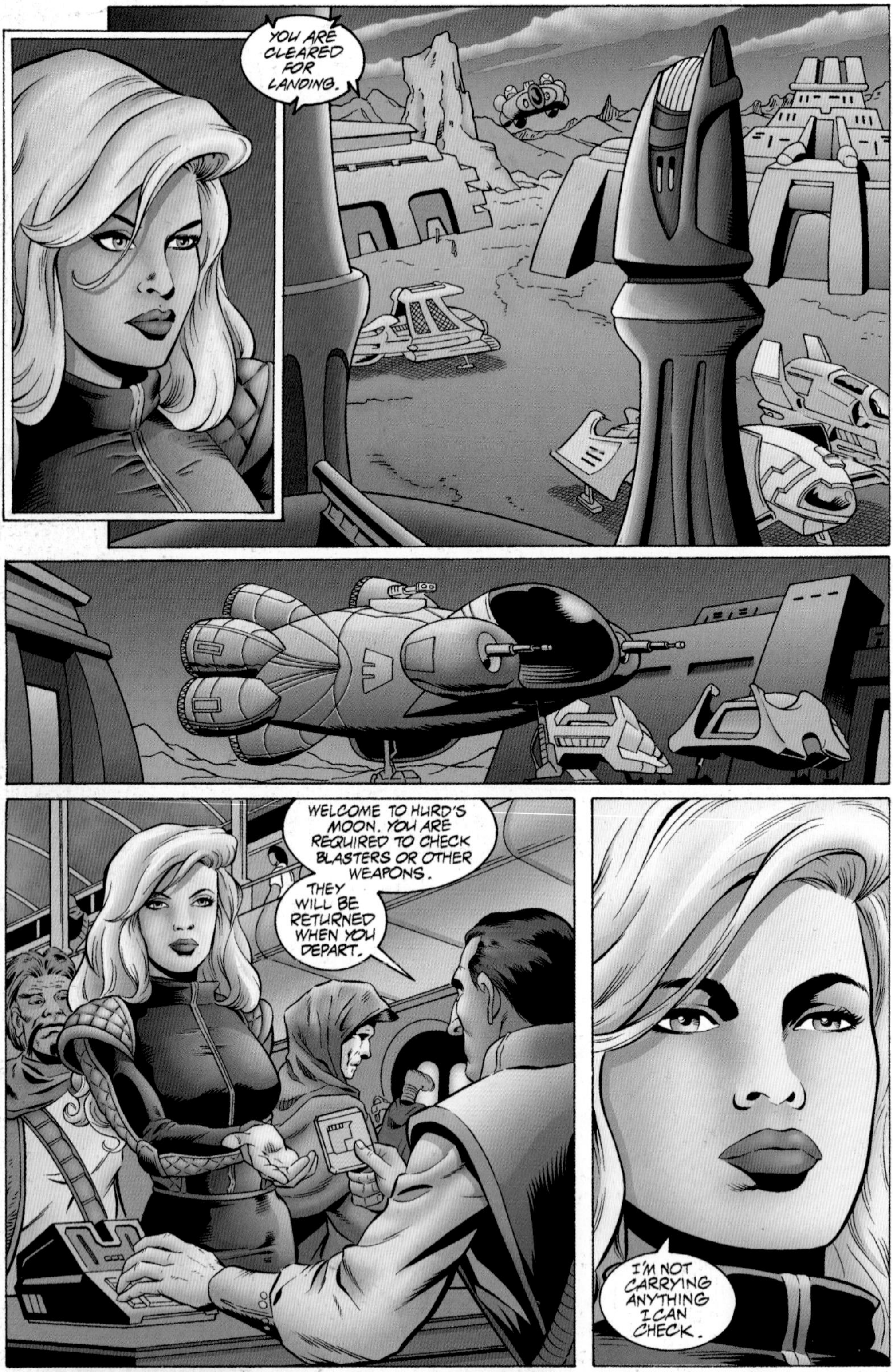
YOU ARE CLEARED FOR LANDING.
WELCOME TO HURD'S MOON. YOU ARE REQUIRED TO CHECK BLASTERS OR OTHER WEAPONS.
THEY WILL BE RETURNED WHEN YOU DEPART.
I'M NOT CARRYING ANYTHING I CAN CHECK.

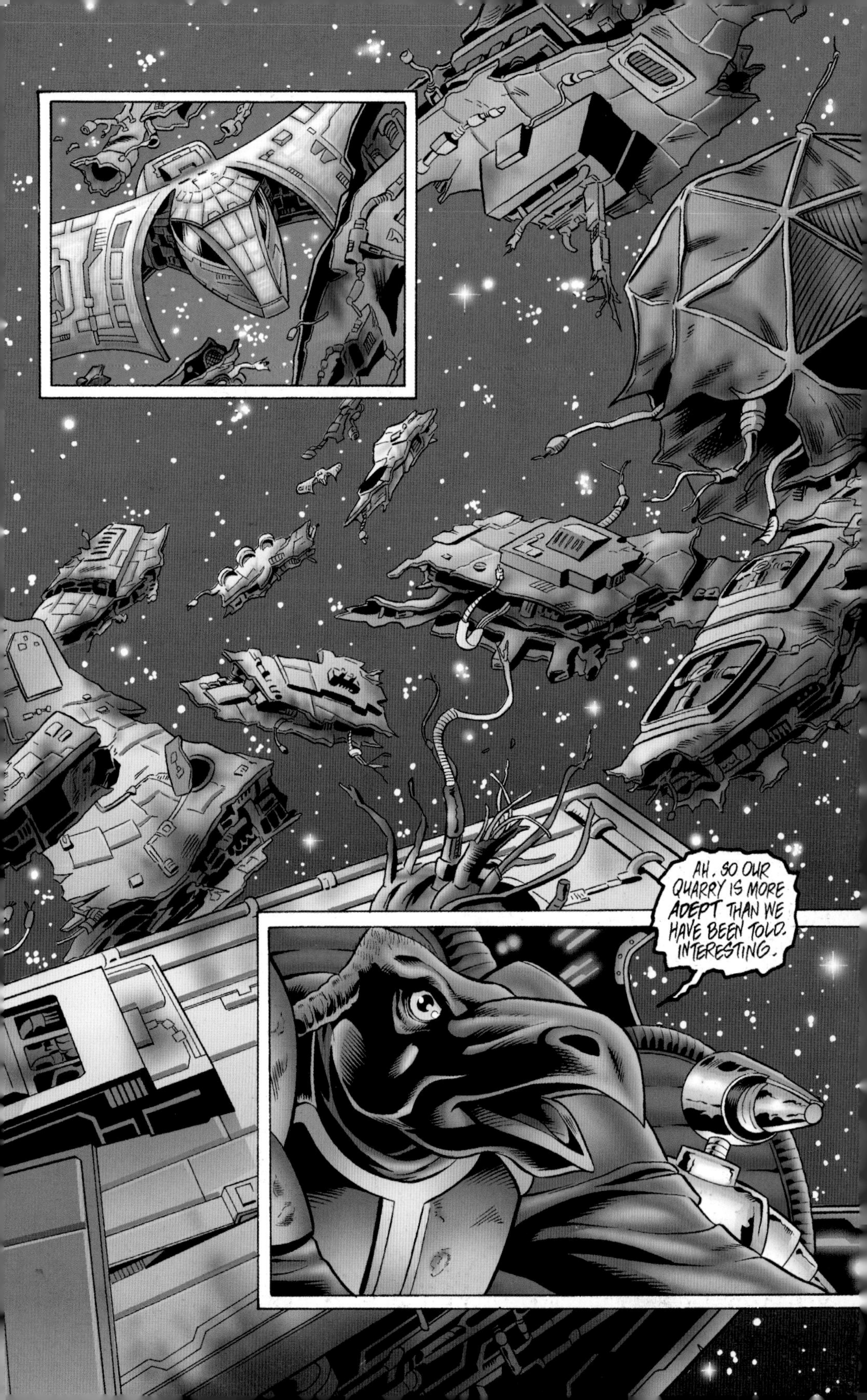
AH. SO OUR QUARRY IS MORE ADEPT THAN WE HAVE BEEN TOLD. INTERESTING.

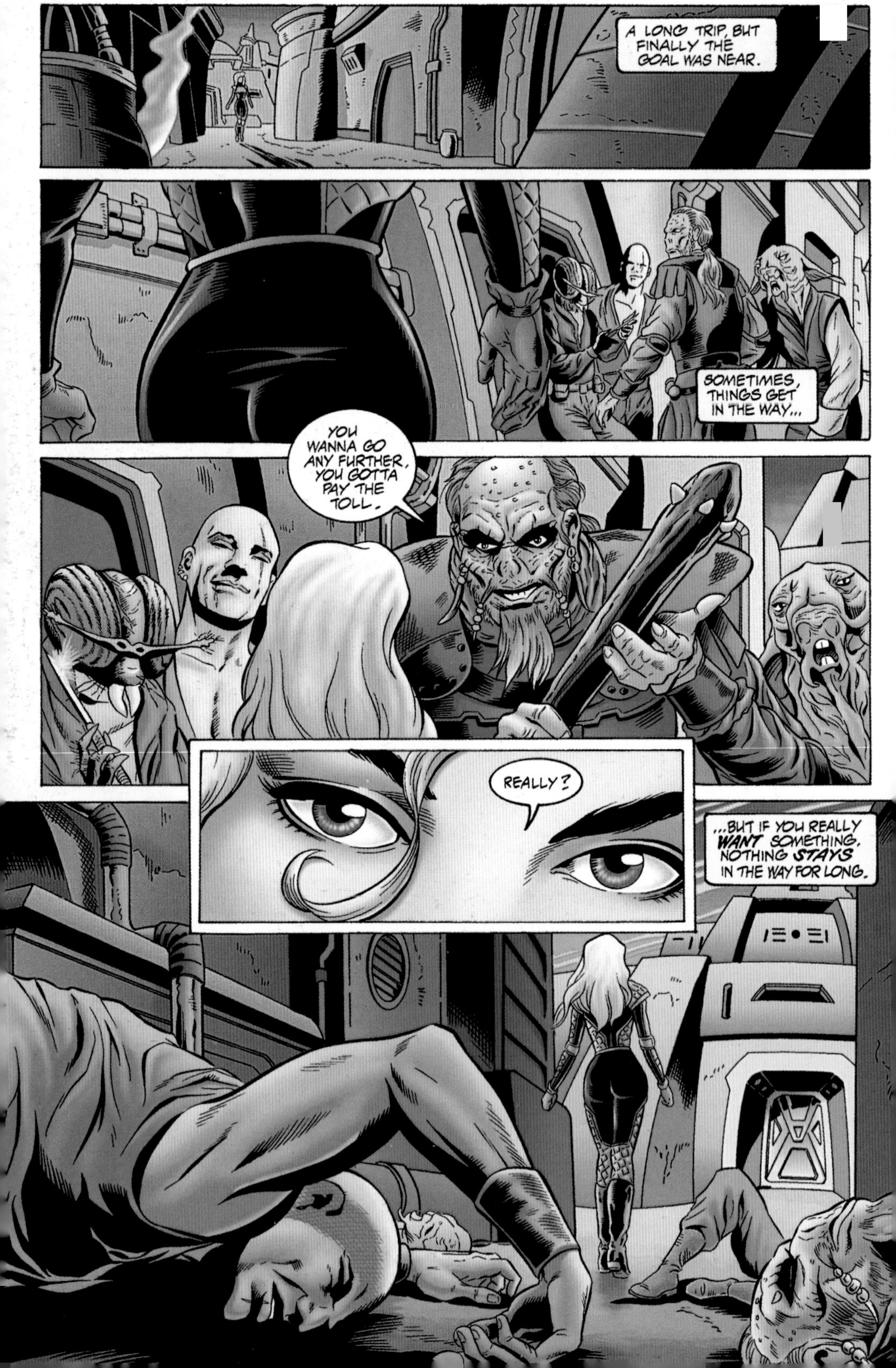
A LONG TRIP, BUT FINALLY THE GOAL WAS NEAR.
SOMETIMES, THINGS GET IN THE WAY...
YOU WANNA GO ANY FURTHER, YOU GOTTA PAY THE TOLL.
REALLY?
...BUT IF YOU REALLY WANT SOMETHING, NOTHING STAYS IN THE WAY FOR LONG.

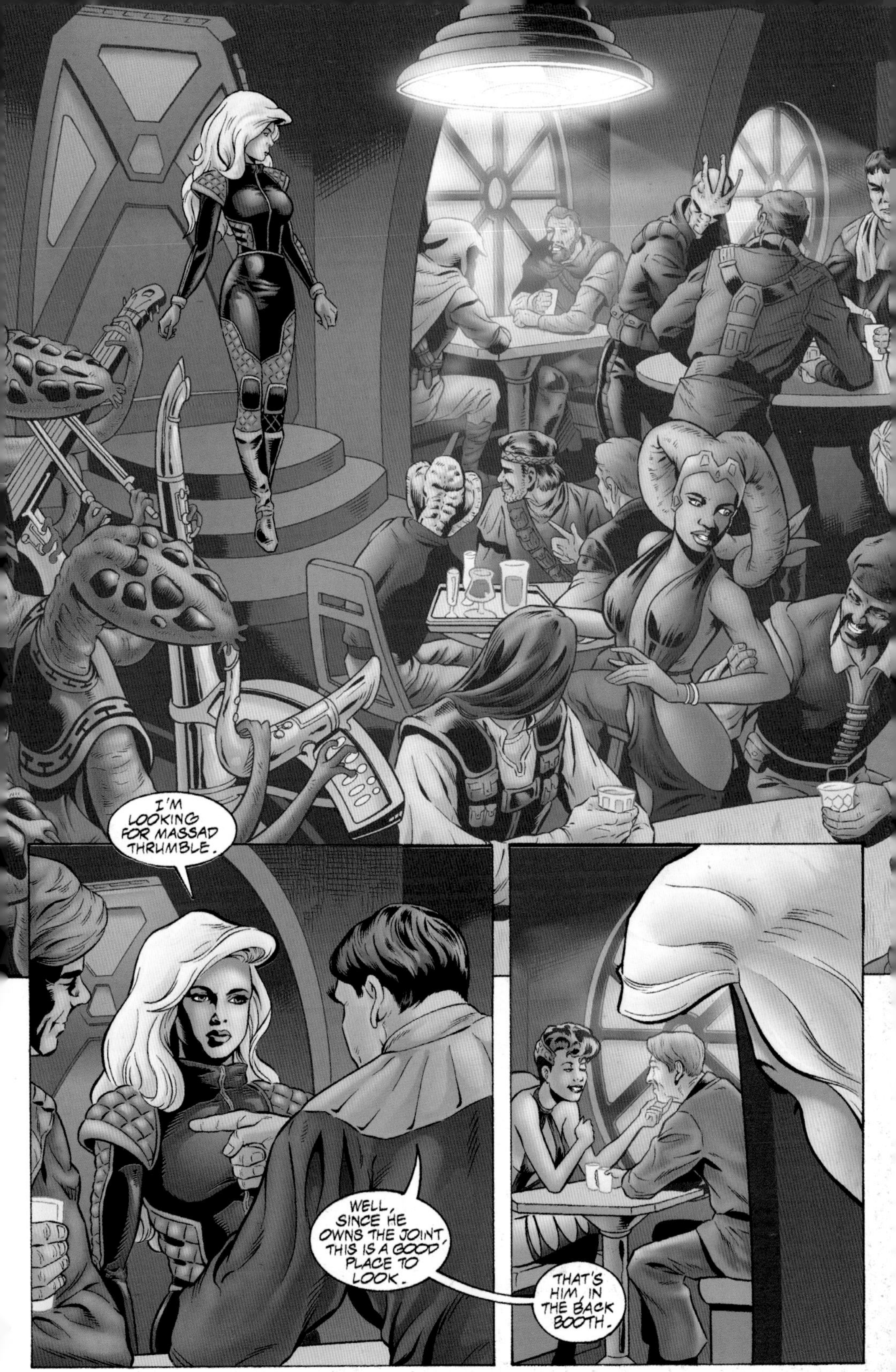
I'M LOOKING FOR MASSAD THRUMBLE.
WELL, SINCE HE OWNS THE JOINT, THIS IS A GOOD PLACE TO LOOK.
THAT'S HIM, IN THE BACK BOOTH.

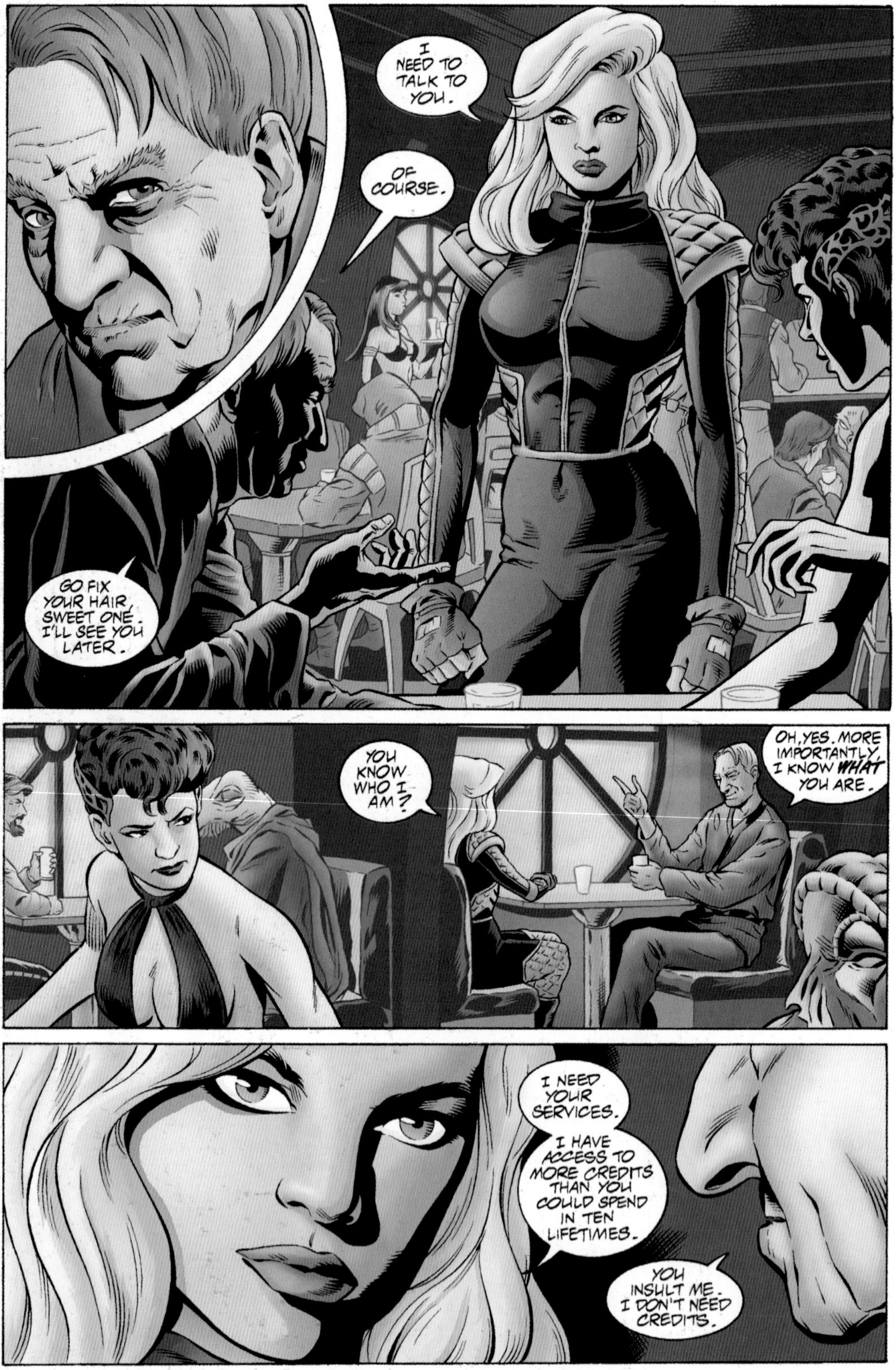
I NEED TO TALK TO YOU.
OF COURSE.
GO FIX YOUR HAIR, SWEET ONE. I'LL SEE YOU LATER.
YOU KNOW WHO I AM?
OH, YES. MORE IMPORTANTLY, I KNOW WHAT YOU ARE.
I NEED YOUR SERVICES.
I HAVE ACCESS TO MORE CREDITS THAN YOU COULD SPEND IN TEN LIFETIMES.
YOU INSULT ME. I DON'T NEED CREDITS.

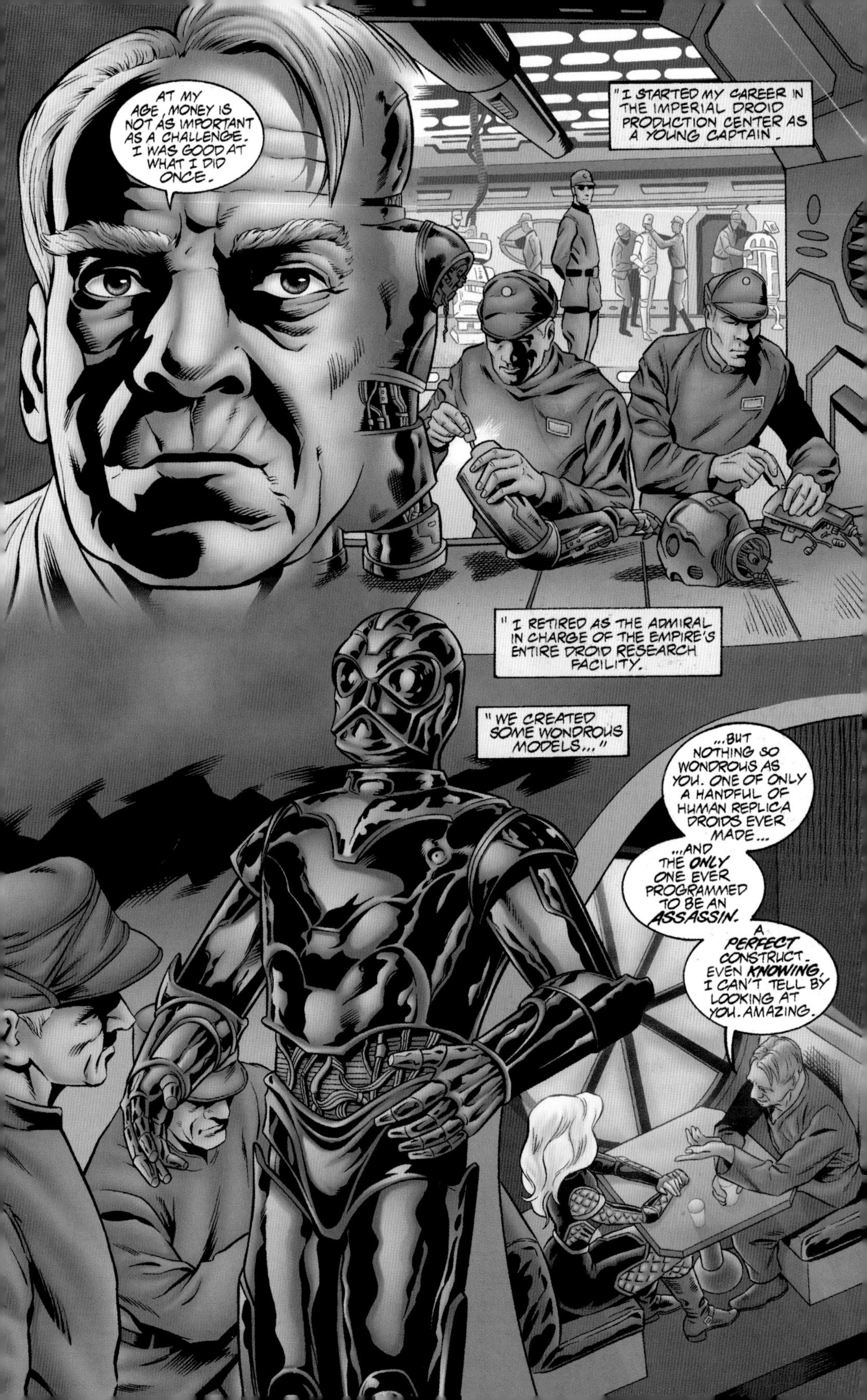
AT MY AGE, MONEY IS NOT AS IMPORTANT AS A CHALLENGE. I WAS GOOD AT WHAT I DID ONCE.
"I STARTED MY CAREER IN THE IMPERIAL DROID PRODUCTION CENTER AS A YOUNG CAPTAIN.
"I RETIRED AS THE ADMIRAL IN CHARGE OF THE EMPIRE'S ENTIRE DROID RESEARCH FACILITY.
"WE CREATED SOME WONDROUS MODELS..."
...BUT NOTHING SO WONDROUS AS YOU. ONE OF ONLY A HANDFUL OF HUMAN REPLICA DROIDS EVER MADE...
...AND THE ONLY ONE EVER PROGRAMMED TO BE AN ASSASSIN.
A PERFECT CONSTRUCT. EVEN KNOWING, I CAN'T TELL BY LOOKING AT YOU. AMAZING.

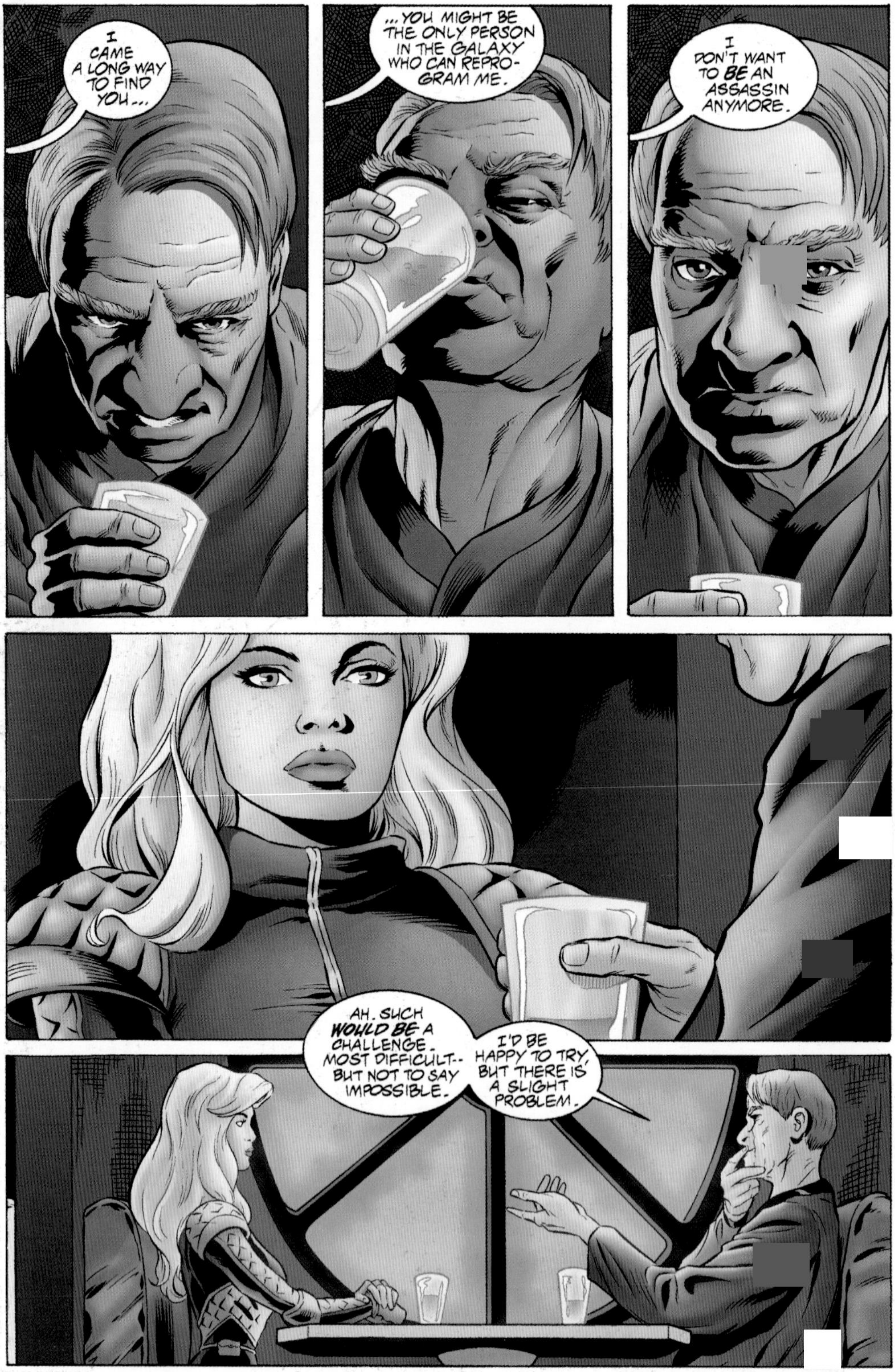
I CAME A LONG WAY TO FIND YOU...
...YOU MIGHT BE THE ONLY PERSON IN THE GALAXY WHO CAN REPRO-GRAM ME.
I DON'T WANT TO BE AN ASSASSIN ANYMORE.
AH. SUCH WOULD BE A CHALLENGE. MOST DIFFICULT-- BUT NOT TO SAY IMPOSSIBLE.
I'D BE HAPPY TO TRY, BUT THERE IS A SLIGHT PROBLEM.

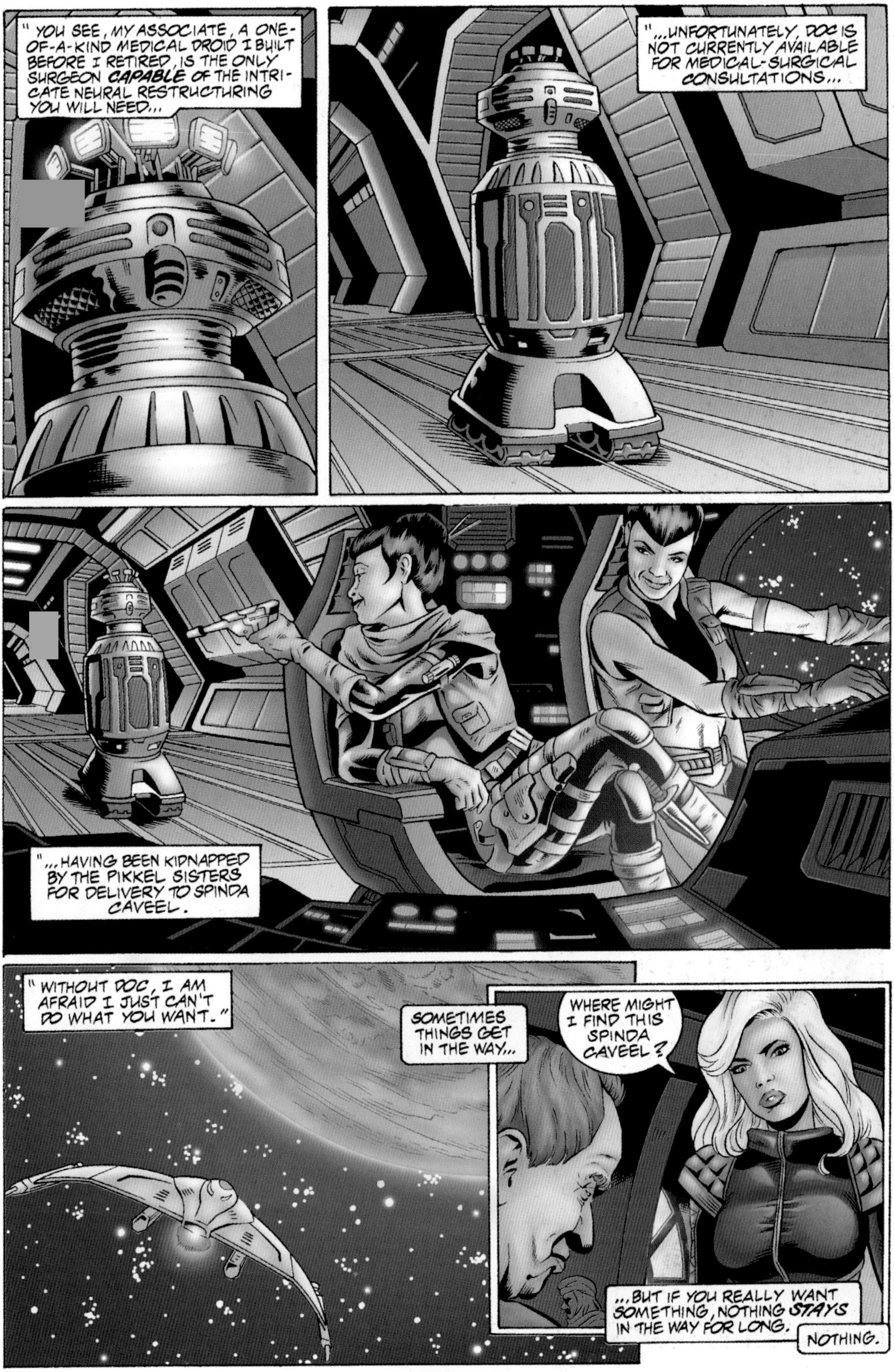
" YOU SEE, MY ASSOCIATE, A ONE-OF-A-KIND MEDICAL DROID I BUILT BEFORE I RETIRED, IS THE ONLY SURGEON CAPABLE OF THE INTRICATE NEURAL RESTRUCTURING YOU WILL NEED...
"...UNFORTUNATELY, DOC IS NOT CURRENTLY AVAILABLE FOR MEDICAL-SURGICAL CONSULTATIONS...
"...HAVING BEEN KIDNAPPED BY THE PIKKEL SISTERS FOR DELIVERY TO SPINDA CAVEEL.
" WITHOUT DOC, I AM AFRAID I JUST CAN'T DO WHAT YOU WANT."
SOMETIMES THINGS GET IN THE WAY...
WHERE MIGHT I FIND THIS SPINDA CAVEEL?
...BUT IF YOU REALLY WANT SOMETHING, NOTHING STAYS IN THE WAY FOR LONG.
NOTHING.

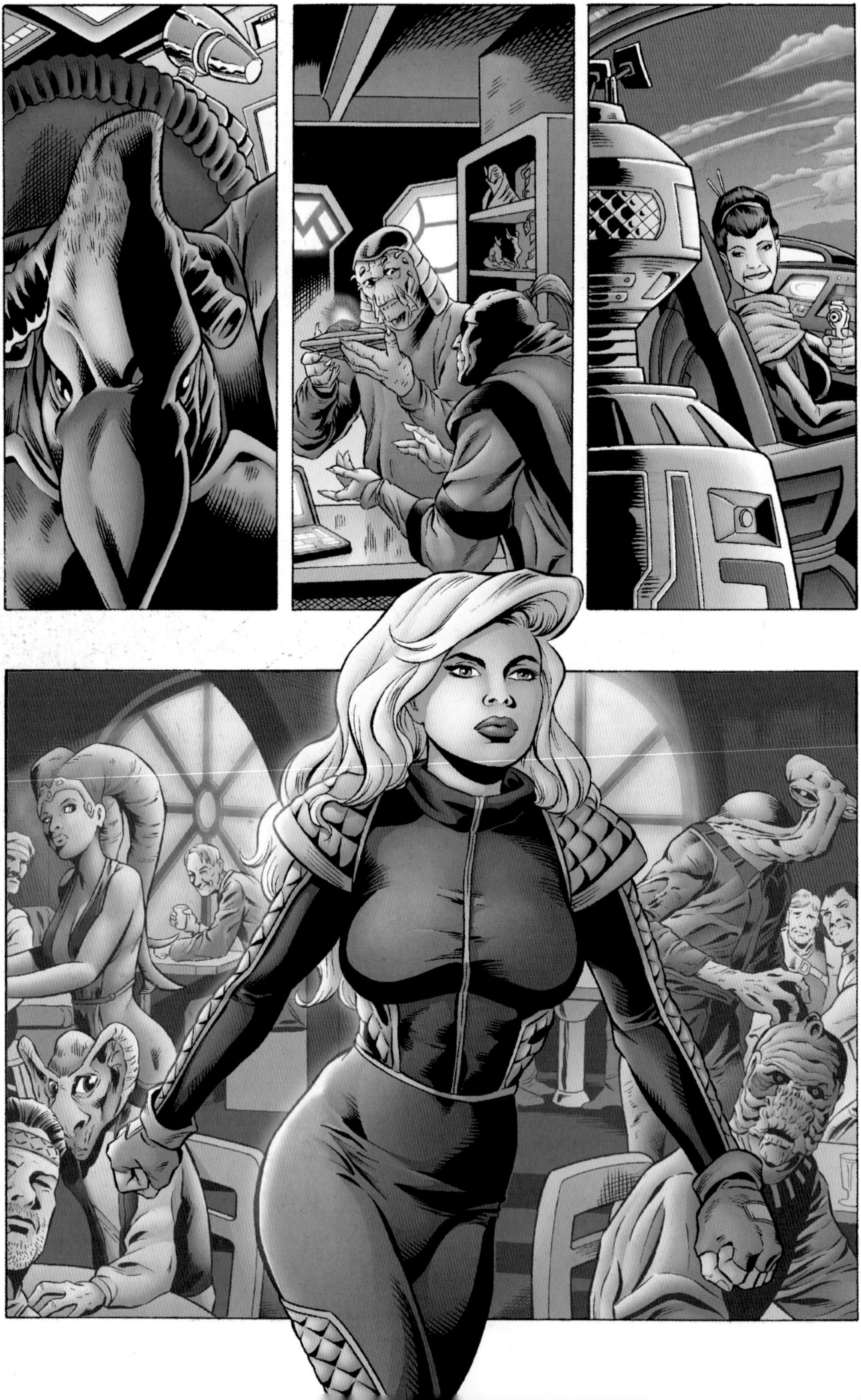

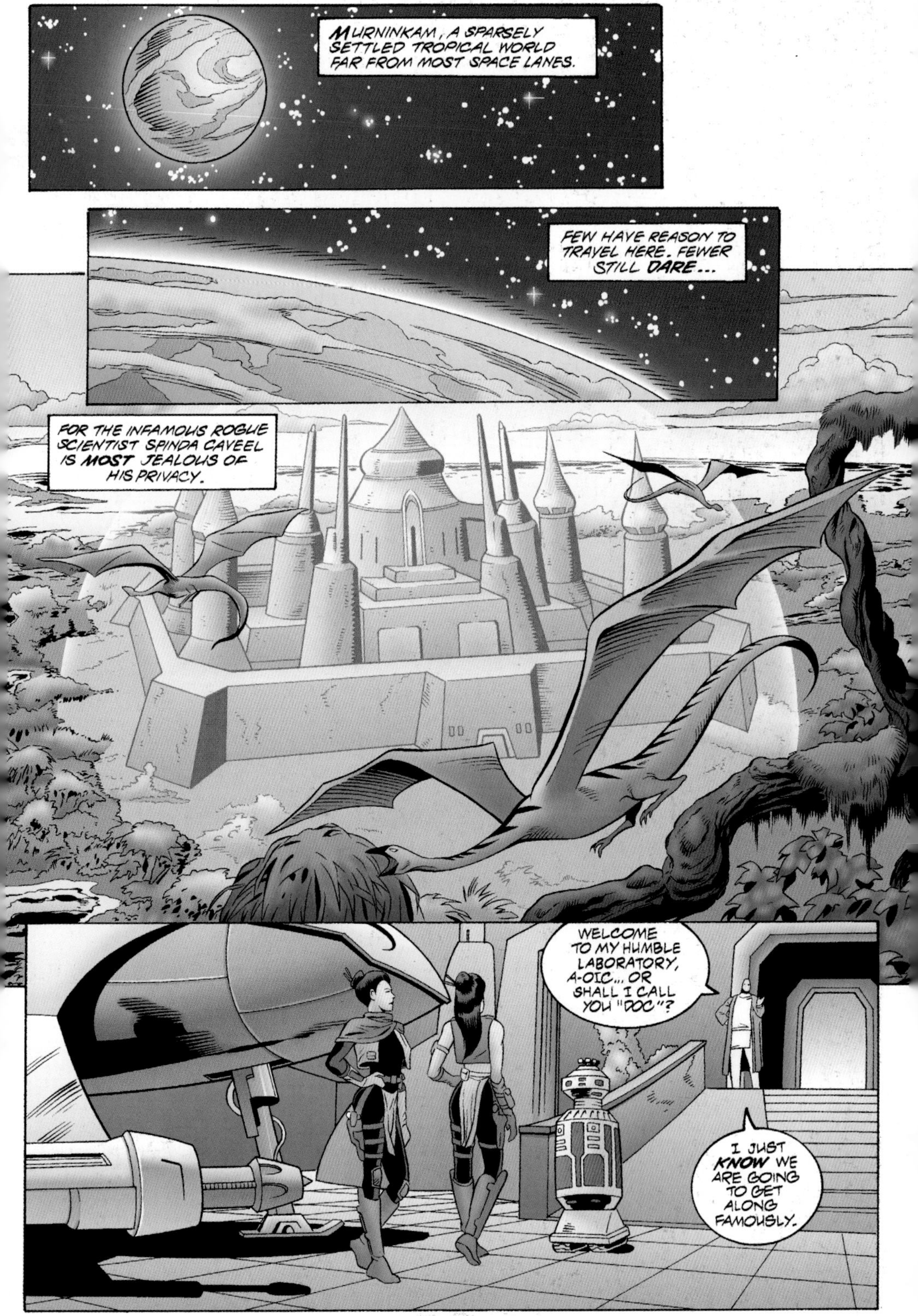
MURNINKAM, A SPARSELY SETTLED TROPICAL WORLD FAR FROM MOST SPACE LANES.
FEW HAVE REASON TO TRAVEL HERE. FEWER STILL DARE...
FOR THE INFAMOUS ROGUE SCIENTIST SPINDA CAVEEL IS MOST JEALOUS OF HIS PRIVACY.
WELCOME TO MY HUMBLE LABORATORY, A-OIC... OR SHALL I CALL YOU "DOC"?
I JUST KNOW WE ARE GOING TO GET ALONG FAMOUSLY.

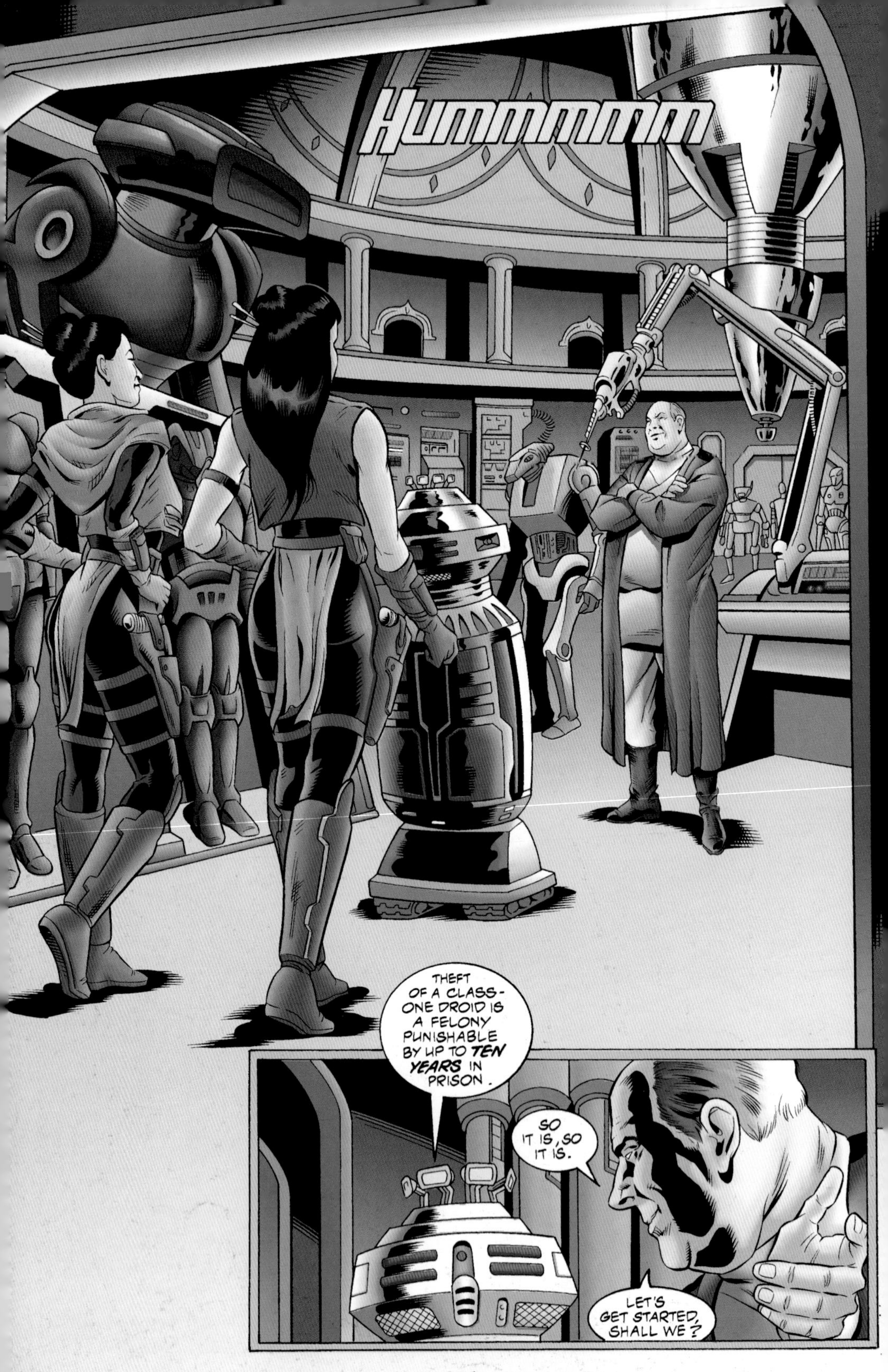
HUMMMMMM
THEFT OF A CLASS-ONE DROID IS A FELONY PUNISHABLE BY UP TO TEN YEARS IN PRISON.
SO IT IS, SO IT IS.
LET'S GET STARTED, SHALL WE?

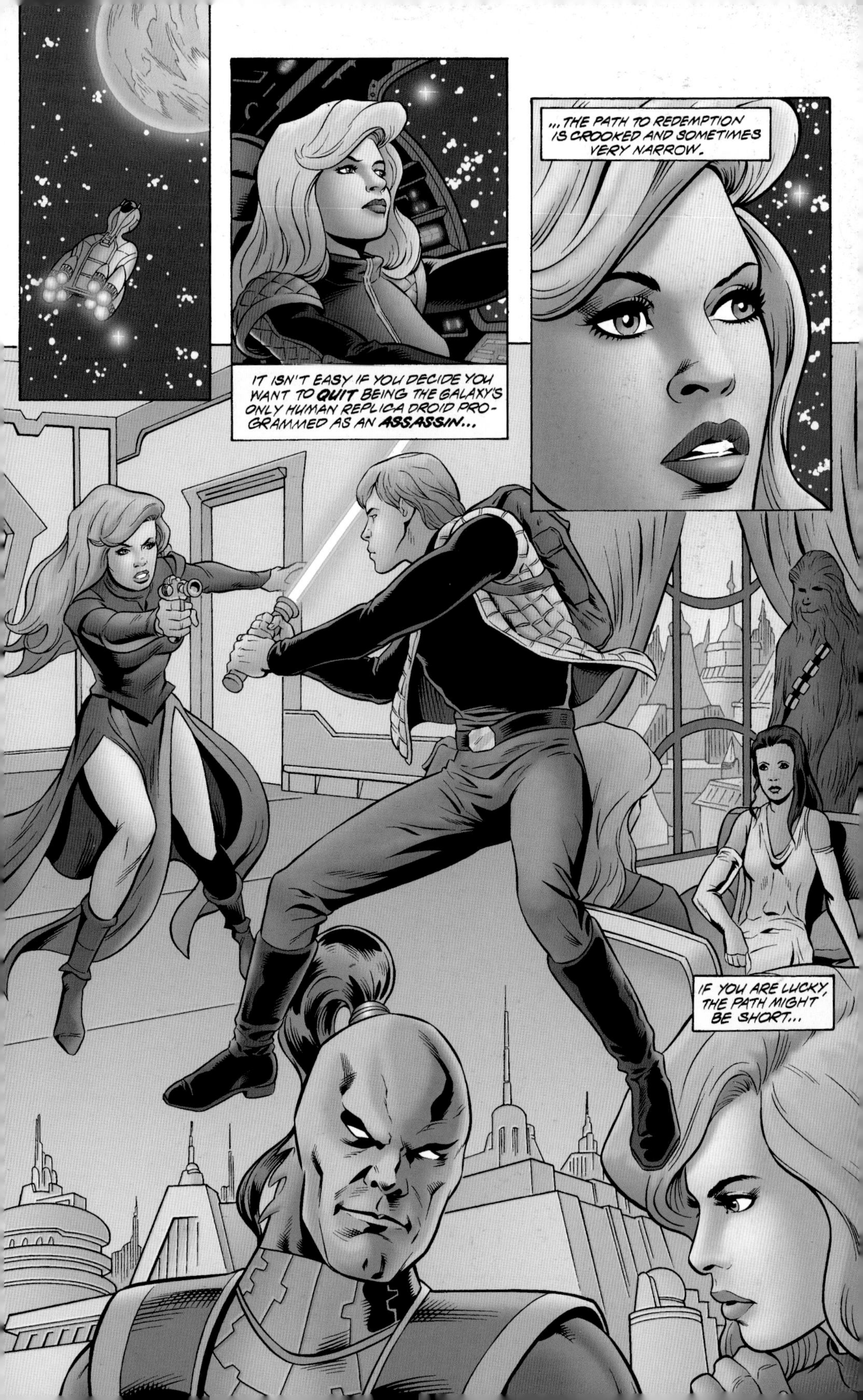

IT ISN'T EASY IF YOU DECIDE YOU WANT TO QUIT BEING THE GALAXY'S ONLY HUMAN REPLICA DROID PRO-GRAMMED AS AN ASSASSIN...
...THE PATH TO REDEMPTION IS CROOKED AND SOMETIMES VERY NARROW.
IF YOU ARE LUCKY, THE PATH MIGHT BE SHORT...

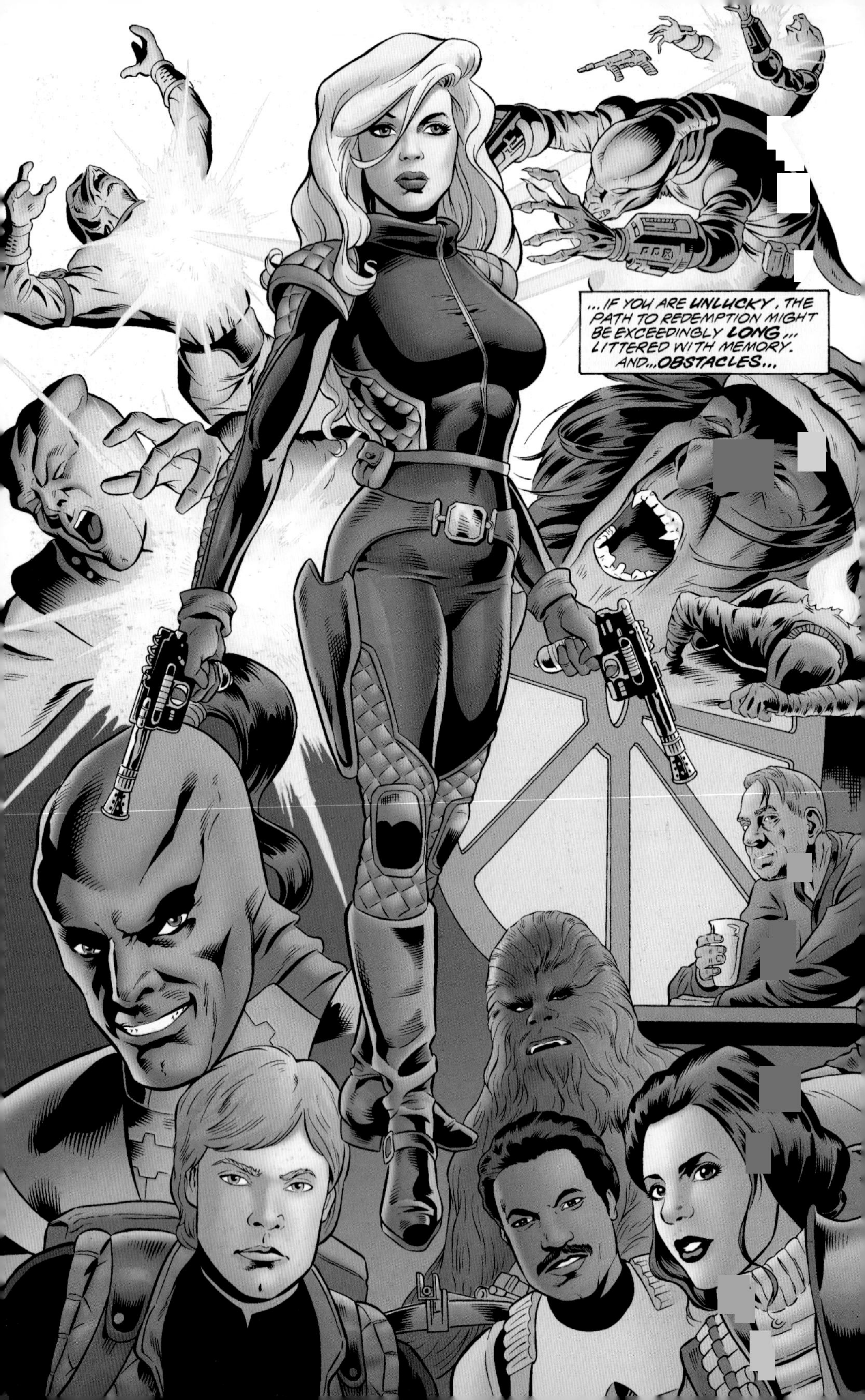
...IF YOU ARE UNLUCKY, THE PATH TO REDEMPTION MIGHT BE EXCEEDINGLY LONG... LITTERED WITH MEMORY. AND...OBSTACLES...

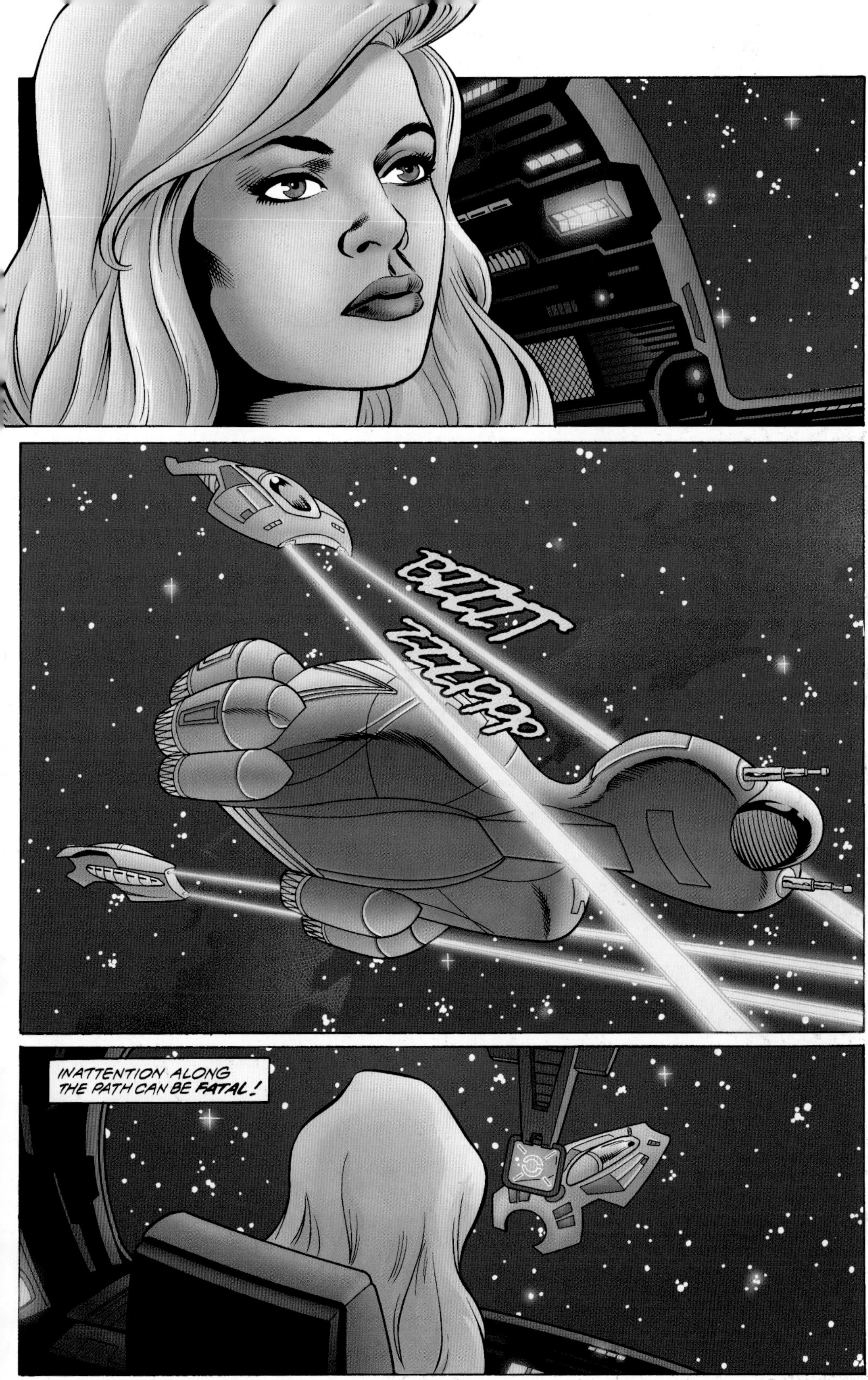
INATTENTION ALONG THE PATH CAN BE FATAL!

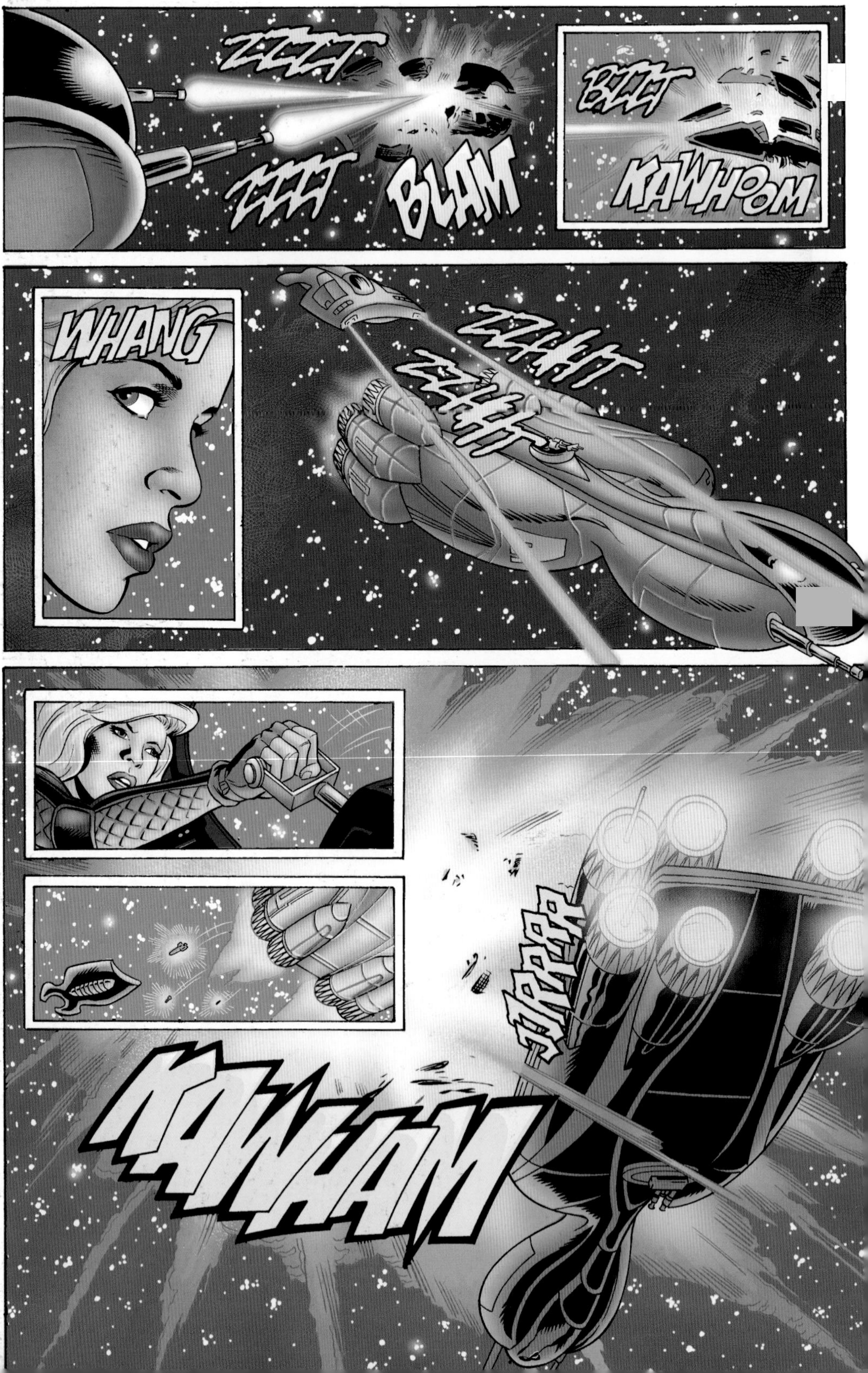
ZZZT
ZZZT
BLAM
BZZT
KAWHOOM
WHANG
ZZHHT
ZZHHT
JRRRR
KAWHAM

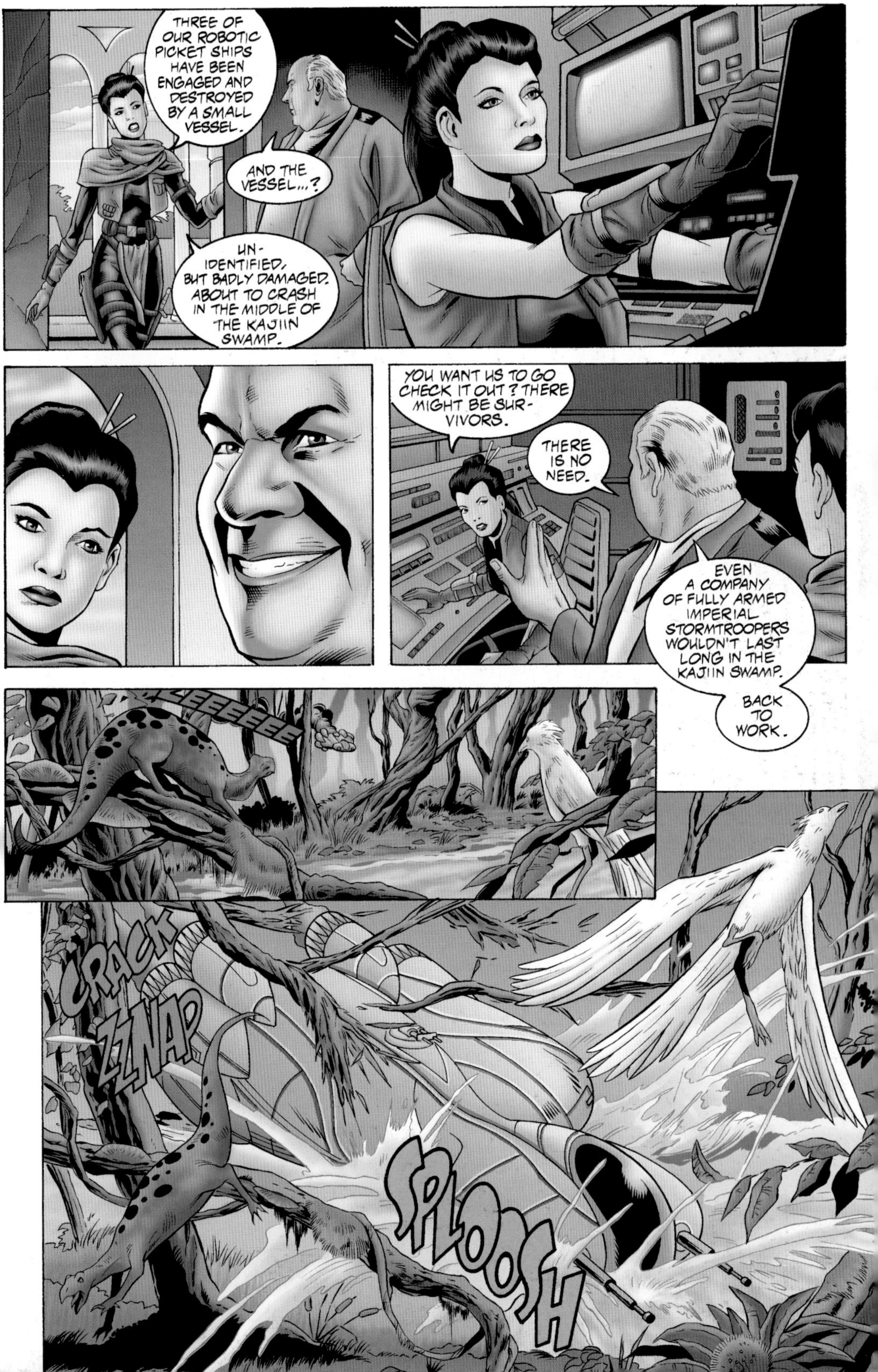
THREE OF OUR ROBOTIC PICKET SHIPS HAVE BEEN ENGAGED AND DESTROYED BY A SMALL VESSEL.
AND THE VESSEL...?
UN-IDENTIFIED, BUT BADLY DAMAGED. ABOUT TO CRASH IN THE MIDDLE OF THE KAJIIN SWAMP.
YOU WANT US TO GO CHECK IT OUT? THERE MIGHT BE SUR-VIVORS.
THERE IS NO NEED.
EVEN A COMPANY OF FULLY ARMED IMPERIAL STORMTROOPERS WOULDN'T LAST LONG IN THE KAJIIN SWAMP.
BACK TO WORK.
EEEEEEE
CRACK
ZZNAP
SPLOOSH

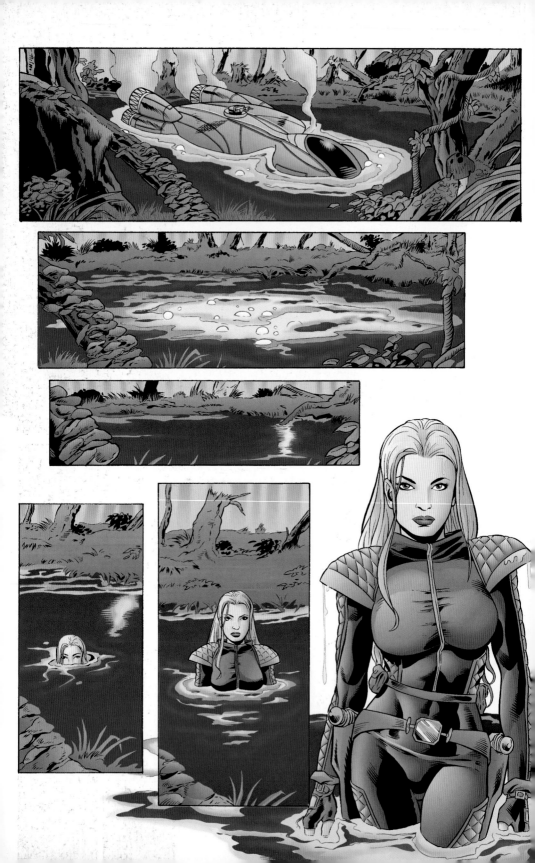

CAN I HELP YOU?

I AM LOOKING FOR THE HUMAN REPLICA DROID KNOWN AS GURI.

SORRY, I DON'T KNOW WHO YOU'RE TALKING ABOUT.

I THINK YOU DO.

IT WOULD BE WISE OF YOU TO TELL ME WHAT I WANT TO KNOW.

OH, REALLY? IS THAT A THREAT?

TAKE IT AS YOU WILL.

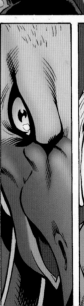

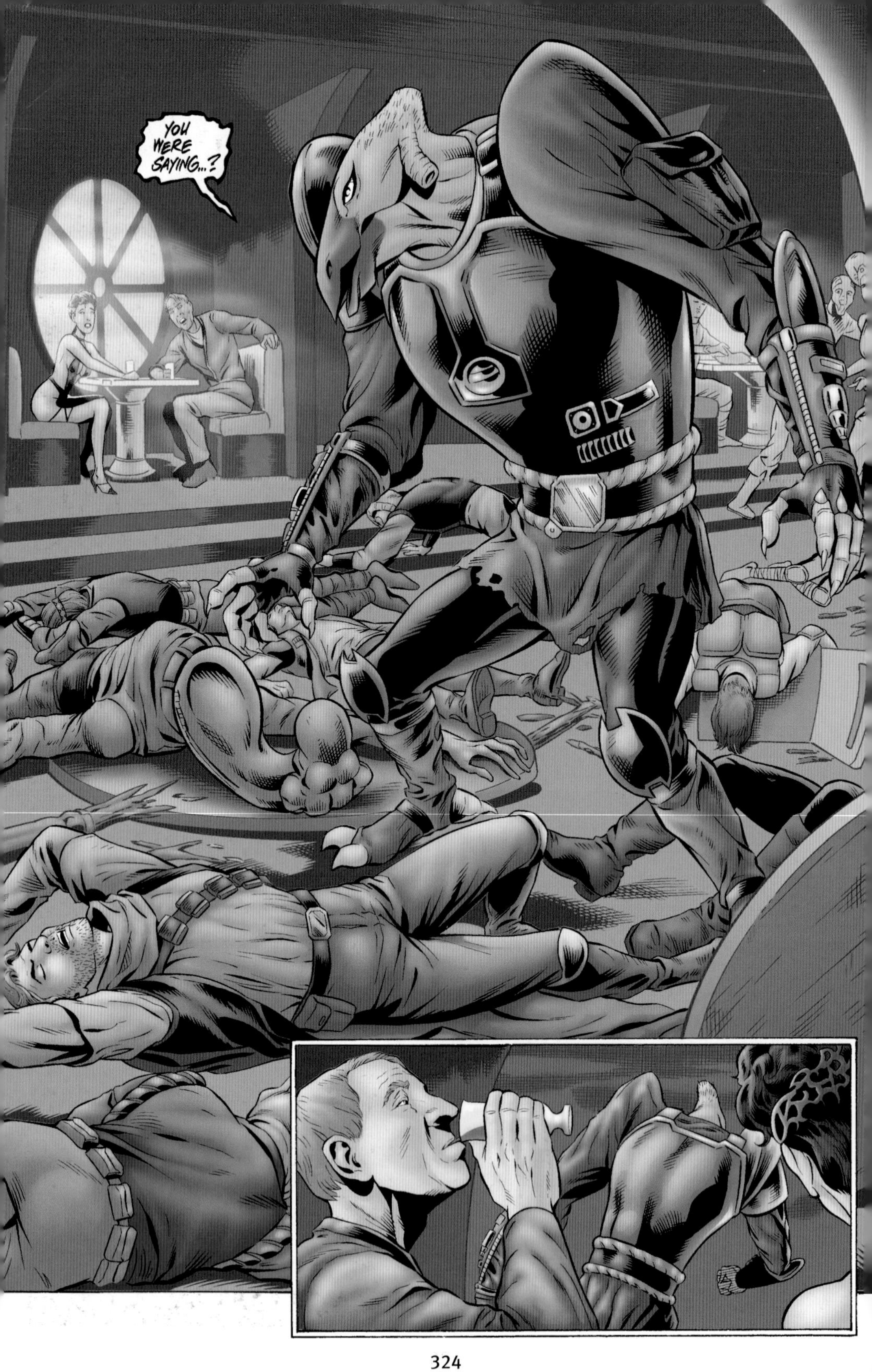
YOU WERE SAYING...?

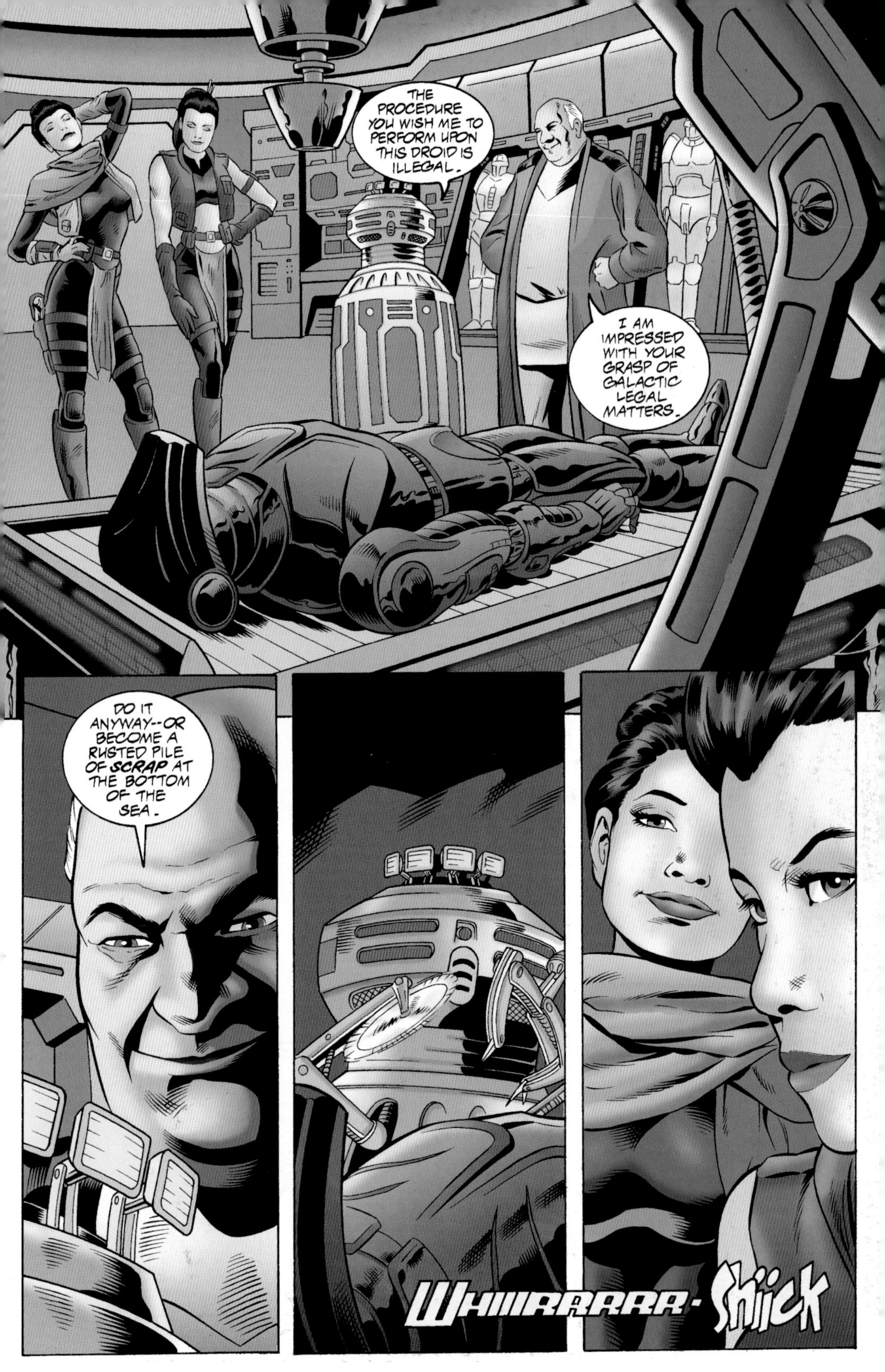
THE PROCEDURE YOU WISH ME TO PERFORM UPON THIS DROID IS ILLEGAL.
I AM IMPRESSED WITH YOUR GRASP OF GALACTIC LEGAL MATTERS.
DO IT ANYWAY--OR BECOME A RUSTED PILE OF SCRAP AT THE BOTTOM OF THE SEA.
WHIIIRRRRRR-SHIICK

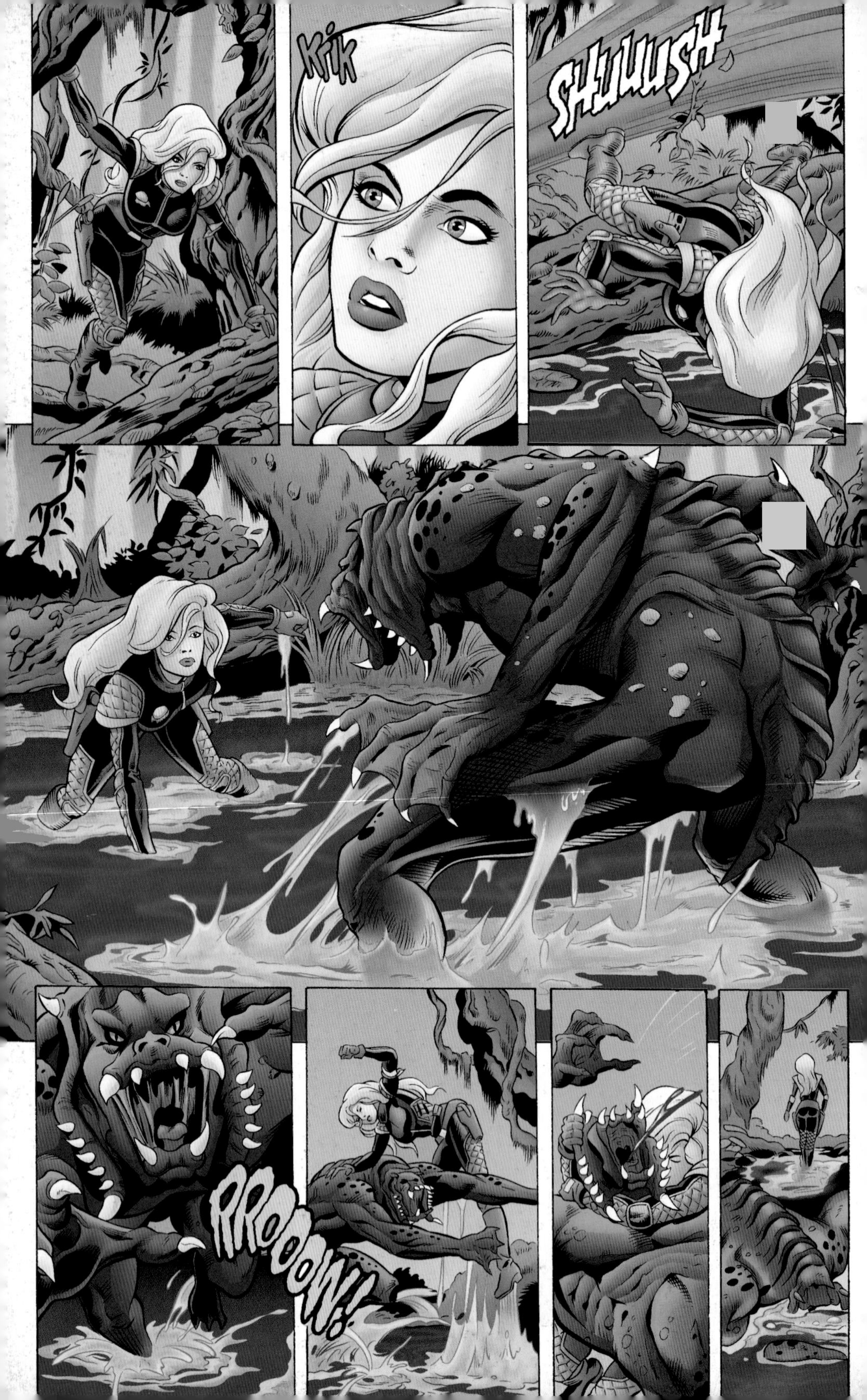
KRIK
SHUUUSH
RROOOWN!!

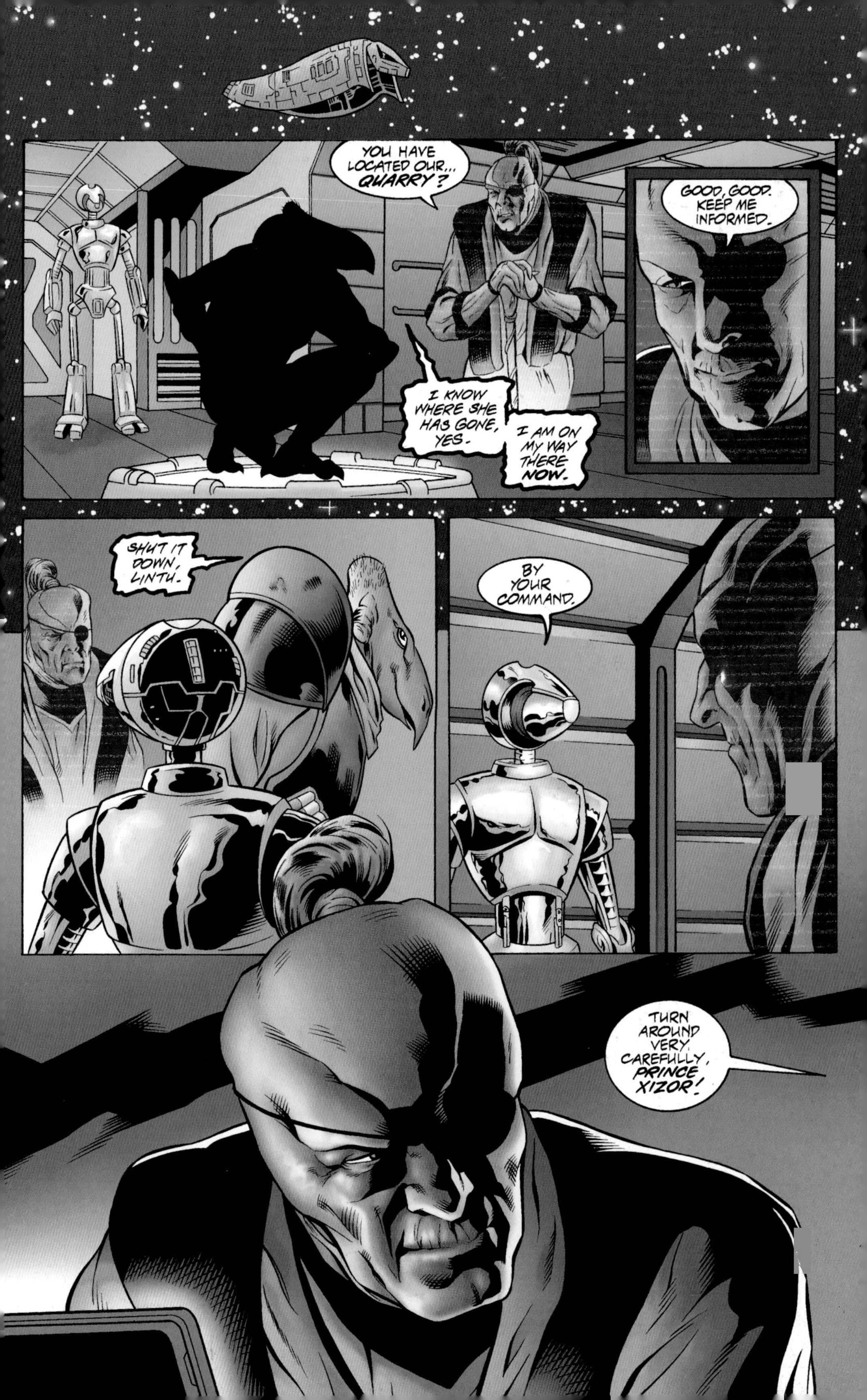
YOU HAVE LOCATED OUR... QUARRY?
GOOD, GOOD. KEEP ME INFORMED.
I KNOW WHERE SHE HAS GONE, YES.
I AM ON MY WAY THERE NOW.
SHUT IT DOWN, LINTU.
BY YOUR COMMAND.
TURN AROUND VERY CAREFULLY, PRINCE XIZOR!

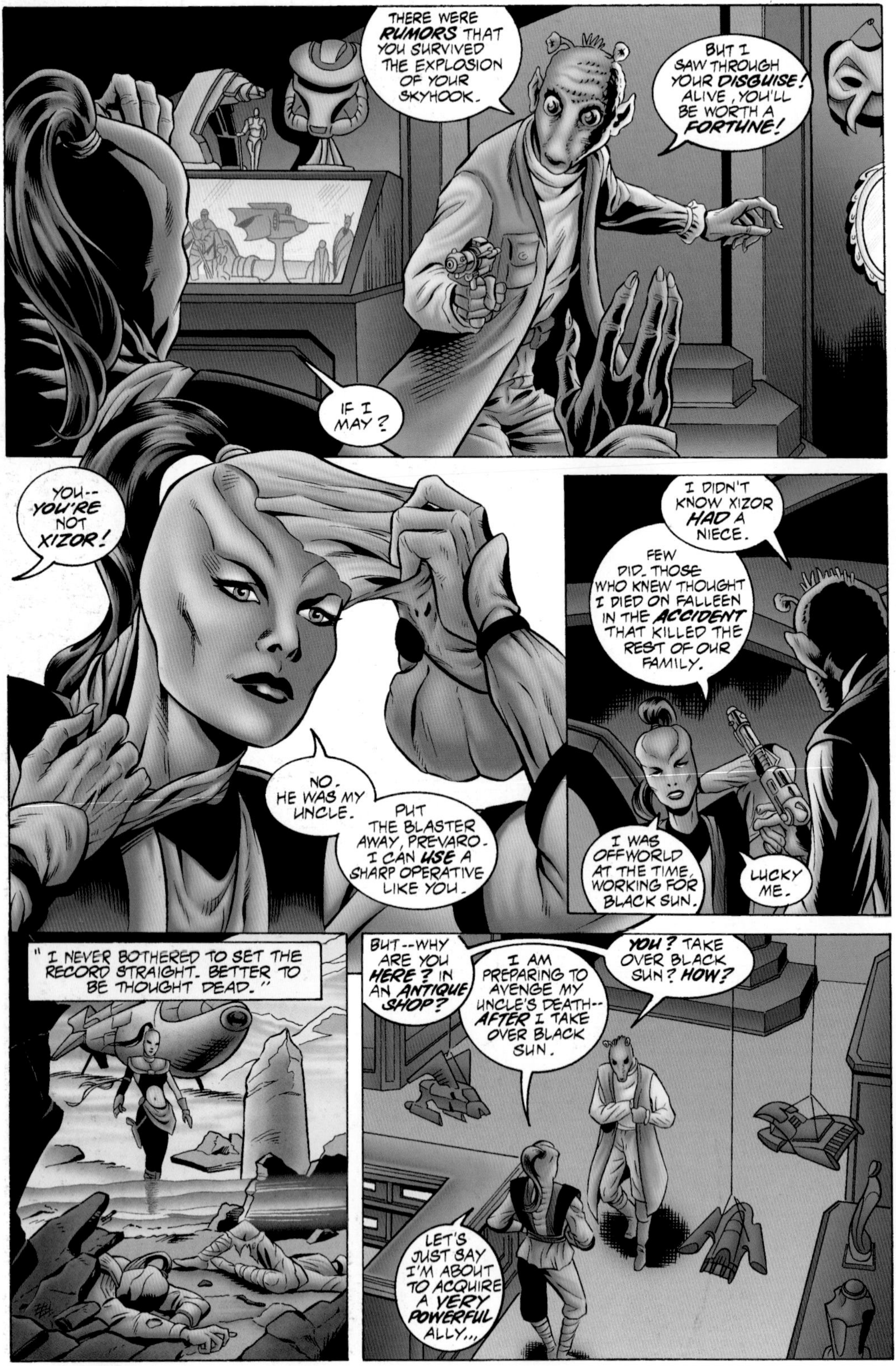
THERE WERE RUMORS THAT YOU SURVIVED THE EXPLOSION OF YOUR SKYHOOK.
BUT I SAW THROUGH YOUR DISGUISE! ALIVE, YOU'LL BE WORTH A FORTUNE!
IF I MAY?
YOU-- YOU'RE NOT XIZOR!
NO. HE WAS MY UNCLE.
PUT THE BLASTER AWAY, PREVARO. I CAN USE A SHARP OPERATIVE LIKE YOU.
I DIDN'T KNOW XIZOR HAD A NIECE.
FEW DID. THOSE WHO KNEW THOUGHT I DIED ON FALLEEN IN THE ACCIDENT THAT KILLED THE REST OF OUR FAMILY.
I WAS OFFWORLD AT THE TIME, WORKING FOR BLACK SUN.
LUCKY ME.
"I NEVER BOTHERED TO SET THE RECORD STRAIGHT. BETTER TO BE THOUGHT DEAD."
BUT--WHY ARE YOU HERE? IN AN ANTIQUE SHOP?
I AM PREPARING TO AVENGE MY UNCLE'S DEATH-- AFTER I TAKE OVER BLACK SUN.
YOU? TAKE OVER BLACK SUN? HOW?
LET'S JUST SAY I'M ABOUT TO ACQUIRE A VERY POWERFUL ALLY...

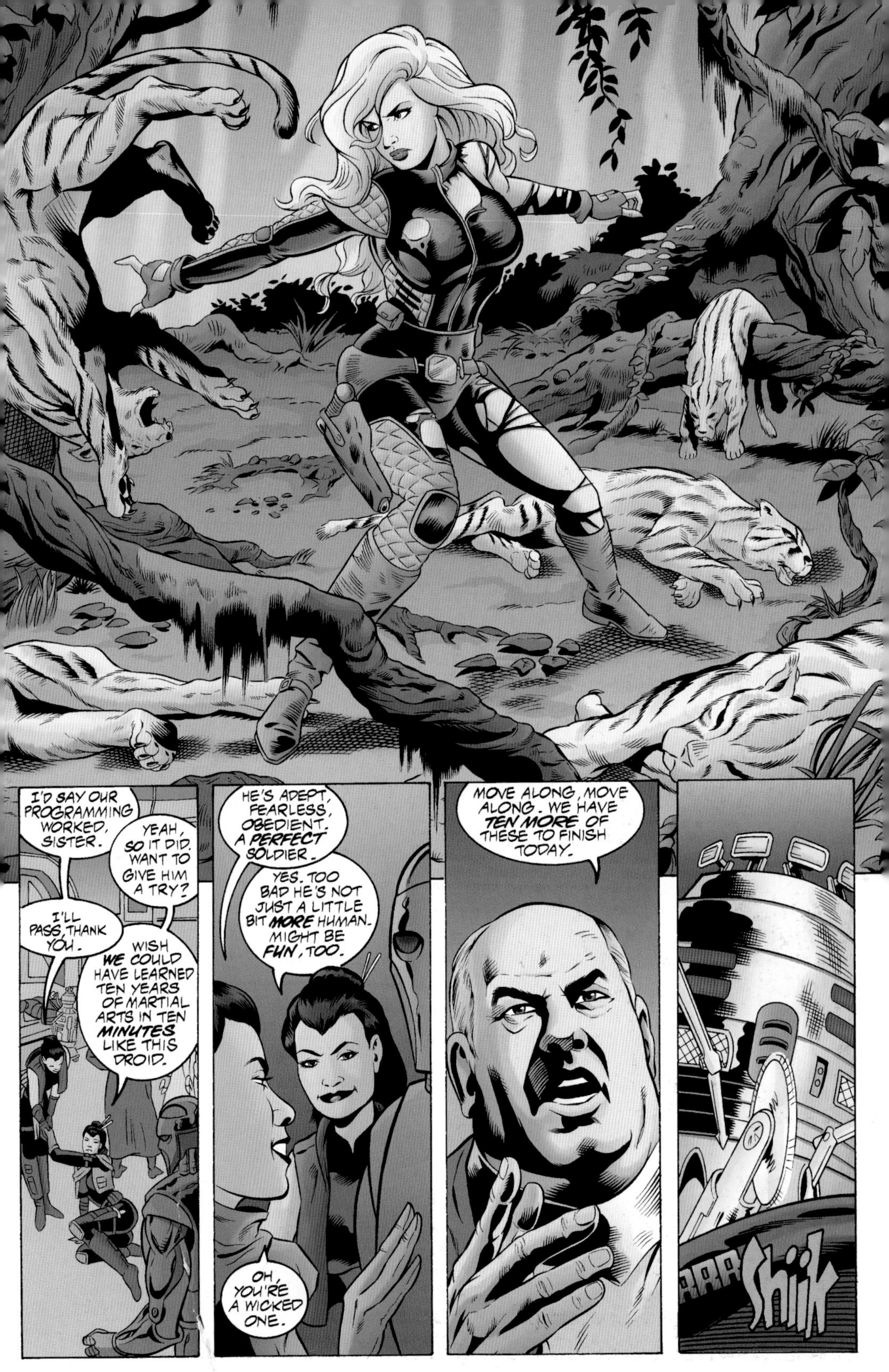

I'D SAY OUR PROGRAMMING WORKED, SISTER.
YEAH, SO IT DID. WANT TO GIVE HIM A TRY?
I'LL PASS, THANK YOU.
WISH WE COULD HAVE LEARNED TEN YEARS OF MARTIAL ARTS IN TEN MINUTES LIKE THIS DROID.
HE'S ADEPT, FEARLESS, OBEDIENT. A PERFECT SOLDIER.
YES. TOO BAD HE'S NOT JUST A LITTLE BIT MORE HUMAN. MIGHT BE FUN, TOO.
OH, YOU'RE A WICKED ONE.
MOVE ALONG, MOVE ALONG. WE HAVE TEN MORE OF THESE TO FINISH TODAY.
SHIIK

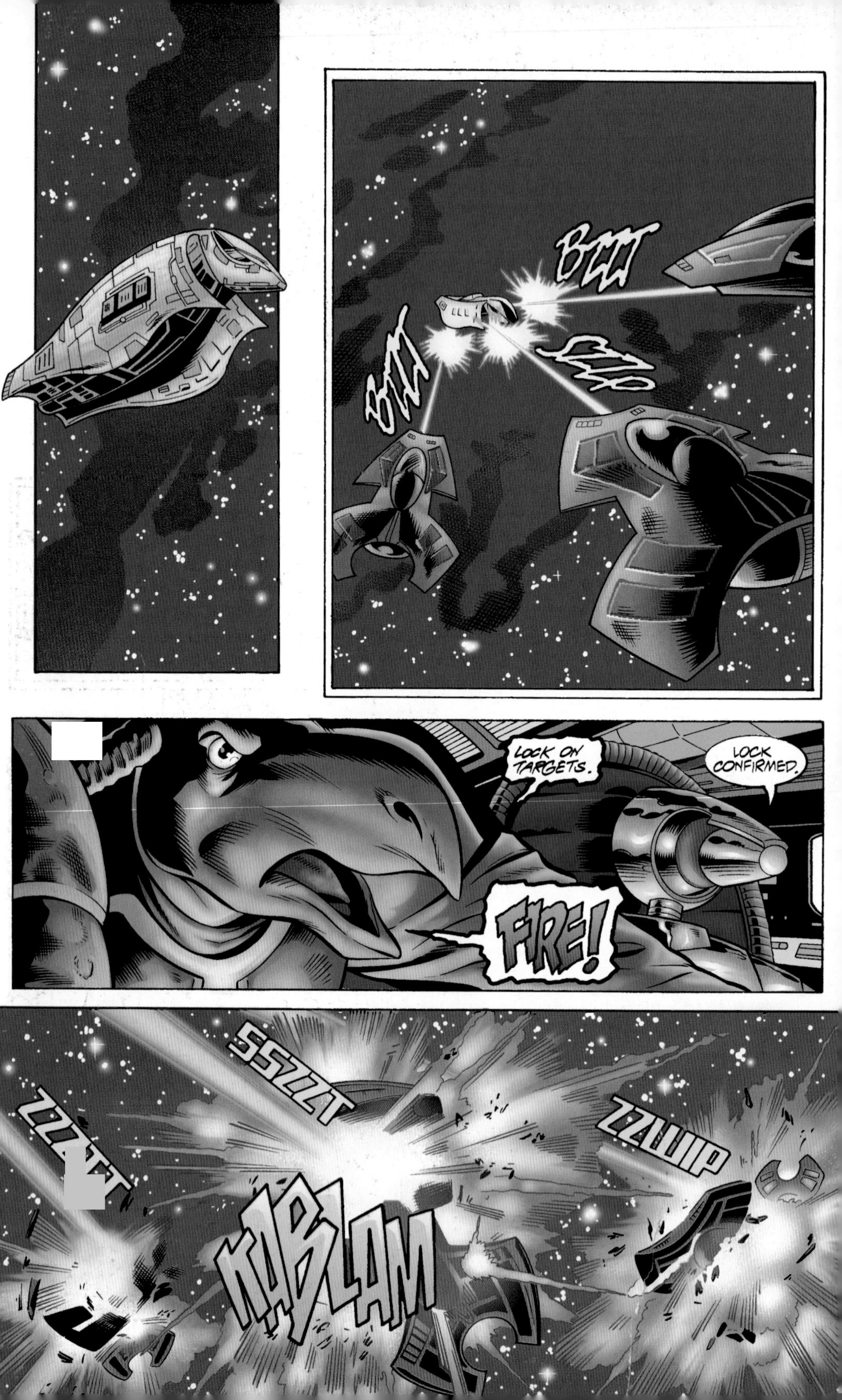

BZZT
BZZT
LOCK ON TARGETS.
LOCK CONFIRMED.
FIRE!
SSZZZT
ZZWIP
KABLAM

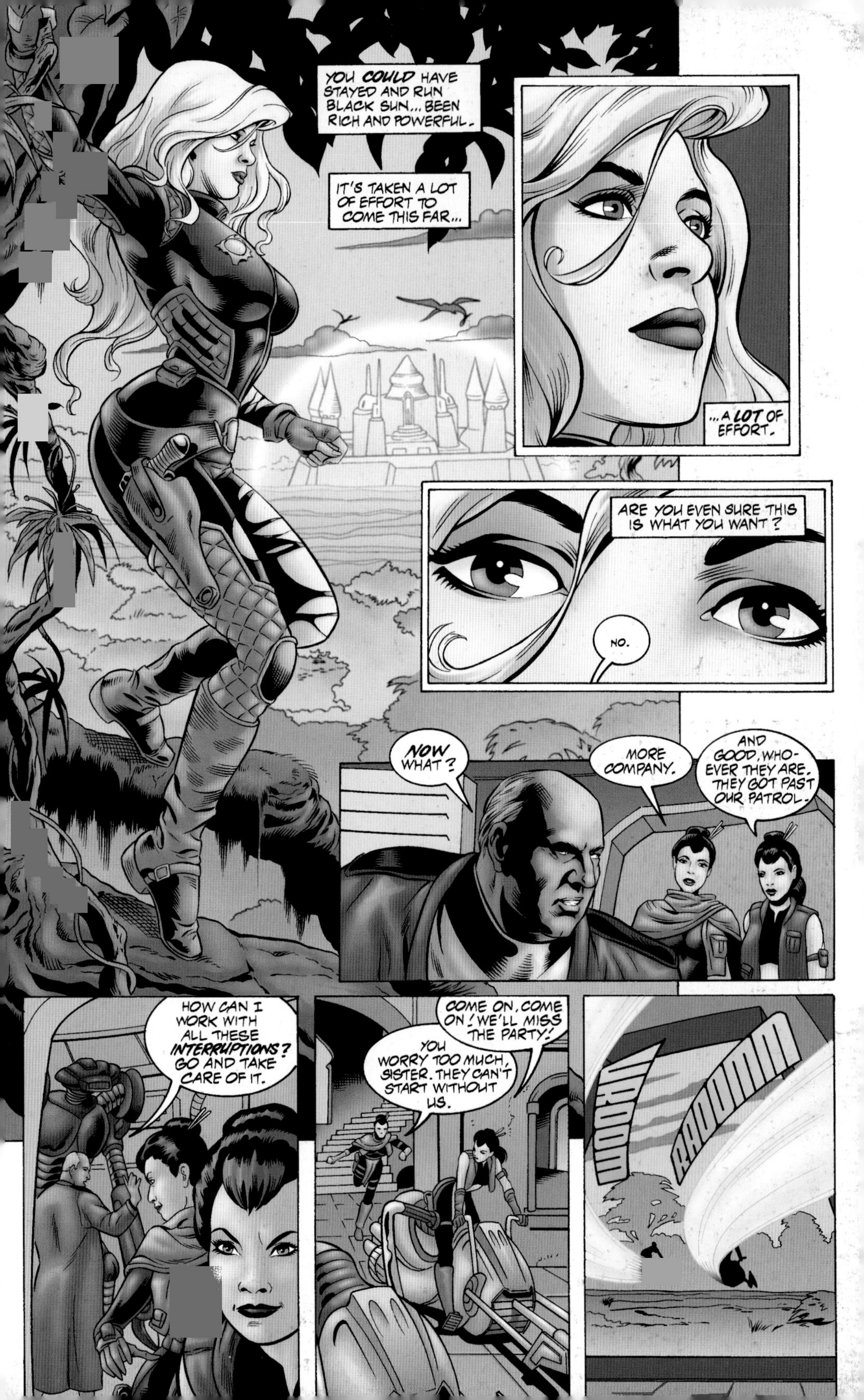
YOU COULD HAVE STAYED AND RUN BLACK SUN... BEEN RICH AND POWERFUL.
IT'S TAKEN A LOT OF EFFORT TO COME THIS FAR...
...A LOT OF EFFORT.
ARE YOU EVEN SURE THIS IS WHAT YOU WANT?
NO.
NOW WHAT?
MORE COMPANY.
AND GOOD, WHOEVER THEY ARE. THEY GOT PAST OUR PATROL.
HOW CAN I WORK WITH ALL THESE INTERRUPTIONS? GO AND TAKE CARE OF IT.
COME ON, COME ON! WE'LL MISS THE PARTY!
YOU WORRY TOO MUCH, SISTER. THEY CAN'T START WITHOUT US.
VROOM

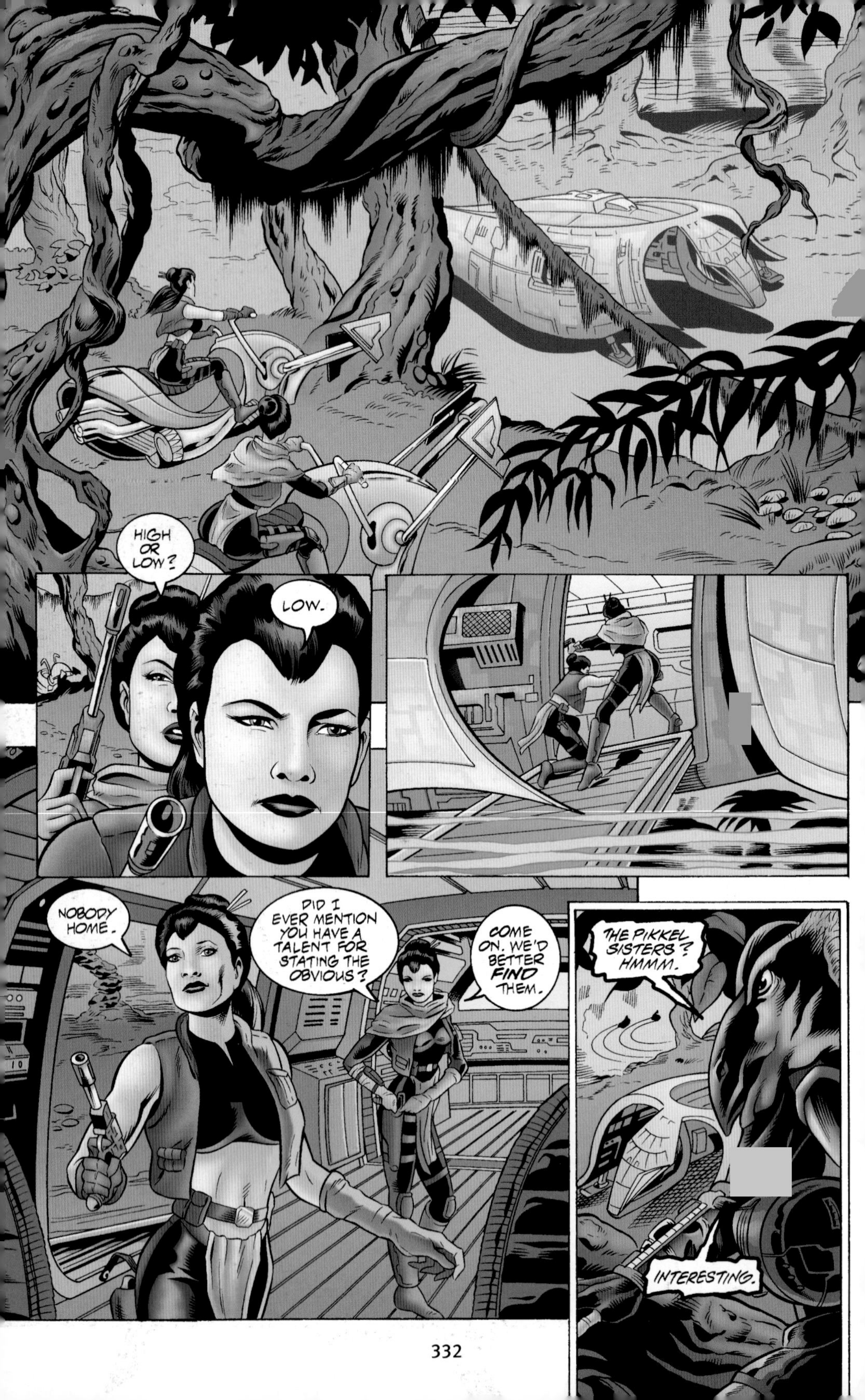
HIGH OR LOW?
LOW.
NOBODY HOME.
DID I EVER MENTION YOU HAVE A TALENT FOR STATING THE OBVIOUS?
COME ON. WE'D BETTER FIND THEM.
THE PIKKEL SISTERS? HMMM.
INTERESTING.

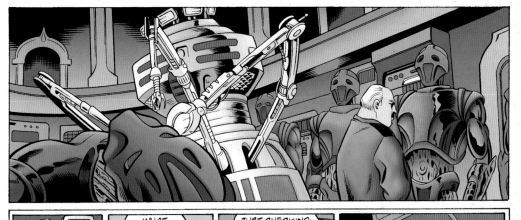

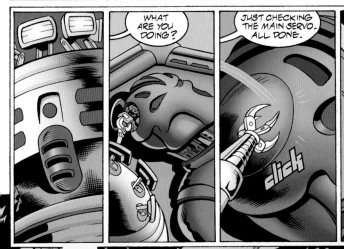

WHAT ARE YOU DOING?

JUST CHECKING THE MAIN SERVO. ALL DONE.

click

"I WONDER WHAT IS TAKING THE SISTERS SO LONG?"

BRUUMM

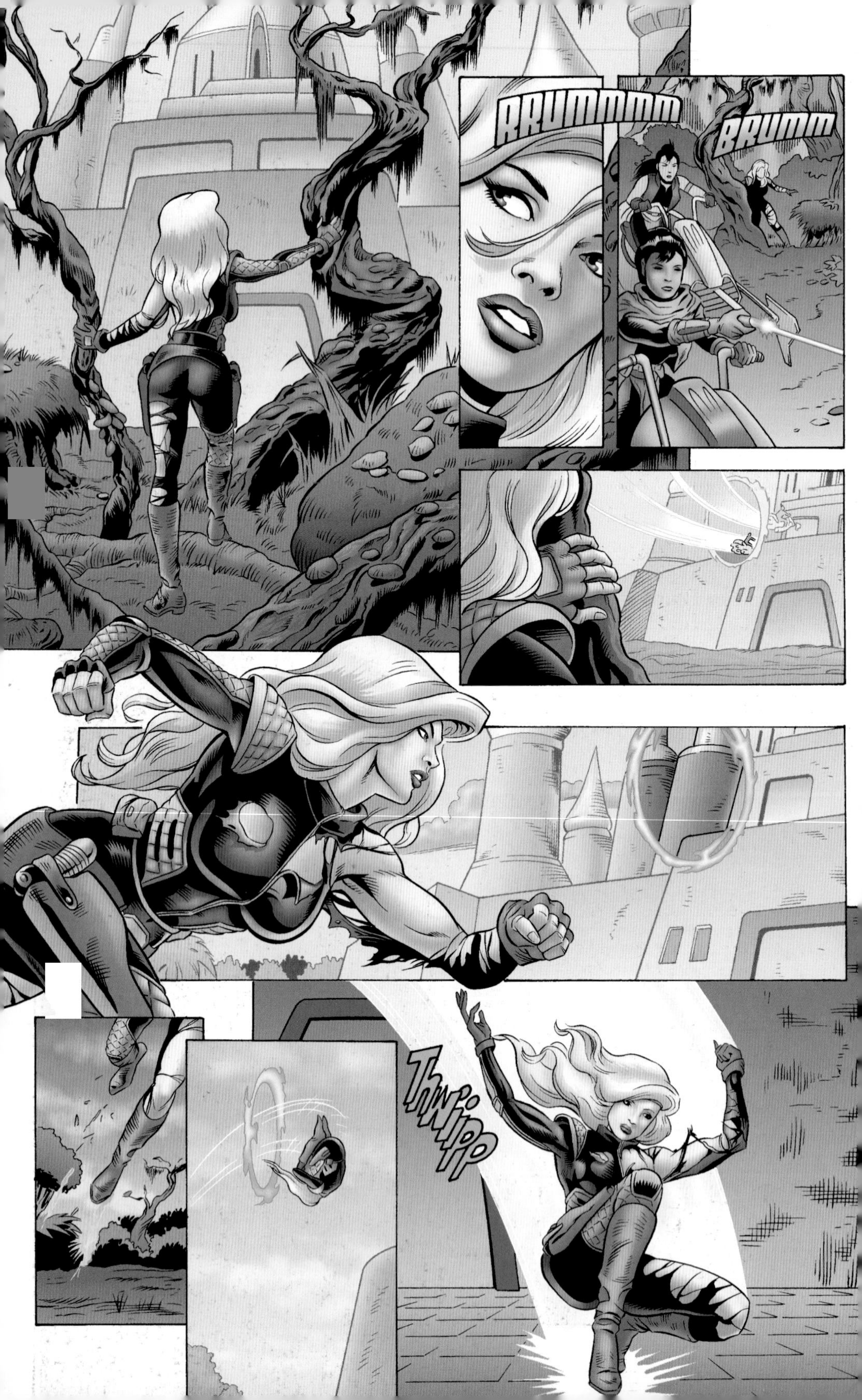
BRUMMMMM
BRUMM
THWIPP

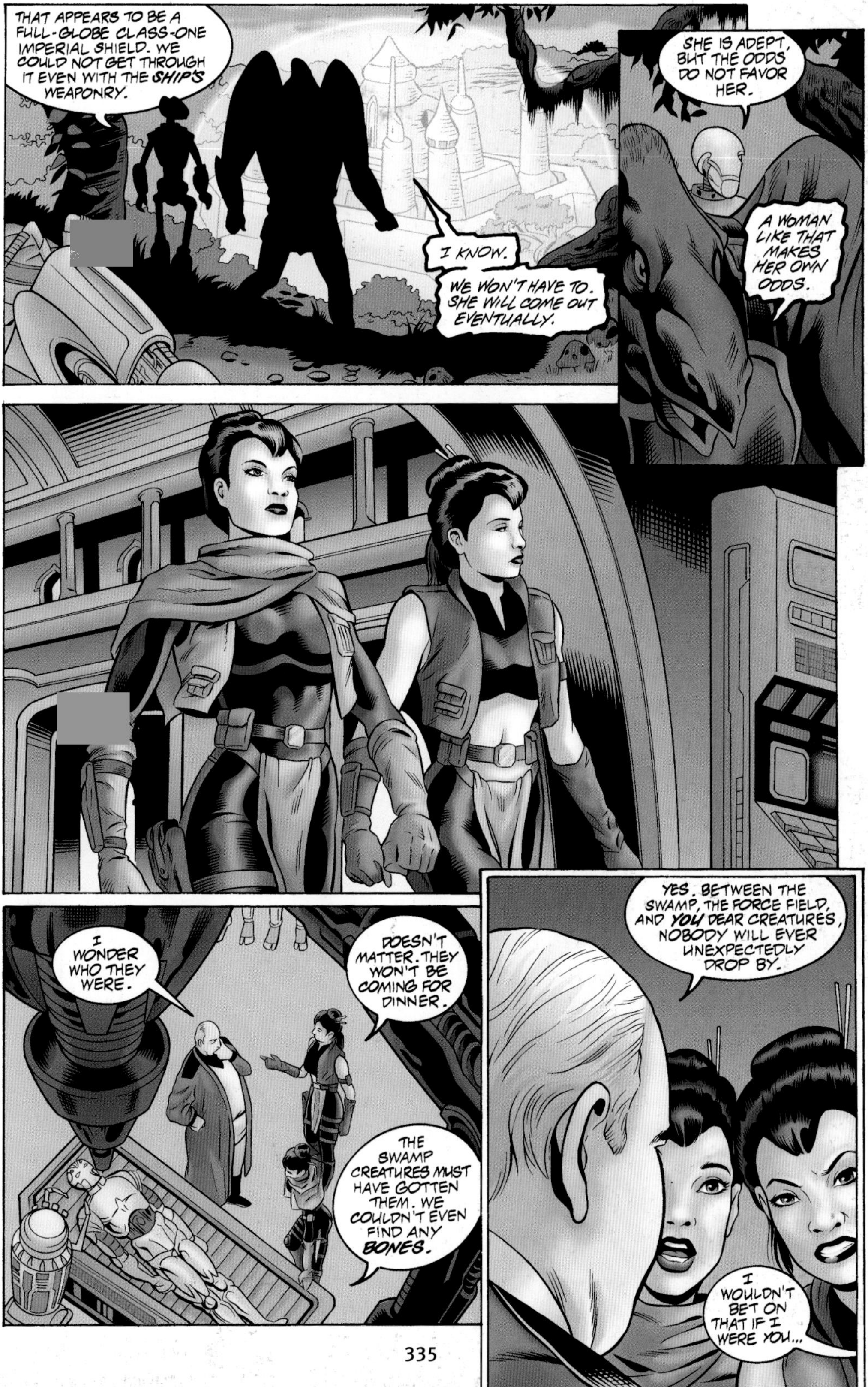
THAT APPEARS TO BE A FULL-GLOBE CLASS-ONE IMPERIAL SHIELD. WE COULD NOT GET THROUGH IT EVEN WITH THE SHIP'S WEAPONRY.
I KNOW.
WE WON'T HAVE TO. SHE WILL COME OUT EVENTUALLY.
SHE IS ADEPT, BUT THE ODDS DO NOT FAVOR HER.
A WOMAN LIKE THAT MAKES HER OWN ODDS.
I WONDER WHO THEY WERE.
DOESN'T MATTER. THEY WON'T BE COMING FOR DINNER.
THE SWAMP CREATURES MUST HAVE GOTTEN THEM. WE COULDN'T EVEN FIND ANY BONES.
YES. BETWEEN THE SWAMP, THE FORCE FIELD, AND YOU DEAR CREATURES, NOBODY WILL EVER UNEXPECTEDLY DROP BY.
I WOULDN'T BET ON THAT IF I WERE YOU...

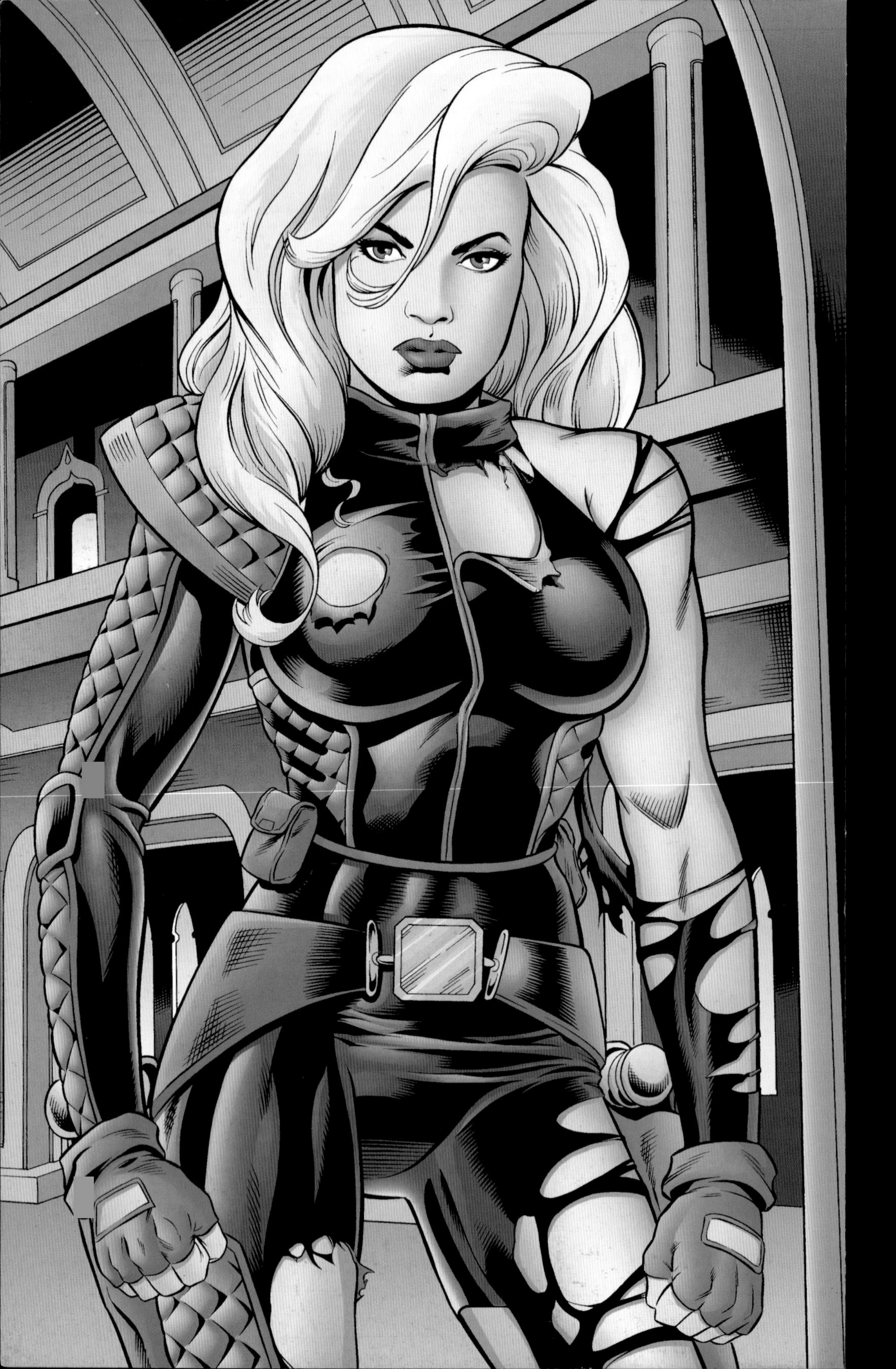

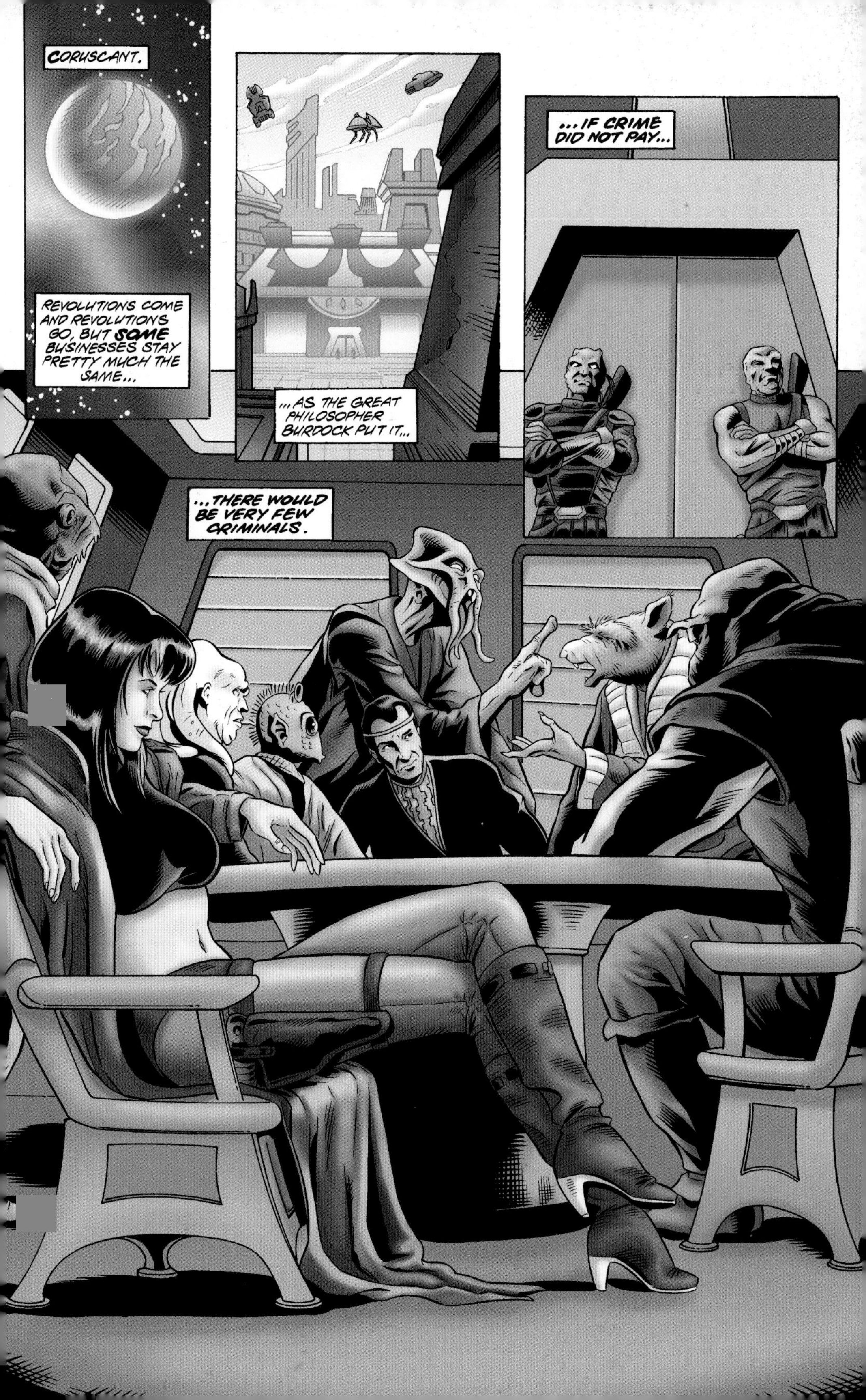
CORUSCANT.
REVOLUTIONS COME AND REVOLUTIONS GO, BUT SOME BUSINESSES STAY PRETTY MUCH THE SAME...
...AS THE GREAT PHILOSOPHER BURDOCK PUT IT...
...IF CRIME DID NOT PAY...
...THERE WOULD BE VERY FEW CRIMINALS.

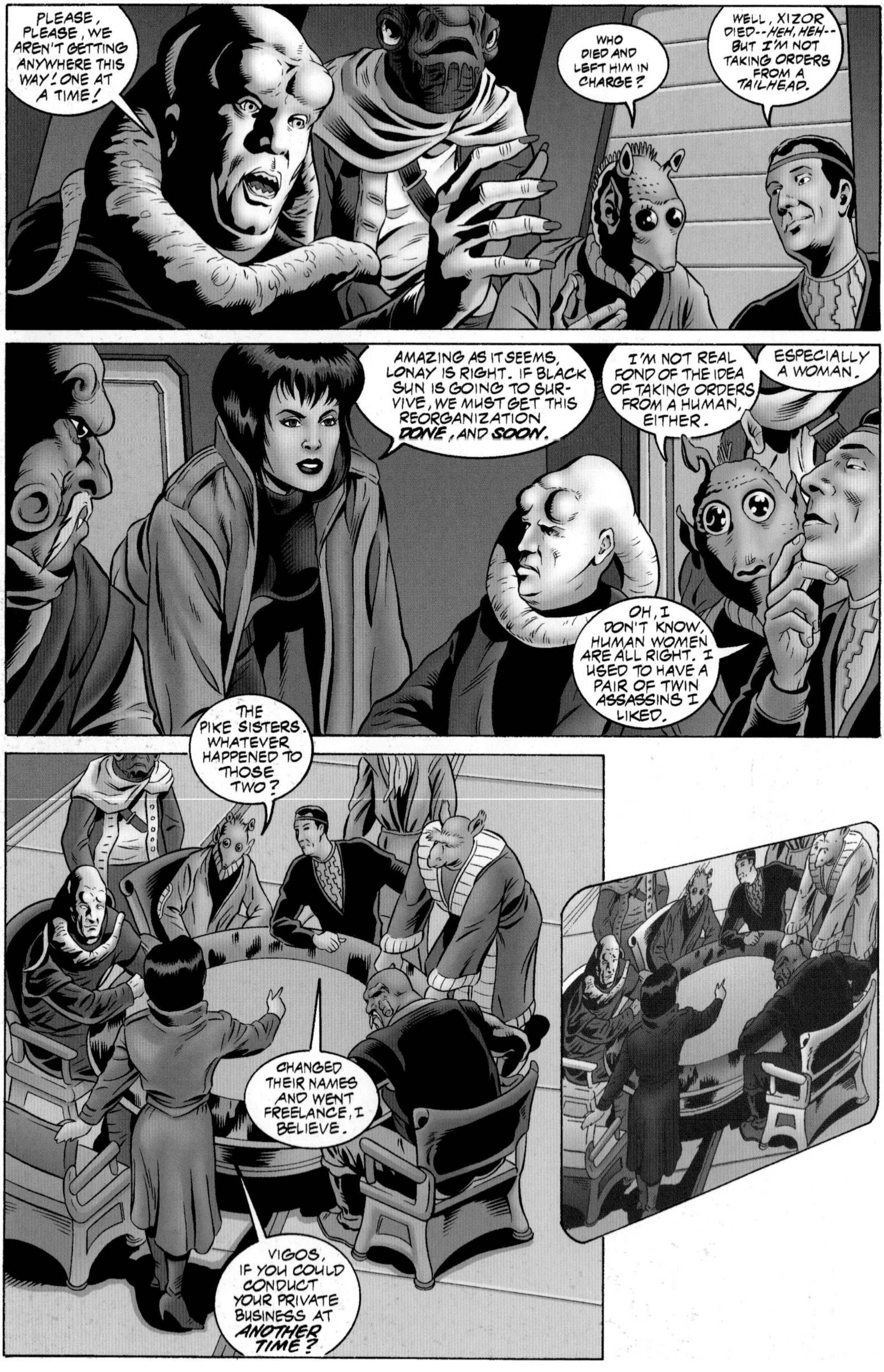
PLEASE, PLEASE, WE AREN'T GETTING ANYWHERE THIS WAY! ONE AT A TIME!
WHO DIED AND LEFT HIM IN CHARGE?
WELL, XIZOR DIED--HEH, HEH--BUT I'M NOT TAKING ORDERS FROM A TAILHEAD.
AMAZING AS IT SEEMS, LONAY IS RIGHT. IF BLACK SUN IS GOING TO SURVIVE, WE MUST GET THIS REORGANIZATION DONE, AND SOON.
I'M NOT REAL FOND OF THE IDEA OF TAKING ORDERS FROM A HUMAN, EITHER.
ESPECIALLY A WOMAN.
OH, I DON'T KNOW, HUMAN WOMEN ARE ALL RIGHT. I USED TO HAVE A PAIR OF TWIN ASSASSINS I LIKED.
THE PIKE SISTERS. WHATEVER HAPPENED TO THOSE TWO?
CHANGED THEIR NAMES AND WENT FREELANCE, I BELIEVE.
VIGOS, IF YOU COULD CONDUCT YOUR PRIVATE BUSINESS AT ANOTHER TIME?

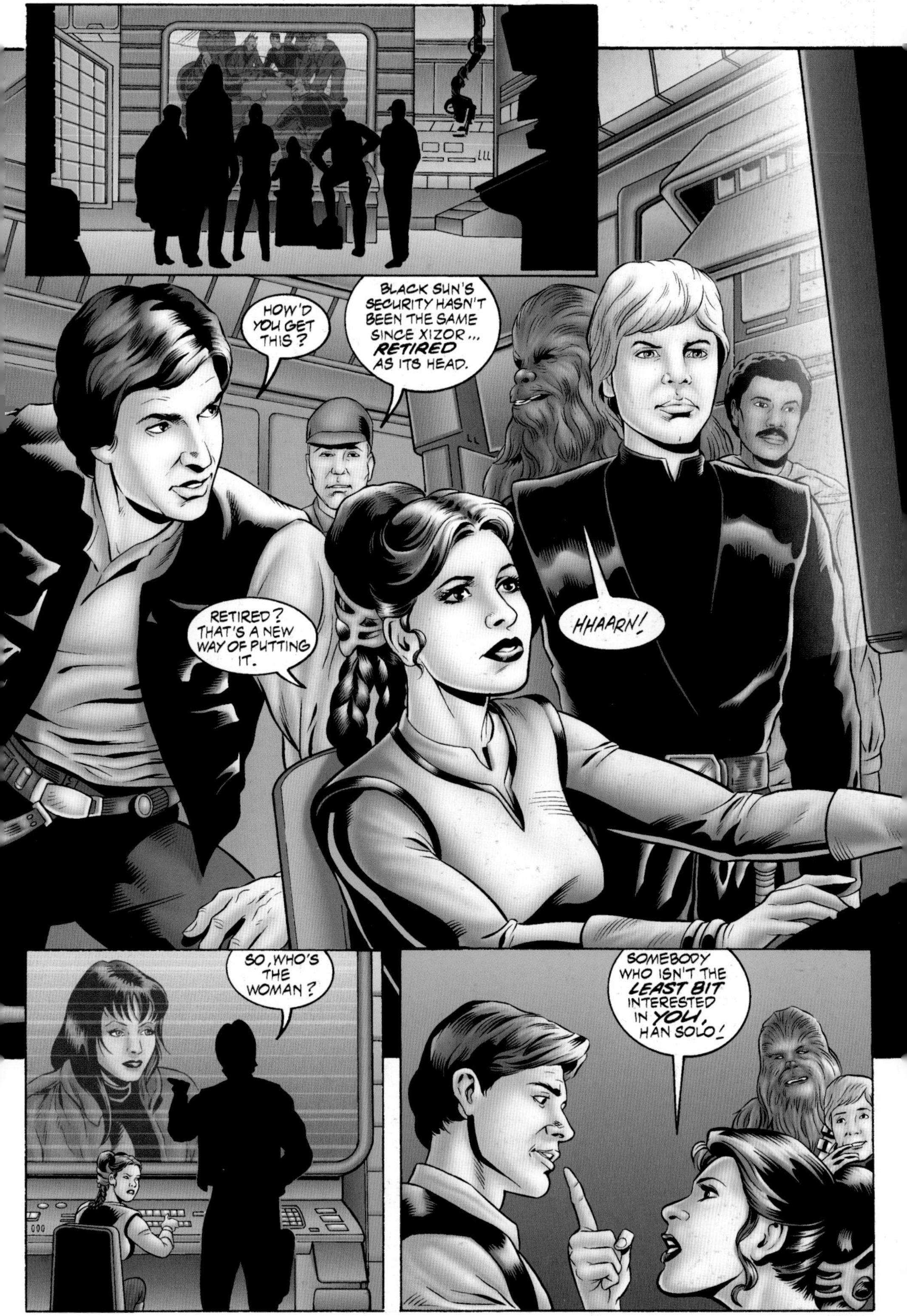
HOW'D YOU GET THIS?
BLACK SUN'S SECURITY HASN'T BEEN THE SAME SINCE XIZOR... RETIRED AS ITS HEAD.
RETIRED? THAT'S A NEW WAY OF PUTTING IT.
HHAARN!
SO, WHO'S THE WOMAN?
SOMEBODY WHO ISN'T THE LEAST BIT INTERESTED IN YOU, HAN SOLO!

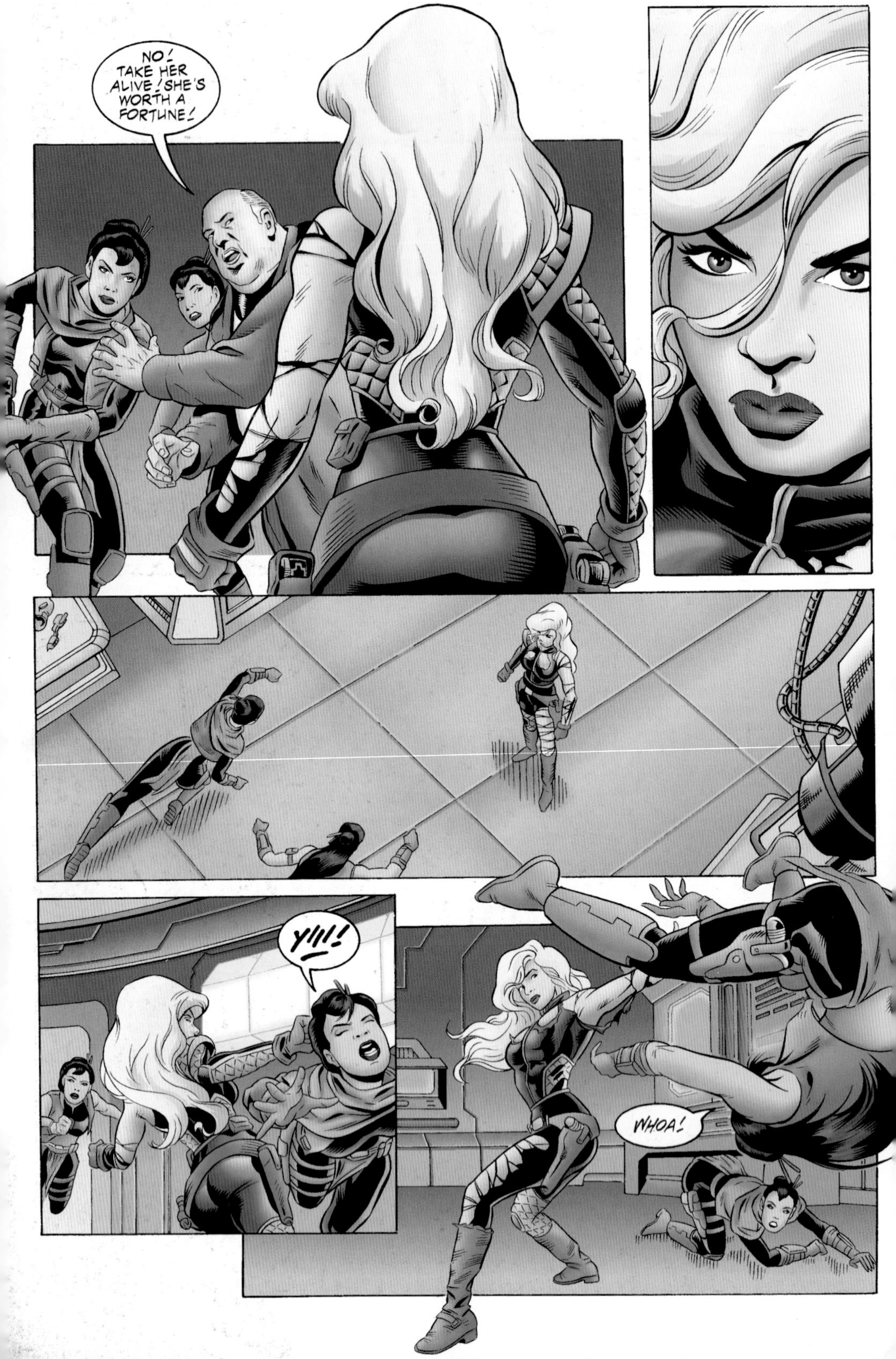
NO! TAKE HER ALIVE! SHE'S WORTH A FORTUNE!
YIII!
WHOA!

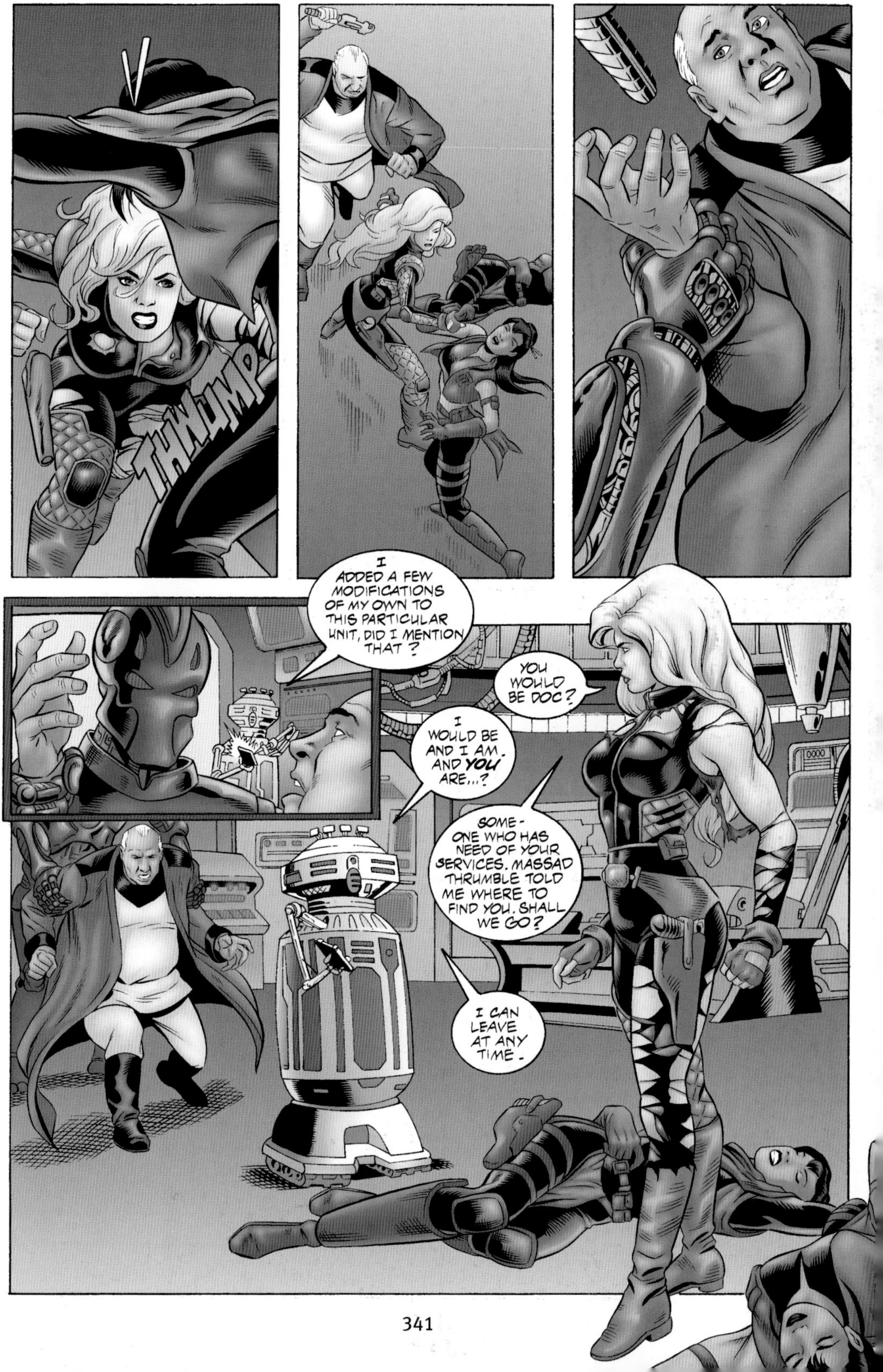
THWUMP
I ADDED A FEW MODIFICATIONS OF MY OWN TO THIS PARTICULAR UNIT, DID I MENTION THAT?
YOU WOULD BE DOC?
I WOULD BE AND I AM. AND YOU ARE...?
SOME-ONE WHO HAS NEED OF YOUR SERVICES. MASSAD THRUMBLE TOLD ME WHERE TO FIND YOU. SHALL WE GO?
I CAN LEAVE AT ANY TIME.

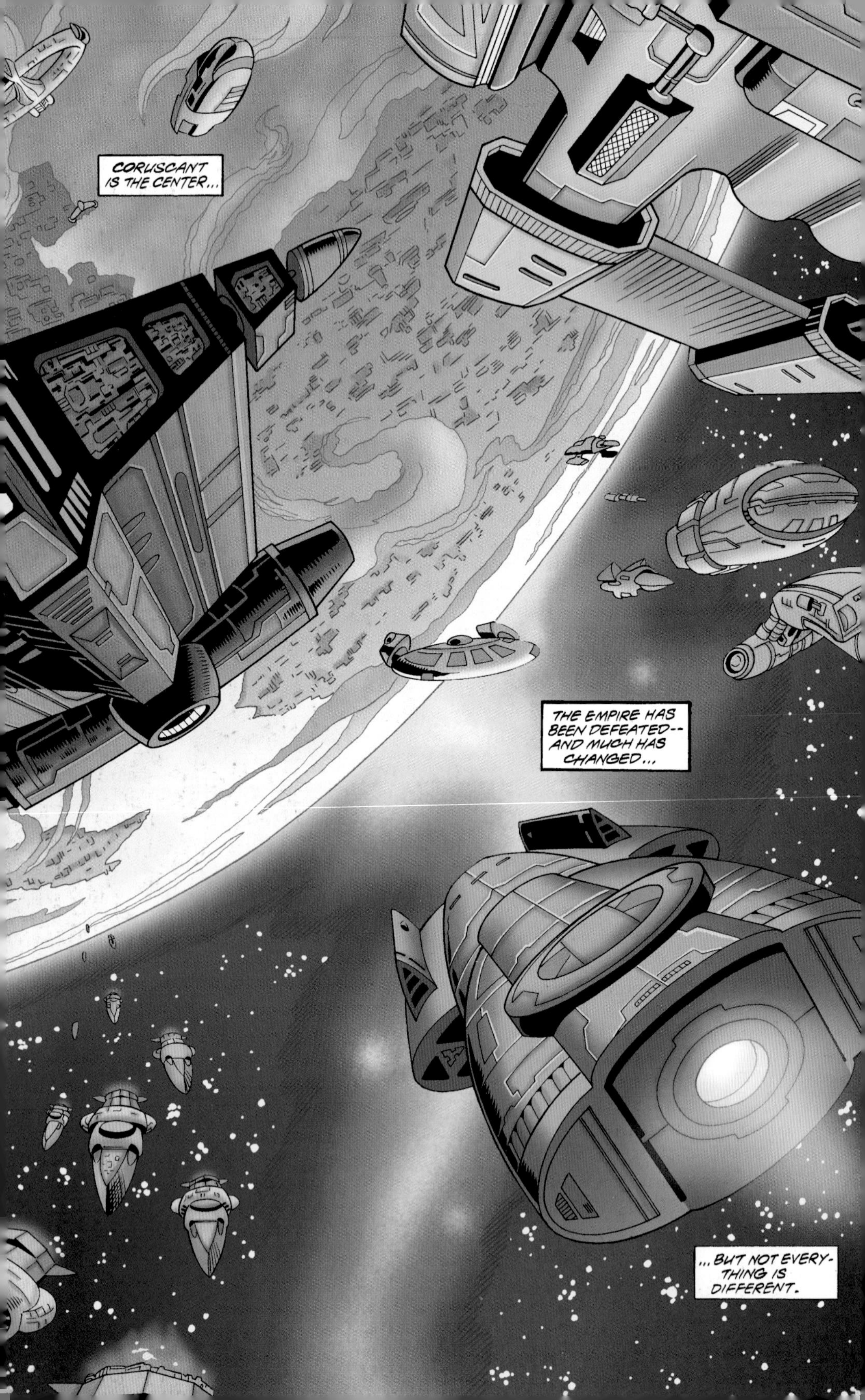
CORUSCANT IS THE CENTER...
THE EMPIRE HAS BEEN DEFEATED-- AND MUCH HAS CHANGED...
...BUT NOT EVERY-THING IS DIFFERENT.

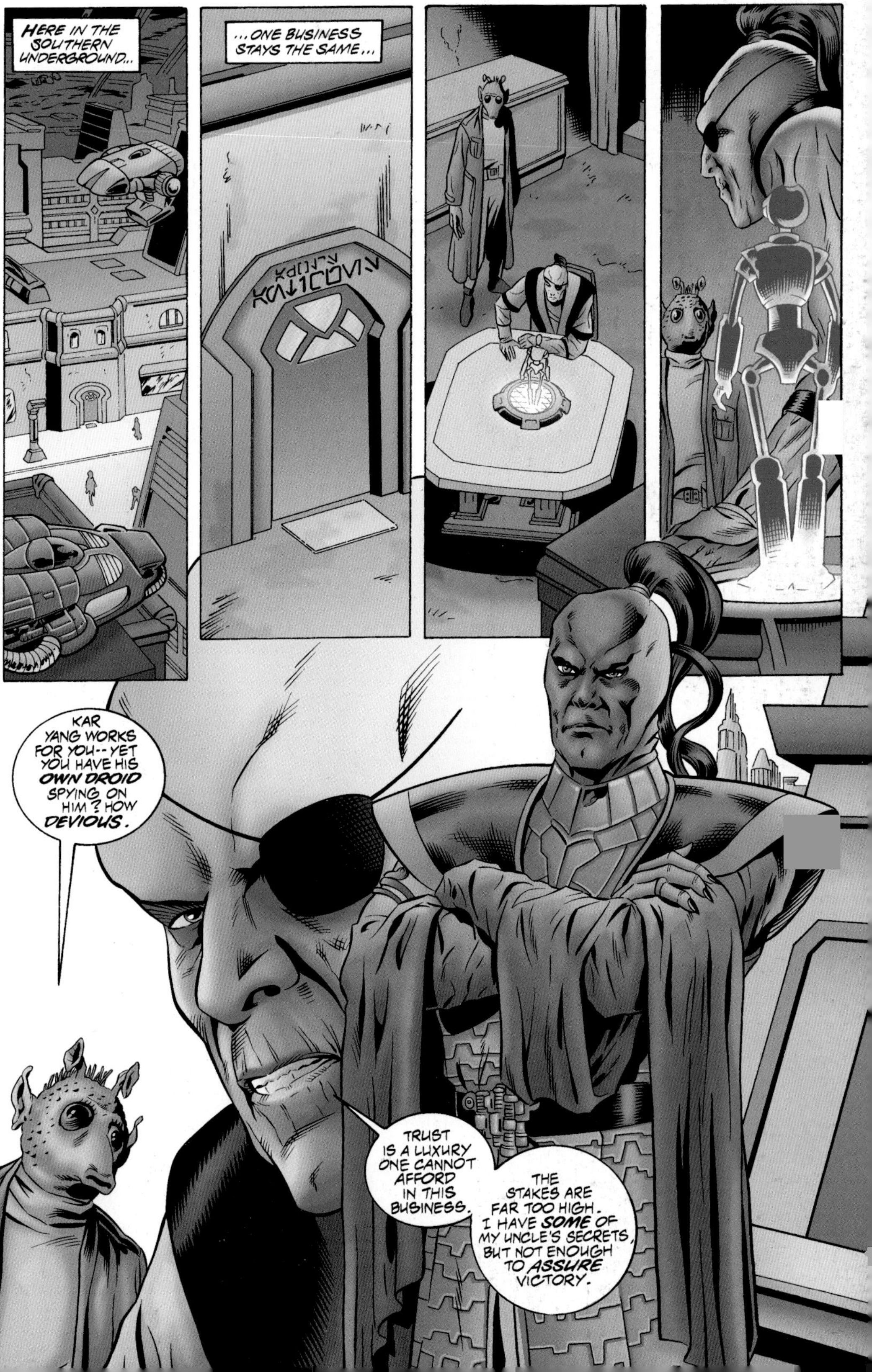
HERE IN THE SOUTHERN UNDERGROUND...
...ONE BUSINESS STAYS THE SAME...
KAR YANG WORKS FOR YOU--YET YOU HAVE HIS OWN DROID SPYING ON HIM? HOW DEVIOUS.
TRUST IS A LUXURY ONE CANNOT AFFORD IN THIS BUSINESS.
THE STAKES ARE FAR TOO HIGH. I HAVE SOME OF MY UNCLE'S SECRETS, BUT NOT ENOUGH TO ASSURE VICTORY.

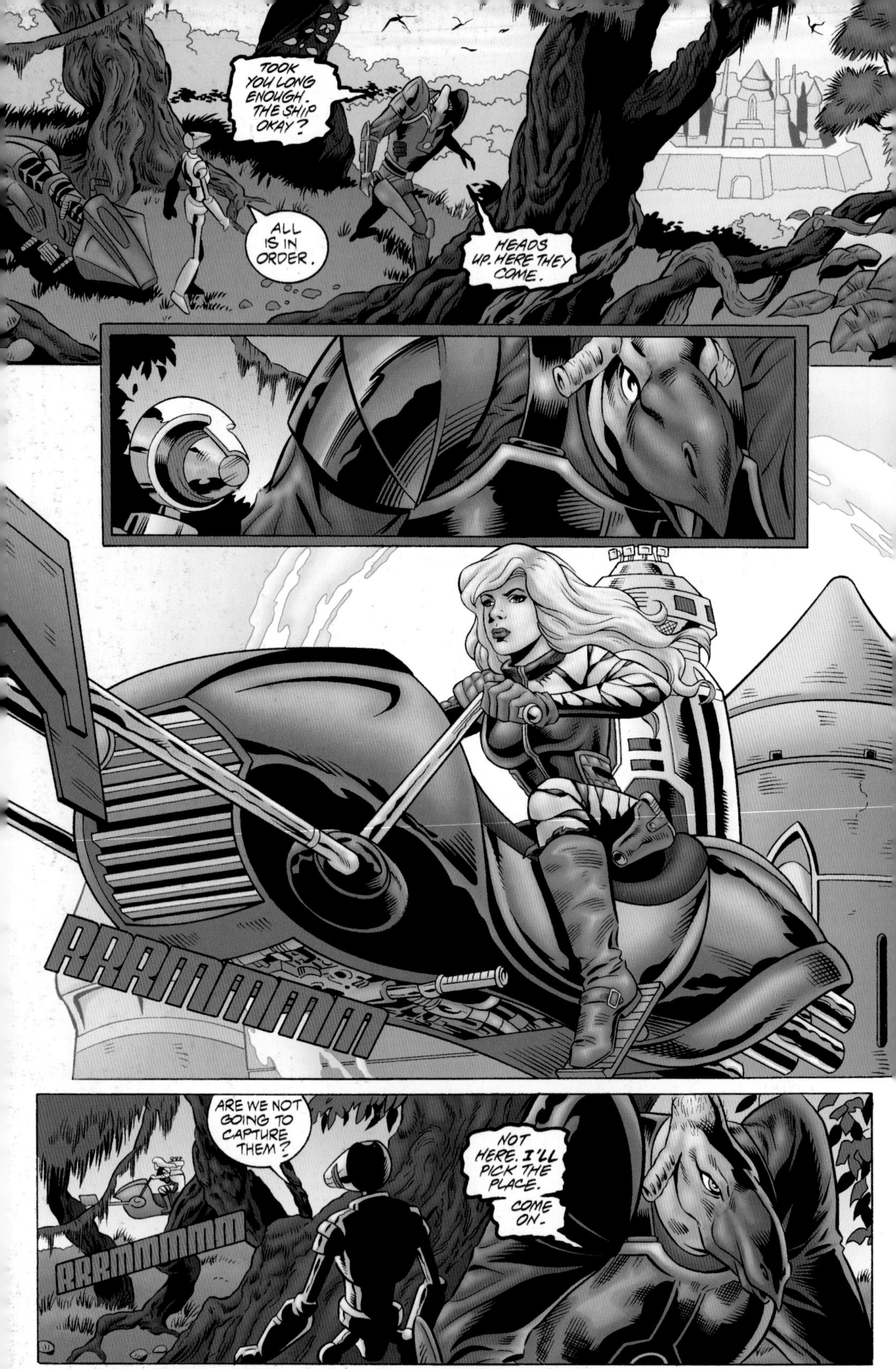
TOOK YOU LONG ENOUGH. THE SHIP OKAY?
ALL IS IN ORDER.
HEADS UP. HERE THEY COME.
RRRMMMMM
ARE WE NOT GOING TO CAPTURE THEM?
NOT HERE. I'LL PICK THE PLACE.
COME ON.
RRRMMMMM

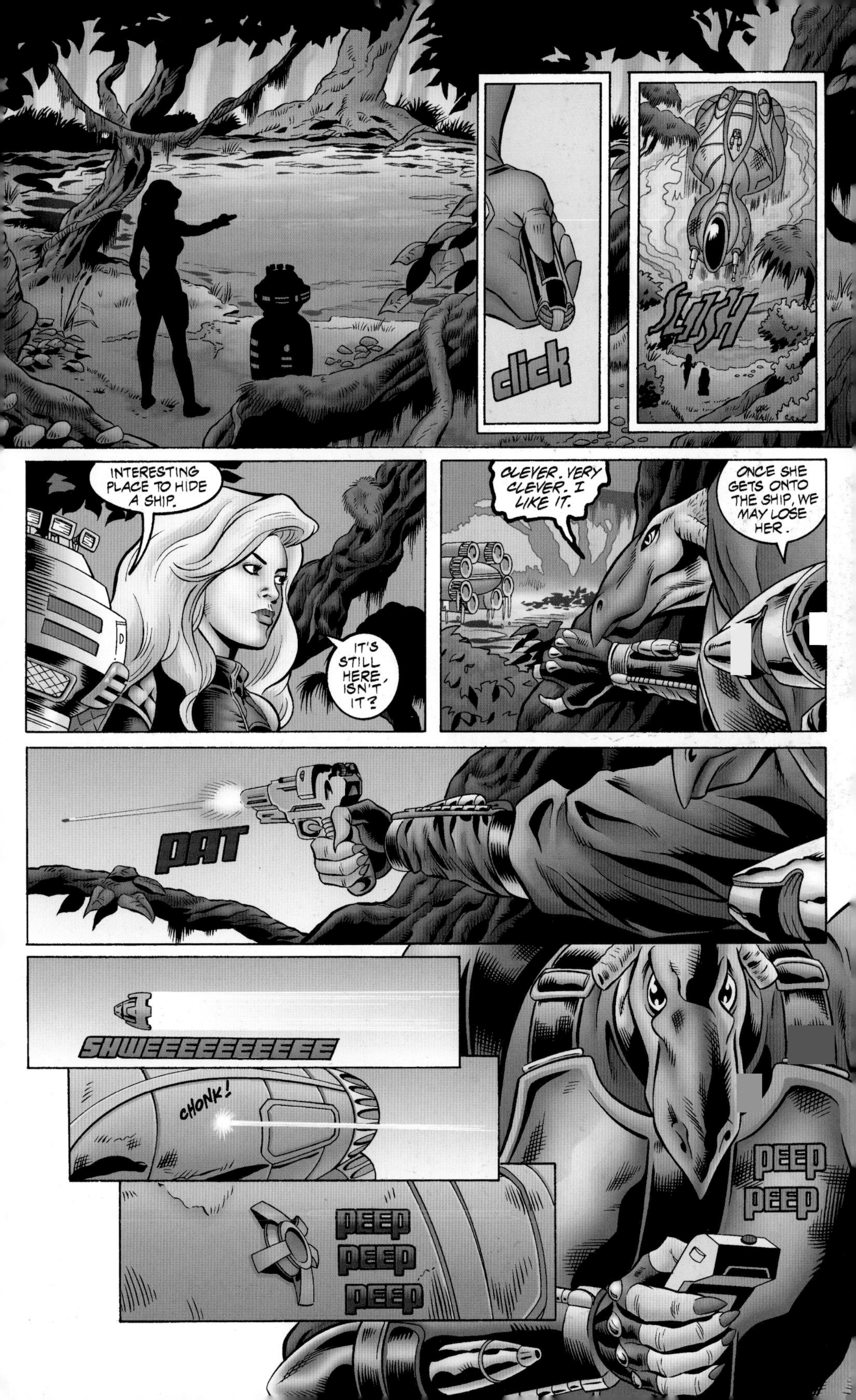
click
SLISH
INTERESTING PLACE TO HIDE A SHIP.
IT'S STILL HERE, ISN'T IT?
CLEVER. VERY CLEVER. I LIKE IT.
ONCE SHE GETS ONTO THE SHIP, WE MAY LOSE HER.
PAT
SHWEEEEEEEEEE
CHONK!
PEEP
PEEP
PEEP
PEEP
PEEP

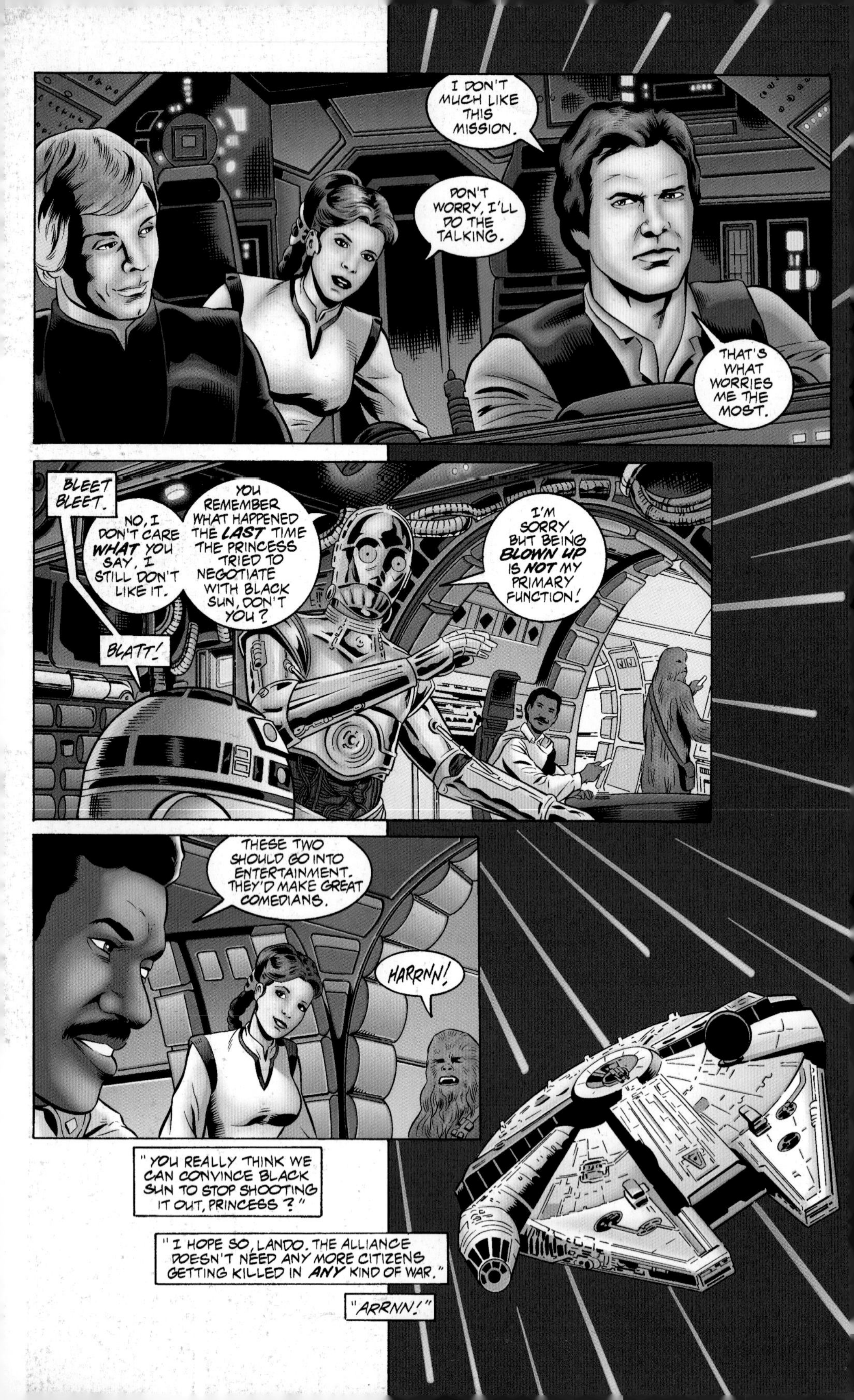

I DON'T MUCH LIKE THIS MISSION.
DON'T WORRY, I'LL DO THE TALKING.
THAT'S WHAT WORRIES ME THE MOST.
BLEET BLEET.
NO, I DON'T CARE WHAT YOU SAY, I STILL DON'T LIKE IT.
YOU REMEMBER WHAT HAPPENED THE LAST TIME THE PRINCESS TRIED TO NEGOTIATE WITH BLACK SUN, DON'T YOU?
BLATT!
I'M SORRY, BUT BEING BLOWN UP IS NOT MY PRIMARY FUNCTION!
THESE TWO SHOULD GO INTO ENTERTAINMENT. THEY'D MAKE GREAT COMEDIANS.
HARRNN!
"YOU REALLY THINK WE CAN CONVINCE BLACK SUN TO STOP SHOOTING IT OUT, PRINCESS?"
"I HOPE SO, LANDO. THE ALLIANCE DOESN'T NEED ANY MORE CITIZENS GETTING KILLED IN ANY KIND OF WAR."
"ARRNN!"

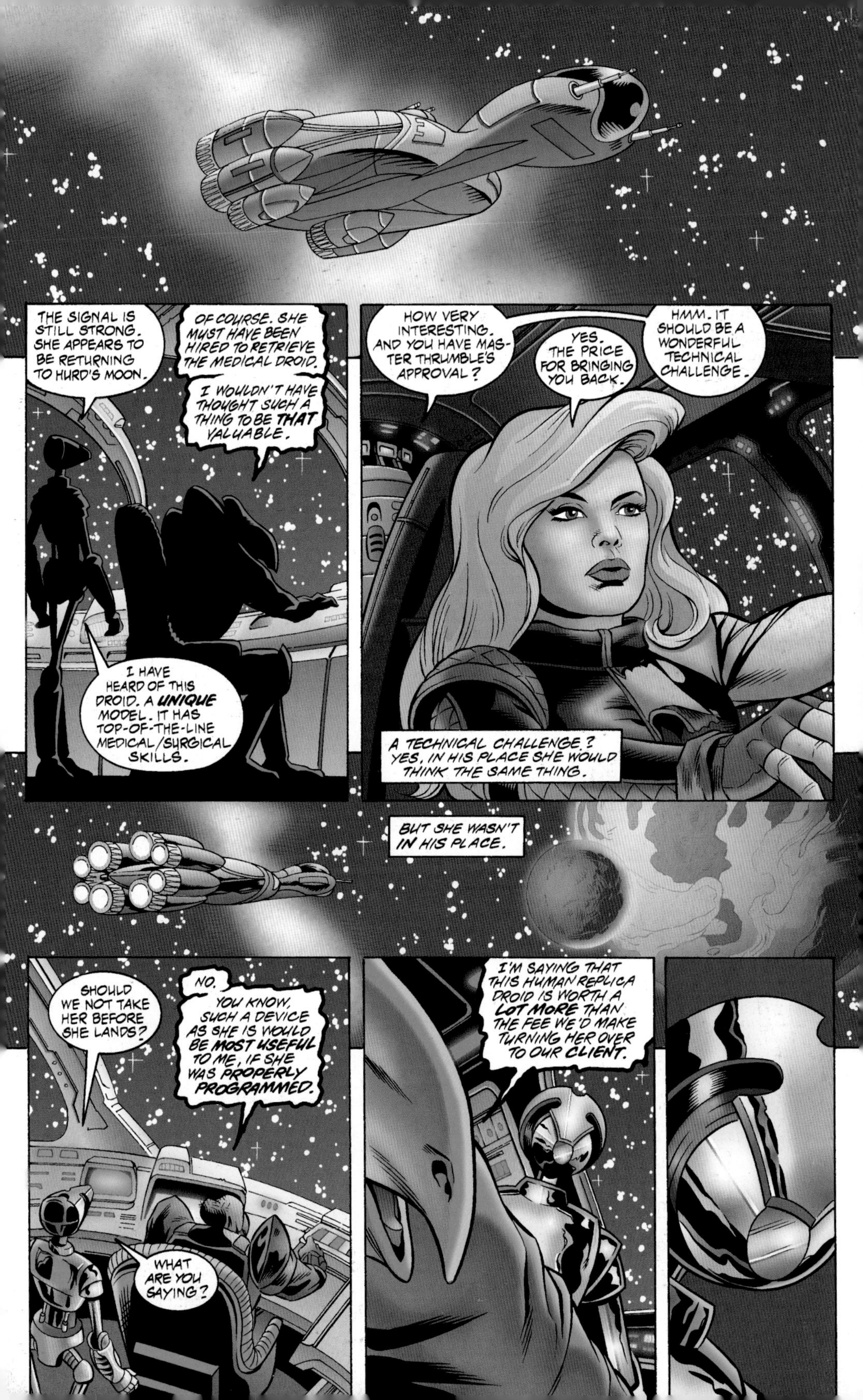
THE SIGNAL IS STILL STRONG. SHE APPEARS TO BE RETURNING TO HURD'S MOON.
OF COURSE. SHE MUST HAVE BEEN HIRED TO RETRIEVE THE MEDICAL DROID.
I WOULDN'T HAVE THOUGHT SUCH A THING TO BE THAT VALUABLE.
I HAVE HEARD OF THIS DROID. A UNIQUE MODEL. IT HAS TOP-OF-THE-LINE MEDICAL/SURGICAL SKILLS.
HOW VERY INTERESTING. AND YOU HAVE MASTER THRUMBLE'S APPROVAL?
YES. THE PRICE FOR BRINGING YOU BACK.
HMM. IT SHOULD BE A WONDERFUL TECHNICAL CHALLENGE.
A TECHNICAL CHALLENGE? YES, IN HIS PLACE SHE WOULD THINK THE SAME THING.
BUT SHE WASN'T IN HIS PLACE.
SHOULD WE NOT TAKE HER BEFORE SHE LANDS?
NO.
YOU KNOW, SUCH A DEVICE AS SHE IS WOULD BE MOST USEFUL TO ME, IF SHE WAS PROPERLY PROGRAMMED.
WHAT ARE YOU SAYING?
I'M SAYING THAT THIS HUMAN REPLICA DROID IS WORTH A LOT MORE THAN THE FEE WE'D MAKE TURNING HER OVER TO OUR CLIENT.

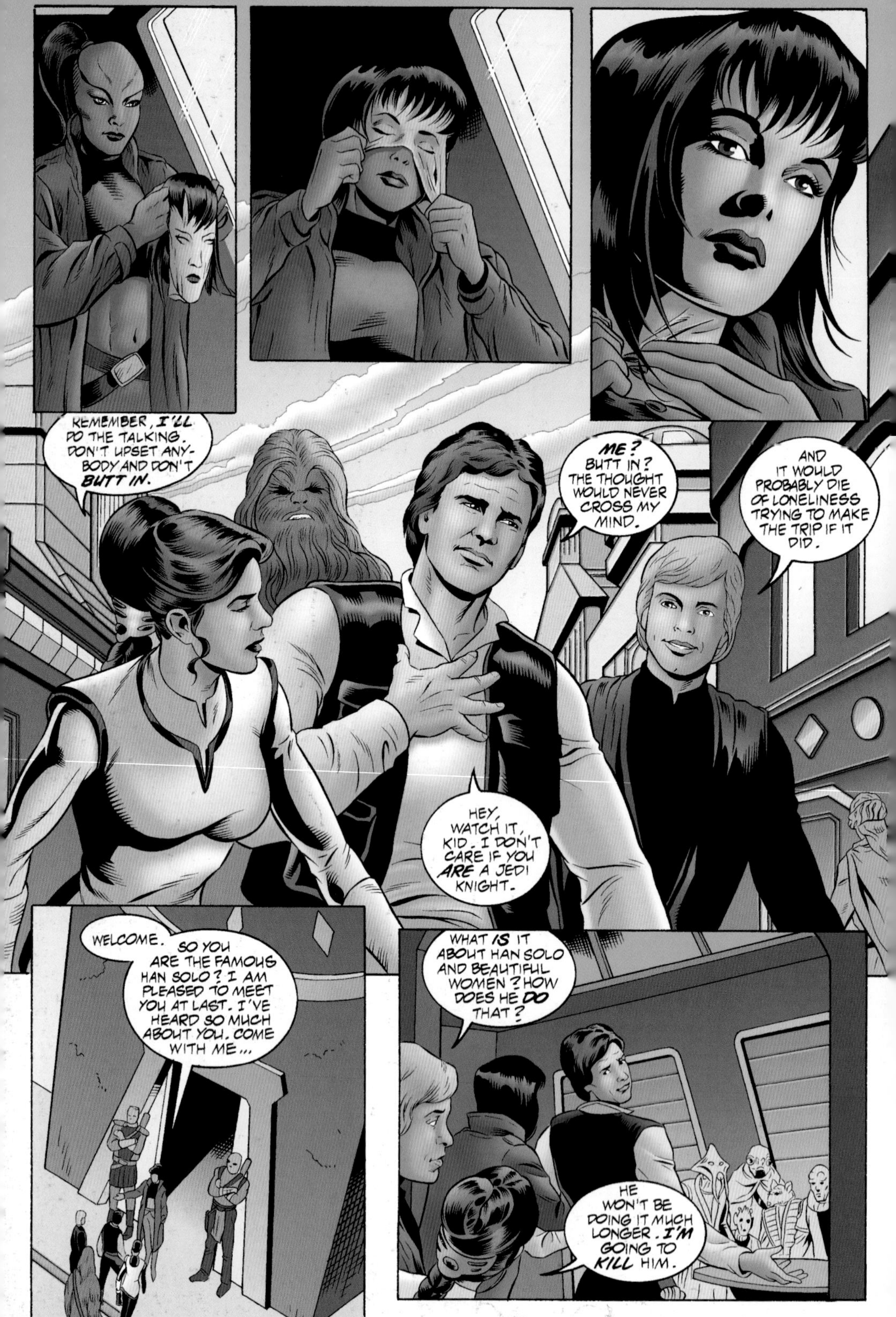
REMEMBER, I'LL DO THE TALKING. DON'T UPSET ANYBODY AND DON'T BUTT IN.
ME? BUTT IN? THE THOUGHT WOULD NEVER CROSS MY MIND.
AND IT WOULD PROBABLY DIE OF LONELINESS TRYING TO MAKE THE TRIP IF IT DID.
HEY, WATCH IT, KID. I DON'T CARE IF YOU ARE A JEDI KNIGHT.
WELCOME.
SO YOU ARE THE FAMOUS HAN SOLO? I AM PLEASED TO MEET YOU AT LAST. I'VE HEARD SO MUCH ABOUT YOU. COME WITH ME...
WHAT IS IT ABOUT HAN SOLO AND BEAUTIFUL WOMEN? HOW DOES HE DO THAT?
HE WON'T BE DOING IT MUCH LONGER. I'M GOING TO KILL HIM.

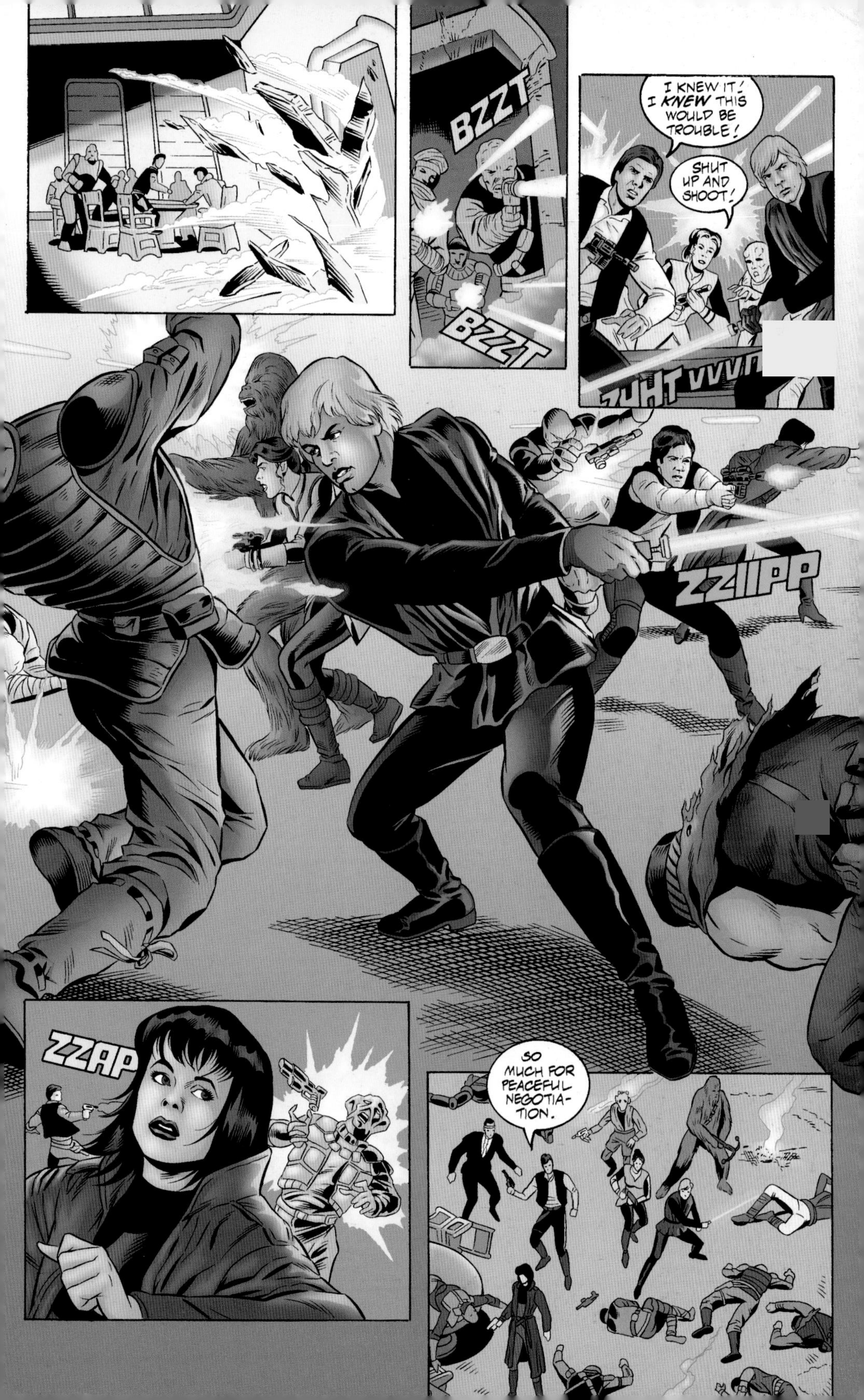
BZZT
BZZT
I KNEW IT! I KNEW THIS WOULD BE TROUBLE!
SHUT UP AND SHOOT!
ZUHT VVVM
ZZIIPP
ZZAP
SO MUCH FOR PEACEFUL NEGOTIA-TION.

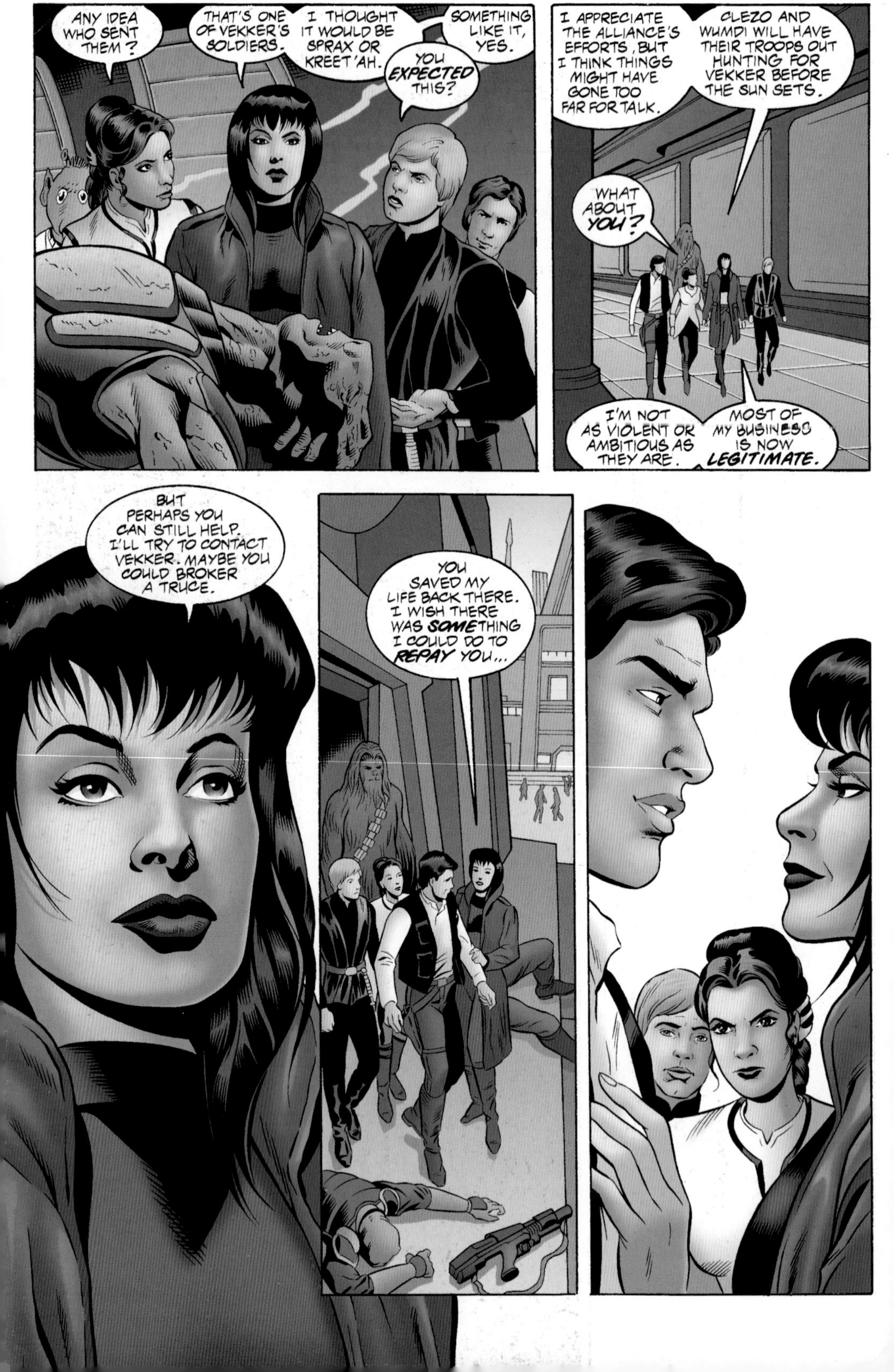
ANY IDEA WHO SENT THEM?
THAT'S ONE OF VEKKER'S SOLDIERS.
I THOUGHT IT WOULD BE SPRAX OR KREET'AH.
YOU EXPECTED THIS?
SOMETHING LIKE IT, YES.
I APPRECIATE THE ALLIANCE'S EFFORTS, BUT I THINK THINGS MIGHT HAVE GONE TOO FAR FOR TALK.
CLEZO AND WUMDI WILL HAVE THEIR TROOPS OUT HUNTING FOR VEKKER BEFORE THE SUN SETS.
WHAT ABOUT YOU?
I'M NOT AS VIOLENT OR AMBITIOUS AS THEY ARE.
MOST OF MY BUSINESS IS NOW LEGITIMATE.
BUT PERHAPS YOU CAN STILL HELP. I'LL TRY TO CONTACT VEKKER. MAYBE YOU COULD BROKER A TRUCE.
YOU SAVED MY LIFE BACK THERE. I WISH THERE WAS SOMETHING I COULD DO TO REPAY YOU...

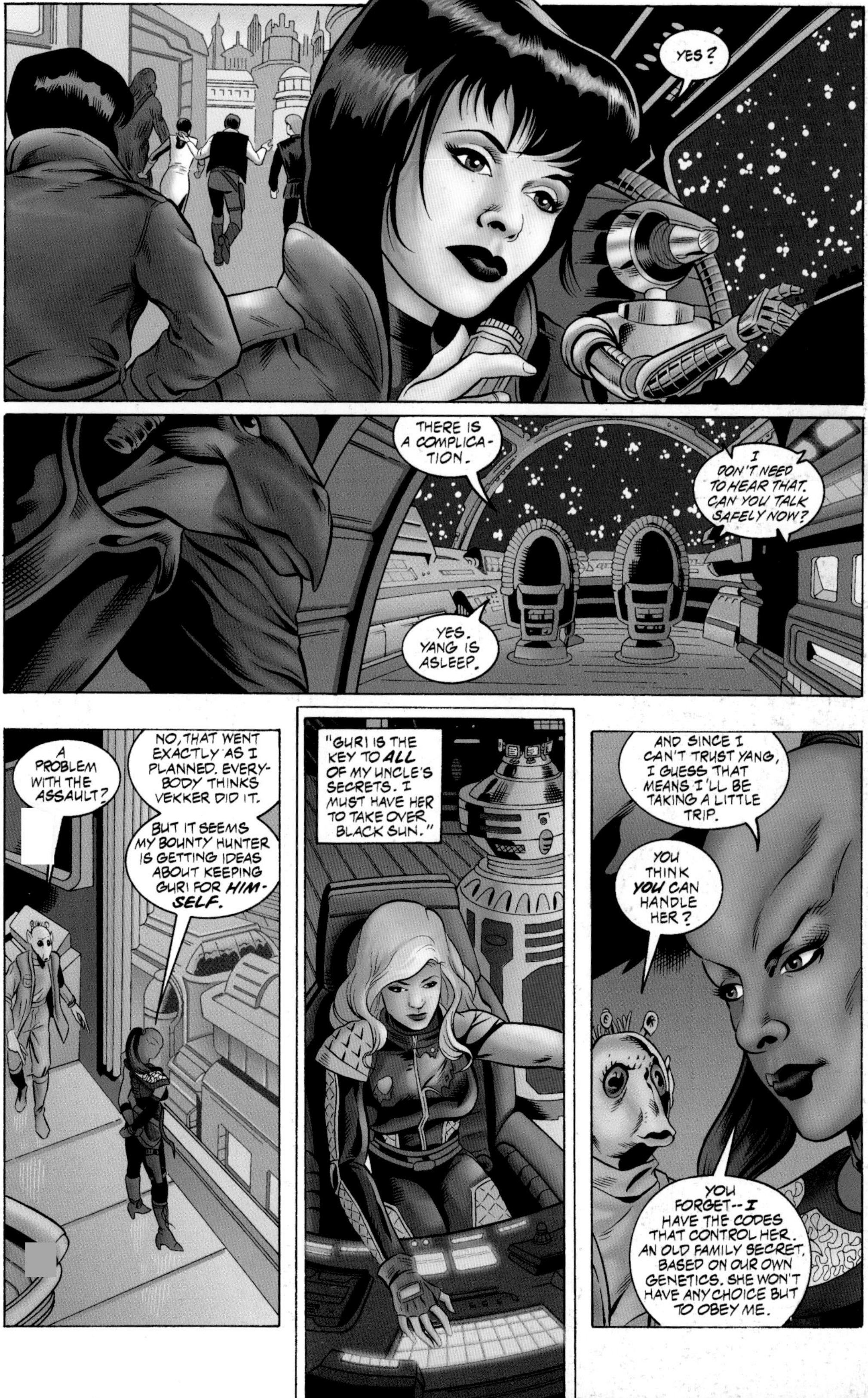
YES?
THERE IS A COMPLICATION.
I DON'T NEED TO HEAR THAT. CAN YOU TALK SAFELY NOW?
YES. YANG IS ASLEEP.
A PROBLEM WITH THE ASSAULT?
NO, THAT WENT EXACTLY AS I PLANNED. EVERYBODY THINKS VEKKER DID IT.
BUT IT SEEMS MY BOUNTY HUNTER IS GETTING IDEAS ABOUT KEEPING GURI FOR HIMSELF.
"GURI IS THE KEY TO ALL OF MY UNCLE'S SECRETS. I MUST HAVE HER TO TAKE OVER BLACK SUN."
AND SINCE I CAN'T TRUST YANG, I GUESS THAT MEANS I'LL BE TAKING A LITTLE TRIP.
YOU THINK YOU CAN HANDLE HER?
YOU FORGET-- I HAVE THE CODES THAT CONTROL HER. AN OLD FAMILY SECRET, BASED ON OUR OWN GENETICS. SHE WON'T HAVE ANY CHOICE BUT TO OBEY ME.

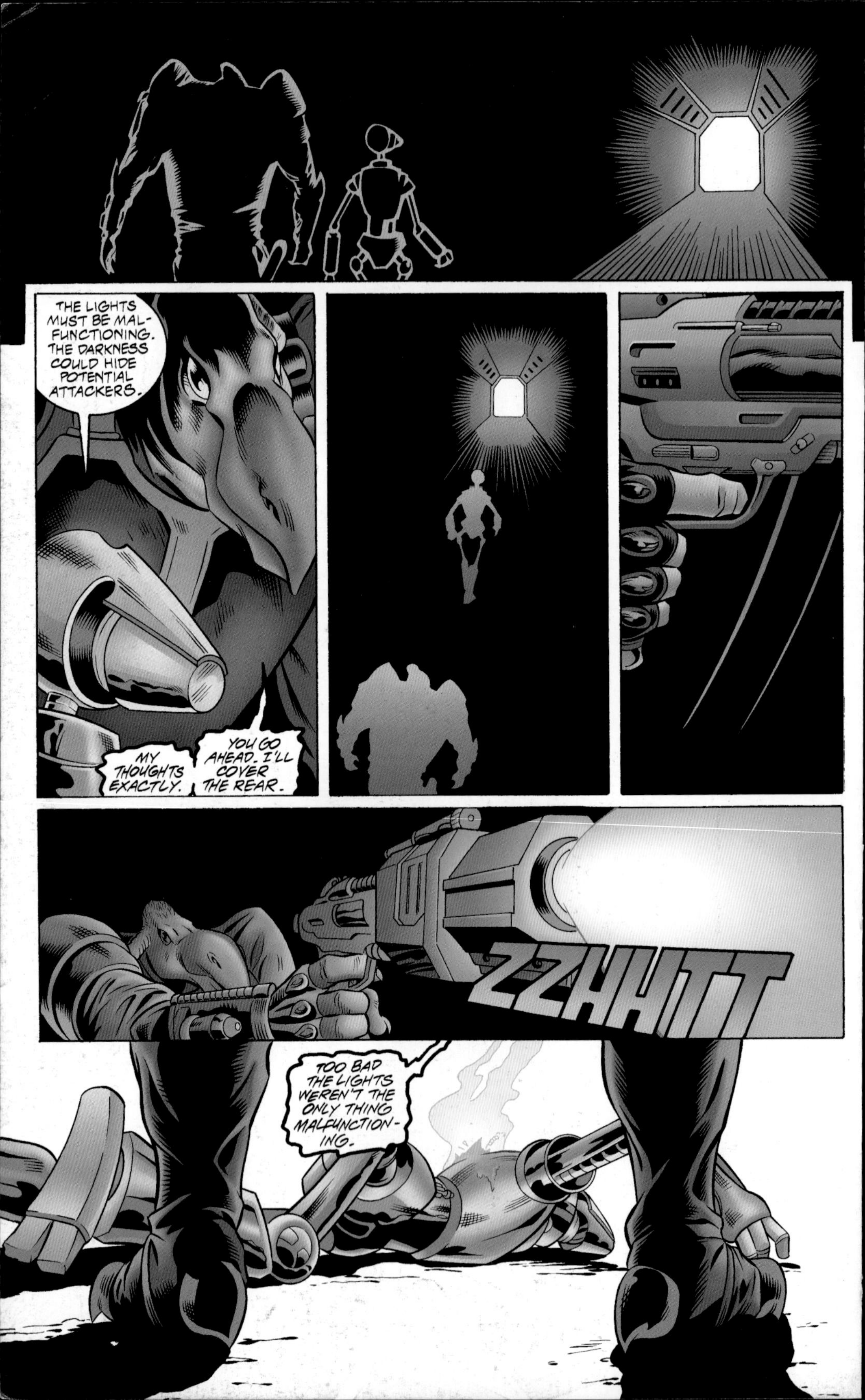
THE LIGHTS MUST BE MAL-FUNCTIONING. THE DARKNESS COULD HIDE POTENTIAL ATTACKERS.
MY THOUGHTS EXACTLY.
YOU GO AHEAD. I'LL COVER THE REAR.
ZZHHTT
TOO BAD THE LIGHTS WEREN'T THE ONLY THING MALFUNCTION-ING.

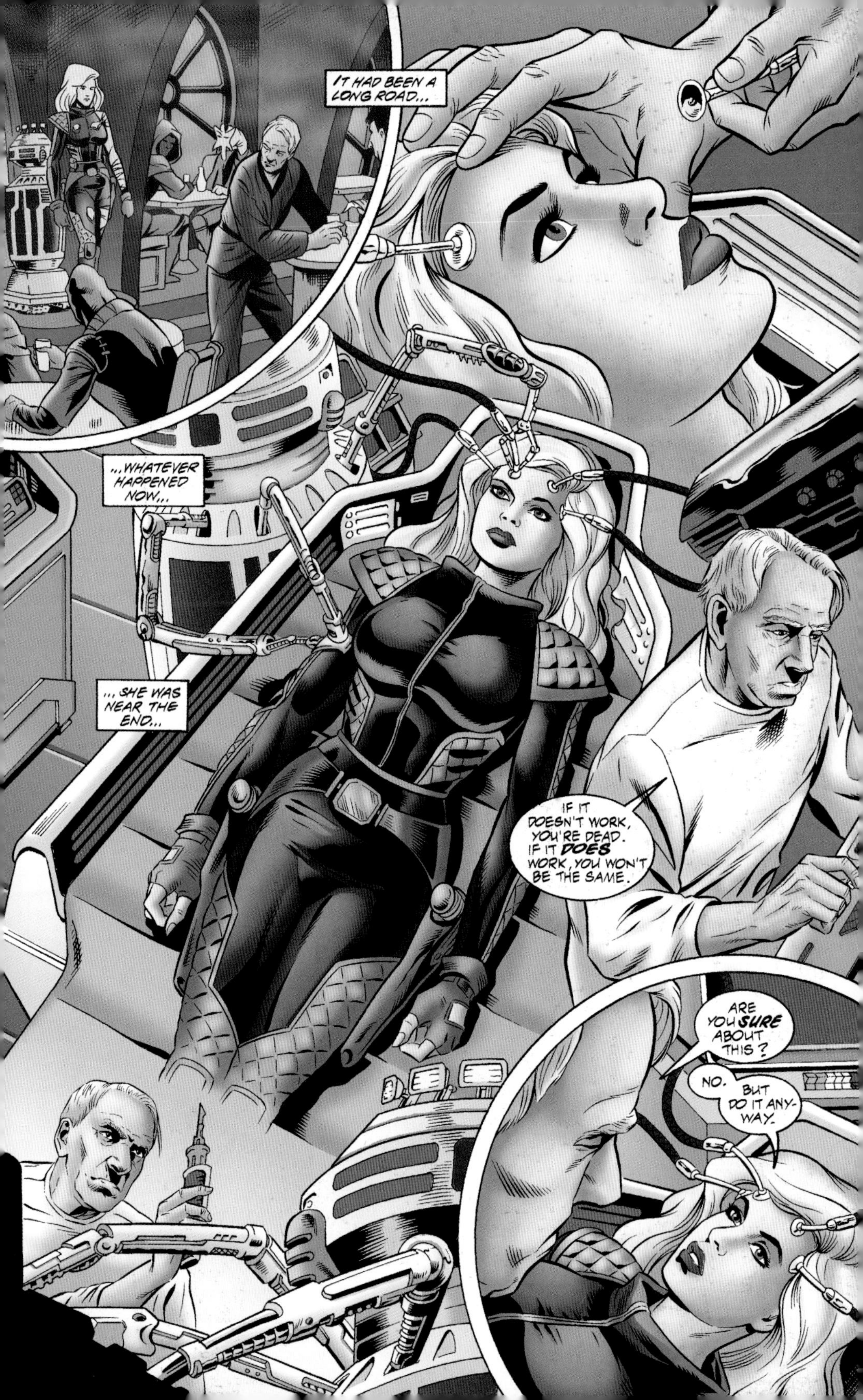
IT HAD BEEN A LONG ROAD...
...WHATEVER HAPPENED NOW...
...SHE WAS NEAR THE END...
IF IT DOESN'T WORK, YOU'RE DEAD. IF IT DOES WORK, YOU WON'T BE THE SAME.
ARE YOU SURE ABOUT THIS?
NO.
BUT DO IT ANYWAY.

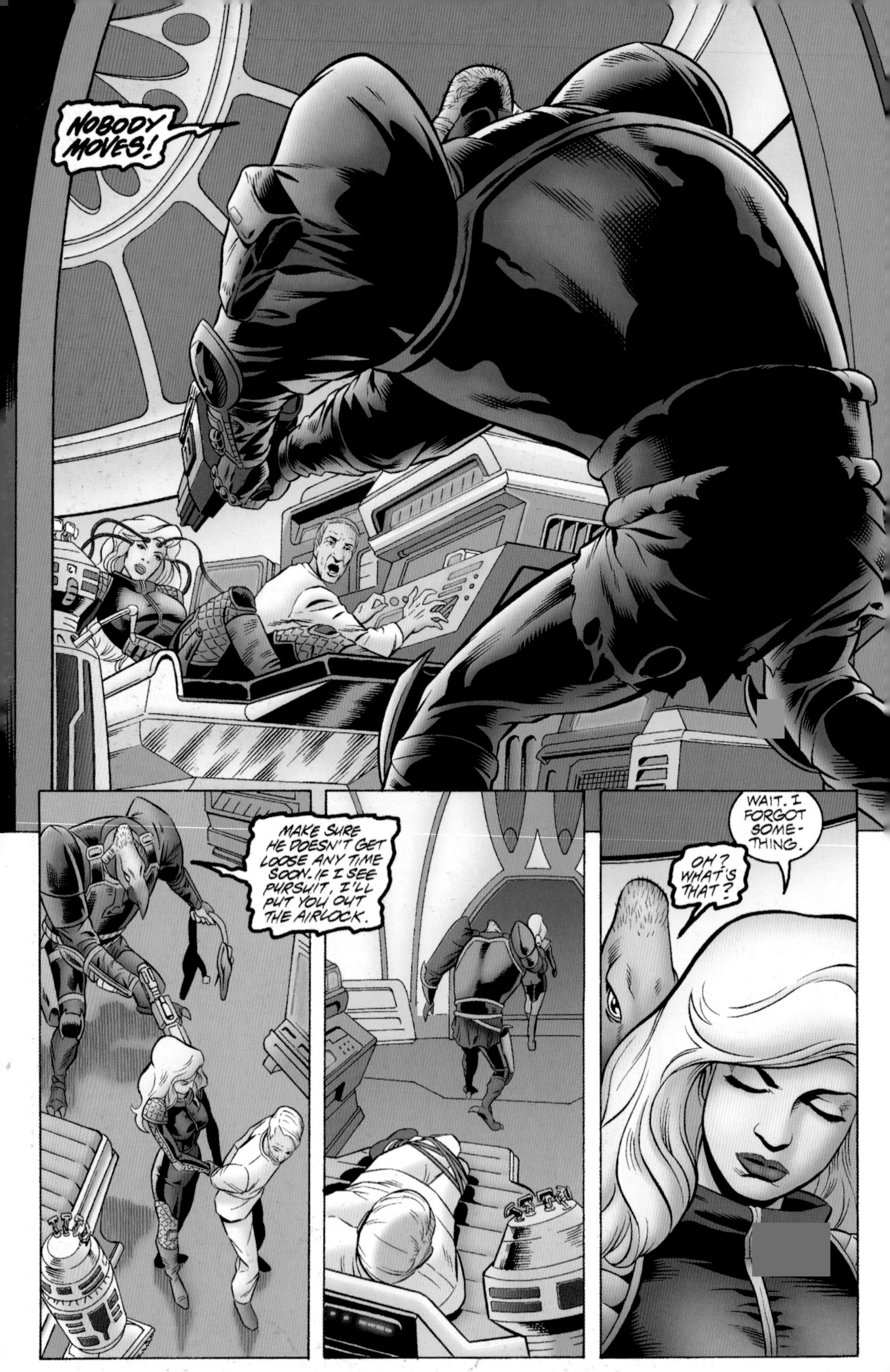
NOBODY MOVES!
MAKE SURE HE DOESN'T GET LOOSE ANY TIME SOON. IF I SEE PURSUIT, I'LL PUT YOU OUT THE AIRLOCK.
WAIT. I FORGOT SOME-THING.
OH? WHAT'S THAT?

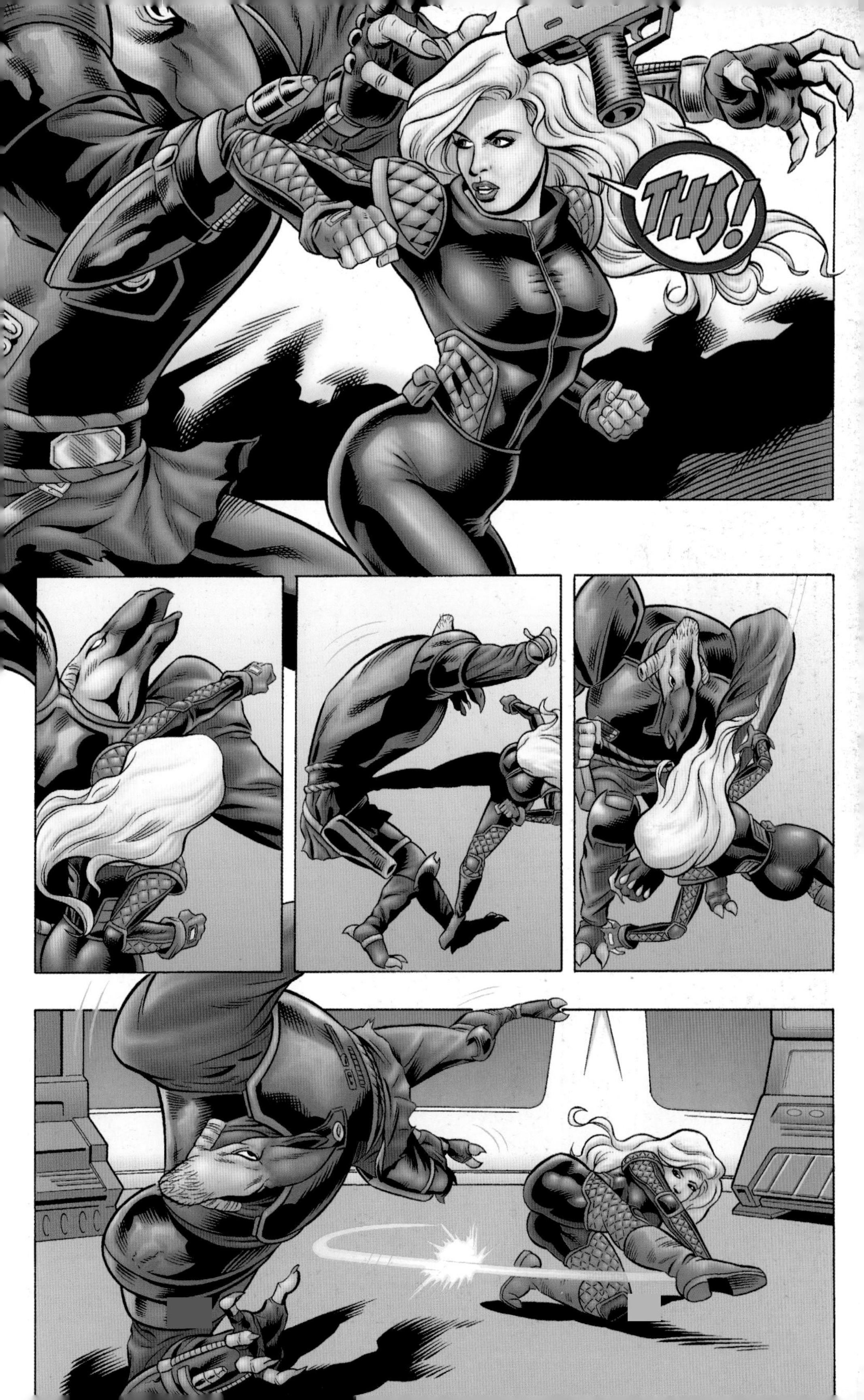
THIS!

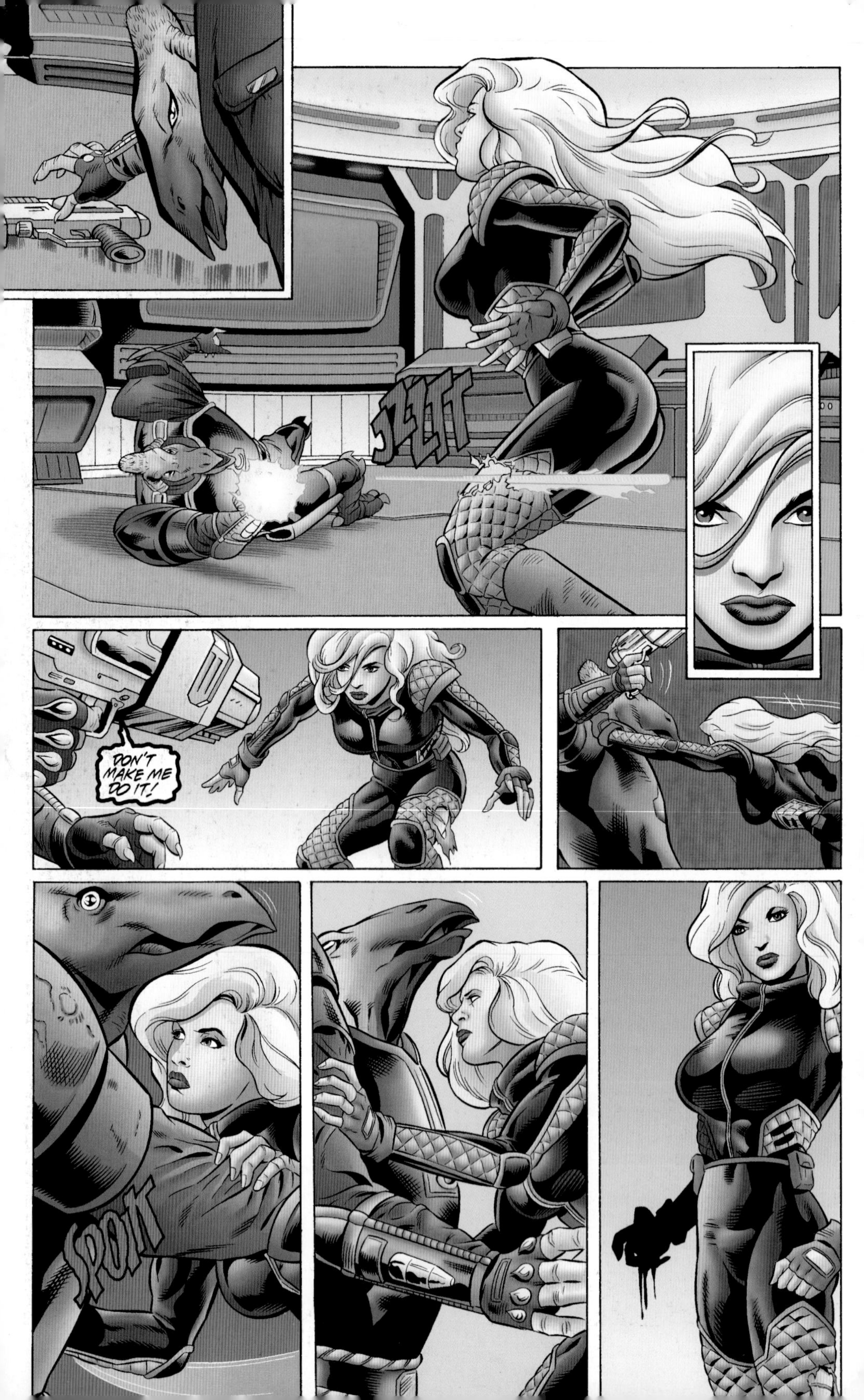

ZZTT
DON'T MAKE ME DO IT!
SPOT

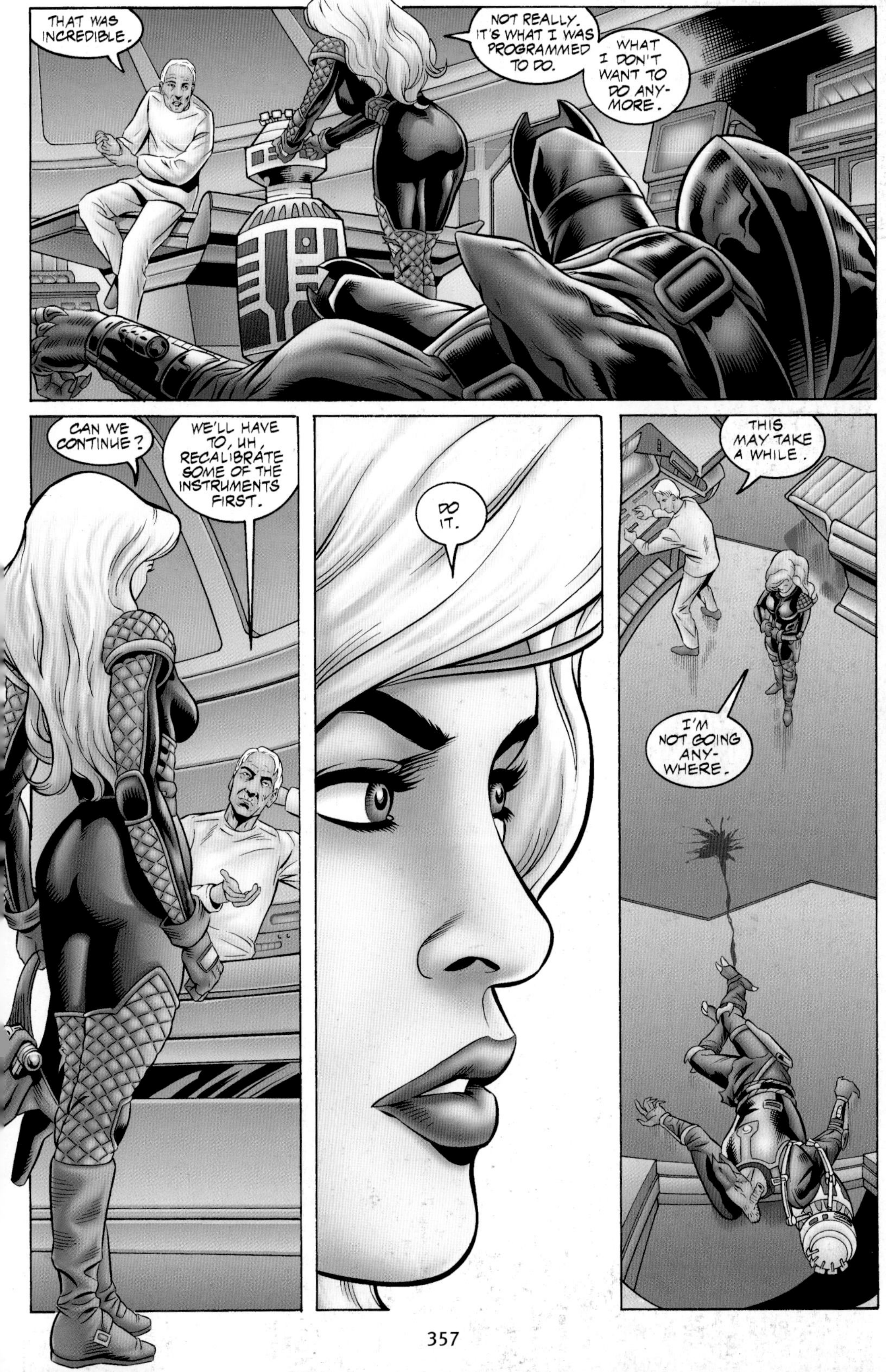
THAT WAS INCREDIBLE.
NOT REALLY. IT'S WHAT I WAS PROGRAMMED TO DO.
WHAT I DON'T WANT TO DO ANYMORE.
CAN WE CONTINUE?
WE'LL HAVE TO, UH, RECALIBRATE SOME OF THE INSTRUMENTS FIRST.
DO IT.
THIS MAY TAKE A WHILE.
I'M NOT GOING ANYWHERE.

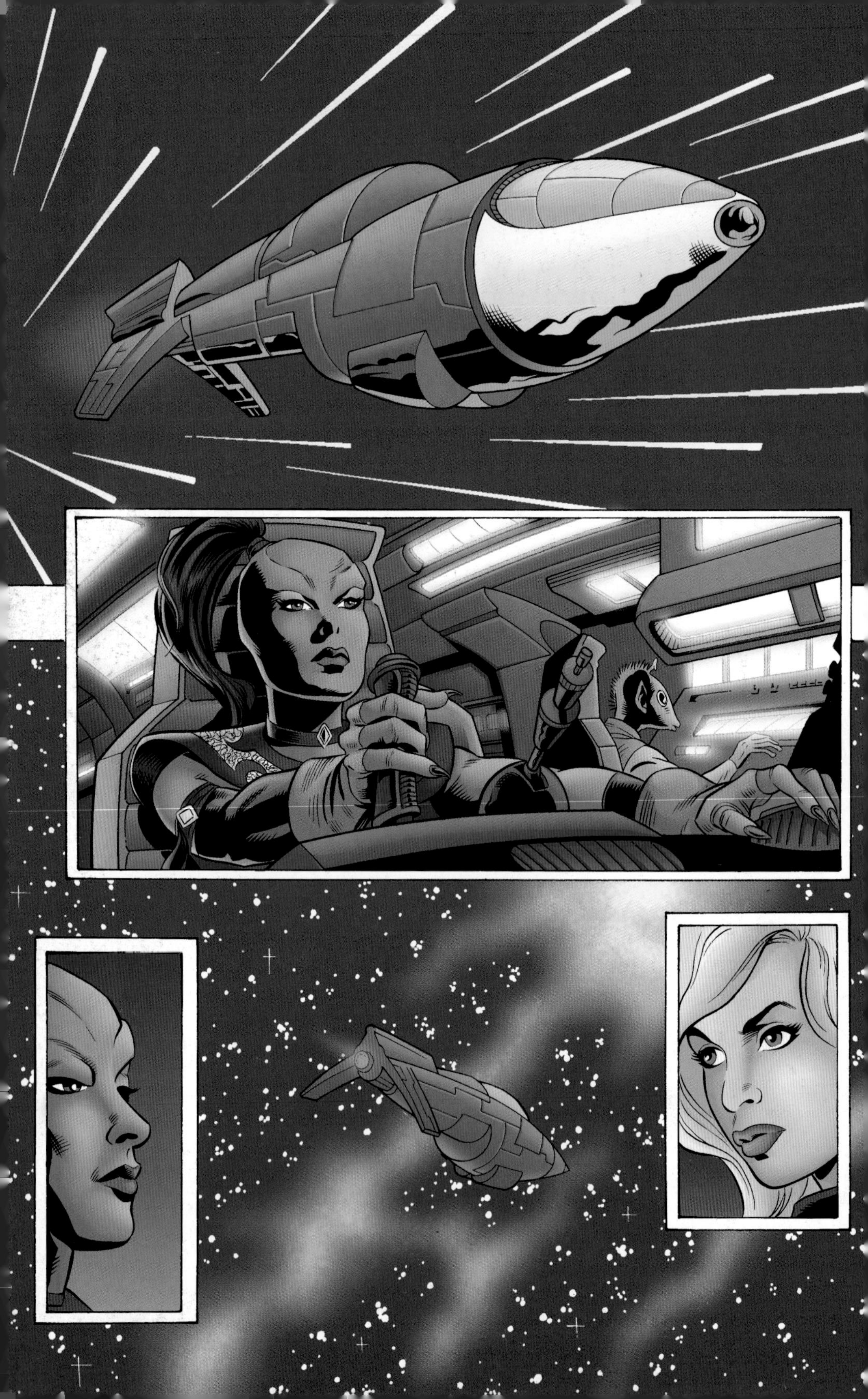

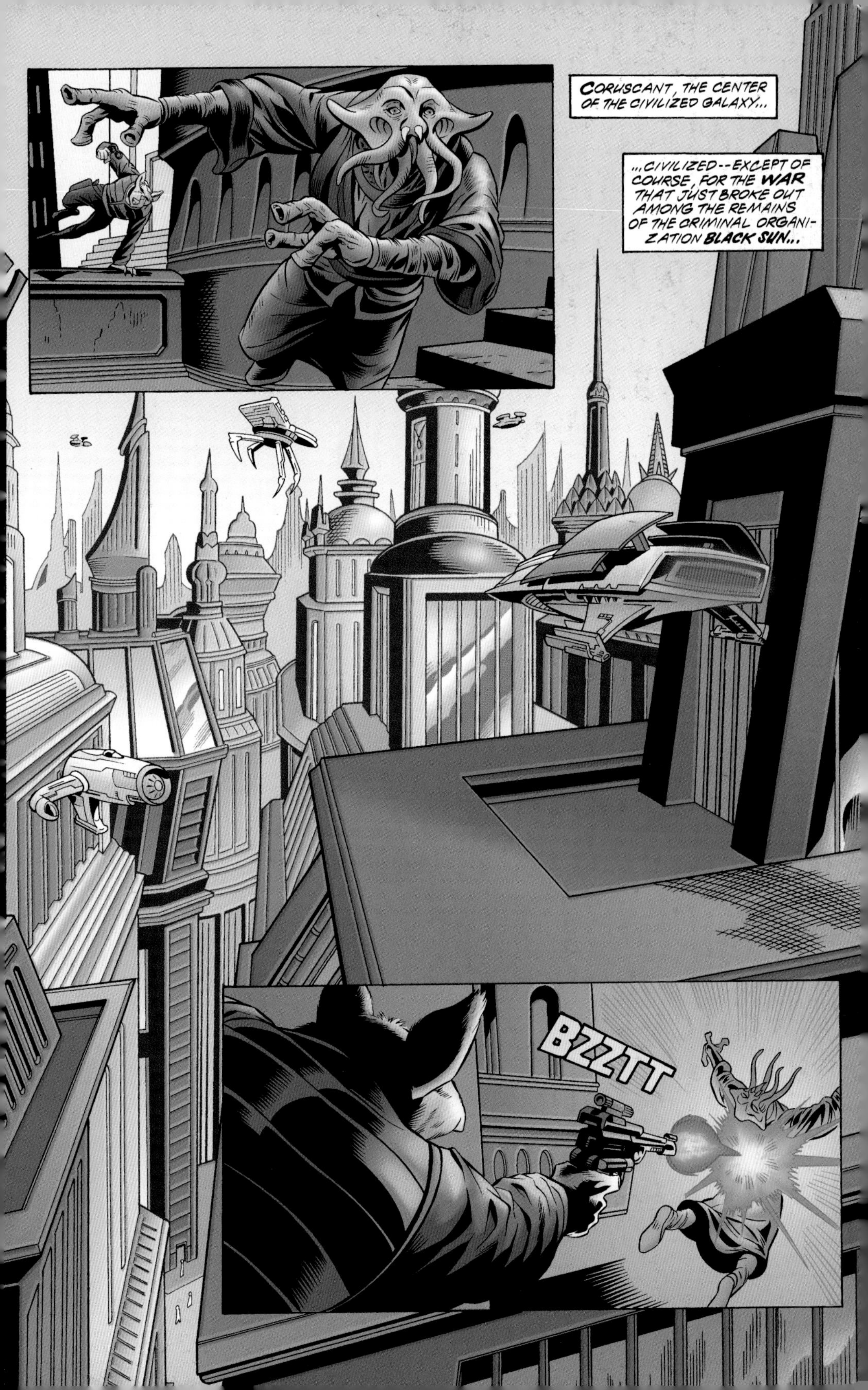
CORUSCANT, THE CENTER OF THE CIVILIZED GALAXY...
...CIVILIZED--EXCEPT OF COURSE, FOR THE WAR THAT JUST BROKE OUT AMONG THE REMAINS OF THE CRIMINAL ORGANIZATION BLACK SUN...
BZZTT

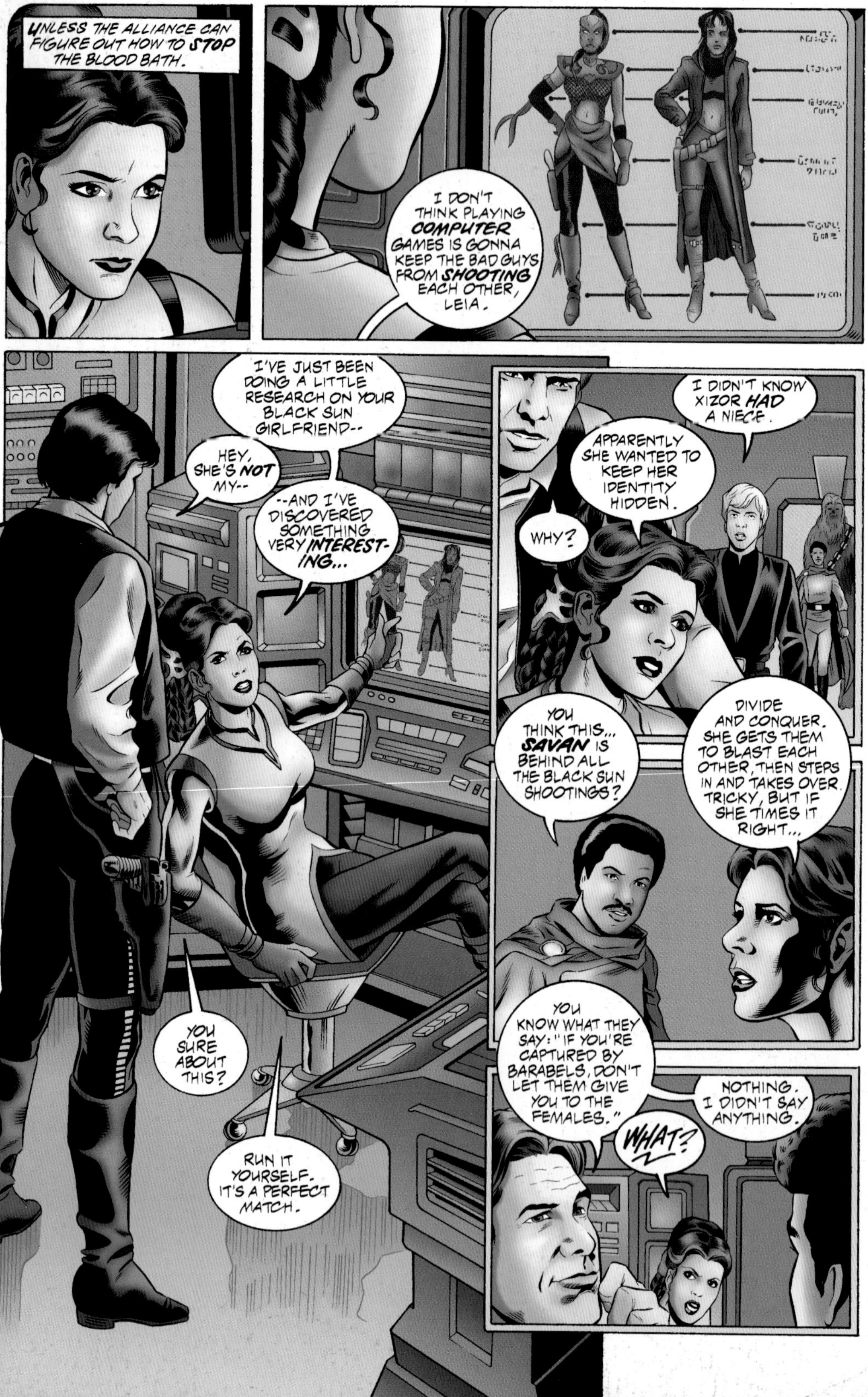
UNLESS THE ALLIANCE CAN FIGURE OUT HOW TO STOP THE BLOOD BATH.
I DON'T THINK PLAYING COMPUTER GAMES IS GONNA KEEP THE BAD GUYS FROM SHOOTING EACH OTHER, LEIA.
I'VE JUST BEEN DOING A LITTLE RESEARCH ON YOUR BLACK SUN GIRLFRIEND--
HEY, SHE'S NOT MY--
--AND I'VE DISCOVERED SOMETHING VERY INTERESTING...
YOU SURE ABOUT THIS?
RUN IT YOURSELF. IT'S A PERFECT MATCH.
I DIDN'T KNOW XIZOR HAD A NIECE.
APPARENTLY SHE WANTED TO KEEP HER IDENTITY HIDDEN.
WHY?
YOU THINK THIS... SAVAN IS BEHIND ALL THE BLACK SUN SHOOTINGS?
DIVIDE AND CONQUER. SHE GETS THEM TO BLAST EACH OTHER, THEN STEPS IN AND TAKES OVER. TRICKY, BUT IF SHE TIMES IT RIGHT...
YOU KNOW WHAT THEY SAY: "IF YOU'RE CAPTURED BY BARABELS, DON'T LET THEM GIVE YOU TO THE FEMALES."
WHAT?
NOTHING. I DIDN'T SAY ANYTHING.

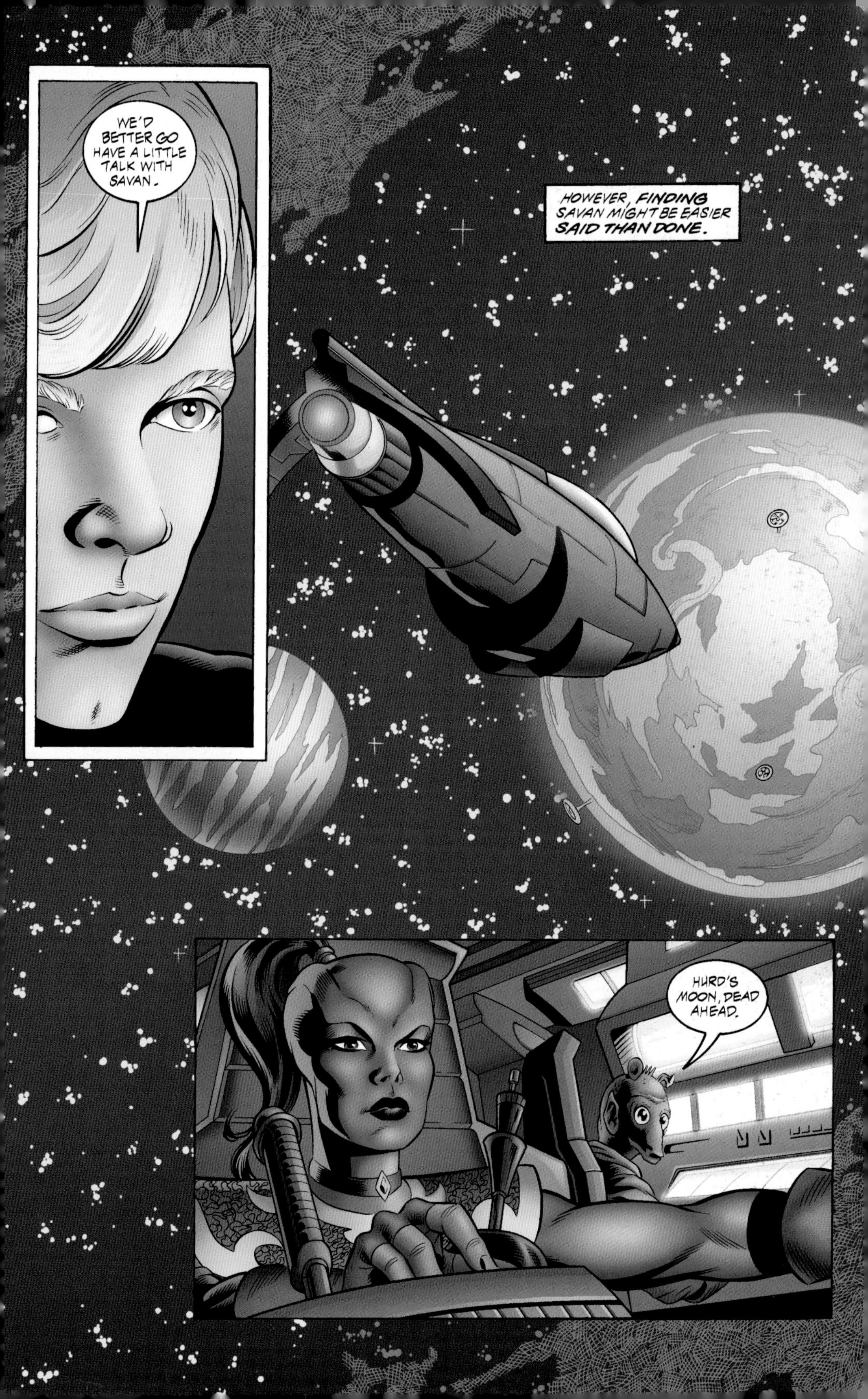
WE'D BETTER GO HAVE A LITTLE TALK WITH SAVAN.
HOWEVER, FINDING SAVAN MIGHT BE EASIER SAID THAN DONE.
HURD'S MOON, DEAD AHEAD.

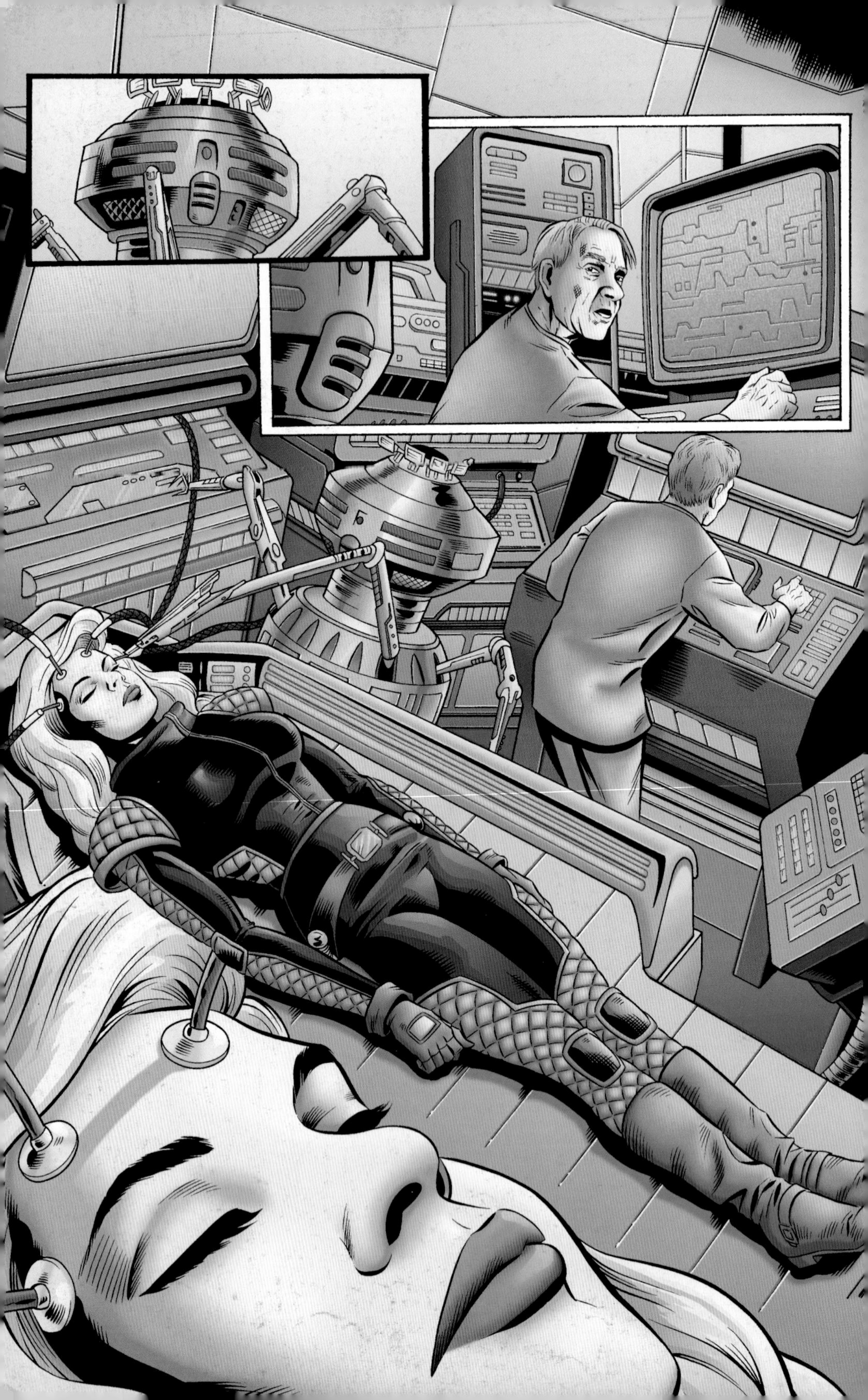

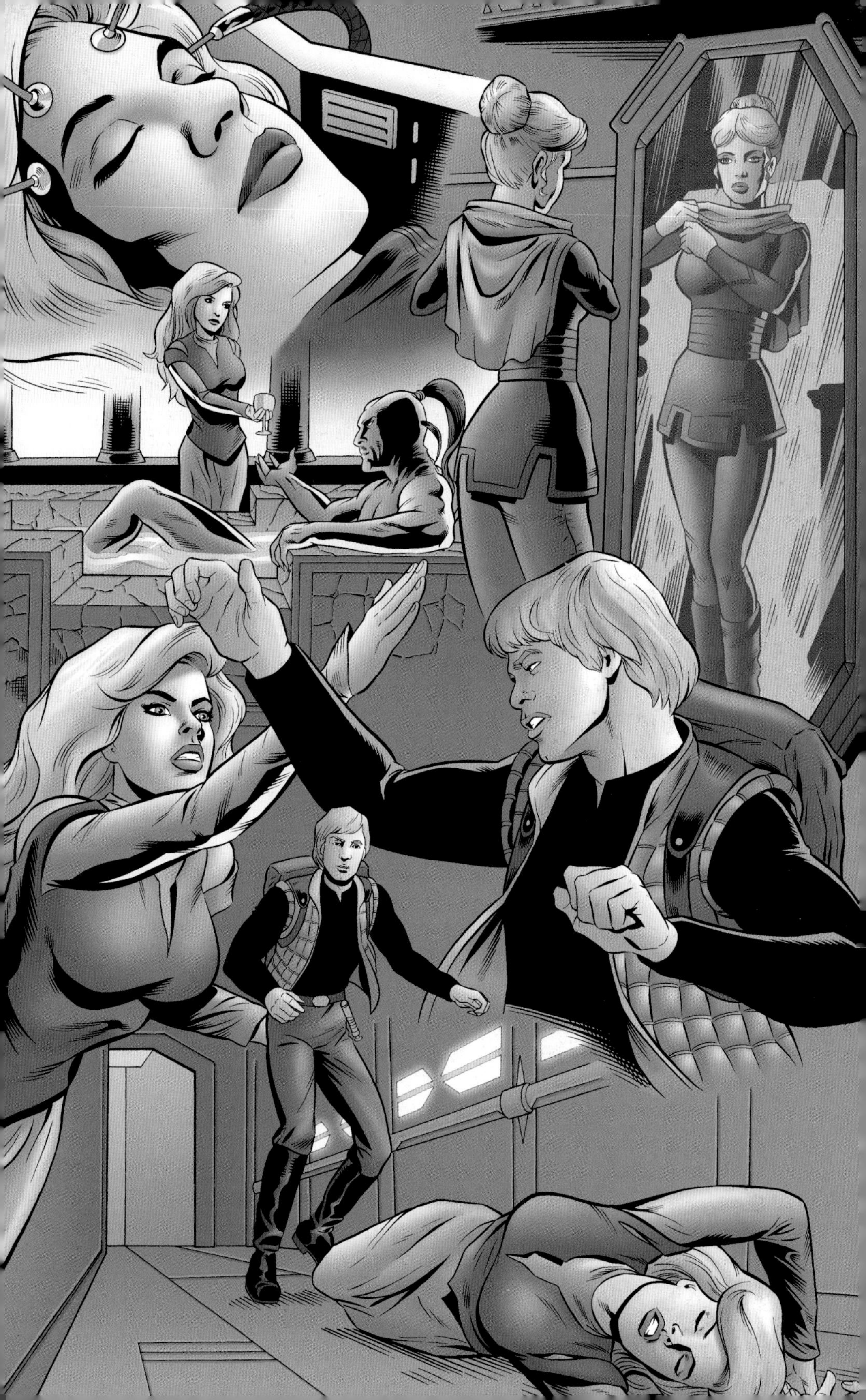

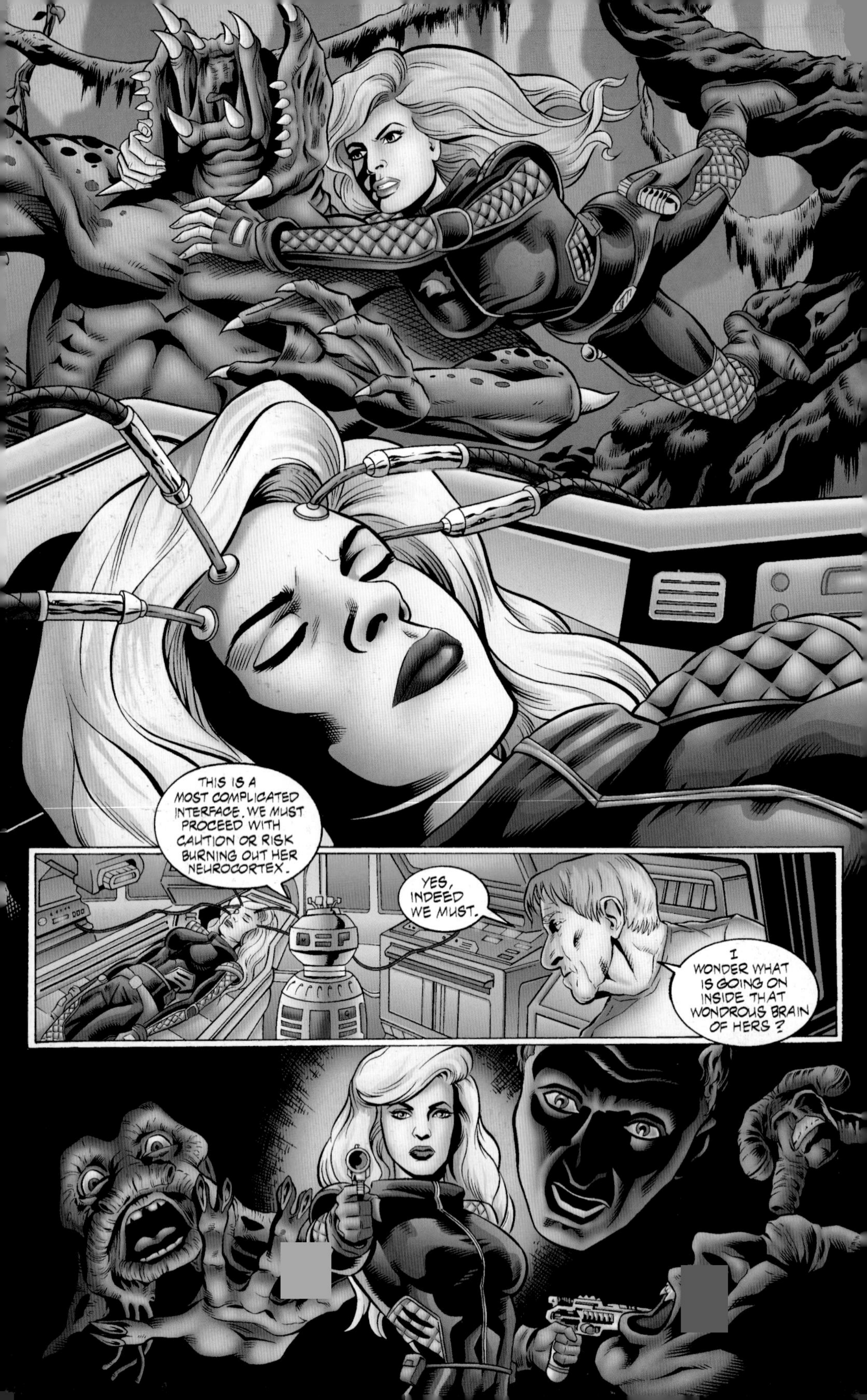
THIS IS A MOST COMPLICATED INTERFACE. WE MUST PROCEED WITH CAUTION OR RISK BURNING OUT HER NEUROCORTEX.
YES, INDEED WE MUST.
I WONDER WHAT IS GOING ON INSIDE THAT WONDROUS BRAIN OF HERS?

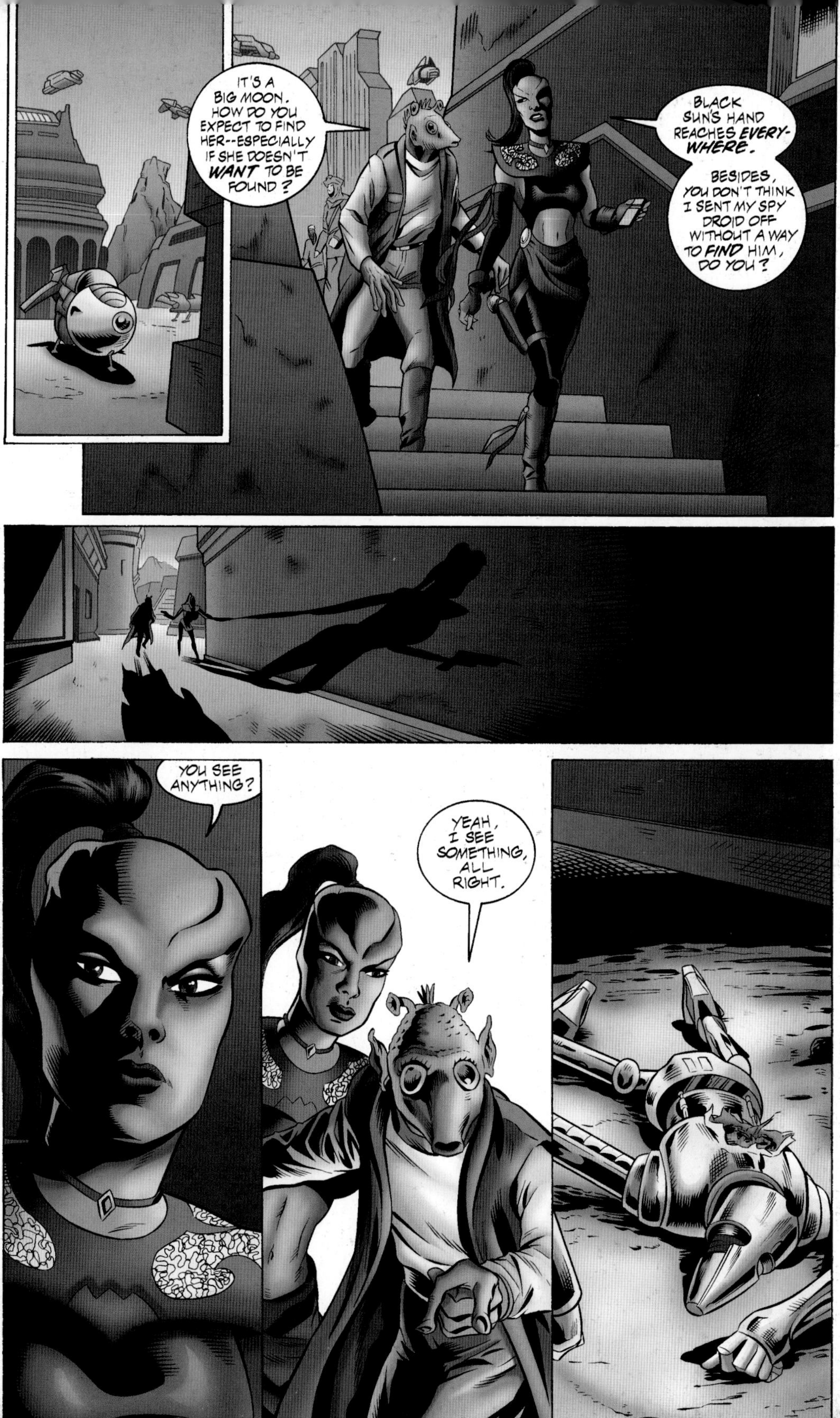
IT'S A BIG MOON. HOW DO YOU EXPECT TO FIND HER--ESPECIALLY IF SHE DOESN'T WANT TO BE FOUND?
BLACK SUN'S HAND REACHES EVERYWHERE.
BESIDES, YOU DON'T THINK I SENT MY SPY DROID OFF WITHOUT A WAY TO FIND HIM, DO YOU?
YOU SEE ANYTHING?
YEAH, I SEE SOMETHING, ALL RIGHT.

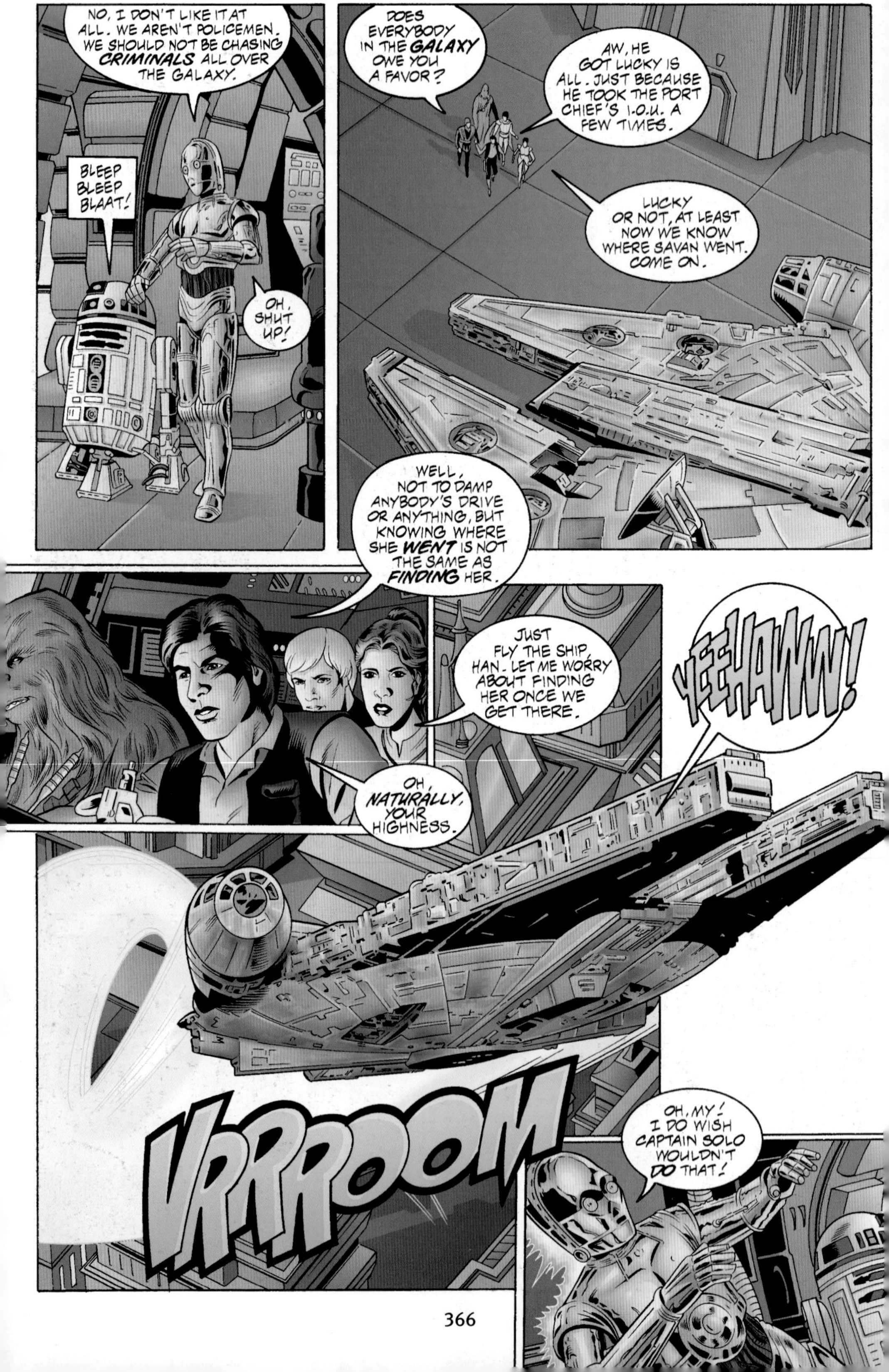

NO, I DON'T LIKE IT AT ALL. WE AREN'T POLICEMEN. WE SHOULD NOT BE CHASING CRIMINALS ALL OVER THE GALAXY.
BLEEP BLEEP BLAAT!
OH, SHUT UP!
DOES EVERYBODY IN THE GALAXY OWE YOU A FAVOR?
AW, HE GOT LUCKY IS ALL. JUST BECAUSE HE TOOK THE PORT CHIEF'S I.O.U. A FEW TIMES.
LUCKY OR NOT, AT LEAST NOW WE KNOW WHERE SAVAN WENT. COME ON.
WELL, NOT TO DAMP ANYBODY'S DRIVE OR ANYTHING, BUT KNOWING WHERE SHE WENT IS NOT THE SAME AS FINDING HER.
JUST FLY THE SHIP, HAN. LET ME WORRY ABOUT FINDING HER ONCE WE GET THERE.
OH, NATURALLY, YOUR HIGHNESS.
YEEHAWW!
VRRROOM
OH, MY! I DO WISH CAPTAIN SOLO WOULDN'T DO THAT!

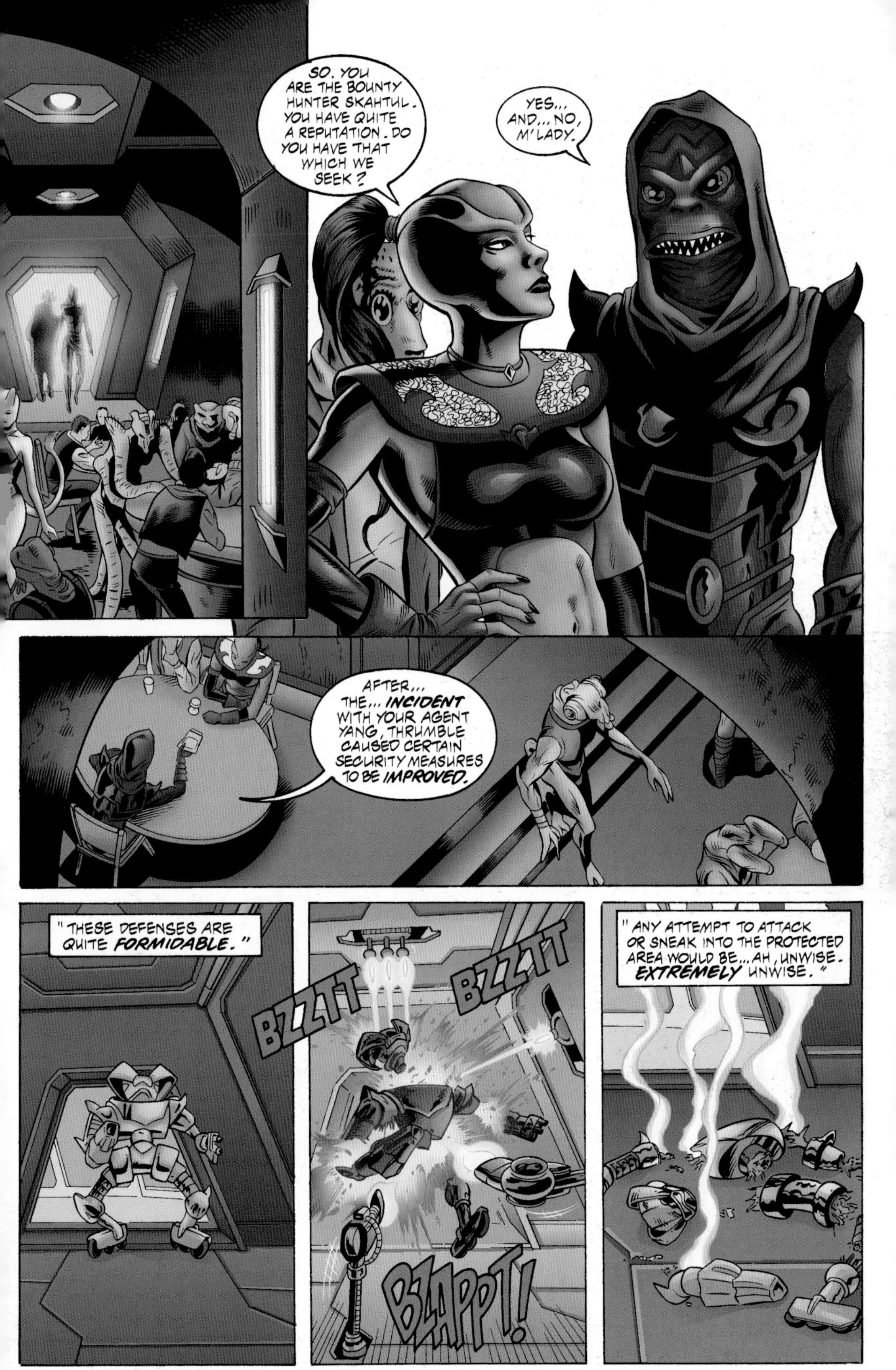
SO. YOU ARE THE BOUNTY HUNTER SKAHTUL. YOU HAVE QUITE A REPUTATION. DO YOU HAVE THAT WHICH WE SEEK?
YES... AND... NO, M'LADY.
AFTER... THE... INCIDENT WITH YOUR AGENT YANG, THRUMBLE CAUSED CERTAIN SECURITY MEASURES TO BE IMPROVED.
"THESE DEFENSES ARE QUITE FORMIDABLE."
BZZTT
BZZTT
BZAPPT!
"ANY ATTEMPT TO ATTACK OR SNEAK INTO THE PROTECTED AREA WOULD BE... AH, UNWISE. EXTREMELY UNWISE."

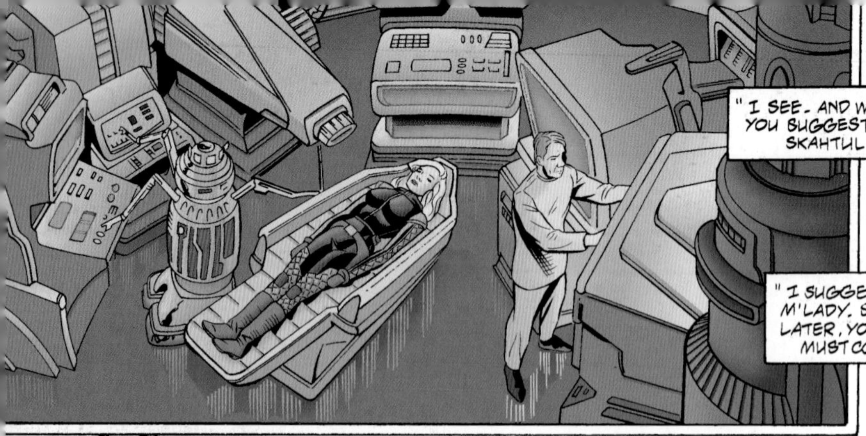
"I SEE. AND WHAT DO YOU SUGGEST WE DO, SKAHTUL?"
"I SUGGEST YOU WAIT, M'LADY. SOONER OR LATER, YOUR QUARRY MUST COME OUT."

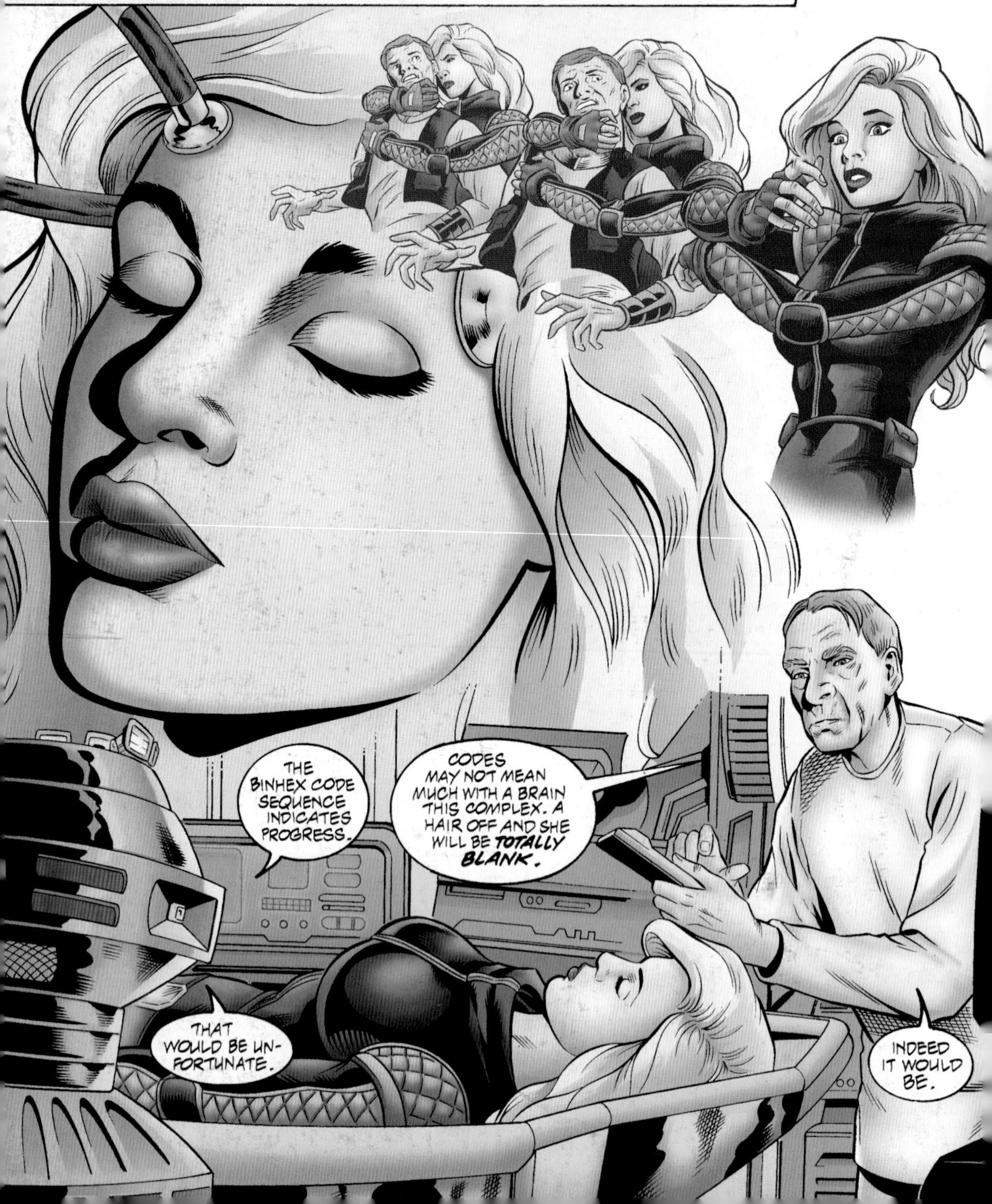
THE BINHEX CODE SEQUENCE INDICATES PROGRESS.
CODES MAY NOT MEAN MUCH WITH A BRAIN THIS COMPLEX. A HAIR OFF AND SHE WILL BE TOTALLY BLANK.
THAT WOULD BE UN-FORTUNATE.
INDEED IT WOULD BE.

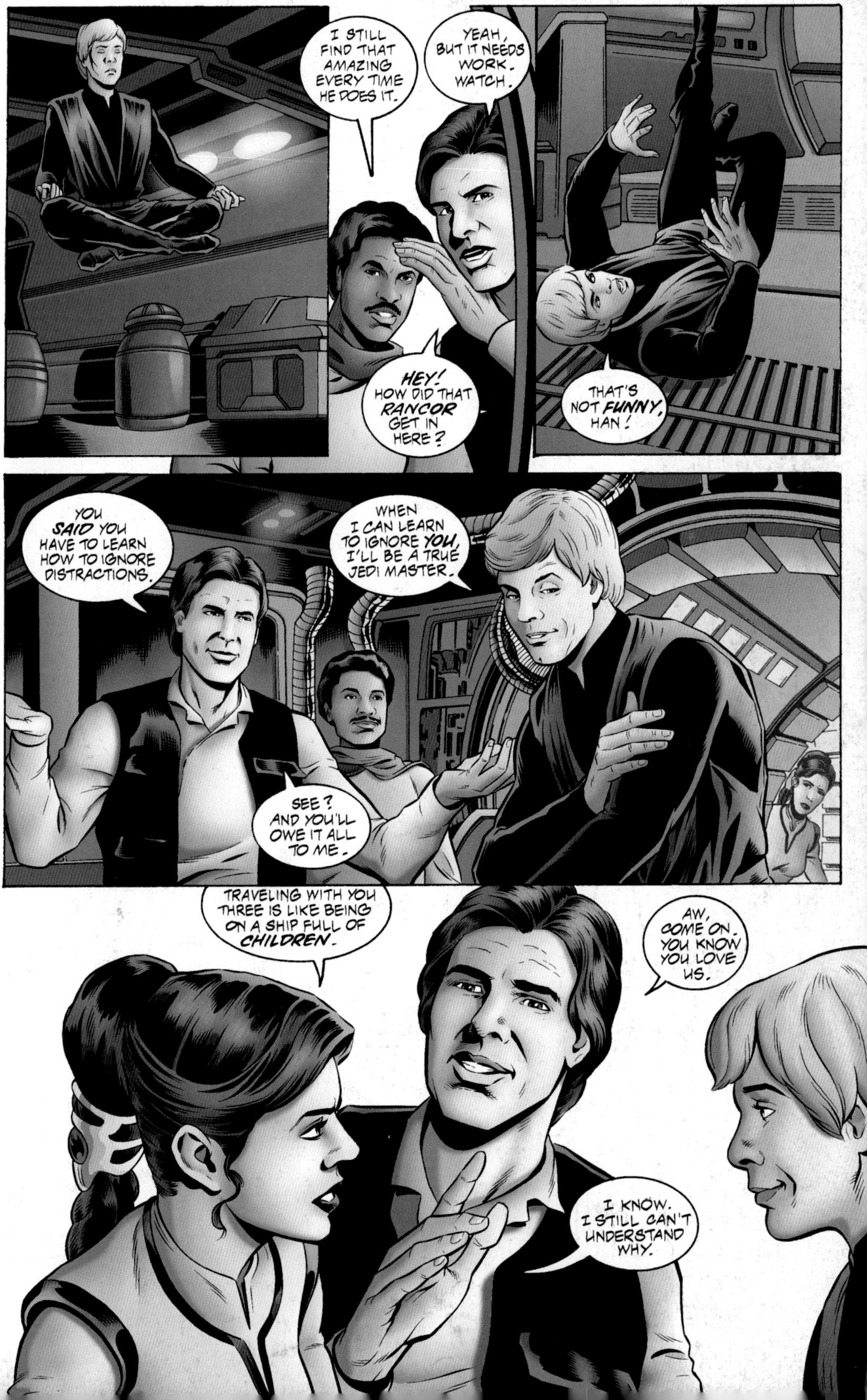
I STILL FIND THAT AMAZING EVERY TIME HE DOES IT.
YEAH, BUT IT NEEDS WORK. WATCH.
HEY! HOW DID THAT RANCOR GET IN HERE?
THAT'S NOT FUNNY, HAN!
YOU SAID YOU HAVE TO LEARN HOW TO IGNORE DISTRACTIONS.
WHEN I CAN LEARN TO IGNORE YOU, I'LL BE A TRUE JEDI MASTER.
SEE? AND YOU'LL OWE IT ALL TO ME.
TRAVELING WITH YOU THREE IS LIKE BEING ON A SHIP FULL OF CHILDREN.
AW, COME ON. YOU KNOW YOU LOVE US.
I KNOW. I STILL CAN'T UNDERSTAND WHY.

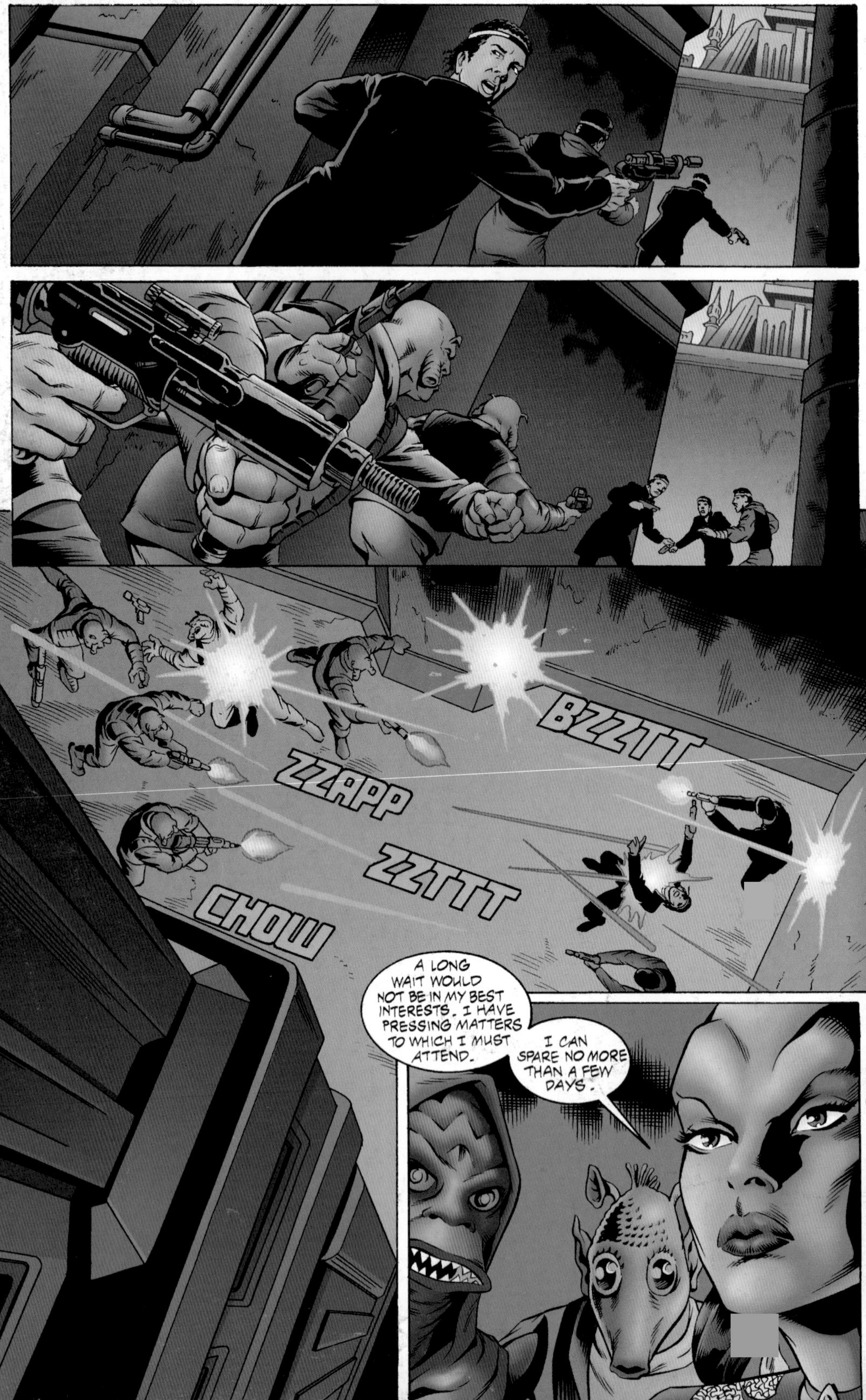
BZZTT
ZZAPP
ZZTTT
CHOW
A LONG WAIT WOULD NOT BE IN MY BEST INTERESTS. I HAVE PRESSING MATTERS TO WHICH I MUST ATTEND.
I CAN SPARE NO MORE THAN A FEW DAYS.

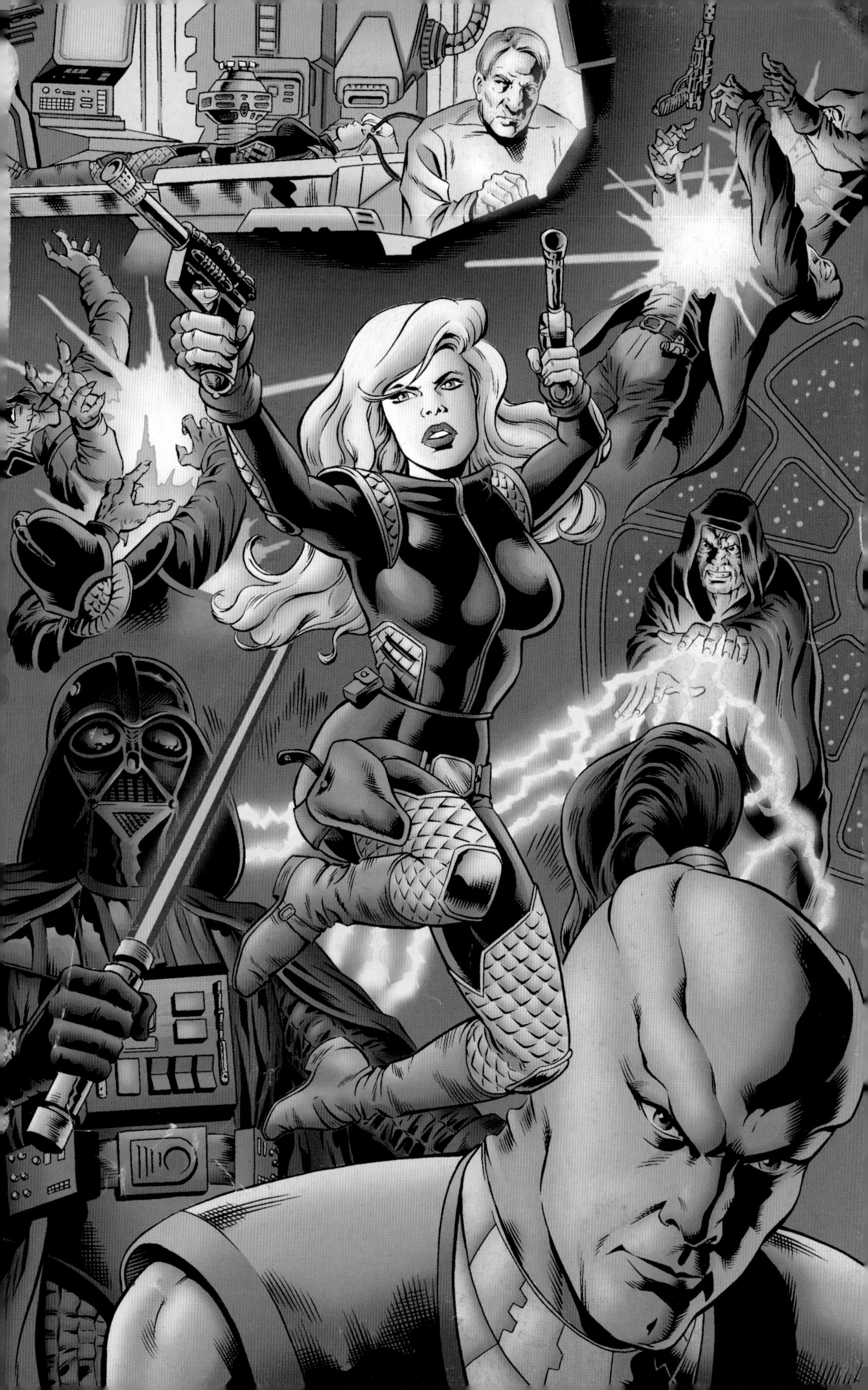

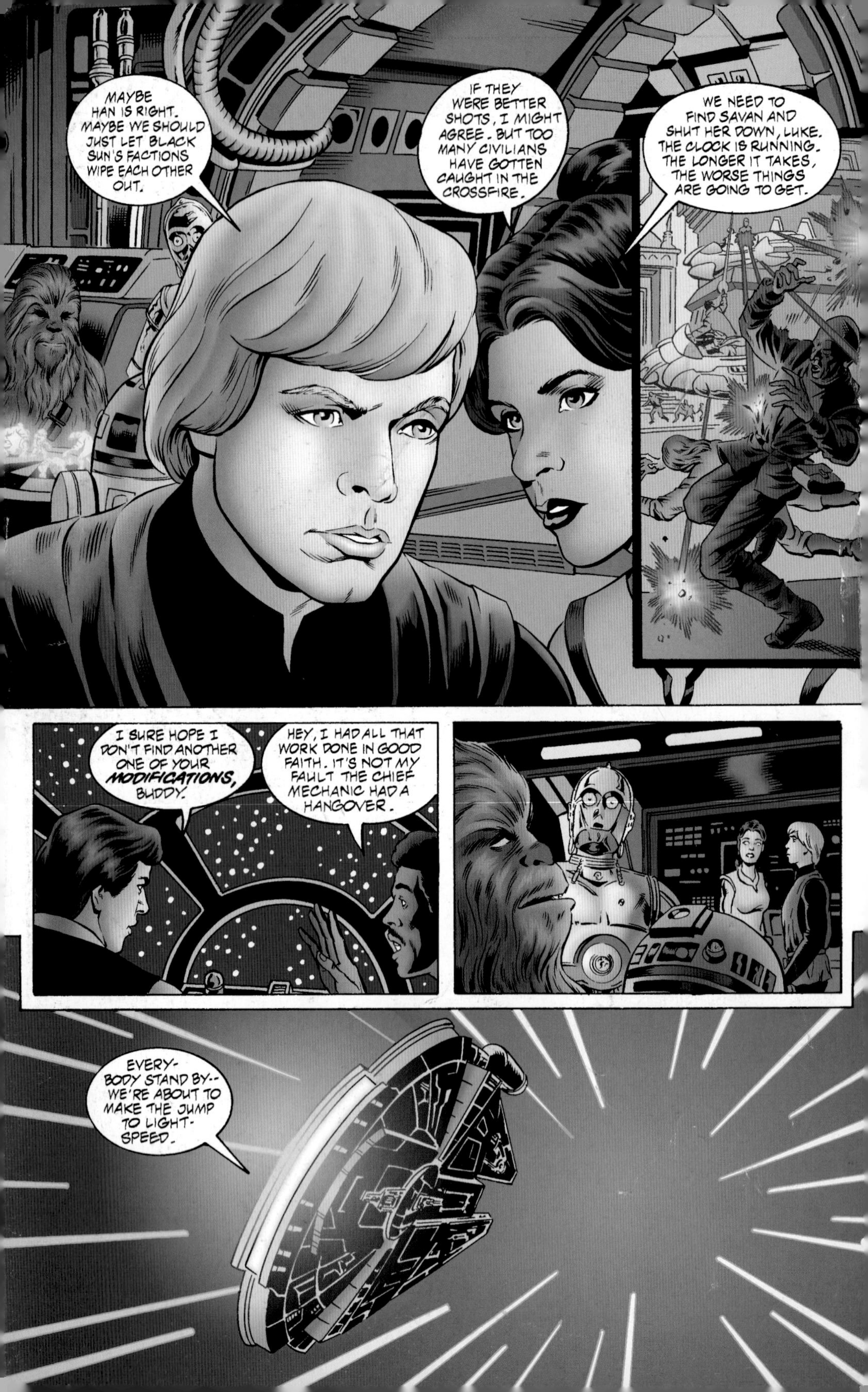
MAYBE HAN IS RIGHT. MAYBE WE SHOULD JUST LET BLACK SUN'S FACTIONS WIPE EACH OTHER OUT.
IF THEY WERE BETTER SHOTS, I MIGHT AGREE. BUT TOO MANY CIVILIANS HAVE GOTTEN CAUGHT IN THE CROSSFIRE.
WE NEED TO FIND SAVAN AND SHUT HER DOWN, LUKE. THE CLOCK IS RUNNING. THE LONGER IT TAKES, THE WORSE THINGS ARE GOING TO GET.
I SURE HOPE I DON'T FIND ANOTHER ONE OF YOUR *MODIFICATIONS*, BUDDY.
HEY, I HAD ALL THAT WORK DONE IN GOOD FAITH. IT'S NOT MY FAULT THE CHIEF MECHANIC HAD A HANGOVER.
EVERY-BODY STAND BY-- WE'RE ABOUT TO MAKE THE JUMP TO LIGHT-SPEED.

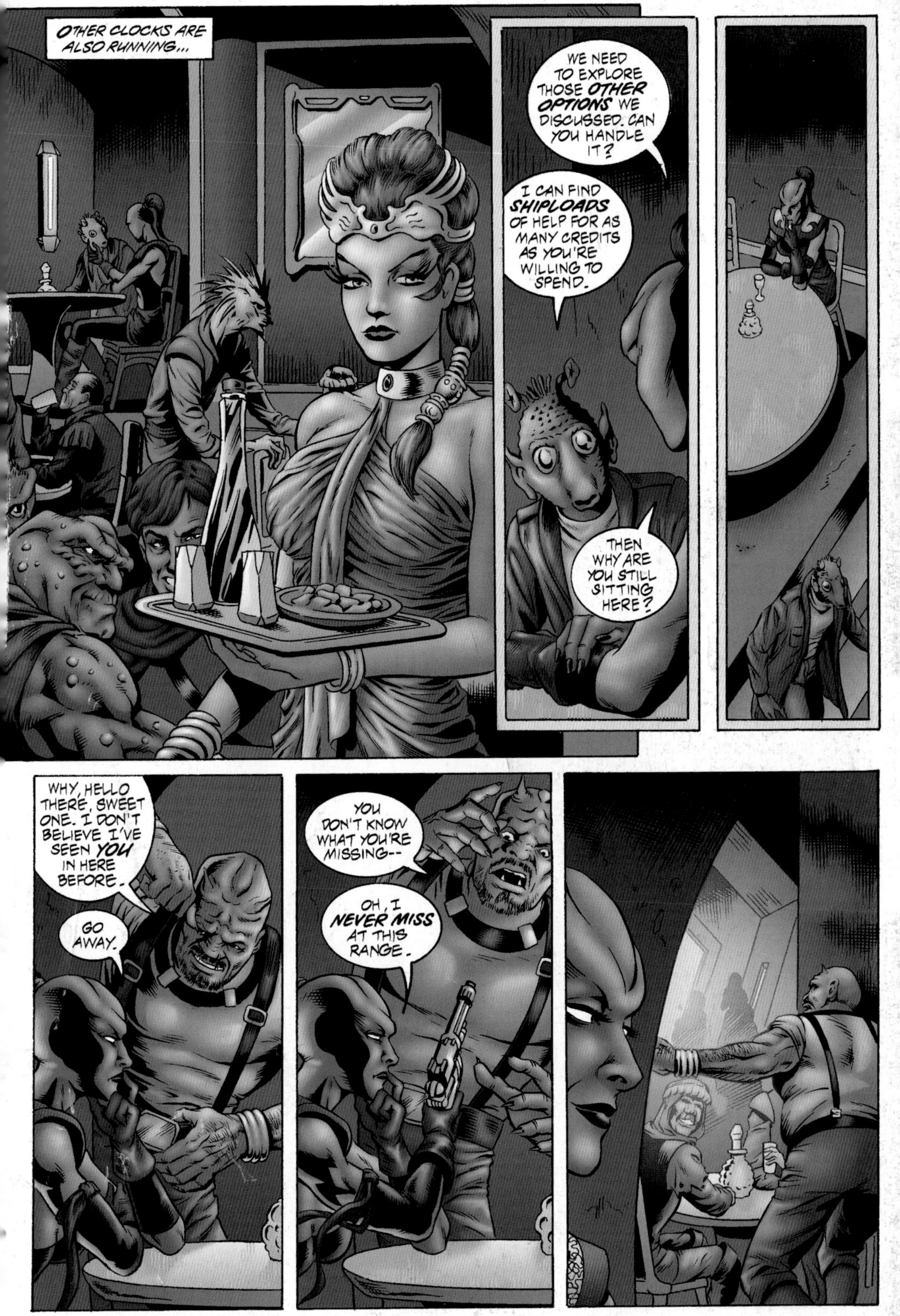
OTHER CLOCKS ARE ALSO RUNNING...
WE NEED TO EXPLORE THOSE OTHER OPTIONS WE DISCUSSED. CAN YOU HANDLE IT?
I CAN FIND SHIPLOADS OF HELP FOR AS MANY CREDITS AS YOU'RE WILLING TO SPEND.
THEN WHY ARE YOU STILL SITTING HERE?
WHY, HELLO THERE, SWEET ONE. I DON'T BELIEVE I'VE SEEN YOU IN HERE BEFORE.
GO AWAY.
YOU DON'T KNOW WHAT YOU'RE MISSING--
OH, I NEVER MISS AT THIS RANGE.

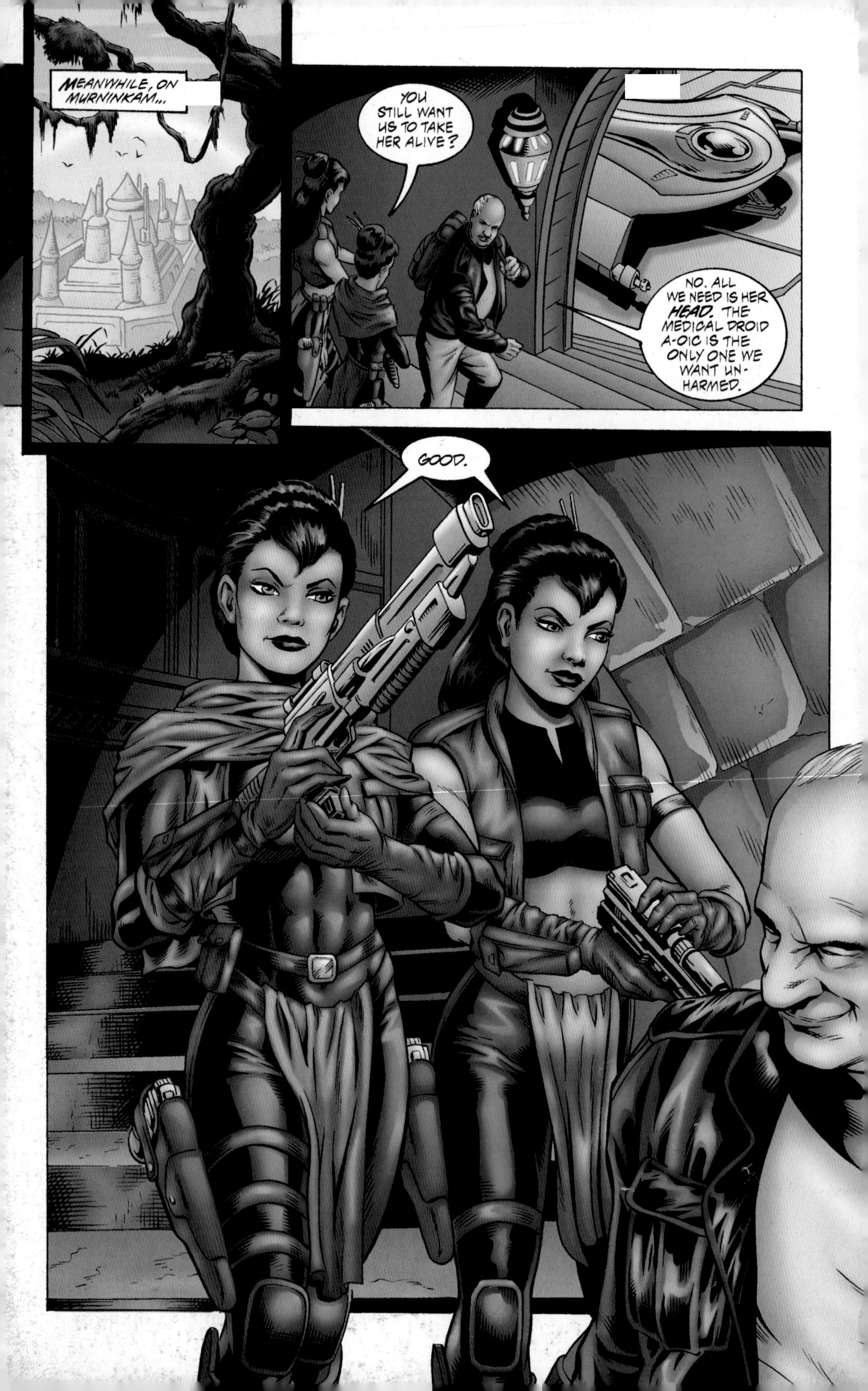

MEANWHILE, ON MURNINKAM...
YOU STILL WANT US TO TAKE HER ALIVE?
NO. ALL WE NEED IS HER HEAD. THE MEDICAL DROID A-OIC IS THE ONLY ONE WE WANT UN-HARMED.
GOOD.

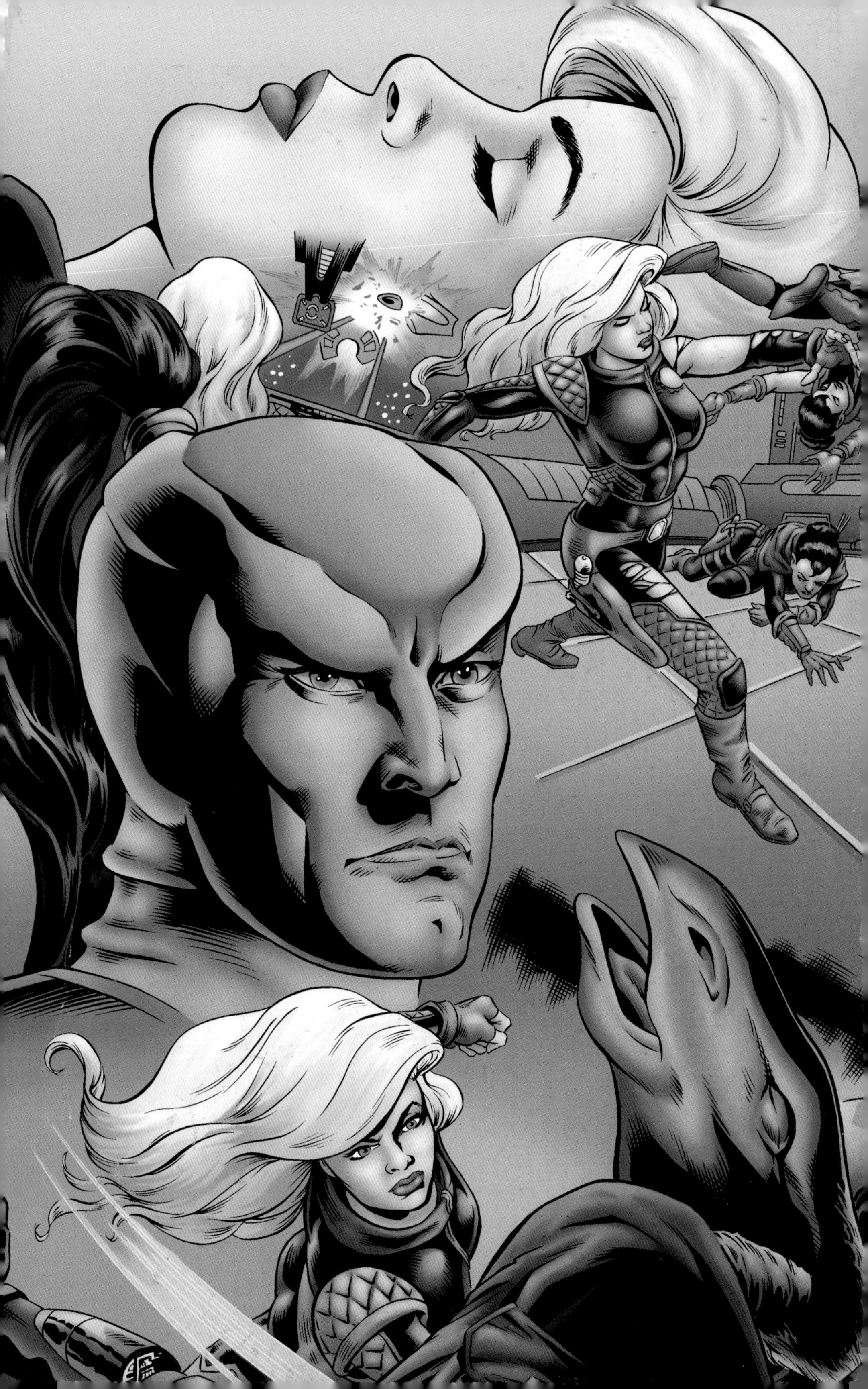

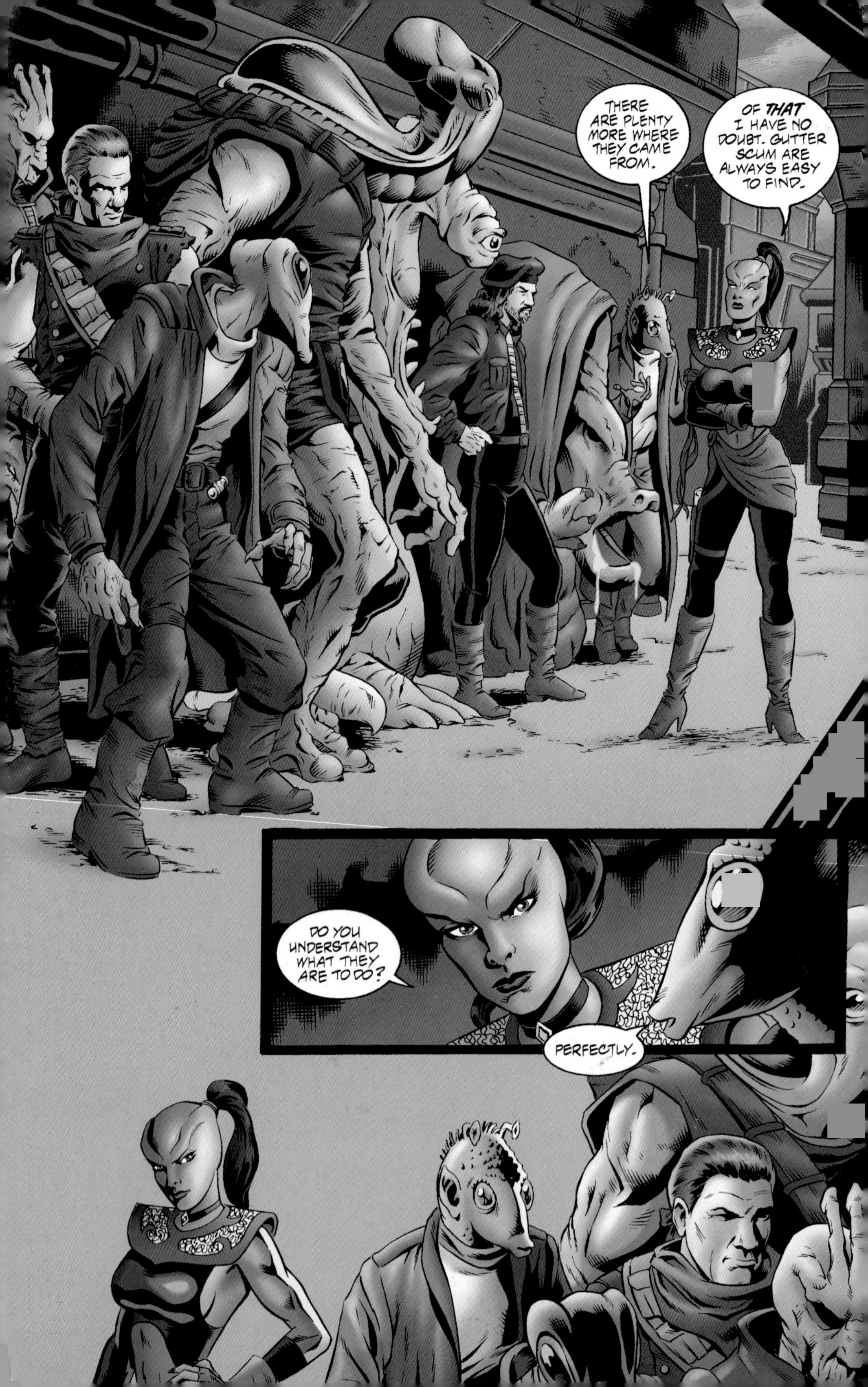
THERE ARE PLENTY MORE WHERE THEY CAME FROM.
OF *THAT* I HAVE NO DOUBT. GUTTER SCUM ARE ALWAYS EASY TO FIND.
DO YOU UNDERSTAND WHAT THEY ARE TO DO?
PERFECTLY.

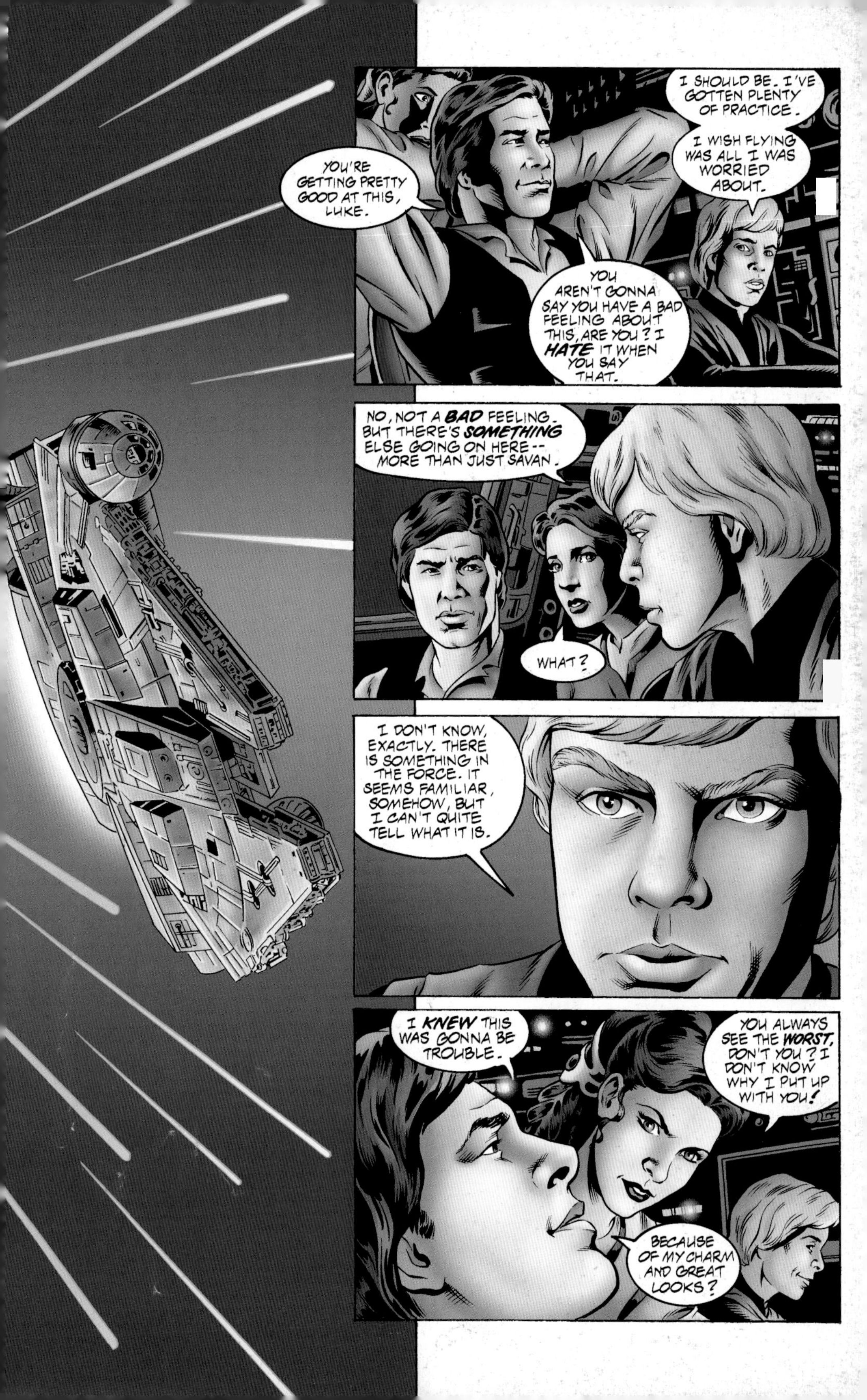
YOU'RE GETTING PRETTY GOOD AT THIS, LUKE.
I SHOULD BE. I'VE GOTTEN PLENTY OF PRACTICE.
I WISH FLYING WAS ALL I WAS WORRIED ABOUT.
YOU AREN'T GONNA SAY YOU HAVE A BAD FEELING ABOUT THIS, ARE YOU? I HATE IT WHEN YOU SAY THAT.
NO, NOT A BAD FEELING. BUT THERE'S SOMETHING ELSE GOING ON HERE-- MORE THAN JUST SAVAN.
WHAT?
I DON'T KNOW, EXACTLY. THERE IS SOMETHING IN THE FORCE. IT SEEMS FAMILIAR, SOMEHOW, BUT I CAN'T QUITE TELL WHAT IT IS.
I KNEW THIS WAS GONNA BE TROUBLE.
YOU ALWAYS SEE THE WORST, DON'T YOU? I DON'T KNOW WHY I PUT UP WITH YOU!
BECAUSE OF MY CHARM AND GREAT LOOKS?

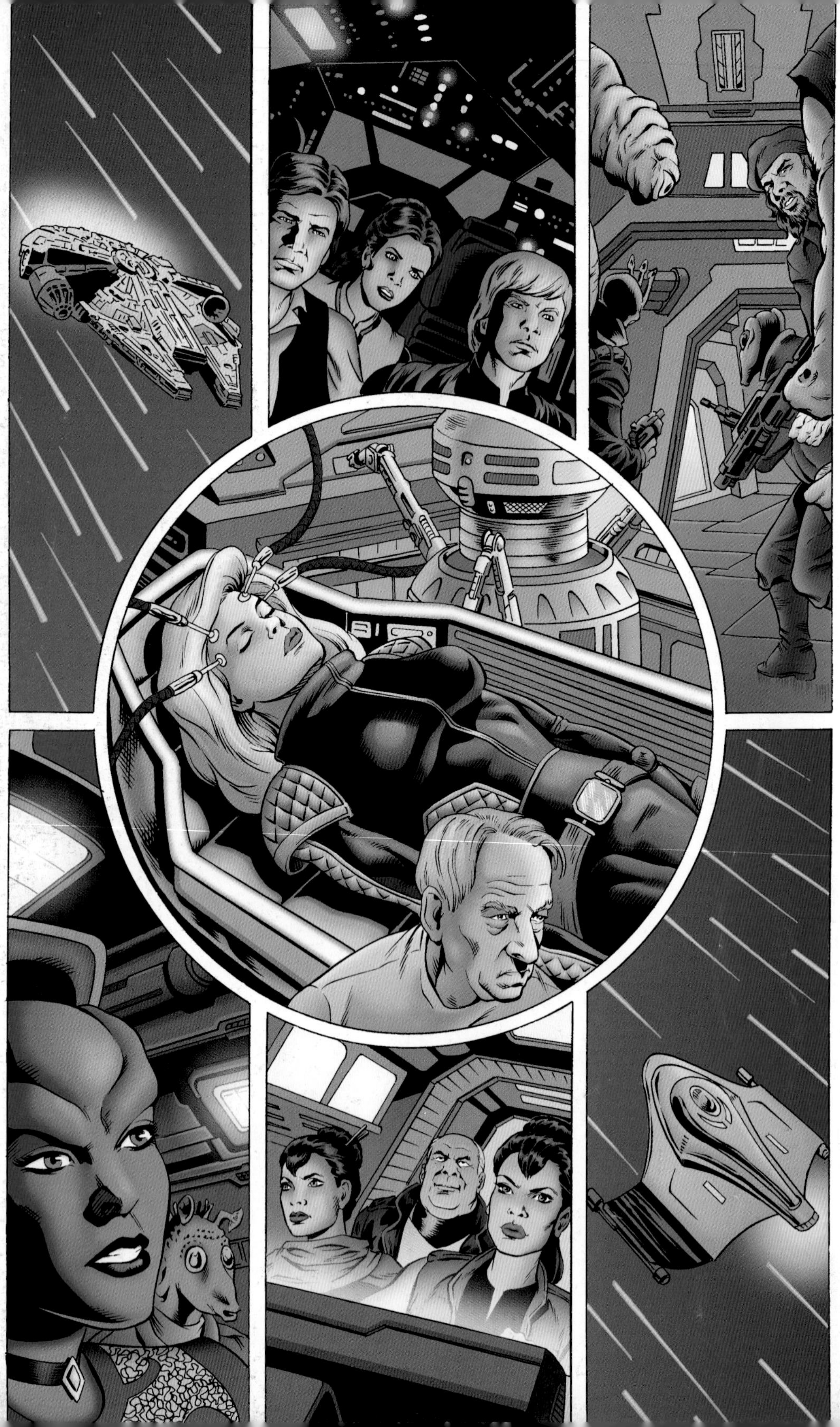

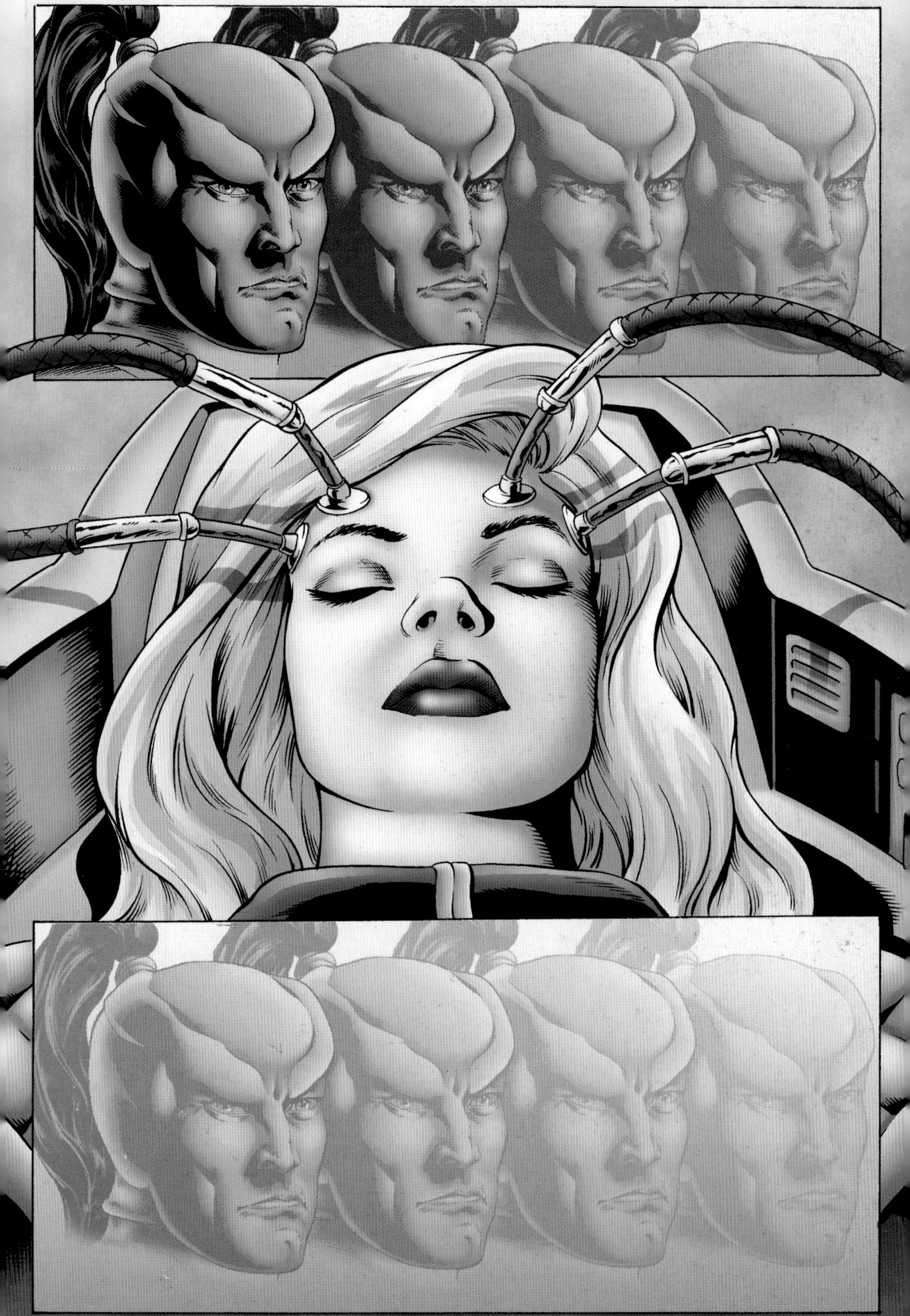

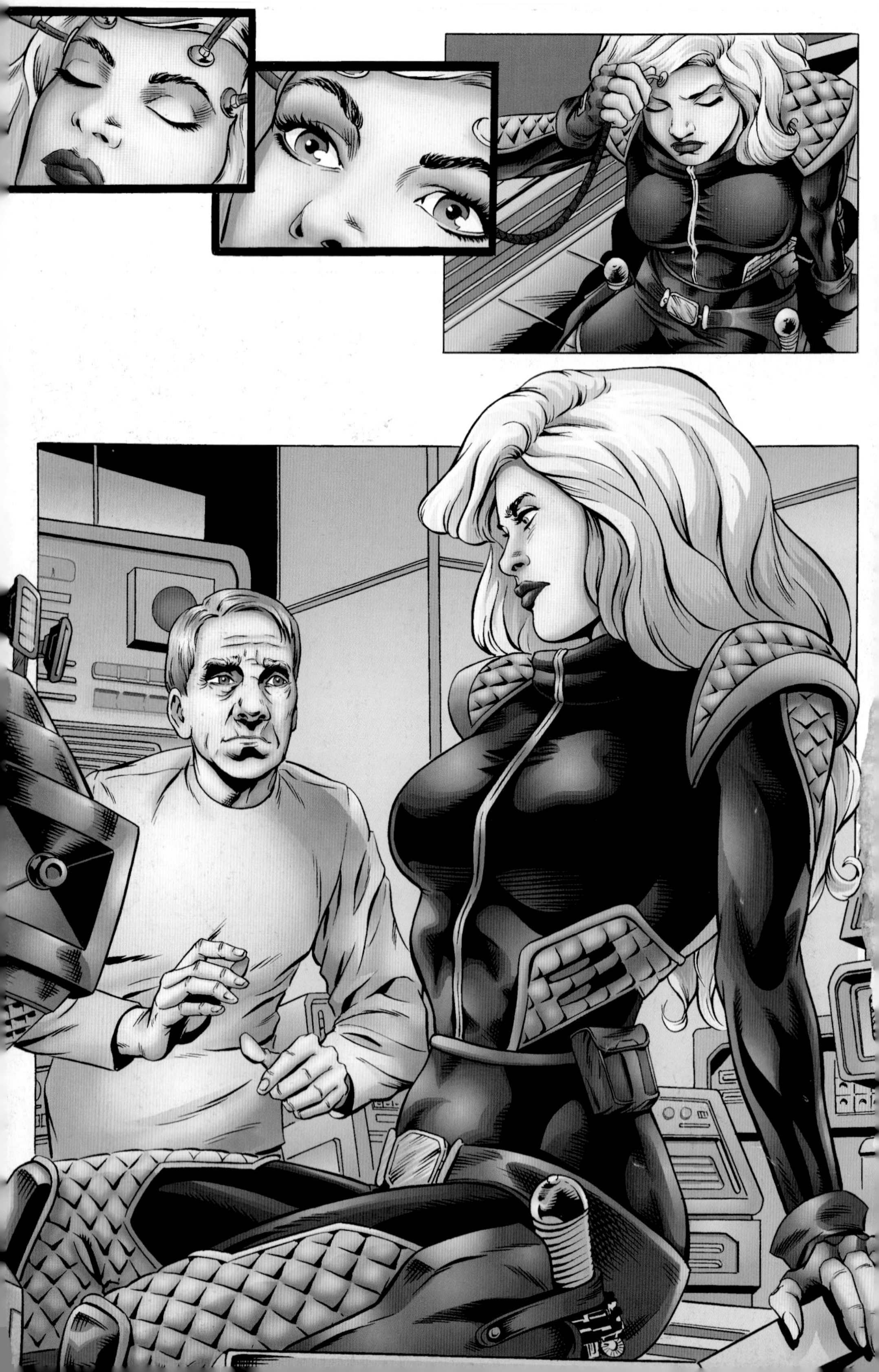

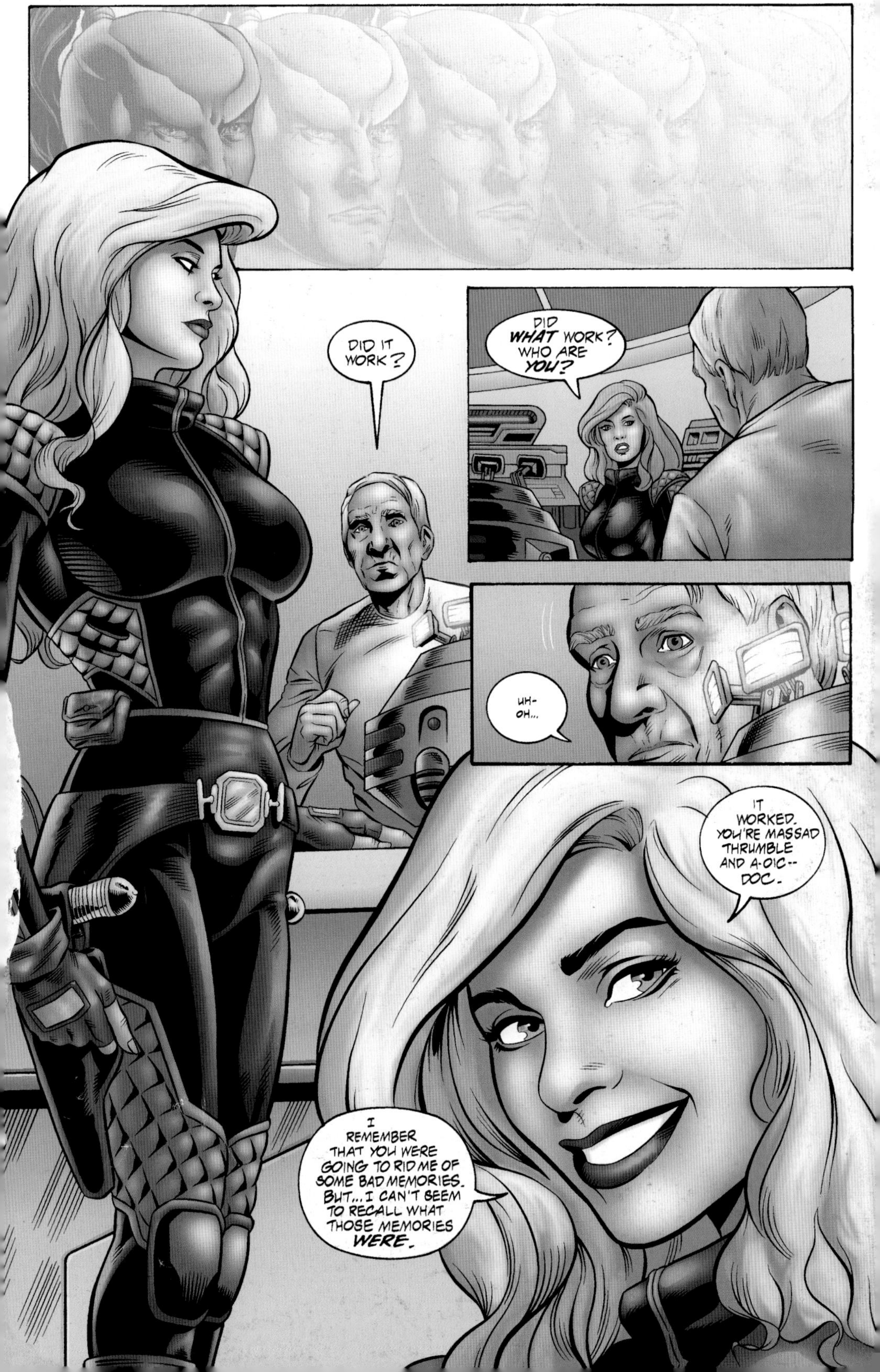
DID IT WORK?
DID WHAT WORK? WHO ARE YOU?
UH-OH...
IT WORKED. YOU'RE MASSAD THRUMBLE AND A-OIC-- DOC.
I REMEMBER THAT YOU WERE GOING TO RID ME OF SOME BAD MEMORIES. BUT... I CAN'T SEEM TO RECALL WHAT THOSE MEMORIES WERE.

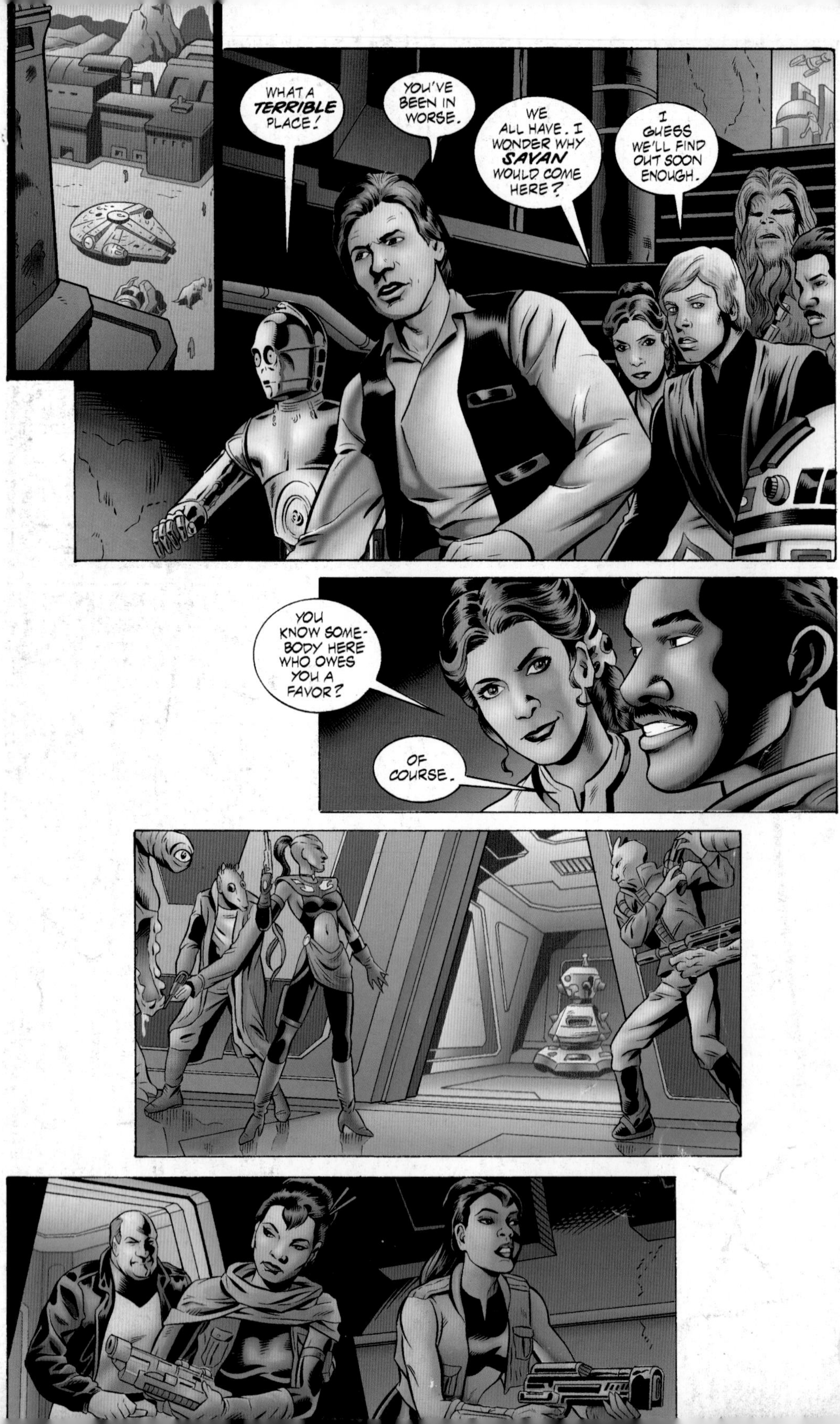
WHAT A TERRIBLE PLACE!
YOU'VE BEEN IN WORSE.
WE ALL HAVE. I WONDER WHY SAVAN WOULD COME HERE?
I GUESS WE'LL FIND OUT SOON ENOUGH.
YOU KNOW SOME-BODY HERE WHO OWES YOU A FAVOR?
OF COURSE.

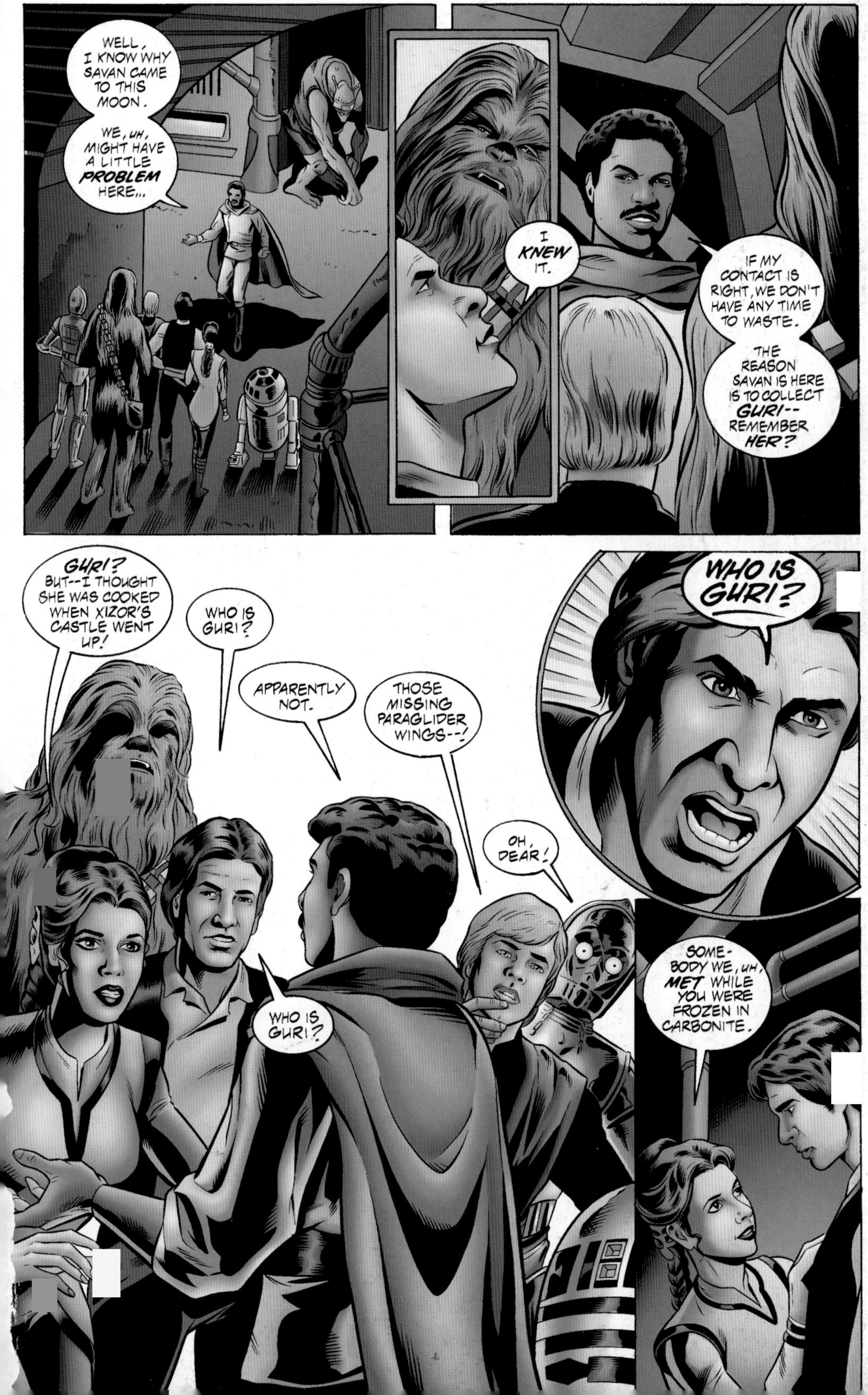
WELL, I KNOW WHY SAVAN CAME TO THIS MOON.
WE, UH, MIGHT HAVE A LITTLE PROBLEM HERE...
I KNEW IT.
IF MY CONTACT IS RIGHT, WE DON'T HAVE ANY TIME TO WASTE.
THE REASON SAVAN IS HERE IS TO COLLECT GURI-- REMEMBER HER?
GURI? BUT--I THOUGHT SHE WAS COOKED WHEN XIZOR'S CASTLE WENT UP!
WHO IS GURI?
APPARENTLY NOT.
THOSE MISSING PARAGLIDER WINGS--!
OH, DEAR!
WHO IS GURI?
WHO IS GURI?
SOME-BODY WE, UH, MET WHILE YOU WERE FROZEN IN CARBONITE.

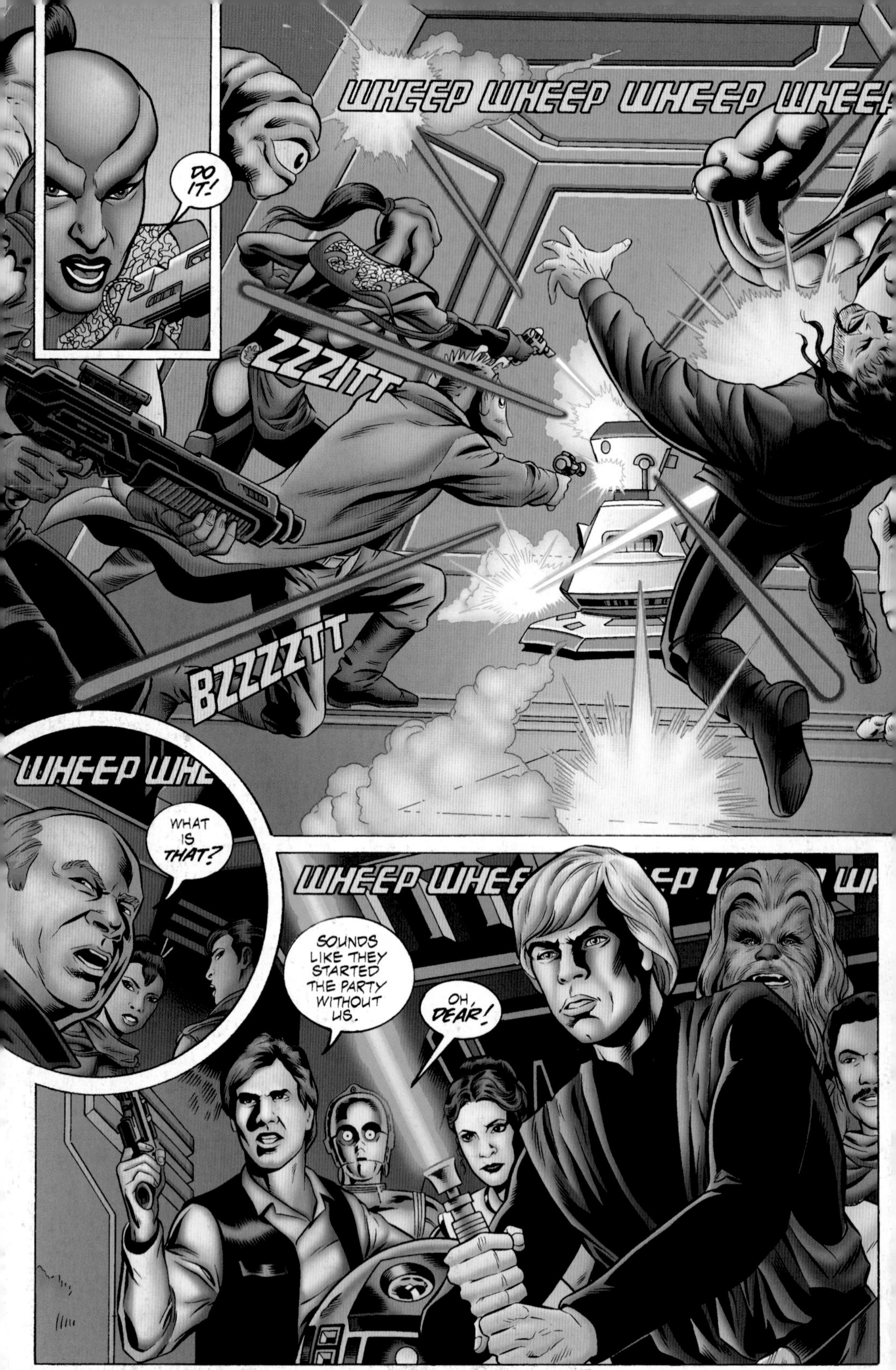
DO IT!
WHEEP WHEEP WHEEP WHEE
ZZZITT
BZZZZTT
WHEEP WHE
WHAT IS THAT?
WHEEP WHEE
SOUNDS LIKE THEY STARTED THE PARTY WITHOUT US.
OH, DEAR!

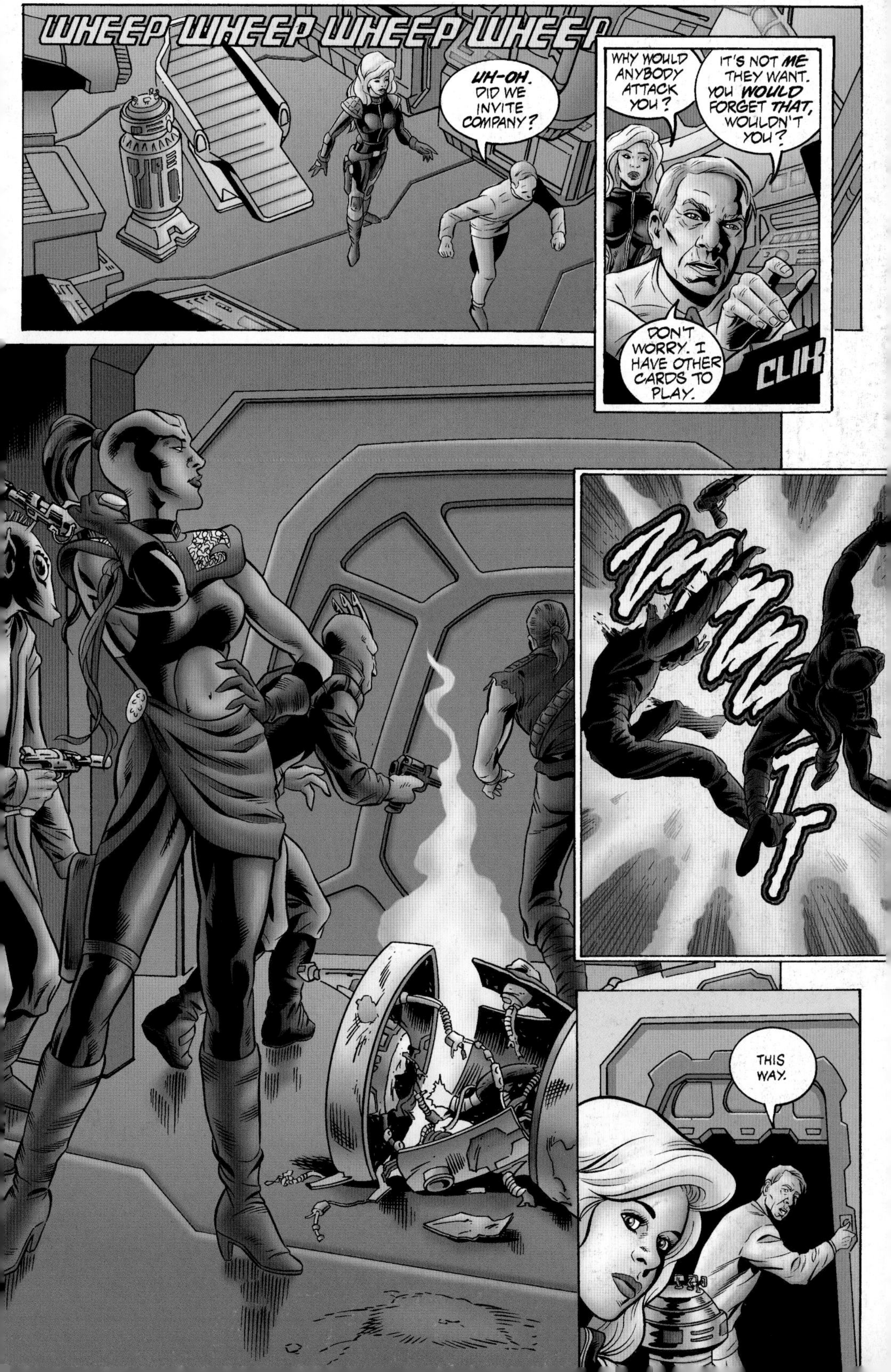
WHEEP WHEEP WHEEP WHEEP
UH-OH. DID WE INVITE COMPANY?
WHY WOULD ANYBODY ATTACK YOU?
IT'S NOT ME THEY WANT. YOU WOULD FORGET THAT, WOULDN'T YOU?
DON'T WORRY. I HAVE OTHER CARDS TO PLAY.
CLIK
THIS WAY.

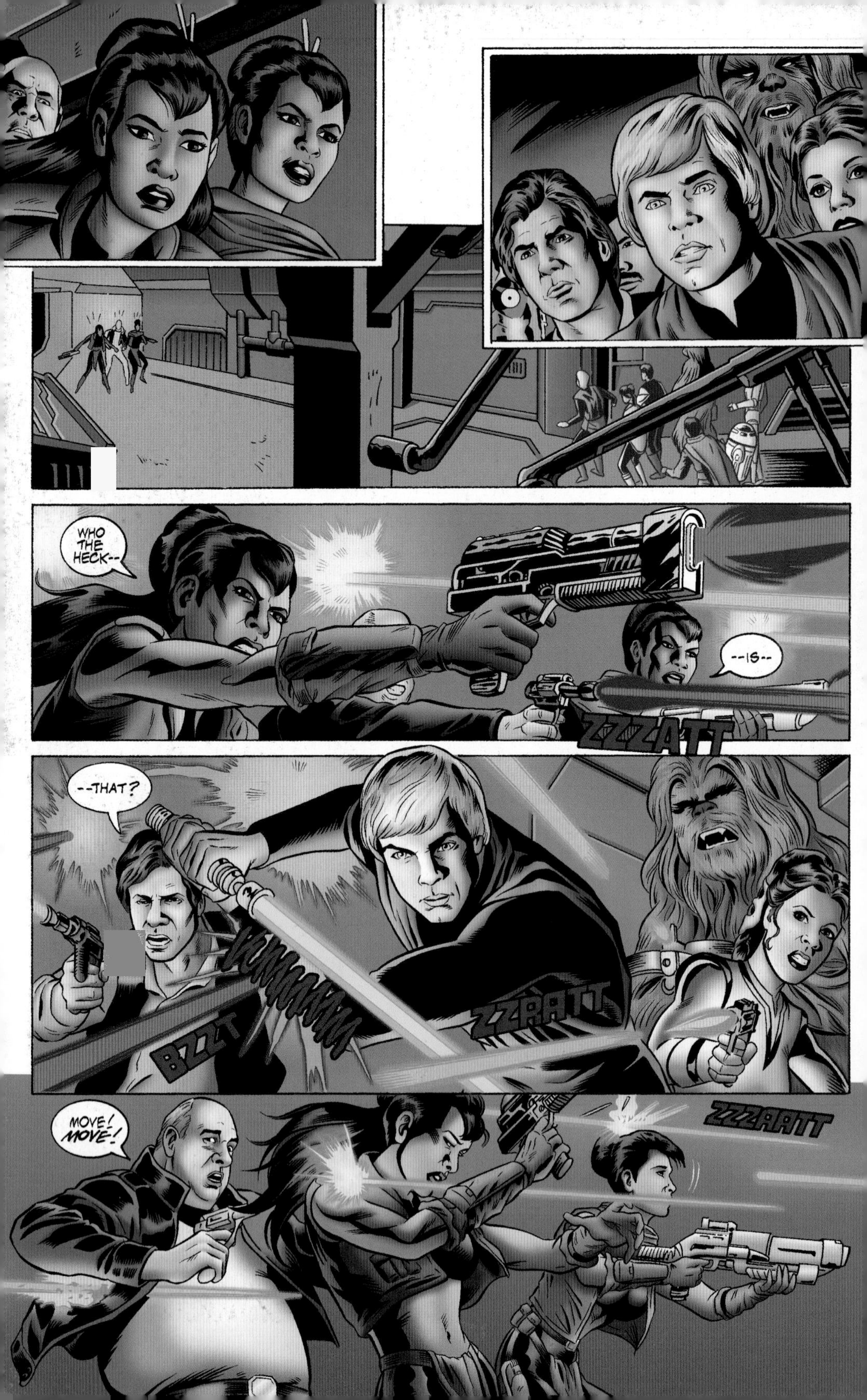
WHO THE HECK--
--IS--
ZZZATT
--THAT?
BZZT
ZZRATT
MOVE! MOVE!
ZZZAATT

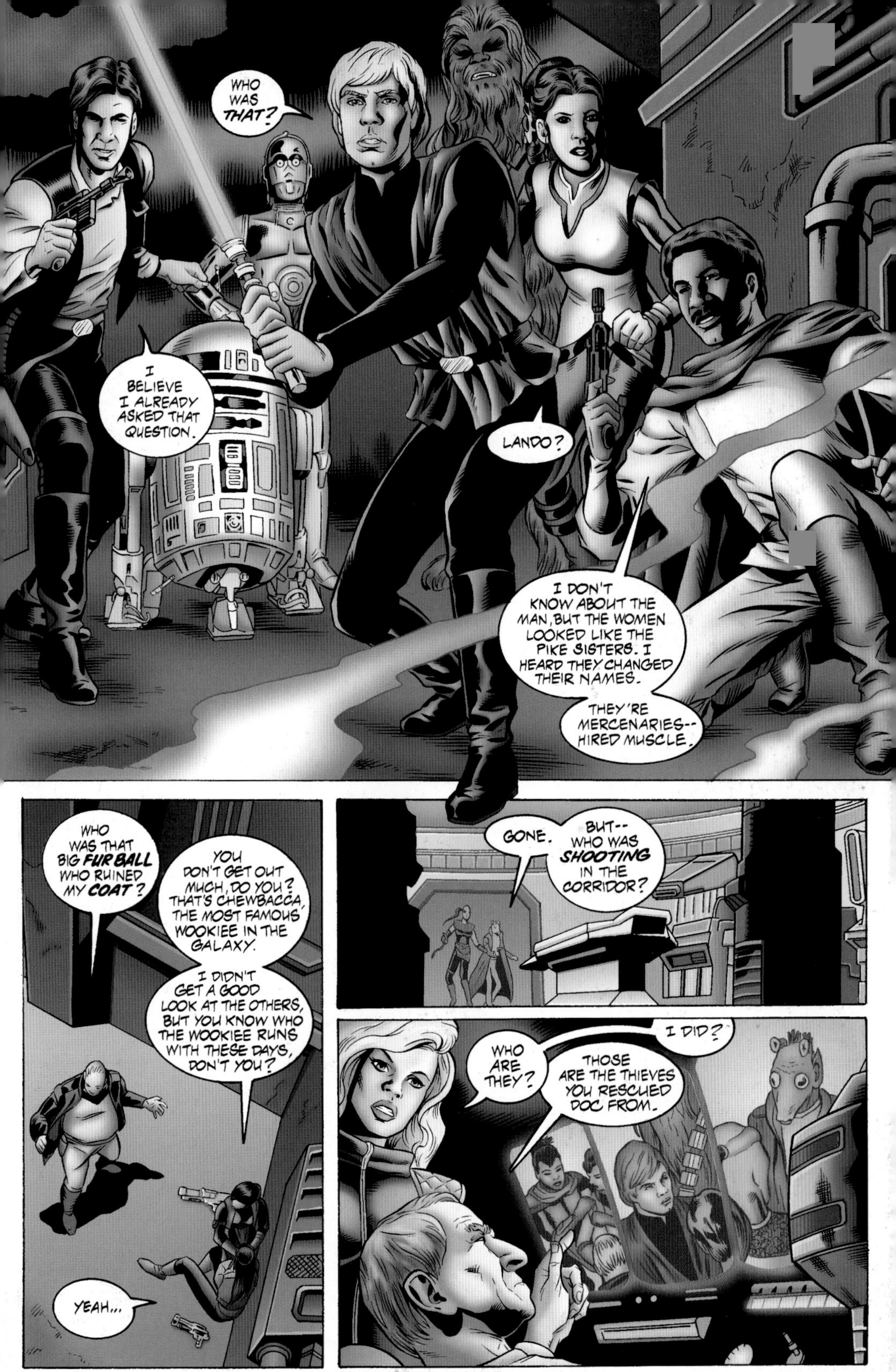
WHO WAS THAT?
I BELIEVE I ALREADY ASKED THAT QUESTION.
LANDO?
I DON'T KNOW ABOUT THE MAN, BUT THE WOMEN LOOKED LIKE THE PIKE SISTERS. I HEARD THEY CHANGED THEIR NAMES.
THEY'RE MERCENARIES-- HIRED MUSCLE.
WHO WAS THAT BIG FUR BALL WHO RUINED MY COAT?
YOU DON'T GET OUT MUCH, DO YOU? THAT'S CHEWBACCA, THE MOST FAMOUS WOOKIEE IN THE GALAXY.
I DIDN'T GET A GOOD LOOK AT THE OTHERS, BUT YOU KNOW WHO THE WOOKIEE RUNS WITH THESE DAYS, DON'T YOU?
YEAH...
GONE.
BUT-- WHO WAS SHOOTING IN THE CORRIDOR?
WHO ARE THEY?
I DID?
THOSE ARE THE THIEVES YOU RESCUED DOC FROM.

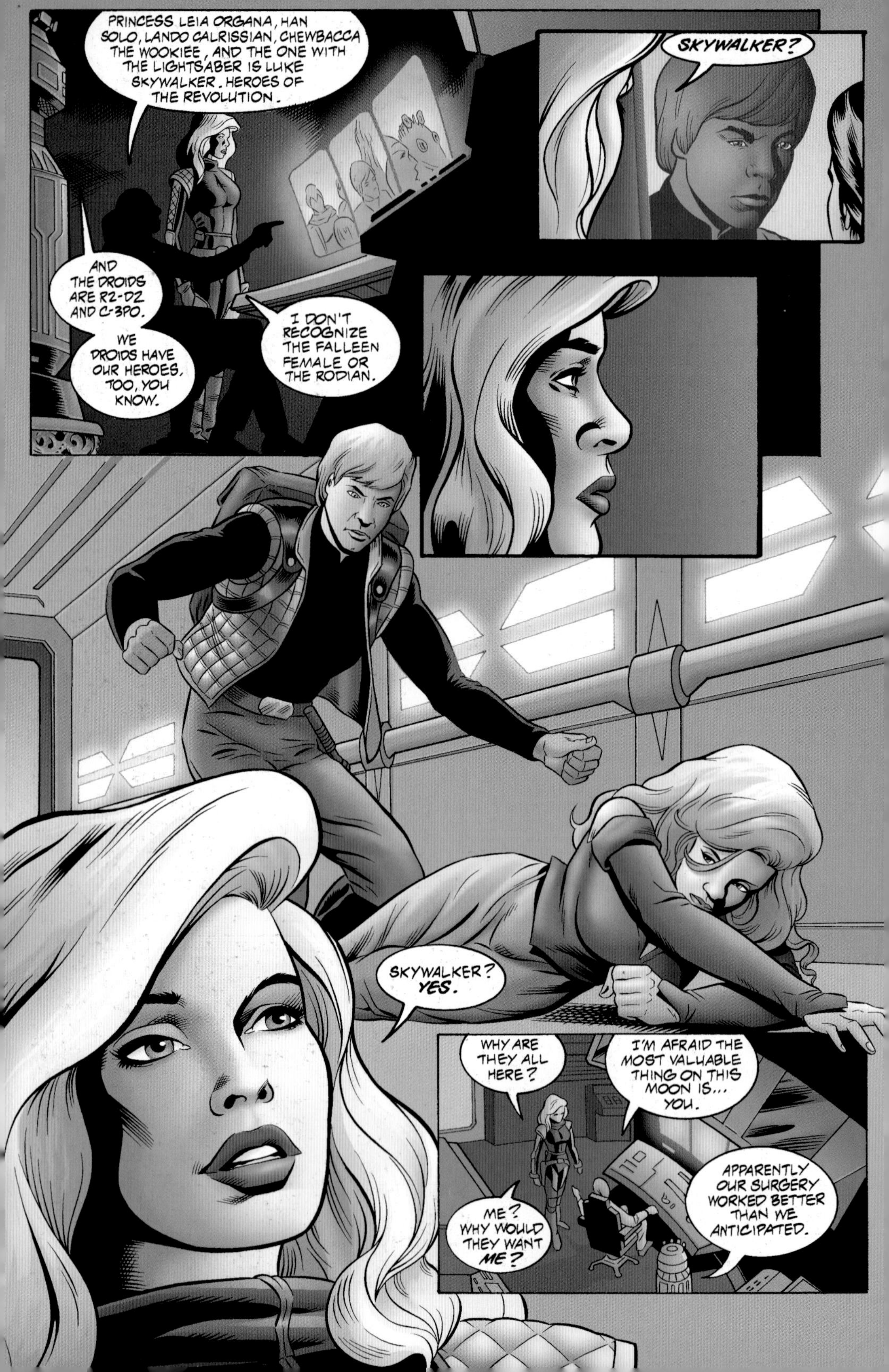
PRINCESS LEIA ORGANA, HAN SOLO, LANDO CALRISSIAN, CHEWBACCA THE WOOKIEE, AND THE ONE WITH THE LIGHTSABER IS LUKE SKYWALKER. HEROES OF THE REVOLUTION.
AND THE DROIDS ARE R2-D2 AND C-3PO.
WE DROIDS HAVE OUR HEROES, TOO, YOU KNOW.
I DON'T RECOGNIZE THE FALLEEN FEMALE OR THE RODIAN.
SKYWALKER?
SKYWALKER? YES.
WHY ARE THEY ALL HERE?
I'M AFRAID THE MOST VALUABLE THING ON THIS MOON IS... YOU.
ME? WHY WOULD THEY WANT ME?
APPARENTLY OUR SURGERY WORKED BETTER THAN WE ANTICIPATED.

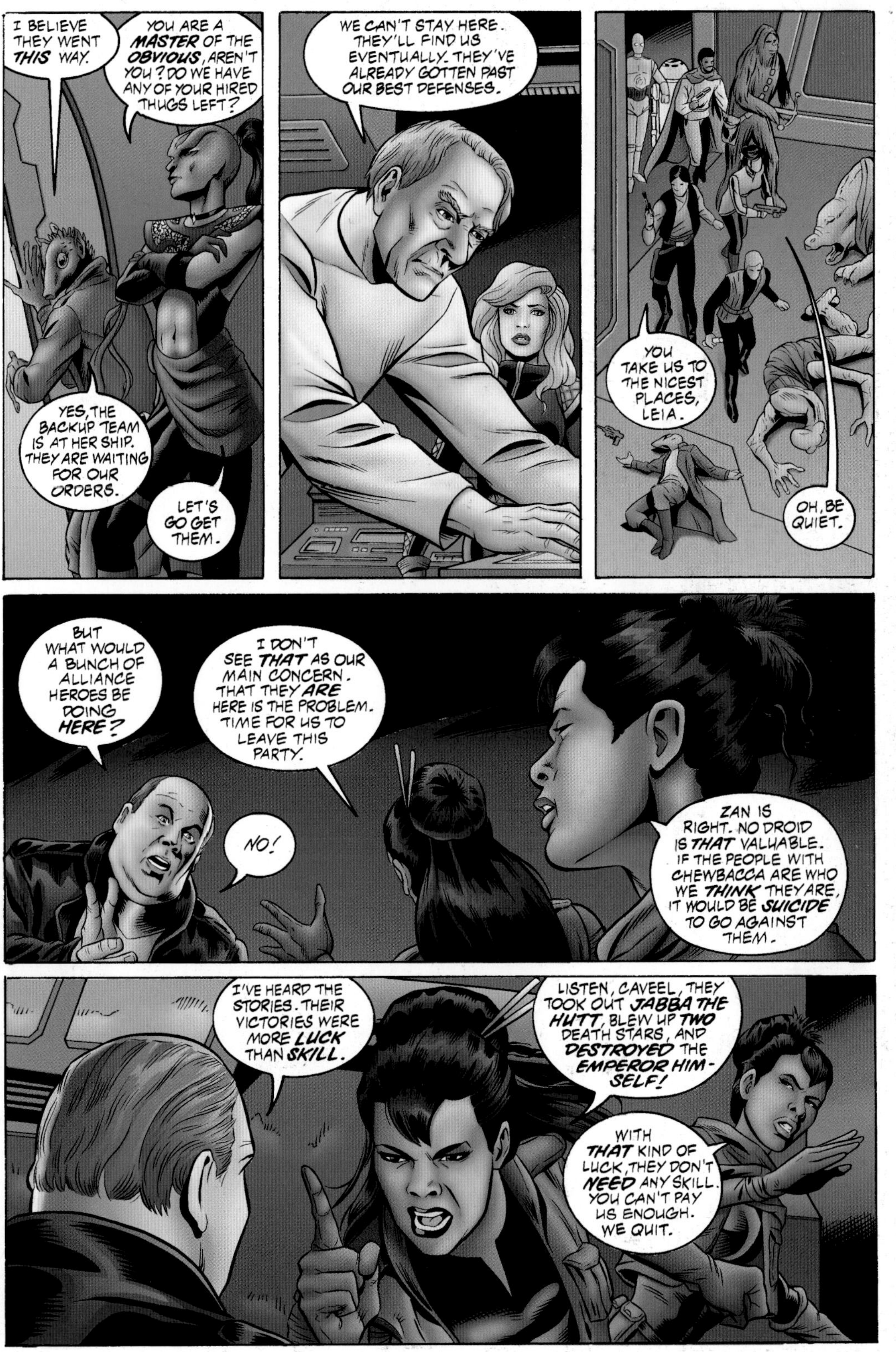
I BELIEVE THEY WENT THIS WAY.
YOU ARE A MASTER OF THE OBVIOUS, AREN'T YOU? DO WE HAVE ANY OF YOUR HIRED THUGS LEFT?
YES, THE BACKUP TEAM IS AT HER SHIP. THEY ARE WAITING FOR OUR ORDERS.
LET'S GO GET THEM.
WE CAN'T STAY HERE. THEY'LL FIND US EVENTUALLY. THEY'VE ALREADY GOTTEN PAST OUR BEST DEFENSES.
YOU TAKE US TO THE NICEST PLACES, LEIA.
OH, BE QUIET.
BUT WHAT WOULD A BUNCH OF ALLIANCE HEROES BE DOING HERE?
I DON'T SEE THAT AS OUR MAIN CONCERN. THAT THEY ARE HERE IS THE PROBLEM. TIME FOR US TO LEAVE THIS PARTY.
NO!
ZAN IS RIGHT. NO DROID IS THAT VALUABLE. IF THE PEOPLE WITH CHEWBACCA ARE WHO WE THINK THEY ARE, IT WOULD BE SUICIDE TO GO AGAINST THEM.
I'VE HEARD THE STORIES. THEIR VICTORIES WERE MORE LUCK THAN SKILL.
LISTEN, CAVEEL, THEY TOOK OUT JABBA THE HUTT, BLEW UP TWO DEATH STARS, AND DESTROYED THE EMPEROR HIMSELF!
WITH THAT KIND OF LUCK, THEY DON'T NEED ANY SKILL. YOU CAN'T PAY US ENOUGH. WE QUIT.

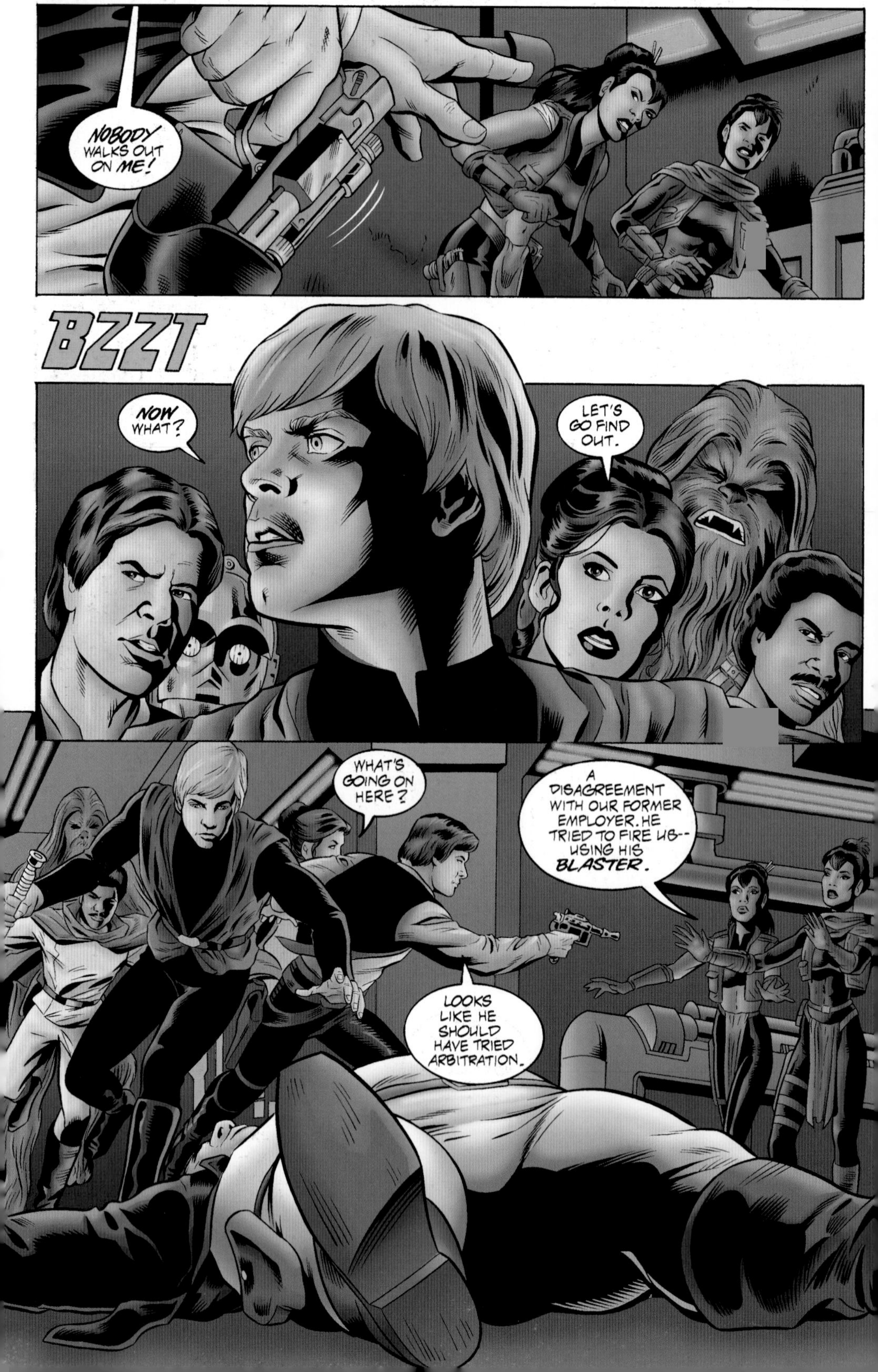
NOBODY WALKS OUT ON ME!
BZZT
NOW WHAT?
LET'S GO FIND OUT.
WHAT'S GOING ON HERE?
A DISAGREEMENT WITH OUR FORMER EMPLOYER. HE TRIED TO FIRE US-- USING HIS BLASTER.
LOOKS LIKE HE SHOULD HAVE TRIED ARBITRATION.

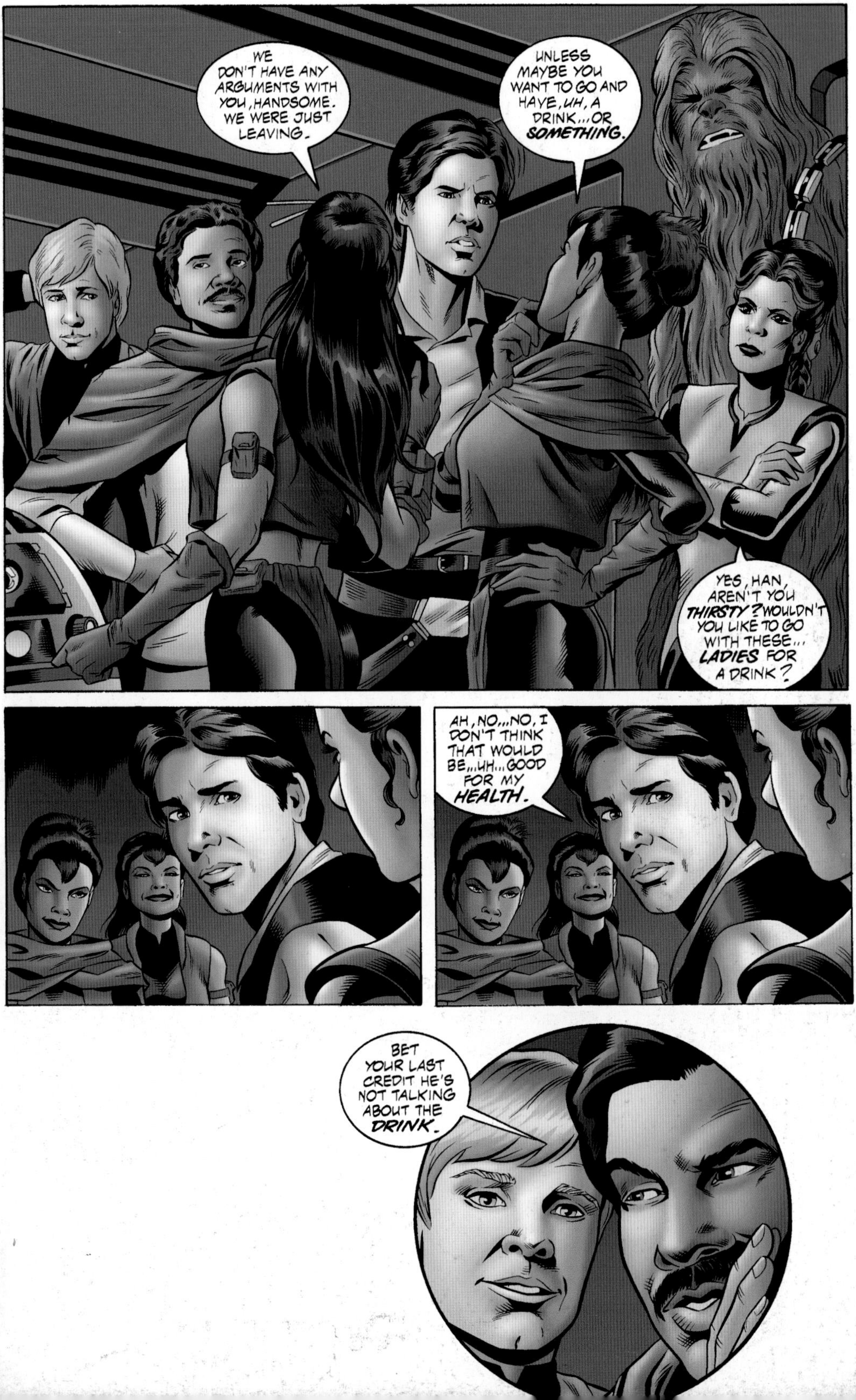
WE DON'T HAVE ANY ARGUMENTS WITH YOU, HANDSOME. WE WERE JUST LEAVING.
UNLESS MAYBE YOU WANT TO GO AND HAVE, UH, A DRINK... OR SOMETHING.
YES, HAN, AREN'T YOU THIRSTY? WOULDN'T YOU LIKE TO GO WITH THESE... LADIES FOR A DRINK?
AH, NO... NO, I DON'T THINK THAT WOULD BE... UH... GOOD FOR MY HEALTH.
BET YOUR LAST CREDIT HE'S NOT TALKING ABOUT THE DRINK.

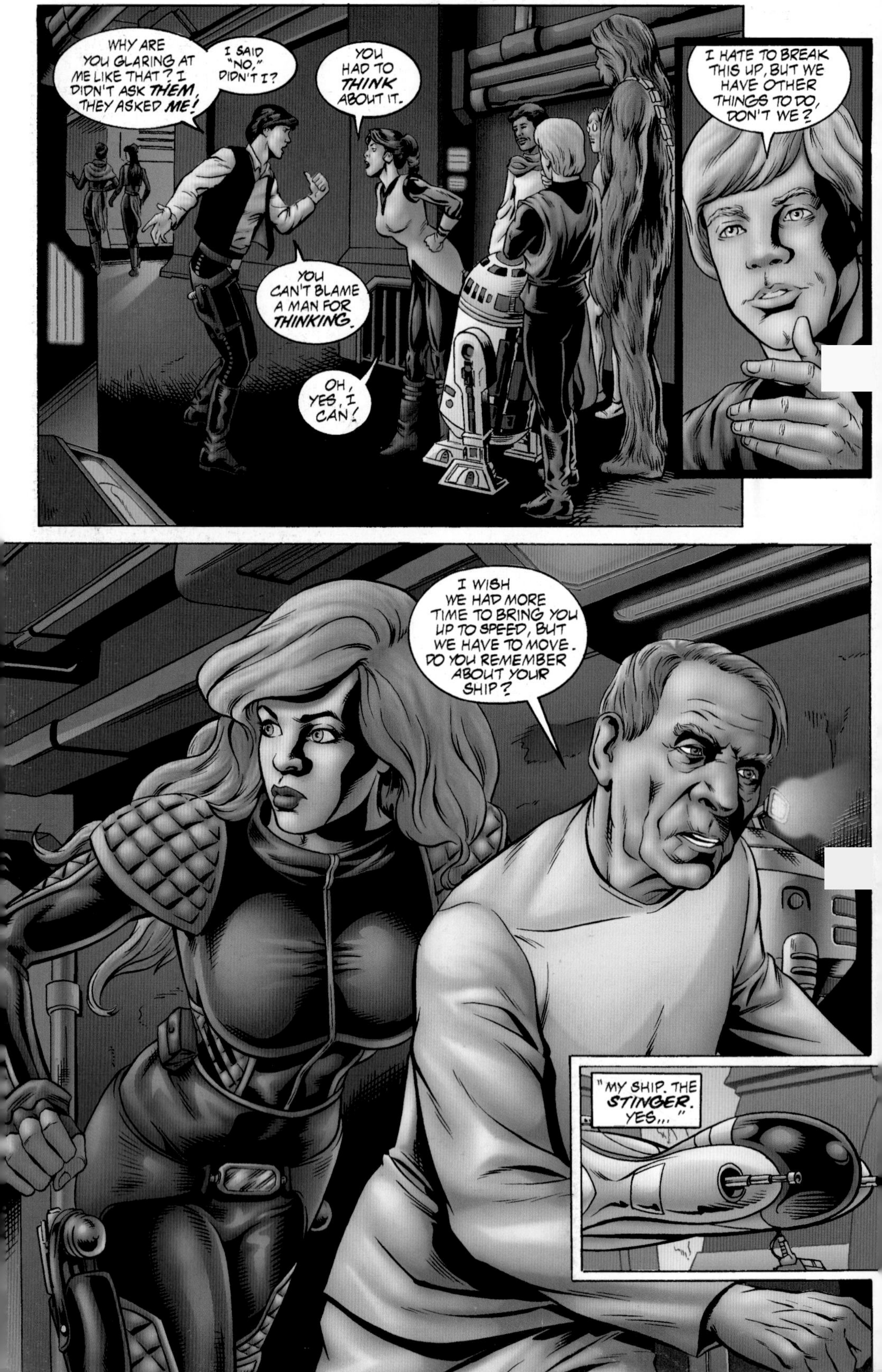
WHY ARE YOU GLARING AT ME LIKE THAT? I DIDN'T ASK *THEM*, THEY ASKED *ME*!
I SAID "NO," DIDN'T I?
YOU HAD TO *THINK* ABOUT IT.
YOU CAN'T BLAME A MAN FOR *THINKING*.
OH, YES, I CAN!
I HATE TO BREAK THIS UP, BUT WE HAVE OTHER THINGS TO DO, DON'T WE?
I WISH WE HAD MORE TIME TO BRING YOU UP TO SPEED, BUT WE HAVE TO MOVE. DO YOU REMEMBER ABOUT YOUR SHIP?
"MY SHIP. THE *STINGER*. YES..."

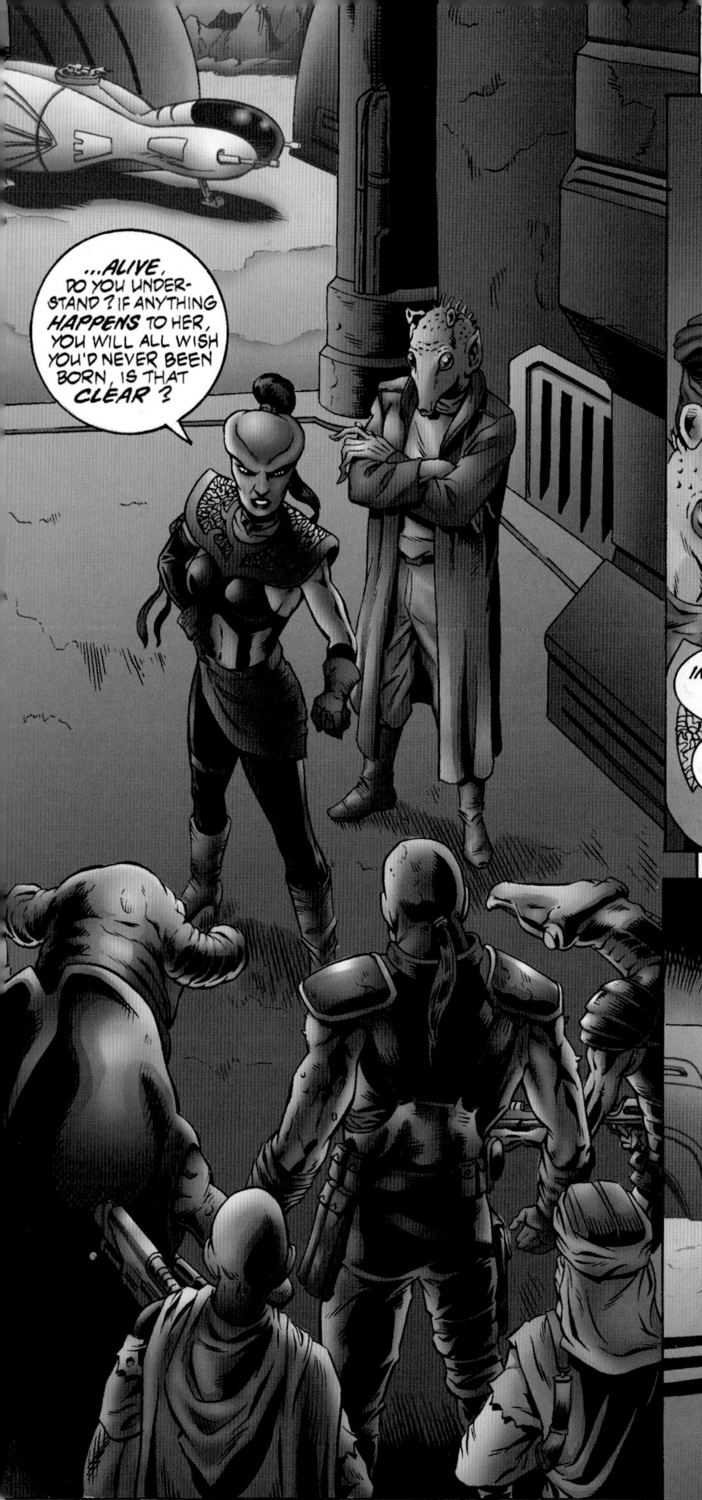
...ALIVE, DO YOU UNDER-STAND? IF ANYTHING HAPPENS TO HER, YOU WILL ALL WISH YOU'D NEVER BEEN BORN, IS THAT CLEAR?

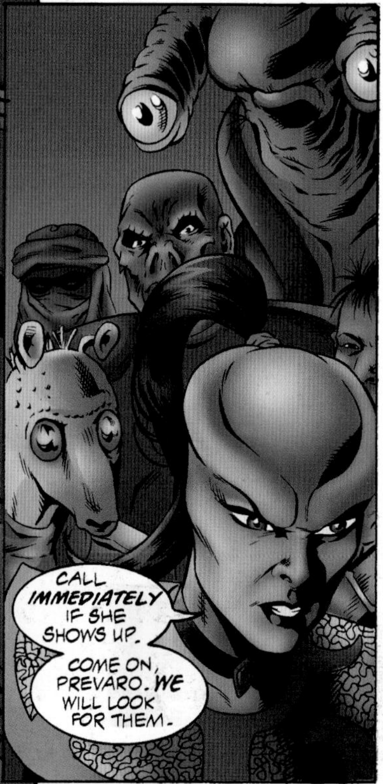
CALL IMMEDIATELY IF SHE SHOWS UP.
COME ON, PREVARO. WE WILL LOOK FOR THEM.

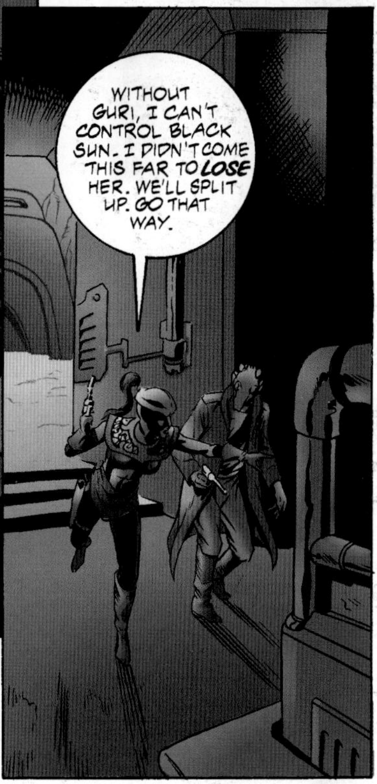
WITHOUT GURI, I CAN'T CONTROL BLACK SUN. I DIDN'T COME THIS FAR TO LOSE HER. WE'LL SPLIT UP. GO THAT WAY.

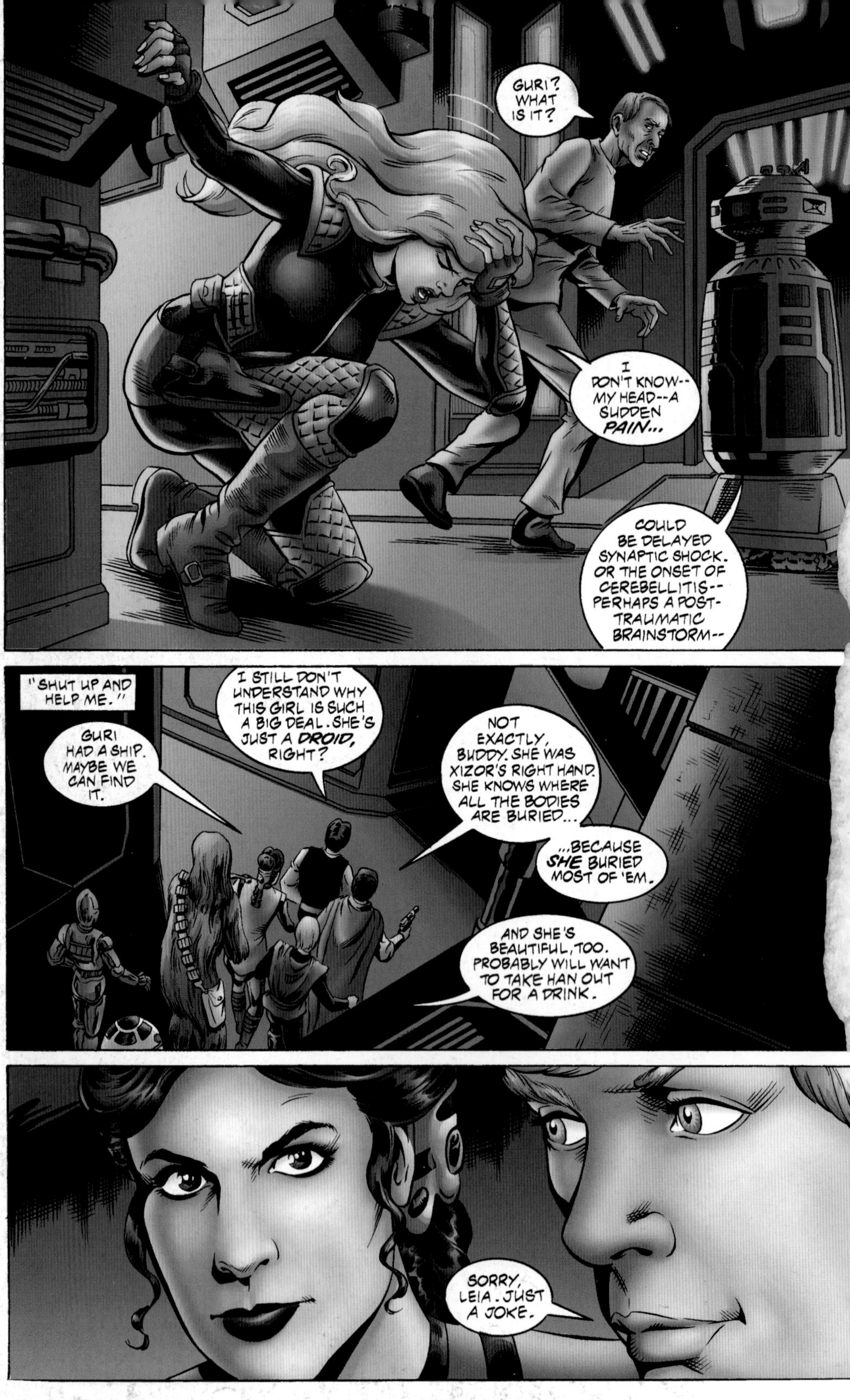
GURI? WHAT IS IT?
I DON'T KNOW-- MY HEAD--A SUDDEN PAIN...
COULD BE DELAYED SYNAPTIC SHOCK. OR THE ONSET OF CEREBELLITIS-- PERHAPS A POST-TRAUMATIC BRAINSTORM--
"SHUT UP AND HELP ME."
GURI HAD A SHIP. MAYBE WE CAN FIND IT.
I STILL DON'T UNDERSTAND WHY THIS GIRL IS SUCH A BIG DEAL. SHE'S JUST A DROID, RIGHT?
NOT EXACTLY, BUDDY. SHE WAS XIZOR'S RIGHT HAND. SHE KNOWS WHERE ALL THE BODIES ARE BURIED...
...BECAUSE SHE BURIED MOST OF 'EM.
AND SHE'S BEAUTIFUL, TOO. PROBABLY WILL WANT TO TAKE HAN OUT FOR A DRINK.
SORRY, LEIA. JUST A JOKE.

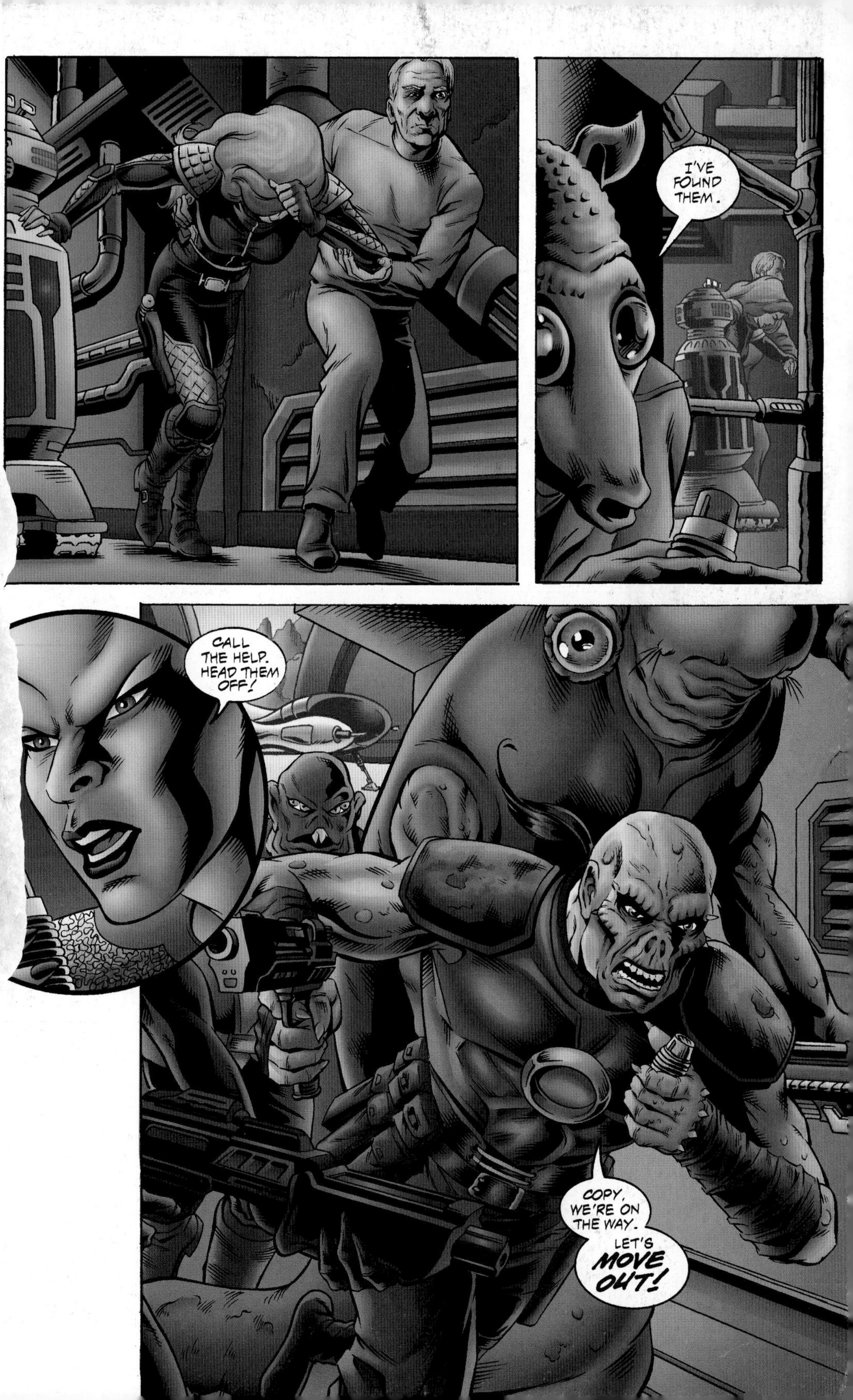
I'VE FOUND THEM.
CALL THE HELP. HEAD THEM OFF!
COPY, WE'RE ON THE WAY.
LET'S **MOVE OUT!**

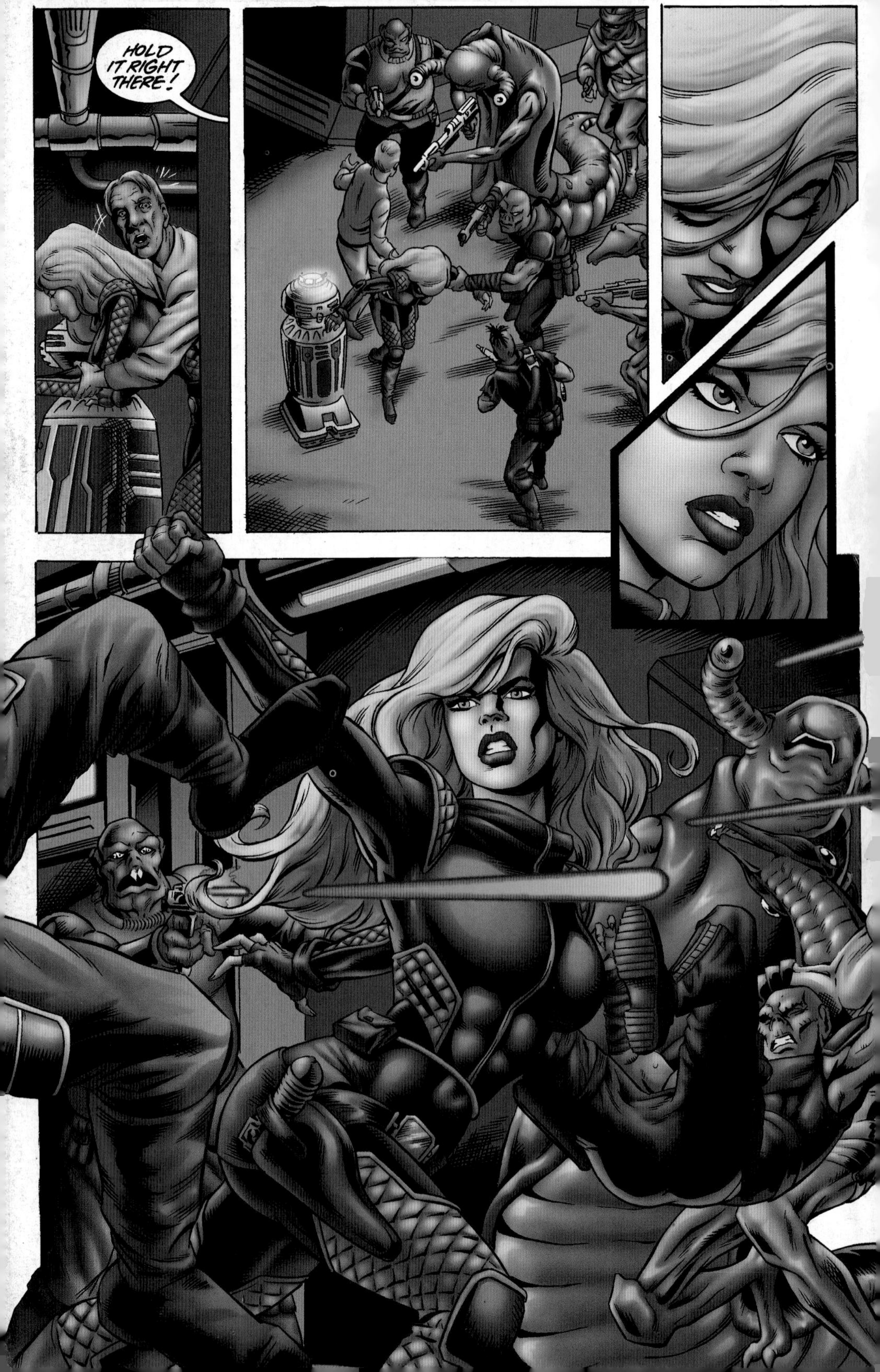
HOLD IT RIGHT THERE!

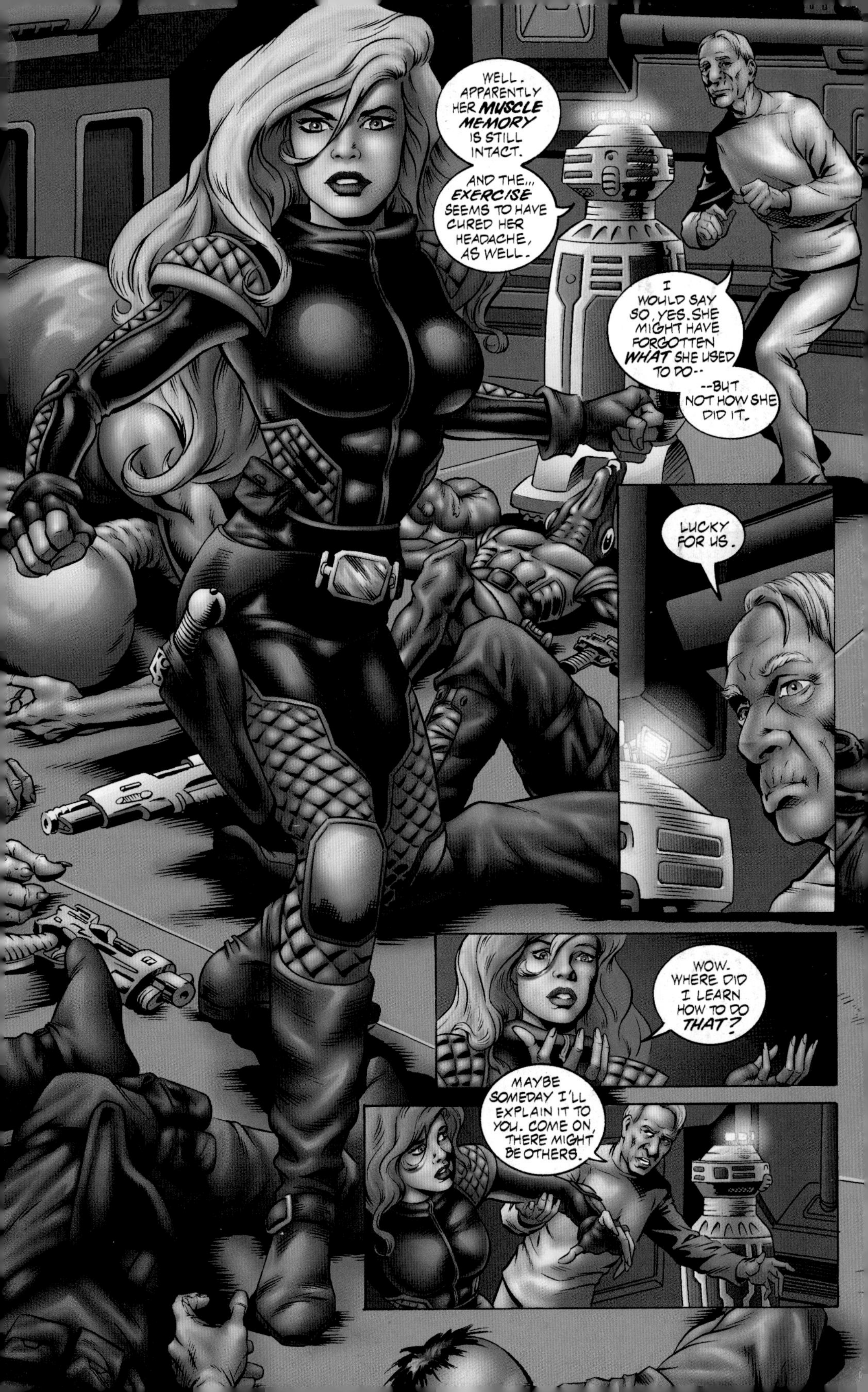
WELL. APPARENTLY HER MUSCLE MEMORY IS STILL INTACT.
AND THE... EXERCISE SEEMS TO HAVE CURED HER HEADACHE, AS WELL.
I WOULD SAY SO, YES. SHE MIGHT HAVE FORGOTTEN WHAT SHE USED TO DO--
--BUT NOT HOW SHE DID IT.
LUCKY FOR US.
WOW. WHERE DID I LEARN HOW TO DO THAT?
MAYBE SOMEDAY I'LL EXPLAIN IT TO YOU. COME ON, THERE MIGHT BE OTHERS.

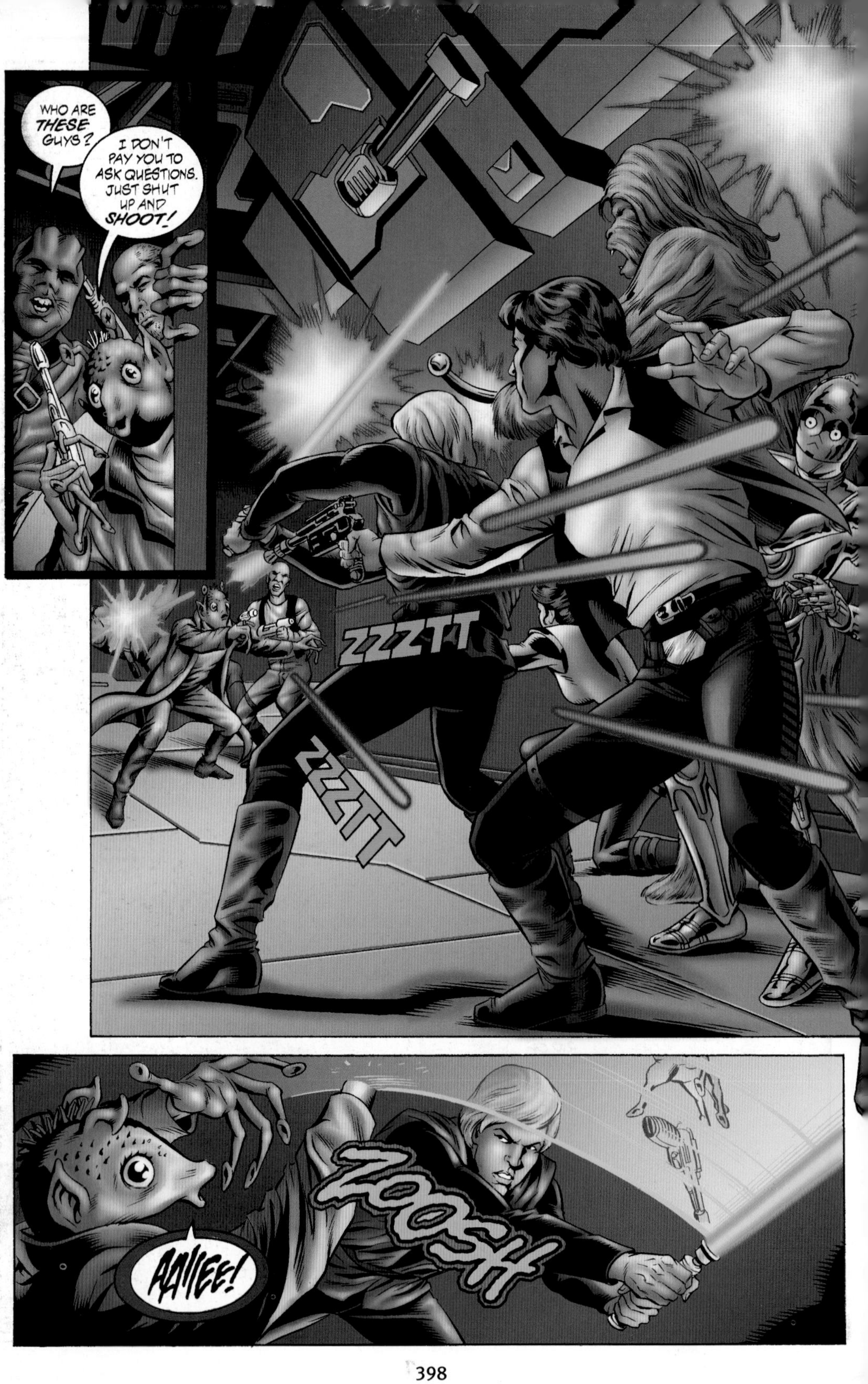
WHO ARE *THESE* GUYS?
I DON'T PAY YOU TO ASK QUESTIONS. JUST SHUT UP AND *SHOOT!*
ZZZTT
ZZZTT
ZOOSH
AAIIEE!

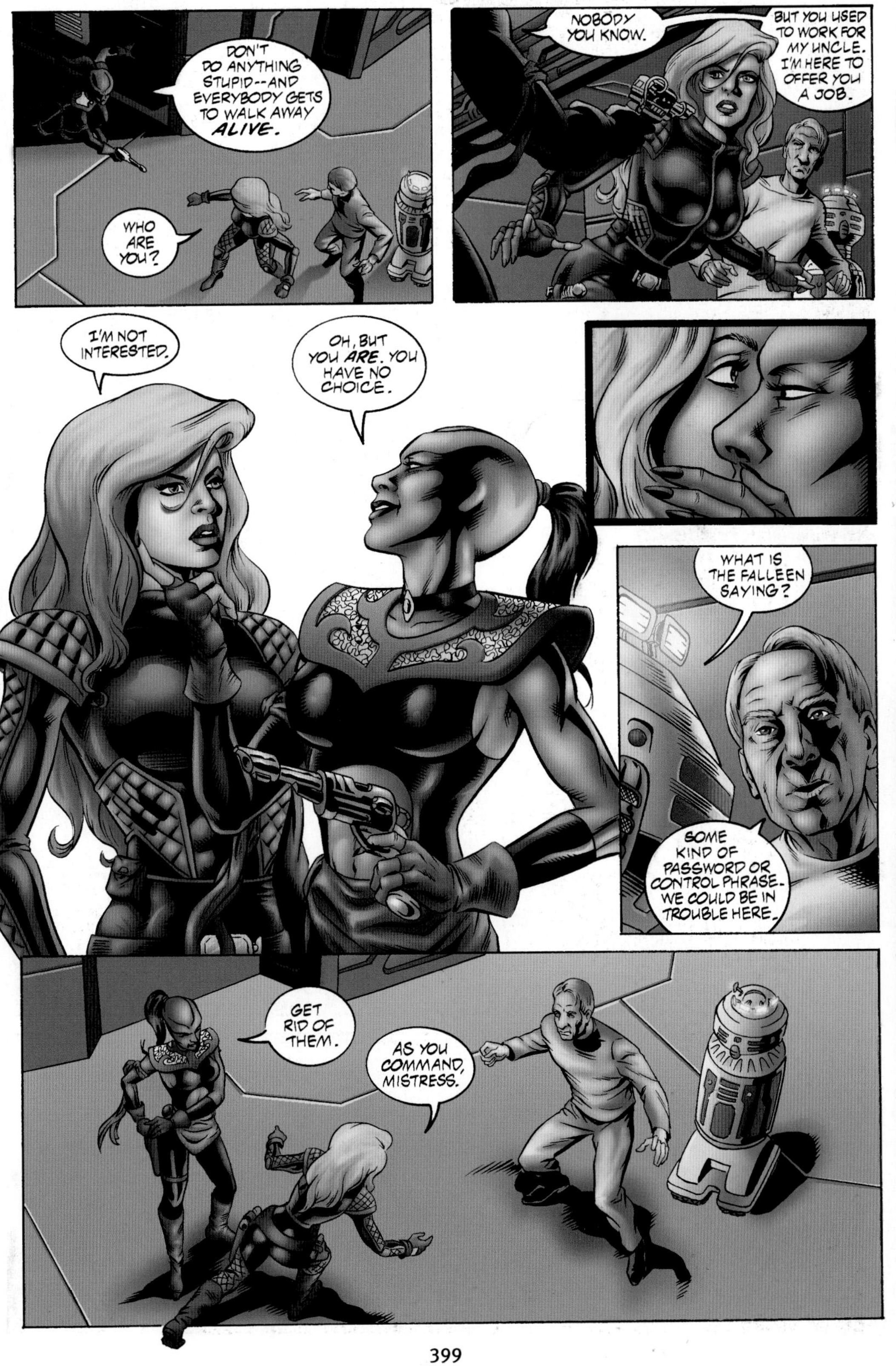
DON'T DO ANYTHING STUPID--AND EVERYBODY GETS TO WALK AWAY ALIVE.
WHO ARE YOU?
NOBODY YOU KNOW.
BUT YOU USED TO WORK FOR MY UNCLE. I'M HERE TO OFFER YOU A JOB.
I'M NOT INTERESTED.
OH, BUT YOU ARE. YOU HAVE NO CHOICE.
WHAT IS THE FALLEEN SAYING?
SOME KIND OF PASSWORD OR CONTROL PHRASE. WE COULD BE IN TROUBLE HERE.
GET RID OF THEM.
AS YOU COMMAND, MISTRESS.

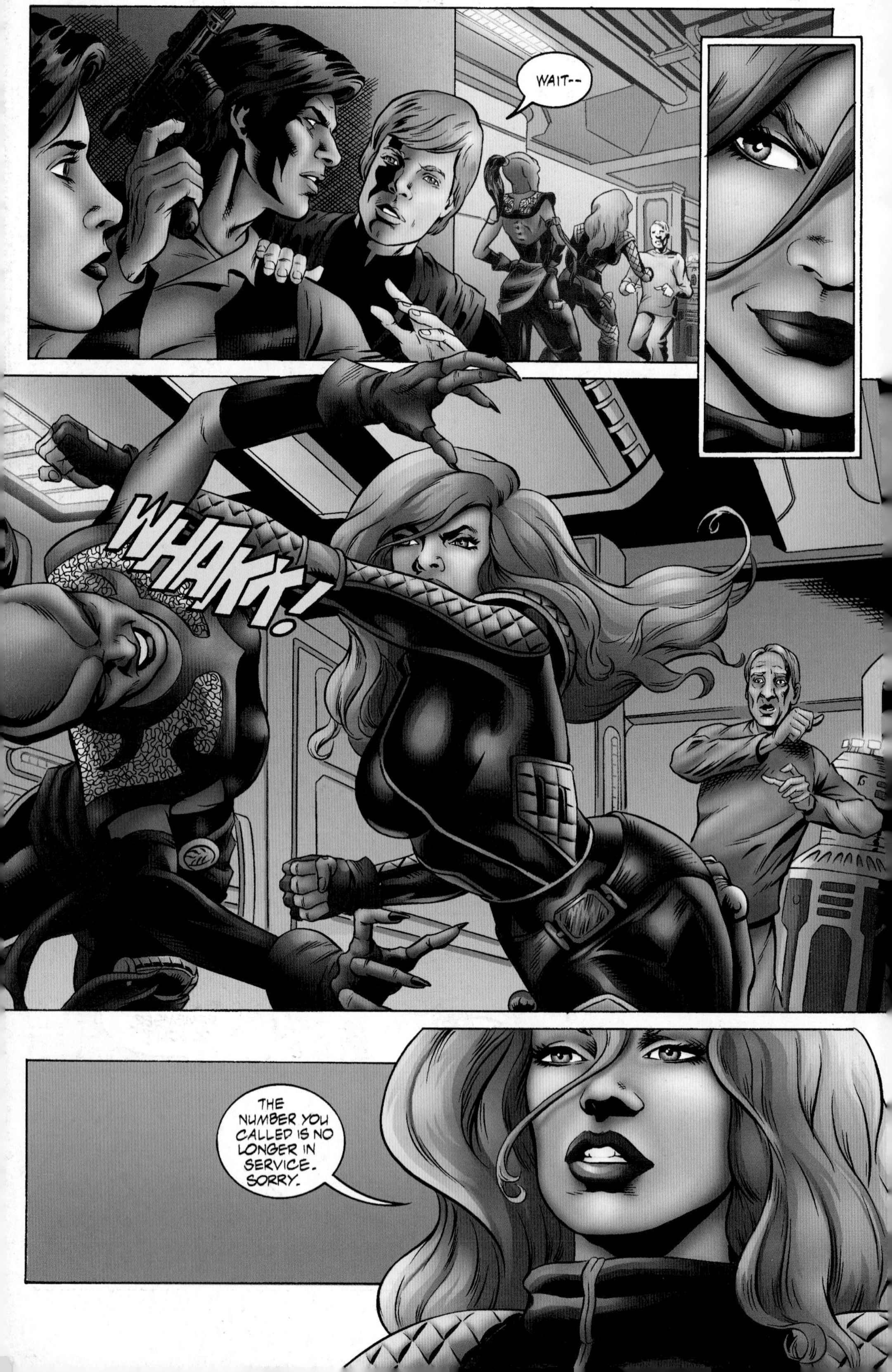
WAIT--
WHAKK!
THE NUMBER YOU CALLED IS NO LONGER IN SERVICE. SORRY.

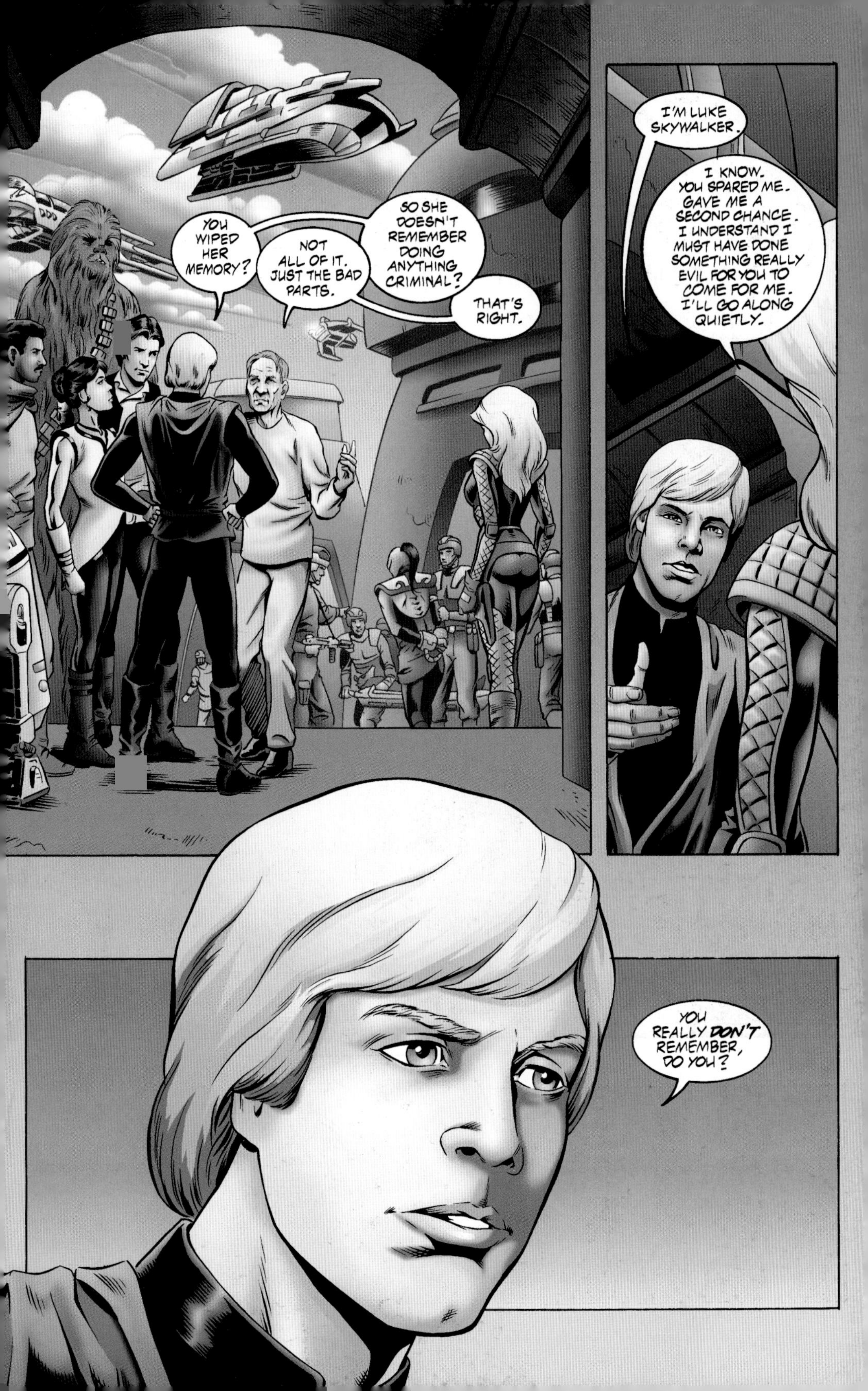
YOU WIPED HER MEMORY?
NOT ALL OF IT. JUST THE BAD PARTS.
SO SHE DOESN'T REMEMBER DOING ANYTHING CRIMINAL?
THAT'S RIGHT.
I'M LUKE SKYWALKER.
I KNOW. YOU SPARED ME. GAVE ME A SECOND CHANCE. I UNDERSTAND I MUST HAVE DONE SOMETHING REALLY EVIL FOR YOU TO COME FOR ME. I'LL GO ALONG QUIETLY.
YOU REALLY DON'T REMEMBER, DO YOU?

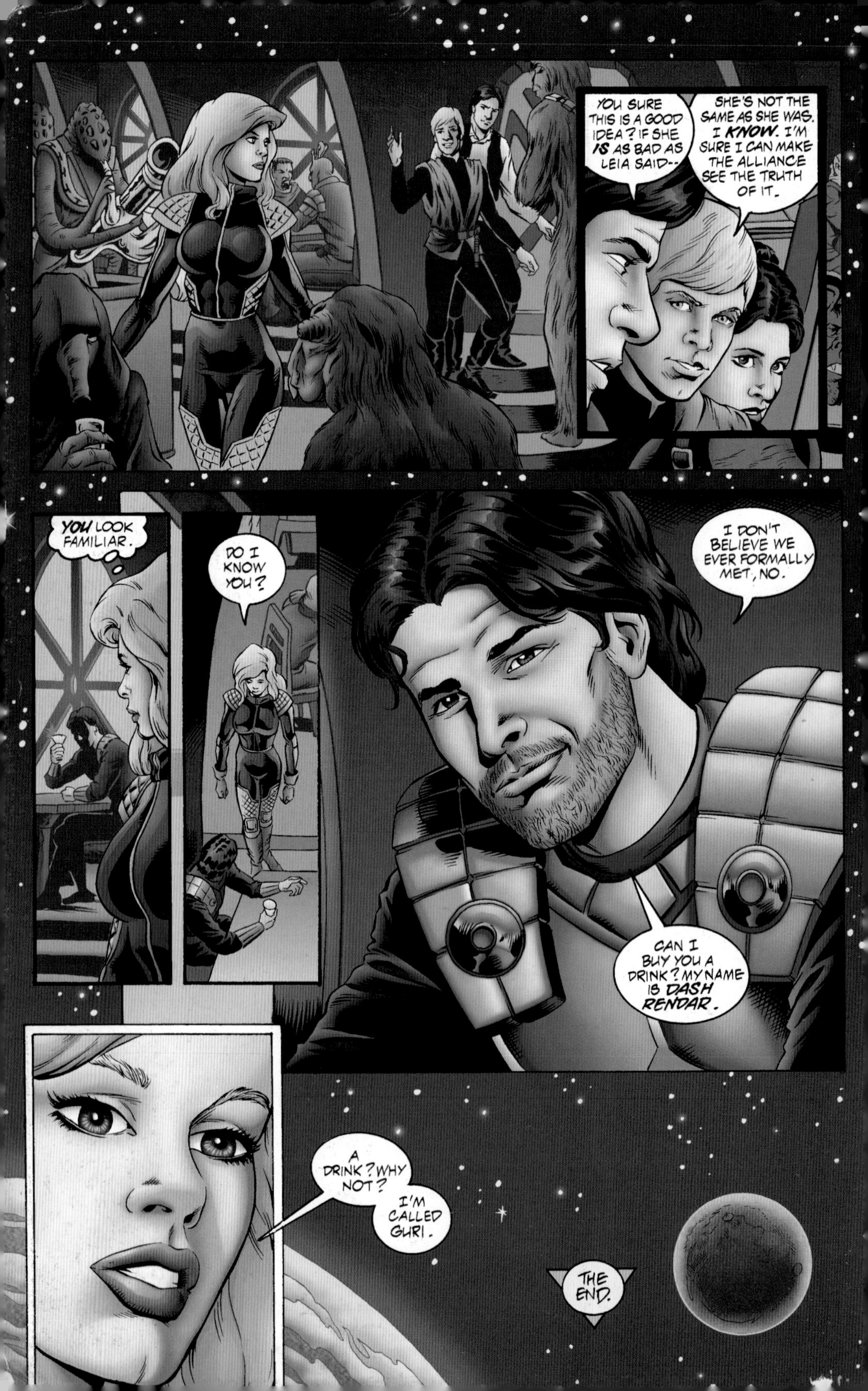
YOU SURE THIS IS A GOOD IDEA? IF SHE IS AS BAD AS LEIA SAID--
SHE'S NOT THE SAME AS SHE WAS. I KNOW. I'M SURE I CAN MAKE THE ALLIANCE SEE THE TRUTH OF IT.
YOU LOOK FAMILIAR.
DO I KNOW YOU?
I DON'T BELIEVE WE EVER FORMALLY MET, NO.
CAN I BUY YOU A DRINK? MY NAME IS DASH RENDAR.
A DRINK? WHY NOT?
I'M CALLED GURI.
THE END.